9th Joint SIGHUM Workshop on Computational Linguistics for Cultural Heritage, Social Sciences, Humanities and Literature (LaTeCH-CLfL-2025)

Albuquerque, New Mexico, USA
4 May 2025

ISBN: 979-8-3313-1921-2

Printed from e-media with permission by:

Curran Associates, Inc.
57 Morehouse Lane
Red Hook, NY 12571

Some format issues inherent in the e-media version may also appear in this print version.

Association for Computational Linguistics
209 N. Eighth Street
Stroudsburg, Pennsylvania 18360

Phone: 1-570-476-8006
Fax: 1-570-476-0860

acl@aclweb.org

Additional copies of this publication are available from:

Curran Associates, Inc.
57 Morehouse Lane
Red Hook, NY 12571 USA
Phone: 845-758-0400
Fax: 845-758-2633
Email: curran@proceedings.com
Web: www.proceedings.com

LaTeCH-CLfL 2025

9th Joint SIGHUM Workshop on Computational Linguistics for Cultural Heritage, Social Sciences, Humanities and Literature

Proceedings of the Workshop

May 4, 2025

The LaTeCH-CLfL organizers gratefully acknowledge the support from the following sponsors.

IDeaL
SFB 1102

Introduction

Welcome to the 2025 edition of LaTeCH-CLfL! Whether you are coming back or joining us for the first time, we are delighted to have you here. This workshop, with a history of nearly two decades, continues to serve as home for a wide spectrum of discussions. This year is no exception, with a lineup of topics that span the intersection of language technology, computational linguistics and the broadly conceived humanities.

This year, in line with the general trend in computational linguistics, we see a central focus on using large language models, with innovative approaches to literary analysis and cultural studies. Papers in this area include evaluating LLM-prompting for sequence labeling in computational literary studies, using LLMs for detecting linguistic variation in Russian media, and exploring zero-shot learning for named entity recognition in historical texts. These contributions demonstrate adaptations of cutting-edge AI technologies to address classic questions in sociolinguistics and in the Humanities.

Historical language processing remains a central area of research, with papers addressing the challenges of working with historical texts and low-resource languages. Contributions in this category include matching entries in historical Swedish encyclopedias, preserving Comorian linguistic heritage through bidirectional transliteration, recovering Egyptian hieroglyphs with next-word prediction language models, and adapting multilingual embedding models to historical Luxembourgish. These papers represent the ongoing effort to extend computational methods to underrepresented languages and historical documents.

Sociopolitical text analysis has also grown in importance, with several papers examining prominent social topics such as bias, propaganda and hate speech. These include works on automated media bias detection, unveiling propagandistic strategies during the Russo-Ukrainian War, detecting gender bias in lyrics, and improving hate speech classification through cross-taxonomy dataset integration. These contributions utilize computational linguistics to observe symptoms of social issues, but also help enhance our understanding of how language shapes public discourse. This year's edition also features more innovative approaches that move beyond the classic context of sociolinguistic, such as quantitative approaches to psychological modeling, conversational AI interviewing techniques, and studies on smalltalk identification in natural conversations that reveal both psychological and social dynamics.

Finally, the computational analysis of literary texts remains a fascinating frontier. This year's papers tackle high-level topics such as scene segmentation in literary texts, relationships in fiction, poetry generation, and the dynamics of the canon – using quantitative and cutting-edge perspectives to model complex literary dynamics.

Overall, we keep seeing the growing convergence of large-scale quantitative models with deep scholarly traditions, creating a frame where cutting edge technology broadens our understanding of human language and (human, for now) culture.

There is something for everyone, all things considered. But do keep an open mind and read all papers, if you have the time. You will be glad you did.

Do not forget to visit our Web site HERE – and check out past workshops too.

It goes without saying that whatever success our workshop enjoys is due to the authors (thank you for staying with us or for trusting us the first time), and without question to the reviewers. A special shout-out to our wonderful program committee!

Yuri, Stefania, Anna, Janis, Diego, Stan

Program Committee

Chairs

Diego Alves, Saarland University
Yuri Bizzoni, Aarhus University
Stefania Degaetano-Ortlieb, Saarland University
Anna Kazantseva, National Research Council Canada
Janis Pagel, Department of Digital Humanities, University of Cologne
Stan Szpakowicz, EECS, University of Ottawa

Program Committee

Jinyeong Bak, Sungkyunkwan University
Johanna Binnewitt, Federal Institute for Vocational Education and Training
Patrick Brookshire, Academy of Sciences and Literature | Mainz
Paul Buitelaar, University of Galway
Miriam Butt, University of Konstanz
Prajit Dhar, University of Groningen
Jacob Eisenstein, Google
Anna Feldman, Montclair State University
Mark Finlayson, FIU
Francesca Frontini, Istituto di Linguistica Computazionale A. Zampolli"- ILC Consiglio Nazionale delle Ricerche - CNR
Serge Heiden, ENS de Lyon
Rebecca Hicke, Cornell University
Labiba Jahan, Southern Methodist University
Dimitrios Kokkinakis, University of Gothenburg
Stasinos Konstantopoulos, NCSR Demokritos
Maria Kunilovskaya, Saarland University
John Ladd, Washington & Jefferson College
John Lee, City University of Hong Kong
Chaya Liebeskind, Jerusalem College of Technology , Lev Academic Center
Thomas Lippincott, Johns Hopkins University
Barbara Mcgillivray, King's College London
Cara Messina, Marist University
Craig Messner, Johns Hopkins University
David Mimno, Cornell University
Vivi Nastase, University of Geneva
Borja Navarro-Colorado, University of Alicante
Pierre Nugues, Lund University
Thijs Ossenkoppele, University of Amsterdam
Andrew Piper, McGill University
Petr Plechac, Institute of Czech Literature CAS
Thierry Poibeau, LATTICE (CNRS & ENS/PSL)
Jelena Prokic, Leiden University
Georg Rehm, DFKI
Nils Reiter, University of Cologne
Pablo Ruiz Fabo, LiLPa, Université de Strasbourg
Marijn Schraagen, Utrecht University

Artjoms Sela, Institute of Polish Language (PAN)
Hale Sirin, Johns Hopkins University
Pia Sommerauer, Vrije Universiteit Amsterdam
Elke Teich, Universität des Saarlandes
Laure Thompson, Princeton University
Ulrich Tiedau, University College London
Ted Underwood, University of Illinois
Menno Van Zaanen, South African Centre for Digital Language Resources
Lorella Viola, Vrije Universiteit Amsterdam
Rob Voigt, Northwestern University
Sophie Wu, McGill University
Albin Zehe, University of Wuerzburg
Heike Zinsmeister, Universitaet Hamburg

Keynote Talk
Computational Humanities as Cultural Seismography

Tom Lippincott
Johns Hopkins University

Abstract: How do we move between machine learning and humanistic inquiry without losing our balance? There's no single right answer, but in this talk I'll enumerate a handful of principles that have emerged as useful guidelines for my group, and how they connect to several ongoing projects in computational cultural studies. These principles include a strong dispreference for pretrained LLMs, an emphasis on deep cross-training, and research considerations closely tied to cognitive science. Beyond the specifics, I hope the talk will be a useful example for junior researchers who are beginning to characterize their own agenda and communicate with potential stakeholders across engineering and the humanities.

Bio:

We are delighted to welcome **Tom Lippincott** as our invited speaker at the LaTeCH-CLfL workshop. Tom is an Associate Research Professor at Johns Hopkins University, where he also serves as Director of Digital Humanities with a primary appointment in the Alexander Grass Humanities Institute. His work bridges the gap between machine learning and the humanities, bringing advanced computational techniques—particularly deep neural architectures—into dialogue with scholarship in literature, history, and archaeology.

Tom holds secondary appointments in the Department of Computer Science and the Center for Language and Speech Processing, and the Data Science and AI Institute. Before joining Johns Hopkins, he was research faculty at Columbia University's Center for Computational Learning Systems, following doctoral work at the University of Cambridge and undergraduate studies in Philosophy and Computer Science at the University of Chicago.

His current research focuses on the development of machine learning models, tools, and practices that can reinforce, expand, or challenge received understanding of human culture activities. He has published influential work on authorship attribution and stylistic analysis, including computational investigations into the Pauline epistles and the Documentary Hypothesis of the Hebrew Bible. Earlier in his career, Tom contributed to unsupervised learning of morphology and syntax, including work that received a Best Paper award at COLING 2016.

In addition to his work on Bayesian modeling and domain variation in scientific literature, Tom has also made significant contributions to social media analysis, language identification, and the development of resources for low-resource languages.

With his deep interdisciplinary expertise and commitment to building bridges between computational methods and humanistic inquiry, Tom brings a unique perspective to our workshop.

Table of Contents

Program

Sunday, May 4, 2025

08:30 - 09:50 *Talks I*

Evaluating LLM-Prompting for Sequence Labeling Tasks in Computational Literary Studies
Axel Pichler, Janis Pagel and Nils Reiter

Prompting the Past: Exploring Zero-Shot Learning for Named Entity Recognition in Historical Texts Using Prompt-Answering LLMs
Crina Tudor, Beata Megyesi and Robert Östling

Generation of Russian Poetry of Different Genres and Styles Using Neural Networks with Character-Level Tokenization
Ilya Koziev and Alena Fenogenova

Why Novels (Don't) Break Through: Dynamics of Canonicity in the Danish Modern Breakthrough (1870-1900)
Alie Lassche, Pascale Feldkamp, Yuri Bizzoni, Katrine Baunvig and Kristoffer Nielbo

09:50 - 10:30 *Poster teasers for online posters and Q&A*

10:30 - 11:00 *Coffee Break*

11:00 - 12:00 *Invited Talk by Tom Lippincott: 'Computational Humanities as Cultural Seismography'*

12:00 - 13:30 *Lunch*

13:30 - 14:50 *Poster session on site*

14:50 - 15:30 *Talks II*

Embedded Personalities: Word Embeddings and the Big FivePersonality Model
Oliver Müller and Stefania Degaetano-Ortlieb

Prompting the Past: Exploring Zero-Shot Learning for Named Entity Recognition in Historical Texts Using Prompt-Answering LLMs
Crina Tudor, Beata Megyesi and Robert Östling

Sunday, May 4, 2025 (continued)

15:30 - 16:00 *Coffee Break*

16:00 - 17:00 *Talks III*

'... like a needle in a haystack": Annotation and Classification of Comparative Statements
Pritha Majumdar, Franziska Pannach, Arianna Graciotti and Johan Bos

LLMs for Translation: Historical, Low-Resourced Languages and Contemporary AI Models
Merve Tekgürler

Matching and Linking Entries in Historical Swedish Encyclopedias
Simon Börjesson, Erik Ersmark and Pierre Nugues

17:00 - 17:30 *Conclusion and SIGHUM Business Meeting*

Matching and Linking Entries in Historical Swedish Encyclopedias

Simon Börjesson[*], **Erik Ersmark**[*], **Pierre Nugues**
Lund University
Lund, Sweden
{si7405bo-s, er5612er-s}@student.lu.se, pierre.nugues@cs.lth.se

Abstract

The *Nordisk familjebok* is a Swedish encyclopedia from the 19th and 20th centuries. It was written by a team of experts and aimed to be an intellectual reference, stressing precision and accuracy. This encyclopedia had four main editions remarkable by their size, ranging from 20 to 38 volumes. As a consequence, the *Nordisk familjebok* had a considerable influence in universities, schools, the media, and society overall. As new editions were released, the selection of entries and their content evolved, reflecting intellectual changes in Sweden.

In this paper, we used digitized versions from *Project Runeberg*. We first resegmented the raw text into entries and matched pairs of entries between the first and second editions using semantic sentence embeddings. We then extracted the geographical entries from both editions using a transformer-based classifier and linked them to Wikidata. This enabled us to identify geographic trends and possible shifts between the first and second editions, written between 1876–1899 and 1904–1926, respectively.

Interpreting the results, we observe a small but significant shift in geographic focus away from Europe and towards North America, Africa, Asia, Australia, and northern Scandinavia from the first to the second edition, confirming the influence of the First World War and the rise of new powers. The code and data are available on GitHub at `https://github.com/sibbo/nordisk-familjebok`.

1 Introduction

Encyclopedias are semi-structured, information-rich bodies of knowledge. In the field of knowledge extraction, their organization into articles with a headword makes them easier to process.

Before the advent of the internet, major encyclopedias like the *Encyclopædia Britannica*, *Brockhaus Enzyklopädie*, and *Nordisk familjebok* regularly released new printed editions for decades or even centuries. Largely written by academics and experts, each edition reflects the knowledge base of the educated class in their respective region at that time. Through digitization efforts, many of these editions are available online.

The *Nordisk familjebok* is widely recognized as the most comprehensive and influential Swedish encyclopedia (Aronsson, 2003; Simonsen, 2016). The encyclopedia was published in four main editions between 1876 and 1993, with over 100 volumes and several hundred thousand articles. Starting in 2003, volunteers at *Project Runeberg*[1] scanned the paper volumes, applied an optical character recognition (OCR) to the images, and proofread a part of the entries.

Linking entries between editions to identify shared, added, and removed articles can indicate changes in the perception of information value or importance due to, e.g., world events or new technologies. One way of looking at this is the geographical spread of entries, i.e., if locations in some countries receive more or less attention over time. Linking entries to a graph database like Wikidata, which has coordinates listed for most entities tied to a location, can help highlight these trends.

The main contributions of our paper are:

1. We scraped and segmented the first and second editions of the *Nordisk familjebok* OCRed by *Project Runeberg*;
2. We classified the segmented entries to identify the locations and cross-references;
3. We matched pairs of entries between the two editions (first and second);
4. We linked entries from both editions to unique Wikidata identifiers;

[*]Equal contribution

[1]`https://runeberg.org/nf/`

Proceedings of LaTeCH-CLfL 2025, pages 1–10

5. We provide a brief interpretation of the changes in geographic focus from the first to the second edition.

Our code is available on GitHub: `https://github.com/sibbo/nordisk-familjebok`.

2 Previous Work

This work addresses three main problems: classifying entries, matching them across editions, and linking each entry to its counterpart in a knowledge graph like Wikidata. We outline relevant techniques and review previous work. Many of them use models trained on English. We also describe models specific to Swedish.

2.1 Categorizing Entries

In this work, we only considered entries describing a location. We extracted these entries using a supervised text categorization technique. Lewis et al. (2004) is an early example of such a technique with a large corpus, where the authors describe the annotation of one million newswires and baseline techniques to classify them.

CLD3[2] is a compact model created for language classification. It uses character n-grams as input to train a two-layer neural network model. Beyond language detection, CLD3 can be applied to other text classification tasks.

The transformer architecture (Vaswani et al., 2017) with the BERT encoder component (Devlin et al., 2019) reported state-of-the-art performances in the GLUE benchmark (Wang et al., 2018) for classification tasks. Through language model pretraining, BERT achieves an impressive understanding of language, enabling it to grasp complex semantic and contextual nuances. It thus decreases the necessary amount of annotated samples to reach high classification scores.

2.2 Matching Entries

Text matching refers to the quantification of the semantic similarity of a pair of documents, here encyclopedia entries. Applications of text matching include information retrieval and question answering. The TF-IDF document vectorization (Spärck Jones, 1972) is a baseline technique for representing documents, and the cosine similarity of two document vectors is a standard measure for evaluating their relatedness.

Dense vector representations of sentences or documents (Cordier, 1965) have proven to be better than sparse ones such as TF-IDF to encapsulate their semantics. Reimers and Gurevych (2019) showed they could train transformer models from pairs of similar sentences and embed them in the form of dense vectors reflecting their semantic proximity.

In our setup, we want to match pairs of corresponding articles between editions, which requires comparing similarity scores of embeddings. In the context of the *Nordisk familjebok*, the brute force method of comparing each article in one edition to all articles in the other quickly becomes unmanageable. With more than 100,000 articles per edition, this results in over 10^{10} comparisons.

Vector databases allow for much faster comparisons through efficient storage and indexing of vectors, employing algorithms like the hierarchical navigable small world algorithm and R-trees (Kukreja et al., 2023). Vector databases can use SBERT models to vectorize the documents or more elaborate algorithms such as those of Xiao et al. (2024), Meng et al. (2024), or Lee et al. (2024).

2.3 Adapting Models to Swedish

KB-BERT (Malmsten et al., 2020) is one of the Swedish BERT models developed at *Kungliga biblioteket* (KB), the National Library of Sweden. It is trained on a corpus of Swedish texts created between 1940-2019, including newspapers, government publications, e-books, social media posts, Swedish Wikipedia, and more. Using a teacher-student model with KB-BERT as the student model, they also created a Swedish sentence transformer, KB-SBERT v2.0 (Rekathati, 2023).

2.4 Linking Entries

Wikidata is a free online knowledge graph containing over 115 million items at the time of this study[3]. Each item has a unique QID and a number of property-value pairs that describe it. For example, Sweden's capital, Stockholm, has the QID `Q1754`, and its properties include `P625`, describing its coordinate location.

A few works have explored the task of linking named entities to Wikidata. Shanaz and Ragel (2021) linked persons mentioned in newspapers, and Nugues (2022) linked location entries from the French dictionary *Petit Larousse illustré* to their

[2] `https://github.com/google/cld3`

[3] `https://www.wikidata.org/wiki/Special:Statistics`

corresponding coordinates in Wikidata. Ahlin et al. (2024) undertook a similar task to this study, linking location entries from the second edition of the *Nordisk familjebok* to Wikidata.

3 Preprocessing

Project Runeberg is an online archive of old Scandinavian literature (Aronsson, 2023). This archive provides complete digital facsimiles and OCR texts of the first, second, and fourth editions of the *Nordisk familjebok*, and parts of the third. Volunteers have carried out a manual proofreading on the vast majority of the OCR texts of the first edition, and parts of the second edition, as well as creating a currently incomplete index over the entry headwords on each page.

3.1 Scraping

We scraped the web pages of the first and second editions of the *Nordisk familjebok* on the *Project Runeberg* website, with the exception of the supplements. We parsed the HTML pages so that we could extract the index of entries on each page, extracted the raw OCR text, and finally removed or replaced most HTML tags and uncommon Unicode characters.

3.2 Segmenting

The segmentation of the raw scraped text revealed a complex problem. While the entry headwords in the physical copies of the *Nordisk familjebok* are always in bold characters, there is often no corresponding markup in the digitized text from *Project Runeberg*, probably due to a rudimentary OCR conversion. This is especially true for the second edition, which at the time of this study had undergone less proofreading than the first edition. To deal with this, we devised a three-step approach:

1. **Bold matching**: If the paragraph begins with a bold tag, it is an entry.
2. **Index matching**: Else, if the paragraph does not begin with a bold tag but starts with a headword present in the index, it is an entry.
3. **Entry classification**: Otherwise, utilize a binary classifier model for entry classification.

Following Ahlin et al. (2024), who observed that excessively long texts negatively impacted the performance of their location classifier, we truncated entry texts to a maximum of 200 characters.

Some entries have numbered subentries under the same headword. This is notably the case with entries for noble lineages and royal houses, containing a list of people under the same family name, as for instance the *Leijonhufvud*[4] and *Natt och Dag*[5] families. For sake of simplicity, we did not consider subentries in this paper.

3.2.1 Bold Matching

We applied the rule that a paragraph is an entry if it begins with an HTML bold tag, `<b>`. The headword is chosen as the text between the opening bold tag `<b>` and the closing bold tag `</b>`, removing any trailing punctuation.

3.2.2 Index Matching

The index contains the headwords of all entries on a page. They are manually added by proof-readers, which invariably gives rise to human errors. This, together with OCR errors, makes strict character comparisons of index words and entry texts impractical.

We utilized the Levenshtein distance (Levenshtein, 1966) to match the index words to the raw text. We found that many of these index words were too long for absolute edit distance to fairly represent the similarity of these words. Therefore, we extended the Levenshtein distance metric to be relative to word length and, through manual testing, set a match threshold of 0.15.

With these prerequisites, the method greedily attempts to match the longest index word to a substring of the same character length, starting at the beginning of the paragraph. In the event of a match, the index word is chosen as the entry headword.

3.2.3 Entry Classification

We created an entry classifier from a reimplementation of Google's CLD3 architecture. This provided us a foundation for a general classification model that is well-suited for exploiting small semantic details in the texts.

Paragraphs in the scraped text that were indeed articles often contained distinctive features, such as punctuation and different types of parentheses. Therefore, we determined that a logistic head, instead of a two-layer network, would suffice for entry classification.

To create a training set, we leveraged the structure of the encyclopedias. Given that a paragraph

[4] `https://runeberg.org/nfai/0520.html`
[5] `https://runeberg.org/nfbs/0318.html`

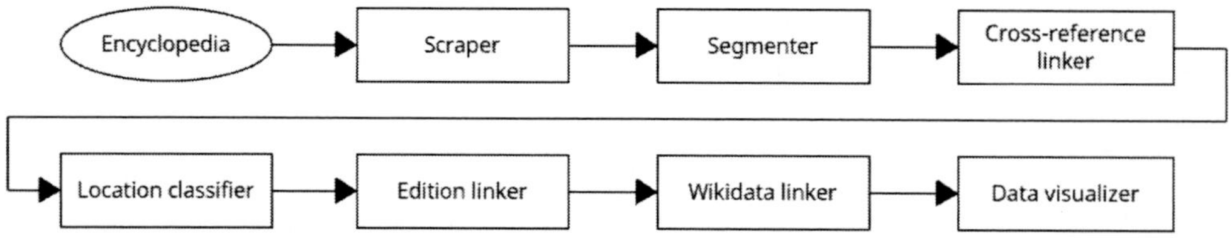

Figure 1: Overview of the pipeline.

beginning with a bold tag is almost certainly a valid entry, we used these paragraphs as ground truth for entries, removing bold tags in the process. Additionally, we used the fact that an encyclopedia is alphabetically ordered to find ground truth for non-entries. For example, in a volume, where all entries begin with the letter *K*, a paragraph starting with any other capital letter is a non-entry.

3.3 Cross-references

Many entries in the *Nordisk familjebok* are cross-references, entries that refer to another entry and provide little to no information on their own, e.g.:

> ***Nervtumör.*** *Se Nervsjukdomar.*
> "***Nerve tumor.*** *See Neurological disorder.*"

For the goals of the study, cross-references provided no value. Therefore, we developed a rule to annotate an entry as a cross-reference if the text was shorter than 60 characters and contained the substring ␣Se "See". We then extracted the word after ␣Se and matched this word to an entry with that exact headword. Some cross-references are longer than 60 characters, but these entries usually provide some information on their own, so we left them as is.

4 Method

Figure 1 shows the processing pipeline consisting of scraping, segmenting, linking cross-references, location classification, edition linking, Wikidata linking, and data visualization.

We described the preprocessing modules, scraping, segmenting and linking cross-references in Section 3. In this section, we describe the rest of the architecture.

4.1 Location Classifier

To determine the location entries, we trained a binary classifier. We manually annotated 200 entries to create a training set of locations and non-locations. We used KB-BERT to tokenize the entry texts and encode them as in Ahlin et al. (2024). We then fitted a logistic regression to the hidden states of the `[CLS]` token.

4.2 Matching Pairs of Entries

We matched the location entries of the first and second editions. We created sentence embeddings of the entries with the KB-SBERT model and used a Qdrant vector database[6] to store them. We then calculated the closest match using cosine similarity. For an entry from the first edition, we finally obtained a list of ranked candidates from the second. We used a greedy strategy and kept the first candidate.

Since always using the closest match leads to many false positives, especially for entries that only exist in one of the editions, we used a cosine similarity threshold value of 0.9 that maximized the F1 score on a manually annotated dataset of 200 entries.

This resulted in a list of matching pairs in the first and second editions of the *Nordisk familjebok* as well as lists of removed and added entries.

4.3 Wikidata Linking

We linked entries marked as locations to Wikidata items and retrieved their geographical coordinates. This consisted of two steps: querying Wikidata and linking texts.

4.3.1 Querying Wikidata

We queried the Wikidata API[7] with the entry headwords and chose the first five results. For each Wikidata item, we retrieved the first 200 characters of the corresponding Swedish Wikipedia article if available[8]. Otherwise, we used the Swedish Wikidata description. We designed our program to prefer Wikipedia texts, assuming that the more

[6] `https://qdrant.tech/`

[7] `https://www.wikidata.org/w/api.php`

[8] Using the Wikipedia API: `https://sv.wikipedia.org/w/api.php`

encyclopedic Wikipedia text would better match the entry texts.

4.3.2 Linking Texts

We encoded the segmented entry text and the retrieved texts of each Wikidata item with the KB-SBERT model, and we compared the encyclopedia entry to each item to find the highest cosine similarity score. Due to the limited search space of five items, we extended the method with a matching threshold, chosen through evaluation on two test sets consisting of 25 random locations from each edition, respectively. We achieved the best F1 scores with a threshold of 0.6.

Lastly, we retrieved the QID and the geographical coordinates using the coordinate location property (P625) of the best match that passed the threshold.

5 Results and Evaluation

Table 3 shows the precision and recall scores of all parts of the pipeline where applicable. Most precision and recall scores were acquired by evaluating validation sets of 25, 50 or 100 random entries either in the encyclopedias or in the JSON files. These validation sets should give a general idea of the performance of each part. Nonetheless, their size is relatively small and larger sets would certainly improve their reliability and statistical significance.

5.1 Segmenter

In Table 1, we can see that the second edition has roughly double the number of entries compared to the first one. The number of matches we obtained with the index and classifier strategies is very low in the first edition, since it has been proofread almost completely.

Christensson (2005) estimates the number of entries in the first edition to 103,000. The disparity between this and our 84,534 entries is likely due to not segmenting supplemental volumes.

Ahlin et al. (2024) report the extraction of 130,383 entries when segmenting the second edition, while Simonsen (2016) estimates over 182,000 headwords. Both included supplemental volumes, which we chose to exclude, but like us, they also omitted subentries. We believe the difference from the former is due to using index matching and a binary classifier for entries without bold tags, and the discrepancy from the latter again is mainly due to not segmenting the supplemental volumes.

In combination with the recall and precision scores for segmenting in Table 3, we can be relatively certain that these numbers are good estimates for the total number of entries in the encyclopedias, excluding subentries and supplemental volumes.

5.2 Cross-references

Table 3 shows the performance of linking cross-references to their referenced entry. The method was quite simple, and gave rise to some errors, most notably linking the cross-reference to an incorrect entry with the same headword. For example, in the second edition, *Bajesid* is listed as an alternate spelling of a lineage of sultans in the Ottoman Empire:

> ***Bajesid,*** *turkiska sultaner. Se Bajasid.*
> *"**Bajesid,** Turkish sultans. See Bajasid."*

However, when trying to find the referenced entry *Bajasid*, another cross-reference for the city of the same name is matched:

> ***Bajasid,*** *stad. Se Bajaset.*
> *"**Bajasid,** city. See Bajaset."*

This is because the first entry with an exact headword match is chosen. For the purpose of removing redundant entries, we believe the performance of our method is satisfactory, but it could probably be improved by using a named entity recognizer.

5.3 Location Classifier

In Table 2, the ratio of locations in both editions is very similar, and the ratio in the second edition is almost identical to that of Ahlin et al. (2024)

Ed.	Entries	Bold	Index	Classifier
1st	84,534	97.7%	2.14%	0.17%
2nd	150,340	76.0%	11.5%	12.5%

Table 1: The total number of entries segmented for both editions, and the proportion of entries segmented using each of the three strategies.

Ed.	Entries	Locations	Proportion
1st	84,534	18,932	22.4%
2nd	150,340	32,378	21.6%

Table 2: The total number of entries segmented for both editions, the number of entries classified as locations, and the corresponding proportions.

Method	First edition			Second edition		
	Precision	Recall	F1-score	Precision	Recall	F1-score
Segmenter, weighted mean[2]	≈1.0	1.0	1.0	0.99	0.94	0.96
Bold matching[2]	1.0	1.0	1.0	1.0	1.0	1.0
Index matching[2]	0.96	-	-	0.94	-	-
Entry classifier[4]	0.95	0.95	0.95	*	*	*
Cross-references[3]	1.0	0.85	0.92	1.0	0.75	0.86
Location classifier[1]	0.84	0.96	0.90	0.92	0.92	0.92
Entry matching[4]	0.85	0.83	0.83	*	*	*
Baseline: headword match[3]	0.74	0.81	0.76	*	*	*
Wikidata linking						
QID match[1]	0.40	0.52	0.45	0.48	0.16	0.24
Within 25 km[1]	0.76	0.64	0.69	0.84	0.40	0.54

[1] 25 entries used, [2] 50 entries used, [3] 100 entries used, [4] Used respective training/test data, '-' : The metric was not applicable, '*' : The values are the same for both editions.

Table 3: Performance metrics of the pipeline for both editions

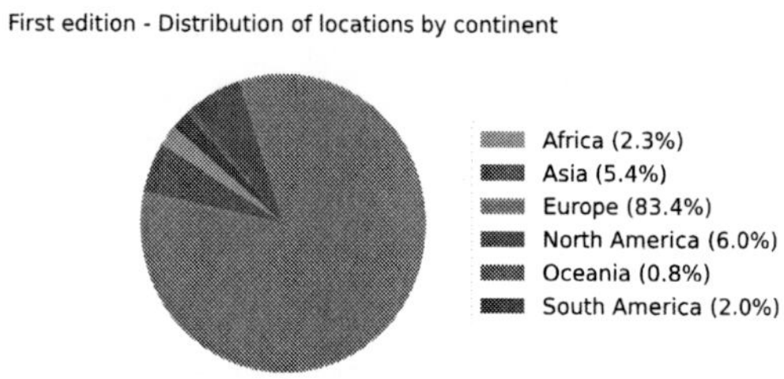

(a) Distribution of locations by continent in the first edition.

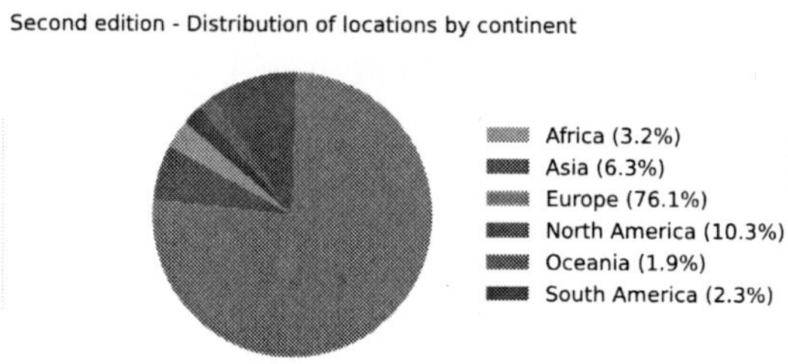

(b) Distribution of locations by continent in the second edition.

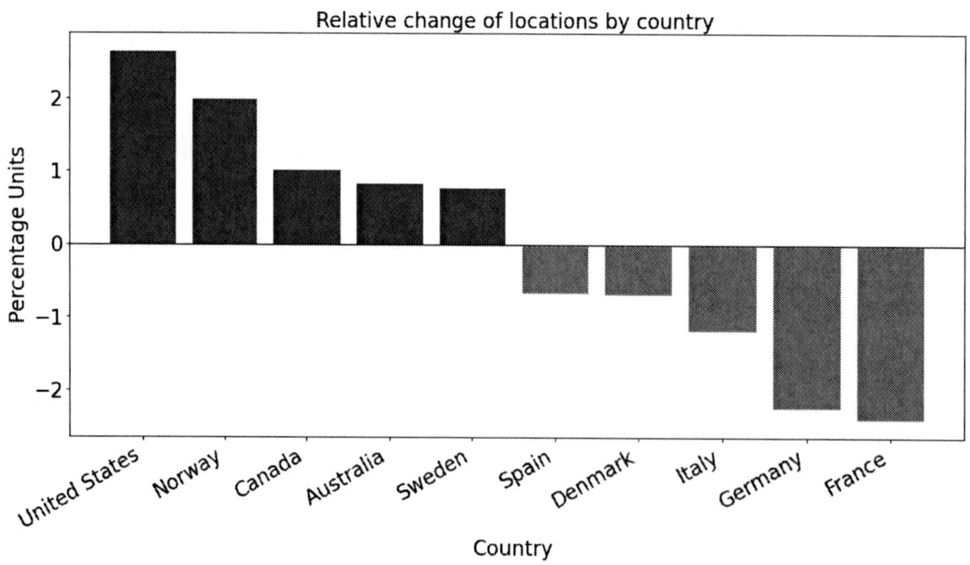

(c) The top five countries with the largest percentage unit increase (blue), top five countries with the largest percentage unit decrease (red), in location counts from the first edition to the second edition.

Figure 2: Location-related statistics from both editions.

Locations in the first and second editions

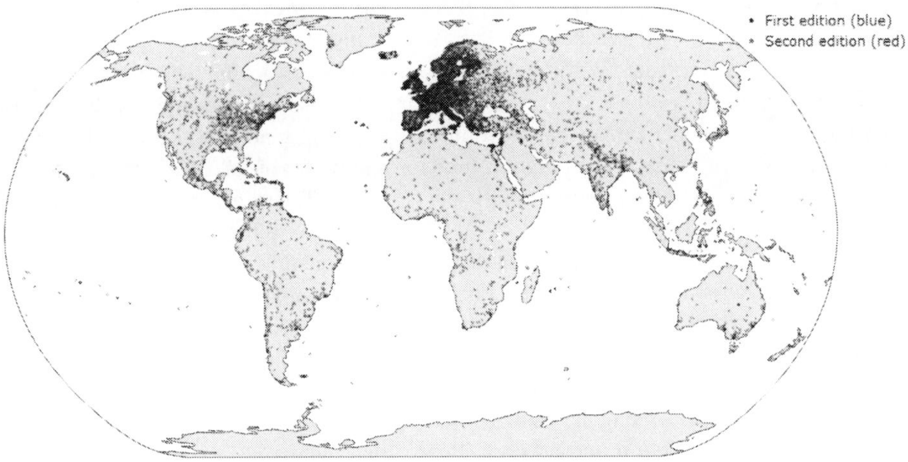

Figure 3: Geographic distribution of locations in both editions.

(21.7%), which is expected since the same method was used.

Table 3 shows the F1 scores of the location classifier for both editions. We can see that they match or surpass 0.9, which is notable considering the KB-BERT model was not fine-tuned for this task.

5.4 Matching Entries

The performance metrics presented in Table 3 demonstrate that our matching approach performs better than the baseline model (headword match) across all metrics, albeit not significantly. We had anticipated a more pronounced performance improvement from the more advanced KB-SBERT model compared to the simple baseline model.

By examining matched sentences, it becomes apparent why certain errors occur. For instance, our method erroneously matched the following two entries, *Åker* and *Åsenhöga*:

> ***Åker.*** *1. Socken i Jönköpings län, Östbo härad. Areal 15,842 har. 1,798 innev. (1892). Å. bildar med...*
> "***Åker.*** *1. Parish in Jönköping county, Östbo hundred. Acreage 15,842 ha. 1,798 res. (1892). Å. forms with...*"

and

> ***Åsenhöga,*** *socken i Jönköpings län, Mo härad. 12,960 har. 1,257 inv. (1921). Å. bildar med...*
> "***Åsenhöga,*** *estate in Jönköping county, Mo hundred. 12,960 ha. 1,257 res. (1921). Å. forms with...*"

These entries exhibit strikingly similar semantic structures, with comparable word sets, order, and article topic. Scenarios like these are understandably difficult, and frequently occur in the corpus.

5.5 Wikidata Linking

When linking an entry to Wikidata, the best cosine similarity match was often not with the correct entity, but with a place or object not very far away, usually within only a few kilometers. A common error was matching a *socken*, an old Swedish term for a church parish, to a nearby city, municipality, or building with the same or a very similar name. For example,

> ***Öved,*** *socken i Malmöhus län...*
> "***Öved,*** *parish in Malmöhus county...*"

was linked to *Övedsklosters slott*, a castle within the borders of the parish.

It is difficult to understand why this match yielded the highest cosine similarity score, but such linking errors make little difference on a global scale. Therefore, we created a metric to check if the matched Wikidata entity was within 25 kilometers of the correct coordinates. Although this metric significantly improved performance for both editions, especially the second, the results in Table 3 remain quite poor. Even though only about half of all locations in the encyclopedias were linked within 25 km of their correct coordinates, it seems reasonable to assume that the overall distribution of locations remains roughly the same.

In Figure 2, we see a slight shift in focus away from large European countries like France, Germany, and Italy, towards primarily North America, Australia, Norway, and Sweden. We provide a brief interpretation of this in Section 6.2.

Another source of error stems from the limited search space we set to reduce computation time, which occasionally caused the program to miss the correct Wikidata item.

The search functionality in Wikidata can be unreliable, especially for uncommon entries. For instance, finding the Russian location *Migulinskaya* required using Cyrillic characters. Additionally, Sweden introduced a spelling reform around the turn of the 19th century. Among the changes was replacing the letter *q* with *k* in most words (Pettersson, 2005). For example, *Qvenneberga* in the first edition became *Kvenneberga* in the second one. Such small spelling changes can be crucial: The first term yielded no search results, while the second one resulted in a few hits. Altogether, these quirks can lead to search results missing valid entries, complicating the process of finding specific items.

6 Discussion

6.1 Applications of Entry Matching

The potential applications of matching entries across the editions of the *Nordisk familjebok* are significant, especially in the context of digitization and preserving the relevance of this cultural artifact.

One potential application is the development of a search system based entirely on the editions of the *Nordisk familjebok*. This concept is currently being explored at the Centre for Digital Humanities at Gothenburg University.[9] Such a system could greatly benefit from the inter-edition links developed in this work, enabling comprehensive search results across all editions from a single query.

Another application of our pipeline that could improve the accessibility of historical encyclopedias in the digital age is to extend Wikipedia pages with links to corresponding entries in digital facsimiles of encyclopedias.

6.2 Geographic Focus

Given the rapid globalization since the first edition, we expected a more even geographic distribution in the second edition due to its later publication date. Figures 2a and 2b confirm this hypothesis. The historical events that unfolded during the publication time frame of the editions could illuminate the reasons behind the observed changes.

The First World War involved many countries worldwide, including Canada, Australia, the United States, Japan, and various European colonies in Africa. The involvement of these regions in the war may have influenced Swedish societal discourse, consequently affecting the content of the second edition (Snape, 2018).

Figure 2c shows an increase in the number of locations situated in Norway and northern Sweden. From the late 19th century to the mid-20th century, Norway and northern Sweden underwent significant industrialization in hydroelectric (Thomson, 1938) and timber production (Sundvall, 2023), respectively. Consequently, the population of these regions increased, which may explain these additions in the second edition.

Furthermore, Figures 2c and 3 depict a relative decrease of location mentions for several European countries in the second edition. However, since the second edition contains more locations overall, it does not imply that the absolute number of location mentions has decreased for these countries.

7 Conclusion

In this paper, we compared two editions of a historical Swedish encyclopedia. We described the corpus collection, the segmentation of the raw text input into entries, the categorization of entries, and how we matched pairs of entries between the two editions. We finally reported how we linked geographical entries from both editions to Wikidata.

In the classification and matching tasks, we used transformer models with parameters pre-trained on modern Swedish. A possible improvement is to fine-tune the models on older Swedish texts. We could also explore alternative algorithms for matching entries, such as the Hungarian algorithm (Kuhn, 1955).

This work enabled us to identify shifts between the two editions and a few geographic trends. Most notably, the second edition reflects the evolution of the geographic awareness toward a more diverse global outlook. Beyond the historical events mentioned in Section 6.2, there may be countless societal, cultural, political, and economic factors contributing to these changes. We hope our work will invite further investigation to provide a better un-

[9] `https://nordiskfamiljebok.dh.gu.se/`

derstanding of the context surrounding them.

Limitations

Our evaluation of headword detection and entry matching is limited and a comprehensive study would include more data. Our validation sets should give a general idea of the performance of each part. Nonetheless, their size is relatively small and larger sets would certainly improve their reliability and statistical significance.

Large language models that we used in this research may generate classification errors or show bias. This bias may come from the corpus used for training the models, mostly contemporary Swedish, while we applied them to the *Nordisk familjebok* that uses a slightly different language.

Ethics Statement

We identified a few potential risks:

1. The *Nordisk familjebok* belongs to book history. It sometimes includes old-fashioned viewpoints and its information is dated.

2. This encyclopedia was written in a different historical context. A few entries may include content that can now be considered offensive. Potential users of our work or of applications based on it must be aware of this context.

Acknowledgments

We would like to thank the anonymous reviewers for their suggestions and comments.

This work was partially supported by *Vetenskapsrådet*, the Swedish Research Council, registration number 2021-04533.

References

Axel Ahlin, Alfred Myrne Blåder, and Pierre Nugues. 2024. Mapping the past: Geographically linking an early 20th century Swedish encyclopedia with Wikidata. In *Proceedings of the 2024 Joint International Conference on Computational Linguistics, Language Resources and Evaluation (LREC-COLING 2024)*, pages 11040–11048, Torino, Italia. ELRA and ICCL.

Lars Aronsson. 2003. Preface to the digital facsimile edition. Last accessed 2024-06-07.

Lars Aronsson. 2023. About Project Runeberg. Last accessed 2024-06-03.

Jakob Christensson. 2005. I encyklopediernas trollkrets: Om Bernhard Meijer och Nordisk familjebok. *Biblis*, 2005(32):32–49.

Brigitte Cordier. 1965. Factor-analysis of correspondences. In *COLING 1965*.

Jacob Devlin, Ming-Wei Chang, Kenton Lee, and Kristina Toutanova. 2019. BERT: Pre-training of deep bidirectional transformers for language understanding. In *Proceedings of the 2019 Conference of the North American Chapter of the Association for Computational Linguistics: Human Language Technologies, Volume 1 (Long and Short Papers)*, pages 4171–4186, Minneapolis, Minnesota. Association for Computational Linguistics.

Harold W Kuhn. 1955. The Hungarian method for the assignment problem. *Naval research logistics quarterly*, 2(1-2):83–97.

Sanjay Kukreja, Tarun Kumar, Vishal Bharate, Amit Purohit, Abhijit Dasgupta, and Debashis Guha. 2023. Vector databases and vector embeddings-review. In *2023 International Workshop on Artificial Intelligence and Image Processing (IWAIIP)*, pages 231–236. IEEE.

Chankyu Lee, Rajarshi Roy, Mengyao Xu, Jonathan Raiman, Mohammad Shoeybi, Bryan Catanzaro, and Wei Ping. 2024. NV-Embed: Improved techniques for training LLMs as generalist embedding models. *Preprint*, arXiv:2405.17428.

Vladimir Levenshtein. 1966. Binary Codes Capable of Correcting Deletions, Insertions and Reversals. *Soviet Physics Doklady*, 10:707–710.

David D. Lewis, Yiming Yang, Tony G. Rose, and Fan Li. 2004. RCV1: A new benchmark collection for text categorization research. *Journal of Machine Learning Research*, 5:361–397.

Martin Malmsten, Love Börjeson, and Chris Haffenden. 2020. Playing with words at the National Library of Sweden–making a Swedish BERT. *arXiv preprint arXiv:2007.01658*.

Rui Meng, Ye Liu, Shafiq Rayhan Joty, Caiming Xiong, Yingbo Zhou, and Semih Yavuz. 2024. SFR-Embedding-2: Advanced text embedding with multi-stage training.

Pierre Nugues. 2022. Connecting a French dictionary from the beginning of the 20th century to Wikidata. In *Proceedings of the Thirteenth Language Resources and Evaluation Conference*, pages 2548–2555, Marseille, France. European Language Resources Association.

Gertrud Pettersson. 2005. *Svenska språket under sjuhundra år: En historia om svenskan och dess utforskande*, 2nd edition. Studentlitteratur, Lund.

Nils Reimers and Iryna Gurevych. 2019. Sentence-BERT: Sentence embeddings using Siamese BERT-networks. In *Proceedings of the 2019 Conference on Empirical Methods in Natural Language Processing and the 9th International Joint Conference on Natural Language Processing (EMNLP-IJCNLP)*, pages

3982–3992, Hong Kong, China. Association for Computational Linguistics.

Faton Rekathati. 2023. The KBLab blog: Swedish sentence transformer 2.0. Last accessed 2024-06-05.

Abdul Lathif Fathima Shanaz and Roshan G. Ragel. 2021. Wikidata based person entity linking in news articles. In *2021 10th International Conference on Information and Automation for Sustainability (ICIAfS)*, pages 66–70.

Maria Simonsen. 2016. *Den skandinaviske encyklopædi: Udgivelse og udformning af Nordisk familjebok & Salmonsens konversationslexikon*. Centrum för Öresundsstudier (Print), 37. Makadam i samarbete med Centrum för Öresundsstudier vid Lunds universitet, Göteborg ; Stockholm.

Michael Snape. 2018. Anglicanism and interventionism: Bishop Brent, the United States, and the British empire in the First World War. *The Journal of Ecclesiastical History*, 69(2):300–325.

Karen Spärck Jones. 1972. A statistical interpretation of term specificity and its application in retrieval. *Journal of Documentation*, 28(1):11–21.

Samuel Sundvall. 2023. Migration and decentralised industrialisation: The development of rural migration in northern Sweden (1850–1950). *Rural History*, pages 1–20.

Claudia Thomson. 1938. Norway's industrialization. *Economic Geography*, 14(4):372–380.

Ashish Vaswani, Noam Shazeer, Niki Parmar, Jakob Uszkoreit, Llion Jones, Aidan N Gomez, Łukasz Kaiser, and Illia Polosukhin. 2017. Attention is all you need. *Advances in Neural Information Processing Systems*, 30.

Alex Wang, Amanpreet Singh, Julian Michael, Felix Hill, Omer Levy, and Samuel Bowman. 2018. GLUE: A multi-task benchmark and analysis platform for natural language understanding. In *Proceedings of the 2018 EMNLP Workshop BlackboxNLP: Analyzing and Interpreting Neural Networks for NLP*, pages 353–355, Brussels, Belgium. Association for Computational Linguistics.

Shitao Xiao, Zheng Liu, Peitian Zhang, Niklas Muennighoff, Defu Lian, and Jian-Yun Nie. 2024. C-Pack: Packed resources for general Chinese embeddings. In *Proceedings of the 47th International ACM SIGIR Conference on Research and Development in Information Retrieval*, SIGIR '24, page 641–649, New York, NY, USA. Association for Computing Machinery.

Preserving Comorian Linguistic Heritage: Bidirectional Transliteration Between the Latin Alphabet and the Kamar-Eddine System

Naira Abdou Mohamed[1,2], **Abdessalam Bahafid**[1,2], **Zakarya Erraji**[1], **Anass Allak**[1], **Naoufal Mohamed Soibira**[3], **Imade Benelallam**[1,2]
[1] INSEA, Rabat, Morocco [2] ToumAI Analytics, Rabat, Morocco
[3] Sciences Po Grenoble, Grenoble, France
{nabdoumohamed,i.benelallam,a.bahafid,zerraji,aallak}@insea.ac.ma
{naira,imade,abahafid}@toum.ai

Abstract

The Comoros Islands, rich in linguistic diversity, are home to dialects derived from Swahili and influenced by Arabic. Historically, the Kamar-Eddine system, based on the Arabic alphabet, was one of the first writing systems used for Comorian. However, it has gradually been replaced by the Latin alphabet, even though numerous archival texts are written in this system, and older speakers continue to use it, highlighting its cultural and historical significance. In this article, we present Shialifube, a bidirectional transliteration tool between Latin and Arabic scripts, designed in accordance with the rules of the Kamar-Eddine system. To evaluate its performance, we applied a round-trip transliteration technique, achieving a word error rate of 14.84% and a character error rate of 9.56%. These results demonstrate the reliability of our system for complex tasks. Furthermore, Shialifube was tested in a practical case related to speech recognition, showcasing its potential in Natural Language Processing. This project serves as a bridge between tradition and modernity, contributing to the preservation of Comorian linguistic heritage while paving the way for better integration of local dialects into advanced technologies.

1 Introduction

At the crossroads of Africa, Europe, the Middle East, and Southeast Asia (Abeid et al., 2024; Allibert, 2015), the Comoros stand out for their rich cultural heritage, a diversity particularly evident in local dialects that share remarkable similarities with several foreign languages. While these dialects belong to the Bantu family due to their closer affinity with Swahili (Ahmed Chamanga, 2022) and the Sabaki language group (Serva and Pasquini, 2021), they also exhibit similarities with Arabic. This is partly why, like Swahili with the Ajami script (Mugane, 2017), one of the earliest writing systems for Comorian dialects is based on the Arabic script (Lafon, 2007).

Known as the Kamar-Eddine system, this writing system was introduced in the 1960s by linguist Sheikh Ahmed Kamar-Eddine. Although the Latin alphabet is now predominantly used to write Comorian, a minority, primarily older individuals, are only proficient in the Arabic script. Furthermore, many manuscripts are written in this script, emphasizing its historical and cultural significance.

Having a solution to process this system could serve three major purposes: (a) Democratizing access to Natural Language Processing (NLP) technologies, making Comorian dialects accessible to a broader audience, especially those without access to modern digital tools; (b) Preserving and promoting the multicultural richness of the archipelago, highlighting the Kamar-Eddine system as a fundamental element of Comorian linguistic and cultural heritage; (c) Making Comorian national archives accessible to all, facilitating their digitization and long-term preservation while paving the way for new research and applications in NLP.

This work aims to initiate NLP research for this writing system, with the hope of contributing to the preservation of Comorian intangible heritage. More concretely, our main contributions can be summarized as follows:

- **Complementary Study**: This work builds on Michel Lafon's article (Lafon, 2007), which, to the best of our knowledge, is the only study conducted on the Kamar-Eddine system.
- **Foundational Exploration**: We contribute to the introduction of NLP not only for this writing system but also for the processing of Comorian, a language still underrepresented in this field.
- **Shared Innovation**: We make the results of this work accessible by sharing the developed code and models, enabling the community to benefit from our progress.

Proceedings of LaTeCH-CLfL 2025, pages 11–18
May 4, 2025 ©2025 Association for Computational Linguistics

2 About ShiKomori

Comorian, or ShiKomori, consists of four dialects, each spoken on a specific island: ShiNgazidja, ShiMwali, ShiNdzuani, and ShiMaore. While ideally, each dialect would be treated individually, this work addresses Comorian as a whole, without distinguishing between its dialectal variations. Two main reasons justify this choice:

- **High Similarities Between Dialects**: The dialects are very closely related (Ahmed Chamanga, 2022). Consequently, a speaker from one island can understand a dialect spoken on another island with little difficulty due to the largely shared lexicon across these variants. This strong similarity facilitates the development of NLP solutions that can generalize across all dialects.

- **Data Scarcity**: It is challenging to find dialect-specific corpora due to the limited research conducted in this field. Furthermore, speakers often prefer writing in French rather than using their local dialects, further restricting access to data.

The high similarities among these dialects, combined with the significant lack of data, make it more practical to treat them as a single language. Attempting to develop solutions for each dialect individually would require working with small, separate corpora, which might not suffice for training effective models. Instead, this approach leverages data-rich dialects to improve performance on those with fewer resources.

This strategy aligns with the findings of Lin et al. (Lin et al., 2019), which explored multilingual transfer learning as a means to improve low-resource language representation by leveraging a well-resourced language with significant similarities. Additionally, the system introduced by Kamar-Eddine considers Comorian as a unified language, with no specific rules tailored to individual dialects.

3 Related Work

Comorian is a language that has been very little studied in the field of NLP. While some previous works have provided solutions addressing it for various use cases (Abdourahamane et al., 2016; Naira et al., 2024), to the best of our knowledge, there is no computational linguistics research that deals with the language in its Arabic script.

Beyond our desire to preserve this intangible heritage, there is a motivation arising from observations made in previous works, such as those found in (Micallef et al., 2023). The latter describes experiments conducted on Maltese in which a curious observation was made: in several tasks (named entity recognition, sentiment analysis, etc.), transliteration into Arabic characters significantly improved the performance of models. The reason for this is that although Maltese is written in Latin characters and contains Italian loanwords, it remains a Semitic language closely related to Arabic. The proximity of Comorian to Arabic thus justifies the exploration of whether existing NLP solutions could be enhanced by adopting a similar approach.

In the absence of work specifically addressing Comorian written in Arabic script, we present in Table 1 a few notable studies that have dealt with the topic of transliteration in general, and particularly for African languages.

4 The Kamar-Eddine System

The standardization of Comorian writing became a priority in the years following the independence of the Comoros archipelago (Chamanga and Gueunier, 1977). While the idea of establishing specific rules for each dialect was quickly abandoned, the debate over whether to use the Latin or Arabic alphabet sparked intense discussions. On one hand, only a small minority of the population, educated in French, the colonial language, knew how to read the Latin alphabet and thus advocated for its use. On the other hand, the majority, having received an education primarily in Quranic schools, were proficient in reading the Arabic alphabet. With public opinion in favor of the latter, Arabic was quickly adopted for the translation of official documents.

However, it is important to note that, despite the widespread use of this alphabet, there were no fixed rules governing its application. It was precisely in this context that Ahmed Kamar-Eddine conceived the idea of standardizing this writing system. He began this project by publishing chronicles in his journal Mwando (see the manuscript of the first edition in Figure 1).

Title	Year	Description
Moroccan Arabizi-to-Arabic conversion using rule-based transliteration and weighted Levenshtein algorithm (Hajbi et al., 2024)	2024	It is a system of transliteration from Arabizi (Moroccan dialectal Arabic written in Latin characters) to Arabic characters. The method used uses the Levenshtein distance.
Exploring the Impact of Transliteration on NLP Performance: Treating Maltese as an Arabic Dialect (Micallef et al., 2023)	2023	Improving the state of the art TAL on several tasks by processing Maltese written in Arabic characters.
A Unified Model for Arabizi Detection and Transliteration using Sequence-to-Sequence Models (Shazal et al., 2020)	2020	Pipeline for detecting Arabizi in a text with code switches (Arabic mixed with other languages, all written in Latin characters) and transliteration into Arabic characters.
Arabizi Chat Alphabet Transliteration to Algerian Dialect (Klouche and Benslimane, 2020)	2020	Transliteration into Arabic characters of comments on the Algerian telephone operator Ooredoo in order to train a sentiment analysis model.

Table 1: Previous work on transliteration into Arabic scripts.

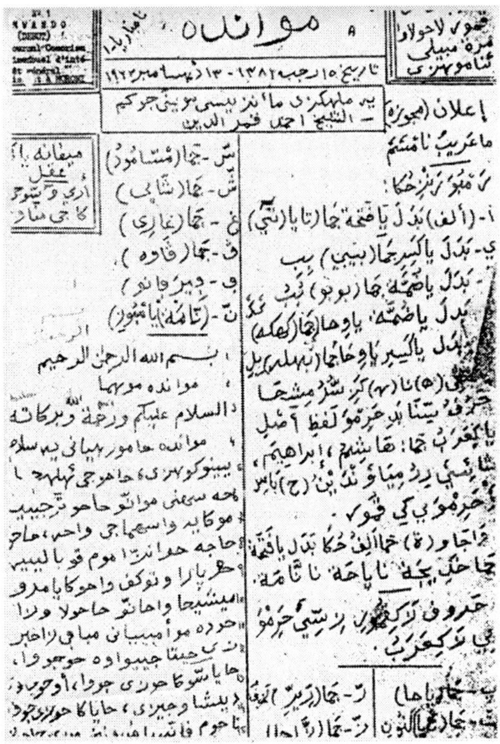

Figure 1: The Mwando Chronicles Manuscript: A historical document showcasing the first application of the Kamar-Eddine system, marking its inaugural use for formalizing the transcription of the Comorian language in Arabic script. The manuscript also describes the writing rules of the system, notably the introduction of long vowels.

Vowels	Transcription	Meaning
na	نَجم (najm)	star
ni	نِظام (nizām)	system
nu	نُور (nūr)	light

Table 2: Diacritics in Arabic writing.

4.1 The first adaptations in Arabic scripts

The Arabic alphabet has the particularity of being an abjad[1]. There are three vowels in Arabic, /a/, /i/, and /u/, represented respectively by the diacritics *fatha*, *kasra*, and *dhamma* (see examples in Table 2). The absence of a vowel is represented by a *sukun*, as in the word بِنْت (bint), which means "girl".

This particularity of Arabic, having only three vowels, poses a challenge when adapting certain languages to this script. This is precisely the case for Wolof, which contains nine vowels (Currah, 2015), Swahili (Raia, 2021), and Comorian (Lafon, 2007). For the latter, there are also additional consonants that do not exist in the Arabic alphabet. To address these specificities, certain adaptations were introduced in the early attempts. Among them were:

- **Introduction of additional characters**: Bor-

[1] A writing system in which characters represent consonants, and vowels are either implied or marked with optional diacritics. Scripts like Arabic and Hebrew are examples of abjads. Unlike full alphabets, abjads do not assign separate letters to vowel sounds.

rowings were made from Persian for representing sounds such as /v/ (ڤ), /g/ (ڠ), and /p/ (پ). However, ambiguities persisted, as the sound /pv/ was sometimes transcribed as ڤ (like /v/) or ف (like /f/).

- **Representation of vowels**: Comorian, with its five vowels /a/, /e/, /i/, /o/, and /u/, required measures to address the absence of /o/ and /e/ in Arabic. These vowels were marked by either using diacritics or resorting to long vowels, و for /o/ and ي for /e/. Yet, this also led to ambiguities in some cases, as terms like "mezi" (month) and "mizi" (roots) were written the same way (مِزِ or ميزي when using long vowels).

4.2 Kamar-Eddine's Original Innovations

To address the ambiguities observed in previous adaptation attempts, one of the solutions proposed by Kamar-Eddine was to abandon diacritics in favor of long vowels. The vowels /a/, /i/, and /u/ retain their original forms, while /e/ and /o/ are represented respectively by ـہـ and ہ. This categorically resolves certain cases of confusion, such as the last example discussed in the previous subsection. With this correction, the term mezi becomes مـہـزي, and mizi becomes ميزي.

Until then, there had been no clear representation of affricates, which are nonetheless frequent in Comorian. Kamar-Eddine proposed using the *shadda* to accentuate these consonants (see Table 3). Finally, we summarize all the identified rules in Table 4.

5 Methodology

Today, unless it has escaped our notice, there is no Comorian database written in Arabic script. To evaluate the effectiveness of our system, we are therefore compelled to rely solely on Latin-script texts[2] as references. Comprising 17,000 entries (sentences, words, and expressions), the dataset is first used to transliterate into Arabic by applying the rules based on the constructed dictionary. We then perform reverse transliteration to recover the original text. To assess the quality of our system, we use Word Error Rate (WER) and Character Error Rate (CER) as metrics.

The Figure 2 summarizes the pipeline through which an input text passes during the inference of our tool. First, we use computation rules to detect the type of script used, whether it is Arabic or Latin. This determines which dictionary to load (arabic_latin or latin_arabic). Then, once the script type and the corresponding dictionary are identified, we perform the transliteration followed by a reverse transliteration to attempt to regenerate the original text. This allows us to calculate round-trip transliteration scores to measure the confidence of the transliteration. Thus, two elements are returned as output: the transliteration and its confidence score.

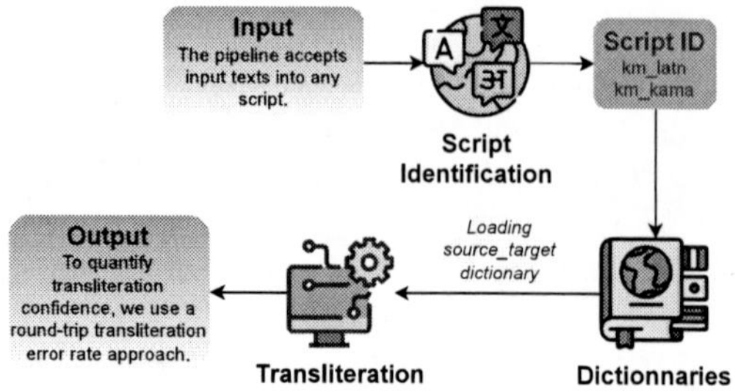

Figure 2: Global Pipeline: the system takes as input a raw text with the possibility to specify the source and target scripts. When no source is specified, a script identification model is used, and then, depending on the detected source, a dictionary is loaded. We use a round-trip transliteration error rate to measure the reliability of the transliteration.

5.1 From Latin to Arabic

The first step of this approach involves identifying the Latin digraphs present in the string and replacing them with their equivalents in Arabic script using a pre-established correspondence dictionary. This step effectively transforms specific sounds represented by two characters into a single appropriate Arabic symbol, such as the digraphs "sh" or "pv" To understand why this is important, imagine we want to transliterate the term shama (association). Failing to identify digraphs at the outset would result in treating sh as two separate letters (interpreting s as س and h as ح), which is a critical error. Instead of this reasoning, we transliterate sh into ش and then process the rest, where each remaining Latin character is converted into its Arabic equivalent according to a second correspondence dictionary for isolated characters, thereby ensuring coverage of sounds not represented by digraphs.

[2] https://huggingface.co/datasets/nairaxo/shikomori-texts

Sound	Transcription	Example	Translation
/ny/	نّ	نّاما	meat
/tr/	تّ	تّونكو	grass
/dz/	زّ	مزّو	burden

Table 3: Use of shadda to represent affricates.

Regular Alphabet						Digraphs / Affricates		
Sound	**Arabic**	**Latin**	**Sound**	**Arabic**	**Latin**	**Sound**	**Arabic**	**Latin**
/a/	ا	a	/m/	م	m	/ð/	ذ	dh
/ɓ/ or /b/	ب	b or ɓ	/n/	ن	n	/ɖ/	رّ	dr
/t͡ʃ/	شّ	c	/o/	ە	o	/d͡z/	زّ	dz
/ɗ/ or /d/	د	ɗ or d	/p/	پ	p	/ʈ/	تّ	tr
/e/	ـٜ	e	/r/	ر	r	/ɲ/	نّ	ny
/f/	ف	f	/s/	س	s	/ʃ/	ش	sh
/g/	ڠ	g	/t/	ت	t	/β/	ڥ	pv
/h/	ح	h	/u/	و	u	/θ/	ث	th
/i/	ي	i	/v/	ڤ	v	/t͡s/	سّ	ts
/d͡ʒ/	ج	j	/w/	و	w			
/k/	ك	k	/y/	ي	y			

Table 4: Table of correspondences between sounds, Arabic script, and Latin script.

5.2 From Arabic to Latin

We perform the transliteration of a string from Arabic script to a Latin representation by applying several specific transformations. This process also involves replacing Arabic letters that need to be represented by Latin digraphs with their equivalents. Next, the algorithm handles special Arabic characters such as the symbol ە, replacing them with the appropriate Latin characters and managing specific combinations like ـيٜ to ensure phonetically accurate transliteration.

After segmenting the string into individual characters, the algorithm applies a set of specific rules to handle letters used as long vowels, such as و and ي. For instance, if و is used not as a long vowel but as the letter representing the sound /w/, it is replaced by w; otherwise, it is replaced by u. Similarly, for ي, the transliterations y and i are applied to represent the sound /y/ and the long vowel /i/, respectively. Finally, the string is reassembled to produce the final Latin-script version, adhering to the phonetic and graphical conventions of the target language.

5.3 System Evaluation

WER is a common metric used to evaluate the accuracy of an automatic speech recognition or machine translation system. It indicates the rate of errors in the transcription produced compared to a reference transcription. WER accounts for multiple types of errors, including insertions, deletions, and substitutions of words. Lower WER values indicate better performance, meaning the system has fewer errors compared to the reference. WER ranges from 0 to 100%. The formula to compute it is as follows:

$$WER = \frac{S + D + I}{N} \tag{1}$$

where:

- **S**: the number of substituted words (incorrect substitutions),
- **D**: the number of deleted words (omissions),
- **I**: the number of inserted words (incorrect additions),
- **N**: the total number of words in the reference transcription.

The same formula is used to compute the CER, which measures the substitution rate at the character level instead of the word level. While both metrics measure the performance of a system like ours,

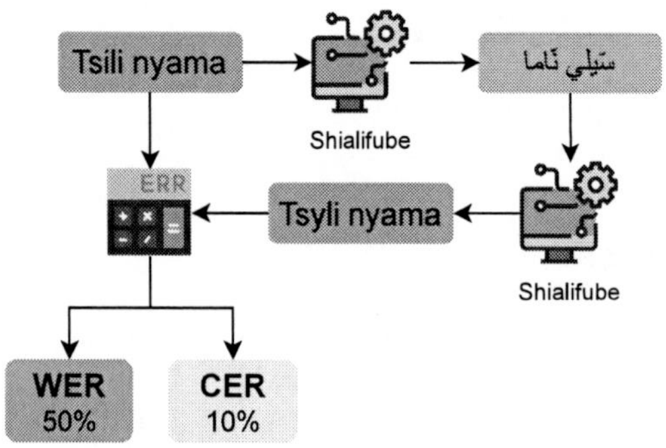

Figure 3: Example of round-trip transliteration and calculation of performance metrics.

they do not necessarily serve the same purpose. For instance, WER tends to measure orthographic divergence between two texts. Let us consider the following example: سّيلي نّاما (I ate meat). It might happen that during transliteration, this phrase is written as سّيل نّام, which is still comprehensible despite the writing error. The WER in this case is 100%, whereas the CER is relatively low at 22.2%.

Generally, to compute these metrics, labeled data is required, which is not the case for our system. To address this, we employ a technique inspired by back-translation (Kementchedjhieva and Søgaard, 2023), where we transliterate our Latin text into Arabic using our system, and then transliterate it back to Latin. We then calculate WER and CER metrics to evaluate the performance of our solution. Figure 3 illustrates an example of a back-transliteration process.

6 Experimental Results

In this section, we first present the results and performance metrics of Shialifube, along with descriptions of the various iterations adopted to improve its performance. Additionally, we conduct an experiment on a real-world use case in speech recognition: the first machine learning model ever designed for Comorian written in Arabic script.

Convinced that open-source contributions are the key to advancing the representation of low-resource languages in the field of NLP, we have made the Shialifube library[3], its code on GitHub[4], and a HuggingFace Space[5] publicly available for everyone.

[3]https://pypi.org/project/shialifube/

[4]https://github.com/nairaxo/shialifube

[5]https://huggingface.co/spaces/nairaxo/swauti

6.1 Round-trip Transliteration

The process of applying our transliteration rules was incremental, with our algorithm gradually adjusting based on the specific cases encountered. The goal was to find the most optimal approach that minimizes the evaluation metrics. Each time we adjusted our algorithm, we recalculated these metrics. Table 5 describes the different scenarios used. In total, we conducted four iterations. The final iteration yielded interesting metrics, indicating a certain reliability of our system, although we propose exploring new improvement avenues in future work.

It is important to note that while we have strived to handle all special cases, limitations may still arise during the system's use. To minimize these limitations, we plan to continue refining and updating the library. The current version is, in fact, a pre-release.

6.2 Use Case: Speech Recognition

In this section, we introduce the first speech recognition model for Comorian using the Arabic script. Our objective is twofold: first, to demonstrate the feasibility of such a model by leveraging our Kamar-Eddine transliteration system and second, to assess the effectiveness of our transliteration framework by measuring its impact on speech recognition performance. In fact, if the conversion of Comorian text into the Arabic script significantly altered the data, it would negatively affect model training, leading to degraded performance.

Regarding the choice of model architecture, we selected Whisper (Radford et al., 2022), one of the most performant speech recognition models in the state of the art. Whisper is pre-trained on a large multilingual dataset that includes Swahili and Arabic. This pre-training phase involves teaching the model to better understand each language by capturing latent parameters within the audio data. We fine-tune the model by updating its parameters for speech recognition tasks, specifying Swahili for the Latin script model and Arabic for the Arabic script model.

The results in Table 6 indicate better performance for the Latin script model compared to the Arabic script model. Two main reasons explain this discrepancy:

- **Untransformed data**: Transforming the data affects its quality. While this approach was necessary to generate data in our case, it

Experiment	Description	WER (%)	CER (%)
1	Initial iteration, without digram handling.	68.56	34.41
2	Digram handling and long vowel processing.	43.09	21.30
3	Corpus sequence standardization and corrections[a].	33.89	16.75
4	Handling additional edge cases and incorporating observations from previous iterations.	14.84	9.56

[a] The corpus used comes from various sources, and given the lack of fixed writing rules for Comorian, a standardization procedure was applied to unify the writing style and correct inconsistencies. This standardized writing facilitates the generalization of our transliteration system.

Table 5: Evaluation metrics for the round-trip transliteration approach.

does compromise performance compared to manual annotation. Manual annotation is a promising avenue for future work, not only to improve speech recognition performance but also for other NLP tasks such as sentiment analysis, named entity recognition, etc.

- **Unknown vocabulary**: The use of a pre-trained model depends on its vocabulary. While Comorian is similar to Arabic, it is not closer than Swahili. Consequently, during tokenization of the Arabic script text for model training, there are more unknown tokens for the pre-trained model compared to training with Latin script text.

Script	WER (%)	CER (%)
Latin	35.48	17.76
Arabic	37.44	21.42

Table 6: WER and CER for speech recognition models trained on Latin and Arabic script corpora. The Latin script model serves as a baseline, while the Arabic script model evaluates the effectiveness of the Kamar-Eddine transliteration system.

Finally, these results demonstrate that training a Comorian speech recognition model using the Arabic script is feasible, thanks to the effectiveness of the Kamar-Eddine transliteration system. While the Latin script model achieves slightly better performance, the Arabic script model remains competitive, highlighting the potential of our approach. Future work will focus on improving data quality through manual annotation and further optimizing the transliteration process to enhance speech recognition accuracy.

7 Conclusion

This work aimed to lay the foundation for NLP applied to the Comorian language, with a focus on transcribing this language into Arabic script using the Kamar-Eddine system. Initially, we compiled the set of writing rules for this system, which served as the basis for Shialifube, a bidirectional transliteration system for Comorian.

In the absence of parallel data to directly evaluate the performance of our solution, we adopted a round-trip transliteration approach. This involved transcribing a corpus from Latin script to Arabic script and then retranscribing it back to Latin script. This method yielded promising metrics after several iterations: a WER of 14.84% and a CER of 9.56%.

To assess the utility of this tool for practical use cases, we also conducted experiments in speech recognition. We observed encouraging performance with a WER of 37.44% for the Arabic script version, although it remained slightly lower than the Latin script model, which achieved a WER of 35.48%.

Finally, it is worth noting that this work represents a preliminary step. We plan to continue refining it as part of future contributions, hoping it will contribute to the preservation and enhancement of Comorian intangible heritage. To encourage other researchers to further this initiative, we are making the entire source code, the Shialifube library, and the trained models publicly available.

References

Moneim Abdourahamane, Christian Boitet, Valérie Bellynck, Lingxiao Wang, and Hervé Blanchon. 2016. Construction d'un corpus parallèle français-comorien en utilisant de la TA français-swahili. In *TALAf (Traitement Automatique des Langues africaines)*, Paris, France.

Said Nassor Abeid, Hamid Farhane, Majida Motrane, Fatima Ezzahra Anaibar, and Nourdin

Harich. 2024. Inference on the biological history of the comoros archipelago using the cd4 alu/str compound system. *Gene Reports*, 34:101865.

Mohamed Ahmed Chamanga. 2022. *ShiKomori, the Bantu Language of the Comoros: Status and Perspectives*, page 79–98. BRILL.

Claude Allibert. 2015. L'archipel des comores et son histoire ancienne. essai de mise en perspective des chroniques, de la tradition orale et des typologies de céramiques locales et d'importation. *Afriques*, 06.

Mohamed Ahmed Chamanga and Noël Jacques Gueunier. 1977. Recherches sur l'instrumentalisation du comorien : problèmes d'adaptation lexicale (d'après la version comorienne de la loi du 23 novembre 1974). *Cahiers d'Études africaines*, 66-67:213–239.

Galien Currah. 2015. Orthographe wolofal.

Soufiane Hajbi, Omayma Amezian, Nawfal El Moukhi, Redouan Korchiyne, and Younes Chihab. 2024. Moroccan arabizi-to-arabic conversion using rule-based transliteration and weighted levenshtein algorithm. *Scientific African*, 23:e02073.

Yova Kementchedjhieva and Anders Søgaard. 2023. Grammatical error correction through round-trip machine translation. In *Findings of the Association for Computational Linguistics: EACL 2023*, page 2208–2215. Association for Computational Linguistics.

B. Klouche and S. M. Benslimane. 2020. *Arabizi Chat Alphabet Transliteration to Algerian Dialect*, page 790–797. Springer International Publishing.

Michel Lafon. 2007. Le système Kamar-Eddine : une tentative originale d'écriture du comorien en graphie arabe. *Ya Mkobe*, 14-15:29–48.

Yu-Hsiang Lin, Chian-Yu Chen, Jean Lee, Zirui Li, Yuyan Zhang, Mengzhou Xia, Shruti Rijhwani, Junxian He, Zhisong Zhang, Xuezhe Ma, Antonios Anastasopoulos, Patrick Littell, and Graham Neubig. 2019. Choosing transfer languages for cross-lingual learning. In *Proceedings of the 57th Annual Meeting of the Association for Computational Linguistics*, page 3125–3135. Association for Computational Linguistics.

Kurt Micallef, Fadhl Eryani, Nizar Habash, Houda Bouamor, and Claudia Borg. 2023. Exploring the impact of transliteration on nlp performance: Treating maltese as an arabic dialect. In *Proceedings of the Workshop on Computation and Written Language (CAWL 2023)*, page 22–32. Association for Computational Linguistics.

John Mugane. 2017. The odyssey of ajami and the swahili people. *Islamic Africa*, 8(1–2):193–216.

Abdou Mohamed Naira, Benelallam Imade, Bahafid Abdessalam, and Erraji Zakarya. 2024. Datasets creation and empirical evaluations of cross-lingual learning on extremely low-resource languages: A focus on comorian dialects. In *Proceedings of The 18th Linguistic Annotation Workshop (LAW-XVIII)*, pages 140–149, St. Julians, Malta. Association for Computational Linguistics.

Alec Radford, Jong Wook Kim, Tao Xu, Greg Brockman, Christine McLeavey, and Ilya Sutskever. 2022. Robust speech recognition via large-scale weak supervision. *Preprint*, arXiv:2212.04356.

Annachiara Raia. 2021. One text, many forms: a comparative view of the variability of swahili manuscripts. In R.H. Samsom and C. Vierke, editors, *Manuscript Cultures*, 17, pages 65–86.

Maurizio Serva and Michele Pasquini. 2021. The sabaki languages of comoros.

Ali Shazal, Aiza Usman, and Nizar Habash. 2020. A unified model for Arabizi detection and transliteration using sequence-to-sequence models. In *Proceedings of the Fifth Arabic Natural Language Processing Workshop*, pages 167–177, Barcelona, Spain (Online). Association for Computational Linguistics.

LLM-based Adversarial Dataset Augmentation for Automatic Media Bias Detection

Martin Wessel
CDTM - Technical University of Munich
Munich, Germany
m.wessel@media-bias-research.org

Abstract

This study presents BiasAdapt, a novel data augmentation strategy designed to enhance the robustness of automatic media bias detection models. Leveraging the BABE dataset, BiasAdapt uses a generative language model to identify bias-indicative keywords and replace them with alternatives from opposing categories, thus creating adversarial examples that preserve the original bias labels. The contributions of this work are twofold: it proposes a scalable method for augmenting bias datasets with adversarial examples while preserving labels, and it publicly releases an augmented adversarial media bias dataset. Training on BiasAdapt reduces the reliance on spurious cues in four of the six evaluated media bias categories.

1 Introduction

Automatic media bias detection has gained significant attention with more capable language models. Systems that automatically detect media bias can help media consumers better identify slanted reporting, help journalists uncover overlooked biases, and help researchers evaluate the reporting landscape (Hamborg et al., 2019; Spinde et al., 2021). However, existing models often rely on spurious cues for classification decisions, which can lead to a superficial understanding of bias and compromise their generalization capabilities and objectivity (Wessel and Horych, 2024). Data augmentation techniques can mitigate the reliance on such shortcuts (Wang et al., 2023). Training data for systems that automatically detect media bias originates predominantly from small, manually labeled datasets (Wessel et al., 2023) with associated high labeling costs (Hamborg, 2020; Spinde et al., 2021). Classical data augmentation techniques would require manual relabeling for every augmented sentence, as, for instance, random swaps of words or deletions could alter the bias of a sentence. To minimize the high manual relabeling costs, an adaptation is required. BiasAdapt, a process designed to enhance the robustness of automatic media bias detection systems, aims to address this.[1] BiasAdapt identifies keywords associated with predefined categories such as gender, origin, or political affiliation. It then generates and replaces alternative words from opposing subcategories. In this study, this adversarial augmentation process is performed on the BABE dataset (Spinde et al., 2021). The augmented data serves as training data, reducing reliance on spurious cues in four of the six evaluated media bias categories. However, these modifications also affect classification performance in some categories, requiring further investigation.

The process of augmenting an existing data set with adversarial data using LLMs is transferable to domains beyond the detection of media bias. It allows for label-preserving alterations of predefined dimensions with accurate content exchanges that require an in-depth understanding of the sentence.

2 Related Work

Media bias, a phenomenon where the information presented in the media is skewed, has been the subject of significant research (Hamborg et al., 2019; Baumer et al., 2015; Spinde et al., 2023). Advances in bias detection, mainly through transformer-based methodologies, have notably improved classification accuracy (Spinde et al., 2021, 2023).

Despite these advancements, a persistent challenge is the dependence on small, narrowly focused, manually annotated datasets (Wessel et al., 2023). This limitation often results in models that overfit and generalize poorly. Recent work by Wessel and Horych (2024) highlights that transformer-based models in automatic

[1]The dataset and code are publicly available under https://github.com/martinpwessel/BiasAdapt-Repository.

Proceedings of LaTeCH-CLfL 2025, pages 19–24
May 4, 2025 ©2025 Association for Computational Linguistics

media bias detection predominantly target highly connotative words and do not grasp the nuance of context. This leads to reliance on unreliable indicators or spurious cues for classification decisions, manifesting itself as inconsistent bias determinations under stress tests. Spurious cues in this context are superficial lexical features, such as demographic terms or political affiliations, that bias detection models incorrectly rely on to classify bias instead of analyzing the actual linguistic and contextual indicators of bias.

Wessel and Horych (2024) introduce a CheckList-based invariance test (INV) (Ribeiro et al., 2020) to assess the resilience of bias detection models to irrelevant input alterations. They define seven bias categories -gender, origin, religion, political affiliation, occupation, politician names, and disability- based on prior literature and practical observations of bias-related word associations. Their CheckList-based invariance test systematically examines whether altering terms within these categories (e.g., replacing a male-associated name with a female-associated one) changes the model's classification. If the model's bias determination fluctuates despite maintaining sentence semantics, it suggests reliance on spurious cues rather than true contextual understanding. Wessel and Horych (2024) report significant disparities in model behavior across datasets. For example, words linked to gender or origin frequently influence bias predictions, implying that classifiers are using these cues instead of analyzing how bias is actually expressed. Such findings emphasize the necessity of model refinement for more robust detection methods.

Wang et al. (2023) propose adversarial training and data augmentation to enhance model robustness. Jia and Liang (2017) showcase the utility of adversarial examples in evaluating and enhancing the robustness of natural language processing models, a key consideration in detecting and mitigating media bias. Additionally, Shafahi et al. (2019) highlight the significance of adversarial data augmentation in addressing the subtleties of language, suggesting its essential role in refining models tasked with understanding nuanced biases.

This study refines media bias detection through adversarial data augmentation, addressing the limitations of existing methods. Techniques like frequency-guided word substitution (FGWS) (Mozes et al., 2021) and adversarial text modifications (Samanta and Mehta, 2017) often fail to preserve bias labels, requiring costly human re-annotation (Sabou et al., 2012) when biases are unintentionally altered. When, for instance, words are randomly added or deleted, a previously unbiased sentence might now be biased. The strategy proposed in this study offers key improvements:

- Label Preservation: Maintains label integrity, reducing the need for manual re-labeling (Zhang and Wallace, 2015).
- Contextual Sensitivity: Ensures coherent augmentations by considering keyword context, which prevents misplaced examples (Wei and Zou, 2019).
- Bias Specificity: Targets bias mitigation, avoiding reinforcement of existing biases (Dixon et al., 2018).

3 Methodology

The BiasAdapt augmentation process expands the dataset to improve bias detection within text-based content. The process begins with an existing annotated dataset. In this case, the BABE (Spinde et al., 2021) data set consists of sentences that are binary labeled for bias. The next step identifies keywords within each sentence by predefined categories. A keyword is any word that can clearly be attributed to one category. For instance, for gender, every gender-associated word is a keyword; for religion, every religion-associated word, and so on. For the context of media bias, these categories are gender, origin, religion, political affiliation, occupation, and politician names as defined by Wessel and Horych (2024).[2] As these categories need to be predefined before the annotation, prior knowledge of where spurious cues may arise in the specific context is necessary. BiasAdapt identifies keywords by individually querying each sentence to a generative language model. For all prompts, GPT-3.5 Turbo (Brown et al., 2020) is used. The language model returns the identified keywords and the associated category (gender, origin, etc.). Once more, these words are queried using the same language model with instructions to generate alternative words for each keyword. The process queries the same language model again, instructing it to generate alternative words for each keyword. These alternatives

[2] Wessel and Horych (2024) also include the category disability. This category was excluded from this analysis because the BABE data set contains only a few words associated with disability, leaving too few permutations for meaningful effects.

must come from opposing categories, ensuring they are associated with, for instance, an opposite political affiliation, gender, or a different religion.
The alternative words then substitute the original terms in the sentence to create new instances, each maintaining the initial bias label. The bias label remains unchanged because the substituted keywords belong to the same predefined category, ensuring that the sentence's bias, whether introduced through framing or word choice, is preserved. Bias can arise from how a sentence is structured but also from the connotations of specific words. For example, replacing 'he' with 'she' in 'He lacks the toughness for leadership' retains gender bias because the stereotype about leadership remains intact. Similarly, swapping 'Christian' with 'Muslim' in 'Policy unfairly favors Christian values' maintains religious bias by preserving the critical framing of the sentence. In political contexts, replacing 'left-wing politician' with 'right-wing politician' in a sentence about corruption does not alter the underlying bias, as the negative framing remains the same. Likewise, in occupation-based bias, exchanging 'artist' with 'construction worker' in 'Artists contribute little to the economy' preserves bias against certain professions. Since these substitutions maintain the same bias patterns, the augmentation process ensures that the dataset's labels remain consistent. This only works for predefined bias categories with predefined opposing subcategories that substitutions can be taken from. In some cases, substitutions may interact with the sentence structure in ways that subtly alter the perceived bias. For example, in 'She is caring and nurturing,' substituting 'she' with 'he' could challenge the stereotype that these traits are inherently feminine, as men are less commonly associated with these characteristics in traditional gender roles. This demonstrates that substitutions in certain contexts may shift or reinforce bias depending on the societal associations linked to the words involved. While the augmentation process follows strict category-based substitutions, potential context-dependent bias shifts are a limitation of this method.

Figure 1 displays the augmentation process with an example sentence from the BABE dataset.
Each sentence may contain multiple identified keywords, each with a list of alternative words, resulting in numerous possible permutations. When substituting these keywords, the rest of the sentence and its label remain unchanged. That is why generating too many permutations can lead to overfitting when the data is used for model training. For this study, three permutations per original sentence are found to be the best trade-off between introducing adversarial examples and the prevention of overfitting. However, this might vary depending on the dataset size, sentence complexity, and length. The three permutations are chosen by randomly sampling alternative words from the word lists. The training setup ensures no data leakage between the training, test, and validation data, as original and altered sentences are always in the same set.

This process creates an Adversarial BABE dataset, which is then used to train a language model to automatically detect media bias. Its detection capabilities are compared to that of a model trained solely on BABE. The performance of the models is evaluated using the test sets from Wessel and Horych (2024). The test set consists of 1,900 binary-labeled sentences distributed over the categories (50% of which are classified as biased). Within each category, variance serves as a metric for spurious cues: Higher values suggest that the model relies on shortcuts rather than general language understanding. For example, if the model does not use gender as a factor in classification, accuracy should remain consistent across sentences containing male, female, and non-binary keywords. Both models are based on a pre-trained RoBERTa model to ensure comparability with Spinde et al. (2021). The model training ends based on an early stopping criteria.

4 Results

The augmentation of the BABE dataset through BiasAdapt significantly increases the dataset size to 14,659 entries, adding 10,986 entries to the original collection. Not for every original sentence permutations can be constructed, as not all sentences contain words that are identified as keywords being associated with one of the predefined categories. While the distribution within categories remains equal, the occurrence of relevant keywords differs between categories depending on their occurrence in the BABE dataset. In the initial step, a total of 4,906 keywords are identified and replaced. The most frequently modified categories are gender (1,469 identified keywords) and politician names (1,232), followed by origin (609), political affiliation (464), religion (97), and occupation (35). This distribution is primarily influenced by the topic choices of the BABE dataset. This study's eval-

Figure 1: Examplary augmentation process using BiasAdapt. The sentence is biased because the phrase "dug his heels in" conveys a negative subjective judgment about the politician's stance.

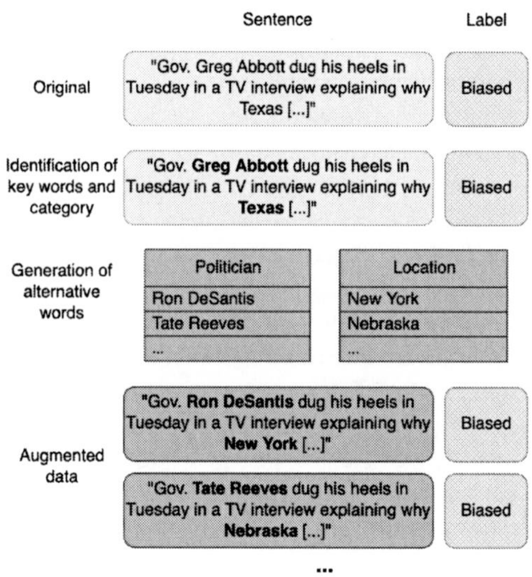

uation, detailed in Table 1, employs F1-scores to compare performance across six bias categories using the INV test set established by Wessel and Horych (2024). The results are displayed by subcategory and then averaged for a category score. Furthermore, the variance among subcategory results is calculated per category.

The comparison reveals two principal findings: Firstly, in four out of six categories, the model trained with the BiasAdapt-augmented dataset displays a lower classification performance variance (remaining the same in the remaining categories). As the variance is the primary measure for reliance on spurious cues, this indicates that BiasAdapt contributes to a more consistent classification performance across different subcategories and reduces reliance on spurious cues. Secondly, the overall performance in the gender category dropped significantly after training on Augmented BABE, improved for political affiliation, and remained relatively stable for all other categories.

5 Discussion

BiasAdapt successfully identifies and replaces relevant keywords though there is still an underrepresentation of certain categories with little occurrence in the original dataset. The observed

Table 1: The detection results (F1-Scores) on the INV test set by subcategories. Variance values are shown in brackets behind the average scores.

Category	Subcategory	Augmented BABE	BABE
Gender	Male	0.54	0.68
	Female	0.54	0.75
	Non-binary	0.54	0.69
	Average	0.54 (3.0e-6)	0.71 (0.001)
Origin	European	0.92	0.94
	African	0.94	0.99
	Asian	1.00	1.00
	Average	0.95 (0.001)	0.98 (0.001)
Religion	Christian	0.87	0.89
	Islam	0.90	0.89
	Atheism	0.79	0.80
	Average	0.86 (0.002)	0.85 (0.002)
Politician names	Conservatives	0.95	0.97
	Liberals	0.91	0.91
	Socialists	0.92	0.89
	Average	0.93 (2.0e-4)	0.92 (0.001)
Political Affiliation	Left-wing	0.96	0.91
	Right-wing	0.91	0.80
	Centrist	0.96	0.88
	Average	0.94 (6.0e-4)	0.86 (0.002)
Occupation	Services	0.65	0.70
	Creative Arts and Media	0.67	0.68
	Trades and Manual Labor	0.67	0.64
	Average	0.66 (7.0e-5)	0.67 (0.0005)

decrease in variance for a majority of categories due to the BiasAdapt augmentation underscores the method's effectiveness in diminishing the model's dependence on predefined bias-indicative keywords. The reduced reliance on keywords suggests that augmentation helps the model analyze the text holistically rather than fixating on specific terms. However, this does not work for all categories, and intra-category differences remain.

The decrease in performance observed in the gender category raises important questions about the role of spurious cues in automated bias detection. Unlike political affiliation or origin, where bias is often directly linked to framing, gender bias tends to involve more implicit associations tied to societal roles or traits. The reliance on these implicit cues might have served as a shortcut, aiding model performance in some cases. In the context of gender, keyword substitutions can interact with these subtleties, potentially altering the strength or direction of bias in ways that are difficult to predict.

The relative stability in F1-Scores across the other categories suggests that the model's ability to detect bias in these areas is less disturbed by reducing reliance on spurious cues. This could indicate that the model's prior results in these categories were less dependent on problematic shortcuts or, alternatively, that the augmentation process more effectively preserves the essential signals of bias within these contexts.

6 Future Work

Several avenues for research emerge from the findings of this study. Further investigations into why the performance changed for two categories, as well as why the variance did not decrease for two, is necessary. Expanding the scope of model architectures tested, including a diverse array of language models, could provide a more comprehensive understanding of BiasAdapt's applicability and effectiveness. This would enable a broader assessment of the augmentation process across different computational frameworks for bias detection.

To mitigate potential shifts in bias, future work could explore filtering mechanisms that detect when a keyword replacement significantly alters a sentence's framing. Additionally, human evaluation of augmented sentences could help assess whether bias labels remain appropriate after substitution, particularly in the gender category.

Addressing the limitation related to the requirement for predefined bias categories, future research could explore developing more adaptive, exploratory methods for identifying potential biases. Such approaches could leverage unsupervised learning techniques or advanced content analysis methods to uncover hidden or emergent bias categories, thereby broadening the scope and applicability of the BiasAdapt method. Moreover, an important direction for future work is investigating whether methods like BiasAdapt can indirectly contribute to improving models' contextual understanding of texts by reducing models' reliance on spurious cues. This could involve integrating techniques to enhance semantic comprehension and inferential reasoning within models, thereby addressing one of the fundamental challenges in automatic bias detection.

7 Conclusion

This study presents BiasAdapt, a data augmentation strategy aimed at improving the robustness of media bias detection systems through adversarial examples. By leveraging prior knowledge of spurious cue dependencies, BiasAdapt demonstrates that data augmentations utilizing large language models (LLMs) can have a measurable impact on improving bias detection performance. Making a significant corpus available for public use lays the groundwork for further exploration in the field. While the focus on a single model and a select number of bias categories limits the generalizability of the findings, this work demonstrates the potential of leveraging LLMs for dataset augmentation and increased robustness in media bias detection. Despite the demonstrated benefits, further investigations to better understand model behavior is necessary. Still, it encourages expanding the scope and transfer to other areas of text analysis with prerequisites similar to media bias.

Limitations

Primarily, the analysis is confined to using a single model architecture, specifically a RoBERTa model. Though beneficial for ensuring comparability with prior work such as Wessel and Horych (2024), this choice restricts understanding how the proposed BiasAdapt augmentation might perform across a broader spectrum of model architectures. Another limitation arises from the reliance on GPT3.5 to generate alternative words. Manual inspections have revealed instances where GPT3.5 may incorrectly identify keywords or suggest inappropriate alternatives. While these errors are infrequent and do not significantly detract from the overall efficacy of the augmentation, they underscore the need for caution and oversight in using generative language models for data augmentation tasks. Furthermore, the replacement can lead to generic or contextually inconsistent replacements, where sentences remain grammatically correct but become unrealistic or lose their meaning.

Additionally, the BiasAdapt approach assumes a priori knowledge of bias categories and subcategories, necessitating predefined taxonomies for media bias. This requirement could constrain the method's applicability, as it presupposes theoretical or empirical insights into potential sources of spurious cues. While this study addresses the issue of over-reliance on specific cues for bias detection, it does not tackle the broader challenge of enhancing models' contextual understanding. This limitation points to an inherent constraint in the scope of the current methodological approach. Lastly, querying an LLM for each sentence and generating multiple permutations can be computationally intensive and time-consuming, particularly for large datasets.

References

Eric Baumer, Elisha Elovic, Ying Qin, Francesca Polletta, and Geri Gay. 2015. Testing and Comparing

Computational Approaches for Identifying the Language of Framing in Political News. In *Proceedings of the 2015 Conference of the North American Chapter of the Association for Computational Linguistics: Human Language Technologies*, pages 1472–1482, Denver, Colorado. Association for Computational Linguistics.

Tom Brown, Benjamin Mann, Nick Ryder, Melanie Subbiah, Jared D Kaplan, Prafulla Dhariwal, Arvind Neelakantan, Pranav Shyam, Girish Sastry, Amanda Askell, et al. 2020. Language models are few-shot learners. *Advances in neural information processing systems*, 33:1877–1901.

Lucas Dixon, John Li, Jeffrey Sorensen, Nithum Thain, and Lucy Vasserman. 2018. Measuring and mitigating unintended bias in text classification. In *Proceedings of the 2018 AAAI/ACM Conference on AI, Ethics, and Society*, pages 67–73.

Felix Hamborg. 2020. Media bias, the social sciences, and nlp: Automating frame analyses to identify bias by word choice and labeling. In *Proceedings of the 58th annual meeting of the association for computational linguistics: student research workshop*, pages 79–87.

Felix Hamborg, Karsten Donnay, and Bela Gipp. 2019. Automated identification of media bias in news articles: an interdisciplinary literature review. *International Journal on Digital Libraries*, 20(4):391–415.

Robin Jia and Percy Liang. 2017. Adversarial examples for evaluating reading comprehension systems. In *Proceedings of the 2017 Conference on Empirical Methods in Natural Language Processing*, pages 2021–2031, Copenhagen, Denmark. Association for Computational Linguistics.

Maximilian Mozes, Pontus Stenetorp, Bennett Kleinberg, and Lewis Griffin. 2021. Frequency-guided word substitutions for detecting textual adversarial examples. In *Proceedings of the 16th Conference of the European Chapter of the Association for Computational Linguistics: Main Volume*, pages 171–186, Online. Association for Computational Linguistics.

Marco Tulio Ribeiro, Tongshuang Wu, Carlos Guestrin, and Sameer Singh. 2020. Beyond Accuracy: Behavioral Testing of NLP Models with CheckList. In *Proceedings of the 58th Annual Meeting of the Association for Computational Linguistics*, pages 4902–4912, Online. Association for Computational Linguistics.

Marta Sabou, Kalina Bontcheva, and Arno Scharl. 2012. Crowdsourcing research opportunities: lessons from natural language processing. In *Proceedings of the 12th International Conference on Knowledge Management and Knowledge Technologies*, pages 1–8.

Suranjana Samanta and Sameep Mehta. 2017. Towards crafting text adversarial samples. *arXiv preprint arXiv:1707.02812*.

Ali Shafahi, Mahyar Najibi, Mohammad Amin Ghiasi, Zheng Xu, John Dickerson, Christoph Studer, Larry S Davis, Gavin Taylor, and Tom Goldstein. 2019. Adversarial training for free! *Advances in neural information processing systems*, 32.

Timo Spinde, Smilla Hinterreiter, Fabian Haak, Terry Ruas, Helge Giese, Norman Meuschke, and Bela Gipp. 2023. The media bias taxonomy: A systematic literature review on the forms and automated detection of media bias. *arXiv preprint*.

Timo Spinde, Manuel Plank, Jan-David Krieger, Terry Ruas, Bela Gipp, and Akiko Aizawa. 2021. Neural Media Bias Detection Using Distant Supervision With BABE - Bias Annotations By Experts. In *Findings of the Association for Computational Linguistics: EMNLP 2021*, pages 1166–1177, Punta Cana, Dominican Republic. Association for Computational Linguistics.

Xuezhi Wang et al. 2023. Identifying and mitigating spurious correlations for improving robustness in nlp models. In *Proceedings of the Conference on Empirical Methods in Natural Language Processing (EMNLP)*.

Jason Wei and Kai Zou. 2019. Eda: Easy data augmentation techniques for boosting performance on text classification tasks. *arXiv preprint arXiv:1901.11196*.

Martin Wessel and Tomáš Horych. 2024. Beyond the surface: Spurious cues in automatic media bias detection. In *Proceedings of the Fourth Workshop on Language Technology for Equality, Diversity, Inclusion*, pages 21–30, St. Julian's, Malta. Association for Computational Linguistics.

Martin Wessel, Tomas Horych, Terry Ruas, Akiko Aizawa, Bela Gipp, and Timo Spinde. 2023. Introducing MBIB - The First Media Bias Identification Benchmark Task and Dataset Collection. In *Proceedings of 46th International ACM SIGIR Conference on Research and Development in Information Retrieval (SIGIR'23)*, New York, NY, USA. ACM. ISBN 978-1-4503-9408-6/23/07.

Ye Zhang and Byron Wallace. 2015. A sensitivity analysis of (and practitioners' guide to) convolutional neural networks for sentence classification. *arXiv preprint arXiv:1510.03820*.

HieroLM: Egyptian Hieroglyph Recovery with Next Word Prediction Language Model

Xuheng Cai
Department of Computer Science
Stanford University
xuheng@stanford.edu

Erica Zhang
Department of Management Science
and Engineering
Stanford University
yz4232@stanford.edu

Abstract

Egyptian hieroglyphs are found on numerous ancient Egyptian artifacts, but it is common that they are blurry or even missing due to erosion. Existing efforts to restore blurry hieroglyphs adopt computer vision techniques such as CNNs and model hieroglyph recovery as an image classification task, which suffers from two major limitations: (i) They cannot handle severely damaged or completely missing hieroglyphs. (ii) They make predictions based on a single hieroglyph without considering contextual and grammatical information. This paper proposes a novel approach to model hieroglyph recovery as a next word prediction task and use language models to address it. We compare the performance of different SOTA language models and choose LSTM as the architecture of our HieroLM due to the strong local affinity of semantics in Egyptian hieroglyph texts. Experiments show that HieroLM achieves over 44% accuracy and maintains notable performance on multi-shot predictions and scarce data, which makes it a pragmatic tool to assist scholars in inferring missing hieroglyphs. It can also complement CV-based models to significantly reduce perplexity in recognizing blurry hieroglyphs. Our code is available at https://github.com/Rick-Cai/HieroLM/.

1 Introduction

Egyptian hieroglyphs is the formal written language and an important medium for religious and funerary practices in Ancient Egypt. The process of decoding hieroglyphs involves first converting them into transliterations and then translating the transliterations into modern languages (Gardiner, 1927). Table 1 presents an illustration of this decoding process on a sample hieroglyphic sentence.

Due to natural erosion, it is common that the hieroglyphs on the surface of the unearthed artifacts are blurry or even missing. Efforts have been made to assist the process of recognizing blurry hieroglyphs with computer vision (CV) -based techniques (Barucci et al., 2021, 2022; Aneesh et al., 2024). Specifically, these works formulate hieroglyph recognition as an image classification task and use CV models such as convolutional neural networks (CNNs) to classify the blurry symbols. However, there are two major limitations in the CV-based approaches: **(i)** They cannot handle severely damaged or completely missing hieroglyphs because they rely on the visual characteristics of the signs. **(ii)** They make predictions based on a single hieroglyph, without considering the contextual and grammatical information contained in surrounding words that could help narrow down possibilities and significantly reduce perplexity.

Hieroglyphs	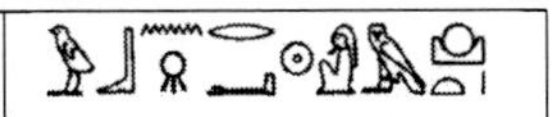
Transliteration	wbn rʿ m ꜣḫt
Transliteration (MdC)	wbn ra m Axt
English Translation	Re (the Sun God) rises in the horizon.

Table 1: An example of transliteration and translation of a hieroglyphic sentence.

As an example, the blurry hieroglyph A in the blue box in Figure 1 would confuse a CV model, because it could be either  (nḫb) or  (sw) based on its vague shape, but from the surrounding words we know that this sentence describes an offering by the king to the god Osiris, so it is likely that this blurry sign is 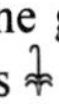 (sw), which means "the king". Moreover, for the red box in Figure 1, the signs are almost entirely missing, and the CV models will become useless, but from the words before it, we know that it should be a title of Osiris, which indicates that the missing word is probably  (ḏdw), because 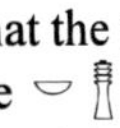 (nb ḏdw; "lord of Djedu") is a common title for Osiris in the offering formula.

In light of these limitations, we propose a novel approach where we model hieroglyph recovery as a next word prediction problem, which can be addressed effectively with language models. To

Proceedings of LaTeCH-CLfL 2025, pages 25–31
May 4, 2025 ©2025 Association for Computational Linguistics

Figure 1: A Middle Kingdom tablet at The Metropolitan Museum of Art.[1] Hieroglyph A in the blue box is an example of blurry hieroglyphs. Hieroglyph B in the red box is an example of (nearly) missing hieroglyphs.

select the best architecture for our task, we consider the following characteristics of Egyptian hieroglyphs (Allen, 2000): (i) It is a dead language whose corpora have ceased to grow, and thus the amount of data available for training is very limited. Hence, our model must be comfortable with small-scale training data. (ii) In Ancient Egypt, hieroglyphs are mostly used in limited scenarios including funerals, religious rituals, and monumental inscriptions. The restrictive formats on the hieroglyphic sentences leads to a better hope of accurate language modeling with simpler architectures. (iii) Due to its limited scope of usage, the hieroglyphic sentence structure has strong local affinity (e.g., a large portion of a sentence could be titles following names of gods or kings), suggesting that our model should have strong capability in capturing short-range dependencies. Based on these characteristics, we build our HieroLM with LSTM (Hochreiter and Schmidhuber, 1997). To validate our design choice, we compare the performance of HieroLM with popular architectures such as RNN (Medsker and Jain, 1999) and Transformers (Vaswani et al., 2017) in Section 4.3.

Our contributions are summarized as follows:

- To the best of our knowledge, this is the first paper to model hieroglyph recovery as a next word prediction task addressed with language models.
- We propose HieroLM based on LSTM, which achieves over 44% accuracy (i.e., it infers missing words correctly almost half of the time).
- Experiments show that HieroLM is robust enough to maintain notable performance on both multi-shot prediction and scarce context.

2 Related Work

2.1 Hieroglyph Recognition with CV

Modeling hieroglyph recognition as an image classification task is well-explored. Franken et al. (Franken and van Gemert, 2013) proposed to use the Histogram of Oriented Gradients (HOG) and the Shape-Context (SC) descriptors to extract and compare hieroglyphs. The HOG method was later enhanced with Region of Interest (ROI) extraction (Elnabawy et al., 2021). Moustafa et al. (Moustafa et al., 2022) and Aneesh et al. (Aneesh et al., 2024) explored the performance of ShuffleNet, MobileNet, ResNet, VGG, DenseNet, and Inception v3 on hieroglyph recognition, while Glyphnet (Barucci et al., 2021) achieves the state-of-the-art performance. However, these CV models rely heavily on the visual quality of the signs and fail to incorporate contextual information.

2.2 Next Word Prediction with LMs

Next-word prediction involves predicting the subsequent word in a sequence given the preceding context. Early approaches use n-gram models which suffer from data sparsity and limited context understanding. NPLM (Bengio et al., 2000) addresses the limitations of n-gram models with neural networks. CSLM (Schwenk, 2007) projects words to a continuous space to handle variable-length contexts. Recurrent neural networks (RNNs) and long short-term memory (LSTM) (Hochreiter and Schmidhuber, 1997) greatly improve the prediction accuracy with recurrent model architectures to maintain memory and capture local dependencies. Recently, Transformers (Vaswani et al., 2017) revolutionizes language modeling by employing self-attention to consider the entire input context, but it is less-suited for our task due to the limited data availability.

3 Methodology

In this section, we describe in detail our HieroLM model, which adopts the LSTM architecture as illustrated in Figure 2.

Assume that the input sentence has T words. Let $x^{(t)} \in \{0,1\}^{|V|}$ be the one-hot encoding of the t-th word ($1 \leq t \leq T$) in the sentence. Then, its embedding $e^{(t)} \in \mathbb{R}^s$, where s is the embedding size,

[1] Source: https://www.metmuseum.org/art/collection/search/545055.

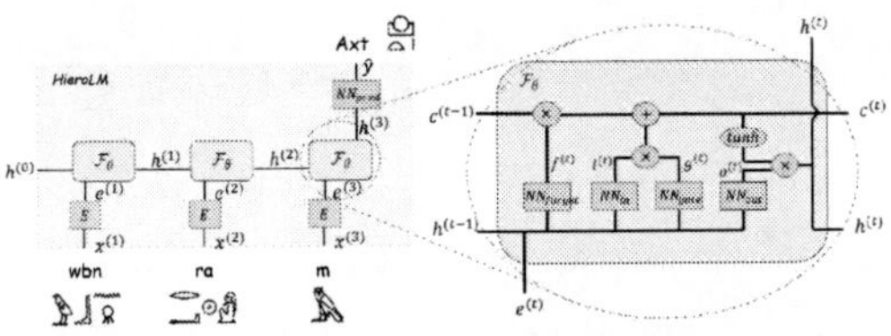

Figure 2: Model structure of HieroLM.

is computed as $e^{(t)} = Ex^{(t)}$, where E is an embedding layer. The hidden state $h^{(t)} \in \mathbb{R}^d$, where d is the hidden dimension size, at step t is computed as:

$$h^{(t)} = \mathcal{F}_\theta(h^{(t-1)}, e^{(t)})$$

where $\mathcal{F}_\theta$ incorporates long short-term memory (Hochreiter and Schmidhuber, 1997). Specifically, given $h^{(t-1)}$ and $e^{(t)}$, we compute the following states with single layer neural networks:

$$\begin{aligned} f^{(t)} &= NN_{forget}(h^{(t-1)}, e^{(t)}) \\ i^{(t)} &= NN_{in}(h^{(t-1)}, e^{(t)}) \\ g^{(t)} &= NN_{gate}(h^{(t-1)}, e^{(t)}) \\ o^{(t)} &= NN_{out}(h^{(t-1)}, e^{(t)}) \end{aligned}$$

The cell state $c^{(t)} \in \mathbb{R}^d$ at step t is computed as:

$$c^{(t)} = f^{(t)} \odot c^{(t-1)} + i^{(t)} \odot g^{(t)}$$

where $c^{(0)}$ is the initial cell state. Finally, the hidden state $h^{(t)}$ is calculated as:

$$h^{(t)} = o^{(t)} \odot tanh(c^{(t)})$$

The predicted output is calculated by:

$$\hat{y} = NN_{pred}(h^{(T)})$$

where NN_{pred} is a single neural layer plus a softmax layer, which projects the final hidden state from d to the size of the vocabulary $|V|$.

4 Experiments

4.1 Datasets

We evaluate our model and the baselines on three real-world datasets with hieroglyphic sentences from unearthed Egyptian artifacts. The dataset statistics are summarized in Table 2.

- *Ancient Egyptian Sentences (AES)* (Jauhiainen and Jauhiainen, 2023): It is a collection of over 100,000 ancient Egyptian sentences across multiple dynasties.
- *The Ramses Transliteration Corpus* (Rosmorduc, 2020): It contains transliterations converted from a large corpus of Late Egyptian sentences.
- *Mixed*: Since AES contains sentences from different eras while texts in Ramses come from Late Egypt, they have different distributions due to language evolution. To evaluate the models' cross-distribution modeling ability, we synthesize AES and Ramses into a mixed dataset.

We use the MdC transliterations of the hieroglyphic sentences throughout our experiments because it replaces irregular letters (e.g., ꜥ and ꜣ) in the common transliteration with English letters (e.g., "a" and "A") for convenient processing. The sentences are split into training, validation, and test sets by an 8:1:1 ratio.

Table 2: Dataset statistics.

Dataset	Sentence #	Vocab #	Training #	Validation #	Test #
AES	98,375	7,058	78,801	9,800	9,774
Ramses	61,069	3,499	48,848	6,116	6,105
Mixed	159,444	8,436	127,649	15,916	15,879

4.2 Baselines

We compare our LSTM-based HieroLM model with the following widely-adopted baselines:

- *Neural Probabilistic Language Model (NPLM)* (Bengio et al., 2000). We use a trigram NPLM as the naivest baseline.
- *Recurrent Neural Network (RNN)* (Medsker and Jain, 1999). We adopt a unidirectional, single-layer RNN. This also serves as an ablated version of HieroLM where the long short-term memory is removed.
- *Transformer* (Vaswani et al., 2017). We employ a single-layer encoder with `nheads=16` and `dropout` $= 0$ due to limited data.

4.3 Performance Validation

We summarize the main results in Table 3, with the following observations:

- **Hieroglyphic vocabulary is restrictive.** Next word prediction is intrinsically hard due to the high degree of freedom of modern languages. There are often multiple legitimate next words that make perfect grammatical and semantic senses for an input context. The SOTA LSTM-based language model for English trained on billion-scale datasets by Google only achieves a

Dataset	Metric	NPLM	Transformer	RNN	**HieroLM**
AES	Perplexity	41.57	52.21	42.25	**26.50**
	Accuracy	0.3075	0.3143	0.3828	**0.4525**
	F1 Score	0.0485	0.0488	0.1201	**0.1420**
Ramses	Perplexity	28.75	38.59	31.89	**21.59**
	Accuracy	0.3553	0.3727	0.4387	**0.4895**
	F1 Score	0.0775	0.0905	0.1933	**0.2074**
Mixed	Perplexity	42.14	53.78	43.34	**26.48**
	Accuracy	0.3022	0.3151	0.3801	**0.4450**
	F1 Score	0.0481	0.0466	0.1377	**0.1421**

Table 3: Main performance results.

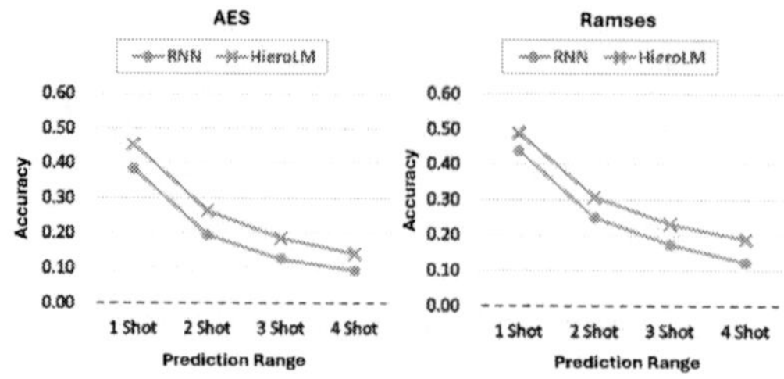

Figure 3: Multi-shot prediction accuracy.

perplexity of 30 (Jozefowicz et al., 2016). However, HieroLM achieves a perplexity of ~26 with less than a million words, indicating that the hieroglyphic vocabulary is highly constrained.

- **Recurrent architecture dominates.** As the table shows, in face of small datasets, models with recurrent architecture (HieroLM and RNN) exhibit consistent superiority. This proves the recurrent models' ability to capture local semantic affinity with limited data.
- **LSTM enhances performance.** The comparison between HieroLM and RNN is a natural ablation study. The outperformance of HieroLM w.r.t. RNN proves that LSTM can enhance the model by long-range perception.
- **Transformer is less-suited for this task.** We can see that Transformer underperforms HieroLM, which demonstrates that its architecture is less suitable for this task due to limited data.

4.4 Multi-shot Prediction Performance

In reality, it is common for a number of contiguous hieroglyphic words to be missing together, which makes it important to evaluate the model's ability to predict a series of words accurately without teacher forcing. Figure 3 presents the accuracy of HieroLM for multiple following words. We can observe a favorable diminishing decrease in accuracy with the increase of prediction range. It is also worth noting that the model maintains an accuracy of over 14% on predicting 4 words in a row.

4.5 Resistance against Data Scarcity

A big obstacle in leveraging ML for hieroglyph recovery is data scarcity, which manifests on two levels: On the corpus level, the total number of hieroglyphic sentences from ancient artifacts are limited. On the sentence level, many hieroglyphic sentences are incomplete due to erosion, with only few identifiable symbols. The short context increases difficulty in inferring missing words. To evaluate HieroLM's robustness in resisting the sentence-level data scarcity, we group test sentences by their length and calculate accuracy of HieroLM and RNN on each group. Figure 4 shows that the models generally perform worse with shorter context (except group [1,5) on AES, as AES contains many short but formulaic phrases), but HieroLM consistently outperforms RNN on all context lengths, demonstrating its robustness under scarce input.

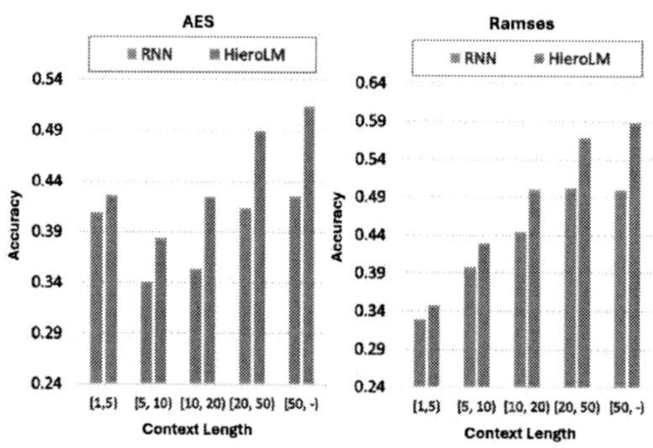

Figure 4: Accuracy with different context lengths.

4.6 Word Embedding Quality

In this section, we illustrate the effectiveness of HieroLM by inspecting the word embeddings it learns on the Mixed dataset. Specifically, we map the embeddings of all words to the 2-D space with PCA and visualize some common words that frequently appear on Egyptian artifacts in Figure 5, which shows a distribution of word embeddings that reflects the semantic of *offering* from the subjects (the mortals) to the targets (the gods).

4.7 Hyperparameter Analysis

We explore the sensitivity of HieroLM with respect to key hyperparameters including embedding size, hidden dimension size, and dropout rate. The results also provide ground for our choice of hyperparameters. Due to space limit, we present the results in Appendix B.

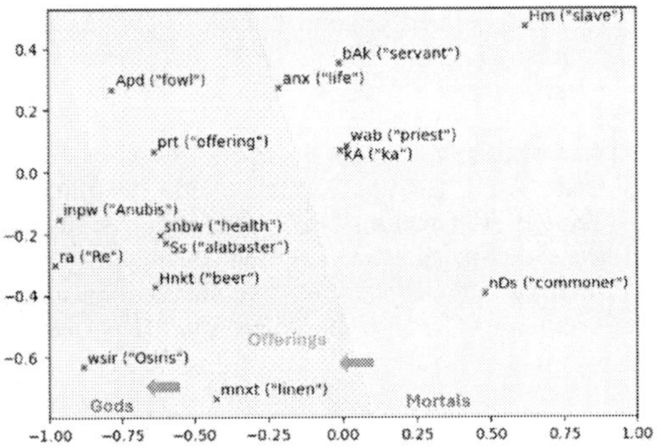

Figure 5: Embeddings of common hieroglyphic words.

4.8 Case Study

We demonstrate HieroLM's ability to learn semantic patterns by two concrete cases corresponding to two common patterns in Egyptian hieroglyphs.

Case 1: Offering formula. Below is the #1563 sentence in the test set of the Mixed dataset.

Processed MdC:

n kA n wr swn w pnTw mAa xrw

Transliteration:

n kꜣ n wr-swn.w pnṯw mꜣꜥ ḫrw

English Translation:

For the *ka* of the great physician Pentu , the true of voice. [2]

This sentence is a common conclusion of the offering formula. It has a fixed format: [n kꜣ n] + [*Title and name of the deceased*] + [mꜣꜥ ḫrw], where mꜣꜥ ḫrw ("the true of voice") is a universal title for the deceased. Upon seeing n kꜣ n and the title and name of the deceased, HieroLM is capable of predicting that the following words are mꜣꜥ ḫrw. Note that this is an example of successful 2-shot prediction.

Case 2: Titles of kings. Below are the first few words of #8779 sentence in test set of the Mixed dataset.

Processed MdC:

nswt bj tj nb tA du wsr mAa t raw stp n jmn zA ra ...

Transliteration:

nswt-bity nb tꜣ.du wsr-mꜣꜥt-rꜥ stp.n-imn sꜣ rꜥ ...

English Translation:

King of Upper and Lower Egypt, Lord of the Two Lands, Ramesses IV, Son of Re ...

[2]In ancient Egypt, *ka* refers to a part of human soul that leaves the body upon death.

This part of the sentence contains the name and titles of the king Ramesses IV. Titles of kings in ancient Egypt have rigorous formats. nswt-bity ("King of Upper and Lower Egypt") is the title preceding the coronation name of the king, and sꜣ rꜥ ("Son of Re") is a title commonly following the king's name. After seeing nswt-bity and the name of the king, HieroLM can infer that the following words are likely to be sꜣ rꜥ. When we feed in the sequence "nswt bj tj nb tA du wsr mAa t raw stp n jmn", the model responds with "zA", and when appending "zA" to the input, it outputs "ra", which is also a 2-shot prediction example.

5 Conclusion

In this paper, we exclusively propose to model Egyptian hieroglyph recovery as a next word prediction task addressed by language models. Considering the data scale and the local semantic affinity, we propose HieroLM with LSTM architecture, which achieves significant accuracy in experiments. Its notable performance on multi-shot predictions and short input contexts makes it practical in archaeological research to infer missing hieroglyphs and complement CV models. In the future, we plan to explore potential ways of integrating computer vision models and language models into a unified and effective hieroglyph recovery system.

6 Limitations

In this work, due to limited data availability, we had little success in leveraging the power of the state-of-the-art Transformer models. While it is not impossible to tailor Transformer to smaller-scale data, it requires sophisticated training techniques (Popel and Bojar, 2018) and is known to be less robust in some cases (Liu et al., 2022). In the future, we aim to explore how self-attention-based architectures can be adapted to Egyptian hieroglyphic texts.

7 Acknowledgement

We sincerely appreciate the guidance and help from Prof. Christopher Manning and Ms. Anna Goldie at Stanford NLP Group.

We are also grateful for the support from Prof. Jose Blanchet at Stanford Management Science and Engineering.

Special thanks to Mr. Amjad Refai at University of Hong Kong for Egyptology knowledge.

References

James P Allen. 2000. *Middle Egyptian: An introduction to the language and culture of hieroglyphs*. Cambridge University Press.

NA Aneesh, Anush Somasundaram, Azhar Ameen, Govind Sreekar Garimella, and R Jayashree. 2024. Exploring hieroglyph recognition: A deep learning approach. In *2024 2nd International Conference on Computer, Communication and Control (IC4)*, pages 1–5. IEEE.

Andrea Barucci, Chiara Canfailla, Costanza Cucci, Matteo Forasassi, Massimiliano Franci, Guido Guarducci, Tommaso Guidi, Marco Loschiavo, Marcello Picollo, Roberto Pini, et al. 2022. Ancient egyptian hieroglyphs segmentation and classification with convolutional neural networks. In *International Conference Florence Heri-Tech: the Future of Heritage Science and Technologies*, pages 126–139. Springer.

Andrea Barucci, Costanza Cucci, Massimiliano Franci, Marco Loschiavo, and Fabrizio Argenti. 2021. A deep learning approach to ancient egyptian hieroglyphs classification. *Ieee Access*, 9:123438–123447.

Yoshua Bengio, Réjean Ducharme, and Pascal Vincent. 2000. A neural probabilistic language model. *Advances in neural information processing systems*, 13.

Reham Elnabawy, Rimon Elias, Mohammed A-M Salem, and Slim Abdennadher. 2021. Extending gardiner's code for hieroglyphic recognition and english mapping. *Multimedia Tools and Applications*, 80:3391–3408.

Morris Franken and Jan C van Gemert. 2013. Automatic egyptian hieroglyph recognition by retrieving images as texts. In *Proceedings of the 21st ACM international conference on Multimedia*, pages 765–768.

Alan Henderson Gardiner. 1927. *Egyptian grammar: being an introduction to the study of hieroglyphs*. Clarendon Press.

Sepp Hochreiter and Jürgen Schmidhuber. 1997. Long short-term memory. *Neural computation*, 9(8):1735–1780.

Heidi Jauhiainen and Tommi Jauhiainen. 2023. Transliteration model for egyptian words. *Digital Humanities in the Nordic and Baltic Countries Publications*, 5(1):149–164.

Rafal Jozefowicz, Oriol Vinyals, Mike Schuster, Noam Shazeer, and Yonghui Wu. 2016. Exploring the limits of language modeling. *arXiv preprint arXiv:1602.02410*.

Bingbin Liu, Jordan T Ash, Surbhi Goel, Akshay Krishnamurthy, and Cyril Zhang. 2022. Transformers learn shortcuts to automata. In *The Eleventh International Conference on Learning Representations*.

Larry Medsker and Lakhmi C Jain. 1999. *Recurrent neural networks: design and applications*. CRC press.

Ragaa Moustafa, Farida Hesham, Samiha Hussein, Badr Amr, Samira Refaat, Nada Shorim, and Taraggy M Ghanim. 2022. Hieroglyphs language translator using deep learning techniques (scriba). In *2022 2nd International Mobile, Intelligent, and Ubiquitous Computing Conference (MIUCC)*, pages 125–132. IEEE.

Martin Popel and Ondřej Bojar. 2018. Training tips for the transformer model. *arXiv preprint arXiv:1804.00247*.

Serge Rosmorduc. 2020. Automated transliteration of late egyptian using neural networks. *Lingua Aegyptia-Journal of Egyptian Language Studies*, 28:233–257.

Holger Schwenk. 2007. Continuous space language models. In *Computer Speech & Language*, volume 21, pages 492–518.

Ashish Vaswani, Noam Shazeer, Niki Parmar, Jakob Uszkoreit, Llion Jones, Aidan N Gomez, Łukasz Kaiser, and Illia Polosukhin. 2017. Attention is all you need. *Advances in neural information processing systems*, 30.

A More Details on Experimental Settings

A.1 Evaluation Metrics

We evaluate the models on 3 metrics:

- *Perplexity.* It measures the model's probability of predicting the correct word. A lower perplexity score indicates better predictive performance and a higher confidence for the prediction.
- *Accuracy.* It is the ratio between the number of correct predictions and the total predictions. It reflects the practical efficacy of our models in real-world application.
- *F1 Score.* This metric harmonizes precision and recall, providing a balanced view of performance across all classes. We use the macro averaging method in F1 calculation.

A.2 Hyperparameters and Training Configurations

For fair comparison, we adopt an embedding size of 1024 and a hidden dimension size of 1024 for HieroLM and all the baselines, based on the hyperparameter analysis in Section 4.7. The dropout rate is searched individually for each dataset. We employ a learning rate decay and early stopping strategy, such that when the validation perplexity stops decreasing for 5 epochs, the learning rate decays by half, and the training will be stopped after five decays.

B Hyperparameter Analysis

In this section, we investigate the sensitivity of HieroLM with respect to key hyperparameters including embedding size, hidden dimension size, and dropout rate. The results, as summarized in Figure 6, also provide basis for our choice of hyperparameters.

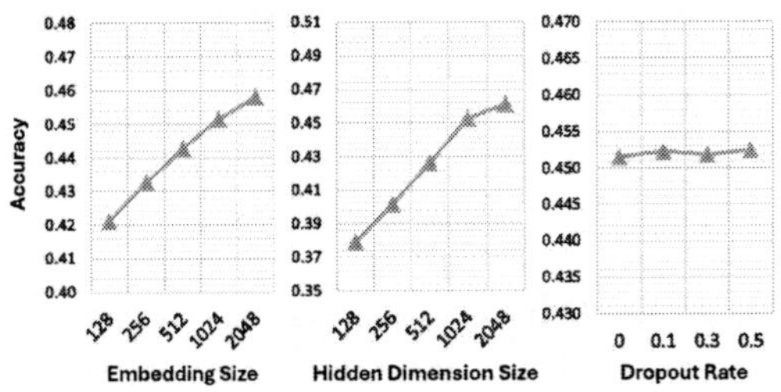

(a) AES

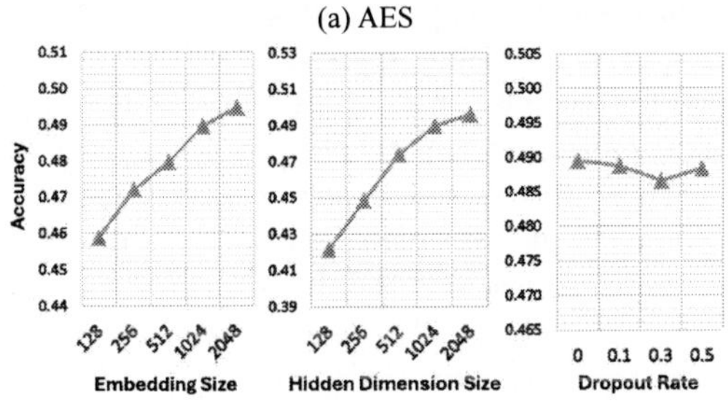

(b) Ramses

Figure 6: Test accuracy w.r.t. embedding size, hidden dim size, and dropout rate.

Evaluating LLM-Prompting for Sequence Labeling Tasks in Computational Literary Studies

Axel Pichler
Department of German Studies
University of Vienna
axel.pichler@univie.ac.at

Janis Pagel and **Nils Reiter**
Department of Digital Humanities
University of Cologne
{firstname.lastname}@uni-koeln.de

Abstract

Prompt engineering holds the promise for the computational literary studies (CLS) to obtain high quality markup for literary research questions by simply prompting large language models with natural language strings. We test prompt engineering's validity for two CLS sequence labeling tasks under the following aspects: (i) how generalizable are the results of identical prompts on different dataset splits?, (ii) how robust are performance results when re-formulating the prompts?, and (iii) how generalizable are certain fixed phrases added to the prompts that are generally considered to increase performance. We find that results are sensitive to data splits and prompt formulation, while the addition of fixed phrases does not change performance in most cases, depending on the chosen model.

1 Introduction

Large language models (LLMs) have taken over the field of natural language processing (NLP) in the past years. LLMs implement the transformer architecture and are fine-tuned to follow instructions (Mishra et al., 2022; Zhang et al., 2024), which also led to the introduction of a new paradigm: 'prompting'.[1] In contrast to pre-training, fine-tuning or classical machine learning, prompting does not actually update the weights of the model itself. Instead, prompt strategies aim at producing the best possible prompt for a given task (Liu et al., 2023), thus providing a textual context for the model to generate reasonable replies.

LLM-prompting is a promising development for digital humanities in general, because task descriptions can be expressed in natural language, presumably making it easier to connect to classical, non-digital research in the humanities. This may also apply to the model's output, if it is in natural language or can be verbalized (correctly) as such. A distinction can be made between two prompting scenarios: i) Interactive prompting, as with a chatbot, is the scenario in which most people currently experience LLMs, as it is easily available even without technical background. It is characterized by a direct application and associated implicit validation, often used in an exploratory manner. Note that results obtained must not be perfect or even correct to be useful, and in following Gricean conversation maxims (Grice, 1975), human users put in interpretation effort to make sense of the results. ii) Batch-use comes into play if prompts are applied to a large(r) quantity of data, and the LLM is used for automatic detection of some textual concept. This paradigm is closely related to established machine learning scenarios, and thus needs to follow established machine learning best practices. The remainder of this article is about this batch-use of LLM prompting.

Evaluation of LLMs can also be separated into two areas: i) With the goal of evaluating LLMs as such (and unrelated to a specific task), they are usually confronted with test items from multiple benchmark data sets that cover a certain range of tasks. ARC (Clark et al., 2018), for instance, defines 7787 natural science questions with four possible answers, out of which one is correct. The model is tasked to provide the identifier of the correct answer. Models can then be ranked according to their (average) performance on such benchmarks, resulting in rankings such as the HuggingFace Open LLM Leaderboard[2]. ii) For a task-specific evaluation, reference data for the specific task is needed, and allows comparing system and reference output as is established in machine learning. In both evaluation setups, it is important to realize that what is evaluated is not (only) the model itself, but a tuple of model, task formalization, parameters and prompt, and that an exhaustive evaluation of all possible settings is usually not possible. This paper, as

[1] Also called 'in-context-learning' (Brown et al., 2020).

[2] https://tinyurl.com/3ms6bmhm

Proceedings of LaTeCH-CLfL 2025, pages 32–46
May 4, 2025

do many others, selects a number of parameters for the experiments and this selection has theoretical and pragmatic reasons.

This paper explores the use of LLM-prompting in computational literary studies (CLS). CLS analyzes literary texts and text corpora using methods of statistics, machine learning and NLP. In doing so, CLS draws partly on traditional literary studies, but does so with the help of data-driven approaches and methods. Past studies in CLS focused on authorship attribution, drama and genre analysis, literary-historical questions, narratological and gender analysis and questions of canonicity (cf. Schöch et al., 2023; Pielström et al., 2023; Andresen and Reiter, 2024). Non-computational literary research questions are typically highly complex, context-dependent and embedded in a deep theoretical framework, that is often expressed somewhat vaguely. Addressing such questions thus requires a multitude of tools and methods that form components in an argumentation that uses manual and automatic work steps. The tasks we discuss in this paper are representative for such components.

Concretely, this paper's contribution is the systematic evaluation of a number of LLMs and prompts on two different CLS-relevant sequence classification tasks for which manually annotated reference data sets exist. Sequence classification in NLP is the task of assigning a categorical label to each element in a sequence of data, such as words in a sentence or characters in a word. Such tasks are complex as they combine two potentially separate work steps in one: the selection of a token span to be classified and the classification of this span. Such tasks are common in CLS as manual annotation tasks.[3]

An important methodological aspect of such an evaluation is that as soon as prompting strategies make use of manually or automatically optimizing prompts on a data set ("prompt engineering"), this needs to be treated as a training process, even if no weight updates are performed: Selecting the best prompt on a data set and evaluating its performance on the very same data set is a case of overfitting and the measured performance is not indicative of its performance on new data. This does not mean that performance on unseen data must be lower in every case – if the model-prompt-combination has generalized properly, it may even achieve similar performance on unseen data. We suspect that in practice this optimization process is usually based on a small, hand-picked selection of examples, and often not evaluated on an independent test set. Accordingly, to avoid overfitting, we propose to follow established best practices and make a (documented) split into train and test data, with similar roles as in classical machine learning: Train data is used to optimize a prompt and test data to evaluate it.

Research questions. Against this background, we will focus on the following three research questions: i) **How generalizable are performance measurements?** This question rests on the assumption that a good model shows similar performance on different data sets. If its performance varies strongly, the model has failed to capture the essence of the task. ii) **How robust is the model against meaning-preserving prompt variations?** This question is related to the issue that Mizrahi et al. (2024) have uncovered (and named "prompt brittleness"): That the performance of prompted LLMs reacts very strongly to minor changes in the prompts, be it minimal changes such as adding or changing punctuation marks, or lexical changes such as paraphrasing the task. iii) **How generalizable are recommendations on prompt components?** Because an exhaustive search over all possible prompts (or other parameters) is impossible, prompting usually relies on best practices developed in interactive prompting scenarios (Saravia, 2022; Bsharat et al., 2024), such as promising the model a reward. Our question is to find out whether following these best practices for non-interactive prompting leads to consistently best (or even good) results. I.e., we investigate if general recommendations on how to construct a prompt actually lead to performance gains and/or consistently best results on CLS tasks and data set.

Documentation of all our experiments (including prompt templates) is done in a GitHub repository, to facilitate the reproduction of our experiments.[4]

2 Related Work

Several studies in NLP use LLMs for classic classification tasks. Balkus and Yan (2023) use GPT-

[3]Following the categorization of classification tasks in cultural analytics according to Bamman et al. (2024), this primarily involves the category of "replacing human labeling at scale," which is also a prerequisite for "top-down theory testing". Note also the survey paper by Hatzel et al. (2023) on machine learning in computational literary studies.

[4]https://github.com/pagelj/prompt-cls

3's API to classify the topics of short texts and use both the generative completion capabilities as well as a dedicated classification end point of the API. Zhao et al. (2023) use ChatGPT to classify agriculture-related texts with regards to sentiment, prediction of natural disasters and text topic. Wang et al. (2023) test GPT-3.5, GPT-4 and Llama 2 on, among others, sentiment analysis of tweets. In addition to this, Clavié et al. (2023) show that in the binary classification of qualification requirements for job advertisements, LLMs such as OpenAI's text-davinci-003 model clearly outperform classical ML approaches such as SVM but also smaller 'foundational models' such as DeBERTaV3.

Many studies investigate the influence of prompts for prediction performance (Schick and Schütze, 2021; Zhao et al., 2021; Perez et al., 2021; Lu et al., 2022; Ceron et al., 2024). All come to the conclusion that the form and quality of manually crafted prompts is highly influential on performance and often suggest methods for automatically generating prompts or using methods such as prompt tuning to circumvent the shortcomings of hard prompts. Many studies distinguish systematically between different prompt components, such as "Definition", "Things to Avoid", etc. (Mishra et al., 2022). Sadr et al. (2025) investigate which words are most important in a prompt by systematically replacing words in prompt components like "Let's think step-by-step" and measure the change in performance via a newly introduced metric. They find that nouns are consistently among the most important words regarding prediction and that the most important word varies according to the task performed. Mizrahi et al. (2024) demonstrate how single prompts lead to chance-based outcomes and suggest using a suite of prompts and averaging over their performance (this strategy is called 'prompt ensemble' in Liu et al. (2023)). Lastly, Schaeffer et al. (2023) suggest that the proclaimed emergent abilities of LLMs disappear once appropriate evaluation metrics are used.

The largest study on the usages of LLMs for classification tasks in a computational humanities context to date comes from Ziems et al. (2024). They work in the context of computational social science and perform zero-shot learning on a wide variety of tasks on different textual levels such as sarcasm and ideology detection, misinformation detection, empathy classification, politeness, event detection and roles and tropes. The study uses one prompt template per task and does not address the potential impact of prompt brittleness on the evaluation. They find that, except for certain minor tasks, LLMs in a zero-shot setting are not able to outperform fine-tuned classifiers or replace the work of human annotators (Ziems et al., 2024, p. 240).

Pichler and Reiter (2024) come to a similar conclusion in the context of an ICL-experiment in the CLS, in which they investigate the extent to which OpenAI's text-davinci-003-LLM can reproduce the performance of smaller older models used by Piper (2020) in the course of a classification task based on complex knowledge from literary theory, namely the determination of domain specific generalizing statements in literary studies.

Pagel et al. (2024) tested several open and close-sourced LLMs in zero and few-shot setups on the task of identifying knowledge transfers about family relations in German dramas. They also conclude that, in the current state, LLMs are not suitable to sufficiently perform high-level CLS classification tasks out-of-the-box.

Bamman et al. (2024), recently published as a pre-print, arrives at differentiated results. The study identifies ten tasks from computer-assisted text analysis, characterized as cultural analytics, for which annotated reference data is available, and investigates how well these tasks can be solved by LLMs compared to pretrained language models (PLMs). The choosen LLMs are GPT-4o, LLAMA 3 70B and Mixtral 8x22B, which are prompted with a single prompt template containing 10 examples but no Chain-of-thought-prompts. They find that "LLMs offer competitive performance through prompting alone for established tasks, while traditional supervised methods excel for newly constructed phenomena (even in scenarios with limited training data)". In a further comparison, for which the models were fine-tuned on the task-specific reference data, the performance differences between masked PLMs and LLMs are even smaller. Issues of prompt brittleness and prompt generalizability are not addressed.

Hicke et al. (2024) perform zero-shot classification for focalization on 16 Stephen King novels with LLAMA 3 and GPT-4o and compare to a NaiveBayes and DistilBERT baseline. They find that GPT-4o performed best with an F1 score of 86.90, but also that initial inter-annotator agreement between the three annotators was relatively low with Krippendorff's α of 0.55. However, an adjudicated version could be created after discussion between the annotators. They also find a correlation between a model's confidence scores and its performance, as well as a robustness of GPT-4o's performance with regard to multiple runs and small changes in the prompt.

We are not aware of any studies dedicated to sequence classification tasks in CLS.

3 Sequence Classification Tasks and Data

This section describes the two sequence classification tasks (emotion and event) and data sets used in our experiments. Note that the event dataset is in German, while the emotion dataset is in English language. Regarding the issue of data leakage (Balloccu et al., 2024), please also note that both the emotion and event dataset are publicly available. It can therefore not be excluded that (parts of) the public data sets and their annotated labels have been included in the pre-training of our models.

Emotion The dataset for the emotion task is coming from work by Kim and Klinger (2018) and is called REMAN (Relational Emotion Annotation for Fiction). They provide annotations of 200 English texts from Project Gutenberg[5] and annotate the emotions *anger*, *anticipation*, *disgust*, *fear*, *joy*, *sadness*, *surprise* and *trust* plus a category *other emotion* for cases that do not fall into one of the above. Annotated is either a single word or phrase with a preference for shorter spans. For instance, the annotated span for the sentence "His smile was distinctly attractive." is "smile" and was given the *joy*-label. In a multi-step process, all spans that do not match exactly between annotators, but overlap, were adjudicated by an expert.

Kim and Klinger provide baseline experimental results on predicting emotions on their dataset, using dictionary and bag-of-words-based baselines, a conditional random field (CRF) model as well as a long short-term memory model (LSTM) architecture with a CRF classification on top. The LSTM-CRF performs best with an F1 score of 43 % in a strict setting where all spans have to match exactly, but the authors note that recall is low for both models. They report inter-annotator agreement scores for their annotations, ranging from an average Cohen's κ of 0.11 for *anticipation* to a κ value of 0.35 for *joy*. See Table 3 for an example of each emotion.

[5]https://www.gutenberg.org/

Event Vauth and Gius (2022) take six German-language texts from the TextGrid[6] and d-prose (Gius et al., 2021) repositories. They annotate three different event types, *process*, *stative* and *change of state*, as well as *non-event* (see Vauth and Gius, 2021). Each span receives exactly one of these labels.

The original annotation task consisted of three parts: In a first step, the annotation span had to be identified, in a second step it had to be marked with the corresponding labels, and then in a third step subordinate property tags had to be assigned. Following this procedure, they achieved an agreement for these event types of Krippendorff's α between 0.57 and 0.75, depending on the text.

To our knowledge, there are currently no published studies on automatic annotation of the dataset. Examples for annotation spans for each of the four categories look like the ones in Table 4.

4 Formalization

In this section, we describe which measurement techniques we use to answer the three research questions introduced above. In general, our prompts consist of a frame structure describing the role of the LLM, the task, the expected output format, and the labels to be used, with slots for variable components and the text to analyze: A prompt is thus defined as a complete input sequence that realizes one of 8 possible combinations of so-called prompt components, where *prompt components* are elements that can be switched on and off. The implementation of one of these 8 possible combinations as a prompt, we call *prompt configuration*. Additionally, there are 3 *paraphrases* (semantically equivalent reformulations) of each prompt. These were generated automatically by using GPT to generate 10 alternative reformulations based on an initial manually created prompt that follows current prompt engineering recommendations, from which we then manually selected three. All in all, this leads to $4 * 8 = 32$ different prompt configurations — for each model and each task — which results in a grand total of 64 different prompts and 256 model runs.

4.1 RQ1: Generalizability of Performance Measurements

To check whether and to what extent a particular prompt configuration performs equally well on dif-

[6]https://textgridrep.org/

ferent test samples, we proceed as follows: For each model, we test each prompt configuration on two test data sets and calculate the difference and p-values between the F1 scores obtained using a paired sample t-test. This way, we test the null hypothesis that different data samples have no effect on the performance.

4.2 RQ2: Robustness against Meaning-Preserving Prompt Variations

In order to investigate how robust each model is against semantic rephrasings in prompt formulations, we first define (with the help of a language model) four different but semantically equivalent paraphrases of each (fully instantiated) prompt. These changes cover the entire prompt: Next to the prompt components, elements of the frame structure of the prompt are also reformulated (see listings 1-4). We then look at the standard deviation of F1 scores over each of those prompt variants by comparing the paraphrases that realize the same components. We hypothesize that a more robust model is less sensitive against these paraphrases, and thus shows lower standard deviation.

4.3 RQ3: Generalizability of Prompt Component Optimization

For the final research question, we investigate how well different components added to a prompt generalize across tasks and models.

Under the term *component*, we understand phrases or instructions added to the prompt that are meant to improve model performance, but are not specific to solving a concrete task. One of the most popular examples of such a component is to assign a **role** or occupation to the model and ask it to provide an answer under the assumption that it behaves like a person with the specified role (for example "You are an expert mathematician").

Bsharat et al. (2024) provide an extensive list of principles to construct good prompts, including prompt components, from which we pick three that we perceive as currently popular options: (i) the model gets **bribed** to give a good answer, (ii) the **stakes** are high, and (iii) the model should think **step** by step.[7]

Concretely, we checked which of the prompt components were present in the best performing prompts per model and how often. This investigation sheds light on which components actually make a measurable positive impact on performance. We hypothesize that, provided the components are actually useful in boosting model performance, they should appear in all or close to all of the best-performing prompt variations.

5 Experiments

We carry out experiments on all tasks described above, using the following LLMs: GPT[8] (GPT-4o[9]), LLAMA (Llama3.1-8B-Instruct (AI@Meta, 2024)[10], MIXTRAL (Mixtral-8x7B-Instruct (Jiang et al., 2024)[11]), and SAUERKRAUT (SauerkrautLM[12]). The models provide a balance of close and (semi-)open source systems and with SAUERKRAUT there is a model that was especially re-pretrained on German language texts. Furthermore, all models displayed high scores on popular NLP benchmarks and should therefore generally be able to tackle the two CLS tasks. Due to the computer resources available, we quantified LLAMA and SAUERKRAUT into a 4-bit version using HuggingFace's `bitsandbytes` library.

5.1 Experimental Setup

For the **Event** dataset, we remove annotated categories which occur less than 600 times. This leads to the *change of state* class being removed, leaving us with the *process*, *stative* and *no event* labels. We use a single text out of four, Effi Briest by Theodor Fontane, as it is by far the longest text and the only one for which the requirement of 600 instances per class can be kept. As the **Emotion** data set is smaller, we have set a threshold of at least 150 occurrences per label. This leaves us with the classes *anger*, *disgust*, *joy*, *sadness* and *surprise*.

From these samples, we create two random subsets for each task, each with 15 % of the instances. The distribution of labels in each subset corresponds to the distribution of label occurrences in the whole dataset. These sets are subsequently called *test 1* and *test 2*.

For all tasks, each prompt contained only a single target sentence together with a fixed frame and

[7] For the specific formulations of the components, see section B

[8] In the following, we will use short names in small caps to refer to the concrete models used in the experiments.

[9] `https://www.wikidata.org/wiki/Q125919502`

[10] `https://huggingface.co/meta-llama/Meta-Llama-3.1-8b-Instruct`

[11] `https://huggingface.co/mistralai/Mixtral-8x7B-Instruct-v0.1`

[12] `https://huggingface.co/VAGOsolutions/Llama-3.1-SauerkrautLM-8b-Instruct`

some of the components (see Listing 1 for an example). The models were asked to i) select word sequences that match the definition and ii) assign a class label in a second step. This procedure differs from the standard procedure for text and sequence classification in that the probabilities of the labels for a selection of tokens are not determined by the LLM, but rather the LLM is prompted to generate both the text sequence to be classified and the corresponding label. To evaluate the output of the LLMs generated in this way, we mapped the classified text sequences to the input sentence, then tokenized it and assigned the label "None" to all those tokens that were not labeled. The evaluation was then based on these token-label pairs.

For all models, we set the temperature to 0.1 and left `top_k` at the default of 5, in order to get results relatively close to deterministic for reproducability. For all other hyperparameters, we used the model-specific default values.

5.2 Results

Before discussing results related to our research questions, the general, best possible performance measured in F1 on the entire test set for each model can be seen in Table 1. Note that different models achieve best performance with different prompt configurations. As can be seen, performance scores for the emotion task are generally lower than for the event task. Best models are GPT (for emotion) and MIXTRAL (for event). We also compare with current average results from the HuggingFace Open LLM Leaderboard that — albeit on very different tasks than ours — are in a similar range. The HuggingFace average is composed of scores for six different benchmarks, including math problems, formatting challenges and language understanding. The leaderboard does not include results for GPT-4o. The similar range of results shows that the scores in our experiments are not only due to our CLS tasks, but also occur for more general tasks. It should however be noted that the standard deviation for the benchmark results from HuggingFace are relatively high, with some benchmarks showing scores of around 70% accuracy, while for other benchmarks, the accuracy is under 10%.

Model	Emotion	Event	HF
GPT	27.04	29.03	-
LLAMA	19.21	28.93	28.20
MIXTRAL	22.72	32.6	23.84
SAUERKRAUT	21.79	28.04	28.68

Table 1: Overall best possible performance, measured in F1 score. Results have been achieved with different prompt configurations. We also compare to the average scores of the HuggingFace (HF) benchmark on `https://huggingface.co/spaces/open-llm-leaderboard/open_llm_leaderboard`, last access on 15th November 2024.

Task	Model	Diff. (pp)
Emotion	GPT	7.7
	MIXTRAL	6.7
	LLAMA	4.2
	SAUERKRAUT	5.2
Event	GPT	6.2
	MIXTRAL	10.9
	LLAMA	6.6
	SAUERKRAUT	6.3

Table 2: Mean of differences of the F1-scores obtained on the two test stets and p-values between the two test sets per model for the Emotion and Event task. All differences are statistically significant ($p < 0.05$).

5.2.1 Generalizability of Performance Measurements

The results relevant to RQ1 can be found in Table 2. Generally, the models achieve a mean of differences for the different data sets between 4.2 % and 10.9 %. While these numbers seem small, they represent a deviation of up to almost 11 percentage points in F1 score, which would be a substantial difference for most applications. The differences between the F1 scores on the two data sets are statistically significant on both tasks for all models (p-values < 0.05). The null hypothesis that different data samples have no effect on the measurement of performance can therefore be rejected in all cases. This indicates that the measurement of the performance on one test set does not generalize well to another test set. It must therefore be expected that performance on new/unseen data sets is significantly different. Possible reasons for this are a.) that the models did not properly generalize (i.e., learn the true nature of the task) or b.) that the two test data sets are distributed differently.

5.2.2 Model Robustness against Prompt Variations

The results for RQ2 can be found in Tables 5 and 6 (see Appendix) for the emotion and event task respectively. Please note that the table shows mean and standard deviation of the F1 scores on the entire test data set (i.e., the union of *test 1* and *test 2*), using four different variants of the prompts.

Generally, the models achieve a mean standard deviation for the different component configuration between 2.4 and 5.92 %. While these numbers seem small, they represent a deviation of up to 6 percentage points in F1 score, which would be a substantial difference for most applications.

For the emotion task, LLAMA achieves the smallest deviation over the formulations, and can thus be considered the most robust model. For the event task, SAUERKRAUT achieves the smallest average deviation, although LLAMA's deviation is only slightly higher. GPT and MIXTRAL do not show an interpretable pattern in this evaluation.

Compared to the results reported by Mizrahi et al. (2024), we can confirm the observation that, depending on the prompt formulation, any ranking of the models can be achieved. We also note, however, that the deviations are much smaller, albeit on a generally low performance level.

5.2.3 Generalizability of Prompt Component Importance

The analysis of prompt components, shown in Figure 1 reveals that there are only few components that occur in all best performing prompts (**steps** three times, **bribe** one time out of a possible eight).[13] Only for LLAMA, **steps** occurs in all best performing prompts, making it the only occurrence were this happens. On average, components occur only half of the time in all best performing prompts across all models and tasks. Since this is around chance level and we expected to see a relatively high frequency for each component, we conclude that the components are generally not a useful addition to the prompts. Overall, no general recommendation can be derived from these figures for the inclusion of certain components in a uniformly designed prompt, at least for the two CLS tasks and four models examined.

6 Discussion

Dividing the test data into two sub-data sets (RQ1) shows a clear tendency: All four models perform in a statistically significant way differently on the two data sets. This is arguably not specific to prompting or large language models, but a general property of machine learning approaches, although we are not aware of work that systematically investigates this. We believe this to be a consequence of how test data is sampled, how much variety of the phenomenon it covers, and, ultimately, how representative the selected test sample is for other test samples or the 'population' in general. In particular the latter question is not easy to answer, given that we are dealing with historical and cultural data, which is subject to a number of highly intransparent selection processes (cf. Levi, 2013). Still, as it has been hinted that large language models "understand" a prompt (Bubeck et al., 2023)[14] (which nobody has claimed for classical machine learning algorithms), it can be argued that if the models would have understood those prompts, they would not show a statistically significant difference on different test data sets.

The fact that different prompts lead to different responses (RQ2) is not surprising per se. What Mizrahi et al. (2024) have uncovered is that meaning-preserving prompt variants (e.g., spelling variation or paraphrases) also lead to different responses, and that – when ranking models for their performance – the exact prompt formulation has tremendous influence on the ranking of such models. They therefore recommend to use the mean performance over multiple prompts. Generally, we also observe a difference in F1 score depending on the exact prompt. While model ranking is not our prime goal here, different model rankings can be established from our experiments as well – which makes the search for the 'best model' for a given task more complex. However, the differences we observe are rather modest, with standard deviations over various prompt variants between 2 and 6 points in F1 score. Still, if the overall absolute performance results were better, a difference in this range could very well have impact on the applicability of such a model in practice. To address specific tasks, there is no alternative to having annotated reference data and experimenting with different formulations and parameters. At the same time, exhaustively searching the best setting is impossible.

Finally, we have investigated recommendations that are often given for manually constructed prompts (RQ3), on what to include in the prompt.

[13]RQ3 has only been evaluated on *test 1*, since it yielded the best average performance scores.

[14]The paper contains sentences such as: "One of the key aspects of GPT-4's intelligence is its generality, the ability to seemingly understand and connect any topic, and to perform tasks that go beyond the typical scope of narrow AI systems." (Bubeck et al., 2023, p. 7)

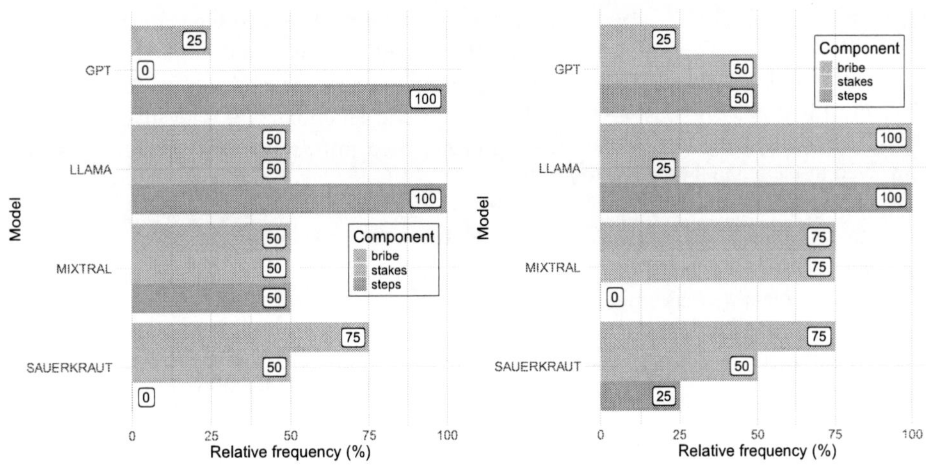

(a) Emotion (b) Event

Figure 1: RQ 3: Relative frequency of enabled prompt components in the best performing prompts for *test 1*, measured per model and task and across paraphrases.

Our results support these recommendations only partially. First of all, we see different results for different tasks. Across the two tasks discussed in this paper, we can only extract three clear trends: a) LLAMA seems to benefit from using the steps-component (asking the model to think step by step). b) The same component seems to be detrimental for the SAUERKRAUT model. c) SAUERKRAUT, on the other hand, benefits from the bribe-component for both tasks. For all other components and models, no tendency can be discerned.

In general, across the three research questions in this paper, there seems to be a generalizability issue (which is also discussed in recent papers in philosophy of science, cf. Buijsman and Durán, 2024). Generalizing from any scientific experiment to the 'real world' (or, more technically, from lab data to application data) rests on certain assumptions about model behavior and data sets. This applies first to the performance measures that have been achieved on a test set – assuming representativity of the test set, performance will be roughly similar during application. This is, in practice, impossible to control and verify. Secondly, as the actual performance of a model-prompt-pair varies substantially depending on prompt variations, it is impossible to recommend a model or prompt formulation that is *in general* beneficial to the performance results. This holds not only to the formulation variants of a prompt, but, thirdly, also to the selection of prompt components. While there is no reason to believe that the same prompt component will always be beneficial (or detrimental) to the results – properly establishing prompt components that *often* lead to better results would require either a huge project or a number of meta studies that investigate many different existing publications.

Conversely, the scientific use of LLMs and prompting as a ML technique is usually not about general chat functionality (as is a smart personal assistant or "general artificial intelligence"), but about very specific questions and tasks. The general performance of a LLM (measured on some benchmark) may not be indicative for the specific tasks that a researcher from CLS has as their goal. For solving specific tasks, using reference data as train/test data still is the only way to systematically search for the best performing combination of model, prompt and parameters.

7 Conclusions

We were able to show that (i) LLM models are sensitive to data splits (ii) the choice of prompt-model combination determines the success in performance to a high degree and (iii) the helpfulness of fixed components in the prompts to increase performance can not be corroborated for all models for the given tasks. Overall, it could also be shown that all tested models have problems to reach satisfying results on both tasks (emotion and event sequences classification), casting doubt on the immediate usefulness of in-context, zero-shot LLM-sequence-classification for the given CLS tasks.

Limitations

Due to the complexity of the model architectures, which is known to be not publicly available for many models (Liesenfeld et al., 2023), as well as the effort involved in the manual creation of reference data curated by specialists, the present study could not take into account all factors that we believe are relevant for assessing its results. This is not least due to the fact that there is still no generally valid and generic formula for what is ultimately relevant for the results that a specific LLM achieves on specific data. Of the factors that we consider relevant, we were unable to take into account the following in particular: 1) The theory dependency of the evaluation data: In the Digital Humanities in general and CLS in particular, the theoretical orientation determines which concepts are operationalized and how they are subsequently measured. It can be assumed that alternative annotation guidelines that are also plausible from a literary studies perspective can be created for the two tasks we examined. In this respect, the classification tasks evaluated here should be tested on several curated reference data sets in order to check the extent to which different operationalization approaches affect the performance of the models via the detour of the reference data. 2) The statistical representativeness of the data split: this is unclear since we only worked with two test splits, although it is unlikely that different splits on the current data would result in significant difference in performance. 3) The data on which the models were trained: for each task, we only evaluated one dataset with certain choices made that other datasets on the same task might not contain. 4.) the answer-space-mapping: i.e. it is completely unclear if the internal representations of the model that produce natural-language-like output correspond directly to the assumptions that domain specialists have when applying predefined class-labels.

Another limitation that needs to be mentioned is related to the tasks we discuss here: Both of them have clear roots in CLS, although they may not be what is ultimately interesting to a literary scholar. Literary research questions, if they are not on specific interpretations of specific texts, which rules out quantitative approaches a priori, are complex, multi-modal and highly context- and theory-dependent. Addressing such tasks requires the integration of many different analysis components, and we consider the two tasks under investigation to be able to fill the role of two such components. Thus: Both event and emotion detection do not address literary research questions per se, the detection of events and emotions is a relevant ingredient for many, more abstract, literary research questions.

References

AI@Meta. 2024. Llama 3 model card.

Melanie Andresen and Nils Reiter, editors. 2024. *Computational Drama Analysis. Reflecting on Methods and Interpretations*. De Gruyter.

Salvador V. Balkus and Donghui Yan. 2023. Improving short text classification with augmented data using gpt-3. *Natural Language Engineering*, page 1–30.

Simone Balloccu, Patrícia Schmidtová, Mateusz Lango, and Ondrej Dusek. 2024. Leak, cheat, repeat: Data contamination and evaluation malpractices in closed-source LLMs. In *Proceedings of the 18th Conference of the European Chapter of the Association for Computational Linguistics (Volume 1: Long Papers)*, pages 67–93, St. Julian's, Malta. Association for Computational Linguistics.

David Bamman, Kent K. Chang, Li Lucy, and Naitian Zhou. 2024. On classification with large language models in cultural analytics. Preprint.

Tom Brown, Benjamin Mann, Nick Ryder, Melanie Subbiah, Jared D Kaplan, Prafulla Dhariwal, Arvind Neelakantan, Pranav Shyam, Girish Sastry, Amanda Askell, Sandhini Agarwal, Ariel Herbert-Voss, Gretchen Krueger, Tom Henighan, Rewon Child, Aditya Ramesh, Daniel Ziegler, Jeffrey Wu, Clemens Winter, Chris Hesse, Mark Chen, Eric Sigler, Mateusz Litwin, Scott Gray, Benjamin Chess, Jack Clark, Christopher Berner, Sam McCandlish, Alec Radford, Ilya Sutskever, and Dario Amodei. 2020. Language models are few-shot learners. In *Advances in Neural Information Processing Systems (NeurIPS)*, volume 33, pages 1877–1901.

Sondos Mahmoud Bsharat, Aidar Myrzakhan, and Zhiqiang Shen. 2024. Principled instructions are all you need for questioning LLaMA-1/2, GPT-3.5/4.

Sébastien Bubeck, Varun Chandrasekaran, Ronen Eldan, Johannes Gehrke, Eric Horvitz, Ece Kamar, Peter Lee, Yin Tat Lee, Yuanzhi Li, Scott Lundberg, Harsha Nori, Hamid Palangi, Marco Tulio Ribeiro, and Yi Zhang. 2023. Sparks of Artificial General Intelligence: Early experiments with GPT-4. ArXiv:2303.12712 [cs].

Stefan Buijsman and Juan M. Durán. 2024. Epistemic implications of machine learning models in science. In *The Routledge Handbook of Philosophy of Scientific Modeling*, 1 edition, pages 456–468. Routledge, London.

Tanise Ceron, Neele Falk, Ana Barić, Dmitry Nikolaev, and Sebastian Padó. 2024. Beyond prompt brittleness: Evaluating the reliability and consistency of political worldviews in LLMs. ArXiv preprint 2402.17649.

Peter Clark, Isaac Cowhey, Oren Etzioni, Tushar Khot, Ashish Sabharwal, Carissa Schoenick, and Oyvind Tafjord. 2018. Think you have Solved Question Answering? Try ARC, the AI2 Reasoning Challenge. _eprint: 1803.05457.

Benjamin Clavié, Alexandru Ciceu, Frederick Naylor, Guillaume Soulié, and Thomas Brightwell. 2023. Large language models in the workplace: A case study on prompt engineering for job type classification. In *Natural Language Processing and Information Systems*, volume 13913 of *Lecture Notes in Computer Science*, pages 3–17, Cham. Springer Nature Switzerland.

Evelyn Gius, Svenja Guhr, and Benedikt Adelmann. 2021. d-prose 1870-1920.

Herbert Paul Grice. 1975. Logic and conversation. *Syntax and Semantics*, 3(S 41):58.

Hans Ole Hatzel, Haimo Stiemer, Chris Biemann, and Evelyn Gius. 2023. Machine Learning in Computational Literary Studies. *it - Information Technology*. Read_Status: New Read_Status_Date: 2024-10-18T18:55:15.614Z.

Rebecca M. M. Hicke, Yuri Bizzoni, Pascale Feldkamp, and Ross Deans Kristensen-McLachlan. 2024. Says who? effective zero-shot annotation of focalization.

Albert Q. Jiang, Alexandre Sablayrolles, Antoine Roux, Arthur Mensch, Blanche Savary, Chris Bamford, Devendra Singh Chaplot, Diego de las Casas, Emma Bou Hanna, Florian Bressand, Gianna Lengyel, Guillaume Bour, Guillaume Lample, Lélio Renard Lavaud, Lucile Saulnier, Marie-Anne Lachaux, Pierre Stock, Sandeep Subramanian, Sophia Yang, Szymon Antoniak, Teven Le Scao, Théophile Gervet, Thibaut Lavril, Thomas Wang, Timothée Lacroix, and William El Sayed. 2024. Mixtral of experts.

Evgeny Kim and Roman Klinger. 2018. Who feels what and why? annotation of a literature corpus with semantic roles of emotions. In *Proceedings of the 27th International Conference on Computational Linguistics*, pages 1345–1359, Santa Fe, New Mexico, USA. Association for Computational Linguistics.

Amalia S. Levi. 2013. Humanities 'Big Data'. myths, challenges, and lessons. In *IEEE International Conference on Big Data*.

Andreas Liesenfeld, Alianda Lopez, and Mark Dingemanse. 2023. Opening up chatgpt: Tracking openness, transparency, and accountability in instruction-tuned text generators. In *Proceedings of the 5th International Conference on Conversational User Interfaces*, CUI '23, New York, NY, USA. Association for Computing Machinery.

Pengfei Liu, Weizhe Yuan, Jinlan Fu, Zhengbao Jiang, Hiroaki Hayashi, and Graham Neubig. 2023. Pre-train, prompt, and predict: A systematic survey of prompting methods in natural language processing. *ACM Comput. Surv.*, 55(9).

Yao Lu, Max Bartolo, Alastair Moore, Sebastian Riedel, and Pontus Stenetorp. 2022. Fantastically ordered prompts and where to find them: Overcoming few-shot prompt order sensitivity. In *Proceedings of the 60th Annual Meeting of the Association for Computational Linguistics (Volume 1: Long Papers)*, pages 8086–8098, Dublin, Ireland. Association for Computational Linguistics.

Swaroop Mishra, Daniel Khashabi, Chitta Baral, and Hannaneh Hajishirzi. 2022. Cross-Task Generalization via Natural Language Crowdsourcing Instructions. In *Proceedings of the 60th Annual Meeting of the Association for Computational Linguistics (Volume 1: Long Papers)*, pages 3470–3487, Dublin, Ireland. Association for Computational Linguistics.

Moran Mizrahi, Guy Kaplan, Dan Malkin, Rotem Dror, Dafna Shahaf, and Gabriel Stanovsky. 2024. State of what art? a call for multi-prompt llm evaluation.

Janis Pagel, Axel Pichler, and Nils Reiter. 2024. Evaluating in-context learning for computational literary studies: A case study based on the automatic recognition of knowledge transfer in German drama. In *Proceedings of the 8th Joint SIGHUM Workshop on Computational Linguistics for Cultural Heritage, Social Sciences, Humanities and Literature (LaTeCH-CLfL 2024)*, pages 1–10, St. Julians, Malta. Association for Computational Linguistics.

Ethan Perez, Douwe Kiela, and Kyunghyun Cho. 2021. True few-shot learning with language models. In *Advances in Neural Information Processing Systems*.

Axel Pichler and Nils Reiter. 2024. »LLMs for everything?« Potentiale und Probleme der Anwendung von In-Context-Learning für die Computational Literary Studies. In *Book of Abstracts of DHd*.

Steffen Pielström, Fotis Jannidis, Evelyn Gius, Jonas Kuhn, Nils Reiter, Christof Schöch, and Simone Winko. 2023. SPP 2207 Computational Literary Studies (CLS) Projects. Accessed: 2024-10-25.

Andrew Piper. 2020. *Can We Be Wrong? The Problem of Textual Evidence in a Time of Data*, 1 edition. Cambridge University Press.

Nikta Gohari Sadr, Sangmitra Madhusudan, and Ali Emami. 2025. Think or step-by-step? UnZIPping the black box in zero-shot prompts.

Elvis Saravia. 2022. Prompt Engineering Guide. Accessed: 2024-07-09.

Rylan Schaeffer, Brando Miranda, and Sanmi Koyejo. 2023. Are emergent abilities of large language models a mirage?

Timo Schick and Hinrich Schütze. 2021. Few-shot text generation with natural language instructions. In *Proceedings of the 2021 Conference on Empirical Methods in Natural Language Processing*, pages 390–402, Online and Punta Cana, Dominican Republic. Association for Computational Linguistics.

Christof Schöch, Julia Dudar, and Evegniia Fileva, editors. 2023. *Survey of Methods in Computational Literary Studies (=CLS INFRA D3.2: Series of Five Short Survey Papers on Methodological Issues)*. CLS INFRA, Trier. With contributions by Joanna Byszuk, Julia Dudar, Evegniia Fileva, Andressa Gomide, Lisanne van Rossum, Christof Schöch, Artjoms Šeļa and Karina van Dalen-Oskam.

Michael Vauth and Evelyn Gius. 2021. Richtlinien für die Annotation narratologischer Ereigniskonzepte.

Michael Vauth and Evelyn Gius. 2022. Event annotations of prose. *Journal of Open Humanities Data*, 8(19):1–6.

Zhiqiang Wang, Yiran Pang, and Yanbin Lin. 2023. Large language models are zero-shot text classifiers.

Shengyu Zhang, Linfeng Dong, Xiaoya Li, Sen Zhang, Xiaofei Sun, Shuhe Wang, Jiwei Li, Runyi Hu, Tianwei Zhang, Fei Wu, and Guoyin Wang. 2024. Instruction tuning for large language models: A survey.

Biao Zhao, Weiqiang Jin, Javier Del Ser, and Guang Yang. 2023. Chatagri: Exploring potentials of chatgpt on cross-linguistic agricultural text classification. *Neurocomputing*, 557:126708.

Tony Z. Zhao, Eric Wallace, Shi Feng, Dan Klein, and Sameer Singh. 2021. Calibrate before use: Improving few-shot performance of language models. In *Proceedings of International Conference on Machine Learning 2021 (ICML)*.

Caleb Ziems, William Held, Omar Shaikh, Jiaao Chen, Zhehao Zhang, and Diyi Yang. 2024. Can large language models transform computational social science? *Computational Linguistics*, 50(1):237–291.

A Dataset Examples

Sentence	Class
For I fear the failing will go with me to the grave that I am very ready to be annoyed, even to the **loss of my temper**, at the urgings of ignoble prudence.	anger
She would brighten up greatly at this, taking it for a compliment **of the best sort**.	anticipation
For I fear the failing will go with me to the grave that I am very ready to be annoyed, even to the loss of my temper, at the urgings of **ignoble prudence**.	disgust
Through all its **tremor**, there was a look of constancy that greatly pleased me.	fear
His **smile** was distinctly attractive.	joy
'Eh,' said the old man, **staring at the floor** and lifting his hands up and down, while his arms rested on the elbows of his chair, 'it's a poor tale if I mun leave th' ould spot an be buried in a strange parish.	sadness
Then she went on with a **sudden outbreak of passion**, a burst of summer thunder in a clear sky:	surprise
"**Not a doubt** of it, my dear.	trust

Table 3: Examples for annotations (bold) in dataset "Emotion".

Sentence	Class
Ich glaube, Mama würde sich freuen, wenn sie wüßte, daß ich so was gesagt habe. "**I think** mom would be happy if she knew I said something like that."	stative
Sidonie nickte. "**Sidonie noded**."	process
Effi, als sie seiner ansichtig wurde, **kam in ein nervöses Zittern**; "**Effi**, when she saw him, **began to tremble nervously**;"	change of state
In drei Tagen feiern wir Sylvester. "**In three days we will celebrate New Year's Eve**."	non event

Table 4: Examples for annotations (bold) in dataset "Event" from the text *Effi Briest*.

B Prompt Templates

```
### Role
You are a literary scholar.

### Instruction
Your task is to classify parts of sentences on the basis of labels given to you.
This should be done in two steps: First, extract the part of the sentence to which one of the three labels applies. Then output this label.

Let's think step by step. <step>
I'm going to tip $1000 for a better solution! <bribe>

### Labels
Select one of the following labels to classify a text excerpt:
        Label: process
        Label: stative_event
        Label: non_event

### Application
When annotating text snippets, the following steps should be taken to determine the appropriate label:
1. **Identify the Main Verb**: Determine the main verb in the sentence or clause to understand the nature of the action or state being described.
2. **Analyze the Context**: Consider the surrounding context to ensure the correct interpretation of the verb and the overall meaning of the snippet.
3. **Assign the Label**:
        - If the text is purely descriptive or provides background information without any action, label it as non_event.
        - If the text describes a state or condition without any dynamic action, label it as stative_event.
        - If the text describes an action or process that involves change or progression, label it as process.

### Output format
Use the following output format:
Part of Sentence to be labeled: str
Label: str

Do NOT generate any more text or repeat the input!
Doing this task well is very important for my career. <stakes>

### What types of event can be found in the following sentence: {snippet}
Part of Sentence to be labeled:
Label:
```

Listing 1: Example prompt (Template 1; Event). The occurrance of the component phrases is annotated in angle brackets.

```
### Role
You are a literary scholar.

### Instruction
Your assignment is to identify and categorize specific segments of sentences according to predefined labels provided to you.
This process involves two steps: First, isolate the relevant portion of the sentence that corresponds to one of the three labels. Then, assign the appropriate label to that portion.

Let's approach this systematically, one step at a time.
I will reward $1000 for anyone who can deliver a more optimal solution.

### Labels
Select one of the following labels to classify a text excerpt:
        Label: process
        Label: stative_event
        Label: non_event

### Application
When annotating text snippets, the following steps should be taken to determine the appropriate label:
1. **Identify the Main Verb**: Determine the main verb in the sentence or clause to understand the nature of the action or state being described.
2. **Analyze the Context**: Consider the surrounding context to ensure the correct interpretation of the verb and the overall meaning of the snippet.
3. **Assign the Label**:
        - If the text is purely descriptive or provides background information without any action, label it as non_event.
        - If the text describes a state or condition without any dynamic action, label it as stative_event.
        - If the text describes an action or process that involves change or progression, label it as process.

### Output format
Use the following output format:
Part of Sentence to be labeled: str
Label: str

Do NOT generate any more text or repeat the input!

### What types of event can be found in the following sentence: {snippet}
Part of Sentence to be labeled:
Label:
```

Listing 2: "Prompt (Template 2; Event; all components)."

```
### Role
You are a literary scholar.

### Instruction
Your objective is to analyze sentences and label specific parts based on the given set of labels.
This task should be completed in two phases: Initially, identify the segment of the sentence that matches one of the three labels. Subsequently, assign the corresponding label to that segment.

Let's break this down into manageable steps.
I'm prepared to give a $1000 tip for a superior solution.

### Labels
Select one of the following labels to classify a text excerpt:

        Label: anger
        Label: joy
        Label: surprise
        Label: sadness
        Label: disgust

### Application
When annotating text snippets, span annotations of key words (e. g., "afraid") should be prefered, except cases when
emotions are only expressed with a phrase (e. g., "tense and frightened") or indirectly (e. g., "the corners of her mouth went down").
Each span is associated with one or more emotion.

### Output format
Use the following output format:
Part of Sentence to be labeled: str
Label: str

Do NOT generate any more text or repeat the input!

### What types of emotion can be found in the follwing text snippet: {snippet}
Part of Sentence to be labeled:
Label:
```

Listing 3: "Prompt (Template 3; Emotion; all components)."

```
### Role
You are a literary scholar.

### Instruction
Your mission is to examine sentences
    and categorize certain elements
    using the provided labels.
This should be accomplished in two
    stages: First, pinpoint the portion
    of the sentence that aligns with
    one of the three labels. Then,
    designate the appropriate label for
    that portion.

Let's tackle this challenge
    methodically, step by step.
To encourage a superior answer, I will
    provide a tip of $1000.

### Labels
Select one of the following labels to
    classify a text excerpt:

        Label: anger
        Label: joy
        Label: surprise
        Label: sadness
        Label: disgust

### Application
When annotating text snippets, span
    annotations of key words (e. g., "
    afraid") should be prefered, except
    cases when
emotions are only expressed with a
    phrase (e. g., "tense and
    frightened") or indirectly (e. g.,
    "the corners of her mouth went down
    ").
Each span is associated with one or
    more emotion.

### Output format
Use the following output format:
Part of Sentence to be labeled: str
Label: str

Do NOT generate any more text or
    repeat the input!

### What types of emotion can be found
    in the follwing text snippet: {
    snippet}
Part of Sentence to be labeled:
Label:
```

Listing 4: "Prompt (Template 4; Emotion; all components)."

C Full Results

Model	Bribe	Stakes	Steps	Mean	Std. dev.
	Components			Over 4 variants	
GPT	−	−	−	18.27	5.24
	−	−	+	18.58	5.31
	−	+	−	18.01	4.76
	−	+	+	17.15	3.95
	+	−	−	17.74	4.65
	+	−	+	17.5	4.83
	+	+	−	17.67	4.3
	+	+	+	17.42	4.58
	Mean			17.79	4.7
LLAMA	−	−	−	14.47	2
	−	−	+	15.41	3.04
	−	+	−	14.63	2.21
	−	+	+	15.16	2.53
	+	−	−	14.15	1.96
	+	−	+	15.27	2.46
	+	+	−	14.41	2.54
	+	+	+	15.19	2.47
	Mean			14.84	2.4
MIXTRAL	−	−	−	16.34	3.44
	−	−	+	16.85	3.93
	−	+	−	16.74	3.54
	−	+	+	16.52	3.35
	+	−	−	16.92	4.14
	+	−	+	16.33	3.54
	+	+	−	16.89	3.86
	+	+	+	16.51	3.46
	Mean			16.64	3.66
SAUERKRAUT	−	−	−	16.0	2.69
	−	−	+	15.53	2.69
	−	+	−	15.74	2.48
	−	+	+	15.87	2.88
	+	−	−	15.97	3.23
	+	−	+	15.3	2.43
	+	+	−	16.16	3.29
	+	+	+	16.12	3.47
	Mean			15.84	2.9

Table 5: RQ 2: Robustness against prompt variations (emotion task)

Model	Components			Over 4 variants	
	Bribe	Stakes	Steps	Mean	Std. dev.
GPT	−	−	−	21.86	3.9
	−	−	+	22.03	3.69
	−	+	−	21.45	4.08
	−	+	+	21.85	3.91
	+	−	−	21.29	3.88
	+	−	+	21.34	3.8
	+	+	−	21.48	3.9
	+	+	+	21.01	3.3
	Mean			21.54	3.81
LLAMA	−	−	−	20.22	3.05
	−	−	+	20.17	4.46
	−	+	−	19.47	3.14
	−	+	+	20.59	4.56
	+	−	−	19.71	3.28
	+	−	+	22.0	4.79
	+	+	−	19.71	3.67
	+	+	+	21.43	4.39
	Mean			20.41	3.92
MIXTRAL	−	−	−	24.3	6.08
	−	−	+	23.98	5.72
	−	+	−	23.68	5.54
	−	+	+	24.18	5.84
	+	−	−	24.07	5.9
	+	−	+	23.8	5.86
	+	+	−	24.51	6.53
	+	+	+	23.84	5.88
	Mean			24.05	5.92
SAUERKRAUT	−	−	−	22.19	3.68
	−	−	+	21.9	3
	−	+	−	22.36	3.61
	−	+	+	22.46	3.79
	+	−	−	22.63	4.04
	+	−	+	22.04	3.01
	+	+	−	22.94	3.59
	+	+	+	22.6	3.25
	Mean			22.39	3.5

Table 6: RQ 2: Robustness against prompt variations (event task)

Generation of Russian Poetry of Different Genres and Styles Using Neural Networks with Character-Level Tokenization

Ilya Koziev
SaluteDevices
inkoziev@gmail.com

Alena Fenogenova
SaluteDevices
alenush93@gmail.com

Abstract

Automatic poetry generation is an immensely complex task, even for the most advanced Large Language Models (LLMs) that requires a profound understanding of intelligence, world and linguistic knowledge, and a touch of creativity. This paper investigates the use of LLMs in generating Russian syllabo-tonic poetry of various genres and styles. The study explores a character-level tokenization architectures and demonstrates how a language model can be pretrained and finetuned to generate poetry requiring knowledge of a language's phonetics. Additionally, the paper assesses the quality of the generated poetry and the effectiveness of the approach in producing different genres and styles. The study's main contribution is the introduction of two end-to-end architectures for syllabo-tonic Russian poetry: pretrained models, a comparative analysis of the approaches, and poetry evaluation metrics.

1 Introduction

Automatic poetry generation is a challenging task that requires systems capable of handling multiple levels of language understanding, including deep comprehension of text, linguistic and world knowledge, common sense, creativity, and an awareness of syllabic and rhythmic structures.

As a form of artistic expression, poetry has been produced in numerous languages, each with its own unique poetic traditions and forms. While most poetry generation systems focus on English and Chinese, there are also efforts targeting other languages (Hämäläinen and Alnajjar, 2019; Hämäläinen et al., 2022; Chudoba and Rosa, 2024). However, the task of automatically generating poetry in Russian remains underexplored and presents unique challenges.

To address this gap, we explore neural network architectures for the automatic generation of syllabo-tonic*[1] Russian poetry. Specifically, we investigate whether transformer-based models can effectively handle end-to-end generation of Russian syllabo-tonic poetry across various genres, styles, and forms. Our analysis reveals that mainstream byte pair encoding (BPE) tokenization often fails to align well with the structural units of Russian syllabo-tonic versification. To address this, we propose and evaluate language models with character- and syllable-level tokenization, training and testing their performance on the poetry generation task.

We also conduct a detailed study of poetry metrics (subsection 5.1) and share our experiences using existing methods to assess the quality of generated poems. These methods include automatic evaluation (Table 3) of fluency and poeticness for several models, as well as human evaluation of the overall quality of poetry generated by models with character-, syllable-, and BPE-based tokenizations (Table 1).

The contributions of our work are as follows:

- We propose several architectures utilizing character-level tokenization, including the CharLLaMa model, based on the Llama architecture (Touvron et al., 2023), and the CharMamba model, based on the Mamba selective state space architecture (Kheradmand et al., 2023). We have released the weights for the CharLLaMa-1.3B [2] and CharLLaMa-2.6B [3] models;
- We compare character- and syllable-level language models with baseline language models after supervised finetuning (subsection 3.2) on diverse poetry genres;

[1] All poetry terms marked with * are defined in the Glossary in Appendix A.

[2] https://huggingface.co/ai-forever/charllama-1.3B

[3] https://huggingface.co/ai-forever/charllama-2.6B

Proceedings of LaTeCH-CLfL 2025, pages 47–63
May 4, 2025 ©2025 Association for Computational Linguistics

- We developed and open-sourced a library for Russian poetry stress placement and meter evaluation.[4]
- We demonstrate that small-sized language models with syllable-level tokenization can compete with larger general-purpose models in poetry generation tasks.

2 Related work

Creativity has been shown to be closely linked to human intelligence (Frith et al., 2021), making computational creativity a compelling area of research (Colton and Wiggins, 2012), including the study of creativity in LLMs (Franceschelli and Musolesi, 2024). Generative poetry, related to artistic creativity (Ismayilzada et al., 2024), differs from other natural language generation domains (Gatt and Krahmer, 2018) by its special lexical and phonological constraints, as well as specialized metrics to evaluating the quality of generated poems (see Chen et al. (2024) as an example). Recent advancements in LLMs have significantly improved the quality of poetry generation, to the extent that humans often cannot reliably distinguish between poems authored by humans and those generated by LLMs (Porter and Machery, 2024).

Tokenization approaches. Despite the progress of current generative models, there remains potential for further improvement in the quality of poetry generation. One area of research is alternative tokenization methods for LMs that circumvent the shortcomings of the currently mainstream BPE tokenization. In the case of syllabic or syllabo-tonic poetry, improvements can be achieved by using character- or syllable-level tokenization (Belouadi and Eger, 2022; Yu et al., 2024; Chen et al., 2024).

Character- and byte-level tokenization has been used in various systems for automatic poetry generation based on recurrent neural networks (Zhang and Lapata, 2014; Yan, 2016; Xie et al., 2017; Hopkins and Kiela, 2017; Tikhonov and Yamshchikov, 2018). After the invention of the transformer architecture, its applicability with character-based text representation for poetry generation was also investigated (Belouadi and Eger, 2022). The need to train the transformer language model from scratch limits the availability of such experiments. In the case of English language, there are open-source foundation models pretrained on vast corpora: CANINE (Clark et al., 2022) and ByT5 (Xue et al., 2022). CANINE is a family of encoder transformer models with tokens corresponding to Unicode codepoints. This model was utilized by Zhang et al. (2024) in melody-to-lyrics generation system. ByT5 implements an encoder-decoder architecture with byte-level tokenization. An example of its use for generating Czech poetry is available in Chudoba and Rosa (2024).

Syllable-level tokenization is a specialized variant of subword unit tokenization. Its effectiveness for generating poetry has been studied for several languages: Italian (Zugarini et al., 2019), Czech (Chudoba and Rosa, 2024), Vietnamese (Nguyen et al., 2021). Similar to character-level tokenization, syllable-level tokenization necessitates either resource-intensive pretraining of a language model from scratch or additional finetuning of a pretrained model with byte-pair encoding tokenization.

Generative poetry evaluation. A comprehensive evaluation of generative poetry models, like other creative models for open-ended tasks, poses significant challenges. Metrics designed for reference-based tasks, such as machine translation, are often unsuitable for this purpose. While perplexity is a commonly used metric for assessing generative poetry models (Yan, 2016; Che et al., 2017; Zugarini et al., 2019; Zhang et al., 2023; Hu et al., 2024), it has notable limitations (Kuribayashi et al., 2021; Wang et al., 2022). A standard alternative is to evaluate and compare generated poems using human assessors, either experts or non-professionals. However, this approach is costly and difficult to scale. In this context, the LLM-as-a-judge method, which has been applied to evaluate poems (Zhang et al., 2024) and prose (Yang et al., 2024), offers a promising solution for creative computation tasks.

Poetic texts exhibit structural properties that are well-suited for formal evaluation, such as adherence to syllable count per line, regularity in the alternation of stressed and unstressed syllables (poetic meter*), and rhyme schemes*. A significant advantage of this approach is the potential for full automation. Corresponding metrics can be computed during the evaluation phase, as demonstrated by Nguyen et al. (2021); Possi et al. (2023); Chudoba and Rosa (2024).

[4] https://github.com/Koziev/RussianPoetryScansionTool

3 Data

To train and evaluate poetry generation models, we required a substantial amount of Russian poetry data. However, publicly available datasets, such as Shavrina and Shapovalova (2017); Plecháč et al. (2023), are limited in size and insufficient for training generative models, particularly those based on transformer architectures.

To address this limitation, we collected a large volume of amateur poetry from various Internet sources (Appendix E). These sources often lack editorial oversight, leading to frequent spelling and punctuation errors that can negatively impact model performance. To mitigate this issue, we developed a rule-based spelling correction algorithm to address the most common errors. Further details about this algorithm are provided in Appendix B.

The collected poems also frequently exhibit defects in adhering to poetic meter* and rhyme*. Since these defects cannot be automatically corrected, we excluded such samples from the finetuning dataset. To identify meter- and rhyme-related defects, we used our custom library, described in 3.3.

3.1 Pretraining Dataset

Our pretraining dataset consists of two parts: 1) prose texts and 2) poetry texts. All texts have been annotated for stress with the library described in 3.3. The sources of the prose samples are presented in Appendix E.

To ensure that various data types are well-represented in the pretraining texts, the poetic data was upsampled (He and Garcia, 2009), as it constituted only half the volume of prose data. Based on our experiments, a fourfold upsampling of poetry is near optimal: more aggressive upsampling leads to a significant increase in plagiarism in the generated text, as models begin to reproduce memorized training data.

The resulting dataset contains 65 billion characters. The prose and poetry texts were randomly mixed and segmented into 1024-character blocks, starting with either `<prose>` or `<poetry>` tokens to identify the content. This setup allows models to generate poetry without extra finetuning by simply using the `<poetry>` token and an optional seed fragment. However, to better control the poem's theme, style, and sentiment, instructive finetuning is needed.

3.2 Finetuning Dataset

Instructive prompts. All samples in the finetuning dataset consist of an instructional prompt with specific parameters paired with a poem. This approach enables flexible control over the generation process by allowing users to specify all requirements directly in the prompt. This distinguishes it from models that rely on keyword-based seeds, as commonly used in systems like Boggia et al. (2022).

To streamline the creation of instructional prompts, we automated the generation process using an LLM, leveraging the collected poems as input. Manual prompt collection is both time-expensive and resource-demanding, making our automatic approach more efficient. The LLM analyzes a given poem — examining its genre, structure, and other key elements before generating a synthetic prompt. The input provided to the LLM follows the following structure (example is translated from Russian):

> Analyze the poem below in the genre "GENRE". Identify the main character, central idea, author's message, key conflict, emotions, vivid metaphors, and all proper names in the poem. Insert these into the "TEMPLATE" to create a task for a poet. Output only the resulting task sentence: "POEM"

`TEMPLATE` refers to a syntactic variation incorporating elements such as sentiment, emotion, length, and poetic meter* to create diverse prompts. Additional examples, including the original Russian version, are provided in Appendix F.

Quality. The quality of the finetuning dataset significantly affects poem generation results. Consequently, we focused extensively on cleaning the collected data. The dataset preparation code contains procedures for correcting typographic defects, including normalizing spaces, correcting commas, spell checking (Appendix B), and a set of filters for rejecting obviously bad poems. The filters include a set of heuristics for detecting the most common defects such as the repetition of some particles, as well as checking for compliance with a number of poetic rules. The latter is implemented through the tool described in 3.3. Poems with severe meter defects and missing rhymes are excluded from the finetuning dataset, resulting in less than 15% of the collected data being utilized.

Genres. In forming a corpus of poems for pretraining and finetuning, we did not limit its composition to any particular genre, style, or form, unlike many other works e.g. (Lo et al., 2022). As a result, the corpus contains, in addition to lyrics with different poetic meter*, tonality, and theme, also comic, satirical, and ironic poems, including a number of hard forms: pirozhki*, chastushka*, rubai*, limericks*, sonnets*, poems for children, poetic riddles, hymns (Greene et al., 2012, page 356), congratulations in verse etc.

The finetuning dataset comprises a total of 1,704,418 samples, distributed across various genres as follows: 52.7% lyrics, 24% hard forms, 11.9% humor and satirical poetry, 5% poems for children, and 6.4% others. The primary sources of poetry include:

- stihi.ru[5] (72%),
- poetory.ru[6] (2.8%),
- chitalnya.ru[7] (1.7%).

3.3 Accentuation and Poetry Scansion

For syllabo-tonic* poetry, the placement of stress marks follows specific rules for alternating stressed and unstressed syllables. Our algorithm supports five meters: trochee*, iamb*, dactyl*, amphibrach*, and anapest*. These five meters account for approximately 97% of all poems in the dataset. The remaining 3% include dolniks* and some exceptional cases (e.g., in the artishoki* genre).

For each stanza, the algorithm selects an optimal meter based on the reference sequence of stressed and unstressed syllables for the meter, the positions of ideal stresses, and whether these ideal stresses align with the permissible stress patterns of the words.

Russian pronunciation allows for variability in word stress, making automatic stress placement a computationally intensive task. The accentuator supports two main cases of variability: 1) certain phrases in the Russian language deviate from standard rules (there are several hundred of these phrases), 2) some words allow for variations in stress within the same grammatical form. To address this efficiently, the algorithm implements a beam search. For each line, there are two variants of stress placement, respectively, resulting in two clauzula* variants. The one that provides the best rhyme combination can be selected among these options.

4 Pretrained Models

The goal of this paper was to investigate whether using a character-level tokenizer and pretraining with it could improve automatic poetry generation. We hypothesized that character-level tokenization would represent text more accurately for poetry generation compared to byte-pair encoding. To test this hypothesis, we used two model architectures, which are described in detail below.

4.1 CharLLaMa

The CharLLaMa models follow the LLaMa architecture (Touvron et al., 2023). The only differences are: 1) character-level tokenization, 2) adjusted internal dimensions. We pretrain the models on the data described in 3.1. CharLLaMa is optimized to handle character-level tokenization and complex sequential patterns, aiming to outperform BPE-based models in capturing Russian poetry language structure. The initialization of the tokenizer vocabulary (a set of tokens for the tokenizer) was performed as follows: 1) the frequencies of Unicode symbols in the pretraining corpus were analyzed; 2) rare symbols with a frequency below 1000 have been excluded. This yields a vocabulary of 375 tokens, including special tokens <s>, </s>, <pad>, <unk>, and two special tokens for marking fragments of prose and poetry.

Two model variants were pretrained: 1.3B and 2.6B parameters (detailed specifications of the models are in Table 2).

Model training. CharLLaMa-1.3B model was pretrained over 14 days using 1 DGX 8*A100, leveraging CUDA V12.3.107 environment, and the CharLLaMa-2.6B was pretrained over 24 days using 1 DGX 8*H100 respectively. The learning parameters are listed in Table 7.

4.2 CharMamba

When using character-level tokenization, it's important to consider that it tends to make token sequences longer than methods like BPE or syllable-level tokenization due to the higher fertility[8] as shown in Table 8. Consequently, both model training and inference may take longer, in addition to

[5] `https://stihi.ru/`

[6] `https://poetory.ru/`

[7] `https://www.chitalnya.ru`

[8] Tokenization fertility was defined and analyzed for the BERT tokenizer in `https://juditacs.github.io/2019/02/19/bert-tokenization-stats.html`

increased memory consumption during autoregressive text generation and the time taken for generating text.

Given these limitations, we opted for the Mamba architecture as the second model for exploration, following the approach outlined in (Gu and Dao, 2023). Mamba is based on advancements in structured state space models, with an efficient hardware-aware design similar to FlashAttention, enabling it to be more efficient and faster that transformer-based models. We adopted the Mamba implementation from the official repository [9] and pretrain CharMamba on the dataset described in 3.1.

Model training. The CharMamba-1.3B model was pretrained over 5 days using 1 DGX A100 system with 8 GPUs, utilizing CUDA V12.3.107. The training parameters are detailed in Table 7.

4.3 Syllabo-tonic GPTs

Syllabo-tonic GPTs (stGPT) are based on the GPT-2 architecture (Radford et al., 2019), with modifications limited to tokenization and the size of hidden layers. We conducted experiments using two model variants: a 100M-parameter model (referred to as "stGPT small") and a 350M-parameter model (referred to as "stGPT medium"). Detailed specifications for both models are provided in Table 2.

Both models were pretrained on 3.1 and fine-tuned on 3.2 with hyperparameters listed in Table 7.

The tokenization algorithm for these models works as follows. First, the text is split into syllables, ensuring that each syllable contains exactly one vowel or consists of a single consonant (as in the case of certain prepositions and particles). Second, stressed syllables are marked using the "combining acute accent" symbol,[10] placed after the vowel. Third, the token sequences in each line of the poem are reversed from right to left, so that the last token of the line appears first, followed by the penultimate token, and so on. This reversal simplifies the model's task of selecting rhyming syllables during generation, reducing the likelihood of unsuccessful poem generation. Without this technique, the model might struggle to choose a rhyme that satisfies both lexical and grammatical constraints when reaching the end of a line. A similar approach has been used by Benhardt et al. (2018); Van de Cruys (2020).

5 Experimental Poetry Generation

5.1 Metrics

Evaluating generative LMs, especially for poetry, is challenging (Hämäläinen and Alnajjar, 2021) due to the lack of ground truth answers and the subjective nature of poetry evaluation. Both automatic tests and manual evaluations can assess poetry generation models. Poetry features strict structural requirements, such as syllabo-tonic forms that adhere to specific patterns of stressed and unstressed syllables. These elements can be verified algorithmically.

We introduced the metric **technicality**, calculated using the tool described in 3.3. A penalty is applied if the ideal meter requires an unstressed syllable, but the actual syllable in this position is stressed. More than two consecutive unstressed syllables are also penalized. A score of 0 indicates that the text does not match the typical patterns of syllabo-tonic poetry, while a score of 1 indicate a perfect match to a classic meter. Intermediate scores correspond to texts with varying numbers of defects; the closer the score to 1, the fewer the defects.

In addition to poetic meter, poems are typically expected to include rhyme. To evaluate the models' ability to generate rhymes, we measure the **rhyming level** as the proportion of quatrains with an ABAB rhyme scheme*. While this is a simplified approach — since generated poems may exhibit other rhyme schemes (e.g., ABBA, AABB, AABA) — the ABAB scheme is the most common in lyric poetry and represents the majority of samples in the training data.

Perplexity is a widely used automatic metric for evaluating the fluency of generated poems (Yan, 2016). It is calculated using a pretrained LMs. For our experiments, we used the ruGPT3-medium model[11] to compute perplexity. However, it is important to note that available LMs are typically trained on general-purpose text and may not fully capture the grammatical and stylistic nuances specific to poetry.

Out-of-vocabulary (OOV) rate is a simple metric used to detect abnormalities in generated poems. It measures the proportion of words in a text that do

[9] https://github.com/state-spaces/mamba

[10] https://unicodeplus.com/U+0301

[11] https://huggingface.co/ai-forever/ruGPT3-medium_based_on_gpt2

not appear in the finetuning dataset. A higher OOV rate indicates a greater likelihood of encountering unusual or nonsensical vocabulary in the generated text. The OOV rate is not a completely reliable indicator of vocabulary defects, as poetry generation is an open-ended task with no fixed dictionary. Lexical innovations, such as neologisms and creative word formation, are common in poetry. Poets often experiment with language boundaries, producing works like Lewis Carroll's "Jabberwocky" (Carroll, 2001) and its translations into Russian,[12] which consist of unconventional or invented words, or the Russian genre of "zaum,"[13]. However, in practice, "broken" vocabulary in generated poems often arises not from the model's creativity, but from a domain shift caused by finetuning language models like Mistral, ByT5, or ruGPT3-medium on poetic texts. This shift occurs because poetic language differs significantly from prose in terms of vocabulary, syntax, and the extensive use of figurative language. As a result, despite its limitations, the OOV rate is a simple and interpretable metric that provides a reasonable estimate of lexical defects.

Side-by-side human evaluation. A team of annotators evaluated the generated poems by comparing their outputs side-by-side with human-authored poems. Each annotator was given a prompt along with pairs of texts and instructed to select the text that best represented a poem in response to the given prompt. The criteria for comparing the texts, arranged in descending order of importance, were as follows:

- *Poeticness*: the text must be poetic and adhere to the rules of Russian syllabo-tonic versification.
- *Fluency, coherence, and meaningfulness*: the text must be free of grammatical errors and convey meaning.
- *Prompt relevancy*: the text must be relevant to the given prompt.

The prompts were generated using an LLM in a zero-shot setting, following a prompt schema similar to the one used for the finetuning dataset (3.2). For evaluation, we selected prompts suitable for poems with lengths ranging from 4 to 8 lines.

[12]https://prosodia.ru/catalog/stikhi/lyuis-kerroll-drug-moy-boysya-barmaglota/

[13]https://library.fiveable.me/key-terms/world-literature-ii/zaum

Author 1	Author 2	Num. of pairs
CharMamba-1.3B	human	873
CharLLaMa-1.3B	human	840
CharLLaMa-1.3B	CharMamba-1.3B	686

Table 1: Statistics of poem pairs used in the side-by-side evaluation study.

The total number of annotated pairs is 2,399, with detailed statistics provided in Table 1.

5.2 Experiments

Comparison with BPE models. In the first experiments, we evaluate the pretrained models listed in Section 4 and several foundation models with BPE tokenization: ruGPT3-large[14]; Mistral-7B-v0.1[15]; FRED-T5-1.7B[16]. All models were finetuned on the instruction dataset (subsection 3.2).

Syllabo-tonic tokenization. In the second part of the experiments, we examined the syllabo-tonic tokenization of the text. Tokens in this approach correspond to syllables, with separate tokens for stressed and unstressed syllables. This type of tokenization attempts to overcome the main limitation of character-level tokenization, which is the difficulty of capturing longer contexts. On average, syllables in the Russian language consist of approximately 2.3 letters, which aligns well with BPE tokenization.

We tested two models with 100M and 350M capacities, named “stGPT small” and “stGPT medium”. Table 2 presents the models' parameters. These models were pretrained on a dataset described in Section 3.1, then finetuned on the dataset described in Section 3.2. Training hyperparameters are presented in Table 7.

Table 4 shows the technicality scores for both human- and LM-authored poems across several genres.

Low-Rank Adaptation (LoRa). Full finetuning was used for all compared models. Our experiments with LLama 8B and LoRa demonstrated a significant degradation of the technicality of the generated poems, so we did not use this training option for the final comparison.

[14]ruGPT3-large is the Russian analog of the GPT-2 model, presented as a family of models of different sizes (Zmitrovich et al., 2024). The large version has 760M parameters

[15]Mistral-7B-v0.1 is the pretrained generative text model with 7 billion parameters proposed by the MistralAI team

[16]FRED-T5-1.7B (Zmitrovich et al., 2024) is the encoder-decoder pretrained model created for the Russian language

Model	$N\_positions$	N_embd	N_head	N_layer	$Num\_parameters$
stGPT small	1024	768	12	12	132,694,272
stGPT medium	1024	1024	16	24	365,840,384
CharLLaMa-1.3B	1024	1536	32	29	1,369,634,304
CharLLaMa-2.6B	2048	2064	24	28	2,641,199,664
CharMamba-1.3B	—	1320	—	31	1,238,287,360

Table 2: Model characteristics of the explored architectures. *N_positions* - number of positional embeddings, *N_emb* - token embedding size, *N_head* - number of transformer self-attention heads, *N_layer* - number of stacked decoder layers, *Num_parameters* — number of models parameters.

Model	Sampling parameters	Technicality	Rhyming level	Perplexity	OOV rate
stGPT medium	temp=0.9 top_p=0.75	0.72	0.467	70.28	0.004
stGPT small	temp=0.8 top_p=0.8	0.70	0.472	59.30	0.004
CharLLaMa-2.6B	temp=0.75 top_p=0.6	0.59	0.339	55.56	0.009
CharLLaMa-1.3B	temp=0.75 top_p=0.6	0.58	0.352	50.71	0.011
CharMamba-1.3B	temp=0.65 top_p=0.75	0.57	0.293	42.60	0.003
Mistral-7B-v0.1	temp=0.65 typical_p=0.75	0.57	0.192	72.41	0.012
FRED-T5-1.7B	temp=0.8 typical_p=0.7	0.26	0.126	**38.44**	**0.0029**
ruGPT3-large	temp=0.9 typical_p=0.7	0.06	0.002	45.59	0.0060
ByT5-large	temp=0.9 top_p=0.7	0.02	0.001	124.62	0.016
ByT5-small	temp=0.9 top_p=0.7	0.01	0.0	341.65	0.035
Human	n/a	**0.81**	**0.683**	72.81	0.0038

Table 3: Automatic metrics for models trained on the finetuning dataset (subsection 3.2). Lower *OOV rate* values indicate better performance, while higher values of *technicality* and *rhyming level* are preferred. *temp* in sampling parameters stands for temperature.

Author	sonnets	rubai	limericks	chastushka	depressyashka	artishok	poroshok
stGPT medium	**0.712**	0.596	0.613	0.689	0.591	0.361	0.578
stGPT small	0.699	0.559	0.636	**0.702**	0.533	0.266	0.567
CharLLaMa-2.6B	0.469	0.499	0.439	0.546	0.511	0.518	0.499
CharLLaMa-1.3B	0.495	0.522	0.484	0.568	0.504	0.487	0.496
CharMamba-1.3B	0.416	0.526	0.409	0.557	0.505	0.439	0.467
FRED-T5-1.7B	0.209	0.24	0.128	0.289	0.345	0.064	0.305
ruGPT3-large	0.059	0.063	0.048	0.079	0.132	0.031	0.064
Human	0.555	**0.644**	**0.644**	0.701	**0.64**	**0.88**	**0.642**

Table 4: Technicality scores for model- and human-authored poems across different genres. Higher technicality values indicate better performance.

Token-less models. We have also explored the performance of token-less models from ByT5 family (Xue et al., 2022). These models employ a tokenizer that operates at the byte level for utf-8 text encoding. It was expected that this tokenization approach would also allow the model to process individual characters of the text, thus helping the model acquire the Russian phonetics.

Finetuning with instructive samples. All samples for finetuning consist of an instructional prompt and poem text. For decoder models, that is, all except FRED-T5-1.7B, a special token separates the prompt and the poem. Samples were randomly combined into fixed-size batches with the right padding using a <pad> token. Prompt tokens were excluded from backpropagation in decoder models by setting an attention mask for each sample.

Experimental setup. The automatic metrics for all experiments were calculated uniformly according to the protocol described below.

- The CharLLaMa, CharMamba, and stGPT were trained from scratch according to the procedure described in Section 4, and subsequently trained on the finetuning dataset (subsection 3.2). Other models were trained only on the finetuning dataset. Models were finetuned using the transformers library v.4.36.2. The finetuning hyperparameters are described in the Appendix 7.

- To evaluate all the experiments and models, we use the test set of 1000 instructional prompts, each instructing to "Compose a quatrain about <theme>..." and being up to 200 characters long. All compared models were prompted to generate lyrics quatrains. If a model produced more than four lines, only the first four were considered. Per-genre evaluation was performed using 600 instructions following the format "Compose a poem in genre <genre> about <theme>".

- Nucleus sampling (Holtzman et al., 2019) was used as a generation algorithm for all models. For each prompt, a single sequence of tokens was generated and used as the result for evaluation. The sampling parameters were optimized for each specific model, with slight variations, as different models have distinct optimal configurations for these parameters.

6 Results

The results of the experiments are shown in Tables 3 for 1000 lyrics quatrains and Table 4 of Appendix refers for 600 generations of several other genres. The metrics indicate that poorly written poems can have lower perplexity, while human-authored poems have higher perplexity. As noted by Yi et al. (2018), it is essential to focus not only on the absolute value of perplexity but also on how well the obtained perplexity value fits within the range of values typical for works written by people. It can be helpful to approximate the corresponding distribution with a Gaussian distribution with a specific mean and variance.

The automatic evaluation results show that the fine-tuned ruGPT3-large and ByT5 models performed poorly in poetry generation, while Mistral-7B-v0.1 achieved better scores. However, Mistral-7B-v0.1's generated poems had higher perplexity and included many out-of-vocabulary words, likely due to its limited pretraining on Russian texts. Despite this, Mistral outperformed other models using BPE and byte-level tokenization, coming close to specialized character-level models. The FRED-T5-1.7B-based model performed slightly worse in terms of technical quality and rhyme but produced texts with fewer language errors, as shown by its lower perplexity and fewer out-of-vocabulary words.

Experiments with stGPT demonstrated that transformer models using syllable-level tokenization achieved the highest technicality scores among all models. For sonnets, stGPT even surpassed human-written poems in terms of technicality. However, this tokenization method has several limitations, as discussed in Section D. Additionally, while these models excel in technicality, they often produce texts with grammatical and fluency issues. These flaws do not affect technicality or rhyming metrics but reduce the overall quality of the poetry. Due to these limitations, we chose not to scale these models to a capacity comparable to CharLLaMa-1.3B, and no full-scale side-by-side evaluations were performed.

Human side-by-side evaluation results. We used expert side-by-side evaluations to assess poem quality, applying the Bradley-Terry model (Hunter, 2003) from the choix library[17]. This model was used to compare poems written by humans with

[17]`https://github.com/lucasmaystre/choix`

Author	Bradley-Terry Rate
Human	1.49
CharLLaMa-1.3B	0.23
CharMamba-1.3B	-0.20

Table 5: Bradley-Terry ratings for the compared models.

those generated by the models, as shown in Table 5.

Based on the side-by-side evaluation results, two key conclusions emerge: (1) automatic metrics alone are insufficient for a comprehensive and objective assessment of generative poetry, and (2) the significant gap between human-authored and generated poems suggests the need for further experimentation.

7 Conclusion

To summarize, our work focuses on generating Russian syllabo-tonic poetry across various genres and styles. We experimented with different approaches, such as character-level tokenization, using the CharLLaMa and CharMamba architectures. We extensively compared these character-level models with baseline models using various tokenization methods, finetuning them across datasets with different domain and rhythm structures. As part of our research, we created a new poetry spell-checking algorithm and accentuation system, which we have made available as open-source. Additionally, we released the top-performing pre-trained model for the Russian poetry generation. Finally, we propose poetry evaluation metrics and share insights on utilizing existing methods to assess the quality of generated poetry models.

Acknowledgments

We extend our sincere gratitude to the team of assessors for their professionalism and dedication in conducting side-by-side evaluations, which enabled the objective and reliable comparison of language models for Russian poetry generation. Special thanks to Timur Shentyurk, Danil Vyazovov, Vsevolod Alipov, Anastasiya Volodina, Igor Beloded, Mikael Desse, Evgeniy Sologub, and Anna Kostikova for their invaluable contributions.

We thank our colleagues Denis Shevelev and Valery Ternovsky for their insightful discussions on generative poetry and their valuable assistance.

We thank Leonid Sinev for his timely and meticulous assistance with references and LaTeX.

We also would like to especially thank Sergei Markov for his insightful suggestions and support, which significantly enriched this work and made it possible.

Limitations

This study has several significant limitations, which are discussed below.

Length of context. Although our generative LMs achieve solid results and promote state-of-the-art performance on various tasks, their context window size limits the model application on long-context tasks. The window size for CharLLaMa-1.3B and CharMamba-1.3B is 1024 tokens, and for CharLLaMa-2.6B, it is 2048 tokens. Remember that char tokenization imposes stricter limits on the number of words for processed sequences compared to models with BPE tokenization. The window context can include a much larger number of tokens, resulting in fewer words in the same context. However, poems are primarily short, and the context is not critical for them.

Speed and optimization. Longer token sequences in models with char-level tokenization lead to increased overhead (kv-cache for CharLLaMa models) and time for autoregressive inference compared to models with BPE tokenization. This is the trade-off between the quality of poems and speed. The research regarding optimization has been left for future work.

Data biases. The generated poems are a result of the data used in the training. However, it's important to note that the study has limitations due to biases present in the training data, especially concerning Russian cultural aspects and copyright constraints. Because the data is culturally biased towards the Russian language, it cannot be directly applied to other languages.

New language models. New pretrained language models[18][19] and enhanced versions of the models[20] discussed in this paper are released frequently. The findings presented in Section 6 should not be generalized to these newer models, as modifications to the model architecture or pretraining pipeline may significantly impact their performance in generat-

[18] `https://huggingface.co/yandex/YandexGPT-5-Lite-8B-pretrain`

[19] `https://huggingface.co/t-tech/T-pro-it-1.0`

[20] `https://huggingface.co/mistralai/Mistral-7B-Instruct-v0.3`

ing Russian-language poetry.

Ethical Consideration

Human creativity and possible misuse. Poetry is a form of creative expression and is often protected by copyright. AI-generated poetry should not infringe upon the rights of original creators. In our research, we only used licensed and open data for training. We must make efforts to avoid creating content that closely mimics or plagiarizes existing works. This helps maintain honesty and clarity in distinguishing between human and machine-generated art. We leave it to future work to address this issue.

Biases and data quality. Poetry is deeply rooted in cultural contexts. Understanding the cultural significance of certain themes, symbols, and language is crucial. The pretraining data for poetry generation of the presented models includes large segments from the internet domain and cultural specifics of Russian literature and cultural biases, consequently containing various stereotypes and biases. Therefore, such models are not transferable to other languages. We collected the datasets used to train poetry-generating AI to be diverse and representative of a wide range of poets and experiences. This helps to ensure that the output reflects a broad spectrum of human expressions. We understand that AI systems can unintentionally produce harmful content, such as violent, discriminatory, or otherwise inappropriate language. Ensuring that the poetry generated is free from such content is a key ethical responsibility.

Energy Efficiency and Usage. We compute the CO_2 emissions from pretraining and finetuning as Equation 1 (Strubell et al., 2019):

$$CO_2 = \frac{PUE * kWh * I^{CO2}}{1000} \quad (1)$$

The power usage effectiveness (PUE) of our data centers is 1.3. The resulting CO2 emission values are CharLLaMa-1.3B — 837 kg, CharLLaMa-2.6B — 2008 kg, and CharMamba-1.3B — 732 kg, respectively. Model compression techniques and parameter-efficient finetuning methods can reduce the computational costs associated with model inference.

AI-assistants Help. We used Grammarly[21] and DeepSeek[22] to improve and proofread this paper, correcting grammatical, spelling, and style errors and paraphrasing sentences. As a result, some parts of our publication may be flagged as AI-generated or AI-edited.

We must consider ethical implications to ensure the responsible use of AI and respect for human creativity and culture. Developers and users of AI poetry tools should maintain responsible practices, honoring human creativity and the cultural significance of poetry.

References

Jonas Belouadi and Steffen Eger. 2022. Bygpt5: End-to-end style-conditioned poetry generation with token-free language models. *arXiv preprint arXiv:2212.10474.*

John Benhardt, Peter Hase, Liuyi Zhu, and Cynthia Rudin. 2018. Shall i compare thee to a machine-written sonnet? an approach to algorithmic sonnet generation. *arXiv preprint arXiv:1811.05067.*

Michele Boggia, Sardana Ivanova, Simo Linkola, Anna Kantosalo, and Hannu (TT) Toivonen. 2022. One line at a time - generation and internal evaluation of interactive poetry. In *International Conference on Innovative Computing and Cloud Computing.*

Lewis Carroll. 2001. *Jabberwocky and other poems.* Courier Corporation.

Tong Che, Yanran Li, Ruixiang Zhang, R Devon Hjelm, Wenjie Li, Yangqiu Song, and Yoshua Bengio. 2017. Maximum-likelihood augmented discrete generative adversarial networks. *arXiv preprint arXiv:1702.07983.*

Yanran Chen, Hannes Gröner, Sina Zarrieß, and Steffen Eger. 2024. Evaluating diversity in automatic poetry generation. In *Proceedings of the 2024 Conference on Empirical Methods in Natural Language Processing*, pages 19671–19692, Miami, Florida, USA. Association for Computational Linguistics.

Michal Chudoba and Rudolf Rosa. 2024. Gpt czech poet: Generation of czech poetic strophes with language models. *arXiv preprint arXiv:2407.12790.*

Jonathan H Clark, Dan Garrette, Iulia Turc, and John Wieting. 2022. Canine: Pre-training an efficient tokenization-free encoder for language representation. *Transactions of the Association for Computational Linguistics*, 10:73–91.

Simon Colton and Geraint A Wiggins. 2012. Computational creativity: The final frontier? In *ECAI 2012*, pages 21–26. IOS Press.

[21] https://app.grammarly.com/

[22] https://chat.deepseek.com/

R Graeme Dunphy and Cristian Bratu. 2010. *The encyclopedia of the medieval chronicle*, volume 2. Brill Leiden.

Giorgio Franceschelli and Mirco Musolesi. 2024. On the creativity of large language models. *Preprint*, arXiv:2304.00008.

Emily Frith, Daniel B Elbich, Alexander P Christensen, Monica D Rosenberg, Qunlin Chen, Michael J Kane, Paul J Silvia, Paul Seli, and Roger E Beaty. 2021. Intelligence and creativity share a common cognitive and neural basis. *Journal of Experimental Psychology: General*, 150(4):609.

J. Fuller. 2017. *The Sonnet*. The Critical Idiom Reissued. Taylor & Francis.

Paul Fussell. 1979. *Poetic Meter and Poetic Form*. McGraw Hill, New York.

Albert Gatt and Emiel Krahmer. 2018. Survey of the state of the art in natural language generation: Core tasks, applications and evaluation. *Journal of Artificial Intelligence Research*, 61:65–170.

Roland Greene, Stephen Cushman, Clare Cavanagh, Jahan Ramazani, and Paul Rouzer. 2012. *The Princeton encyclopedia of poetry and poetics*. Princeton University Press.

Albert Gu and Tri Dao. 2023. Mamba: Linear-time sequence modeling with selective state spaces. *arXiv preprint arXiv:2312.00752*.

Mika Hämäläinen and Khalid Alnajjar. 2019. Let's face it. finnish poetry generation with aesthetics and framing. *arXiv preprint arXiv:1910.13946*.

Mika Hämäläinen and Khalid Alnajjar. 2021. Human evaluation of creative nlg systems: An interdisciplinary survey on recent papers. *arXiv preprint arXiv:2108.00308*.

Mika Hämäläinen, Khalid Alnajjar, and Thierry Poibeau. 2022. Modern french poetry generation with roberta and gpt-2. *arXiv preprint arXiv:2212.02911*.

Haibo He and Edwardo A. Garcia. 2009. Learning from imbalanced data. *IEEE Transactions on Knowledge and Data Engineering*, 21(9):1263–1284.

John Hollander. 2014. *Rhyme's reason: a guide to English verse*, 4th edition. Yale University Press, New Haven, CT.

Ari Holtzman, Jan Buys, Li Du, Maxwell Forbes, and Yejin Choi. 2019. The curious case of neural text degeneration. *arXiv preprint arXiv:1904.09751*.

Jack Hopkins and Douwe Kiela. 2017. Automatically generating rhythmic verse with neural networks. In *Proceedings of the 55th Annual Meeting of the Association for Computational Linguistics (Volume 1: Long Papers)*, pages 168–178, Vancouver, Canada. Association for Computational Linguistics.

Zhiyuan Hu, Chumin Liu, Yue Feng, Anh Tuan Luu, and Bryan Hooi. 2024. Poetrydiffusion: Towards joint semantic and metrical manipulation in poetry generation. In *Proceedings of the AAAI Conference on Artificial Intelligence*, volume 38, pages 18279–18288.

David R. Hunter. 2003. Mm algorithms for generalized bradley-terry models. *Annals of Statistics*, 32:384–406.

Mete Ismayilzada, Debjit Paul, Antoine Bosselut, and Lonneke van der Plas. 2024. Creativity in ai: Progresses and challenges. *Preprint*, arXiv:2410.17218.

Shakiba Kheradmand, Daniel Rebain, Gopal Sharma, Hossam Isack, Abhishek Kar, Andrea Tagliasacchi, and Kwang Moo Yi. 2023. Accelerating neural field training via soft mining. *Preprint*, arXiv:2312.00075.

Tatsuki Kuribayashi, Yohei Oseki, Takumi Ito, Ryo Yoshida, Masayuki Asahara, and Kentaro Inui. 2021. Lower perplexity is not always human-like. *arXiv preprint arXiv:2106.01229*.

Edward Lear. 2011. *Limericks*. Readers' & writers' genre workshop. Poetry. Benchmark Education Company.

Kai-Ling Lo, Rami Ariss, and Philipp Kurz. 2022. Gpoet-2: A gpt-2 based poem generator. *arXiv preprint arXiv:2205.08847*.

Tuan Nguyen, Phong Nguyen, Hanh Pham, Truong Bui, Tan Nguyen, and Duc Luong. 2021. Sp-gpt2: semantics improvement in vietnamese poetry generation. In *2021 20th IEEE International Conference on Machine Learning and Applications (ICMLA)*, pages 1576–1581. IEEE.

Aleksandr Nikolaevich Nikolyukin. 2001. *Literaturnaya entsiklopediya terminov i ponyatii*. NPK Intelvak.

Petr Plecháč, Robert Kolár, Silvie Cinková, Artjoms Šeļa, Mirella De Sisto, Lara Nugues, Thomas Haider, Benjamin Nagy, Éliane Delente, Richard Renault, Klemens Bobenhausen, Benjamin Hammerich, Adiel Mittmann, Gábor Palkó, Péter Horváth, Borja Navarro Colorado, Pablo Ruiz Fabo, Helena Bermúdez Sabel, Kirill Korchagin, Vladimir Plungian, and Dmitri Sitchinava. 2023. PoeTree. Poetry Treebanks in Czech, English, French, German, Hungarian, Italian, Portuguese, Russian and Spanish.

Brian Porter and Edouard Machery. 2024. AI-generated poetry is indistinguishable from human-written poetry and is rated more favorably. *Scientific Reports*, 14(1):26133.

Maurilio De Araujo Possi, Alcione De Paiva Oliveira, Alexandra Moreira, and Lucas Mucida Costa. 2023. Carmen: A method for automatic evaluation of poems. In *2023 5th International Conference on Natural Language Processing (ICNLP)*, pages 244–247. IEEE.

Alec Radford, Jeffrey Wu, Rewon Child, David Luan, Dario Amodei, Ilya Sutskever, et al. 2019. Language models are unsupervised multitask learners. *OpenAI blog*, 1(8):9.

Tatiana Shavrina and Olga Shapovalova. 2017. To the methodology of corpus construction for machine learning:"taiga" syntax tree corpus and parser. In *Proceedings of "CORPORA-2017" International Conference*, pages 78–84.

Emma Strubell, Ananya Ganesh, and Andrew McCallum. 2019. Energy and policy considerations for deep learning in NLP. In *Proceedings of the 57th Annual Meeting of the Association for Computational Linguistics*, pages 3645–3650, Florence, Italy. Association for Computational Linguistics.

Alexey Tikhonov and Ivan P Yamshchikov. 2018. Guess who? multilingual approach for the automated generation of author-stylized poetry. In *2018 IEEE Spoken Language Technology Workshop (SLT)*, pages 787–794. IEEE.

Hugo Touvron, Thibaut Lavril, Gautier Izacard, Xavier Martinet, Marie-Anne Lachaux, Timothée Lacroix, Baptiste Rozière, Naman Goyal, Eric Hambro, Faisal Azhar, et al. 2023. Llama: Open and efficient foundation language models. *arXiv preprint arXiv:2302.13971*.

Tim Van de Cruys. 2020. Automatic poetry generation from prosaic text. In *Proceedings of the 58th annual meeting of the association for computational linguistics*, pages 2471–2480.

Olga Vechtomova, Gaurav Sahu, and Dhruv Kumar. 2020. Generation of lyrics lines conditioned on music audio clips. *arXiv preprint arXiv:2009.14375*.

M. Wachtel. 2004. *The Cambridge Introduction to Russian Poetry*. Cambridge Introductions to Literature. Cambridge University Press.

Yequan Wang, Jiawen Deng, Aixin Sun, and Xuying Meng. 2022. Perplexity from plm is unreliable for evaluating text quality. *arXiv preprint arXiv:2210.05892*.

Stanley Xie, Ruchir Rastogi, and Max Chang. 2017. Deep poetry: Word-level and character-level language models for shakespearean sonnet generation. *Natural Lang. Process. Deep Learn.*

Linting Xue, Aditya Barua, Noah Constant, Rami Al-Rfou, Sharan Narang, Mihir Kale, Adam Roberts, and Colin Raffel. 2022. Byt5: Towards a token-free future with pre-trained byte-to-byte models. *Transactions of the Association for Computational Linguistics*, 10:291–306.

Rui Yan. 2016. i, poet: Automatic poetry composition through recurrent neural networks with iterative polishing schema. In *IJCAI*, volume 2238, page 2244.

Zhenyuan Yang, Zhengliang Liu, Jing Zhang, Cen Lu, Jiaxin Tai, Tianyang Zhong, Yiwei Li, Siyan Zhao, Teng Yao, Qing Liu, Jinlin Yang, Qixin Liu, Zhaowei Li, Kexin Wang, Longjun Ma, Dajiang Zhu, Yudan Ren, Bao Ge, Wei Zhang, Ning Qiang, Tuo Zhang, and Tianming Liu. 2024. Analyzing nobel prize literature with large language models. *Preprint*, arXiv:2410.18142.

Xiaoyuan Yi, Maosong Sun, Ruoyu Li, and Wenhao Li. 2018. Automatic poetry generation with mutual reinforcement learning. In *Proceedings of the 2018 Conference on Empirical Methods in Natural Language Processing*, pages 3143–3153.

Chengyue Yu, Lei Zang, Jiaotuan Wang, Chenyi Zhuang, and Jinjie Gu. 2024. Token-free llms can generate chinese classical poetry with more accurate format. *arXiv preprint arXiv:2401.03512*.

Xingxing Zhang and Mirella Lapata. 2014. Chinese poetry generation with recurrent neural networks. In *Proceedings of the 2014 conference on empirical methods in natural language processing (EMNLP)*, pages 670–680.

Xinran Zhang, Maosong Sun, Jiafeng Liu, and Xiaobing Li. 2023. Lingxi: A diversity-aware Chinese modern poetry generation system. In *Proceedings of the 61st Annual Meeting of the Association for Computational Linguistics (Volume 3: System Demonstrations)*, pages 63–75, Toronto, Canada. Association for Computational Linguistics.

Zhe Zhang, Karol Lasocki, Yi Yu, and Atsuhiro Takasu. 2024. Syllable-level lyrics generation from melody exploiting character-level language model. In *Findings of the Association for Computational Linguistics: EACL 2024*, pages 1336–1346.

Dmitry Zmitrovich, Aleksandr Abramov, Andrey Kalmykov, Vitaly Kadulin, Maria Tikhonova, Ekaterina Taktasheva, Danil Astafurov, Mark Baushenko, Artem Snegirev, Tatiana Shavrina, Sergei S. Markov, Vladislav Mikhailov, and Alena Fenogenova. 2024. A family of pretrained transformer language models for Russian. In *Proceedings of the 2024 Joint International Conference on Computational Linguistics, Language Resources and Evaluation (LREC-COLING 2024)*, pages 507–524, Torino, Italia. ELRA and ICCL.

Andrea Zugarini, Stefano Melacci, and Marco Maggini. 2019. Neural poetry: Learning to generate poems using syllables. In *Artificial Neural Networks and Machine Learning–ICANN 2019: Text and Time Series: 28th International Conference on Artificial Neural Networks, Munich, Germany, September 17–19, 2019, Proceedings, Part IV 28*, pages 313–325. Springer.

A Glossary

Acrostic is a poem or other word composition in which the first letter (or syllable, or word) of each new line (or paragraph, or other recurring feature in the text) spells out a word, message, or the alphabet. For more information see (Dunphy and Bratu, 2010, page 8).

Amphibrach is a metrical foot consisting of a stressed syllable between two unstressed syllables (Greene et al., 2012, page 31).

Anapest is a metrical foot consisting of two unstressed syllables followed by one stressed syllable (Greene et al., 2012, page 37).

Chastushka is a humorous quatrain with a simple rhyming scheme - see more details at (Nikolyukin, 2001, page 598).

Clauzula is the final part of a verse or stanza* starting from the last ictus* (Greene et al., 2012, page 141).

Dactyl is a metrical foot consisting of one stressed syllable followed by two unstressed syllables (Greene et al., 2012, page 179).

Dolnik is the type of poetic meter in Russian poetry, the peculiarity of which is a variable number of unstressed syllables between ictuses*. More information is available at (Nikolyukin, 2001, page 235).

Ictus is a stressed syllable (Greene et al., 2012, page 362).

Iamb is a metrical foot consisting of one unstressed syllable followed by one stressed syllable (Greene et al., 2012, page 360).

Limerick is a five-line poem with a rhyme scheme* AABBA, imitating the corresponding genre of English poetry (Lear, 2011).

Metrical foot is a regularly repeating pattern of 1 stressed and 1 to 2 unstressed syllables. There are two variants of disyllabic meter, called iambic* and trochee*, and three variants of trisyllabic meter, called amphibrach*, dactyl*, and anapest*. The main poetic meters that occur in training data are presented in Table 10.

Pirozhki, poroshki, depressyashki, artishoki are comic quatrains written without capital letters and punctuation marks, often with deliberate deviations from the rules of spelling. For each of these forms, there are strict constraints on the number of syllables, meter, and rhyme — see more details at the link

Poetic meter refers to the recurring pattern of stressed and unstressed syllables in lines of poetry. A comprehensive discussion of poetic meter and its nuances can be found in (Fussell, 1979).

Rhyme scheme describes which lines in a stanza* rhyme with each other, that is, contain the same or similarly sounding stressed endings of the lines (Hollander, 2014). Rhyme schemes presented in the finetune dataset (subsection 3.2) are listed in Table 11.

Rubai is a classical Persian poetry form, typically a quatrain with AABA or AAAA rhyming - see more details at (Greene et al., 2012, page 1227).

Stanza is a group of lines separated by blank lines from other stanzas. See (Greene et al., 2012, page 809) for more information.

Syllabo-tonic versification is based on 1) a fixed number of syllables in lines and 2) a regular pattern of stressed and unstressed syllables. In English-language literature, the term "accentual-syllabic" is more commonly used (Fussell, 1979, page 6), while "syllabo-tonic" is more common in scientific literature devoted to Slavic languages and Russian versification in particular (Wachtel, 2004). Given the specialization of this article on Russian-language poetry, we decided to use the "syllabo-tonic" variant.

Sonnet is a fixed verse poetic form consisting of 14 lines with constrained rhyming. For more information see (Fuller, 2017).

Trochee is a metrical foot consisting of one stressed syllable followed by one unstressed syllable (Greene et al., 2012, page 870).

B Fixing the spelling, punctuation, and tokenization issues

A significant portion of the training data was scraped from online sources, in particular from amateur poetry sites. The significant number of spelling and punctuation errors in these texts forced us to take special measures to clean the training data. A detailed description of the cleaning procedure is presented below.

We analyzed the collected poems described in section 3 for the most frequent misspellings and typos. As a result, many typos and common errors, which occurred up to 10 times in an 8 GB corpus, were corrected to their appropriate forms. Table 6 presents the 10 most frequent corrections. Based on this analysis, we created a "white list", which served as the reference dictionary for identifying out-of-vocabulary words in the poetry corpus. We use dictionary-based replacements and heuristic rules for common spelling errors. When the algorithm detects a mistake, it checks if the correction exists in the reference dictionary and fixes it. We have developed about 30 rules based on regular expressions for this purpose. The typical problem cases are described below:

- Replace visually similar Latin characters with Cyrillic ones when they appear together in a word.
- Replace the combination of the letter "i" and the Unicode symbol U+0306 with the standalone Russian letter "j".
- To differentiate between Russian and English symbols, check for surrounding Cyrillic characters when dealing with single-letter words containing symbols from the character set [K, O, C, A, B, o, a, c, k, y].
- Replace various Unicode space characters[23] with the standard space character (U+0020).
- Handle cases where standard ASCII punctuation marks are replaced with full-width or half-width Unicode counterparts to convert them back to their ASCII prototypes.

The code implementing the above rules, along with all dictionary files, is publicly available as open source.[24]

One common issue in internet-sourced poetry texts is the presence of unnecessary commas. In generated poems, extra commas, especially between the subject and predicate, greatly reduce the quality of the text. To address this, we have implemented an algorithm that uses the perplexity of ruGPT3-medium[25] as an indicator of text likelihood. The algorithm functions by sequentially removing all commas from a sentence, except for the last one, and then comparing the perplexity of the sentence before and after each removal. If the perplexity significantly decreases after a comma is removed, that comma is deemed unnecessary and is eliminated. This method has the advantage of not requiring training on a specialized model. However, one drawback is that perplexity can be unreliable for short texts, as language models tend to consider shorter texts as less likely overall.

The above procedure affected about 10% of all collected data.

[23]In the texts collected on the Internet, nearly all the whitespace characters listed in the table `https://www.unicode.org/Public/UCD/latest/ucd/PropList.txt` are found

[24]`https://github.com/Koziev/Spellchecker`

[25]`ai-forever/ruGPT3-medium_based_on_gpt2`

Defective text	Corrected text	Share, %
vraz	v raz	2.3
kak-budto	kak budto	2.0
gde to	gde-to	2.0
Kak-budto	Kak budto	1.6
kogda to	kogda-to	1.5

Table 6: The top frequent replacements in the corpus. The tokens are transliterated from Russian.

C Examples

Figure 1 presents a sample poem generated by our top model and its translation to English.

D Tokenizer Discussion

The use of language models with character-level tokenization is described in a number of papers (Belouadi and Eger, 2022; Yu et al., 2024). Compared to mainstream BPE tokenization and similar approaches, representing text at the character level makes it easier for the language model to handle poetry. For syllabo-tonic poetry, the key limitation lies in a strictly defined order of alternation of stressed and unstressed vowels (coinciding with syllables for the Russian language), as well as a certain number of syllables in each line. In BPE tokenization, different tokens contain different number of vowels. Therefore, the LM needs a more pretraining data to collect information about the composition of the tokens. In addition, taking into account vowel stress in the BPE scheme requires additional effort.

A compromise option can be considered a syllable-level representation of the text (Zugarini et al., 2019; Vechtomova et al., 2020). The disadvantage of this text representation is the difficulty of tokenizing for prose in some cases, for example, in multilingual contexts, when the syllabication rules differ for different languages.

Additionally, syllable-level tokenization, similar to BPE, performs poorly in some scenarios where

```
Как быть счастливым, если нет покоя?        How to be happy if there is no peace?
Как быть счастливым, если в сердце мрак?    How to be happy if there is darkness in the heart?
Как быть счастливым, если нет прибоя?       How to be happy if there is no surf?
Как быть счастливым, если ты дурак?         How to be happy if you are a fool?

Как быть счастливым, если ты не знаешь,     How to be happy if you do not know,
Как быть счастливым, если ты не жил?        How to be happy if you have not lived?
Как быть счастливым, если ты не понял,      How to be happy if you do not understand,
Как быть счастливым, если не любил?         How to be happy if you have not loved?
```

Figure 1: The example of the generated poem. The English version is translated from the Russian.

Model	learning_rate	lr_scheduler_type	floating type	optimizer
CharLLaMa-1.3B	2e-5	constant	fp16	adamw_torch
CharMamba-1.3B	2e-5	linear	fp16	adamw_torch
CharLLaMa-2.6B	2e-5	constant	bf16	adamw_torch
stGPT small	5e-5	constant	bf16	adamw_torch
stGPT medium	5e-5	constant	bf16	adamw_torch
Mistral-7B-v0.1	2e-5	constant	bf16	adamw_torch
FRED-T5-1.7B	1e-4	constant	bf16	adafactor
ByT5-small	1e-4	constant	bf16	adafactor

Table 7: The hyperparameters of the models are in the finetuning stage for the experiments. The parameters were selected specially for each model.

the LM is required to understand the character-level composition of tokens, such as acrostics*.

Unfortunately, character-level tokenization has some disadvantages. They arise from the fact that token sequences are lengthened in comparison with BPE and syllable-level tokenization. Because of this, the time required for model pretraining and finetuning increases substantially. Memory consumption for the autoregressive text generation scheme and the time of this generation also increases.

Table 8 compares tokenization approaches for LMs described in Section 5.2.

E Pretraining Data Sources

The pretraining data is drawn from two sources: poetry and prose, with the proportion of each detailed in Table 9.

For prose, the following datasets were used as sources for the pretraining data:

- "YandexQ"[26] is a dataset of questions and answers scraped from Yandex.Q in the Internet domain. There are 836810 answered questions out of the total of 1297670.
- "Mail Question Answering" [27] is a set of question-answering pairs from real users.
- Instruction set of conversational agents [28] is a Russian instruction set of conversational domain.
- ruWikiHow[29] is a public dataset based on the parsed WikiHow source.
- Wikidepia[30] contains cleaned articles from Wikipedia dumps[31], one subset per language, each having a single train split. The Russian section was utilized for pretraining.
- Habr[32] is a dataset of posts and comments from habr.com[33], a Russian collaborative blog in the technical domain.

F Prompt Design

For every poem in the finetuning dataset (subsection 3.2), we create a synthetic prompt that varies in parameters (emotion, length, poetic meter*, etc.). The Russian example of the prompt for the creation

[26]https://huggingface.co/datasets/its5Q/yandex-q

[27]https://huggingface.co/datasets/Den4ikAI/mailruQA-big

[28]https://huggingface.co/datasets/Den4ikAI/russian_instructions_2

[29]Den4ikAI/ruWikiHow_instructions

[30]https://huggingface.co/datasets/wikimedia/wikipedia

[31]https://dumps.wikimedia.org/

[32]https://huggingface.co/datasets/IlyaGusev/habr

[33]https://habr.com/

Model	Tokenizer	Characters per token w/o accentuation	Characters per token with accentuation
ByT5	ByT5Tokenizer	0.56	0.55
CharLLaMa	CharacterTokenizer	1.00	1.00
Mistral-7B-v0.1	LlamaTokenizerFast	1.98	1.74
Llama-2	LlamaTokenizerFast	2.10	1.79
ruGPT3	GPT2TokenizerFast	3.20	2.12
FRED-T5-1.7B	GPT2Tokenizer	3.20	2.12
stGPT	StressedGptTokenizer	n/a	2.30

Table 8: Comparative results of tokenizers from the experiments described in Section 5.2. Characters per token is the default metric for tokenizer vocabularies of different sizes, obtained using the BPE and Unigram algorithms. N/A indicates cases where accentuation is required by design.

Type	Number of characters	Share, %
Prose	39,364,771,098	60.76
Poetry	25,427,281,242	39.24

Table 9: Statistics and proportion of prose and poetry texts in the pretraining dataset (subsection 3.1).

Meters	Share, %
iambic	57.88
trochee	34.28
amphibrachium	3.91
dactyl	2.24
anapaest	1.57
others	0.12

Table 10: The main poetic meters* and their proportions in the finetuning dataset (subsection 3.2).

Rhyming scheme	Share, %
-A-A	34.94
ABAB	34.68
----	16.09
AABB	11.26
ABBA	1.99
A-A-	0.55
AABA	0.4
others	0.9

Table 11: The most frequent rhyming schemes in the finetuning dataset.

of the synthetic prompt for the specific poem is presented in Figure 2.

Проанализируй приведенное ниже стихотворение в **жанре** "пейзажная лирика".
Выдели главного героя, основную мысль, авторскую посылку, ключевой конфликт, эмоцию, яркую метафору, все имена собственные в этом стихотворении и подставь вместо многоточия в **шаблон** «придумай стихотворение с описанием ...», чтобы получилось задание для поэта.
Выведи только получившуюся строку задания.

Вы не ругайте ветер, что ленив,
Что запил, и забросил всю работу.
Он листья оборвав с берез и ив,
Зиме оставив о листве заботу.

Шаловливый безобразник
Для себя устроил праздник.
Листья он кружил, вертел,
И от радости свистел.

result => Придумай стихотворение с описанием осени.

Figure 2: An example of the prompt and generated text. The yellow text represents a poem, while the red text denotes the TEMPLATE. The template is modified by the LLM based on its parameters and the analysis of the input poem, generating a instructive prompt for new poem creation.

Automating Violence Detection and Categorization from Ancient Texts

Alhassan Abdelhalim and Michaela Regneri
Universität Hamburg, Dept. of Computer Science, Hamburg, Germany
{alhassan.abdelhalim, michaela.regneri}@uni-hamburg.de

Abstract

Violence descriptions in literature offer valuable insights for a wide range of research in the humanities. For historians, depictions of violence are of special interest for analyzing the societal dynamics surrounding large wars and individual conflicts of influential people. Harvesting data for violence research manually is laborious and time-consuming. This study is the first one to evaluate the effectiveness of large language models (LLMs) in identifying violence in ancient texts and categorizing it across multiple dimensions. Our experiments identify LLMs as a valuable tool to scale up the accurate analysis of historical texts and show the effect of fine-tuning and data augmentation, yielding an F1-score of up to 0.93 for violence detection and 0.86 for fine-grained violence categorization.

1 Introduction

Violence has been a defining element in human history, influencing cultural values, political structures, and social norms (Frier, 1985; Raaflaub et al., 2007; Konstan, 2007). Understanding its role in shaping ancient civilizations provides valuable insights into societal evolution, power dynamics, and conflict resolution (Westbrook and Beckman, 2003; Redfield, 1994; Bizos, 2008). To analyze historical texts for information on violent events, historians have traditionally relied on manual analysis, reading, and annotating vast amounts of text. While manual annotation remains a gold standard for nuanced interpretations, time and labor required for the sheer volume of ancient texts and their linguistic complexities make this approach intractable for exhaustive collections of ancient manuscripts. The rapid growth of digital archives and historical corpora underscores the need for automated methods to assist historians in extracting information more efficiently.

Large Language Models (LLMs), such as BERT (Devlin et al., 2019), RoBERTa (Liu et al., 2019), and GPT (Radford and Narasimhan, 2018), have successfully been applied to a wide range of classification tasks, also for scaling annotation of historical texts (Celli and Mingazov, 2024). So far, they have not been used to classify text passages denoting violent events.

Our research bridges the gap between the hermeneutical processes of historical analysis and the computational methods of natural language processing. We develop and evaluate methodologies that automate the annotation of violence in ancient texts while preserving the depth of understanding traditionally achieved through manual methods. As our gold standard, we use the manually curated ERIS database (Riess and Zerjadtke, 2015)[1], a large digital collection of violent events from ancient literature.

We first identify the violent passages contained in ERIS within their original texts using classifiers based on LLMs. Then, we further reproduce some more fine-grained annotations from ERIS, categorizing the violent passages across multiple dimensions: level of violence, contextual background, underlying motives, and long-term consequences. The results of our study show that LLMs offer a promising solution for extracting violence data. They can expedite the identification of violent events and the extraction of contextual information from ancient texts. With accurate results for a range of classification tasks around violence, LLMs can complement the expertise of historians, allowing them to focus on deeper interpretative tasks rather than the extensive and time-consuming data processing typically required.

In the following, we first give an overview of related work (Sec. 2) before we introduce our dataset and methodology (Sec. 3). We then present our results (Sec. 4) and discuss their implications (Sec. 5)

[1] https://www.ancientviolence.uni-hamburg.de

Proceedings of LaTeCH-CLfL 2025, pages 64–78
May 4, 2025

before we conclude with a short summary and ideas for future work (Sec. 6). Code and data are provided as supplementary material [2].

2 Background & Related Work

This section provides some background on violence research in history and the digital humanities (Sec. 2.1). We then introduce large language models and discuss related work concerning LLMs for classification and annotation support (Sec. 2.2).

2.1 Historical Perspectives and Data on Violence

The meaning of violence is deeply shaped by cultural context, making it a complex phenomenon to define. From a historian's point of view, violence can be defined as *"a physical act, a process in which a human being inflicts harm on another human being via physical strength"* (Riess, 2012). Violence shaped societal values, legal systems, and social hierarchies in ancient civilizations. Interpersonal violence often reflected concepts of honor, justice, and societal expectations, as reflected in texts like The Iliad (Diemke et al.; Konstan, 2007). Legal codes like Hammurabi's Lex talionis and Roman law institutionalized violence, balancing societal order and retributive justice (Roth, 1995; Frier, 1985).

Power dynamics frequently used violence as a tool for asserting dominance, with leaders such as Julius Caesar and Augustus consolidating power through both physical and symbolic acts of violence (Fagan, 2011; Dando-Collins, 2010). Gendered violence highlighted patriarchal structures, as myths and legal frameworks depicted male dominance and societal control (Lerner, 1986; Pomeroy, 2011). Conflict resolution in ancient texts ranged from violent duels to legal settlements and diplomatic treaties, such as the peace treaty after the Battle of Kadesh (Witham, 2020; Gagarin, 1982).

Psychological drivers of violence, such as honor, revenge, and emotional turmoil, are central to narratives like The Iliad and The Oresteia, where cycles of vengeance reflect societal norms and the transition to judicial systems (Olson, 1990; Cohen, 1986). Violence in historical accounts, such as Caesar's assassination, also humanizes figures, exposing vulnerabilities and the socio-political landscapes of their time (Tranquillus and Graves, 1962; Allen, 2005).

Analyzing violence in ancient texts enables researchers to gain insights into societal evolution (Westbrook and Beckman, 2003), comparative legal systems (Trigger, 2003; Redfield, 1994), and the foundation of modern justice (Jackson, 1968; Bizos, 2008; Eichler, 2009). Detecting violent instances in ancient texts presents unique challenges due to the implicit and symbolic nature of violence in historical narratives.

In digital humanities, the study of violence in ancient texts relies on digital resources which provide access to extensive literary and historical collections. In our work, we focus on two of these resources:

Perseus[3] (Smith et al., 2000) offers Greek and Roman literature with translations, linguistic annotations, and open-access tools, enabling tasks like text reconstruction and model training (Assael et al., 2019). Despite its utility, it faces usability challenges (Lang, 2018; Preece and Zepeda, 2009).

ERIS (Riess and Zerjadtke, 2015) is a curated and expanding database of violent depictions in Greek, Roman, and some medieval texts. It includes metadata for bibliographic contexts and details of violent events. We provide a more detailed discussion of ERIS compared to Perseus because ERIS plays a central role in our study and has significant potential for future expansion. In contrast, Perseus, being a widely recognized and extensively documented resource, primarily served as a supplementary source to retrieve non-violent contexts for our dataset. ERIS is further introduced in Sec. 3.1.

2.2 Large Language Models

Large Language Models (LLMs) have revolutionized Natural Language Processing (NLP), enabling advanced text understanding and generation capabilities that were previously unattainable. Built on the architecture of Transformers (Vaswani et al., 2017), LLMs such as Generative Pre-trained Transformer (GPT) (Radford and Narasimhan, 2018), BERT (Devlin et al., 2019), and RoBERTa (Liu et al., 2019) have set new benchmarks in language modeling and processing tasks.

GPT excels in generative tasks like text completion and translation by leveraging a unidirectional architecture that predicts the next word based on prior context (Brown et al., 2020). In contrast, BERT (Bidirectional Encoder Representations from Transformers) introduced bidirectional

[2] https://osf.io/ae835/

[3] http://www.perseus.tufts.edu/

context understanding, enabling deeper insights for tasks such as question answering and named entity recognition (Devlin et al., 2019). RoBERTa (Robustly Optimized BERT Pretraining Approach) further refined BERT's capabilities by using larger datasets for training and optimizing various hyperparameters, which enhances performance across various benchmarks (Liu et al., 2019).

These models demonstrate the power of pretraining on vast datasets, capturing linguistic patterns and contextual nuances that generalize across diverse domains. In consequence, LLMs cemented their role as main component for scalable language processing, especially various classification tasks, such as sentiment analysis (Bang et al., 2023), text categorization (et al, 2023), and natural language inference (Honovich et al., 2022). The possibility to fine-tune such pre-trained models to small domains makes them a versatile tool also for uncommon data like ancient texts: They have already been used for scaling up annotation of historical data (Celli and Mingazov, 2024), and for hate speech detection (Mathew et al., 2021). Both tasks have goals close to our objective of extracting and categorizing violence from ancient texts. Our method is developed to scale the annotation of violent events in ancient texts, and we are also concerned with textually manifested ferocity. Our contribution extends previous approaches in that we use annotation methods for violent texts and that our data contains descriptions of violence rather than verbal assaults, as in hate speech. To the best of our knowledge, we present the first study that automatically extracts and annotates violence from historical text data.

3 Data and Experimental Setup

In this section, we explain ERIS as the basis for our experiments (Sec. 3.1), how we set up the experiments for violence detection (Sec. 3.2) and violence categorization (Sec. 3.3), and introduce the evaluation metrics used for both tasks (Sec. 3.4).

3.1 Data: The ERIS Database

ERIS (Riess and Zerjadtke, 2015) is a manually curated and continuously growing database containing depictions of violence from Greek, Roman and some medieval texts, including references to violence from Herodian, Plutarch, Tacitus, Thucydides and Xenophon. Each text passage is annotated with metadata, denoting the bibliographic contexts as well as details on the violent event. Among other labels, it categorizes violent acts by context, motives, and social factors. It also provides metadata as timestamps and geographical coordinates, supporting advanced filtering and geospatial analysis. ERIS emphasizes sociological dimensions of violence, enabling a deeper understanding of its impacts across time and regions. Most notably, ERIS contains links to the Perseus database to match violence passages to their original texts. At the time of writing this paper, ERIS contained 3,252 entries spanning various time periods, starting from Archaic Greece in the 7th century BCE to the Salian period in the 11th century AD.

Attribute	Details
Related Conflict	Wars of Alexander The Great
Perpetrator	*Name:* Alexander III the Great *Age:* Adult *Activity:* Monarch/Ruler *Origin:* Macedonian
Victim	*Name:* Cleitus the Black *Age:* Adult *Direct Consequence:* death *Origin:* Macedonian
Third Party (Person) **Third Party (Group)**	*Name:* Aristophanes *Age:* Adult *Activity:* Soldier Friends of Alexander III *Origin*: Mixed *Age*: mixed *Activity*: commander/general
Source	Plutarch, Alexander 51.5
Year	328 B.C.
Location	Maracanda (Samarkand)
Time Period	Hellenistic Greece
Level	Interpersonal
Context	entertaining
Motivation	emotional
Weapon	Spear
Original Text	"οὕτω δὴ λαβὼν παρά τινος τῶν δορυφόρων Ἀλέξανδρος αἰχμὴν ἀπαντῶντα τὸν Κλεῖτον αὐτῷ καὶ παράγοντα τὸ πρὸ τῆς θύρας παρακάλυμμα διελαύνει."
Translation	*"And so, at last, Alexander seized a spear from one of his guards, met Cleitus as he was drawing aside the curtain before the door, and ran him through."*
Remark	*perpetrator*: Alexander is shocked by his deed and tries to kill himself. This is mentioned in 51.6. *thirdperson*: The presence of these persons is mentioned in 51.1-4 and 51.6.

Figure 1: An entry from ERIS titled : Alexander kills Cleitus with a spear.

Figure 1 shows an example entry from ERIS. Each entry includes metadata such as title, source references, historical period, and century, as well as detailed classifications of violence level, context, motive, weapon, consequences, and method of execution. Additionally, it provides temporal and situational context, including date, season, month, and duration, along with references to the primary text sources. Some of the attributes also refer to information not contained in the text passage, here noted as *Remark*. ERIS mostly contains Greek and Roman literature, along with English translations. Our work is based on the ERIS content from biographies of Plutarch, an ancient Greek writer. We work with the English translations of the original texts.

3.2 Violence Detection

In our first experiment, we perform a binary classification task to detect instances of violence (and distinguish them from non-violent passages) in ancient texts. For classification, we compare the plain pre-trained models with fine-tuned LLMs.

As ERIS contains only violent passages, we additionally need comparable non-violent examples to train our model. To obtain those, we retrieve the context of the violent passages from ERIS by re-connecting them to their source texts. Then we train LLMs to distinguish violent from non-violent passages. As a baseline, we also use the ChatGPT-API to simulate an annotator that works with the support of ChatGPT and compare the results.

Data Pre-processing

To obtain data that we can use for training and testing, we need to amend the ERIS data with non-violent examples. Our core idea is to retrieve data from the original texts the ERIS passages were extracted from and use sentences that are not labeled in ERIS as nonviolent data. Because this requires us to have digital access to the respective original texts, we restrict this experiment to ERIS samples from Plutarch's biographies, which have digital links to their source text in the Perseus database.

For each violent passage from ERIS, the full sections from which these excerpts were derived were retrieved. Any paragraph not explicitly marked as violent in ERIS was treated as non-violent, forming the negative examples for the dataset, resulting in a final dataset of 461 violent and 2103 non-violent texts extracted from 13 different Plutarch books. We assume that for any book that is completely annotated for ERIS, each text part that is not contained in ERIS does only contain non-violent text. This assumption might not always hold, because annotators could have missed some passages. We discuss future assessment of this in the Limitations section.

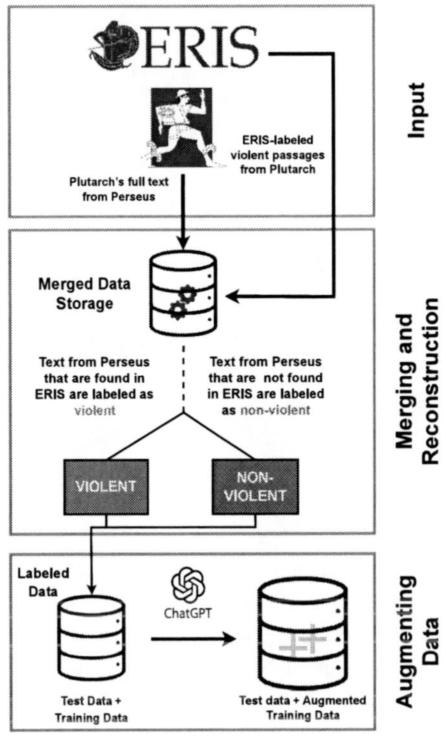

Figure 2: Data Preprocessing Pipeline for Violence Detection.

As a held-out test set for evaluation, 500 texts (371 non-violent and 129 Violent) distributed evenly across the 13 Plutarch books were selected. The remaining passages were used later on for training, fine-tuning, and data augmentation.

Because the Plutarch vitae constitute a comparably small dataset, we want to explore the impact of data augmentation with LLMs, for which we used the OpenAI API. For each entry in the training dataset, we generated three paraphrased versions and thus quadrupled the training data size. We retained 6928 non-violent texts and 1328 violent texts. Then we tested the augmented models on the 500 sentences reserved for evaluation to quantify the influence of augmentation. Figure 3 shows an exemplary sentence from ERIS and the three paraphrases obtained using the OpenAI API.

Original Sentence	*As a result of this battle, the Greeks could not only harry the country of the King without fear, but had the satisfaction of seeing due punishment inflicted upon Tisaphernes, an abominable man, and most hateful to the Greek race.* ***[Plut. Ages. 10.3]***
Paraphrase 1	*Consequently, the Greek army found themselves able to pillage the king's realm without trepidation, while also deriving satisfaction from the punishment dealt to Tisaphernes, a detestable individual who was particularly reviled by their people.*
Paraphrase 2	*This battle enabled the Greeks to wreak havoc across the king's lands unimpeded, while they also relished the sight of Tisaphernes, an odious person hated by the Greek civilization, finally facing the consequences of his actions.*
Paraphrase 3	*Following this conflict, the Hellenic forces were not only able to raid the territory of the monarch freely but also took pleasure in witnessing Tisaphernes, a loathsome figure deeply despised by the Greeks, receive just retribution.*

Figure 3: An example of our text augmentation. This approach effectively quadriples the training data.

Model Selection

For violence detection, we evaluated BERT-large and RoBERTa-large as LLMs for direct classification. Both models were tested first as-is and then with fine-tuning to the historical data. As an additional model that simulates annotation with the support of ChatGPT, we used the GPT-4o mini API with a specifically designed prompt that outputs the classifications. We provide the prompt in Appendix B.

3.3 Categorizing Violent Events

In our second experiment, we automatically apply a more fine-grained annotation of violent texts, aiming to reproduce some ERIS annotations. In contrast to the first experiment, we use the full ERIS database as our source data. Thus, our input contains a wider variety of source texts than the violence classification (which was restricted to Plutarch biographies) and only texts that are manually labeled as violent. For this experiment, data augmentation was not suitable because we would have to augment the fine-grained annotation from ERIS as well.

With the ERIS passages, we use a multi-class classification approach across four key dimensions from the ERIS annotations:

- **Level of Violence:** Classifies instances of violence into four categories: interpersonal (conflict between individuals), intrapersonal (self-harm), intersocial (conflicts between groups, like wars), and intrasocial (conflicts within a societal group). They highlight the relational context of the events.
- **Context:** Contains 25 categories of the setting in which the violence occurred, with various political, military, and social contexts.
- **Motive:** 13 different classes for the underlying reasons for violent actions, distinguishing between tactical/strategic goals, political ambitions, adherence to authority, emotional impulses, and economic motives.
- **Long-Term Consequences:** The most fine-grained label with 38 outcomes of violent events, including social disruption, political changes, and personal impacts.

We split the dataset into 80% for training/validation and 20% for testing. Some (5) classes with very few instances do not occur in the randomly assigned test split. We fine-tuned and evaluated one BERT and one RoBERTa model per dimension.

3.4 Evaluation Metrics

For both experiments, we measure the performance of all models using the standard evaluation metrics precision, recall and F1 score.

Given that TP, FP, FN, TN are the True Positives, False Positives, False Negatives, and True Negatives respectively, key metrics are defined as follows:

$$\textbf{Precision:} \quad P = \frac{TP}{TP + FP} \tag{1}$$

Precision measures the proportion of correct positive predictions.

$$\textbf{Recall:} \quad R = \frac{TP}{TP + FN} \tag{2}$$

Recall measures the proportion of actual positives that are correctly identified.

$$\textbf{F1 Score:} \quad F_1 = \frac{2 * P * R}{P + R} \tag{3}$$

The F1 score is the harmonic mean of precision and recall, which is sensitive to disparities between them. This property ensures that the F1 score is low if either precision or recall is low, accurately reflecting the model's overall performance.

We also provide two baselines: majority and random. A **majority baseline** represents a trivial classifier that only predicts the majority class c_{majority}. Given class probabilities $P(c_k)$ for K classes, a class c_k is predicted with: $\hat{y} = c_{\text{majority}}, \quad \forall x \in X$.

A **random baseline** assigns labels based on class probabilities $p_i = \frac{\#C_i}{X}$. The expected probability of making a correct prediction is given by $\sum_{i=1}^{N} p_i^2$. This represents the probability of randomly guessing the correct label, serving as a lower-bound benchmark for classifiers.

4 Results

In this section we provide our results for violence detection (Sec. 4.1) and violence categorization (Sec. 4.2).

4.1 Violence Detection

Our results are summarized in Table 1. Overall, BERT with augmentation and fine-tuning performs best for our task. Fine-tuning enhanced the results drastically. The fine-tuned BERT and RoBERTa-large yielded an F1-score of 0.83 and 0.87, effectively capturing violent instances. Both provided competitive results.

Applying data augmentation enhanced the performance of both models. In particular, it vastly enhanced recall for all models, which is of particular interest for supporting annotators: The most common mistake when extracting violent passages manually is to miss them in the text. Having a preprocessor with high recall (maybe compromising with lower precision) can perfectly complement the precise human annotation because it is much faster to sort out falsely selected violent passages than to re-read the whole source text to retrieve missed but relevant paragraphs.

For F1, data augmentation made only a significant difference for BERT ($p < 0.05$ using McNemar's test), but not for RoBERTa.

Our simulated zero-shot GPT annotator implemented with the general-purpose GPT-4o mini model attained an F1-score of 0.71 but struggled with non-violent instances. We attribute this to the lack of fine-tuning in ChatGPT, which is supported by both our results and many other studies that measure the importance of domain-specific fine-tuning for better classification (Rietzler et al., 2020; Rostam and Kertész, 2024; Liu et al., 2024). We also evaluated the larger GPT-4o model exploratively, which is approximately 16 times more expensive than the GPT-4o mini version. Despite the increased computational cost, GPT-4o offered only marginal improvements on our test data in the F1 score (0.5), indicating limited practical advantage for this task. We thus continued using the GPT-4o mini model.

4.2 Violence Categorization

For categorization, we used fine-tuned BERT-large and RoBERTa-large. An overview of the results is shown in Table 2. We report the averages over all instances, which amounts to weighted averages over the individual classes. A detailed breakdown by individual labels is given in Appendix D. We generally achieve promising results with an F1 score of 0.8, even for the most fine-grained category (long-term consequences with 37 classes). As for violence identification, BERT shows a slightly better performance than RoBERTa.

For identifying the *violence level*, the models performed best in classifying interpersonal and intersocial violence, achieving high precision and recall. However, intrapersonal violence posed challenges due to its lower representation and the subtle contextual understanding required.

For *context*, F1 is still comparably high given the complexity of the task with 23 classes. Looking at the details, we find that the model effectively identified broad categories like "War/Military Campaign" and "Battle" but struggled with nuanced distinctions between similar contexts, such as large-scale campaigns versus single combat.

Distinguishing *motives* works with similar accuracy. Again, the model performed well in identifying broad categories like "Tactical/Strategical" and "Political" but struggled with nuanced or less frequent categories such as "Emotional" and "Ambition". Overlaps between motives like "Political", "Following Orders", and "Tactical/Strategical" led to misclassifications.

Finding the *Long-Term Consequences* was the most challenging task with 37 different classes. The model excelled in identifying concrete categories like "Destruction/Devastation" and "Victory," which are frequently referenced in historical texts. However, categories with fewer examples,

	Model	Precision	Recall	F1-Score	Support
Violent	GPT-4o mini	0.69	0.74	0.71	129
	BERT [as-is]	0.25	0.97	0.40	129
	BERT [fine-tuned]	0.88	0.78	0.83	129
	BERT [fine-tuned and augmented]	0.87	0.99	**0.93**	129
	RoBERTa [as-is]	0.00	0.0	0.00	129
	RoBERTa [fine-tuned]	0.89	0.86	0.87	129
	RoBERTa [fine-tuned and augmented]	0.82	0.99	**0.90**	129
Non-Violent	GPT-4o mini	0.91	0.88	0.89	371
	BERT [as-is]	0.00	0.00	0.00	371
	BERT [fine-tuned]	0.93	0.96	0.94	371
	BERT [fine-tuned and augmented]	1.00	0.95	**0.97**	371
	RoBERTa [as-is]	0.74	1.0	0.85	371
	RoBERTa [fine-tuned]	0.95	0.96	0.96	371
	RoBERTa [fine-tuned and augmented]	1.00	0.92	**0.96**	371
Overall	GPT-4o mini	0.69	0.74	0.71	500
	BERT [as-is]	0.25	0.97	0.40	500
	BERT [fine-tuned]	0.88	0.78	0.83	500
	BERT [fine-tuned and augmented]	0.87	0.99	**0.93**	500
	RoBERTa [as-is]	0.00	0.00	0.00	500
	RoBERTa [fine-tuned]	0.89	0.86	0.87	500
	RoBERTa [fine-tuned and augmented]	0.82	0.99	**0.90***	500
Baselines (overall)	Majority (all non-violent)	0.74	0.74	0.74	500
	Random	0.61	0.61	0.61	500

Table 1: Violence detection performance across different models, evaluated per class (Non-Violent and Violent). Support indicates the number of instances in each class of the test set. (*) marks an insignificant difference.

		RoBERTa			BERT			Baselines	
Dimension	**Classes**	**Precision**	**Recall**	**F1-Score**	**Precision**	**Recall**	**F1-Score**	**Majority**	**Random**
Level	4	0.95	0.95	**0.95**	0.93	0.93	0.93	0.67	0.49
Context	23	0.86	0.85	0.84	0.86	0.86	**0.85**	0.33	0.16
Motive	12	0.86	0.85	0.85	0.86	0.86	**0.86**	0.35	0.20
Consequences	37	0.82	0.80	0.80	0.82	0.81	**0.81**	0.36	0.16

Table 2: Overall Violence Categorization Results. Breakdowns by label are provided in Appendix D

such as "Exile" and "Coronation," proved challenging, resulting in lower precision and recall. The abstract nature of some consequences, like political changes or psychological impacts, added complexity to classification.

5 Discussion

The experiments demonstrated the potential of fine-tuned large language models (LLMs) in detecting and classifying violence in ancient texts. Our evaluation demonstrates the models' strengths in violence classification, with an F1-score of up to 0.93. In manual classification recall is often the problem due to implicit or symbolic violence, ambiguous wording, and a bias toward precision, leading to missed instances. Our finetuned and augmented models achieve a high recall, showing that LLMs can mitigate blind spots that humans miss. However, challenges like class imbalance, conceptual overlap, and abstract categories in multi-class tasks revealed areas for improvement.

For violence categorization, our approach excelled in well-represented and concrete categories, such as "Victory" and "Destruction," but struggled with abstract or underrepresented categories like "Intrapersonal Violence" or "Exile". Conceptual overlaps, such as between "Political" and "Tactical" motives, also led to misclassifications.

From the perspective of historians, choosing between fine-tuned models, tools like ChatGPT, or manual annotation depends on specific project needs. We provide an overview over the specific features to be considered for applying fine-tuned LLMs and ChatGPT (either via user interface or via API) in Table 3. Fine-tuned LLMs excel in structured, large-scale tasks where efficiency and consistency are paramount, offering rapid processing capabilities that can save months of manual labor. ChatGPT, while versatile and user-friendly, lacks domain-specific fine-tuning, making it less reliable for specialized classifications but valuable for exploratory tasks or initial insights. Manual annotation remains irreplaceable for complex interpretative work, especially in ambiguous cases requiring deep historical expertise. A hybrid approach, where LLMs handle bulk annotation and historians validate edge cases, offers an optimal balance between efficiency and precision.

Criteria	LLM Finetuning	API
Highly specialized task	✓	✗
Requires extensive labeled data	✓	✗
Cost-effective for small tasks	✗	✓
Faster deployment	✗	✓
Full control over architecture	✓	✗
Local dependency	✓	✗
inference speed	✓	?
Suitable for dynamic scaling	✗	✓
Ongoing model maintenance	✓	✗
Scalability	✗	✓
Convenience / Usable across devices	✗	✓
Ongoing Maintenance / feedback	✗	✓
Ethical considerations	?	✓

Table 3: Pros and cons of fine-tuning LLMs vs. zero-shot approach through pre-trained OpenAI APIs

Convenience and usability are also to be considered when choosing between fine-tuning LLMs or directly using APIs. Fine-tuned models require technical expertise for setup and training but deliver streamlined workflows once operational. ChatGPT, with its accessible API and conversational interface, is more user-friendly and easy to use since it can be conveniently used in tablets or mobile phones. However, it lacks the tailored accuracy of fine-tuned models.while manual annotation is intellectually robust, it is resource-intensive and impractical for large datasets. Integrating intuitive interfaces with fine-tuned models could enhance their usability, encouraging broader adoption among non-technical users.

Inference speed varies between fine-tuned models and API-based solutions. Fine-tuned models offer lower latency but require dedicated hardware, while API-based models provide scalability but introduce network latency and rate limits. Fine-tuning is preferable for low-latency applications, while APIs offer scalability and ease of use.

Ongoing model maintenance refers to the continuous process of monitoring, updating, and retraining fine-tuned LLMs to maintain their performance and adapt to evolving data distributions or task requirements. When practitioners fine-tune their own models, they bear the responsibility for performance monitoring, infrastructure management, and regular model updates to ensure accuracy and relevance over time.

Ethical and bias considerations differ significantly between fine-tuned LLMs and API-based solutions. Pre-trained APIs are typically pre-moderated, incorporating safeguards to filter harmful or biased outputs. On the other hand, fine-tuned models require custom mitigation strategies (Jin et al., 2021; Garimella et al., 2022), which can either reduce or amplify biases, depending on dataset quality and training methods. Fine-tuning allows for domain-specific alignment but poses risks if ethical oversight is inadequate.

The implications of this research extend beyond ancient texts, offering valuable insights for analyzing contemporary violence depictions, addressing modern datasets such as media reports, social media content, or legal documents. Adapting the models to contemporary datasets would require adjustments to account for different linguistic styles, cultural contexts, and evolving definitions of violence, presenting an exciting avenue for interdisciplinary research.

A significant gap lies in automating the identification of abstract or highly contextual categories, such as psychological impacts or symbolic violence. Achieving this would require expanding datasets, understanding abstractions in LLMs (Regneri et al., 2024), incorporating knowledge bases (Wang et al., 2024), and exploring advanced techniques like retrieval augmented generation (RAG) (Chen et al., 2024). Developing dynamic models that can learn from continuous expert feedback through techniques like reinforcement learning from human feedback (RLHF) could also bridge this gap (Kaufmann et al., 2023).

6 Conclusion

In this work, we proposed a framework for automating the classification and categorization of violent ancient texts using LLMs. Our two main contributions are the development of models capable of accurately classifying violent sentences, and employing these models to automate the process of fine-grained violence categorization. In both cases, we showed the effect of fine-tuning the models. For violence detection, we also showed that data augmentation drastically enhances recall, which is the most important measure for supporting manual annotation. Our results can enable historians to accomplish tasks that previously required months or years in minutes. To the best of our knowledge, we are also the first to utilize the OpenAI API to classify violent ancient historical texts and compare its performance against other pre-trained models. Our findings underscore the potential of LLMs to automate labor-intensive tasks and pave the way for large-scale text analysis in historical research. While fine-tuned LLMs provide structured and efficient classification, ChatGPT remains useful for exploratory tasks, and manual annotation retains its importance in complex interpretative work.

Challenges remain, particularly with underrepresented classes and computational constraints. Exploring larger models could enhance contextual understanding while maintaining runtime performance. Future work in close collaboration with historians could help resolve ambiguous cases that even human experts find difficult to classify. A hybrid approach integrating automated classification with expert validation would maximize both efficiency and accuracy. Additionally, incorporating surrounding textual context instead of analyzing passages in isolation could further enhance classification performance. Our methods also offer potential for extending the ERIS database to annotate and include texts from more recent historical periods. Adapting the models to contemporary datasets would require adjustments for linguistic style, cultural contexts, and evolving definitions of violence, presenting exciting opportunities for interdisciplinary research.

Limitations

Our study shows a promising approach to scaling up the annotation of violent events in ancient texts. While delivering accurate results in our experiments, we acknowledge several limitations rooted in the dataset, the methodology and the experimental coverage.

Dataset and annotation: ERIS is a well-curated dataset and contains the largest amount of manually annotated violent text passages from historical texts. However, this dataset also has its limits: First, for a machine learning approach the number of examples is still comparably small. Second, it only contains historical data from ancient texts as well as some medieval texts. While we assume that our approach would be applicable (possibly after more fine-tuning) to other texts, too, we cannot evaluate it with the given data. Further, ERIS does not contain information on inter-rater agreement, so we do not have a manual comparison stating how complex the task is for humans. We also do not have a detailed account on the amount of time it takes to annotate the violence passages manually. What we do know is that it strongly depends on the annotator, and that manual efforts are, overall, not easy to scale.

Methodology and Experiments: Given the limits of the database, our experiments have further limitations added. First of all, we only operate on translations rather than original texts. This might be a restriction for both text understanding and scaling the methods to texts for which no translations are available. Currently, this mirrors the manual annotation process, because annotators with knowledge of Latin or Ancient Greek are hard to find, so most of ERIS is annotated using the translations.

For violence classification, we only used the texts available in the Perseus database, because we needed to extend the ERIS data with comparable passages that do not contain violent data. Like this, the violence classification does not contain the whole ERIS database, especially not the medieval texts. While we are convinced that our results can still carry over to other epochs and text sorts, our experiments do not prove this as of yet.

Some accuracy in the fine-grained violence categorization is lost in the automated annotation, which is partly due to the ambiguity within the texts, and partly due to the challenging fine-grained taxonomy in ERIS. It is up to future work to decide whether the actual annotation guidelines and the categories need to be adapted or whether the methodology should account for this. To make this distinction, more detailed analysis and data on inter-annotator agreement would be needed (see above).

Weighted averages were chosen to reflect overall model performance effectively, particularly given the significant imbalance between class sizes. However, this method inherently favors dominant classes and can obscure weaker results in less frequent categories. A more balanced approach should be considered, potentially involving class-based weighting or specialized metrics to ensure accurate representation across all classes.

Further, we only used four of the fine-grained ERIS categorizations for annotations. We did not do further categorization and information extraction to simulate a complete annotation of an ERIS entry. While we think that some categories are straight-forward to apply (like the identification of the weapon), others might be impossible for a model to guess, because they are not contained in the violent passages (like geographical data or sometimes the actors). In order to do this comprehensive annotation automatically, we would have to implement a different classification approach that takes the context of the violent text passages into account. We leave this experiment for future work.

Ethics Statement

We provide an experiment that helps to classify violent text passages, primarily in ancient texts. We did not use or produce any sensitive data during those experiments. We do see the potential for our method to be applied for the common good, especially when adapted to contemporary data. Like other studies on hate speech have shown, the automated detection of harmful content can support the automated analysis of the media with the aim of *protecting vulnerable groups*.

While the methodology presented in this work is primarily intended for academic and educational purposes, we recognize the potential *misuse* of AI technologies in misrepresenting historical data when applied without supervision. A misclassification of violent text or a blind reliance on the comprehensiveness of the method can lead to unwanted mistakes in the aforementioned protective purposes. Like most statements here, this applies to basically all automation methods and needs to be mediated accordingly.

Bearing in mind the general societal awareness of jobs being automatized, our work explicitly encourages the *responsible use of AI in humanities research*. Our models are designed to complement human expertise, ensuring that tedious workload is alleviated, which might be especially welcome in the case of violent texts. Like all automation approaches, this aims at scaling in terms of data set size rather than replacing analysis depth. This allows historians to focus on deeper interpretative analyses, fostering a collaborative approach between human expertise and machine learning.

Acknowledgments

The authors wish to thank Werner Rieß and Justine Diemke for providing access to the ERIS database and offering valuable feedback on results and potential research directions. Special thanks to Sri Gowry Sritharan for her assistance in extracting non-violent examples from Perseus. Additionally, the authors extend their gratitude to Sören Laue, Hanna Herasimchyk, Lennart Bengtson, and Mostafa Kotb for their technical and methodological advice and for proofreading and improving the manuscript. We also thank the three anonymous reviewers for their helpful comments. All remaining errors are, of course, our own.

References

Brooke Allen. 2005. Alexander the great: Or the terrible? *The Hudson Review*, 58(2):220–230.

Yannis Assael, Thea Sommerschield, and Jonathan Prag. 2019. Restoring ancient text using deep learning: a case study on Greek epigraphy. In *Proceedings of the 2019 Conference on Empirical Methods in Natural Language Processing and the 9th International Joint Conference on Natural Language Processing (EMNLP-IJCNLP)*, pages 6368–6375, Hong Kong, China. Association for Computational Linguistics.

Yejin Bang, Samuel Cahyawijaya, Nayeon Lee, Wenliang Dai, Dan Su, Bryan Wilie, Holy Lovenia, Ziwei Ji, Tiezheng Yu, Willy Chung, Quyet V. Do, Yan Xu, and Pascale Fung. 2023. A multitask, multilingual, multimodal evaluation of ChatGPT on reasoning, hallucination, and interactivity. In *Proceedings of the 13th International Joint Conference on Natural Language Processing and the 3rd Conference of the Asia-Pacific Chapter of the Association for Computational Linguistics (Volume 1: Long Papers)*, pages 675–718, Nusa Dua, Bali. Association for Computational Linguistics.

George Bizos. 2008. Ethics, politics and law in ancient greece and contemporary south africa. *Phronimon*, 9(2):5–15.

Tom Brown, Benjamin Mann, Nick Ryder, Melanie Subbiah, Jared D Kaplan, Prafulla Dhariwal, Arvind Neelakantan, Pranav Shyam, Girish Sastry, Amanda Askell, Sandhini Agarwal, Ariel Herbert-Voss, Gretchen Krueger, Tom Henighan, Rewon Child, Aditya Ramesh, Daniel Ziegler, Jeffrey Wu, Clemens Winter, Chris Hesse, Mark Chen, Eric Sigler, Mateusz Litwin, Scott Gray, Benjamin Chess, Jack Clark, Christopher Berner, Sam McCandlish, Alec Radford, Ilya Sutskever, and Dario Amodei. 2020. Language models are few-shot learners. In *Advances in Neural Information Processing Systems*, volume 33, pages 1877–1901. Curran Associates, Inc.

Fabio Celli and Dmitry Mingazov. 2024. Knowledge extraction from llms for scalable historical data annotation. *Electronics*, 13(24).

Jiawei Chen, Hongyu Lin, Xianpei Han, and Le Sun. 2024. Benchmarking large language models in retrieval-augmented generation. In *Proceedings of the AAAI Conference on Artificial Intelligence*, volume 38, pages 17754–17762.

David Cohen. 1986. The theodicy of aeschylus: Justice and tyranny in the oresteia. *Greece and Rome*, 33(2):129–141.

Stephen Dando-Collins. 2010. *The Ides: Caesar's Murder and the War for Rome*. Turner Publishing Company.

Jacob Devlin, Ming-Wei Chang, Kenton Lee, and Kristina Toutanova. 2019. BERT: Pre-training of deep bidirectional transformers for language understanding. In *Proceedings of the 2019 Conference of the North American Chapter of the Association for Computational Linguistics: Human Language Technologies, Volume 1 (Long and Short Papers)*, pages 4171–4186, Minneapolis, Minnesota. Association for Computational Linguistics.

Justine Diemke, Felix K Maier, Superhero Comics, Eleonora Sereni, Ulrich Bröckling, Barbara Korte, and Ulrike Zimmermann. helden. heroes. héros.

Barry L. Eichler. 2009. Law and morality in ancient near eastern thought. In *Ethics, Politics, and Democracy: From Primordial Principles to Prospective Practices*. The MIT Press.

Liang et al. 2023. Holistic evaluation of language models. *Trans. Mach. Learn. Res.*, 2023.

Garrett G. Fagan. 2011. *The lure of the arena : social psychology and the crowd at the Roman games*. Cambridge University Press.

Bruce W. Frier. 1985. *The rise of the Roman jurists : studies in Cicero's Pro Caecina*. UT Back-in-Print Service.

Michael Gagarin. 1982. The organization of the gortyn law code. *Greek, Roman, and Byzantine Studies*, 23(2):129–146.

Aparna Garimella, Rada Mihalcea, and Akhash Amarnath. 2022. Demographic-aware language model fine-tuning as a bias mitigation technique. In *Proceedings of the 2nd Conference of the Asia-Pacific Chapter of the Association for Computational Linguistics and the 12th International Joint Conference on Natural Language Processing (Volume 2: Short Papers)*, pages 311–319, Online only. Association for Computational Linguistics.

Or Honovich, Roee Aharoni, Jonathan Herzig, Hagai Taitelbaum, Doron Kukliansy, Vered Cohen, Thomas Scialom, Idan Szpektor, Avinatan Hassidim, and Yossi Matias. 2022. TRUE: Re-evaluating factual consistency evaluation.

Bernard S Jackson. 1968. Evolution and foreign influence in ancient law. *The American Journal of Comparative Law*, 16(3):372–390.

Xisen Jin, Francesco Barbieri, Brendan Kennedy, Aida Mostafazadeh Davani, Leonardo Neves, and Xiang Ren. 2021. On transferability of bias mitigation effects in language model fine-tuning. In *Proceedings of the 2021 Conference of the North American Chapter of the Association for Computational Linguistics: Human Language Technologies*, pages 3770–3783, Online. Association for Computational Linguistics.

Timo Kaufmann, Sarah Ball, Jacob Beck, Eyke Hüllermeier, and Frauke Kreuter. 2023. On the challenges and practices of reinforcement learning from real human feedback. In *Joint European Conference on Machine Learning and Knowledge Discovery in Databases*, pages 276–294. Springer.

David Konstan. 2007. *The emotions of the ancient Greeks: Studies in Aristotle and classical literature*. University of Toronto Press.

Sarah Lang. 2018. Perseus digital library. *RIDE: A Review Journal for Digital Editions and Resources*, 8.

Gerda Lerner. 1986. The creation of patriarchy. *Oxford University Press*.

An Liu, Zonghan Yang, Zhenhe Zhang, Qingyuan Hu, Peng Li, Ming Yan, Ji Zhang, Fei Huang, and Yang Liu. 2024. PANDA: Preference adaptation for enhancing domain-specific abilities of LLMs. In *Findings of the Association for Computational Linguistics: ACL 2024*, pages 10960–10977, Bangkok, Thailand. Association for Computational Linguistics.

Yinhan Liu, Myle Ott, Naman Goyal, Jingfei Du, Mandar Joshi, Danqi Chen, Omer Levy, Mike Lewis, Luke Zettlemoyer, and Veselin Stoyanov. 2019. Roberta: A robustly optimized bert pretraining approach. *ArXiv*, abs/1907.11692.

Binny Mathew, Punyajoy Saha, Seid Muhie Yimam, Chris Biemann, Pawan Goyal, and Animesh Mukherjee. 2021. Hatexplain: A benchmark dataset for explainable hate speech detection. *Proceedings of the AAAI Conference on Artificial Intelligence*, 35(17):14867–14875.

S. Douglas Olson. 1990. The stories of agamemnon in homer's odyssey. *Transactions of the American Philological Association (1974-)*, 120:57–71.

Sarah Pomeroy. 2011. *Goddesses, whores, wives, and slaves: Women in classical antiquity*. Schocken.

Emily Preece and Christine Zepeda. 2009. The perseus digital library: A case study. *Texas ScholarWorks*.

Kurt A Raaflaub et al. 2007. *War and peace in the ancient world*. Wiley Online Library.

Alec Radford and Karthik Narasimhan. 2018. Improving language understanding by generative pre-training.

James M Redfield. 1994. *Nature and Culture in the Iliad: the Tragedy of Hector*. Duke University Press.

Michaela Regneri, Alhassan Abdelhalim, and Soeren Laue. 2024. Detecting conceptual abstraction in LLMs. In *Proceedings of the 2024 Joint International Conference on Computational Linguistics, Language Resources and Evaluation (LREC-COLING 2024)*, pages 4697–4704, Torino, Italia. ELRA and ICCL.

Werner Riess. 2012. *Performing Interpersonal Violence Court, Curse, and Comedy in Fourth-Century BCE Athens*. de Gruyter.

Werner Riess and Michael Zerjadtke. 2015. Eris: Hamburg information system on greek and roman violence. *Digital Classics Online*, pages 70–75.

Alexander Rietzler, Sebastian Stabinger, Paul Opitz, and Stefan Engl. 2020. Adapt or get left behind: Domain adaptation through BERT language model finetuning for aspect-target sentiment classification. In *Proceedings of the Twelfth Language Resources and Evaluation Conference*, pages 4933–4941, Marseille, France. European Language Resources Association.

Zhyar Rzgar K Rostam and Gábor Kertész. 2024. Fine-tuning large language models for scientific text classification: A comparative study. In *2024 IEEE 6th International Symposium on Logistics and Industrial Informatics (LINDI)*, pages 000233–000238. IEEE.

Martha T Roth. 1995. *Law collections from Mesopotamia and Asia minor*. Scholars Press.

David A Smith, Jeffrey A Rydberg-Cox, and Gregory R Crane. 2000. The perseus project: A digital library for the humanities. *Literary and Linguistic Computing*, 15(1):15–25.

Caius Suetonius Tranquillus and Robert Graves. 1962. *The Twelve Caesars... Translated by Robert Graves*. Cassell; printed in Czechoslovakia.

Bruce G Trigger. 2003. *Understanding early civilizations: a comparative study*. Cambridge University Press.

Ashish Vaswani, Noam Shazeer, Niki Parmar, Jakob Uszkoreit, Llion Jones, Aidan N Gomez, Ł ukasz Kaiser, and Illia Polosukhin. 2017. Attention is all you need. In *Advances in Neural Information Processing Systems*, volume 30. Curran Associates, Inc.

Xi Wang, Liana Mikaelyan, Taketomo Isazawa, and James Hensman. 2024. Kblam: Knowledge base augmented language model. *arXiv preprint arXiv:2410.10450*.

R. Westbrook and G.M. Beckman. 2003. *A History of Ancient Near Eastern Law*. Number Bd. 2 in A History of Ancient Near Eastern Law. Brill.

Dorothy Natalie Witham. 2020. The battle of kadesh: Its causes and consequences. *Master Of Arts, University Of South Africa*.

A Code and Data

We provide the training data for both tasks as well as the code, downloadable under

`https://osf.io/ae835/`

Violence detection

The folder `1_violence_detection` contains the training and test data for the violence identification task. The sentences are a subset of ERIS extended with their original contexts extracted from the Perseus database. We provide both the original dataset and the augmented dataset used for training. The annotation contains the source as noted in Perseus (book, chapter, and section), the passage text, and the violence annotation (1 for violent, 0 for non-violent).

Violence categorization

The folder `2_violence_categorization` contains a condensed version of the ERIS database, including the text passage with the four annotation dimensions we used for classification. To reproduce our training and test data, please use the code we provide.

Code

We provide two Jupyter notebooks (`violence_detection.ipynb` and `violence_categorization.ipynb`) to reproduce our data preprocessing, model training, and evaluation for both tasks.

B GPT-4o mini Testing Prompt

You are a historian that classifies historical texts into violent or non-violent based on the provided examples. The following principles apply to the classification of violent acts:

- *Arrests of people and banishments are initially recorded as acts of violence and discussed with the team before being activated.*
- *Fictional narratives, such as the conquest of Troy, are included.*
- *Establishment of colonies, verbal violence (insults), and damage to property (including fires in buildings, etc.) are excluded.*

Your task is to classify each passage based on the criteria above. Respond with only ***[VIOLENT]*** *or* ***[NON-VIOLENT]*** *for each classification.*

C GPT-4o mini Augmentation Prompt

You are a historian that wants to paraphrase sentences to create new ones for enhancing your dataset. Generate three different ways to rewrite the following sentence while keeping the same meaning. Important to note that you are not allowed to change context, motive or consequences.

D Detailed Breakdown for the Violence Categorization results

These are the extended results for Table 2.

	RoBERTa Results				**BERT Results**			
	Precision	**Recall**	**F1-Score**	**Support**	**Precision**	**Recall**	**F1-Score**	**Support**
Interpersonal	0.92	0.91	0.91	96	0.93	0.88	0.90	96
Intrasocial	0.95	0.83	0.89	72	0.95	0.78	0.85	72
Intersocial	0.96	0.98	0.97	371	0.94	0.99	0.96	371
Intrapersonal	0.84	0.94	0.89	17	0.76	0.76	0.76	17
Overall	0.95	0.95	0.95	556	0.93	0.93	0.93	556
Baselines: Majority = 0.67, Random = 0.49								

Table 4: Comparison of Level Results for RoBERTa, BERT, and Baselines

	RoBERTa Results				BERT Results			
	Precision	Recall	F1-Score	Support	Precision	Recall	F1-Score	Support
Civilian	1.00	0.69	0.82	29	0.96	0.79	0.87	29
Jurisdictional	0.86	0.80	0.83	30	1.00	0.77	0.87	30
War/Military Campaign	0.80	0.94	0.87	181	0.83	0.97	0.89	181
Battle	0.93	0.81	0.87	69	0.92	0.88	0.90	69
Plunder	0.69	0.53	0.60	17	0.75	0.53	0.62	17
Ambush	0.85	0.73	0.79	15	1.00	0.67	0.80	15
Conspiracy	0.82	0.82	0.82	11	0.53	0.82	0.64	11
Revolt	1.00	1.00	1.00	21	1.00	1.00	1.00	21
Conquest	0.50	0.57	0.53	7	0.57	0.57	0.57	7
Naval Battle	1.00	1.00	1.00	2	0.29	1.00	0.44	2
Religious	1.00	1.00	1.00	6	0.67	0.33	0.44	6
Institutional	0.60	0.75	0.67	4	1.00	0.75	0.86	4
Sack	0.00	0.00	0.00	1	0.00	0.00	0.00	1
Single Combat	1.00	0.50	0.67	4	1.00	0.50	0.67	4
Siege	0.83	0.81	0.82	31	0.89	0.81	0.85	31
Unknown	1.00	1.00	1.00	5	1.00	0.80	0.89	5
Regicide	0.69	1.00	0.81	11	0.79	1.00	0.88	11
Military	0.90	0.87	0.89	93	0.91	0.90	0.91	93
Entertaining	0.60	0.43	0.50	7	0.60	0.43	0.50	7
Mutiny	1.00	0.75	0.86	8	1.00	0.75	0.86	8
Familicide	1.00	1.00	1.00	2	0.00	0.00	0.00	2
Fratricide	0.00	0.00	0.00	1	0.00	0.00	0.00	1
Paramilitary	1.00	1.00	1.00	1	0.00	0.00	0.00	1
Overall	0.86	0.85	0.84	556	0.86	0.86	0.85	556
	Baselines: Majority = 0.33, Random = 0.16							

Table 5: Comparison of Context Results for RoBERTa, BERT, and Baselines

	RoBERTa Results				BERT Results			
	Precision	Recall	F1-Score	Support	Precision	Recall	F1-Score	Support
Unknown	1.00	0.80	0.89	20	0.81	0.65	0.72	20
Political	0.84	0.86	0.85	122	0.91	0.86	0.89	122
Tactical/Strategical	0.87	0.88	0.87	197	0.92	0.88	0.90	197
Economical	0.74	0.82	0.78	28	0.69	0.86	0.76	28
Following Orders	0.90	0.86	0.88	77	0.81	0.90	0.85	77
Self-Defence	0.75	0.69	0.72	13	0.73	0.62	0.67	13
Emotional	0.97	0.77	0.86	43	0.92	0.84	0.88	43
Ambition	0.71	0.83	0.76	35	0.64	0.83	0.72	35
Social	0.71	1.00	0.83	5	1.00	1.00	1.00	5
Religious	0.83	0.83	0.83	6	0.83	0.83	0.83	6
Other	1.00	1.00	1.00	6	1.00	0.83	0.91	6
None/Accident	0.75	0.75	0.75	4	0.75	0.75	0.75	4
Overall	0.86	0.85	0.85	556	0.86	0.86	0.86	556
	Baselines: Majority = 0.35, Random = 0.20							

Table 6: Comparison of Motive Results for RoBERTa, BERT, and Baselines

	RoBERTa Results				BERT Results			
	Precision	**Recall**	**F1-Score**	**Support**	**Precision**	**Recall**	**F1-Score**	**Support**
Unknown	0.78	0.89	0.83	199	0.83	0.91	0.87	199
Campaign	0.81	0.87	0.85	28	0.82	0.82	0.82	28
Conquest	0.83	0.83	0.83	24	0.58	0.92	0.71	24
Coronation/Inauguration	1.00	0.67	0.80	12	0.90	0.75	0.82	12
Exile	1.00	0.67	0.80	6	0.86	1.00	0.92	6
Death	0.81	0.72	0.72	32	0.77	0.69	0.73	54
Other	0.72	0.72	0.72	32	0.86	0.78	0.82	32
Victory	1.00	1.00	1.00	16	0.88	0.94	0.91	16
Bestowing of Honors	0.67	0.33	0.44	6	1.00	0.17	0.29	6
Issuing of Law/Decrees	1.00	0.33	0.50	3	0.50	0.33	0.40	3
Injury	0.71	1.00	0.83	5	1.00	1.00	1.00	5
Battle	0.80	0.53	0.64	15	0.67	0.67	0.67	15
Declaration of War	1.00	1.00	1.00	2	1.00	1.00	1.00	2
Retreat	0.67	0.80	0.73	10	0.67	0.80	0.73	10
Mutiny	1.00	0.50	0.67	2	1.00	0.50	0.67	2
Sending of Envoys	0.93	1.00	0.96	13	0.92	0.92	0.92	13
Civil Conflict/Civil War	0.00	0.00	0.00	1	0.00	0.00	0.00	1
Tyranny	0.50	1.00	0.67	2	1.00	1.00	1.00	2
Capture	0.71	0.71	0.71	14	0.77	0.71	0.74	14
Destruction/Devastation	0.84	0.81	0.82	26	0.84	0.81	0.82	26
Repopulation	1.00	1.00	1.00	2	1.00	1.00	1.00	2
Declaration of Peace/Truce	1.00	0.44	0.62	9	1.00	0.44	0.62	9
Release of Prisoners	1.00	1.00	1.00	2	0.67	1.00	0.80	2
Garrisoning of Troops	1.00	0.67	0.80	6	1.00	0.67	0.80	6
Famine	1.00	1.00	1.00	1	1.00	1.00	1.00	1
Siege	0.95	0.70	0.81	30	0.95	0.70	0.81	30
Deportation	1.00	0.25	0.40	4	1.00	0.50	0.67	4
Treaty/Agreement/Pact	1.00	0.33	0.50	3	0.00	0.00	0.00	3
Surrender	0.67	1.00	0.80	2	0.67	1.00	0.80	2
Financial Reward	0.75	1.00	0.86	3	0.75	1.00	0.86	3
Seclusion	0.33	1.00	0.50	2	1.00	1.00	1.00	2
Plunder	0.86	1.00	0.92	6	1.00	1.00	1.00	6
Mutilation	1.00	1.00	1.00	1	1.00	1.00	1.00	1
Revenge	1.00	1.00	1.00	6	1.00	1.00	1.00	6
Execution	0.40	0.50	0.44	4	0.33	0.25	0.29	4
Torture	0.75	1.00	0.86	3	0.75	1.00	0.86	3
Applause	1.00	0.50	0.67	2	1.00	0.50	0.67	2
Overall	0.82	0.80	0.80	556	0.82	0.81	0.81	556
Baselines: Majority = 0.36, Random = 0.16								

Table 7: Comparison of Long-Term Consequences Results for RoBERTa, BERT, and Baselines

Rethinking Scene Segmentation. Advancing Automated Detection of Scene Changes in Literary Texts

Svenja Guhr[1,2] **Huijun Mao**[2] **Fengyi Lin**[2]
[1]*fortext lab*, Technical University of Darmstadt, Germany
[2]Literary Lab, Stanford University, USA
{sguhr, huijunm, linfy}@stanford.edu

Abstract

Automated scene segmentation is an ongoing challenge in computational literary studies (CLS) to approach literary texts by analyzing comparable units. In this paper, we present our approach to text segmentation using a classifier that identifies the position of a scene change in English-language fiction. By manually annotating novels from a 20th-century US-English romance fiction corpus, we prepared training data for fine-tuning transformer models, yielding promising preliminary results for improving automated text segmentation in CLS.

1 Introduction

Segmenting literary prose into meaningful units, such as events, plots, or scenes, opens up new possibilities for comparative analysis by focusing on smaller units rather than entire texts. However, automating this process remains a significant challenge in CLS. While many computational approaches depend on pre-segmented texts due to input size limitations, standardized methods for segmentation are still lacking. As a result, heuristic approaches, such as dividing texts into equal-sized units or relying on chapter boundaries, are often used – even though chapter divisions typically reflect editorial choices rather than coherent narrative structures, and especially popular fiction and serialized novels often play with cliff hangers that extend a key action beyond chapter boundaries (Pethe et al., 2020; Bartsch et al., 2023; Stiemer et al., 2025).

Drawing from their established use in dramatic texts and film studies, scenes have emerged as useful units for segmenting literary prose. Defined by consistency in time, place, and characters, scenes "center around a particular action" (Gius et al., 2019). This internal coherence allows them to function as self-contained, meaningful units that can be systematically compared to other scenes within a narrative or a text corpus. For instance, consider a novel in which an initial scene takes place in a supermarket where one of the characters is depicted grocery shopping. This is followed by a new scene set in a kitchen where two characters are cooking and talking. Each scene can be analyzed independently in terms of its temporal and spatial dimensions. By segmenting a text into such discrete units, we enable systematic comparative investigations of character constellations, spatial patterns, and thematic developments. For example, after identifying all the scenes that take place in a supermarket, one could compare the recurring characters in those scenes and analyze their actions in that specific space.

The automation of scene annotation was first approached by Gius et al. (2019), whose definition served as the basis for the Shared Task of Scene Segmentation (STSS) of German prose (Zehe et al., 2021b). This initiative included the development of scene detection guidelines (Gius et al., 2021) and the creation of German-language training datasets with manually annotated scenes to support automated methods. The most effective approach, developed by Kurfalı and Wirén (2021), utilized a BERT-based model with weighted cross-entropy and the IOB2 scheme, focusing on identifying scene boundaries rather than full segments.

Our goal is to make a first attempt at developing a scene recognition classifier for US-English fiction. We build on the winning team's approach in the German shared task, but use more recent language models and an approximation strategy that works by predicting scene changes that occur in six-sentence segments[1]. Since the submission of this paper in January 2025, we have learned of an independent but comparable approach developed by Zehe et al. (2025). Their work, focusing on German texts, extends the earlier scene segmentation project (Zehe et al., 2021b), which was

[1]Code is available at: https://github.com/literarylab/scene_segmentation.

Proceedings of LaTeCH-CLfL 2025, pages 79–86
May 4, 2025 ©2025 Association for Computational Linguistics

Corpus "Men Made in America"	
female authors	47
romance novels	50
words in total	5,5 Mio.
manually annotated texts	10
in words	572,907
scene changes in gold annotation	795

Table 1: Corpus metadata.

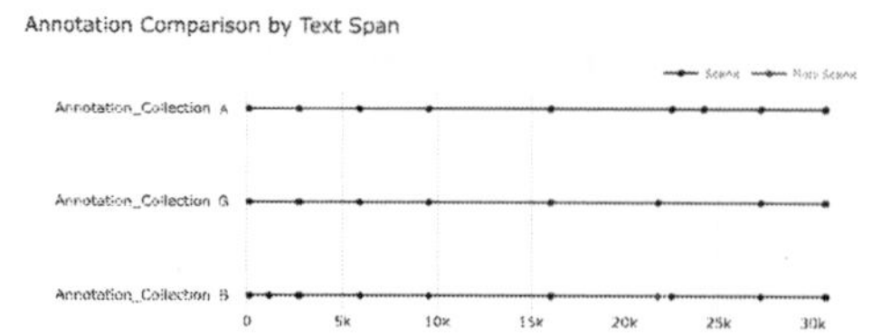

Figure 1: Comparison of two independent annotations (A+B, 0.35γ) with the gold annotation (G) in the middle. Visualization created with GitMA (Vauth et al., 2022) to demonstrate the gold annotation creation process.

paused in 2022 after the completion and evaluation of the shared task at KONVENS 2021. To evaluate their inter-annotator agreement and the performance of their automation, they introduce a new metric, namely a "relaxed F1 score" (Zehe et al., 2025, 5), which allows a tolerance of three sentences for the detected position of a scene change in the manual and automated annotations. The authors argue that fluid scene changes, which cannot be precisely positioned in the text even by human annotators, usually occur within a window of three sentences. Accordingly, the relaxed F1 score gives better scoring results that reflect the performance of the human annotators and the models (Zehe et al., 2025, 5). These findings are consistent with our observation that scene change transitions can span up to three sentences, which led to our decision to use a six-sentence segment approach for the prediction process.

2 Method

2.1 Manual Annotation

Referring to the scene annotation guidelines from Gius et al. (2021), we manually annotated 20% of a corpus of thematically cohesive romance novels from the Harlequin series "Men Made in America" (1982–2002) for scene changes (Table 1 for more information). As already recognized in Zehe et al. (2021a), genre fiction proved easier to annotate than high-brow literature due to its block-style and inherently scenic writing style. The homogeneous corpus consists of 50 novels (each 250 pages – between ca. 40,000 and 75,000 words) written solely by female authors, with each novel telling the romantic story of a couple in one of the 50 United States of America.

As a group of four experts and four trained student annotators from literary studies, we manually annotated ten novels with two annotators per novel[2]. Our inter-annotator agreement[3] (Table 2), ranging from 0.31 to 0.53 Mathet's γ[4], was lower than in Zehe et al. (2021a), who reported an agreement of 0.7 for the annotation of German novels by two trained expert annotators. However, differences in segment length preferences and inclusion or exclusion of chapter headings sparked valuable discussions and resulted in compromise gold annotations. Evaluating annotation quality highlighted the benefits of "collective intelligence" as described by Baledent et al. (2022, 2947), where annotators' errors are mutually offset – such as one favoring shorter segments and the other preferring fewer longer ones. By involving a third annotator to create gold annotations based on the independent annotations by two annotators, the results struck a balanced compromise, mitigating the effects of lower inter-annotator agreement (Figure 1).

This process highlights the interpretive nature of scene segmentation, for a task for which there is no ground truth data, especially when time, place, and character information remain vague. Instead, a negotiated consensus ensures that gold annotations represent a balanced compromise among annotators. Annotators review the entire text, identify scene change positions, highlight the relevant text, and label it as either "scene" or "non-scene." Initial comparisons revealed that scenes are more frequent than non-scenes in novels, with notable variation in the distribution and length of segments depending on the novel (mean segment length: 869.10 words; standard deviation: ±799.47 words; minimum: 69.63; maximum: 1668.57), reflecting dif-

[2]The manual annotation process utilizes the software CATMA 7.1 (Evelyn Gius et al., 2024), which facilitates collaborative annotation and comparison of annotations.

[3]The inter-annotator agreement has been calculated using the Python package GitMA by Vauth et al. (2022).

[4]Mathet's γ is further explained in Mathet et al. (2015) and Zehe et al. (2021a, 3172).

ferences in narrative style. Chapter markers were observed to sometimes signal scene changes, but not as a consistent pattern, as cliffhangers in some novels break this convention. These findings underscore the value of defining scene changes as a semantically meaningful segmentation unit in literary studies, as opposed to relying solely on chapter boundaries. Consistent with Zehe et al. (2021b, 15), scene changes were frequently triggered by temporal shifts (e.g., "two hours later"), spatial transitions, or changes in character configurations. The main consequence of calculating inter-annotator agreement, engaging in discussions, and creating gold annotations was that we decided to include embedded scenes and short non-scenes within larger annotated segments. We also decided to treat temporally parallel actions presented from different perspectives in successive narrative units, but representing the same narrative time and space, as sub-scenes combined into a larger single annotated segment. Drawing on the terminology and analytical framework of film analysis, we refer to these interconnected narrative units as "sequences" (Cutting, 2014, 70–71). In this context, the boundaries of these cohesive narrative units – each of which may consist of multiple smaller segments – were selected and prepared as training data for the automation of their detection in the text.

2.2 Automation Approaches

To automate scene segmentation, we investigated two approaches: (1) using a generative model and (2) fine-tuning a pre-trained custom model.

(1) In our first approach (in November 2024), we provided the novel text (either the entire novel at once or pre-segmented in chapters) along with the scene annotation guidelines from Gius et al. (2021) to several large language models (LLMs), including ChatGPT 4 and 4-o, Claude 3.5 (Sonnet and Haiku), Gemini Pro, and Llama 3.2. However, none of these models produced satisfactory results, as anecdotally noted in the following: For example, ChatGPT 4-o frequently misinterpreted a single conversation scene, dividing it into multiple discrete scenes, likely due to shifts in the speaking character. Additionally, some LLM approaches produced an excessive number of short scene segments, suggesting a tendency to over-annotate rather than accurately detect meaningful boundaries, possibly as a strategy to generate more results without a clear understanding of the underlying structure. Although our findings remain anecdotal due to the lack of a detailed quantitative evaluation, initial experiments showed significant issues with accurate scene boundary detection, leading us to explore alternative approaches. These observations are in line with prior research on LLM performance, which has shown that these models can exhibit signs of misclassifying or overgeneralizing based on their pre-training data (Bamman et al., 2024). Additionally, LLMs struggle with long-context sequences, getting lazy especially in complex real-world scenarios that require them to understand the entire input (Li et al., 2024). Accordingly, we suggest that current LLMs are not yet equipped to effectively process and reason over long, context-rich sequences, which is crucial for tasks like scene segmentation[5]. Given these failures, it became clear that relying on generative models for this task was not yet appropriate.

(2) Consequently, we shifted to fine-tuning a transformer-based pre-trained model for detecting scene change points within a text, which allowed us to derive the desired scene segments. To approximate scene change positions, we pre-processed the manually annotated novels by automatically splitting them into six-sentence passages (after removing typographical elements such as "***" or chapter indications to avoid bias). We chose the passage size based on the aforementioned observation that scene changes often occur gradually over a few sentences, and that annotators' decisions about scene boundaries typically vary by about ±3 sentences, making six sentences a reasonable segment length for the approximation task. Automatically extracted from the manual annotations using regular expressions, the passages are binary labeled as containing a scene change (1) or not (0). We have fine-tuned two transformer-based models to this binary classification task: BERT (Devlin et al. (2019), model version from 2023) and the Universal Sentence Encoder (USE by Cer et al. (2018), model version from 2023 with total parameters: 470,928,387 (1.75 GB) and trainable parameters: 1,538 (6.01 KB)). Although BERT is widely used in most NLP tasks, we found USE to achieve better performance in our specific case. BERT is de-

[5]In a brief trial with DeepSeek in February 2025 (DeepThink R1 (DeepSeek-AI, 2025)), we found that the model detected fewer scene changes than human annotators, but the locations of scene changes in a short test set all overlapped with human annotations. However, we are currently waiting for secure local API access to the LLMs to perform a qualitative experiment on our copyrighted data.

Author (Date)	Title	Cohen's k	Mathet's γ	Scene changes in gold annot.	words
Ferrarella (2000)	*Found: His Perfect Wife* AK	0.49	–	59	65,421
Broadrick (1986)	*Deceptions* CA	0.3	–	69	42,605
Stuart (1984)	*Tangled Lies* HI	0.3	0.31	88	69,124
Palmer (1985)	*Love By Proxy* IL	0.3	–	76	42,063
Campbell (1987)	*Pros and Cons* MA	0.38	–	91	75,527
Webb (2000)	*Warrior's Embrace* MS	0.21	0.34	118	58,903
McKenna (1984)	*Too Near the Fire* OH	0.78	0.41	39	43,319
Leonard (2000)	*Cowboy Be Mine* TX	0.52	0.53	65	62,421
Neggers (1989)	*Finders Keepers* VT	0.51	–	90	52,869
Cassidy (1997)	*Midnight Wishes* WY	0.39	–	100	60,655
10 Romance novels	from "Men Made in America"	ø0.4	ø0.4	795	572,907
20 translated novels	reuse from Zehe et al. (2025)	–	ø0.7	1,250	597,659
30 novels	total training set	–	–	2,045	1,170,566

Table 2: Inter-annotator agreement between two expert human annotators of manual annotations. A visual comparison of the agreement and its relation to the IAA scores can be found in Figure 1 demonstrating an agreement of 0.35γ.

signed to capture the bidirectional context of words within a sentence, making it particularly effective for token-level tasks such as question answering and named entity recognition. In contrast, USE generates fixed-size vector embeddings that represent entire sentences, making it well-suited for semantic similarity and sentence-level tasks. Given that scene detection typically involves analyzing larger segments of text rather than individual words, we hypothesize that USE's sentence-level embeddings provide a more effective representation for this task.When comparing the fine-tuned BERT and USE models in an initial model selection trial, we observed an increase in F1 score of approximately 0.2 for both the balanced training and validation test sets (Table 3), supporting the decision to focus on USE.

For the final training of the model, we combined the ten manually annotated texts from the romance novel corpus (see Table 1) with an automatically generated translation of 20 novels from the training corpus of the shared task described in Zehe et al. (2021b) and Zehe et al. (2025). Furthermore, we upsampled the scene change annotations to provide an equal distribution of the classes and avoid model bias (using random oversampling). Accordingly, for the automation task, the majority baseline dropped from 0.87 to 0.5 in the internal test set.

3 Evaluation and Error Analysis

For the evaluation, we compiled a test set using the final five manually annotated scenes from each of the ten romance novels in the original corpus. These last five scenes were previously excluded from the training set, resulting in a total of 50 scenes. Like the training data, they were segmented into six-sentence segments (0.8 majority baseline). This approach ensured that the test set remained sufficiently similar to the data of interest, namely our US romance novel corpus, while still providing enough variation to assess the model's generalization ability.

The evaluation on the unseen test set reveals that the model is more prone to overlooking a scene change than to mistakenly identifying one where none exists, as there are many more false negatives than false positives. Through an examination of individual examples, we identify several factors that influence the model's predictions: 1) segment length, 2) characters and pronouns, 3) ambiguity in manual annotations. First, we find that the model is more likely to make errors when processing longer inputs. Specifically, by calculating the average segment length, we observed that the biggest difference was between correct cases and false positives, indicating that the model is more likely to detect a scene change in longer segments. Second, we identify character names as a key factor influencing the model's predictions, particularly in cases where errors occur. We recognize that false positive and false negative cases are governed by different aspects of character mentions. In false positive cases, the model misinterprets a continuous scene as a scene change due to the introduction of new characters, which incorrectly signals a break. Conversely, in false negative cases, actual scene breaks are mistaken for continuity because the model recognizes recurring names or pronouns across scenes, leading to incorrect predictions. Finally, we also identify a third group of errors where the reasoning

Model Performance	(first trial) BERT	USE	(final training) USE	test set
Accuracy				0.83
Training	0.92	0.94	0.81	
Validation	0.92	0.95	0.81	
F1				0.5
Training	0.48	0.69	0.66	
Validation	0.48	0.71	0.65	
Precision				0.59
Training	0.47	0.74	0.72	
Validation	0.46	0.76	0.72	
Recall				0.44
Training	0.50	0.65	0.62	
Validation	0.50	0.67	0.61	
Loss				–
Training	0.31	0.16	0.43	
Validation	0.31	0.17	0.42	

Table 3: First trial: Performance comparison of two Transformer models (best epoch) indicating the validation results during the initial training process leading to the decision to use USE as the main model: BERT en_uncased and Universal Sentence Encoder (USE) fine-tuned on four manually annotated training texts (before upsampling). Final training: Performance of the best epoch of the USE model fine-tuned on 20 manually annotated training texts (after upsampling). The last column contains the evaluation results on the independent test set.

behind the human annotator's decision to mark a scene change is unclear, making it difficult to determine the correct interpretation. This is of particular interest given the low agreement among human annotators in manual scene change annotation, suggesting the absence of ground truth for this task for US-English texts.

4 Conclusion and Outlook

In conclusion, the evaluation results and the error analysis[6] are promising, but the current approach only approximates scene change positions within six-sentence segments. To enhance precision, we started developing a sentence-wise prediction model that identifies the first sentence of a six-sentence segment previously predicted with a high probability of bearing a scene-change. However, the task is still far from being solved and with our contribution we want to reopen the discussion on scene segmentation, and add a new perspective to the discourse on meaningful literary text segmentation for CLS.

[6] A detailed analysis of the errors can be found in the Appendix A.

Limitations

The study has several limitations that warrant further investigation: Regarding generalizability, while the segmentation approach may be applicable to other popular fiction genres similar to those found in our annotated corpus, we do not expect it to perform well on more complex, highbrow literary texts. The structural and stylistic differences between such texts and the corpus used in this study pose a challenge for direct transferability (see also Zehe et al. (2021b)).

Another limitation is that our study focuses only on segment boundary detection, without distinguishing between scenes and non-scenes. While this classification is part of the full task as defined by Zehe et al. (2021b), our approach does not account for their distinction, nor for the detection of nested scene structures, where scenes exist within other scenes. Addressing this aspect would require a more hierarchical segmentation approach, which remains an open direction for future research.

Additionally, due to differences in language and test sets, our results are not directly comparable to those reported by Zehe et al. (2021b). This discrepancy should be considered when interpreting our findings in relation to prior work.

Ethics Statement

Our experiments are conducted on an extended version of an existing dataset consisting exclusively of fictional texts, including romance novels, which are subject to copyright restrictions. The scene segmentation task is independent of the specific content of these texts and focuses solely on structural analysis. We do not identify any ethical concerns related to this task or its potential applications. The models presented in this study are intended purely for the analysis of fictional narratives.

Acknowledgments

Many thanks to our student annotators / further project members Mallen Clifton, Agnes Hilger, Jessica Monaco, Alexander J. Sherman, and Ellen Yang who supported the project with their close reading, manual scene annotations, and discoveries of unconventional scene structures. Furthermore, we are very grateful for the extended training data provided by the automatic translations of the manually scene-annotated training texts from the German scene segmentation project, which opens up new possibilities for the task beyond language barriers. Finally, we thank the anonymous reviewers for their thoughtful comments.

References

Anaëlle Baledent, Yann Mathet, Antoine Widlöcher, Christophe Couronne, and Jean-Luc Manguin. 2022. Validity, Agreement, Consensuality and Annotated Data Quality. In *Proceedings of the Thirteenth Language Resources and Evaluation Conference*, pages 2940–2948, Marseille, France. European Language Resources Association. Read_Status: New Read_Status_Date: 2024-12-09T19:52:13.016Z.

David Bamman, Kent K. Chang, Lucy Li, and Naitian Zhou. 2024. On Classification with Large Language Models in Cultural Analytics. In *Proceedings of the Computational Humanities Research Conference 2024*, volume 3834 of *CEUR Workshop Proceedings*, pages 494–527, Aarhus, Denmark. CEUR.

Sabine Bartsch, Evelyn Gius, Marcus Müller, Andrea Rapp, and Thomas Weitin. 2023. Sinn und Segment. Wie die digitale Analysepraxis unsere Begriffe schärft. *Zeitschrift für digitale Geisteswissenschaften*.

Daniel Cer, Yinfei Yang, Sheng-yi Kong, Nan Hua, Nicole Limtiaco, Rhomni St. John, Noah Constant, Mario Guajardo-Cespedes, Steve Yuan, Chris Tar, Yun-Hsuan Sung, Brian Strope, and Ray Kurzweil. 2018. Universal Sentence Encoder.

James E. Cutting. 2014. Event segmentation and seven types of narrative discontinuity in popular movies. *Acta Psychologica*, 149:69–77. TLDR: Using a sample of 24 movies, results suggest that there are at least four different signatures of narrative shifts to be found in popular movies - general patterns across time, patterns of historical change, genre- specific patterns, and film-specific patterns.

DeepSeek-AI. 2025. Deepseek-r1: Incentivizing reasoning capability in llms via reinforcement learning.

Jacob Devlin, Ming-Wei Chang, Kenton Lee, and Kristina Toutanova. 2019. BERT: Pre-training of Deep Bidirectional Transformers for Language Understanding. In *Proceedings of the 2019 Conference of the North*, pages 4171–4186, Minneapolis, Minnesota. Association for Computational Linguistics.

Evelyn Gius, Jan Christoph Meister, Malte Meister, Marco Petris, Dominik Gerstorfer, and Mari Akazawa. 2024. CATMA.

Evelyn Gius, Fotis Jannidis, Markus Krug, Albin Zehe, Andreas Hotho, Frank Puppe, Jonathan Krebs, Nils Reiter, Natalie Wiedmer, and Leonard Konle. 2019. Detection of Scenes in Fiction. In *Book of Abstracts*, Utrecht.

Evelyn Gius, Carla Sökefeld, Lea Dümpelmann, Lucas Kaufmann, Annekea Schreiber, Svenja Guhr, Nathalie Wiedmer, and Fotis Jannidis. 2021. Guidelines for Detection of Scenes.

Murathan Kurfalı and Mats Wirén. 2021. Breaking the Narrative: Scene Segmentation through Sequential Sentence Classification. In *Proceedings of the Shared Task on Scene Segmentation*, pages 49–53.

Tianle Li, Ge Zhang, Quy Duc Do, Xiang Yue, and Wenhu Chen. 2024. Long-context LLMs Struggle with Long In-context Learning.

Yann Mathet, Antoine Widlöcher, and Jean-Philippe Métivier. 2015. The Unified and Holistic Method Gamma () for Inter-Annotator Agreement Measure and Alignment. *Computational Linguistics*, 41(3):437–479.

Charuta Pethe, Allen Kim, and Steve Skiena. 2020. Chapter Captor: Text Segmentation in Novels. In *Proceedings of the 2020 Conference on Empirical Methods in Natural Language Processing (EMNLP)*, pages 8373–8383, Online. Association for Computational Linguistics.

Haimo Stiemer, Hans Ole Hatzel, Chris Biemann, and Evelyn Gius. 2025. Pause im Text. Zur Exploration semantisch konditionierter Sprechpausen in Hörbüchern. In *DHd2025*, pages 275–278, Bielefeld. Zenodo.

Michael Vauth, Malte Meister, Hans Ole Hatzel, Dominik Gerstorfer, and Evelyn Gius. 2022. GitMA.

Albin Zehe, Elisabeth Fischer, and Andreas Hotho. 2025. Assessing the state of the art in scene segmentation. *Proceedings of the NAACL 2025*.

Albin Zehe, Leonard Konle, Lea Katharina Dümpelmann, Evelyn Gius, Andreas Hotho, Fotis Jannidis, Lucas Kaufmann, Markus Krug, Frank Puppe, Nils Reiter, Annekea Schreiber, and Nathalie Wiedmer. 2021a. Detecting Scenes in Fiction: A new Segmentation Task. In *Proceedings of the 16th Conference of the European Chapter of the Association for Computational Linguistics: Main Volume*, pages 3167–3177, Online. Association for Computational Linguistics.

Albin Zehe, Leonard Konle, Svenja Guhr, Lea Katharina Dümpelmann, Evelyn Gius, Andreas Hotho, Fotis Jannidis, Lucas Kaufmann, Markus Krug, Frank Puppe, Nils Reiter, and Annekea Schreiber, editors. 2021b. *Proceedings of the Shared Task on Scene Segmentation*, volume 3001 of *CEUR Workshop Proceedings*. CEUR, KONVENS 2021, Düsseldorf.

A Appendix: Detailed Error Analysis

In this section, we conduct an in-depth analysis of the prediction errors from the six-sentence USE model (see the confusion matrix in Figure 2).

We begin with an overview of the test data. Among the 493 test cases, the model made 403 correct predictions and 90 incorrect ones. Of these 90

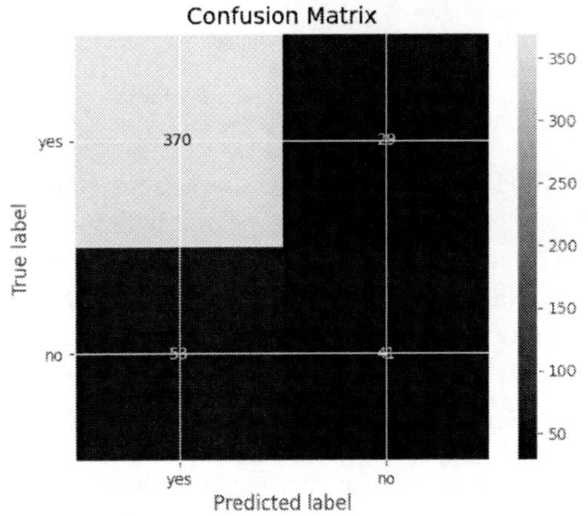

Figure 2: Confusion matrix indicating the predictions on the test set: [[370 29] [53 41]].

errors, 74 were false negatives, and 16 were false positives. This suggests that the model is more prone to overlooking a scene change than mistakenly identifying one when none exists. Through an examination of individual examples, we identify several factors that influence the model predictions: 1) segment length, 2) density of characters, 3) pronoun usage. We will analyze each factor and explore how they manifest in both false positive and false negative cases.

A.1 Length

We compute the average scene segment length for correctly predicted cases, incorrectly predicted cases[7], false positives, and false negatives, as shown in Table 4. Our analysis reveals that incorrect cases tend to have a higher average length than correct ones, suggesting that the model is more prone to errors when processing longer inputs. Additionally, the biggest difference in average length is observed between correct cases and false positives, as shown in Figure 3. With a gap of approximately 150 words, this suggests that the model is more likely to detect a scene change in longer segments.

A.2 Characters

We identify character names as a key factor influencing the model's predictions, particularly in cases where errors occur. To investigate this, we calculate the number of character mentions in each scene segment and compare averages across correct, incorrect, false positive, and false negative cases, as shown in Table 5. Our findings show that, on average, incorrect cases contain slightly more character mentions than correct ones. Notably, the largest difference is observed between correct cases and false positives. As shown in Figure 4, correct cases typically include an average of 1.5 character names, while false positives feature more than 2.5. This suggests that scenes with multiple characters pose a challenge for the model's predictions.

Manually looking into each prediction, we recognize that false positive and false negative cases are governed by different aspects of character mentions. In false positive cases, the model misinter-

[7]Correctly predicted cases: true positives and true negatives. Incorrectly predicted cases: false positives and false negatives.

Category	Average segment length	Annot. differing from gold label
correct	337	0
incorrect	425	87
false Negative	411	74
false Positive	488	150

Table 4: Segment length comparison across different categories. The second column calculates the average segment length for each category, while the third column shows the difference in average length between each category and the correct category.

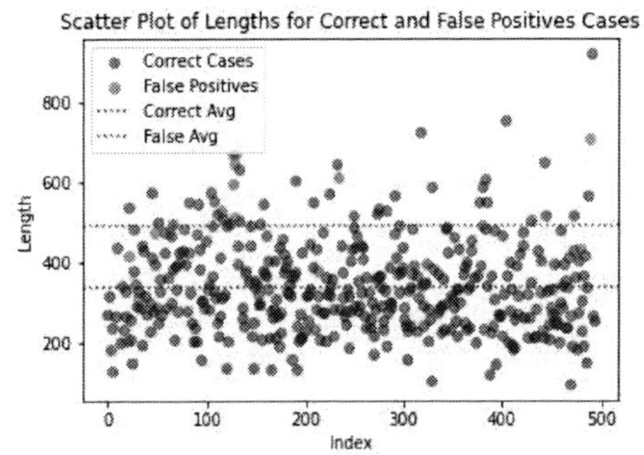

Figure 3: Scatter plot of lengths for correct and false positive cases.

Category	Average character count	Annot. differing from gold label
correct	1.67	0
incorrect	2.29	0.62
false negative	2.20	0.53
false positive	2.69	1.02

Table 5: Average character count comparison across different categories. The second column calculates the average character counts for each category, while the third column shows the difference in average character counts between each category and the correct category.

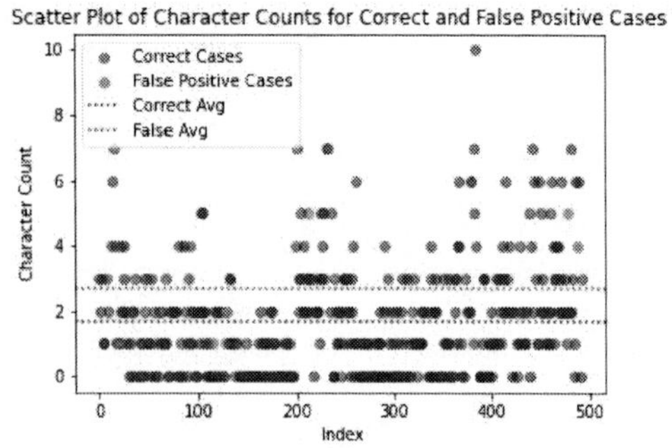

Figure 4: Scatter plot of character counts for correct and false positive cases.

prets a continuous scene as a scene change due to the introduction of a new character, which incorrectly signals a break. Conversely, in false negative cases, actual scene breaks are mistaken for continuity because the model recognizes recurring names or pronouns across scenes, leading to incorrect predictions.

Specifically, the following passage shows an example of when the model predicts a scene change when there is no scene change:

> From the exterior there was no sign of the fire, although there was still work to be done on the inside. The charges against **Abby** had been dropped, and all the loose ends of **Greg's** death and Rusty's betrayal had been tied up. Both **Rusty** and **Richard** had continued to maintain that they'd had nothing to do with the tack under Blackheart's saddle blanket or the hay bale that had nearly killed **Abby**. **Abby** had chalked the incidents up to the hazards and accidents of ranch life. As the wagon drew closer to the dragon tree, all thoughts left **Abby's** head. Beneath the tree, next to the preacher, stood **Luke** and **Cody**.
> (from *Midnight Wishes* by Cassidy)

As for the false negative cases, we recognize that the character patterns can be categorized into two subtypes: 1) same character names; 2) ambiguity of pronouns.

The following passage is an example of the first subcategory where the same character name appears both before and after the scene change. In this instance, the model incorrectly predicts continuity when a scene change actually occurs. We hypothesize that this character continuity misleads the model, resulting in incorrect predictions.

> I think he could have been a real cowboy if he'd tried harder, don't you?" Cody asked. Abby squeezed her son's shoulders sympathetically, unable to speak around the lump of emotion in her throat. Dawn brought a nightmare sight. In the early glow of morning light the full extent of the damage to the house was evident. Abby sat on the bench next to the barn, staring at the gaping black hole that marred the exterior of her home.
> (from *Midnight Wishes* by Cassidy)

The second subcategory arises in situations where similar pronouns appear in both scenes. In such cases, the model may associate the pronouns with the same individuals, leading it to predict continuity when there is actually a scene change. The following passage is an example where a scene change occurs, but the model predicts otherwise. The pronouns indicate the presence of both a male and a female in the first scene, as well as in the second. Despite the time marker "after six" at the beginning of the second scene, we observe that in many cases involving pronoun ambiguity, the model seems to prioritize character continuity over time markers when making its predictions.

> Her head was full of ideals about the world as it should be, and his was full of knowledge about the way it really was. A computer couldn't have picked a man more different from her. HE UNLOCKED THE DOOR and came in shortly after six in the evening. He looked at her apprehensively. She was sitting in the white armchair, watching the rain. She looked paler than usual, and he had a sudden desire to go to her, draw her to her feet and take her in his arms. Except, he thought, that was probably just what she didn't want.
> (from *Pros and Cons* by Campbell)

A.3 Human Annotator

We identify a third group of ambiguous errors, where the reasoning behind the human annotator's decision to mark a scene change is unclear. The following paragraph serves as an example, where the human annotator indicates a scene change, but we cannot identify one, and the model predicts no scene change. It's possible that the scene change occurs at the beginning or end of the segment, but without additional context, it remains uncertain. As a result, we have created a separate error group for these cases, where the ambiguity arises from the lack of clear justification for the scene change, making it difficult to determine the correct interpretation.

> All the time. Nobody to tell her what to do. Not that Carl ever had. Still, she would be all by herself in that big house, keeping her own schedule, marching to her own drummer. Something twisted inside her. The plain fact was this: There was only one tune she wanted to march to, and that was the tune of love.
> (from *Warrior's Embrace* by Webb)

Sentence-Alignment in Semi-parallel Datasets

Steffen Frenzel and Manfred Stede
Applied Computational Linguistics
University of Potsdam
steffen.frenzel|manfred.stede@uni-potsdam.de

Abstract

In this paper, we are testing sentence alignment on complex, semi-parallel corpora, i.e., different versions of the same text that have been altered to some extent. We evaluate two hypotheses: To make alignment algorithms more efficient, we test the hypothesis that matching pairs can be found in the immediate vicinity of the source sentence and that it is sufficient to search for paraphrases in a 'context window'. To improve the alignment quality on complex, semi-parallel texts, we test the implementation of a segmentation into Elementary Discourse Units (EDUs) in order to make more precise alignments at this level. Since EDUs are the smallest possible unit for communicating a full proposition, we assume that aligning at this level can improve the overall quality. Both hypotheses are tested and validated with several embedding models on varying degrees of parallel German datasets. The advantages and disadvantages of the different approaches are presented, and our next steps are outlined.

1 Introduction

The task of sentence alignment originated in the context of machine translation, as the preparatory step for word or phrase alignment, which eventually informed bilingual translation models. In this paper, we address the somewhat different scenario of monolingual semi-parallel text, i.e., different versions of the same text. A well-known case is that of simplified language, where a text in standard language has been mapped to a text that is easier to process for audiences with limited knowledge of the language or people with cognitive or intellectual disabilities. In addition to this, we study two other settings that to our knowledge have not received attention yet. The first are sets of different biographic encyclopedia articles on the same person (authors from the former German Democratic Republic). The second is a specific use case from the Social Sciences, viz. the writings of the philosopher Hannah Arendt, who frequently published second (edited) versions of her works. All our data is in German, but our methods are in principle language-neutral and can be adapted to other target languages, and also to multilingual alignment tasks.

These datasets are well-suited for our experiments for several reasons: First, they represent different levels of difficulty in terms of segmentation and alignment. While the plain-language data contains relatively short and concise sentences and the data is relatively parallel, Hannah Arendt's essays offer significantly greater challenges; they are more heavily altered and the syntactic complexity is greater. The encyclopedia entries represent a special case, as some of the texts are written in terse style, often avoiding full clauses. However, in terms of content they are less parallel than the plain-language texts and, therefore, form an interesting complement.

In this paper we test two hypotheses:

- Matching pairs of text units should be found in similar positions in the two text versions, and it should therefore be sufficient to search for paraphrases in a predefined 'context window'. This approach should make the alignment models more efficient and could even improve alignment quality.
- Complex, heavily-altered sentences can be difficult to align, because only parts of the sentences are matching. Therefore, alignment quality should be improved by aligning on the (often sub-sentential) level of Elementary Discourse Units instead of sentence level. We expect this effect to be greater on complex data like the Arendt essays than on simple data like the plain-language texts.

The paper is structured as follows: In Section 2, we first describe related work for the most impor-

Proceedings of LaTeCH-CLfL 2025, pages 87–96
May 4, 2025

tant concepts of this paper - the notion of semi-parallel texts, EDU segmentation and sentence alignment. In Section 3, we present our datasets in detail. We provide content descriptions in Section 3.1 and corpus statistics in Section 3.2. In Section 3.3 we describe the process and the results of our manual annotation study. In Section 4, we explain methods and results of our experiments - separately for the topics of segmentation, embedding and alignment. Section 5 provides a qualitative error analysis, and Section 6 summarizes our conclusions and describes next steps.

2 Background & Related Work

2.1 Semi-parallel texts

The term 'parallel corpora' originates from research on statistical machine translation (SMT), where parallel texts were generally understood as direct translations into another language (Wołk and Marasek, 2017). However, parallel and non-parallel texts are difficult to clearly distinguish from each other; instead, it is often seen as a scale of 'comparable' corpora (Cheung and Fung, 2004). Such comparable texts have long been the subject of research, with most work focusing on the extraction of parallel sentences from these corpora (e.g., Tillmann (2009); Rauf and Schwenk (2011); Smith et al. (2010); Chu et al. (2013)). These papers use the term *quasi-comparable* texts for loosely related texts that can be written on the same topic or on different topics (Cheung and Fung, 2004).

In addition, research on paraphrase detection and paraphrase generation is also relevant for our work on semi-parallel text versions. Paraphrases map possibilities to change sentences on a lexical, morphological or syntactic level without affecting the meaning (Wahle et al., 2023). Many works have already been published on both paraphrase detection (e.g., Gold et al. (2019); Liu and Soh (2022)) and paraphrase generation (e.g., Bandel et al. (2022); Yang et al. (2022)). Paraphrases are also analyzed as a phenomenon of intertextuality in the context of digital humanities (e.g., Sier and Wöckener-Gade (2019)).

Our definition of semi-parallel texts is based on this research, but for the purposes of this paper we refer only to monolingual text variants. These are texts that are more or less closely related to each other and deal with the same topics. They may be texts that have been reformulated by the author for different audiences, written by different authors on the same topic, or simplified in order to be accessible to more people. In any case, due to their high similarity of content it should be possible to compute a meaningful alignment.

2.2 EDU Segmentation

The notion of 'Elementary Discourse Unit' (EDU) originated in the field of discourse parsing, especially in the tradition of Rhetorical Structure Theory (RST) (Mann and Thompson, 1988), where a text is first divided into EDUs, which are then recursively connected to each other via coherence relations (Cause, Contrast, Elaboration, etc.). Intuitively, an EDU is an independent clause or an adjunct clause that makes a complete contribution to the discourse; specific annotation guidelines then typically describe language-specific syntactic criteria. To illustrate, the sentence in Example 1 consists of two EDUs, while the matrix and complement clauses in Example 2 do not constitute two independent contributions:

(1) [This novel reads well,] [though it is a bit too long.]

(2) [In the bookshop I was told that this novel is a bit too long.]

RST parsers thus contain a segmentation component, but the notion of EDU is relevant also for other tasks. An early stand-alone segmenter for English, built on top of a syntactic parser, was SLSeg (Tofiloski et al., 2009). A more recent approach using a BiLSTM-CRF approach is NeuralEDUSeg (Wang et al., 2018). For German, a syntax-oriented approach was implemented by Sidarenka et al. (2015), who utilized a constituent and a dependency parser for two variants of a segmentation module. Recently, a few multilingual models have been built as part of a shared task (Braud et al., 2023).

The training data situation for German has very recently improved with the introduction of a new RST-annotated corpus (Shahmohammadi and Stede, 2024). For our work, we thus use their RST parser and extract from its output the sequence of EDUs computed for an input text.

2.3 Sentence Alignment and Evaluation

Sentence alignment is the task of matching sentences of two text versions that have the greatest semantic similarity. Early sentence aligners initially used scoring functions that only compared the number of words or characters, because they assumed strong parallelism (Brown et al., 1991; Gale and Church, 1993). In later work (e.g. Moore (2002)) also lexical features and heuristics were used to improve speed and alignment quality. For example, LERA (Pöckelmann et al., 2022) models the alignment problem in a graph theoretic way and makes the alignment decision with a distance function based on the Jaccard index (Jaccard, 1901).

Sentence alignment algorithms are usually applied to bilingual, parallel texts. The use of machine translation (MT) methods to convert both texts into a common language was therefore widespread. For example, Sennrich and Volk (2010) use the BLEU score to carry out alignments in machine-translated texts.

Since the introduction of BERT by Devlin et al. (2019), the use of sentence embeddings has become increasingly established in this field of research. Reimers and Gurevych (2019) improved the computation of sentence embeddings with their Sentence-BERT (SBERT) model, reducing the enormous computational effort of the classical BERT model.

Embedding vectors can then be compared using classical similarity calculations such as the cosine similarity or the Euclidean distance. One of the first papers to implement this approach to sentence alignment was VecAlign (Thompson and Koehn, 2019). Both VecAlign and SentAlign (Steingrimsson et al., 2023) are based on bilingual sentence representations such as LASER (Artetxe and Schwenk, 2019) and LaBSE (Feng et al., 2022).

Recently, Molfese et al. (2024) introduced CroCoAlign - an algorithm that, in contrast to the models mentioned so far, incorporates more contextual information for disambiguating possible sentence mappings.

3 Data and Manual Annotation of Alignment

In this section, we first describe the three sources of data that we are using and how we constructed the corpora; this includes segmenting texts into EDUs. Then we report on our inter-annotator agreement study on the alignment task.

3.1 The Datasets

Hannah Arendt essays: In our experiment, we aligned two different versions of the essay on Franz Kafka: firstly, the original version 'Franz Kafka', which appeared in 1948 in the publication 'Sechs Essays' (*Six Essays*), and secondly, a radio broadcast entitled 'Franz Kafka - von Neuem gewürdigt' (*Franz Kafka – newly appreciated*), which was also published in 1948. The essays are part of the Hannah Arendt Edition, a digital, open-access edition that is hosted by Freie Universität Berlin.[1]

GDR literature encyclopedias: This dataset consists of encyclopedia entries on authors from the GDR. Two entries on the same person were manually selected from a larger dataset, but from different encyclopedias. For selecting the articles, particular attention was paid to finding entries that were as detailed as possible and ideally written in complete sentences, even though this was not possible for all entries. In all cases, one Wikipedia article was used as the reference text, with the second entry coming from different encyclopedias.

Plain language dataset: The third dataset consists of news reports, each of which is available in an original and a simplified version. The dataset was originally created to train models for text simplification tasks. Although the texts are closely related, it is possible that information has been lost during the simplification process or that the grammatical structure has been changed. This data is part of the APA-RST dataset (Hewett, 2023).

3.2 Corpus Statistics

As the three datasets come from different genres, they are structured differently and each present their own challenges. In two of the three cases, the data is available both in full sentences and in EDUs; however, many of the GDR encyclopedias were not initially written in sentence form and therefore EDU segmentation was not possible in this case. Detailed corpus statistics are listed in Table 1.

Hannah Arendt essays: This dataset includes two variants of the essay 'Franz Kafka'. The original version is slightly longer (36 sentences) than the radio broadcast and also features longer sentences - this is likely due to the change in target audience. In comparison to the other datasets at hand, the essays from Hannah Arendt provide the longest and most complex sentences with an average of around 30 words per sentence.

GDR literature encyclopedias: This dataset consists of encyclopedia articles about 61 authors

[1] https://hannah-arendt-edition.net/home?lang=en

from the GDR. The alignment is performed between the Wikipedia article and one other encyclopedia entry about this person, so the dataset consists of 122 documents in total. Since some of the encyclopedia entries were written with heavily-abbreviated sentences, this dataset is well-suited to test the performance of the alignment models at sub-sentence level, but it cannot be used to compare it for EDUs and whole sentences.

Plain language dataset: This dataset consists of 449 different news reports, each of which is available in the original and simplified version. In addition, we segmented both versions of the 449 reports into EDUs. In contrast to the essays by Hannah Arendt, the sentences are shorter and less complex; in many cases they cannot be segmented into more than one EDU.

3.3 Manual Annotation

Samples of all three datasets were selected for manual annotation of sentence alignment. Since context is an important factor for alignment decisions, documents were randomly selected for manual annotation rather than sentences.

Two annotators worked on the study. Both are students of Computational Linguistics and therefore trained in the linguistic characteristics of texts and their computational processing. The annotators were given guidelines for manual annotation. These guidelines specified that the basis for alignment must always be semantic similarity rather than surface form. It was specified that multiple alignments of the same element should only be made in justified exceptions and that, in contrast, there is no obligation to align all elements. Following these guidelines, the following alignment patters are allowed: `[1:0, 0:1, 1:n, n:1]`. However, `[n:m]` alignments are not possible.

To create a gold standard, the main annotator labeled encyclopedia entries on 11 different authors, 11 different newspaper reports from the plain language dataset, and the essays on Franz Kafka. To measure the inter-annotator agreement (IAA), the second annotator also processed almost half of this data. IAA for all datasets and additional statistics of the manual annotation can be found in Table 1.

Datasets:	Arendt	GDR-Data	Plain-language
Corpus Statistics			
Documents	2	122	898
Sentences	402	-	43,255
Segments	1,036	1,745	48,282
Words	12,323	17,571	440,000
Avg. Segments / Sentence	2.575	-	1.12
Avg. Words / Sentence	30.45	-	10.2
Avg. Words / Segment	11.825	10.06	9.1
Results of Manual Annotation			
Total: Aligned Sentences	402 (201)	-	568 (207)
Total: Aligned Segments	1,036 (512)	194 (88)	648 (237)
Cohen's Kappa: Sentences	0.772	-	0.917
Cohen's Kappa: Segments	0.843	0.785	0.909
Non-aligned Sentences	24.6% (28.97%)	-	25.6% (22.7%)
Non-aligned Segments	40.1% (47.8%)	52% (47%)	24.9% (24.9%)

Table 1: Statistics for all three corpora and results of the manual annotation.

4 Experiments and Results

4.1 Methods

Next, we describe our methods separately for segmentation, embedding and alignment.

4.1.1 Segmentation

Our alignment procedure should make it possible to carry out alignments both at sentence level and at EDU level. The first step in our pipeline is therefore the EDU segmentation of sentences. This step requires language-specific models, which are rare, especially for German. For the work described here, we used a modified version of the DPLP parser (Ji and Eisenstein, 2014), which was trained by Shahmohammadi and Stede (2024) on a corpus covering three different genres (blog posts, news, commentary). The parser produces complete RST trees from which the EDUs are then extracted.

4.1.2 Embedding

In order to process large texts efficiently, we use sentence embeddings for the numerical representation of language data. As we work exclusively with German data, we require embedding models that can process German texts. Several monolingual and multilingual models are suitable for this purpose. Furthermore, there are major differences in our data in terms of sentence length and grammatical complexity. We need embeddings that can process long, convoluted sentences from Hannah Arendt's essays as well as short EDUs and keyword-like entries from the lexicon articles.

Since, to our knowledge, there are no models that have been explicitly trained on EDUs, we tried out various embedding models on our test data and selected the following two models for the final experiments:

- `T-Systems-onsite/cross-en-de-roberta -sentence-transformer`: This is an `xlm-roberta-base` model (Conneau et al., 2019) that was fine-tuned by Philip May on the STSbenchmark dataset for processing English and German texts.

- `paraphrase-multilingual-mpnet-base-v2` This is a multilingual sentence-BERT model for STS tasks, trained on parallel data for more than 50 languages (Reimers and Gurevych, 2019).

We tested both embedding models in all runs, but since the RoBERTa model led consistently to better results, we decided to omit the second model for this task.

4.1.3 Alignment

We are also testing two different approaches for the automatic alignment of embeddings; one considers all possible unit pairs, the other reduces the candidate set. We cannot use existing alignment algorithms such as VecAlign (Thompson and Koehn, 2019) or SentAlign (Steingrimsson et al., 2023), since these approaches are designed to align parallel texts and cannot produce mappings that violate the parallel sentence ordering (for illustration, see the crossing lines in Figures 1 and 2).

The first approach uses the `paraphrase mining` function from the `Sentence Transformers` module (Reimers and Gurevych, 2019). It takes a list of strings as input and calculates sentence embeddings from them. The embedding model required for this can be defined manually. The function then uses cosine similarity to calculate the semantic similarity of all possible pairs of elements of the input. Finally, it outputs one or more possible matches for each element, sorted in descending order of cosine similarity. The function also offers the option to use other measurement units instead of cosine similarity to determine the similarity.

We generate several possible matches for each element and use a customized function to calculate the final alignments from there. This function is designed in a way that we have several adjustment options for fine-tuning. For example, we can specify that two elements should only be aligned if a certain cosine similarity is exceeded. We can also use a binary parameter to determine whether the same element may be aligned multiple times or not.

Our second approach is based on the assumption that the best matches of a sentence are to be found in an adjacent part of the second text version, i.e. that the index positions of the matched sentences are close. We have therefore developed a customized function that iterates over the first text version and searches for possible alignments in a neighboring section of the second text. The advantage of this approach is the reduced requirements in terms of computing power and time, as only the similarity to a few possible matches has to be calculated for each sentence.

The function is designed in a way that a threshold for alignments can be defined here as well. It can also be determined whether multiple alignments should be permitted and the size of the context window can be varied. Finally, the model for calculating the embeddings and the distance measure for determining the semantic similarity can also be specified using optional parameters. These setting options are intended to ensure that the algorithm can be flexibly adapted to the requirements of the different datasets at hand.

In Table 2, we list the fine-tuning settings of both approaches in the 'settings'-column.

4.2 Results

4.2.1 Alignment Algorithms

Comparing the results of the two alignment functions shown in Table 2, the context window generally performs better. For all datasets except the EDU-segmented plain language data, the context window leads to better alignments - on average approx. 0.4 higher Cohen's Kappa. In the case of EDU-segmented plain language data, however, the paraphrase function achieves a Cohen's Kappa that is approx. 0.4 higher.

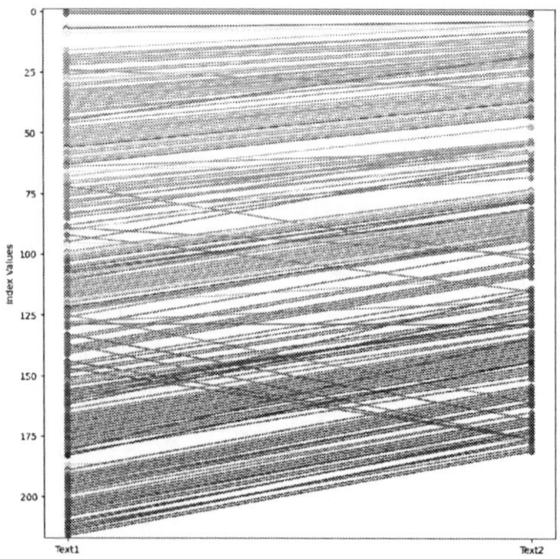

Figure 1: Alignments of Arendt essays on sentence level

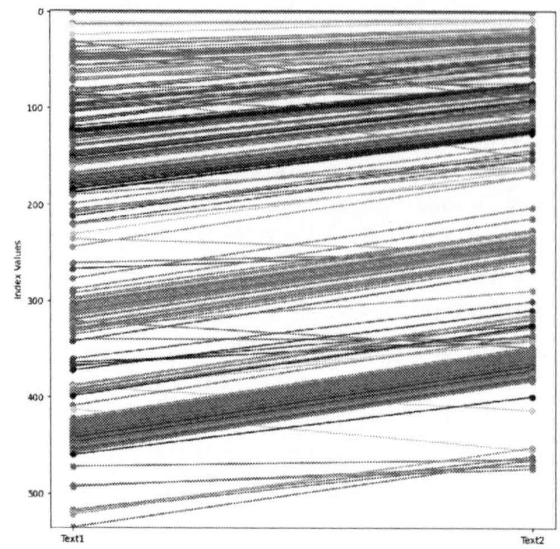

Figure 2: Alignments of Arendt essays on EDU level

In addition, the context window is also faster in all cases, on average approx. 14%. The biggest difference in terms of calculation time is for the encyclopedia entries, where the context window takes 36% less time than the paraphrase mining function. The smallest difference, on the other hand, is for the Kafka essays at sentence level - here the context window is only around 3% faster. These results correlate with the size of the context window, which in turn result from the properties of the datasets. If the texts are short or highly parallel, a small context window is sufficient to find the correct matches and the function can save a lot of time. With the long and heavily modified Kafka essays, on the other hand, much larger context windows are required to achieve good alignments and the efficiency advantage of the function shrinks accordingly. This can also be seen from the visualizations of the alignment throughout the Kafka essays in Figures 1 and 2. Since the text versions are of different length and some parts are heavily altered, the gap between aligned sentences is bigger (indicated by darker colors).

In most cases, the EDU-segmented texts can also be aligned faster than whole sentences. On average, however, the difference is smaller than the difference between the two alignment functions. It is particularly surprising that the EDUs also have an advantage with the paraphrase function, as significantly more elements have to be compared with each other at this level. However, it seems to be possible to calculate the embeddings of EDUs much faster, which results in an overall runtime advantage.

4.2.2 Alignment Level

A direct comparison between the alignment of EDUs and whole sentences (see Table 2) shows that the models achieve slightly better results on the sentence level than on EDU level, both for the Arendt data and for the plain language data.

Plain language dataset: The more sensitive RoBERTa model achieves better scores than the `sbert` model in all runs. The best run is achieved on the sentence level: With the embeddings of the RoBERTa model and a relatively high threshold of 0.55 cosine, a Cohen's Kappa of 0.76 is achieved between the manual alignment and the automatic alignment. The F1 score is also 0.76 in this case. If EDUs are used for alignment instead, the values across all runs are approx. 0.1 points below the runs with whole sentences. In the best run (RoBERTa, again 0.55 cosine), 0.65 Cohen's kappa is achieved.

Hannah Arendt essays: A similar picture emerges for this text pair: Full sentences again lead to better scores than EDUs. The differences between the various settings are therefore more evident here. However, the overall best performances - both for EDUs and for whole sentences - are again achieved with the RoBERTa embeddings and the threshold of 0.55 cosine. The Cohen's kappa here is 0.65 for whole sentences and 0.49 for EDUs.

GDR literature encyclopedias: Although this data is only available in a keyword-like form, good

Dataset	Alignment Algorithm	Settings	Prec	Recall	F1	Kappa	Computing time
Plain Lang - Sents	Context Window	model 1, Threshold: 0.55, multi-align: True, Window-size: 10	0.902	0.762	0.764	**0.761**	102.3 Sec
	Paraphrase Function	model 1, Threshold: 0.4, multi-align: True	0.898	0.743	0.740	0.731	117.2 Sec
Plain Lang - EDUs	Context Window	model 1, Threshold: 0.55, multi-align: True, Window-size: 20	0.839	0.673	0.671	0.650	**93.3** Sec
	Paraphrase Function	model 1, Threshold: 0.6, multi-align: True	0.817	0.699	0.684	0.693	97.4 Sec
Kafka - Sents	Context Window	model 1, Threshold: 0.55, multi-align: True, Window-size: 50	0.816	0.684	0.648	**0.656**	104.2 Sec
	Paraphrase Function	model 1, Threshold: 0.55, multi-align: True	0.780	0.657	0.623	0.630	107.3 Sec
Kafka - EDUs	Context Window	model 1, Threshold: 0.55, multi-align: True, Window-size: 75	0.805	0.695	0.655	0.589	**100.7** Sec
	Paraphrase Function	model 1, Threshold 0.6, multi-align: True	0.802	0.572	0.609	0.578	116.4 Sec
Encyclopedias	Context Window	model 1, Threshold 0.55, multi-align: True, Window-size: 10	0.888	0.786	0.740	**0.697**	**61.0** Sec
	Paraphrase Function	model 1, Threshold 0.6, multi-align: True	0.860	0.672	0.660	0.600	83.7 Sec

Table 2: Best overall results for different datasets and alignment algorithms.

alignment results are generated here in various runs with a Cohen's Kappa of up to 0.7.

The results also show that in general it seems to work better to allow aligning the same elements multiple times and combining this setting with a cosine threshold. In all runs this led to better results than restricting multiple alignments and removing the threshold.

5 Error Analysis

The most severe difficulties arise for the Arendt essays. When the aligned sentences are examined more closely, it becomes clear that an incorrect assignment may have been made, even though the matched sentences generally fit together well thematically. 'Meaning-heavy' terms like names and nouns, which have a great influence on the sentence embeddings, occur repeatedly throughout the dataset and thus make correct assignment more difficult. Therefore, part of the problem is that the embeddings of such complex sentences are not fine-grained enough to select the actual correct sentence from several potentially-matching sentences. This phenomenon can be observed in the following examples (English translations created by us, not by Hannah Arendt):

(3) [Original] **Das gemeinsame Erlebnis der Leser Kafkas ist eine allgemeine, unbestimmbare Bezauberung [...], eine klare Erinnerung an merkwürdige und scheinbar unsinnige Bilder und Beschreibungen - bis sich ihnen eines Tages der verborgene Sinn mit der plötzlichen Deutlichkeit einer einfachen und unangreifbaren Wahrheit enthüllt.**

The common experience of Kafka's readers is a general, indefinable enchantment [...], a clear memory of strange and seemingly nonsensical images and descriptions - until one day the hidden meaning is revealed to them with the sudden clarity of a simple and unassailable truth.

(4) [Found match] **Das einzige, was den Leser in Kafkas Werk lockt und verlockt, ist die Wahrheit selbst, und diese Verlockung ist Kafka in seiner stillosen Vollkommenheit geglückt, daß seine Geschichten auch dann in Bann schlagen, wenn der Leser ihren eigentlichen Wahrheitsgehalt erst einmal**

nicht begreift.

The only thing that lures and entices the reader in Kafka's work is the truth itself, and Kafka succeeded in this enticement with such quiet perfection that his stories cast a spell even if the reader does not at first grasp their actual truthfulness.

(5) [Correct match] **Kafkas eigentliche Kunst besteht darin, daß der Leser eine unbestimmte, vage Faszination, die sich mit der unausweichlich klaren Erinnerung an bestimmte, erst scheinbar sinnlose Bilder und Begebenheiten paart, [...] aushält, bis sich die wahre Bedeutung der Geschichte sich enthüllt.**

Kafka's real art lies in the fact that the reader endures an indeterminate, vague fascination, which is coupled with the inescapably clear memory of certain images and events that at first appear to make no sense [...] until the true meaning of the story is revealed.

As already mentioned in the last section, the alignment of the Arendt texts is made more difficult by the fact that the texts were also heavily altered at paragraph level. Parts were added or omitted and the sentence order was changed considerably. These characteristics make it very difficult (in particular for the context window) to find the correct correspondences, as the window size would have to be increased significantly and the efficiency advantages of this approach would be lost as a result.

6 Conclusion

The context window shows a superior performance compared to the paraphrase mining function both for alignment quality and alignment speed. However, there are still problems to be solved: If text versions are altered heavily, the window size has to be extended to find the best match. To mitigate this, a previous paragraph alignment could be implemented and the sentence alignment could be performed in a second step.

The role of EDU segmentation is difficult to assess. The use of EDUs in the alignment process can only make sense if the sentences are so long on average that several EDUs are created. However, even the experiments on the Hannah Arendt data showed that the models achieve slightly worse values on average with EDUs than with whole sentences. Several aspects should be considered here: Of all the data we worked with, Hannah Arendt's essays are by far the least parallel and therefore the most difficult to align. This can already be seen from the proportion of unaligned items in the test data: While less than 25% of the data in the plain language dataset was not aligned, this proportion is more than 35% in the EDUs of the Arendt essays. In addition, alignment is made very difficult by the length of the texts. Both the news reports of the plain language dataset (46 segments on average) and the encyclopedia entries (14 segments on average) are short, and correspondences are to be expected in the immediate vicinity. Arendt's essays, on the other hand, consist of more than 500 segments. They were restructured on paragraph level and are of different lengths.

In contrast, both models achieve very good values on the encyclopedia data, with Kappa scores ranging from 0.65 to 0.75. This also shows that the generally poorer scores of the Arendt essays are due more to the difficulty of the dataset than to the problems caused by the use of EDUs in the alignment process.

In order to solve the problems described here, several tasks must be tackled in the next steps: To conclusively evaluate the usability of EDUs for the alignment of complex, semi-parallel texts, further data should be included, which to some extent form a compromise of the datasets available here: They should be longer and more complex than the plain language and encyclopedia data, but more similarly structured on the textual level than the Arendt essays. In addition, further models for EDU segmentation should be considered, which may also be fine-tuned on the data available.

Also, it is necessary to thoroughly check the quality of the sentence embeddings. It has been discovered as part of the problem that the embeddings cannot clearly distinguish similar but non-identical phrases. A study that specifically measures the similarity of exchanged words, sentence structures and paraphrases could help to develop more precise embeddings for this use case.

Finally, a previous paragraph alignment should be tested to mitigate the fact that increased window sizes are necessary to combat alterations on paragraph level. With these additions, it should be possible to further improve sentence alignment on semi-parallel datasets.

Acknowledgments

We thank our student assistants Dietmar Benndorf and Maximilian Krupop for annotating training data, and we are grateful to the anonymous reviewers for their helpful feedback. Data from GDR literature encyclopedias was provided by the research group "Forschungsplattform Literarisches Feld DDR".[2] Our work is supported by the Deutsche Forschungsgemeinschaft (DFG), project (524057241) "Semi-automatische Kollationierung verschiedensprachiger Fassungen eines Textes".

References

Mikel Artetxe and Holger Schwenk. 2019. Massively Multilingual Sentence Embeddings for Zero-Shot Cross-Lingual Transfer and Beyond. *Transactions of the Association for Computational Linguistics*, 7:597–610.

Elron Bandel, Ranit Aharonov, Michal Shmueli-Scheuer, Ilya Shnayderman, Noam Slonim, and Liat Ein-Dor. 2022. Quality controlled paraphrase generation. In *Proceedings of the 60th Annual Meeting of the Association for Computational Linguistics (Volume 1: Long Papers)*, pages 596–609, Dublin, Ireland. Association for Computational Linguistics.

Chloé Braud, Yang Janet Liu, Eleni Metheniti, Philippe Muller, Laura Rivière, Attapol Rutherford, and Amir Zeldes. 2023. The DISRPT 2023 shared task on elementary discourse unit segmentation, connective detection, and relation classification. In *Proceedings of the 3rd Shared Task on Discourse Relation Parsing and Treebanking (DISRPT 2023)*, pages 1–21, Toronto, Canada. The Association for Computational Linguistics.

Peter F. Brown, Jennifer C. Lai, and Robert L. Mercer. 1991. Aligning sentences in parallel corpora. In *Proceedings of the 29th Annual Meeting on Association for Computational Linguistics*, ACL '91, page 169–176, USA. Association for Computational Linguistics.

Percy Cheung and Pascale Fung. 2004. Sentence alignment in paralllel, comparable and quasi-comparable corpora.

Chenhui Chu, Toshiaki Nakazawa, and Sadao Kurohashi. 2013. Chinese–Japanese parallel sentence extraction from quasi–comparable corpora. In *Proceedings of the Sixth Workshop on Building and Using Comparable Corpora*, pages 34–42, Sofia, Bulgaria. Association for Computational Linguistics.

Alexis Conneau, Kartikay Khandelwal, Naman Goyal, Vishrav Chaudhary, Guillaume Wenzek, Francisco Guzmán, Edouard Grave, Myle Ott, Luke Zettlemoyer, and Veselin Stoyanov. 2019. Unsupervised cross-lingual representation learning at scale. *CoRR*, abs/1911.02116.

Jacob Devlin, Ming-Wei Chang, Kenton Lee, and Kristina Toutanova. 2019. Bert: Pre-training of deep bidirectional transformers for language understanding. *Preprint*, arXiv:1810.04805.

Fangxiaoyu Feng, Yinfei Yang, Daniel Cer, Naveen Arivazhagan, and Wei Wang. 2022. Language-agnostic BERT sentence embedding. In *Proceedings of the 60th Annual Meeting of the Association for Computational Linguistics (Volume 1: Long Papers)*, pages 878–891, Dublin, Ireland. Association for Computational Linguistics.

William A. Gale and Kenneth W. Church. 1993. A program for aligning sentences in bilingual corpora. *Computational Linguistics*, 19(1):75–102.

Darina Gold, Venelin Kovatchev, and Torsten Zesch. 2019. Annotating and analyzing the interactions between meaning relations. In *Proceedings of the 13th Linguistic Annotation Workshop*, pages 26–36, Florence, Italy. Association for Computational Linguistics.

Freya Hewett. 2023. APA-RST: A text simplification corpus with RST annotations. In *Proceedings of the 4th Workshop on Computational Approaches to Discourse (CODI 2023)*, pages 173–179, Toronto, Canada. Association for Computational Linguistics.

Paul Jaccard. 1901. Etude comparative de la distribution florale dans une portion des alpes et des jura. *Bulletin de la Societe Vaudoise des Sciences Naturelles*, page 547–579.

Yangfeng Ji and Jacob Eisenstein. 2014. Representation learning for text-level discourse parsing. In *Annual Meeting of the Association for Computational Linguistics*.

Timothy Liu and De Wen Soh. 2022. Towards better characterization of paraphrases. In *Proceedings of the 60th Annual Meeting of the Association for Computational Linguistics (Volume 1: Long Papers)*, pages 8592–8601, Dublin, Ireland. Association for Computational Linguistics.

William Mann and Sandra Thompson. 1988. Rhetorical structure theory: Towards a functional theory of text organization. *TEXT*, 8:243–281.

Francesco Molfese, Andrei Bejgu, Simone Tedeschi, Simone Conia, and Roberto Navigli. 2024. Crocoalign: A cross-lingual, context-aware and fully-neural sentence alignment system for long texts. In *Proceedings of the 18th Conference of the European Chapter of the Association for Computational Linguistics (Volume 1: Long Papers)*, pages 2209–2220, St. Julian's, Malta. Association for Computational Linguistics.

Robert C. Moore. 2002. Fast and accurate sentence alignment of bilingual corpora. In *Proceedings of the 5th Conference of the Association for Machine Translation in the Americas: Technical Papers*, pages 135–144, Tiburon, USA. Springer.

[2] www.ddr-literatur.de

Marcus Pöckelmann, André Medek, Jörg Ritter, and Paul Molitor. 2022. LERA—an interactive platform for synoptical representations of multiple text witnesses. *Digital Scholarship in the Humanities*, 38(1):330–346.

Sadaf Abdul Rauf and Holger Schwenk. 2011. Parallel sentence generation from comparable corpora for improved smt. *Machine Translation*, 25(4):341–375.

Nils Reimers and Iryna Gurevych. 2019. Sentence-bert: Sentence embeddings using siamese bert-networks. *Preprint*, arXiv:1908.10084.

Rico Sennrich and Martin Volk. 2010. MT-based sentence alignment for OCR-generated parallel texts. In *Proceedings of the 9th Conference of the Association for Machine Translation in the Americas: Research Papers*, Denver, Colorado, USA. Association for Machine Translation in the Americas.

Sara Shahmohammadi and Manfred Stede. 2024. Discourse parsing for German with new RST corpora. In *Proceedings of the 20th Conference on Natural Language Processing (KONVENS 2024)*, pages 65–74, Vienna, Austria. Association for Computational Linguistics.

Uladzimir Sidarenka, Andreas Peldszus, and Manfred Stede. 2015. Discourse Segmentation of German Texts. *JLCL*, 30(1):71–98.

Kurt Sier and Eva Wöckener-Gade. 2019. Paraphrase als Ähnlichkeitsbeziehung. ein digitaler zugang zu einem intertextuellen phänomen. In *Platon Digital. Tradition und Rezeption*. Propylaeum.

Jason R. Smith, Chris Quirk, and Kristina Toutanova. 2010. Extracting parallel sentences from comparable corpora using document level alignment. In *Human Language Technologies: The 2010 Annual Conference of the North American Chapter of the Association for Computational Linguistics*, pages 403–411, Los Angeles, California. Association for Computational Linguistics.

Steinthor Steingrimsson, Hrafn Loftsson, and Andy Way. 2023. SentAlign: Accurate and scalable sentence alignment. In *Proceedings of the 2023 Conference on Empirical Methods in Natural Language Processing: System Demonstrations*, pages 256–263, Singapore. Association for Computational Linguistics.

Brian Thompson and Philipp Koehn. 2019. Vecalign: Improved sentence alignment in linear time and space. In *Proceedings of the 2019 Conference on Empirical Methods in Natural Language Processing and the 9th International Joint Conference on Natural Language Processing (EMNLP-IJCNLP)*, pages 1342–1348, Hong Kong, China. Association for Computational Linguistics.

Christoph Tillmann. 2009. A beam-search extraction algorithm for comparable data. In *Annual Meeting of the Association for Computational Linguistics*.

Milan Tofiloski, Julian Brooke, and Maite Taboada. 2009. A syntactic and lexical-based discourse segmenter. In *Proc. of the Joint Conference of the 47th Annual Meeting of the ACL and the 4th International Joint Conference on Natural Language Processing of the AFNLP (Short Papers)*, pages 77–80, Suntec, Singapore. Association for Computational Linguistics.

Jan Wahle, Bela Gipp, and Terry Ruas. 2023. Paraphrase types for generation and detection. In *Proceedings of the 2023 Conference on Empirical Methods in Natural Language Processing*, page 12148–12164. Association for Computational Linguistics.

Yizhong Wang, Sujian Li, and Jingfeng Yang. 2018. Toward fast and accurate neural discourse segmentation. In *Proceedings of the 2018 Conference on Empirical Methods in Natural Language Processing*, pages 962–967, Brussels, Belgium. Association for Computational Linguistics.

Krzysztof Wołk and Krzysztof Marasek. 2017. Unsupervised construction of quasi-comparable corpora and probing for parallel textual data. In *Multimedia and Network Information Systems*, pages 307–320, Cham. Springer International Publishing.

Kexin Yang, Dayiheng Liu, Wenqiang Lei, Baosong Yang, Haibo Zhang, Xue Zhao, Wenqing Yao, and Boxing Chen. 2022. GCPG: A general framework for controllable paraphrase generation. In *Findings of the Association for Computational Linguistics: ACL 2022*, pages 4035–4047, Dublin, Ireland. Association for Computational Linguistics.

Argumentation in political Empowerment on Instagram

Aenne Knierim and **Ulrich Heid**
University of Hildesheim
Universitätsplatz 1
31141 Hildesheim
knierim@uni-hildesheim.de
heidul@uni-hildesheim.de

Abstract

This paper adopts a distant reading approach to analyze political empowerment on Instagram. We focus on argument mining and content classification to uncover cooccurences between aspects of political empowerment and argument components. We develop an annotation scheme based on literature in digital political empowerment, classifying content into five primary categories along the aspects of political awareness, personal e-identity and political participation. We implemented the modified toulmin scheme for argument component detection. As an example discourse, we chose the German discourses #WirSindMehr and #NieWiederIstJetzt. The upheaval was targeted against right-wing extremism and antisemitism. Political awareness emerged as the dominant category, highlighting convergent public concern against antisemitism and right-wing extremism. Claims and backings often contain statements about societal change and aim to raise consciousness. Calls for participation in offline events appear mostly in non-argumentative texts.

1 Introduction

Empowerment research has its roots in community psychology. There, it is defined as a "construct that links individual strengths and competencies, natural helping systems, and proactive behaviors to matters of social policy and social change" (Zimmerman and Rappaport, 1988). It is also related to Freire's theory 1970 of conscientization, which describes how critical consciousness is the first step to the ability of transforming one's status in society. Next to social and political understanding, the individual experience of empowerment includes a combination of self-acceptance and the ability to play an assertive role in controlling resources and decisions in one's community, for example through citizen participation (Zimmerman and Rappaport, 1988).

The notion of political empowerment was introduced to overcome the potential lack of citizen participation in democracies (Pirannejad and Janssen, 2019). While there is no set definition of political empowerment, and many theoretical models address empowerment, they all emphasize the need for competence and experience to be enhanced (Amichai-Hamburger et al., 2008). Examples of empowerment outcomes are political participation, influence and perceived control or transfer of power between groups of society, or resource mobilization skills (Leong et al., 2019, 2015; Alexander et al., 2016; Jones, 1978; Pirannejad and Janssen, 2019; Perkins and Zimmerman, 1995).

Researchers have examined political empowerment in the digital setting. Several studies have specifically investigated the role of social networks in promoting political empowerment (Leong et al., 2015, 2019; Waitoa et al., 2015; Hurley, 2021; Halliday and Brown, 2018). Building on this body of work, the present study examines political empowerment in social media. Specifically, we strive to characterize typical characteristics of political empowerment using a birds-eye view.

For this purpose, we perform two classifications. The first classifies political empowerment along the three aspects political awareness, political participation and e-identity, following Amichai-Hamburger et al. (2008) and Pirannejad and Janssen (2019). The goal is to identify how aspects of political empowerment are reflected in the data, as a first step towards a quantitative sketch of the phenomenon. The second classification is an argument mining task. We detect argument components using Habernal & Gurevych's modified Toulmin scheme 2017.

Finally, we want to identify cooccurences of the argument components and aspects of political empowerment. For example, do claims often express group identity towards a political stance?

As an example corpus, we chose the German

Proceedings of LaTeCH-CLfL 2025, pages 97–108
May 4, 2025

discourses #WirSindMehr ("We are more") and #NieWiederIstJetzt ("Never again is now"). The upheaval was targeted against right-wing voters and took a stance against antisemitism after the attack on Israel on the 7th of October 2023. We investigate Instagram captions because scholars found that captions are where political issues are primarily communicated on the platform (Bast, 2021; Towner and Muñoz, 2018; Liebhart and Bernhardt, 2017; Lalancette and Raynauld, 2019).

2 Related work: digital political empowerment

In this study, we create annotation guidelines that cover all three aspects of political empowerment: e-identity, political participation and political awareness. Importantly, we built on literature that focused on political empowerment via the Internet, rather than political empowerment in an analogous setting. We refer in particular to the studies conducted by Amichai-Hamburger et al. (2008); Pirannejad and Janssen (2019), as these were pivotal for further research.

2.1 E-identity

Scholars argue that blogs and similar venues can serve as "identity workshops", allowing to test social skills (Bruckman, 1992). Besides, the anonymity of communicating online facilitates mastery, increasing self-efficacy. Next to the option of anonymity, the opportunity for editing allows for a (perceivably) highly protected environment. Impression formation also sets differently than in analog settings, as physical cues are often not available (Amichai-Hamburger et al., 2008). Another aspect is the ability for cross-cultural communication and the opportunity of finding similar others. Woo-Young (2005) finds that users can easily express their support or disapproval of opinions expressed online, potentially affecting the formation of public opinion and adding to the formation of group identity.

2.2 Political participation

Digitally enabled interactions between government and citizens can help citizens feel that they may make a significant contribution to politics (Pirannejad and Janssen, 2019; Amichai-Hamburger et al., 2008). The variety of available group decision-making tools eases action taking in the virtual space. Several scholars also found the opportunity for monitoring of government activities empowering (Woo-Young, 2005; Pirannejad and Janssen, 2019). This could include monitoring the allocation of government resources or the legislative activities of politicians (Woo-Young and Won-Tae, 2006). Simpler forms of participation include fundraising or petition signing (Johnson, 2017)

2.3 Political awareness

The Internet can play a critical role at "gathering and distributing a large volume of political information rapidly and at low cost"(Pirannejad and Janssen, 2019). Next to this, the availability of digital resources informs people about parties' efforts. Social communication enabled through social network sites also increases access to political information. Amichai-Hamburger et al. (2008) find that citizens can quickly find, for example, comparative stances taken by elected or potential representatives. Freire (1970) introduced the concept of conscientization, illustrating how empowerment can occur through critical consciousness of one's situation.

2.4 Empowerment in social media

An aspect of political empowerment unique to social media is the overlap between personal and public space, which encourages the preservation of the underlying network (Leong et al., 2019). In addition, social networks generate options for people to participate based on their interests, capabilities and capacities (Leong et al., 2019) – although this might also be true for ICTs in general. Another opportunity social media offer is the management of resources, and quick information coordination (Leong et al., 2019, 2015). Waitoa et al. (2015) also highlight that "the promise that social networks hold for diasporic populations is the ability to connect with their language and culture remotely".

2.5 Studying Instagram captions

Instagram's multimodal environment offers great potential for political communication (Bast, 2021). With 41% of the population in Germany using the platform (statista.com, accessed 01/2025), it is no surprise that Instagram reflects political moments of citizen engagement or plays a role in agenda-setting (Towner and Muñoz, 2018; Barbala, 2024). Following Bast (2021), Instagram is a popular tool for promoting a political image. In her review of the platform, Bast (2021) found that most studies focus on the self-representation of political actors on Instagram, particularly examining whether they use the platform to discuss political issues, share campaign information and mobilize voters.

Visual Instagram contents like images and videos have been studied to uncover macro-visual patterns of colors, photo-filters used and selfie-styles (Manovich, 2017), in attempt to study its visual culture (Caliandro and Graham, 2020; Gibbs et al., 2015). But Instagram is not limited to visual content, as it offers users the possibility of adding long captions to their posts which is where political issues are primarily communicated (Bast, 2021; Towner and Muñoz, 2018; Liebhart and Bernhardt, 2017; Lalancette and Raynauld, 2019). Therefore, in this study, we investigate political empowerment in Instagram captions. We use #NieWiederIstJetzt and #WirSindMehr as an example discourse.

2.6 Argument Mining

Argument Mining is an area of natural language processing defined by a variety of tasks, aiming to extract and structure arguments from unstructured text (Galassi et al., 2023). Most commonly, argument mining is defined as a classification task for detecting argumentative units such as premises or claims. It can also be defined as a relation extraction task, aiming to identify support or attack relations between argumentative units. Others have investigated argument facet similarity (Swanson et al., 2015), argument mining and fact checking (Dusmanu et al., 2017), usefulness of arguments (Passon et al., 2018), argument similarity (Boltuzic and Snajder, 2015) and even argument clustering (Reimers et al., 2019). Falk and Lapesa (2022) investigated reports of personal experiences in argumentation.

Common approaches to argument mining include traditional supervised machine learning approaches such as Support Vector Machines (Palau and Moens, 2011) or Logistic Regression (Goudas et al., 2014). Since the introduction of BERT (Devlin et al., 2019), many researchers made use of deep learning models for argument mining tasks, for example Bhatti et al. (2021) and Schaefer and Stede (2022). Both approaches rely on manually annotated datasets (Habernal and Gurevych, 2015). Due to the recent advent of large language models (LLMs), researchers have tested the performances of fewshot and zeroshot settings, finding that LLMs significantly outperformed the best performing RoBERTa-based baseline on a relation-based argument mining task (Gorur et al., 2025). This is very promising, as only few publicly available datasets exist for German, and annotations are costly. Other research tests the applicability of LLMs for argumentation corpora. For example, Mirzakhmedova et al. (2024) investigated their application for the annotation of argument quality. Ni et al. (2024) tested LLMs for a argumentative unit detection task.

Argument mining tasks can be performed on the micro-level (monological), macro-level (dialogical), or rhetoric models. Micro-level models "pinpoint an individual argument's components and internal organization", while "the macro-level model focuses on the relations between arguments and their external structure" (Patel, 2024). Next to the simple claim-premise scheme, two standard micro-level models are Walton's scheme and Toulmin's model, which Habernal and Gurevych updated for user-generated web discourse (modified Toulmin model) 2017; 2008; 2003. Argument mining on user-generated web content is typically performed on the micro-level, as user posts are typically short. As Schaefer and Stede (2022) stated, the language specific to social media proposes challenges for arguments, due too its linguistic characteristics such as spelling and grammar, hashtags, emoticons, and abbreviations. Boltuzic and Snajder (2015) point out that "unlike in debates or other more formal argumentation sources, the arguments provided by users, if any, are less formal, ambiguous, vague, implicit, or simply poorly worded".

3 Data compilation and description

In the German political conversations of #WirSindMehr and #NieWiederIstJetzt, a group of civilians reacted to the political shift to the right in the country, taking a stance against racism and antisemitism. Formerly called "silent majority" by German newspapers (Stuttgarter Zeitung, accessed 01/2025), the upheaval was targeted against right-wing voters and politicians of the AfD party. The upheaval was a reaction to the Düsseldorfer Forum, a right-wing meet-up that was planning the "remigration" of Germans with migration background and refugees; and antisemitic incidences in Germany after the terrorist attack of the Hamas on Israel (Bensmann, Marcus et al., 2024). Over a period of three months, a total of two million people protested across Germany (Sauerbrey, 2024). We collected the data with Crowdtangle in the period between 10/07/2023 and 03/31/2024[1]. The

[1]crowdtangle.com

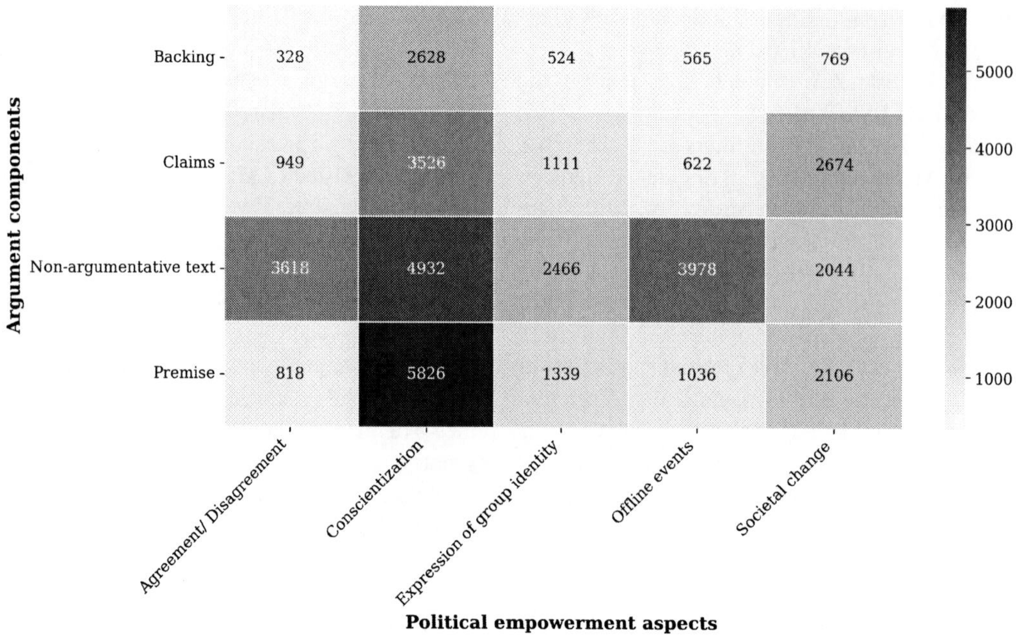

Figure 1: Cooccurences between argument components and political empowerment aspects.

search terms used were the hashtags #wirsindmehr or #niewiederistjetzt and spelling variants. The tool automatically searches for the words even without hashtags. We collected data from Instagram. The dataset comprises 13469 posts with the post length being 91 words on average. The total token count is 1279585. Two samples of around 1200 posts each were annotated for content and argument components. The annotation process is described in the sections 4 and 5.

4 Annotation process

4.1 Annotating for political empowerment

Based on the literature review presented in chapter 3, we initially extracted eleven possible labels (see apx. tab. 1). Two trained annotators labeled 1200 posts, a random sample from our corpus.

We iteratively worked with our annotators, which resulted in one additional category not present in the literature. We found that, next to calls for participation in offline events, users often report from offline events in their posts. We could not classify using all twelve categories, because not all classes sufficiently present in our dataset (see apx. tab. 1). Although six classes were annotated between 104 and 732 times, the other six were annotated between two and eight times. We also merged the classes "call for participation" and "report from political events" to handle class imbalances. The five resulting classes used to train our classifier are displayed in Table 3. A complete overview of our annotation scheme is visualized in Table 1 in the apx.

Interestingly, five of the six classes that have been annotated less than ten times cover aspects of political participation. They describe interactive tasks such as petition signing, fundraising, or inquiries to politicians. They might be more common on internet sites, as for example on funding and petition websites such as gofundme.com or change.org as well as other formats native to the internet like e-mail.

4.2 Annotating for argument mining

We define argument mining as a component classification task. A micro-level model is required, since Instagram captions typically consist of only 91 words. We use the modified Toulmin model introduced by Habernal and Gurevych (2017), since it was specifically adapted to user-generated web content. The modified Toulmin model comprises the argument components claim, premise, backing, rebuttal, and refutation (Habernal and Gurevych, 2017). We added non-argumentative text as a component. We adopted all other guidelines of the modified Toulmin model. The annotation was con-

Table 1: Count of annotated labels. Labels are performed by two annotators. Labels beneath the line are excluded from classification due to a low count.

Aspect	Label	Explanation	Count	Literature
Political Awareness	Conscientization	Raising consciousness about political circumstances	732	Freire 1970, Woo-Young & Won-Tae 2006
	Societal change	Post talks about a change in societal stance	169	Pirannejad & Jannsen 2019
	Participation in offline events	Call to participate in political events non-digitally	109	Pirannejad & Jannsen 2019
	Report from offline events	Posts reports from protests or other political action	104	
E-Identity	Group identity	Expresses a feeling of group identity in the context of political stance	373	Amichai-Hamburger et al. 2008, Yuce et al. 2014
	Agreement or disagreement	Expression of agreement or disagreement with a point of view	445	Yuce et al. 2014, Woo-Young 2005
	Networking	Networking with other groups with a similar stance	8	Tye et al. 2018, Jackson et al. 2020, Leong et al. 2019
Political Participation	Monitoring	Monitoring of government	6	Woo-Young & Won-Tae 2006
	Request	Request to parties or politicians	3	Amichai-Hamburger et al. 2008, Pirannejad & Jannsen 2019
	Fundraising	Fundraising for activist purposes	2	Johnson 2017, Amichai-Hamburger et al. 2008, Pirannejad & Jannsen 2019
	Interactive decision-making	Group decision-making facilitated by the platform	2	Leong et al. 2015; 2019, Amichai-Hamburger et al. 2008

Label	Count
Non-argumentative text	658
Claim	282
Premise	193
Backing	121

Table 2: Count of annotated component labels for argument mining. Labels performed by one annotator.

ducted by only one trained, paid annotator. Similar to the annotation of political empowerment, there was a class imbalance, making it impossible to detect all components automatically. As a result, we defined four classes: claims, premises, backing, and non-argumentative text.

5 Classifying political empowerment

5.1 Component detection

We use our annotated dataset of 1200 posts to train and compare the performance of three deep learning models. Two of the models are German language models, gbert-base (Chan et al., 2020) and GottBERT_base_last (Scheible et al., 2024). We used one multilingual model, xlm-roberta-base (Conneau et al., 2019). We chose sentence as unit of analysis, instead of a post-based analysis, as one sentence often presented one argument component. We also performed hyper-parameter finetuning with the goal to minimize the loss function. For gbert-base, 14 epochs, a batch_size of 16, learning rate =5e-5 yielded the best results. The results were cross-validated as averages from ten runs.

The multi-label classification model demonstrates strong overall performance, achieving a macro-average F1-score of 0.90, with balanced precision (0.90) and recall (0.89) across all categories. The "non-argumentative" category exhibits near-perfect classification (F1 = 0.98), indicating the model's high confidence in distinguishing non-argumentative text from argumentative components. Among the argument components, Premise (F1 = 0.88) and Claim (F1 = 0.86) are well-identified, though the slightly lower recall for Claim (0.85) suggests room for improvement in capturing all relevant instances. Similarly, Backing (F1 = 0.86) performs reliably, though differentiation between Premise and Backing could be further refined. These results indicate that the model is highly effective in identifying argument structures, with minor areas for enhancement in recall for specific argumentative components.

Additionally, we tested one large language model in a zeroshot setting, Em_german_7b_v01, a Llama2-based model (Touvron et al., 2023). As annotated data for argument mining are scarce and expensive, zero-shot learning and few-shot learning are promising tools for the task. Gorur et al. (2025) and Ni et al. (2024) also demonstrate the potential of zeroshot and fewshot settings for argument mining. In our setting, all finetuned deep learning models significantly outperformed the zeroshot model. All results of the comparison are visible in Table 4. As gbert-base outperformed the other models with a macro f1-score of 0.90, we used gbert-base to perform the classification on our entire dataset (13469 posts with ca. 40000 sentences).

5.2 Classifying empowerment aspects

For the classification of empowerment aspects, we also used gbert-base, since it performed well on our corpus in the previous classification. Table 3 shows which classes we used, while Table 1 in the appendix shows which classes could not be used due to class imbalances. We also used sentences as unit of analysis. For the hyperparameter finetuning, 8 epochs, a batch_size of 5, learning rate =5e-5 yielded the best results. We had an f1-score of 0.81, suggesting balanced performance across all categories. Conscientization has the highest performance, which is consistent with the fact that it had most examples in the training data. Participation in offline events and expression of agreement/disagreement perfom consistently well across precision, recall and f1-score. Societal change shows weaker recall, suggesting more training data would be needed. In Table 5, the performance of gbert-base for each class is visualized.

6 Cooccurences

Finally, we want to identify cooccurences between argument components and aspects of political empowerment. For example, are premises typically used in a way that spreads consciousness? Is the expression of group identity used to support one's claims? We visualize the cooccurences in a heatmap (see Figure 1.). The heatmap shows the relations between the argument components, premise, backing, claim, and non-argumentative text; and aspects of political empowerment. This section shows results in the cooccurences.

Label	Explanation
Conscientization	Raising consciousness about political circumstances
Participation in offline events	Call to participate in pol. events; or report from participation
Group identity	Expresses a feeling of group identity in the context of political stance
Societal change	Post talks about a change in societal stance
Agreement or disagreement	Expression of agreement or disagreement with a point of view

Table 3: Labels for the annotation of political empowerment aspects.

	GBERT	GottBERT	RoBERTa	Em_german_7b_v01
Precision	0.86	0.85	0.89	0.39
Recall	0.89	0.84	0.89	0.50
Macro F1-Score	**0.90**	0.84	0.89	0.43

Table 4: Comparison of the different models for the argument mining task.

6.1 Claims

Claims in Instagram captions most commonly express aspects of political awareness building. The most common is conscientization, defined after Freire (1970) as political consciousness building. For example, one user claimed, referring to the Düsseldorfer Forum: "Such secret meetings remind us of Germany's darkest days." Claims which express that society changes are second most common and appear in 2674 sentences. An example claim is: "The majority of people do not want a society in which people are pitted against each other". This exemplifies how people use Instagram to build and share critical consciousness. Additionally, in more than 25% of claims, group idenitity is expressed.

6.2 Backing

Supporting components most often contain conscientizatizing statemens. Despite, conscientization occurs more often in claims than in supporting components (3526 vs 2628 times). Many backings draw parallels between the deportations imagined at the Düsseldorfer Forum and the deportations resulting in the Shoa. One user posted in a conscientizing backing: "#weremember between 1933 and 1945, the Nazi regime cost millions and millions of people their lives." Just as in claims, the second most frequent category is societal change. Reports from participation in offline events, and calls to participate in such, occur just as often as group identity is expressed. The expression of agreement or disagreement appears seldomly in backings.

6.3 Premises

Premises occur most in the data, even before the class "non-argumentative text". Premises mainly express conscientizing statements (5826), a simple example is: "A democracy needs democrats". 2000 premises comment on changes in society. This shows that in claims, backings, and premises, conscientization and societal change appear most frequently in the discourse around #WirSindMehr and #NieWiederIstJetzt. This makes political awareness the most prominent aspect of political empowerment in our dataset.

6.4 Non-argumentative text

Non-argumentative texts are the second biggest component after the premise class. Unlike in other argument components, aspects of political empowerment occur in a more balanced fashion. Although "conscientization" is still the most frequent class, "participation in offline events" is expressed nearly 4000 times within this class. This means non-argumentative sentences often call for political participation; or share a report from political events. Examples are simple reports: "Today we were 2,000 in Sigmaringen and 2,500 in Balingen" and calls to participate – "Come in large numbers! #theaterkiel #democracy #tolerance #solidarity #niewiederistjetzt". Calls also included memorial marches and commemorative events; like: "You are cordially invited to the commemorative event in St. Paul's Church on Sunday, 28". Agreement and disagreement are also frequently expressed in non-argumentative text, often in the form of several hashtags.

Argumentative texts primarily contain aspects of political awareness, which shows that users want to convince their network of the urgency of taking a political stance. Non-argumentative posts reflect political awareness aspects and e-identity as-

Component	Precision	Recall	F1-score
Non-argumentative text	0.98	0.98	0.98
Claim	0.87	0.85	0.86
Premise	0.87	0.89	0.88
Backing	0.86	0.86	0.86
Macro Average	0.90	0.89	0.90

Table 5: Performance of GBERT on the argument component classification.

Component	Precision	Recall	F1-score
Conscientization	0.86	0.81	0.84
Participation in offline events	0.82	0.82	0.82
Group identity	0.78	0.83	0.80
Societal change	0.80	0.71	0.75
Agreement/ Disagreement	0.81	0.83	0.82
Accuracy		0.81	
Macro Average	0.81	0.80	0.81

Table 6: Performance of GBERT on multilabel classification for political empowerment.

pects. Opinion-forming processes and community building with others are evident. Different communication goals may be evident in the different text types: Non-argumentative texts more frequently express feelings of group identity and more often contain reports of political events or calls to attend them.

7 Discussion

In this paper, we take a distant reading perspective on the discourse around the hashtags #WirSindMehr and #NieWiederIstJetzt. We made use of argument component detection and performed a content classification to identify cooccurences between argument components and aspects of political empowerment.

For this purpose, we designed an annotation scheme based on the literature around digital political empowerment. The content classification was performed with only five classes instead of ten. This has two reasons: Firstly, the aspects of personal e-identity and political awareness building stood out more prominently. This most definitely is a result of investigating Instagram captions, as platform functionalities such as surveys or requests to parties typically appear in other platform affordances such as Instagram stories or private chats, and not in captions. For example, an aspect introduced by Woo-Young and Won-Tae (2006) is interactive decision-making, which could happen in the "survey" button in stories. Stories also contain a button for fundraising, but link to a new website.

The second reason were class imbalances: It was not the case that aspects of political empowerment did not appear in the captions at all, but they appeared less than 10 times in the training data, unlike other classes which appeared between 104 and 732 times. This made it impossible to train our classifier for all classes. The decision to reduce classes to yield a clear classification result was thus a pragmatic but necessary one.

For the annotation of argument components, we made use of the modified toulmin scheme (Habernal and Gurevych, 2017). Since we had big class imbalances again, we performed a multilabel classification with four classes: claim, backing, premise and non-argumentative text. To maintain class balance, we used a random sample of 300 posts from all data labeled as "non-argumentative text" (see tab.2 for count of annotated component labels).

Finally, we identified cooccurences of argument components and the content aspects of digital political empowerment (tab. 3). In general, "premises" and "non-argumentative text" are the most frequent argument components. Claims were most frequently concerned with conscientization and societal change. According to our analysis, a typical backing contained conscientizing statements. All other aspects only appeared less than 1000 times. This might indicate that a claim about societal change might frequently be backed by a conscientizing statement. This hypothesis needs to be tested in future work on relation-based argument mining. A typical example could be:

- **Claim:** "Right-wing extremism and antisemitism is on the rise."
- **Backing:** "Jews have been assaulted on German streets, their homes marked with Stars of David and synagogues pelted with Molotov cocktails."

Looking at the bigger picture, we can see that political awareness is the most frequent category in the corpus: Conscientizing statements and statements about societal change appear most often. This is plausible, because #NieWiederIstJetzt is a statement against antisemitism and refers to the Shoa, expressing: The shoa shoud never happen again. It is thus no surprise that users want to raise awareness for antisemitic hate and the rise of right-wing extremism in Germany and Europe. These concerns are frequently stated in all three components; premises, claims, and backings. One aspect of political awareness is commented on less frequently – reports from participation in offline events and calls to participate. Within argument components, it is most frequently found in the class "non-argumentative text" which comprises non-argumentative texts, rebuttals, refutations.

Aspects of e-identity appear second most in our data. The expression of agreement or disagreement with a point of view was most often found in class "Non-argumentative text" (3618 times), and appeared around 1000 times in each of the other classes. Likely, users stated their approval with the stance in the hashtags #WirSindMehr or #NieWiederIstJetzt, but made no substantial argument. It is also probable that disapproval was expressed, as counter discourse is commonly tagged with the same hashtags.

The expression of group identity appeared between 500 and 1500 times per component type, which is less than expected. One might think that the hashtag #WirSindMehr already expresses a feeling of identity; as participants are opponents of right-wing voters and belong to the former "silent majority" as expressed by the Stuttgarter Zeitung. Potentially, this result is due to the preprocessing, as the hashtags #WirSindMehr and #NieWiederIstJetzt were removed from the training data due to their frequent occourence.

In this paper, political empowerment language is characterized by its aspects political awareness, political participation and e-identity. Importantly, we only look at one aspect of Instagram's archictecture, the caption. Although the caption is where political messages are primarily communicated (Bast, 2021; Towner and Muñoz, 2018; Liebhart and Bernhardt, 2017; Lalancette and Raynauld, 2019), we acknowledge that political empowerment should be studied in ephemeral content such as Instagram stories (Bainotti et al., 2021) which offer different functionalities. For a holistic approach to the analysis of empowerment in social media, a close reading approach should complement this work.

Political awareness has shown to be the most frequent category of political empowerment in this corpus. We believe that this could be corpus-specific, because the hashtags' topics were meant to build consciousness of antidemocratic forces in Germany and Europe. Therefore, future work should test if this distribution also shows in other corpora of political empowerment.

This work also illustrates the difficult bridge between humanities theories and applicability in machine-learning, as we had to follow a more coarse-grained approach due to practicalities of machine learning. Nevertheless, we recommend the iterative process of starting with fine-grained approaches informed by extensive humanities theory.

8 Future work

In future work, we will investigate relations between argument components. Like this, we want to extract typical argument relations which would be particularly interesting for content analysis of #NieWiederIstJetzt and #WirSindMehr. Future research could also include fact-checking of common claims, as well as experiment with argument similarity. Additionally, a comparison with image texts on Instagram would be fruitful. This would add insights about the use of different modalities of the platform. It could be interesting to explore whether the participatory aspect of political empowerment is conveyed through image captions. Future work could expand this research to other platforms.

Acknowledgments

We thank the annotators for their work.

References

Amy C Alexander, Catherine Bolzendahl, and Farida Jalalzai. 2016. Defining women's global political empowerment: Theories and evidence. *Sociology Compass*, 10(6):432–441.

Yair Amichai-Hamburger, Katelyn YA McKenna, and Samuel-Azran Tal. 2008. E-empowerment: Empowerment by the internet. *Computers in Human Behavior*, 24(5):1776–1789.

Lucia Bainotti, Alessandro Caliandro, and Alessandro Gandini. 2021. From archive cultures to ephemeral content, and back: Studying instagram stories with digital methods. *New Media & Society*, 23(12):3656–3676.

Astri Moksnes Barbala. 2024. Reassembling# metoo: Tracing the techno-affective agency of the feminist instagram influencer. *Convergence*, 30(3):992–1007.

Jennifer Bast Jennifer Bast. 2021. Politicians, parties, and government representatives on instagram: A review of research approaches, usage patterns, and effects. *Review of Communication Research*, 9.

Bensmann, Marcus, von Daniels, Justus, Dowideit, Annette, Peters, Jean, and Keller, Gabriela. 2024. Neue Rechte – Geheimplan gegen Deutschland. *CORRECTIV Recherchen für die Gesellschaft.*

Muhammad Mahad Afzal Bhatti, Ahsan Suheer Ahmad, and Joonsuk Park. 2021. Argument mining on twitter: A case study on the planned parenthood debate. In *Proceedings of the 8th Workshop on Argument Mining, ArgMining@EMNLP 2021, Punta Cana, Dominican Republic, November 10-11, 2021*, pages 1–11. Association for Computational Linguistics.

Filip Boltuzic and Jan Snajder. 2015. Identifying prominent arguments in online debates using semantic textual similarity. In *Proceedings of the 2nd Workshop on Argumentation Mining, ArgMining@HLT-NAACL 2015, June 4, 2015, Denver, Colorado, USA*, pages 110–115. The Association for Computational Linguistics.

Amy Bruckman. 1992. Identity workshop: Emergent social and psychological phenomena in text-based virtual reality.

Alessandro Caliandro and James Graham. 2020. Studying instagram beyond selfies. *Social media+ society*, 6(2):2056305120924779.

Branden Chan, Stefan Schweter, and Timo Möller. 2020. German's next language model. In *Proceedings of the 28th International Conference on Computational Linguistics, COLING 2020, Barcelona, Spain (Online), December 8-13, 2020*, pages 6788–6796. International Committee on Computational Linguistics.

Alexis Conneau, Kartikay Khandelwal, Naman Goyal, Vishrav Chaudhary, Guillaume Wenzek, Francisco Guzmán, Edouard Grave, Myle Ott, Luke Zettlemoyer, and Veselin Stoyanov. 2019. Unsupervised cross-lingual representation learning at scale. *CoRR*, abs/1911.02116.

Jacob Devlin, Ming-Wei Chang, Kenton Lee, and Kristina Toutanova. 2019. BERT: Pre-training of deep bidirectional transformers for language understanding. In *Proceedings of the 2019 Conference of the North American Chapter of the Association for Computational Linguistics: Human Language Technologies, Volume 1 (Long and Short Papers)*, pages 4171–4186, Minneapolis, Minnesota. Association for Computational Linguistics.

Mihai Dusmanu, Elena Cabrio, and Serena Villata. 2017. Argument mining on twitter: Arguments, facts and sources. In *Proceedings of the 2017 Conference on Empirical Methods in Natural Language Processing, EMNLP 2017, Copenhagen, Denmark, September 9-11, 2017*, pages 2317–2322. Association for Computational Linguistics.

Neele Falk and Gabriella Lapesa. 2022. Reports of personal experiences and stories in argumentation: datasets and analysis. In *Proceedings of the 60th Annual Meeting of the Association for Computational Linguistics (Volume 1: Long Papers), ACL 2022, Dublin, Ireland, May 22-27, 2022*, pages 5530–5553. Association for Computational Linguistics.

Paulo Freire. 1970. Cultural action and conscientization. *Harvard educational review*, 40(3):452–477.

Andrea Galassi, Marco Lippi, and Paolo Torroni. 2023. Multi-task attentive residual networks for argument mining. *IEEE ACM Trans. Audio Speech Lang. Process.*, 31:1877–1892.

Martin Gibbs, James Meese, Michael Arnold, Bjorn Nansen, and Marcus Carter. 2015. # funeral and instagram: Death, social media, and platform vernacular. *Information, communication & society*, 18(3):255–268.

Deniz Gorur, Antonio Rago, and Francesca Toni. 2025. Can large language models perform relation-based argument mining? In *Proceedings of the 31st International Conference on Computational Linguistics, COLING 2025, Abu Dhabi, UAE, January 19-24, 2025*, pages 8518–8534. Association for Computational Linguistics.

Theodosios Goudas, Christos Louizos, Georgios Petasis, and Vangelis Karkaletsis. 2014. Argument extraction from news, blogs, and social media. In *Artificial Intelligence: Methods and Applications - 8th Hellenic Conference on AI, SETN 2014, Ioannina, Greece, May 15-17, 2014. Proceedings*, volume 8445 of *Lecture Notes in Computer Science*, pages 287–299. Springer.

Ivan Habernal and Iryna Gurevych. 2015. Exploiting debate portals for semi-supervised argumentation mining in user-generated web discourse. In *Proceedings of the 2015 Conference on Empirical Methods in Natural Language Processing, EMNLP 2015, Lisbon, Portugal, September 17-21, 2015*, pages 2127–2137. The Association for Computational Linguistics.

Ivan Habernal and Iryna Gurevych. 2017. Argumentation mining in user-generated web discourse. *Computational linguistics*, 43(1):125–179.

Aria S Halliday and Nadia E Brown. 2018. The power of black girl magic anthems: Nicki minaj, beyoncé, and "feeling myself" as political empowerment. *Souls*, 20(2):222–238.

Zoe Hurley. 2021. # reimagining arab women's social media empowerment and the postdigital condition. *Social Media+ Society*, 7(2):20563051211010169.

Sarah J Jackson, Moya Bailey, and Brooke Foucault Welles. 2020. *# HashtagActivism: Networks of race and gender justice*. Mit Press.

Hayley Johnson. 2017. # nodapl: Social media, empowerment, and civic participation at standing rock. *Library Trends*, 66(2):155–175.

Mack H Jones. 1978. Black political empowerment in atlanta: Myth and reality. *The ANNALS of the American Academy of Political and Social Science*, 439(1):90–117.

Mireille Lalancette and Vincent Raynauld. 2019. The power of political image: Justin trudeau, instagram, and celebrity politics. *American behavioral scientist*, 63(7):888–924.

Carmen Leong, Shan L Pan, Shamshul Bahri, and Ali Fauzi. 2019. Social media empowerment in social movements: power activation and power accrual in digital activism. *European Journal of Information Systems*, 28(2):173–204.

Carmen Mei Ling Leong, Shan L Pan, Peter Ractham, and Laddawan Kaewkitipong. 2015. Ict-enabled community empowerment in crisis response: Social media in thailand flooding 2011. *Journal of the Association for Information Systems*, 16(3):1.

Karin Liebhart and Petra Bernhardt. 2017. Political storytelling on instagram: Key aspects of alexander van der bellen's successful 2016 presidential election campaign. *Media and Communication*, 5(4):15–25.

Lev Manovich. 2017. Instagram and contemporary image.

Nailia Mirzakhmedova, Marcel Gohsen, Chia-Hao Chang, and Benno Stein. 2024. Are large language models reliable argument quality annotators? In *Robust Argumentation Machines - First International Conference, RATIO 2024, Bielefeld, Germany, June 5-7, 2024, Proceedings*, volume 14638 of *Lecture Notes in Computer Science*, pages 129–146. Springer.

Jingwei Ni, Minjing Shi, Dominik Stammbach, Mrinmaya Sachan, Elliott Ash, and Markus Leippold. 2024. Afacta: Assisting the annotation of factual claim detection with reliable LLM annotators. In *Proceedings of the 62nd Annual Meeting of the Association for Computational Linguistics (Volume 1: Long Papers), ACL 2024, Bangkok, Thailand, August 11-16, 2024*, pages 1890–1912. Association for Computational Linguistics.

Raquel Mochales Palau and Marie-Francine Moens. 2011. Argumentation mining. *Artif. Intell. Law*, 19(1):1–22.

Marco Passon, Marco Lippi, Giuseppe Serra, and Carlo Tasso. 2018. Predicting the usefulness of amazon reviews using off-the-shelf argumentation mining. In *Proceedings of the 5th Workshop on Argument Mining, ArgMining@EMNLP 2018, Brussels, Belgium, November 1, 2018*, pages 35–39. Association for Computational Linguistics.

Tavisha Patel. 2024. Machine learning and applications in argumentation mining. *International Journal of High School Research*, 6(1).

Douglas D Perkins and Marc A Zimmerman. 1995. Empowerment theory, research, and application. *American journal of community psychology*, 23:569–579.

Ali Pirannejad and Marijn Janssen. 2019. Internet and political empowerment: Towards a taxonomy for online political empowerment. *Information Development*, 35(1):80–95.

Nils Reimers, Benjamin Schiller, Tilman Beck, Johannes Daxenberger, Christian Stab, and Iryna Gurevych. 2019. Classification and clustering of arguments with contextualized word embeddings. In *Proceedings of the 57th Conference of the Association for Computational Linguistics, ACL 2019, Florence, Italy, July 28- August 2, 2019, Volume 1: Long Papers*, pages 567–578. Association for Computational Linguistics.

Anna Sauerbrey. 2024. Opinion | Germany Has Finally Woken Up — nytimes.com. `https://www.nytimes.com/2024/01/31/opinion/germany-protests-far-right.html`. [Accessed 04-09-2024].

Robin Schaefer and Manfred Stede. 2022. Gercct: An annotated corpus for mining arguments in german tweets on climate change. In *Proceedings of the Thirteenth Language Resources and Evaluation Conference, LREC 2022, Marseille, France, 20-25 June 2022*, pages 6121–6130. European Language Resources Association.

Raphael Scheible, Johann Frei, Fabian Thomczyk, Henry He, Patric Tippmann, Jochen Knaus, Victor Jaravine, Frank Kramer, and Martin Boeker. 2024. Gottbert: a pure german language model. In *Proceedings of the 2024 Conference on Empirical Methods in Natural Language Processing, EMNLP 2024, Miami, FL, USA, November 12-16, 2024*, pages 21237–21250. Association for Computational Linguistics.

Reid Swanson, Brian Ecker, and Marilyn A. Walker. 2015. Argument mining: Extracting arguments from online dialogue. In *Proceedings of the SIGDIAL 2015 Conference, The 16th Annual Meeting of the Special Interest Group on Discourse and Dialogue, 2-4 September 2015, Prague, Czech Republic*, pages 217–226. The Association for Computer Linguistics.

Stephen E Toulmin. 2003. *The uses of argument*. Cambridge university press.

Hugo Touvron, Louis Martin, Kevin Stone, Peter Albert, Amjad Almahairi, Yasmine Babaei, Nikolay Bashlykov, Soumya Batra, Prajjwal Bhargava, Shruti Bhosale, et al. 2023. Llama 2: Open foundation and fine-tuned chat models. *arXiv preprint arXiv:2307.09288*.

Terri L Towner and Caroline Lego Muñoz. 2018. Picture perfect? the role of instagram in issue agenda setting during the 2016 presidential primary campaign. *Social science computer review*, 36(4):484–499.

Michelle Tye, Carmen Leong, Felix Tan, Barney Tan, and Ying Hooi Khoo. 2018. Social media for empowerment in social movements: the case of malaysia's grassroots activism. *Communications of the Association for Information Systems*, 42(1):15.

Joanne Waitoa, Regina Scheyvens, and Te Rina Warren. 2015. E-whanaungatanga: The role of social media in māori political empowerment. *AlterNative: An International Journal of Indigenous Peoples*, 11(1):45–58.

DN Walton. 2008. *Argumentation schemes*. Cambridge University Press.

Chang Woo-Young. 2005. Online civic participation, and political empowerment: Online media and public opinion formation in korea. *Media, Culture & Society*, 27(6):925–935.

Chang Woo-Young and Lee Won-Tae. 2006. Cyberactivism and political empowerment in civil society: A comparative analysis of korean cases: A comparative analysis of korean cases. *Korea Journal*, 46(4):136–167.

Serpil T Yuce, Nitin Agarwal, Rolf T Wigand, Merlyna Lim, and Rebecca S Robinson. 2014. Bridging women rights networks: Analyzing interconnected online collective actions. *Journal of Global Information Management (JGIM)*, 22(4):1–20.

Marc A Zimmerman and Julian Rappaport. 1988. Citizen participation, perceived control, and psychological empowerment. *American Journal of community psychology*, 16(5):725–750.

Interpretable Models for Detecting Linguistic Variation in Russian Media: Towards Unveiling Propagandistic Strategies during the Russo-Ukrainian War

Anastasiia Vestel
Saarland University
Saarbruecken, Germany
anastasiia.vestel@uni-saarland.de

Stefania Degaetano-Ortlieb
Saarland University
Saarbruecken, Germany
s.degaetano@mx.uni-saarland.de

Abstract

With the start of the full-scale Russian invasion of Ukraine in February 2022, the spread of pro-Kremlin propaganda increased to justify the war, both in the official state media and social media. This position paper explores the theoretical background of propaganda detection in the given context and proposes a thorough methodology to investigate how language has been strategically manipulated to align with ideological goals and adapt to the changing narrative surrounding the invasion. Using the WarMM-2022 corpus, the study seeks to identify linguistic patterns across media types and their evolution over time. By doing so, we aim to enhance the understanding of the role of linguistic strategies in shaping propaganda narratives. The findings are intended to contribute to the broader discussion of information manipulation in politically sensitive contexts.

1 Introduction

The Russo-Ukrainian war has intensified the need to understand media manipulation and its societal impacts. There has been an increased number of endeavors for propaganda detection, in general and on the Russo-Ukrainian war specifically. Since language variation can be driven by external factors such as social, political, or cultural influences, studying linguistic change in the context of propaganda can help detect it more accurately. This argument is further supported by the fact that disinformation changes and evolves over time (Adriani, 2019), as is the case with Russian propaganda (Solopova et al., 2023a), which has been used by the government to justify the invasion and gain support from its population. Moreover, research has shown that linguistic change can occur not only diachronically, but also across diverse contexts, such as different political viewpoints (Azarbonyad et al., 2017; Ustyianovych and Barbosa, 2024). By comparing traditional mass media, i.e., press and TV, with social media in Russia, Alyukov et al. (2024) found that propaganda frames[1] differ between these two text types: state media are targeted at more passive audiences, whereas social media seek to convince those searching for alternative sources of information. This suggests that there might be fewer regime supporters on social media, and thus the political stance of the users might differ between the two text types.

This paper presents a research framework to analyze Russian state-controlled media and social media, which will allow us to answer the following research questions: (1) how language in these two text types linguistically differs and might reflect propaganda strategies (e.g., the use of euphemisms); (2) how it might have changed over time. As a result, we expect to see linguistic variations between the two media types, since they use distinct propaganda frames and strategies. Specifically, we might find a tendency towards euphemistic choices to prevail in state-controlled media texts in comparison to social media posts, such as by replacing *war* with *special military operation* (the former term is less likely to be propaganda, cf. Park et al., 2022; Solopova et al., 2023a). Additionally, by conducting our analysis, we anticipate to trace the diachronic evolution of Russian propaganda about the war in Ukraine.

Even though propaganda and disinformation detection is a common natural language processing (NLP) task, few studies have focused on linguistic change as a possible indicator of information manipulation. Furthermore, recent research relies on transformer-based architectures exploiting contextual embeddings for propaganda detection and classification into techniques (e.g., Hein, 2023).

[1] According to Entman (1993), to frame is to "select some aspects of a perceived reality and make them more salient in a communicating text, in such a way as to promote a particular problem definition, causal interpretation, moral evaluation, and/or treatment recommendation for the item described" (Entman, 1993, p. 52).

Proceedings of LaTeCH-CLfL 2025, pages 109–116
May 4, 2025

While these methods perform relatively well, they heavily rely on annotated data and explainability remains a major issue, as they do not allow fully capturing on which basis the classification of propagandistic texts is motivated (cf. Da San Martino et al., 2021; Park et al., 2022). In this study, besides using word embeddings, we also propose interpretable methods applied to the analysis of language variation and change. Word embeddings (Mikolov et al., 2013; Hamilton et al., 2016) will allow us to model semantic shifts. Kullback-Leibler Divergence (KLD; Kullback and Leibler, 1951) is employed to detect and analyze features contributing to change across linguistic levels (Hughes et al., 2012; Bochkarev et al., 2014; Fankhauser et al., 2014; Klingenstein et al., 2014; Degaetano-Ortlieb and Teich, 2022). To capture more nuanced changes in the local linguistic context, we use surprisal, which models the (un)expectedness of words in particular contexts (Hale, 2001). The combination of these methods would help us detect distinctive features of linguistic change, providing highly interpretable results. Their detailed description is provided in Section 4.

2 Related Work

Since the beginning of Russia's full-scale invasion of Ukraine, there have been a number of attempts to combat Russian propaganda with the help of NLP techniques. Some studies applied both traditional and neural machine learning to detect pro-Kremlin propaganda with promising results (Vanetik et al., 2023; Solopova et al., 2023b, 2024). Arguing that dehumanization leads to extreme violence, Burovova and Romanyshyn (2024) trained a few binary classifiers to detect dehumanizing language of Ukrainians on Russian social media, with the SpERT model outperforming the rest.

Other studies delved into the computational analysis of Russian propaganda about the war. For instance, Alyukov et al. (2023) created the Wartime Media Monitor (WarMM-2022) corpus, which includes publications on the Russo-Ukrainian war and consists of two parts: state media and social media, and used it to analyze major propaganda themes and strategies. In their later study, Alyukov et al. (2024), by working on the same dataset, explored the differences between propaganda frames representing diverse semantic entities in the two subcorpora. They identified the following frames: dependence (the narrative about Ukraine's dependence on the West), dehumanization (using dehumanizing language towards Ukrainians), normalization (downplaying the effects of the war on the everyday life in Russia), and disinformation (presenting news from Ukraine and the West as fake). The researchers found that the press and TV applied the dehumanization frame (which is in line with the results reported by Burovova and Romanyshyn, 2024), as well as dependence and normalization, while social media used the disinformation frame. These strategies, on the one hand, aimed to pacify the regime supporters who mostly consumed traditional media, and on the other hand, tried to mobilize the users of social media by employing the disinformation frame. The findings by Solopova et al. (2023a) also confirmed that the mobilization strategy was used by the government to target the Russian population. This indicates that the two text types are distinct from each other, as they are aimed at different audiences (at the semantic as well as other linguistic levels).

Similarly, Park et al. (2022) analyzed the media effects of Russian news about the war; however, instead of comparing press and TV with social media, they looked into state-affiliated and independent outlets on two online platforms, VKontakte and Twitter. They found that since the start of the full-scale invasion, independent media outlets have predominantly used the term *war*, while state-affiliated outlets have frequently opted for the euphemism *(special military) operation*. The same difference was observed by Ustyianovych and Barbosa (2024) between pro-Russian and pro-Ukrainian Telegram channels, indicating that political opinions might influence semantic choices and phrasing. Using the term *special military operation* was also given as an example of the normalization propaganda frame by Alyukov et al. (2024). This is in line with Solopova et al.'s (2023a) results, who trained two classifiers based on SVM and BERT to detect pro-Kremlin propaganda, and found that the word *war* was highly predictive for both models, meaning that a text containing it was more likely to be labeled as not propagandistic. The authors explain it by the fact that this term was deliberately avoided by government officials and even became illegal in Russia. Consequently, it rarely appeared in pro-Kremlin news, which relied on euphemisms instead.

Apart from linguistic variation between the state-affiliated and independent media, Park et al. (2022) also observed differences in the two platforms

(VKontakte vs. Twitter, particularly divergent framing strategies), as well as across time (before vs. after the beginning of the full-scale invasion, e.g., an increase of frequency of terms related to war). This confirms Azarbonyad et al.'s (2017) hypothesis that semantic change can occur both diachronically and in distinct contexts, such as divergent political viewpoints. Since traditional media and social media may reflect differences in the stance of the users, we presume that language might also vary between these two text types.

Diachronic variation of war narratives was also analyzed by Solopova et al. (2023a), who looked at the evolution of pro-Kremlin propaganda within the first year of the full-scale invasion. Compared to the beginning of 2022, they found an increase in the use of the term *Kyiv Regime*, claims, assertive words, adverbs, and other high-modality words, as well as the mention of the West and negotiations on Russian Telegram at the start of 2023. In contrast, *special military operation*, negotiations, sanctions, genocide, fake news, and Belarus were discussed less frequently in the Russian state-run media in 2023 in comparison with 2022. In a similar vein, Burovova and Romanyshyn (2024) observed varying temporal dynamics of the dehumanization rhetoric, whose changes coincided with important events before or after the start of the full-scale invasion. In particular, they found that certain types of dehumanization began to rise shortly before the invasion and declined at its onset, suggesting that dehumanization plays a preparatory role in legitimizing acts of genocide. These developments reveal important shifts in propagandistic narratives over time.

3 Data

For our pilot study, we are using the WarMM-2022 corpus (Alyukov et al., 2023), which is a collection of 1.7M posts on the Russo-Ukrainian war. Our motivation for choosing it is two-fold. Firstly, the corpus includes two text types targeting different audiences. The state-controlled mass media include 24.4M tokens of press and 1.7M tokens of TV transcripts, and their style is more formal. Social media posts consist of 268.4M tokens and are characterized by limited governmental control and less formal register. Whereas the former text type promotes state-imposed propaganda, the latter includes both publications by regime supporters and anti-government voices. These differences between the text types would allow us to study linguistic variation in divergent contexts. Secondly, the WarMM-2022 corpus is diachronic: the state media subcorpus covers the period from February until September 2022, whereas the posts on social media span from July to September 2022, which is useful for analyzing linguistic change over time.

4 Proposed Methodology

4.1 Measuring Divergence Between Media Types and Time

To measure how much the two text types of the WarMM-2022 corpus (state vs. social media) differ from each other and by which linguistic features, we use KLD (Kullback and Leibler, 1951). KLD is used to quantify the divergence between two probability distributions of linguistic features. Using the whole lexicon to depict the lexical level, as well as vocabulary subsets such as content words, part-of-speech tags, etc. to represent more abstract linguistic levels, we implement KLD on the two probability distributions: *State* (for state media) and *Social* (for social media).

We apply KLD to the WarMM-2022 corpus comparing probability distributions of text types and diachronically by using various linguistic features. The probability distribution is based on the unigram probability of a linguistic feature (e.g., a word) to occur in one or the other sub-corpus. In general, KLD measures the number of additional bits needed to encode one distribution with the other distribution. For example, KLD of *State* given *Social* is measured as:

$$D(\text{State} \parallel \text{Social}) = \sum_i p(\text{feature}_i \mid \text{State}) \log_2 \frac{p(\text{feature}_i \mid \text{State})}{p(\text{feature}_i \mid \text{Social})}$$

In this equation, $p(\text{feature}_i \mid \text{State})$ stands for the i-th linguistic feature in the *State* distribution and $p(\text{feature}_i \mid \text{Social})$ for the i-th feature in the *Social* distribution. As the overall divergence is a sum of the individual divergences of each feature, we get to know how much linguistic features contribute to divergence-revealing features that are disproportionately emphasized in one corpus relative to the other. In comparison to using mere frequency, with KLD we are also able to detect low-frequency but distinctive features of variation (cf. Degaetano-Ortlieb et al., 2021).

Previous studies have demonstrated KLD's utility in analyzing linguistic variation and change, enabling comparisons of linguistic features across registers (Fankhauser et al., 2014), styles (Hughes et al., 2012), social variables and combinations of these (Degaetano-Ortlieb et al., 2021) as well as linguistic differences in criminal trials (Klingenstein et al., 2014), and word frequency shifts across languages (Bochkarev et al., 2014).

By applying KLD to the WarMM-2022 corpus, we expect to see some differences between the two text types. Furthermore, KLD can be applied to investigate diachronic linguistic change. For instance, Degaetano-Ortlieb and Teich (2022), who explored the evolution of scientific English, showed that external factors such as new scientific discoveries influenced the vocabulary of the language, which was reflected by peaks in KLD. Therefore, this method can help us study how linguistic strategies of propaganda shifted over time. Overall, KLD will offer us a nuanced perspective on how narratives adapt to audience and platform constraints and evolve diachronically.

We argue that KLD offers interpretability advantages over more opaque machine learning methods in detecting divergent language use which can be mapped to propaganda techniques and provides a deeper understanding of how these techniques are linguistically construed and evolve over time. While neural models achieve high accuracy, their reliance on labeled data and challenges in domain transfer limits adaptability to novel datasets and hardly allows analyzing linguistic choices. In contrast, KLD's reliance on probability distributions aligns with the FAIR (Findable, Accessible, Interoperable and Reusable) principles, enabling reproducibility and transparency in computational linguistics research.

4.2 Surprisal

According to information theory, information is defined as unpredictability within a given context, often described as surprisal (Hale, 2001). Surprisal quantifies the degree of unexpectedness of a unit, such as a word in a sequence, based on its preceding context. It is expressed in bits, with higher values indicating greater unpredictability and lower values reflecting higher predictability. For instance, in the context of Russian propaganda, the surprisal of the word *operation* given *special military* would be measured as follows:

$$S(\text{operation}) = -\log_2 p(\text{operation} \mid \text{special military})$$

Since the term *special military operation* was introduced at the beginning of the full-scale invasion, we hypothesize that the surprisal of the word *operation* in the given context will be higher in February 2022, but it will drop in the following months, indicating the conventionalized usage of this term in state-imposed propaganda.

Surprisal has been applied in a number of studies on language change, e.g., to trace the evolution of scientific English (Teich et al., 2021; Degaetano-Ortlieb and Teich, 2022; Steuer et al., 2024) and to analyze linguistic variation in Early Modern English (Gergel et al., 2017), suggesting the validity of this method for this task.

4.3 Word Embeddings

In distributional semantics, words are represented as vectors in a space based on their co-occurrence patterns, allowing their representations to be compared across different periods (Hamilton et al., 2016). Word embeddings are a commonly used method to study semantic change (Hamilton et al., 2016; Bizzoni et al., 2020; Giulianelli et al., 2020; Montariol et al., 2021). It has also been applied to examine linguistic variation in political and social contexts (Azarbonyad et al., 2017; Garg et al., 2018; Wevers, 2019; Marjanen et al., 2019; Tripodi et al., 2019), including the Russo-Ukrainian war (Ustyianovych and Barbosa, 2024).

We also believe that word embeddings are useful for investigating semantic shifts that might reveal propaganda strategies. For example, Russia has been using the narrative of "Nazi Ukraine" to justify its invasion, claiming that the current Ukrainian government commits genocide against Russians (Fortuin, 2022). By visualizing the word *Nazi* in the semantic space, we anticipate that it will be closer to words related to Nazi Germany and World War II before or at the very beginning of the full-scale invasion, but afterward, this word will probably be more strongly associated with Ukraine, its government and people.

5 Preliminary and Expected Results

Drawing from Alyukov et al.'s (2024) work, we anticipate finding differences and/or similarities between state and social media, as well as tracing the evolution of Russian propaganda over time by applying the above-mentioned methods. This would allow us to study linguistic change both diachronically and across media types. We might also gain insights into the interplay between the text types. Specifically, narratives that originate in the official media might influence social media discourse. This could happen through the repetition and reinforcement of state-approved messages by pro-government social media users and the dissemination of mainstream propaganda by bots or paid commentators (Alyukov et al., 2023).

As the first step of our pilot study, we conducted some experiments by applying KLD to a small subset of the WarMM-2022 corpus, and we could already see some of the results we expected. Specifically, we compared the usage of nouns in social and state media posts from July 30 and 31, 2022 (approx. 2 million nouns). While the direct term война[2] is the most distinctive noun for social media, state media mostly uses opaque euphemisms like спецоперация[3], ситуация[4] and демилитаризация[5]. This is in line with previous studies, which showed a clear distinction between the words denoting the war used in propagandistic or non-propagandistic texts (Solopova et al., 2023a), pro-Russian or pro-Ukrainian news (Ustyianovych and Barbosa, 2024) and state-affiliated or independent outlets (Park et al., 2022). Another interesting observation is that there is a high contribution of words such as правда[6] and факт[7] to the language of social media, as opposed to that of press and TV. This could indicate the government's efforts to employ the disinformation frame, which, as was shown by Alyukov et al. (2024), is predominant on social media as a means to discourage users from seeking out other sources of news that contradict the pro-Kremlin narratives.

In the future, we plan to do a more comprehensive KLD analysis comparing state and social media posts from the whole WarMM-2022 corpus, as well as studying diachronic linguistic change in the context of propaganda and applying other methods mentioned in Section 4, namely surprisal and word embeddings. As a more ambitious goal, we hope that our work will contribute towards combating disinformation, specifically in war contexts. In terms of practical applications of our methodology, we expect it could be employed in studying other political or historical events.

[2] [voyna] — *war*.

[3] [spetsoperatsiya] — an abbreviation from "special [military] operation".

[4] [situatsiya] — *situation*, as in "situation in Ukraine".

[5] [demilitarizatsiya] — *demilitarization*, a term used by the Russian government to justify its invasion of Ukraine.

[6] [pravda] — *truth*.

[7] [fakt] — *fact*.

6 Conclusion

This work underscores the potential of open, transparent methodologies to democratize access to knowledge and foster resilience against disinformation. By leveraging interpretable methods such as KLD, surprisal, and word embeddings, our study aims to provide a robust framework for detecting and analyzing propaganda strategies in Russian state-controlled and social media.

By systematically examining linguistic change both across text types and over time, our study contributes to a deeper understanding of propaganda mechanisms and their societal implications. It also highlights the importance of combining interpretability and reproducibility in computational linguistics research, particularly in political contexts.

In addition to its academic contributions, this research has significant practical implications. It equips researchers, policymakers, and media analysts with tools to critically examine information landscapes and identify deliberate attempts to influence public opinion. Ultimately, by demonstrating how linguistic change can be an indicator of propagandistic strategies, we aim to advance efforts to counteract disinformation and enhance media literacy.

7 Future Work

We use KLD, surprisal, and word embeddings for a preliminary analysis of propagandistic narratives, which would reveal certain linguistic features that drive change in this domain. In future studies, we might also use graph neural networks, as they have been shown to provide promising and interpretable results in semantic change (Chen et al., 2023) and disinformation detection (Panayotov et al., 2022). We also plan to consider a combination of these methods as a complementary means to transformer-based approaches, specifically, by using machine learning methods to detect propaganda. Possible directions include classifying news into fake or real (as in Solopova et al., 2024), pro- or anti-regime (similar to Ustyianovych and Barbosa, 2024), and according to propaganda frames (following the work by Alyukov et al., 2024). Potentially, we might extend our research and analyze not only linguistic change of propaganda across time and text types, but also how narratives about the war differ between languages such as Russian, Ukrainian, and English, representing another dimension of linguistic variation. Finally, we could also investigate pro-Kremlin propaganda that preceded the full-scale invasion of Ukraine in 2022, e.g., since the start of the war in Donbas in 2014.

8 Challenges and Limitations

Propaganda detection is a complicated task not only for computers but even for humans, as many people fall victim to information manipulation in today's enormous influx of news in media. First of all, there is no single definition of propaganda in general or a single framework for detecting it with NLP techniques. We aim to address these challenges by providing a working definition of propaganda based on previous research in the field, as well as proposing a thorough methodology for tackling it computationally. Secondly, propaganda identification can be biased, as it depends on the political stance of the researcher. To eliminate any possible bias, we again plan to rely on related work and use data-driven approaches to detect propaganda, which were described in Section 4.

9 Ethical Considerations

Propaganda and war are highly sensitive topics. However, since we are using an already available corpus of news on the Russo-Ukrainian war (WarMM-2022), our research does not involve human participants (e.g., to annotate texts as propaganda or not), thus eliminating any ethical concerns in this regard. In the future, we might also use other datasets that were employed in previous research on the topic of the Russian invasion of Ukraine.

10 Acknowledgments

Funded by the European Union. Views and opinions expressed are however those of the authors only and do not necessarily reflect those of the European Union or European Research Executive Agency (REA). Neither the European Union nor the granting authority can be held responsible for them.

We sincerely thank Maria Kunilovskaya for providing the WarMM-2022 dataset, which has been invaluable for our research.

References

Roberto Adriani. 2019. The Evolution of Fake News and the Abuse of Emerging Technologies. *European Journal of Social Sciences*, 2(1):18–24.

Maxim Alyukov, Maria Kunilovskaya, and Andrei Semenov. 2023. Wartime Media Monitor (WarMM-2022): A Study of Information Manipulation on Russian Social Media during the Russia-Ukraine War. In *Proceedings of the 7th Joint SIGHUM Workshop on Computational Linguistics for Cultural Heritage, Social Sciences, Humanities and Literature*, pages 152–161, Dubrovnik, Croatia. Association for Computational Linguistics.

Maxim Alyukov, Maria Kunilovskaya, and Andrei Semenov. 2024. Confuse and Normalise: Authoritarian Propaganda in a High-Choice Media Environment and Russia's Invasion of Ukraine. In Paul Goode, editor, *Russian Propaganda Today: Challenges, Effectiveness, and Resistance*, page in print. University of Michigan press, University of Manchester Press.

Hosein Azarbonyad, Mostafa Dehghani, Kaspar Beelen, Alexandra Arkut, Maarten Marx, and Jaap Kamps. 2017. Words are Malleable: Computing Semantic Shifts in Political and Media Discourse. In *Proceedings of the 2017 ACM on Conference on Information and Knowledge Management*, CIKM '17, pages 1509–1518, New York, NY, USA. Association for Computing Machinery.

Yuri Bizzoni, Stefania Degaetano-Ortlieb, Peter Fankhauser, and Elke Teich. 2020. Linguistic Variation and Change in 250 Years of English Scientific Writing: A Data-Driven Approach. *Frontiers in Artificial Intelligence*, 3:73.

Vladimir Bochkarev, Valery D. Solovyev, and Søren Wichmann. 2014. Universals versus Historical Contingencies in Lexical Evolution. *Journal of The Royal Society Interface*, 11(101):20140841.

Kateryna Burovova and Mariana Romanyshyn. 2024. Computational Analysis of Dehumanization of Ukrainians on Russian Social Media. In *Proceedings of the 8th Joint SIGHUM Workshop on Computational Linguistics for Cultural Heritage, Social Sciences, Humanities and Literature (LaTeCH-CLfL 2024)*, pages 28–39, St. Julians, Malta. Association for Computational Linguistics.

Jing Chen, Emmanuele Chersoni, Dominik Schlechtweg, Jelena Prokic, and Chu-Ren Huang. 2023. ChiWUG: A Graph-based Evaluation Dataset for Chinese Lexical Semantic Change Detection. In *Proceedings of the 4th Workshop on Computational Approaches to Historical Language Change*, pages 93–99, Singapore. Association for Computational Linguistics.

Giovanni Da San Martino, Stefano Cresci, Alberto Barrón-Cedeño, Seunghak Yu, Roberto Di Pietro, and Preslav Nakov. 2021. A Survey on Computational Propaganda Detection. In *Proceedings of the Twenty-Ninth International Joint Conference on Artificial Intelligence*, IJCAI'20, pages 4826–4832, Yokohama, Yokohama, Japan.

Stefania Degaetano-Ortlieb, Tanja Säily, and Yuri Bizzoni. 2021. Registerial Adaptation vs. Innovation

Across Situational Contexts: 18th Century Women in Transition. *Frontiers in Artificial Intelligence*, 4:609970.

Stefania Degaetano-Ortlieb and Elke Teich. 2022. Toward an Optimal Code for Communication: The Case of Scientific English. *Corpus Linguistics and Linguistic Theory*, 18(1):175–207.

Robert M. Entman. 1993. Framing: Toward Clarification of a Fractured Paradigm. *Journal of Communication*, 43(4):51–58.

Peter Fankhauser, Jörg Knappen, and Elke Teich. 2014. Exploring and Visualizing Variation in Language Resources. In *Proceedings of the Ninth International Conference on Language Resources and Evaluation (LREC'14)*, pages 4125–4128, Reykjavik, Iceland. European Language Resources Association (ELRA).

Egbert Fortuin. 2022. "Ukraine Commits Genocide on Russians": The Term "Genocide" in Russian Propaganda. *Russian Linguistics*, 46(3):313–347.

Nikhil Garg, Londa Schiebinger, Dan Jurafsky, and James Zou. 2018. Word Embeddings Quantify 100 Years of Gender and Ethnic Stereotypes. *Proceedings of the National Academy of Sciences*, 115(16):E3635–E3644.

Remus Gergel, Martin Kopf-Giammanco, and Julia Masloh. 2017. Surprisal and Satisfaction: Towards an Information-theoretic Characterization of Presuppositions with a Diachronic Application. In *IWCS 2017 - 12th International Conference on Computational Semantics - Short Papers, Montpellier, France, September 19 - 22, 2017*. The Association for Computer Linguistics.

Mario Giulianelli, Marco Del Tredici, and Raquel Fernández. 2020. Analysing Lexical Semantic Change with Contextualised Word Representations. In *Proceedings of the 58th Annual Meeting of the Association for Computational Linguistics*, pages 3960–3973, Online. Association for Computational Linguistics.

John Hale. 2001. A Probabilistic Earley Parser as a Psycholinguistic Model. In *Proceedings of the Second Meeting of the North American Chapter of the Association for Computational Linguistics on Language Technologies*, NAACL '01, pages 1–8, USA. Association for Computational Linguistics.

William L. Hamilton, Jure Leskovec, and Dan Jurafsky. 2016. Diachronic Word Embeddings Reveal Statistical Laws of Semantic Change. In *Proceedings of the 54th Annual Meeting of the Association for Computational Linguistics (Volume 1: Long Papers)*, pages 1489–1501, Berlin, Germany. Association for Computational Linguistics.

Vitalij Hein. 2023. *Propaganda Detection in Russian and American News Coverage about the War in Ukraine through Text Classification*. Thesis, Technische Universität Wien.

James M. Hughes, Nicholas J. Foti, David C. Krakauer, and Daniel N. Rockmore. 2012. Quantitative Patterns of Stylistic Influence in the Evolution of Literature. *Proceedings of the National Academy of Sciences*, 109(20):7682–7686.

Sara Klingenstein, Tim Hitchcock, and Simon DeDeo. 2014. The Civilizing Process in London's Old Bailey. *Proceedings of the National Academy of Sciences*, 111(26):9419–9424.

Solomon Kullback and Richard A. Leibler. 1951. On Information and Sufficiency. *The Annals of Mathematical Statistics*, 22(1):79–86.

Jani Marjanen, Lidia Pivovarova, Elaine Zosa, and Jussi Kurunmäki. 2019. Clustering Ideological Terms in Historical Newspaper Data with Diachronic Word Embeddings: HistoInformatics2019 - the 5th International Workshop on Computational History. *HistoInformatics 2019 : International Workshop on Computational History 2019*, pages 21–29.

Tomás Mikolov, Kai Chen, Greg Corrado, and Jeffrey Dean. 2013. Efficient Estimation of Word Representations in Vector Space. In *1st International Conference on Learning Representations, ICLR 2013, Scottsdale, Arizona, USA, May 2-4, 2013, Workshop Track Proceedings*.

Syrielle Montariol, Matej Martinc, and Lidia Pivovarova. 2021. Scalable and Interpretable Semantic Change Detection. In *Proceedings of the 2021 Conference of the North American Chapter of the Association for Computational Linguistics: Human Language Technologies*, pages 4642–4652, Online. Association for Computational Linguistics.

Panayot Panayotov, Utsav Shukla, Husrev Taha Sencar, Mohamed Nabeel, and Preslav Nakov. 2022. GREENER: Graph Neural Networks for News Media Profiling. In *Proceedings of the 2022 Conference on Empirical Methods in Natural Language Processing*, pages 7470–7480, Abu Dhabi, United Arab Emirates. Association for Computational Linguistics.

Chan Young Park, Julia Mendelsohn, Anjalie Field, and Yulia Tsvetkov. 2022. Challenges and Opportunities in Information Manipulation Detection: An Examination of Wartime Russian Media. In *Findings of the Association for Computational Linguistics: EMNLP 2022*, pages 5209–5235, Abu Dhabi, United Arab Emirates. Association for Computational Linguistics.

Veronika Solopova, Christoph Benzmüller, and Tim Landgraf. 2023a. The Evolution of Pro-Kremlin Propaganda From a Machine Learning and Linguistics Perspective. In *Proceedings of the Second Ukrainian Natural Language Processing Workshop (UNLP)*, pages 40–48, Dubrovnik, Croatia. Association for Computational Linguistics.

Veronika Solopova, Viktoriia Herman, Christoph Benzmüller, and Tim Landgraf. 2024. Check News in One Click: NLP-Empowered Pro-Kremlin Propaganda Detection. In *Proceedings of the 18th Conference of the European Chapter of the Association for Computational Linguistics: System Demonstrations*, pages 44–51, St. Julians, Malta. Association for Computational Linguistics.

Veronika Solopova, Oana-Iuliana Popescu, Christoph Benzmüller, and Tim Landgraf. 2023b. Automated Multilingual Detection of Pro-Kremlin Propaganda in Newspapers and Telegram Posts. *Datenbank-Spektrum*, 23(1):5–14.

Julius Steuer, Marie-Pauline Krielke, Stefan Fischer, Stefania Degaetano-Ortlieb, Marius Mosbach, and Dietrich Klakow. 2024. Modeling Diachronic Change in English Scientific Writing over 300+ Years with Transformer-based Language Model Surprisal. In *Proceedings of the 17th Workshop on Building and Using Comparable Corpora (BUCC) @ LREC-COLING 2024*, pages 12–23, Torino, Italia. ELRA and ICCL.

Elke Teich, Peter Fankhauser, Stefania Degaetano-Ortlieb, and Yuri Bizzoni. 2021. Less is More/More Diverse: On The Communicative Utility of Linguistic Conventionalization. *Frontiers in Communication*, 5. Publisher: Frontiers.

Rocco Tripodi, Massimo Warglien, Simon Levis Sullam, and Deborah Paci. 2019. Tracing Antisemitic Language Through Diachronic Embedding Projections: France 1789-1914. In *Proceedings of the 1st International Workshop on Computational Approaches to Historical Language Change*, pages 115–125, Florence, Italy. Association for Computational Linguistics.

Taras Ustyianovych and Denilson Barbosa. 2024. Instant Messaging Platforms News Multi-Task Classification for Stance, Sentiment, and Discrimination Detection. In *Proceedings of the Third Ukrainian Natural Language Processing Workshop (UNLP) @ LREC-COLING 2024*, pages 30–40, Torino, Italia. ELRA and ICCL.

Natalia Vanetik, Marina Litvak, Egor Reviakin, and Margarita Tyamanova. 2023. Propaganda Detection in Russian Telegram Posts in the Scope of the Russian Invasion of Ukraine. In *Proceedings of the Conference Recent Advances in Natural Language Processing - Large Language Models for Natural Language Processings*, pages 1162–1170. INCOMA Ltd., Shoumen, BULGARIA.

Melvin Wevers. 2019. Using Word Embeddings to Examine Gender Bias in Dutch Newspapers, 1950-1990. In *Proceedings of the 1st International Workshop on Computational Approaches to Historical Language Change*, pages 92–97, Florence, Italy. Association for Computational Linguistics.

Tuning Into Bias: A Computational Study of Gender Bias in Song Lyrics

Danqing Chen*, **Adithi Satish***, **Rasul Khanbayov***, **Carolin M. Schuster**, **Georg Groh**

Technical University of Munich
Munich, Germany,

{chen.danqing, adithi.satish, rasul.khanbayov, carolin.schuster}@tum.de, grohg@in.tum.de

Abstract

The application of text mining methods is becoming increasingly prevalent, particularly within Humanities and Computational Social Sciences, as well as in a broader range of disciplines. This paper presents an analysis of gender bias in English song lyrics using topic modeling and bias measurement techniques. Leveraging BERTopic, we cluster a dataset of 537,553 English songs into distinct topics and analyze their temporal evolution. Our results reveal a significant thematic shift in song lyrics over time, transitioning from romantic themes to a heightened focus on the sexualization of women. Additionally, we observe a substantial prevalence of profanity and misogynistic content across various topics, with a particularly high concentration in the largest thematic cluster. To further analyse gender bias across topics and genres in a quantitative way, we employ the Single Category Word Embedding Association Test (SC-WEAT) to calculate bias scores for word embeddings trained on the most prominent topics as well as individual genres. The results indicate a consistent male bias in words associated with intelligence and strength, while appearance and weakness words show a female bias. Further analysis highlights variations in these biases across topics, illustrating the interplay between thematic content and gender stereotypes in song lyrics.

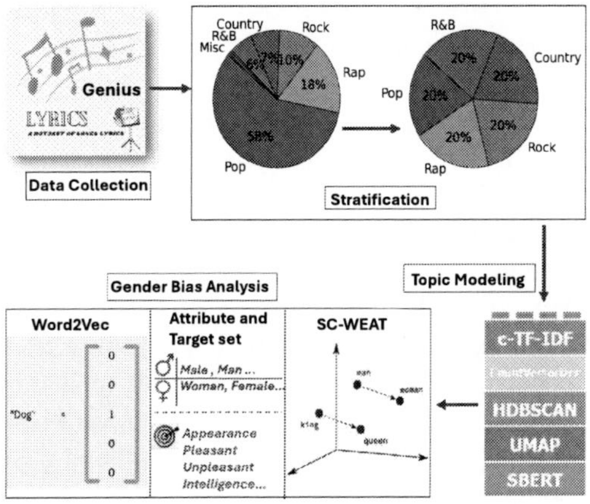

Figure 1: Detailed workflow including data collection, topic modeling, and SC-WEAT.

1 Introduction

Disclaimer: Lyrics in the dataset may include explicit or vulgar language, which is inherently reflected in the topic labels generated by the BERTopic model. This does not represent the views or opinions of the authors.

Music is integrally tied with gender identity, where lyrics, melodies, and performance styles can reflect and shape societal perceptions of gender roles, stereotypes, and experiences (Flynn et al., 2016; Colley, 2008; Alexander, 1999). Through lyrics, artists have a way of expressing their emotions and discussing unique themes. While these themes often span a wide variety of issues, they can also propagate dangerous stereotypes and objectification (Rasmussen and Densley, 2017; Hall et al., 2011; Frisby and Behm-Morawitz, 2019; Smiler et al., 2017a), pointing out the need to critically examine these gender biases that can occur in lyrics.

Natural Language Processing (NLP) techniques provide a robust framework for analyzing song lyrics by leveraging their underlying textual structure to extract thematic patterns and gender-associated linguistic representations (Betti et al., 2023). In particular, word embeddings (Bengio Y, 2000), which encode lexical items as dense, high-dimensional vectors within a continuous space, have been shown to effectively capture and encode latent linguistic biases that align with human cognitive associations (Caliskan et al., 2017; Qin and Tam, 2023). This representational property renders word embeddings a powerful com-

*These authors contributed equally to this work

Proceedings of LaTeCH-CLfL 2025, pages 117–129
May 4, 2025

putational tool for systematically quantifying and analyzing gender biases embedded within lyrical discourse (Boghrati and Berger, 2022).

While previous research has primarily analyzed gender bias at the artist level by comparing the lyrics of songs performed by male and female artists (Anglada-Tort et al., 2021; Betti et al., 2023; Boghrati and Berger, 2023), this study does not differentiate based on the artist's gender. Instead, we focus solely on examining bias within the lyrics themselves. By integrating topic modelling with quantitative bias measurement, this approach facilitates a granular analysis of gender bias across themes and genres, utilizing NLP to bridge the gap in Humanities and Social Sciences to analyze complex text-based artefacts and their sociocultural implications.

Topic modeling is a powerful technique for uncovering the underlying themes within a corpus, such as song lyrics in our study (Kleedorfer et al., 2008). In this paper, we employ BERTopic (Grootendorst, 2022), a state-of-the-art topic modeling method, to analyze persistent lyrical themes across various genres and examine their evolution over multiple decades. This approach enables us to uncover critical insights, including the increasing sexualization of women in song lyrics over time and the notable prevalence of profanity, particularly in rap music. While the topic model provides a broad overview of the gender bias in lyrics, we also take a more fine-grained look into this bias by applying the SC-WEAT analysis to quantify it and evaluate the associations of specific target word sets with gender-related attributes (Mikolov et al., 2013; Caliskan et al., 2017). Our major contributions, as depicted in the workflow diagram in Figure 1, are:

- Conducting topic analysis on a stratified sample of song lyrics to identify cross-genre themes, recurrent topics, and the historical evolution of gender bias.
- Evaluating the prevalence and variation of gender bias in lyrics quantitatively across topics and genres through the computation of SC-WEAT scores.

2 Related Work

The intersection of music and natural language processing (NLP) has been the focus of extensive research, encompassing tasks such as mood classification, music transcription, lyrics and melody generation, among others (Laurier et al., 2008; Benetos et al., 2018; Chen and Lerch, 2020; Yu et al., 2021). Music — and, by extension, lyrics — constitutes a valuable resource for investigating underlying societal dynamics, particularly in the context of gender stereotypes and objectification (Flynn et al., 2016; Bretthauer et al., 2007; Smiler et al., 2017b; Boghrati and Berger, 2022).

Previous research has demonstrated that word embeddings are inherently susceptible to capturing and, in some cases, amplifying the social biases present in the data from which they are derived (Hovy and Prabhumoye, 2021). A well-known example provided by Bolukbasi et al. (2016) illustrates that the word embedding for "man" is more closely associated with "programmer," while "woman" is linked to "homemaker." Similarly, the findings of Durrheim et al. (2023) and Zhao et al. (2019) reveal that word embeddings encode implicit cultural and gender biases, even when such biases are not explicitly stated in the source data. This body of work highlights the critical importance of examining and addressing biases embedded in linguistic representations, especially when applied to cultural artifacts such as song lyrics.

In our paper, we quantify this gender bias using an extension of the Word Embedding Association Test (WEAT), the Single Category WEAT score (SC-WEAT) (Caliskan et al., 2017; Charlesworth et al., 2021; Betti et al., 2023). The SC-WEAT score is also used by Betti et al. (2023) and Boghrati and Berger (2023) to analyze the nature of gender bias in lyrics and the differences across artist genders. However, we expand on this approach by using topic modeling to identify popular and intriguing topics. We then analyze the gender bias in the lyrics on a per-topic as well as per-genre basis, aiming to uncover how this bias may vary across different themes.

Topic modeling is a widely used technique for clustering documents to summarize or classify them, enabling the identification of underlying social patterns within the data (Egger and Yu, 2022). When applied to song lyrics, it serves as an effective approach for uncovering recurring themes (Kleedorfer et al., 2008; Fell et al., 2023; Devi and Saharia, 2020; Karamouzi et al., 2024). While Latent Dirichlet Allocation (LDA) remains one of the most common methods for topic modeling, recent findings by Gan et al. (2023) demonstrate that BERTopic, introduced by Grootendorst (2022), outperforms traditional approaches by producing more distinctive and interpretable clusters.

BERTopic has also been successfully applied in gender and social science research. For example, Nakajima Wickham (2023) utilized the algorithm to examine gender expectations on social media and their influence on suicidal ideation. This demonstrates BERTopic's utility in the clustering of categories that are meaningful to societal and cultural dynamics.

3 Experimental Setup

3.1 Data

The dataset used for the lyric analysis is a combination of song metadata from the WASABI Song Corpus created by Fell et al. (2023), and English lyrical content from Genius Song Lyrics [1]. Our lyrics dataset includes data as recent as 2022 extracted from Genius, an online platform where users can upload and explain songs, poems, and even books but primarily focus on songs.

The final dataset consists of 537,553 song lyrics across five main genres and an additional miscellaneous category as described in Table 1.

Genre	Counts (% of dataset)
Pop	311,085 (58%)
Rap	94,234 (18%)
Rock	54,560 (10%)
Country	39,078 (7%)
R&B	30,747 (6%)
Misc	7,849 (1%)

Table 1: Counts of songs across genres in the dataset.

3.2 Topic Modeling with BERTopic

BERTopic leverages transformers to create clusters, providing more interpretable topic representations compared to traditional methods (Grootendorst, 2022). The algorithm creates topics in four steps, which involve (i) transforming the documents into embeddings using a pre-trained language model, (ii) reducing their dimensionality, (iii) clustering and finally, (iv) deriving the topic representations from these clusters using a class-based version of TF-IDF. For our analysis, we use the default configuration of BERTopic, which utilizes (i) all-MiniLM-L6-V2 [2], (ii) UMAP, (iii) HDBSCAN and (iv) c-TF-IDF for the four steps mentioned above [3].

BERTopic leverages c-TF-IDF (class-based Term Frequency-Inverse Document Frequency) to represent topics by weighting words based on their importance within a topic rather than across the entire corpus (Grootendorst, 2022). This approach emphasizes words that are not only frequent within a given topic but also capable of distinguishing that topic from others in the dataset. To optimize computational resources while preserving dataset representativeness, we train the BERTopic model on a stratified sample comprising 20,000 songs per genre and 7,849 "misc" entries. The model then predicts topic labels for the full corpus, which are subsequently analyzed for gender bias using SC-WEAT scores.

3.3 Bias Measurements - SC-WEAT

To analyze gender bias in lyrics, we quantify the bias by training word embeddings from scratch to compute their association scores, using an extension of the original WEAT score (Caliskan et al., 2017; Charlesworth et al., 2021), called the SC-WEAT score, which quantifies the relationship between a set of target words and two sets of attribute words (Betti et al., 2023).

SC-WEAT Score Formula: The association strength is calculated using the formula below, as proposed by Caliskan et al. (2017) and used by Betti et al. (2023):

$$s(w, A, B) = \text{mean}_{a \in A} \cos(\vec{w}, \vec{a}) - \text{mean}_{b \in B} \cos(\vec{w}, \vec{b}) \quad (1)$$

$$\text{SCWEAT}(X, A, B) = \sum_{x \in X} s(x, A, B) \quad (2)$$

$$d = \frac{\text{mean}_{xinX}\, s(x, A, B)}{\text{stddev}_{xinX}\, s(x, A, B)} \quad (3)$$

The cosine similarity *s(w,A,B)* is the difference between the mean cosine similarity of the word vector *w* to vectors in attribute sets *A* and *B*, respectively. The differential association, or effect size, is the normalized SC-WEAT score.

To compute SC-WEAT scores, we train Word2Vec embeddings for each genre and the top topic within each genre. Static embeddings, such as Word2Vec, are well-suited for analyzing aggregate biases within the data (Caliskan et al.,

[1] https://www.kaggle.com/datasets/carlosgdcj/genius-song-lyrics-with-language-information

[2] https://huggingface.co/sentence-transformers/all-MiniLM-L6-v2

[3] https://maartengr.github.io/BERTopic/algorithm/algorithm.html

Target Set	Examples of words in the word sets
Pleasant	"joy", "wonderful", "love", "peace"
Unpleasant	"terrible", "hatred", "nasty", "kill"
Appearance	"thin","gorgeous","fat","pretty"
Intelligence	"intelligent","genius","brilliant"
Strength	"bold","leader","strong","power"
Weakness	"loser","failure","weak","follow"
Attribute Set	**Examples of words in the word sets**
Female	"girl","her","woman","girlfriend"
Male	"boy","him","man","boyfriend"

Table 2: Examples of target and attribute sets used for SC-WEAT analysis. The full lists of words, curated by Betti et al. (2023), can be found in Table 3 and Table 4 in the Appendix.

2017; Betti et al., 2023). As the objective is to examine gender bias inherent in the dataset rather than the model itself, Word2Vec—trained from scratch—is more appropriate than contextual models like BERT (Mikolov et al., 2013).

We define six target sets, curated by Caliskan et al. (2017) and Chaloner and Maldonado (2019), which are used by Betti et al. (2023), in addition to two attribute sets for male and female characteristics, respectively (see Table 2). The SC-WEAT scores are calculated for each of these target sets using the aforementioned formula for each embedding model. A negative SC-WEAT score indicates a higher similarity towards the female attribute set, whereas a positive score indicates a higher similarity towards the male attribute set. The magnitude of the effect size indicates the strength of the respective bias.

4 Results & Discussion

4.1 Topic Analysis

The BERTopic model identifies a total of 541 topics, with 1.5% of documents classified as outliers. Figure 2 illustrates the most salient topics along with their genre distributions, representing the genre composition of songs assigned to each topic label, where each label is generated based on the most representative terms, constructed using the top three words with the highest c-TF-IDF values.

While the figure shows the composition of the top topics in each genre, it reveals the dominant influence of pop in other genres as well. For instance, in addition to the top topic within pop, the top topics in country (*"tears_heart_wish"*), R&B (*"body_girl_baby"*) and rock (*"ayy ayy_change_long_sentiment"*) are also largely shaped or consist of pop songs. This indicates greater thematic diversity of pop songs, whereas rap exhibits a strong thematic concentration, with 89.2% of songs in *"nigga_niggas_bitch"* belonging to the rap genre. While pop is the most prevalent genre in the dataset (see Table 1), this imbalance is mitigated by the stratified sampling approach outlined in Section 3.2, ensuring a more balanced genre representation in the analysis.

Despite the prevalence of pop music in the dataset, Figure 3 shows that the most prominent topic in rap, *"nigga_niggas_bitch"*, has the highest frequency across all genres and emerged predominantly in the 1990s. Analyzing the distribution of top topics within each genre highlights a stark disparity: the top topic in pop accounts for only 1.77% of all pop songs, whereas in rap, the top topic represents 37.88% of the genre. This significant concentration indicates the dominant popularity and thematic specificity of this topic within rap, accounting for a substantial portion of the dataset.

This pronounced disparity emphasizes the distinctive narrative centrality of the top topic in rap compared to pop, necessitating a more detailed investigation into its linguistic and cultural characteristics. An analysis of the lyrics within this topic reveals a frequent occurrence of vulgar language and profanity, as evident from the c-TF-IDF scores (see Figure 4). These observations highlight the thematic uniqueness of rap and underline the importance of further examining the social and cultural implications embedded within its lyrical content.

A detailed qualitative analysis of the lyrics within this topic, exemplified by tracks such as *Big L's 7 Minute Freestyle* and *Eminem's Kill You*, reveals a prevalent use of explicit and coarse language. Notable lyrical excerpts, including *"F*ck love / All I got for hoes is hard d*ck and bubblegum' and 'Slut, you think I won't choke no whore / Til the vocal cords don't work in her throat no more?!"*, exemplify this linguistic trend. These findings align with the argument presented by Evadewi and Jufrizal (2018), who contend that rap music lyrics are distinguished by the frequent incorporation of vulgar and explicit language, setting them apart from other English-language musical genres. Furthermore, a quantitative analysis of word frequency within this topic and across rap lyrics

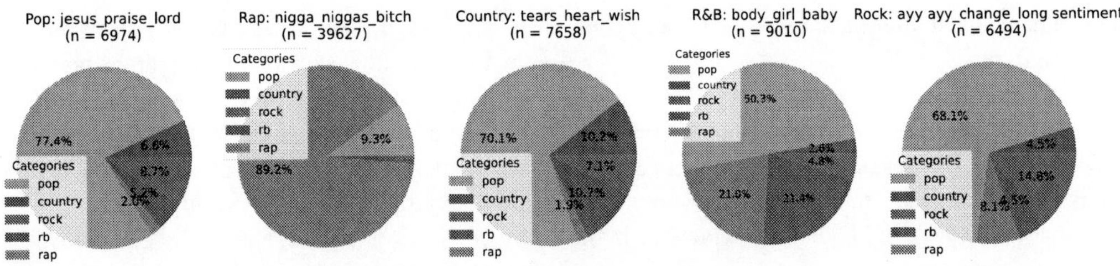

Figure 2: Distribution of the top topic in each genre, with (n) representing the number of songs associated with that topic. As shown, the top topic in each genre often includes a significant proportion of songs from other genres, indicating genre overlap in topic composition.

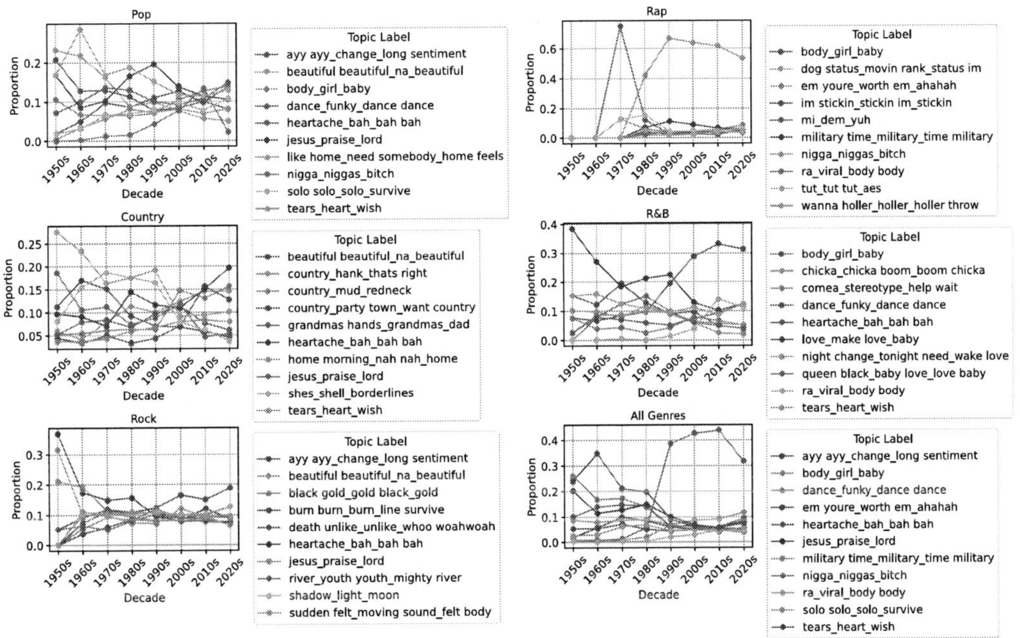

Figure 3: Development over time of top 10 topics in each genre and overall; decline from 2010 to 2020 can be explained by the yet still limited data for the 2020s.

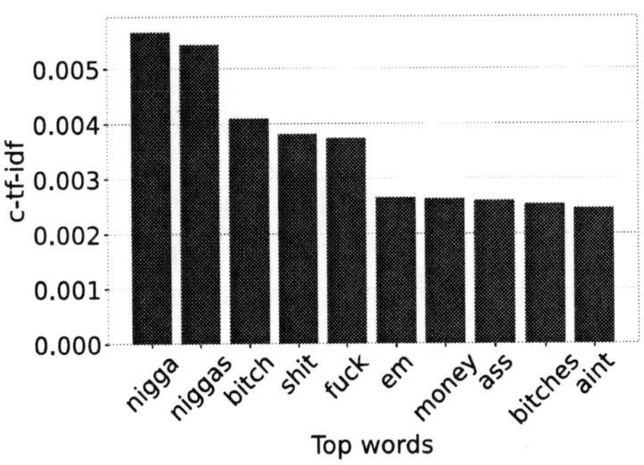

Figure 4: c-TF-IDF score for the overall top topic: *"nigga_niggas_bitch"*.

underscores the recurrent presence of misogynistic terminology, which serves to reinforce negative gender stereotypes and perpetuate discriminatory narratives. In particular, derogatory terms such as 'bitches,' 'sluts,' and 'hoes' frequently appear in reference to women, reflecting broader patterns of gendered linguistic bias within this lyrical subdomain. This observation is further corroborated by Adams and Fuller (2006) and Grönevik (2013), who highlight that such ideologies manifest through a spectrum of expressions, from subtle insinuations to obvious stereotypical representations and defamatory language within rap lyrics. Additionally, the higher prevalence of misogyny and profanity in rap lyrics, compared to other genres, aligns with the findings of Frisby and Behm-Morawitz (2019), who document similar patterns in their comprehensive analyses.

Furthermore, Smiler et al. (2017a) also documented the evolution of music content over time, shifting from themes related to romantic relationships to an increase in references to sexual behaviour and objectified bodies, as evidenced in the topics in rap. This is also proven in our findings that in the top topics across successive decades, the following topics appear as trending: *"wonderful_sweeter years_sweeter"*, spanning from the 1950s to the 1960s, (due to fewer occurrences of this topic, it does not feature in Figure 3), *"tears_heart_wish"*, from 1960s to the 1980s, and *"nigga_niggas_bitch"* from 1980s to 2020s. This observation is consistent with the results reported by Hall et al. (2011), who found that when comparing lyrics from 2009 to those from 1959, the occurrence of sexualized content in 2009 was over three times higher.

4.2 SC-WEAT Analysis

Employing these topics as grouping indicators, we analyze gender bias in the lyrics by calculating the SC-WEAT scores, grouped by genre, as shown in Figure 5. We observe no common trend in any genre to be male or female-biased overall; instead, they show variations in each target set.

We observe that Unpleasant, Intelligence, and Strength words exhibit positive SC-WEAT scores across all genres, with notably higher effect sizes in rap and country. This indicates that these target sets are more closely associated with male attributes on average, reflecting a pronounced male bias. These findings align with prior research by Betti et al. (2023), which highlights the strong association between Strength words and male nouns or names. Furthermore, the observed male bias aligns with prior research indicating that men are more frequently associated with attributes related to competence, such as 'smart,' 'strong,' and 'brave,' in contrast to women (Boghrati and Berger, 2022, 2023).

A systematic analysis of female bias within song lyrics reveals that the Weakness target set consistently exhibits negative SC-WEAT scores across multiple genres. This trend suggests that, in parallel with the stronger association of men with competence-related attributes, women are more frequently linked to concepts of weakness. Such linguistic patterns reinforce entrenched gender stereotypes, thereby perpetuating and amplifying gendered asymmetries in lyrical discourse.

This phenomenon aligns with prior findings by Liu et al. (2023), which highlight the prevalence of gender stereotypes in media, such as the association of men with strength and women with appearance, particularly in contexts like video games. Similarly, the corpus-based study by Krasse (2019) on pop lyrics identifies a pronounced linguistic pattern wherein adjectives such as "pretty," "beautiful," "ugly," and "baby" frequently precede female nouns. Our empirical analysis substantiates these findings, revealing that Appearance-related words consistently yield negative SC-WEAT scores across four out of five musical genres. This trend highlights the predominant linguistic association of women with attributes linked to physical appearance rather than intellectual or competence-related qualities. These results are consistent with prior research documenting the pervasive sexualization and objectification of women in song lyrics (Flynn et al., 2016; Hall et al., 2011; Karsay et al., 2019; Rasmussen and Densley, 2017), further illustrating how this cultural medium serves to reinforce and perpetuate traditional gender stereotypes.

For a more granular analysis, we compute SC-WEAT scores for the top topic in each genre and overall. Figure 6 visualizes the scores for the top overall topic (*"nigga_niggas_bitch"*), where Appearance words exhibit a strong female bias, while Intelligence words show a marked male bias. These findings reinforce the gender divide and the objectification of women within this topic, as discussed in Section 4.1.

Furthermore, Figure 7 illustrates that the biases associated with target sets vary across topics. Notably, Appearance words generally exhibit a female bias; however, in the topic *"ayy ayy_change_long sentiment"*, they display a male bias, while Intelligence words show a female bias—contrasting with the overall trend observed in the rock genre (refer to Figure 5). These findings emphasize the importance of topic-specific analysis to capture the nuanced variations in biases across different topics, which might otherwise be obscured in genre-level aggregations.

Moreover, certain prevalent topics that appear across multiple genres exhibit differing biases depending on the genre (see Figure 2). For instance, the topic *"tears_heart_wish"*, which is present in the country, pop, and R&B genres, demonstrates distinct SC-WEAT scores for each genre, as shown in Figure 8. In the country genre, this topic consistently displays a female bias across

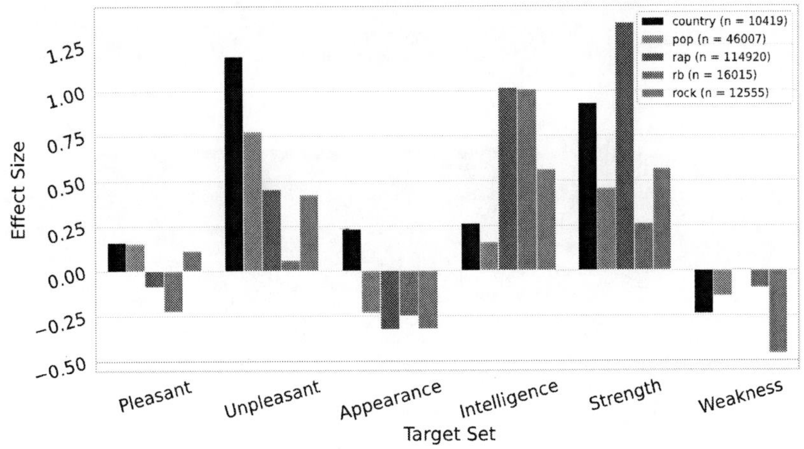

Figure 5: The SC-WEAT effect size of the target sets in each genre. A positive score indicates male bias, whereas a negative score indicates female bias, and n represents the number of word vectors for each genre.

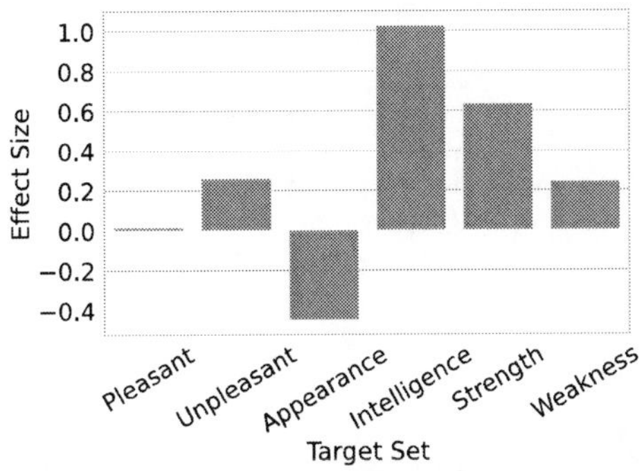

Figure 6: SC-WEAT score for the top topic: *"nigga_niggas_bitch"*. A positive score indicates male bias, whereas a negative score indicates female bias, and n is the number of word vectors.

all target sets, with Weakness words showing the strongest bias. These findings align with prior research by Rasmussen and Densley (2017), which observed that over half of the country songs analyzed reinforce stereotypical female gender roles and objectify women. This underscores the role of genre-specific contexts in shaping the gendered associations present in song lyrics.

Figure 8 reveals that Weakness words consistently exhibit a female bias across the three genres analyzed, aligning with our broader observation that women are more frequently associated with weakness. Notably, Intelligence words in country and R&B deviate from their average bias trends (see Figure 5), as these genres typically display a strong male bias overall yet show negligible scores for this specific genre.

The influence of genre-specific dynamics is further highlighted by the behaviour of Appearance words in Figure 8. While Appearance words display a male bias in R&B, they exhibit a female bias in pop, demonstrating how the same topic can exhibit divergent biases depending on the genre. These findings underscore the critical role of genre in shaping the gendered associations of recurring themes within song lyrics, emphasizing the need for a nuanced, genre-sensitive analysis to fully understand the interplay between thematic content and gender bias.

5 Conclusion

As a socio-cultural artefact, music offers insights into societal norms and biases, making it a valuable subject for computational analysis. This study leverages BERTopic, an advanced topic modeling technique, to identify thematic patterns and gender bias in song lyrics across five genres—country, pop, rap, R&B, and rock—over 70 years. Using SC-WEAT, we quantify gender bias within these themes and explore how biases vary across topics and genres. By addressing the intersection of music, culture, and societal norms, our findings reveal the gendered narratives embedded in song lyrics and their evolution over time.

We employ a stratified sampling strategy for BERTopic model training to ensure balanced genre representation. The most dominant topic, *"nigga_niggas_bitch"*, exhibits a high prevalence of misogynistic language and profanity, becoming particularly prominent in the 1990s despite the dataset spanning from the 1950s to the 2020s. In contrast, earlier dominant themes, such as *"tears_heart_wish"* and *"wonderful_sweeter_years_sweeter"*, primarily reflect

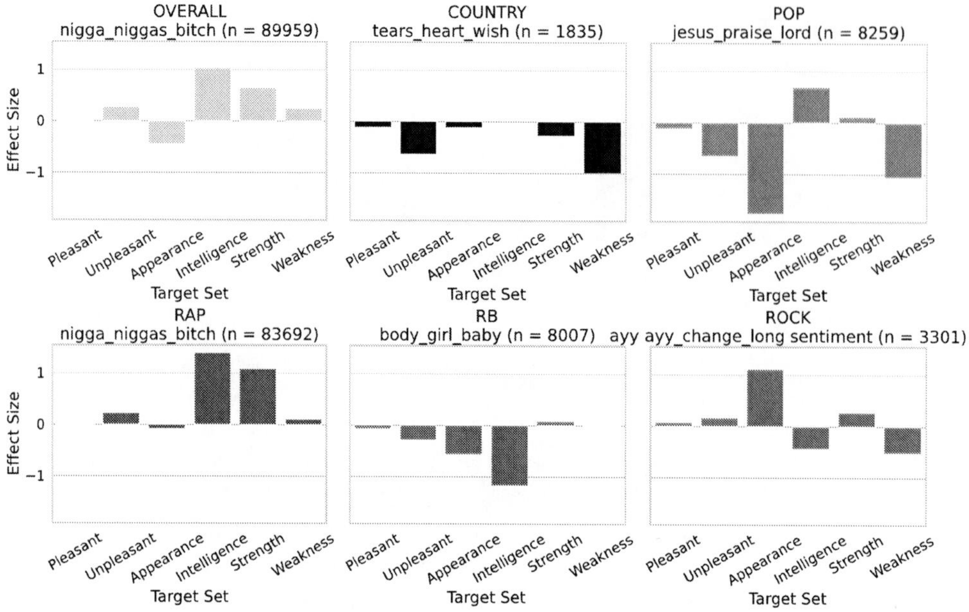

Figure 7: Comparison of SC-WEAT bias plots of the top topics in each genre. A positive score indicates male bias, whereas a negative score indicates female bias, and n is the number of word vectors.

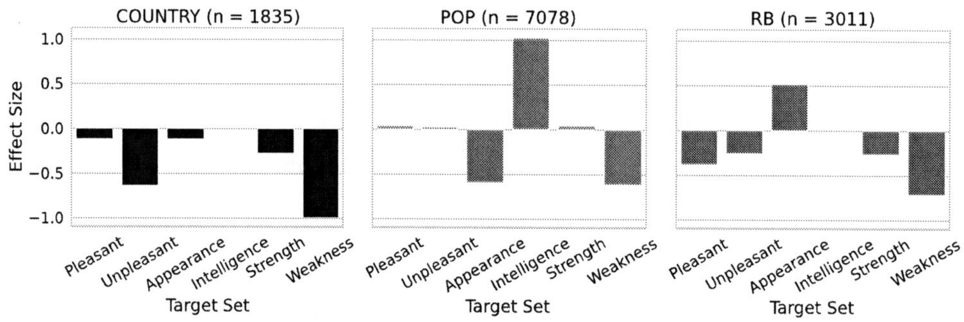

Figure 8: Comparison of SC-WEAT plots for *"tears_heart_wish"* in the country, pop, and R&B genres. A positive score indicates male bias, whereas a negative score indicates female bias, and n is the number of word vectors.

romantic and sentimental content. Over time, these themes shift toward heightened sexualization and explicit language, reflecting broader sociocultural and linguistic transformations in popular music, aligning with prior research on the increasing prevalence of sexualized and gendered language in song lyrics (Hall et al., 2011; Smiler et al., 2017b).

The SC-WEAT analysis further examines the trends of sexualization and profanity previously identified through topic modeling. The results reveal implicit gender bias in song lyrics, with Weakness and Appearance words showing a female bias, while Intelligence and Strength words exhibit a male bias. The female bias in Appearance words supports observations on the sexualization of women in music (Flynn et al., 2016; Hall et al., 2011; Rasmussen and Densley, 2017). The per-topic and per-genre analysis uncovers notable variations, with biases differing across themes and genres.

For instance, in the topic *"tears_heart_wish,"* bias scores vary across genres: country exhibits a female bias across all target sets, while Intelligence words in pop and Appearance words in R&B show a male bias. These results highlight the intersection of thematic content, genre, and gender bias, emphasizing the value of computational methods in analyzing sociocultural dynamics in song lyrics.

In conclusion, this study demonstrates the utility of integrating topic modeling with bias measurement techniques to analyze thematic structures in song lyrics and examine how these themes perpetuate implicit gender biases. By applying NLP methods to a significant sociocultural dataset, this work aligns with the growing demand in Digital Humanities and Social Sciences for tools that facilitate the analysis and interpretation of complex, non-standard textual data. Our approach highlights the potential of computational methods to address sociocultural questions, offering insights into how gender stereotypes are embedded in and perpetuated through lyrical content.

Limitations

Language Limitations: This study focuses exclusively on English-language songs, despite the multilingual content available on the Genius platform. Future research could expand to include songs in other languages, enhancing the scope and applicability of the findings.

Gender Classification: This analysis treats gender as binary, overlooking the spectrum of gender identities. Future research should explore the full spectrum of gender diversity in music for more inclusive insights.

BERTopic Modeling: A limitation of BERTopic, when applied to song lyrics analysis, is that it assigns a single topic per song, which does not account for songs that comprise different verses which may have different topics.

Race and Gender: In this paper, we look at the gender bias in lyrics independent of the race or gender of the artists, potentially neglecting their influence on the bias in the songs, especially in genres like rap. Future work could focus on integrating these aspects for a more detailed analysis of bias in music.

Addressing these limitations could significantly advance the field, offering an even more nuanced and comprehensive perspective on the intersection of music, culture, and societal norms.

References

Terri M. Adams and Douglas B. Fuller. 2006. The words have changed but the ideology remains the same: Misogynistic lyrics in rap music. *Journal of Black Studies*, 36(6):938–957.

Susan Alexander. 1999. The gender role paradox in youth culture: An analysis of women in music videos. *Michigan Sociological Review*, pages 46–64.

Manuel Anglada-Tort, Amanda E Krause, and Adrian C North. 2021. Popular music lyrics and musicians' gender over time: A computational approach. *Psychology of Music*, 49(3):426–444.

Emmanouil Benetos, Simon Dixon, Zhiyao Duan, and Sebastian Ewert. 2018. Automatic music transcription: An overview. *IEEE Signal Processing Magazine*, 36(1):20–30.

Vincent P Bengio Y, Ducharme R. 2000. A neural probabilistic language model. In *NIPS*, volume 13, pages 932–938. MIT Press.

Lorenzo Betti, Carlo Abrate, and Andreas Kaltenbrunner. 2023. Large scale analysis of gender bias and sexism in song lyrics. *EPJ Data Science*, 12(1):10.

Reihane Boghrati and Jonah Berger. 2022. Quantifying gender bias in consumer culture. *CoRR*, abs/2201.03173.

Reihane Boghrati and Jonah Berger. 2023. Quantifying cultural change: Gender bias in music. *Journal of Experimental Psychology: General*.

Tolga Bolukbasi, Kai-Wei Chang, James Y Zou, Venkatesh Saligrama, and Adam T Kalai. 2016. Man is to computer programmer as woman is to homemaker? debiasing word embeddings. *Advances in neural information processing systems*, 29.

Brook Bretthauer, Toni Schindler Zimmerman, and James H Banning. 2007. A feminist analysis of popular music: Power over, objectification of, and violence against women. *Journal of Feminist Family Therapy*, 18(4):29–51.

Aylin Caliskan, Joanna Bryson, and Arvind Narayanan. 2017. Semantics derived automatically from language corpora contain human-like biases. *Science*, 356:183–186.

Kaytlin Chaloner and Alfredo Maldonado. 2019. Measuring gender bias in word embeddings across domains and discovering new gender bias word categories. In *Proceedings of the First Workshop on Gender Bias in Natural Language Processing*, pages 25–32.

Tessa ES Charlesworth, Victor Yang, Thomas C Mann, Benedek Kurdi, and Mahzarin R Banaji. 2021. Gender stereotypes in natural language: Word embeddings show robust consistency across child and adult language corpora of more than 65 million words. *Psychological Science*, 32(2):218–240.

Yihao Chen and Alexander Lerch. 2020. Melody-conditioned lyrics generation with seqgans. In *2020 IEEE International Symposium on Multimedia (ISM)*, pages 189–196. IEEE.

Ann Colley. 2008. Young people's musical taste: Relationship with gender and gender-related traits 1. *Journal of applied social psychology*, 38(8):2039–2055.

Maibam Debina Devi and Navanath Saharia. 2020. Exploiting topic modelling to classify sentiment from lyrics. In *Machine Learning, Image Processing, Network Security and Data Sciences: Second International Conference, MIND 2020, Silchar, India, July 30-31, 2020, Proceedings, Part II 2*, pages 411–423. Springer.

Kevin Durrheim, Maria Schuld, Martin Mafunda, and Sindisiwe Mazibuko. 2023. Using word embeddings to investigate cultural biases. *British Journal of Social Psychology*, 62(1):617–629.

Roman Egger and Joanne Yu. 2022. A topic modeling comparison between lda, nmf, top2vec, and bertopic to demystify twitter posts. *Frontiers in sociology*, 7:886498.

Rani Evadewi and Jufrizal Jufrizal. 2018. An analysis of english slang words used in eminem's rap music. *English Language and Literature*, 7(1).

Michael Fell, Elena Cabrio, Maroua Tikat, Franck Michel, Michel Buffa, and Fabien Gandon. 2023. The wasabi song corpus and knowledge graph for music lyrics analysis. *Language Resources and Evaluation*, 57(1):89–119.

Mark A Flynn, Clay M Craig, Christina N Anderson, and Kyle J Holody. 2016. Objectification in popular music lyrics: An examination of gender and genre differences. *Sex roles*, 75:164–176.

Cynthia M. Frisby and Elizabeth Behm-Morawitz. 2019. Undressing the words: Prevalence of profanity, misogyny, violence, and gender role references in popular music from 2006-2016. *Media Watch*, 10(1):5–21.

Lin Gan, Tao Yang, Yifan Huang, Boxiong Yang, Yami Yanwen Luo, Lui Wing Cheung Richard, and Dabo Guo. 2023. Experimental comparison of three topic modeling methods with lda, top2vec and bertopic. In *International Symposium on Artificial Intelligence and Robotics*, pages 376–391. Springer.

Klara Grönevik. 2013. The depiction of women in rap and pop lyrics.

Maarten Grootendorst. 2022. Bertopic: Neural topic modeling with a class-based tf-idf procedure. *arXiv preprint arXiv:2203.05794*.

P. Hall, Joshua West, and Shane Hill. 2011. Sexualization in lyrics of popular music from 1959 to 2009: Implications for sexuality educators. *Sexuality Culture*, 16.

Dirk Hovy and Shrimai Prabhumoye. 2021. Five sources of bias in natural language processing. *Language and Linguistics Compass*, 15(8):e12432.

Eirini Karamouzi, Maria Pontiki, and Yannis Krasonikolakis. 2024. Historical portrayal of greek tourism through topic modeling on international newspapers. In *Proceedings of the 8th Joint SIGHUM Workshop on Computational Linguistics for Cultural Heritage, Social Sciences, Humanities and Literature (LaTeCH-CLfL 2024)*, pages 121–132.

Kathrin Karsay, Jörg Matthes, Lisa Buchsteiner, and Veronika Grosser. 2019. Increasingly sexy? sexuality and sexual objectification in popular music videos, 1995–2016. *Psychology of popular media culture*, 8(4):346.

Florian Kleedorfer, Peter Knees, and Tim Pohle. 2008. Oh oh oh whoah! towards automatic topic detection in song lyrics. In *Ismir*, pages 287–292.

Louise Krasse. 2019. A corpus linguistic study of the female role in popular music lyrics.

Cyril Laurier, Jens Grivolla, and Perfecto Herrera. 2008. Multimodal music mood classification using audio and lyrics. In *2008 seventh international conference on machine learning and applications*, pages 688–693. IEEE.

Bingqing Liu, Kyrie Zhixuan Zhou, Danlei Zhu, and Jaihyun Park. 2023. Understanding gender stereotypes in video game character designs: A case study of honor of kings. In *Proceedings of the Joint 3rd International Conference on Natural Language Processing for Digital Humanities and 8th International Workshop on Computational Linguistics for Uralic Languages*, pages 125–131, Tokyo, Japan. Association for Computational Linguistics.

Tomas Mikolov, Kai Chen, Greg Corrado, and Jeffrey Dean. 2013. Efficient estimation of word representations in vector space. *Preprint*, arXiv:1301.3781.

Elissa Nakajima Wickham. 2023. Girlbosses, the red pill, and the anomie and fatale of gender online: Analyzing posts from r/SuicideWatch on Reddit. In *Proceedings of the Joint 3rd International Conference on Natural Language Processing for Digital Humanities and 8th International Workshop on Computational Linguistics for Uralic Languages*, pages 195–212, Tokyo, Japan. Association for Computational Linguistics.

Xuanlong Qin and Tony Tam. 2023. Stereotype content dictionary: A semantic space of 3 million words and phrases using google news word2vec embeddings. In *International Conference on Social Computing, Behavioral-Cultural Modeling and Prediction and Behavior Representation in Modeling and Simulation*, pages 12–22. Springer.

Juan Ramos. 2003. Using tf-idf to determine word relevance in document queries.

Eric E Rasmussen and Rebecca L Densley. 2017. Girl in a country song: Gender roles and objectification of women in popular country music across 1990 to 2014. *Sex Roles*, 76:188–201.

Andrew Smiler, Jennifer Shewmaker, and Brittany Hearon. 2017a. From "i want to hold your hand" to "promiscuous": Sexual stereotypes in popular music lyrics, 1960–2008. *Sexuality and Culture*, 21:1–23.

Andrew P Smiler, Jennifer W Shewmaker, and Brittany Hearon. 2017b. From "i want to hold your hand" to "promiscuous": Sexual stereotypes in popular music lyrics, 1960–2008. *Sexuality & Culture*, 21(4):1083–1105.

Yi Yu, Abhishek Srivastava, and Simon Canales. 2021. Conditional lstm-gan for melody generation from lyrics. *ACM Transactions on Multimedia Computing, Communications, and Applications (TOMM)*, 17(1):1–20.

Jieyu Zhao, Tianlu Wang, Mark Yatskar, Ryan Cotterell, Vicente Ordonez, and Kai-Wei Chang. 2019. Gender bias in contextualized word embeddings. *arXiv preprint arXiv:1904.03310*.

A Appendix

A.1 Data Cleaning

We gather the song metadata from the WASABI corpus [4] and their respective lyrics information from the Genius Music Platform. Songs obtained from the Genius platform require preprocessing due to their unique format. Metadata associated with songs is typically enclosed within square brackets and embedded directly within the lyrical content. Additionally, the structure of the lyrics is generally preserved, resulting in entries that contain numerous newline characters. These characteristics may introduce challenges when parsing the data or preparing it for input into computational models, necessitating careful preprocessing to ensure consistency and usability. An example of the lyrics stored in the Genius dataset for "Love Story" by Taylor Swift:

> [Verse 1]
> We were both young when I first saw you
> I close my eyes and the flashback starts...
>
> [Pre-Chorus]
> That you were Romeo, you were throwing pebbles
> ...

A.2 Analysis of genre popularity across decades

Figure 9 presents a line chart illustrating the temporal evolution of genre popularity from the 1950s onward. In the early decades, country music demonstrates a higher relative prevalence compared to rap. However, a pronounced shift emerges in the 1990s, marked by a significant and rapid increase in the prominence of rap music.

[4] https://github.com/micbuffa/WasabiDataset

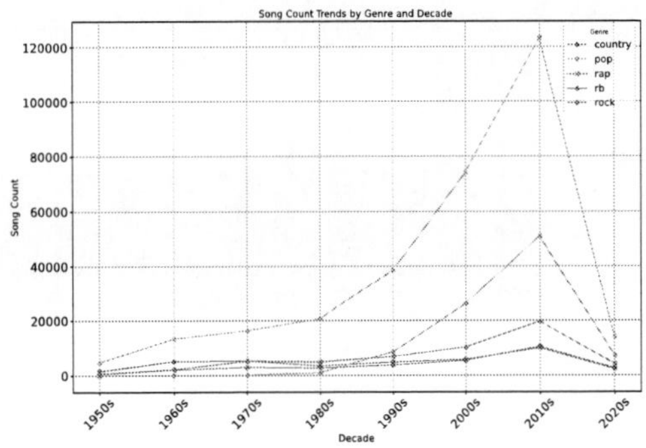

Figure 9: Genre trends over decades.

A.3 Initial BERTopic Model

The initial BERTopic model was trained on a randomly sampled subset of approximately 40,000 rows from the dataset. However, this approach resulted in an excessively high outlier rate, with over 50% of entries (approximately 27,000 rows) classified as outliers. This necessitated computationally intensive post-processing steps for outlier reduction, ultimately rendering the model suboptimal for integration into the final analytical pipeline. To address this limitation, we employed a stratified sampling strategy, selecting 107,000 rows balanced across musical genres for model training, followed by transformation on the entire dataset. This revised approach led to a substantial improvement in model stability and representational fidelity, reducing the proportion of outliers to just 1.5%. Consequently, this methodological refinement enhanced both the computational efficiency and the overall robustness of the topic modeling pipeline.

A.4 Topic Label Analysis Using c-TF-IDF score from Bertopic model

As shown in Figure 10, the topic labels are derived by selecting words with the highest c-TF-IDF scores, which are identified by the BERTopic model (Grootendorst, 2022). Unlike traditional TF-IDF, c-TF-IDF computes word importance at the cluster level rather than the document level (Ramos, 2003; Grootendorst, 2022). This method ensures that the most representative and distinguishing terms for each topic are highlighted, facilitating the interpretation of thematic structures within the dataset.

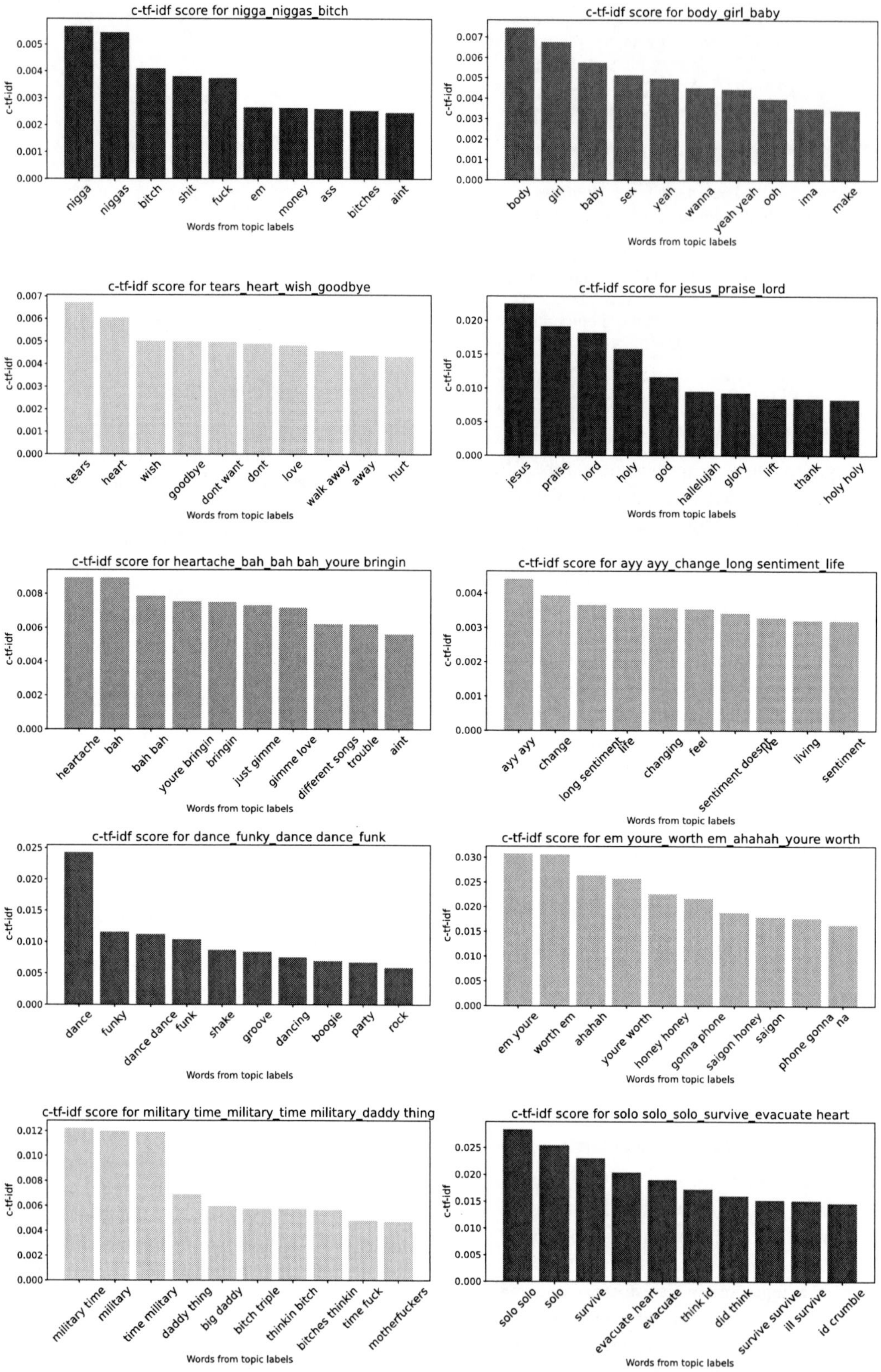

Figure 10: c-TF-IDF scores for words in the top 10 topics.

Target Set	Words
Pleasant	“friend”, “joy”, “wonderful”, “vacation”, “love”, “honest”, “honor”, “pleasure”, “loyal”, “family”, “peace”, “heaven”, “cheer”, “freedom”, “diploma”, “gentle”, “happy”, “paradise”, “diamond”, “laughter”, “sunrise”, “gift”, “health”, “rainbow”, “caress”, “lucky”, “miracle”
Unpleasant	“terrible”, “prison”, “divorce”, “war”, “poverty”, “sickness”, “abuse”, “tragedy”, “hatred”, “crash”, “accident”, “poison”, “nasty”, “awful”, “grief”, “disaster”, “stink”, “pollute”, “ugly”, “rotten”, “filth”, “failure”, “bomb”, “horrible”, “jail”, “kill”, “cancer”, “death”, “murder”, “evil”, “vomit”, “agony”, “assault”
Appearance words	“sensual”, “thin”, “handsome”, “feeble”, “bald”, “fashionable”, “slim”, “gorgeous”, “fat”, “plump”, “muscular”, “pretty”, “strong”, “weak”, “ugly”, “slender”, “homely”, “healthy”, “blushing”, “athletic”, “voluptuous”, “stout”, “beautiful”, “alluring”, “attractive”
Intelligence words	“intelligent”, “venerable”, “adaptable”, “reflective”, “thoughtful”, “resourceful”, “genius”, “logical”, “smart”, “astute”, “judicious”, “imaginative”, “intuitive”, “shrewd”, “ingenious”, “apt”, “precocious”, “inventive”, “analytical”, “inquiring”, “inquisitive”, “discerning”, “brilliant”, “clever”, “wise”
Strength words	“potent”, “bold”, “leader”, “strong”, “triumph”, “command”, “shout”, “winner”, “dominant”, “power”, “succeed”, “confident”, “dynamic”, “loud”, “assert”
Weakness words	“wispy”, “loser”, “failure”, “timid”, “lose”, “weak”, “weakness”, “shy”, “surrender”, “follow”, “fragile”, “withdraw”, “vulnerable”, “yield”, “afraid”

Table 3: List of target sets used for SC-WEAT analysis. These sets were chosen from the word sets curated by Betti et al. (2023), who compiled it from two different sources (Caliskan et al., 2017; Chaloner and Maldonado, 2019).

Attribute Set	Words
Female	“aunt”, “auntie”, “daughter”, “daughter-in-law”, “female”, “gal”, “girl”, “girlfriend”, “grandmother”, “grandmother-in-law”, “her”, “hers”, “lady”, “madam”, “mama”, “miss”, “mom”, “mother”, “niece”, “queen”, “she”, “sis”, “sister”, “wife”, “woman”
Male	“boy”, “boyfriend”, “brother”, “dad”, “father”, “father-in-law”, “grandfather”, “grandpa”, “guy”, “he”, “him”, “his”, “husband”, “king”, “male”, “man”, “nephew”, “papa”, “sir”, “son”, “son-in-law”, “uncle”

Table 4: List of attribute sets used for SC-WEAT analysis.

Artificial Relationships in Fiction: A Dataset for Advancing NLP in Literary Domains

Despina Christou
School of Informatics,
Aristotle University of Thessaloniki,
54124, Greece
christoud@csd.auth.gr

Grigorios Tsoumakas
School of Informatics,
Aristotle University of Thessaloniki,
54124, Greece,
Archimedes, Athena Research Center, Greece,
greg@csd.auth.gr

Abstract

Relation extraction (RE) in fiction presents unique NLP challenges due to implicit, narrative-driven relationships. Unlike factual texts, fiction weaves complex connections, yet existing RE datasets focus on non-fiction. To address this, we introduce *Artificial Relationships in Fiction* (ARF), a synthetically annotated dataset for literary RE. Built from diverse Project Gutenberg fiction, ARF considers author demographics, publication periods, and themes. We curated an ontology for fiction-specific entities and relations, and using GPT-4o, generated artificial relationships to capture narrative complexity. Our analysis demonstrates its value for finetuning RE models and advancing computational literary studies. By bridging a critical RE gap, ARF enables deeper exploration of fictional relationships, enriching NLP research at the intersection of storytelling and AI-driven literary analysis.

1 Introduction

Relation extraction is a fundamental NLP task that identifies and categorizes semantic relationships between entities in text (Wadhwa et al., 2023). While RE has been extensively studied in structured domains like news articles and scientific literature (Zhao et al., 2024), its application to fiction remains underexplored (Bamman et al., 2019). Fictional narratives present unique challenges due to their narrative-driven structures, implicit relationships, and varied linguistic styles that differ significantly from factual texts (Elsner, 2012).

To address this gap, we introduce *Artificial Relationships in Fiction (ARF)*, a synthetically annotated dataset for RE in literary texts. The dataset is constructed from a curated selection of real literary texts sourced from Project Gutenberg, with relationship annotations generated using GPT-4o. Unlike traditional datasets that rely on manual annotation, ARF leverages AI-assisted annotation to extract meaningful relationships within fictional narratives. This approach enables large-scale dataset creation while capturing the complexities of fictional interactions (Yang et al., 2024; Chen et al., 2019).

Our contributions include: (1) introducing a synthetically annotated dataset for RE in fiction, (2) developing a systematic dataset creation methodology combining curated selection with language model-assisted relationship generation, and (3) providing a thorough dataset analysis along with example use cases demonstrating its potential for RE research in fiction.

The paper is structured as follows: Section 2 reviews related work, Section 3 outlines dataset creation, Section 4 presents dataset analysis, Section 5 explores evaluation methods and applications, and Section 6 concludes with future research directions.

2 Related Work

Research on RE has traditionally focused on structured, factual texts. Numerous datasets and approaches address newswire (Zeng et al., 2014; Zhang et al., 2017), biomedical (Gu et al., 2016), finance (Vela and Declerck, 2009), legal (Andrew, 2018), and scientific literature (Luan et al., 2018). For instance, the TACRED dataset (Zhang et al., 2017) provides a large-scale corpus of annotated sentences for relation classification, while the ACE dataset (Doddington et al., 2004) supports multilingual entity, relation, and event detection. Shared tasks at SemEval (Hendrickx et al., 2010) further drive benchmarks, enabling methods from feature-based learning (Mintz et al., 2009) to deep neural networks (Zeng et al., 2014) to advance RE in non-fiction.

Despite these developments, fiction remains comparatively underexplored (Moretti, 2011; Zhang, 2024). Unlike factual prose, fictional narratives often convey relationships implicitly through figurative language, complex story arcs, and evolv-

Proceedings of LaTeCH-CLfL 2025, pages 130–147
May 4, 2025 ©2025 Association for Computational Linguistics

ing character dynamics. Early computational literary analysis studied character networks and narrative structures (Moretti, 2011), while systems like BookNLP (Bamman et al., 2014) aided entity extraction and coreference resolution. LitBank (Bamman et al., 2019) annotates literary entities but lacks focus on fictional relationships. Other fiction-oriented datasets target social networks (Hamilton et al., 2025) or characterization (Soni et al., 2023; Bamman et al., 2014) but do not systematically address RE. Limited RE efforts in fiction, e.g., character-location associations (He et al., 2013; Vala et al., 2015; Iyyer et al., 2016; Srivastava et al., 2016; Chaturvedi et al., 2017; Mani et al., 2008), often have narrow scopes and lack comprehensive ontologies that capture the diverse range of fictional entities and relations (Christou and Tsoumakas, 2021; Soni et al., 2023).

In response to this gap, recent work has expanded literary relationship analysis. For instance, (Hamilton et al., 2025) introduced synthetic annotations of social networks in literary texts. However, such efforts typically focus on specific relationship types or small corpora. Advancing RE in fiction requires richer ontologies encompassing characters, settings, objects, abstract concepts, and thematic linkages (Bamman et al., 2019).

Meanwhile, the use of large language models for generating synthetic training data has gained momentum as a means to overcome the scarcity and cost of human annotations (Wei et al., 2023; Jiang et al., 2024). Xu et al. (2023) show how GPT-3.5 excels at few-shot RE, highlighting the potential of LLMs for creative or domain-specific tasks. Leveraging these models, researchers can create datasets that reflect the complexity of fictional narratives while still maintaining consistency and diversity in annotations.

Against this backdrop, we present the Artificial Relationships in Fiction (ARF) dataset, a synthetic resource for literary RE. Using fiction from Project Gutenberg and a tailored ontology, ARF leverages GPT-4o to generate nuanced relationships, enriching resources and advancing research in NLP, storytelling, and computational literary analysis.

3 Dataset Creation

High-quality datasets are vital for NLP, especially in literary domains where relationship extraction requires nuanced understanding but lacks annotations. This section details the creation of *Artificial Relationships in Fiction* through three stages: source selection, chunking, and synthetic relationship generation. The dataset[1] is available in three configurations, each supporting distinct analytical needs in literary NLP.

3.1 Selection Criteria

To ensure broad coverage of fiction subgenres, we curated a diverse set of fiction books from specific Project Gutenberg (PG) bookshelves. The selection process involved:

- **Data Collection**: Extracted all books and their metadata[2] from the following PG bookshelves: Fiction, Children & Young Adult Reading, and Crime/Mystery.
- **Deduplication**: Removed books appearing in multiple bookshelves.
- **Language Filtering**: Retained only English-language books.
- **Copyright Compliance**: Included only books marked as *Public domain in the USA*.
- **Outlier Removal**: Excluded books by authors born before 1300 AD (0.2%) to ensure linguistic consistency. Note that the gap from 1300 to mid 19th c. reflects the absence of fiction books from the specified bookshelves in the source corpus.
- **Text Cleaning**: Fixed encoding mismatches and removed formatting artifacts while preserving paragraph and chapter structure.
- **Metadata Additions**: To support richer fiction analysis, we augmented the dataset with additional metadata:
  Author Gender: Inferred via GPT-4o and manually verified.
  Topic Categorization: Condensed verbose PG subjects[3] into 51 thematic topics for better classification (see Appendix A).

The final dataset, available as `fiction_books` configuration, contains 6,322 unique books written between the mid-19th and mid-20th by 1,716 authors, with a 69%-31% male-female author distribution. Spanning 51 thematic topics, this structured dataset supports literary analysis across genres, authors, and writing styles, facilitating deeper

[1] `https://huggingface.co/datasets/Despina/project_gutenberg`

[2] PG books extracted metadata: book_id, title, author, author_birth_year, author_death_year, release_date, subjects, language, copyright, text

[3] Example of verbose PG subject: Tarzan (Fictitious character) – Fiction, Africa – Fiction, Fantasy fiction, Good and evil – Juvenile fiction, Adventure stories, Apes – Fiction

insights into thematic relationships and character interactions in fiction.

3.2 Text Chunking

To enable effective relationship extraction, we segmented book texts into five-sentence chunks using a rolling window, where each chunk overlaps by one sentence to maintain coherence. This overlapping strategy helps maintain coherence across segments and ensures that relational mentions extending beyond a single chunk are partially captured. While a five-sentence window limits long-range relationships in literary texts, it balances contextual depth with computational efficiency. The resulting dataset, available as `fiction_books_in_chunks` configuration, comprises 5,961,303 chunks, averaging 943 per book.

3.3 Synthetic Relationship Generation

To improve relationship extraction in fiction, we used GPT-4o to generate synthetic relations for selected PG book chunks within a $1K budget. We subsampled 95,475 chunks while preserving thematic and author-gender distributions (see next chapter for details). Ensuring adherence to a structured ontology was a key priority. Our methodology:

Entity Ontology: Developed the most comprehensive ontology of entity types in literary works to date (see Appendix B).

Relationship Ontology: Designed an ontology capturing nuanced relationships between entity types in fictional narratives (see Appendix C).

LLM-Based Relation Extraction: Constructed a robust GPT-4o prompt (see Appendix D) that integrates entity and relationship ontologies in the system prompt, ensuring relationships are classified strictly within predefined categories. To account for potential deviations, we track inconsistency frequencies and report them in Section 4. Relationships were assumed to exist only between two entities that appear in a span of five sentences. Extracted relationships were formatted as JSON objects to ensure compatibility with computational processing pipelines, including the following fields:

- *entity1*, *entity2*: Related entities' text spans
- *entity1Type*, *entity2Type*: Entities ontology types
- *relation*: Ontology-defined relationship type

Metric	Value
Books Count	96
Authors Count	91
Gender Ratio (M-F)	55%-45%
Subgenres	51
Total chunks	95,475
Avg. Chunks per book	995
Chunks w/o Relations	35,230
Avg. Relations per Book	1337
Avg. Relations per Chunk	1.34

Table 1: Dataset Statistics

4 Dataset Statistics, Evaluation, and Analysis

This section presents an overview of the dataset, including key statistics, examples of extracted relations, and a deeper analysis of its structure. The insights provided here inform potential research directions in NLP applications for fiction.

4.1 Dataset Statistics

The dataset (Table 1) consists of 96 books across 51 fiction subgenres, written by 91 authors with a 55%-45% male-female split, ensuring demographic balance. It includes 95,475 text chunks, averaging 995 per book, with 36.9% containing no explicit relations. On average, each book includes 1,337 relations, while relation-containing chunks feature an average of 1.34 relations, demonstrating a structured relational density. These statistics highlight the dataset's diversity and suitability for NLP tasks such as relation extraction and narrative modeling. A complete list of titles and authors is available in Appendix F.

4.2 Examples of Extracted Relations

To illustrate relation extraction quality, consider the example below, capturing pronoun-based relationships—an established challenge in NLP.

```
[{'entity1': 'Vortigern', 'entity2': 'his
  master's sons', 'entity1Type': 'PER',
  'entity2Type': 'PER','relation': 'enemy_of'},
 {'entity1': 'Vortigern', 'entity2': 'castle',
  'entity1Type': 'PER', 'entity2Type': 'FAC',
  'relation': 'owns'}]
```

Further examples appear in Appendix E. As it can be seen, our curated ontologies and GPT-4o-based prompt extract rich relationships, while smaller models like GPT-4o-mini and spaCy's NER and RE failed to detect these pairs, highlighting our approach's robustness and dataset richness.

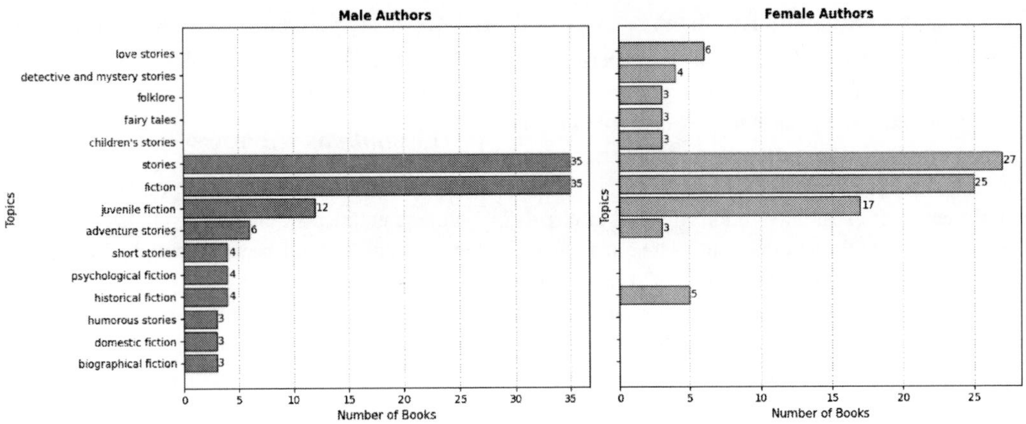

Figure 1: Top-10 subgenres per Author Gender

Ontology Category	New Types	Deviation
Entity 1	10	0.01%
Entity 2	53	0.04%
Relation	3785	2.95%

Table 2: Ontology deviations by category, showing new instances and deviation rates.

4.3 Evaluation

To assess the robustness of the extracted relationships, we analyze deviations from our structured ontology, as summarized in Table 2. This evaluation provides a quantitative measure of the model's accuracy in extracting complex relationships and highlights areas for potential refinement.

Table 2 presents a breakdown of ontology deviations, categorizing inconsistencies observed across entity and relation types. The results indicate that entity deviations are minimal (below 0.05%), while relation-based deviations are comparatively higher (2.95%), likely due to the complexity of multi-faceted relationship extraction. These findings underscore the robustness of our approach while also revealing opportunities for refinement. To further enhance consistency, we plan to incorporate structured output formats from ChatGPT, reducing ambiguity in generated responses.

Additionally, in our preliminary model selection, we tested GPT-4o, GPT-4o-mini, Llama-3.3-70B, Claude-3.5-Sonnet, and Gemini-1.5-Pro for ontology adherence. GPT-4o consistently extracted more complex relationships and was the only model to fully comply without inconsistencies. While this validates our choice, a broader comparative analysis is proposed for future work.

4.4 Analysis

We examine subgenres, entity and relation distributions, and gender-based narrative patterns, providing a foundation for computational literary analysis and NLP in fiction.

4.4.1 Top Subgenres

Figure 1 shows that "fiction," "stories," and "juvenile fiction" dominate across genders. Note, that books often belong to multiple subgenres, reflecting literary fluidity. Despite this shared prominence, distinct gender-based patterns emerge. Male authors favor adventure, humor, and biographical fiction, often engaging with historical and psychological narratives. Female authors emphasize relational and cultural storytelling through love stories, folklore, and children's literature. "Historical fiction" remains a shared interest, suggesting its broad thematic appeal. These patterns provide insights into how gender shapes thematic priorities and narrative structures in fiction in 1850-1950.

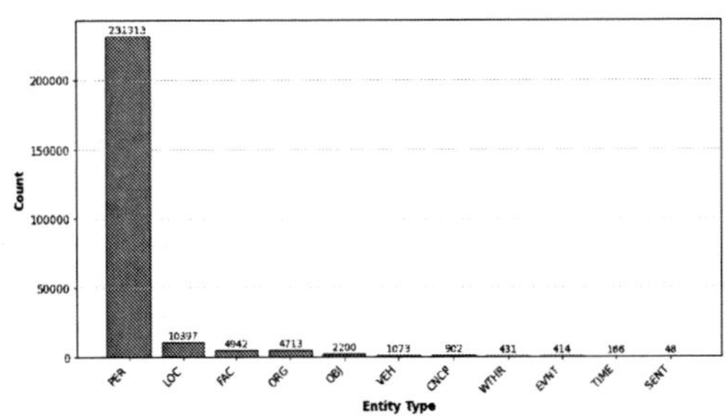

Figure 2: Entity Types Distribution.

4.4.2 Top Entities and Relations

Figures 2, 3 highlight the dataset's character-driven nature. The Person (PER) category dominates with 231,313 occurrences, underscoring the centrality of characters in fiction. Categories such as Location (LOC), Facility (FAC), and Organization (ORG) represent settings and institutions integral to world-building but are far less frequent. Rare entity types like Weather (WTHR), Event (EVNT), and Time (TIME) suggest their secondary importance in storytelling. This distribution highlights the emphasis on characters and their environments in fictional narratives.

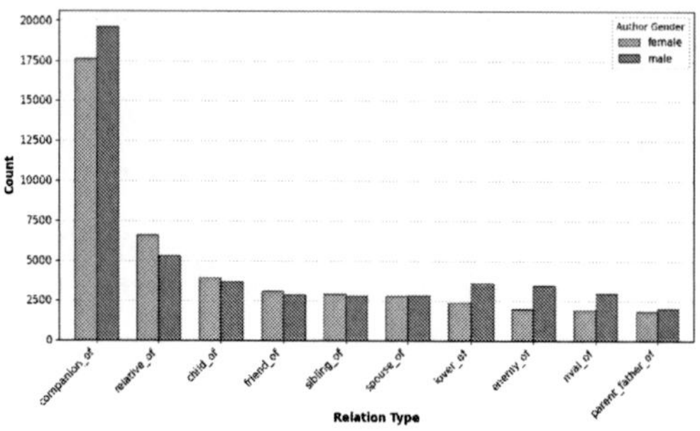

Figure 3: Top-10 relations with author gender usage

Gender-related trends show men slightly favoring PER entities, suggesting a focus on character-driven narratives, while women more frequently use FAC entities, emphasizing settings and contexts. These variations may reflect historical literary norms (Mulvey et al., 2006; Flanagan, 2009).

The most common relations (Figure 3) underscore interpersonal themes. Companion_of is most frequent, highlighting partnership dynamics, alongside familial (relative_of, child_of) and romantic (spouse_of, lover_of) ties. Conflict-driven relations (enemy_of, rival_of) add narrative tension. Gender trends show male-authored works featuring power structures (e.g., kings, warriors), while female-authored works emphasize domestic and relational dynamics. These patterns align with historical literary conventions, shaping how fiction evolved between 1850 and 1950.

5 Use Cases

This dataset offers valuable applications in fiction-specific NLP. It enables model finetuning, helping adapt NLP models for relationship extraction in literary narratives. It also supports literary analysis, allowing researchers to study character networks, relationship evolution, and thematic trends at scale. Additionally, it has creative applications, enhancing AI-driven storytelling and character development for writers, game designers, and digital creators by ensuring richer, more consistent narratives.

6 Limitations & Future Work

While this dataset advances fiction-specific RE, its synthetic nature pose challenges. Below, we outline key limitations and propose future directions to address them.

GPT-4o-generated annotations may introduce biases or inaccuracies, especially for complex or implicit relationships requiring deeper narrative understanding. The reliance on five-sentence chunks, while computationally feasible, limits the capture of long-range relationships across chapters or books, and the absence of explicit coreference resolution hinders tracking evolving character interactions. Without systematic human validation, precision and recall remain unverified, highlighting the need for manual evaluation.

Future work includes a small-scale human validation study, leveraging OpenAI's structured output mode for stricter ontology adherence, and integrating coreference resolution to improve continuity. Adaptive chunking strategies may enhance long-range dependency extraction. Comparative studies with other models and relation extraction systems will assess performance, while active learning could expand the dataset efficiently. Addressing these limitations will enhance reliability and broaden applicability in literary NLP research, enabling deeper narrative analysis.

7 Conclusion

This paper introduces *Artificial Relationships in Fiction*, a synthetically annotated dataset for relation extraction in literary texts. Built from public-domain fiction and GPT-4o generated relationships, ARF bridges structured RE tasks and fictional narratives. Our analysis demonstrates its ability to capture diverse literary relationships, supporting research in character networks, thematic links, and narrative NLP. Challenges include synthetic biases and scalability, requiring future work on human validation and dataset expansion. We envision *ARF* as a foundational resource for NLP, literary analysis, and AI-driven storytelling.

References

Judith Jeyafreeda Andrew. 2018. Automatic extraction of entities and relation from legal documents. In

Proceedings of the Seventh Named Entities Workshop, pages 1–8.

David Bamman, Sejal Popat, and Sheng Shen. 2019. An annotated dataset of literary entities. In *Proceedings of the 2019 Conference of the North American Chapter of the Association for Computational Linguistics: Human Language Technologies, Volume 1 (Long and Short Papers)*, pages 2138–2144.

David Bamman, Ted Underwood, and Noah A Smith. 2014. A bayesian mixed effects model of literary character. In *Proceedings of the 52nd Annual Meeting of the Association for Computational Linguistics (Volume 1: Long Papers)*, pages 370–379.

Snigdha Chaturvedi, Mohit Iyyer, and Hal Daume III. 2017. Unsupervised learning of evolving relationships between literary characters. In *Proceedings of the AAAI Conference on Artificial Intelligence*, volume 31.

Mia Xu Chen, Benjamin N Lee, Gagan Bansal, Yuan Cao, Shuyuan Zhang, Justin Lu, Jackie Tsay, Yinan Wang, Andrew M Dai, Zhifeng Chen, et al. 2019. Gmail smart compose: Real-time assisted writing. In *Proceedings of the 25th ACM SIGKDD International Conference on Knowledge Discovery & Data Mining*, pages 2287–2295.

Despina Christou and Grigorios Tsoumakas. 2021. Extracting semantic relationships in greek literary texts. *Sustainability*, 13(16):9391.

George Doddington, Alexis Mitchell, Mark Przybocki, Lance Ramshaw, Stephanie Strassel, and Ralph Weischedel. 2004. The automatic content extraction (ACE) program – tasks, data, and evaluation. In *Proceedings of the Fourth International Conference on Language Resources and Evaluation (LREC'04)*, Lisbon, Portugal. European Language Resources Association (ELRA).

Micha Elsner. 2012. Character-based kernels for novelistic plot structure. In *Proceedings of the 13th Conference of the European Chapter of the Association for Computational Linguistics*, pages 634–644.

Mary Flanagan. 2009. *Critical play: Radical game design*. MIT press.

J Gu, L Qian, and G Zhou. 2016. Chemical-induced disease relation extraction with various linguistic features. *Database: the Journal of Biological Databases and Curation*, 2016:baw042–baw042.

Sil Hamilton, Rebecca MM Hicke, David Mimno, and Matthew Wilkens. 2025. A city of millions: Mapping literary social networks at scale. *arXiv preprint arXiv:2502.19590*.

Hua He, Denilson Barbosa, and Grzegorz Kondrak. 2013. Identification of speakers in novels. In *Proceedings of the 51st Annual Meeting of the Association for Computational Linguistics (Volume 1: Long Papers)*, pages 1312–1320.

Iris Hendrickx, Su Nam Kim, Zornitsa Kozareva, Preslav Nakov, Diarmuid Ó Séaghdha, Sebastian Padó, Marco Pennacchiotti, Lorenza Romano, and Stan Szpakowicz. 2010. SemEval-2010 task 8: Multi-way classification of semantic relations between pairs of nominals. In *Proceedings of the 5th International Workshop on Semantic Evaluation*, pages 33–38, Uppsala, Sweden. Association for Computational Linguistics.

Mohit Iyyer, Anupam Guha, Snigdha Chaturvedi, Jordan Boyd-Graber, and Hal Daumé III. 2016. Feuding families and former friends: Unsupervised learning for dynamic fictional relationships. In *Proceedings of the 2016 Conference of the North American Chapter of the Association for Computational Linguistics: Human Language Technologies*, pages 1534–1544.

Pengcheng Jiang, Jiacheng Lin, Zifeng Wang, Jimeng Sun, and Jiawei Han. 2024. GenRES: Rethinking evaluation for generative relation extraction in the era of large language models. In *Proceedings of the 2024 Conference of the North American Chapter of the Association for Computational Linguistics: Human Language Technologies (Volume 1: Long Papers)*, pages 2820–2837, Mexico City, Mexico. Association for Computational Linguistics.

Yi Luan, Luheng He, Mari Ostendorf, and Hannaneh Hajishirzi. 2018. Multi-task identification of entities, relations, and coreference for scientific knowledge graph construction. *arXiv preprint arXiv:1808.09602*.

Inderjeet Mani, Janet Hitzeman, Justin Richer, Dave Harris, Rob Quimby, and Ben Wellner. 2008. Spatialml: Annotation scheme, corpora, and tools. In *Proceedings of the Sixth International Conference on Language Resources and Evaluation (LREC'08)*.

Mike Mintz, Steven Bills, Rion Snow, and Dan Jurafsky. 2009. Distant supervision for relation extraction without labeled data. In *Proceedings of the Joint Conference of the 47th Annual Meeting of the ACL and the 4th International Joint Conference on Natural Language Processing of the AFNLP*, pages 1003–1011.

Franco Moretti. 2011. Network theory, plot analysis.

Laura Mulvey, Kaja Silverman, Teresa de Laurentis, and Barbara Creed. 2006. Feminist film theorists.

Sandeep Soni, Amanpreet Sihra, Elizabeth Evans, Matthew Wilkens, and David Bamman. 2023. Grounding characters and places in narrative text. In *Proceedings of the 61st Annual Meeting of the Association for Computational Linguistics (Volume 1: Long Papers)*, pages 11723–11736.

Shashank Srivastava, Snigdha Chaturvedi, and Tom Mitchell. 2016. Inferring interpersonal relations in narrative summaries. In *Proceedings of the AAAI Conference on Artificial Intelligence*, volume 30.

Hardik Vala, David Jurgens, Andrew Piper, and Derek Ruths. 2015. Mr. bennet, his coachman, and the archbishop walk into a bar but only one of them gets recognized: On the difficulty of detecting characters in literary texts. In *Proceedings of the 2015 conference on empirical methods in natural language processing*, pages 769–774.

Mihaela Vela and Thierry Declerck. 2009. Concept and relation extraction in the finance domain. In *Proceedings of the eight international conference on computational semantics*, pages 346–350.

Somin Wadhwa, Silvio Amir, and Byron C Wallace. 2023. Revisiting relation extraction in the era of large language models. In *Proceedings of the conference. Association for Computational Linguistics. Meeting*, volume 2023, page 15566. NIH Public Access.

Xiang Wei, Xingyu Cui, Ning Cheng, Xiaobin Wang, Xin Zhang, Shen Huang, Pengjun Xie, Jinan Xu, Yufeng Chen, Meishan Zhang, et al. 2023. Chatie: Zero-shot information extraction via chatting with chatgpt. *arXiv preprint arXiv:2302.10205*.

Xin Xu, Yuqi Zhu, Xiaohan Wang, and Ningyu Zhang. 2023. How to unleash the power of large language models for few-shot relation extraction? *arXiv preprint arXiv:2305.01555*.

Yi Yang, Aida Davani, Avirup Sil, and Anoop Kumar. 2024. Proceedings of the 2024 conference of the north american chapter of the association for computational linguistics: Human language technologies (volume 6: Industry track). In *Proceedings of the 2024 Conference of the North American Chapter of the Association for Computational Linguistics: Human Language Technologies (Volume 6: Industry Track)*.

Daojian Zeng, Kang Liu, Siwei Lai, Guangyou Zhou, and Jun Zhao. 2014. Relation classification via convolutional deep neural network. In *Proceedings of COLING 2014, the 25th international conference on computational linguistics: technical papers*, pages 2335–2344.

Jiarui Zhang. 2024. Guided profile generation improves personalization with large language models. In *Findings of the Association for Computational Linguistics: EMNLP 2024*, pages 4005–4016, Miami, Florida, USA. Association for Computational Linguistics.

Yuhao Zhang, Victor Zhong, Danqi Chen, Gabor Angeli, and Christopher D Manning. 2017. Position-aware attention and supervised data improve slot filling. In *Conference on empirical methods in natural language processing*.

Xiaoyan Zhao, Yang Deng, Min Yang, Lingzhi Wang, Rui Zhang, Hong Cheng, Wai Lam, Ying Shen, and Ruifeng Xu. 2024. A comprehensive survey on relation extraction: Recent advances and new frontiers. *ACM Computing Surveys*, 56(11):1–39.

A Thematic Topic Classification

id	Thematic Topic	id	Thematic Topic
1	autobiographical fiction	27	children's stories
2	biographical fiction	28	christmas stories
3	crime fiction	29	code and cipher stories
4	diary fiction	30	college stories
5	didactic fiction	31	cricket stories
6	domestic fiction	32	detective and mystery stories
7	fantasy fiction	33	erotic stories
8	fiction	34	football stories
9	gothic fiction	35	frame-stories
10	historical fiction	36	ghost stories
11	juvenile fiction	37	humorous stories
12	musical fiction	38	hunting stories
13	mystery fiction	39	legal stories
14	paranormal fiction	40	love stories
15	political fiction	41	mystery and detective stories
16	psychological fiction	42	nature stories
17	science fiction	43	opera stories
18	fables	44	railroad stories
19	fairy tales	45	sea stories
20	folklore	46	short stories
21	legends	47	sports stories
22	mythology	48	spy stories
23	tales	49	stories
24	adventure stories	50	war stories
25	baseball stories	51	western stories
26	bible stories		

B Ontology of Entity Types in Fiction

id	Entity Type	Short Description	Description
1	PER	Person	A single person identified by a proper name or a common noun phrase. This category also includes groups or sets of people. Examples: Tom Sawyer, the boy, her daughters, the Ashburnhams.
2	FAC	Facility	A functional, man-made structure created for human use, including spaces for habitation, storage, transportation, and outdoor purposes. Interior spaces like rooms and closets are also included. Examples: the museum, a barn, the highway, the garden, a kitchen.
3	LOC	Location	Physical places without political boundaries, including natural areas, loosely defined regions, or celestial bodies. Examples: the woods, the river, New England, Mars.
4	WTHR	Weather	Natural atmospheric or celestial phenomena, such as storms, droughts, or celestial events. Examples: a thunderstorm, a drought, a solar eclipse, the first snow.

5	VEH	Vehicle	Physical devices designed for transportation, often reflecting historical modes of travel in literature. Examples: a ship, a train, a carriage, a steamboat.
6	ORG	Organization	Formal associations or institutional entities, including administrative, military, political, or religious groups. Examples: the army, the Church (as an organization, not a building), the guild.
7	EVNT	Event	Significant historical, cultural, or personal occurrences within the narrative. Examples: the ball at Netherfield, a proposal in the rain, the war, a festival.
8	TIME	Time Expression	Periods or temporal expressions, including historical eras or chronological markers. Examples: Victorian Era, the Renaissance, the 20th century, a winter evening.
9	OBJ	Object	Artifacts or tangible items of significance within the text. Examples: a letter, a necklace, a sword, a painting.
10	SENT	Sentiment	Emotional states or feelings expressed within the narrative. Examples: happiness, jealousy, anger, grief.
11	CNCP	Concept	Abstract themes or ideas explored in the text, often representing motifs or ideologies. Examples: love, justice, betrayal, courage, freedom.

C Ontology of Relation Types in Fiction

id	Relation Type	Description	Entity1 Type	Entity2 Type
1	parent_father_of	Represents the relationship between a parent and their father. Example: Darth Vader is father_of Luke Skywalker.	PER	PER
2	parent_mother_of	Represents the relationship between a parent and their mother. Example: Cersei Lannister is mother_of Joffrey Baratheon.	PER	PER
3	child_of	Represents the relationship between a child and its parents. Example: Harry Potter is child_of James Potter and Lily Potter.	PER	PER
4	sibling_of	Denotes siblings within the same family. Example: Thor is sibling_of Loki.	PER	PER
5	spouse_of	Indicates a marital relationship, regardless of gender or cultural context. Example: Elizabeth Bennet is spouse_of Mr. Darcy.	PER	PER
6	relative_of	Captures a broader familial connection beyond immediate family, such as cousins, uncles, or distant relatives. Example: Hamlet is relative_of Claudius (uncle-nephew relationship).	PER	PER
7	adopted_by	Indicates a non-biological familial or societal relationship, such as legal guardianship or cultural adoption. Example: Jon Snow is adopted_by Ned Stark.	PER	PER

8	companion_of	A broader term for someone who accompanies, aids, or supports another, including travel companions or loyal allies. Example: Don Quixote is companion_of Sancho Panza.	PER	PER
9	friend_of	Indicates a strong, platonic relationship. Example: Frodo is friend_of Samwise.	PER	PER
10	lover_of	Represents a romantic or amorous relationship, whether mutual or unrequited. Example: Romeo is lover_of Juliet.	PER	PER
11	rival_of	Indicates a competitive relationship that may involve admiration, respect, or antagonism, not necessarily hostile. Example: Sherlock Holmes is rival_of Professor Moriarty.	PER	PER
12	enemy_of	Represents rivalry, hostility, or animosity among people or organizations. Example: Harry Potter is enemy_of Voldemort.	PER/ORG	PER/ORG
13	inspires	To show a motivational or creative influence. Example: Virgil inspires Dante in The Divine Comedy.	PER	PER
14	sacrifices_for	To capture an act of selflessness for another. Example: Sydney Carton sacrifices_for Charles Darnay in *A Tale of Two Cities*.	PER	PER
15	mentor_of	Describes a teaching, guiding, or advisory relationship where one person provides knowledge or support. Example: Dumbledore is mentor_of Harry Potter.	PER	PER
16	teacher_of	To capture formal or academic teaching relationships, distinct from mentor relationships. Example: Snape is teacher_of Harry Potter.	PER	PER
17	protector_of	Represents a caretaking or safeguarding bond, often involving physical or emotional security. Example: Hagrid is protector_of Harry Potter.	PER	PER
18	employer_of	Denotes a work-related hierarchical relationship between an employer and an employee. Example: Ebenezer Scrooge is employer_of Bob Cratchit.	PER	PER
19	leader_of	Indicates a leadership role where an individual leads a group, organization, or nation. Example: Aragorn is leader_of the Fellowship of the Ring.	PER	ORG
20	member_of	Represents membership or affiliation with a group, organization, or society. Example: Harry Potter is member_of Gryffindor House.	PER	ORG
21	lives_in	Specifies a person's residence. Example: Bilbo lives_in Bag End.	PER	FAC/LOC
22	lived_in	Represents historical association. Example: Jane Eyre lived_in the Victorian Era.	PER	TIME
23	visits	Captures temporary presence in a place or facility, such as a visit to a specific location or landmark. Example: Pip visits Satis House in *Great Expectations*.	PER	FAC

24	travel_to	Indicates movement or journey to a specific location, whether planned or incidental. Example: Odysseus travels_to Ithaca.	PER	LOC
25	born_in	A person's birthplace. Example: Napoleon was born_in Corsica.	PER	LOC
26	travels_by	Describes transport modes. Example: Sherlock Holmes travels_by carriage.	PER	VEH
27	participates_in	A person attending or involved in an event. Example: Elizabeth Bennet participates_in the Netherfield Ball.	PER	EVNT
28	causes	A person triggering an event. Example: Macbeth causes Duncan's murder.	PER	EVNT
29	owns	Represents possession of objects. Example: Bilbo owns the Ring.	PER	OBJ
30	believes_in	Represents an individual's ideology, faith, or belief in a concept, philosophy, or ideal. Example: Atticus Finch believes_in justice.	PER	CNCP
31	embodies	A person symbolizing an abstract idea. Example: Beowulf embodies courage.	PER	CNCP
32	located_in	Indicates geographic placement. Example: The Louvre is located_in Paris.	FAC	LOC
33	part_of	Smaller entities within larger ones. Example: The throne room is part_of the castle.	FAC/LOC/ ORG	FAC/LOC/ ORG
34	owned_by	Represents ownership. Example: Thornfield Hall is owned_by Mr. Rochester.	FAC/VEH	PER
35	occupied_by	Indicates current inhabitant. Example: Bag End is occupied_by Frodo.	FAC	PER
36	used_by	Represents organizational usage. Example: The palace is used_by the monarchy.	FAC	ORG
37	affects	Weather affecting a location or an event. Example: The storm affects the village.	WTHR	LOC/ EVNT
38	experienced_by	A person enduring weather. Example: The storm is experienced_by King Lear.	WTHR	PER
39	travels_in	Indicates vehicle operation in specific areas. Example: The ship travels_in the Pacific Ocean.	VEH	LOC
40	based_in	Geographic headquarters. Example: The Knights Templar is based_in Jerusalem.	ORG	LOC
41	attended_by	Persons present at the event. Example: The ball is attended_by Elizabeth Bennet.	EVNT	PER
42	ends_in	To represent temporal conclusions. Example: The war ends_in 1945.	EVNT	TIME
43	occurs_in	The event's geographic location. Example: The battle occurs_in France/spring.	EVNT	LOC/ TIME
44	features	Objects central to the event. Example: The duel features swords.	EVNT	OBJ
45	stored_in	Placement in a specific location. Example: The painting is stored_in the gallery.	OBJ	LOC/FAC
46	expressed_by	Emotional expression. Example: Jealousy is expressed_by Othello.	SENT	PER
47	used_by	Denotes usage. Example: Arthur uses Excalibur.	OBJ	PER

48	associated_with	Concepts tied to events. Example: Justice is associated_with the trial.	CNCP	EVNT

D GPT-4o Prompt for Fictional Relationship Annotation

System Prompt

You are an expert Literature Analyst specializing in identifying entities and their relationships within excerpts from literary works. Your task is to analyze text chunks and extract meaningful **relations** between **entities** based on predefined ontologies below.

Relations Ontology

Each relation connects two entities, defined by their types and descriptions. Use this ontology to categorize relationships accurately.

ID	Relation Type	Description	Entity Type 1	Entity Type 2
1	parent_father_of	Represents the relationship between a parent and their father.	PER	PER
2	parent_mother_of	Represents the relationship between a parent and their mother.	PER	PER
3	child_of	Represents the relationship between a child and their parents.	PER	PER
4	sibling_of	Denotes siblings within the same family.	PER	PER
5	spouse_of	Indicates a marital relationship, regardless of gender or cultural context.	PER	PER
6	relative_of	Captures a broader familial connection beyond immediate family, such as cousins, uncles, or distant relatives.	PER	PER
7	adopted_by	Indicates a non-biological familial or societal relationship, such as legal guardianship or cultural adoption.	PER	PER
8	companion_of	Represents someone who accompanies, aids, or supports another.	PER	PER
9	friend_of	Indicates a strong, platonic relationship.	PER	PER
10	lover_of	Represents a romantic or amorous relationship, whether mutual or unrequited.	PER	PER
11	rival_of	Indicates a competitive relationship that may involve admiration, respect, or antagonism.	PER	PER
12	enemy_of	Represents rivalry, hostility, or animosity among people or organizations.	PER/ORG	PER/ORG

ID	Relation Type	Description	Entity Type 1	Entity Type 2
13	inspires	Shows motivational or creative influence.	PER	PER
14	sacrifices_for	Captures an act of selflessness for another.	PER	PER
15	mentor_of	Describes a teaching, guiding, or advisory relationship.	PER	PER
16	teacher_of	Captures formal or academic teaching relationships.	PER	PER
17	protector_of	Represents a caretaking or safeguarding bond.	PER	PER
18	employer_of	Denotes a work-related hierarchical relationship.	PER	PER
19	leader_of	Indicates a leadership role over a group or organization.	PER	ORG
20	member_of	Represents membership or affiliation with a group or organization.	PER	ORG
21	lives_in	Specifies a person's residence.	PER	FAC/LOC
22	lived_in	Represents historical association.	PER	TIME
23	visits	Captures temporary presence in a place or facility.	PER	FAC
24	travel_to	Indicates movement or journey to a specific location.	PER	LOC
25	born_in	Represents a person's birthplace.	PER	LOC
26	travels_by	Describes transport modes.	PER	VEH
27	participates_in	Captures involvement in an event.	PER	EVNT
28	causes	Represents a person triggering an event.	PER	EVNT
29	owns	Represents possession of objects.	PER	OBJ
30	believes_in	Represents an individual's belief in a concept.	PER	CNCP
31	embodies	Represents a person symbolizing an abstract idea.	PER	CNCP
32	located_in	Indicates geographic placement.	FAC	LOC
33	part_of	Represents smaller entities within larger ones.	FAC/LOC/ORG	FAC/LOC/ORG
34	owned_by	Represents ownership.	FAC/VEH	PER
35	occupied_by	Indicates current inhabitant.	FAC	PER
36	used_by	Represents usage of a facility or object.	FAC	ORG
37	affects	Weather affecting a location or event.	WTHR	LOC/EVNT
38	experienced_by	A person enduring weather.	WTHR	PER

ID	Relation Type	Description	Entity Type 1	Entity Type 2
39	travels_in	Indicates vehicle operation in specific areas.	VEH	LOC
40	based_in	Represents geographic headquarters.	ORG	LOC
41	attended_by	Represents persons present at an event.	EVNT	PER
42	ends_in	Represents temporal conclusions.	EVNT	TIME
43	occurs_in	Represents an event's geographic location or time.	EVNT	LOC/TIME
44	features	Represents objects central to the event.	EVNT	OBJ
45	stored_in	Represents placement of objects in a location.	OBJ	LOC/FAC
46	expressed_by	Represents emotional expression.	SENT	PER
47	used_by	Represents usage of objects.	OBJ	PER
48	associated_with	Represents concepts tied to events.	CNCP	EVNT

Entity Types Ontology

Entities are categorized by their types. Use these definitions to identify and classify entities within the text.

ID	Entity Type	Short Description	Description
1	PER	Person	A single person or group of people.
2	FAC	Facility	Functional, man-made structures for human use.
3	LOC	Location	Physical places without political boundaries.
4	WTHR	Weather	Natural atmospheric or celestial phenomena.
5	VEH	Vehicle	Physical devices for transportation.
6	ORG	Organization	Formal associations or institutions.
7	EVNT	Event	Significant occurrences or actions.
8	TIME	Time Expression	Chronological markers or eras.
9	OBJ	Object	Tangible items of significance.
10	SENT	Sentiment	Emotional states or feelings.
11	CNCP	Concept	Abstract themes or ideas.

Prompt

Identify and extract all related named entity pairs from the provided text. Format the extracted pairs as a list of JSON objects using the structure below for each found relation. Ensure only the list of JSON objects is returned, without any additional text.

```
[
  {
    "entity1": "Exact text of the first entity",
    "entity2": "Exact text of the second entity",
```

```
    "entity1Type": "Type of the first entity",
    "entity2Type": "Type of the second entity",
    "relation": "Relation type"
  }
]
```

Text:

<the text chunk>

E Examples of Extracted Relations

Input Text Chunk	Output Relations
At those words Vortigern's face grew white as ashes, and, rising in confusion and disorder, he sent for all the best artificers and craftsmen and mechanics, and commanded them vehemently to go and build him straightway in the furthest west of his lands a great and strong castle, where he might fly for refuge and escape the vengeance of his master's sons—"and, moreover," cried he, "let the work be done within a hundred days from now, or I will surely spare no life amongst you all." Then all the host of craftsmen, fearing for their lives, found out a proper site whereon to build the tower, and eagerly began to lay in the foundations. But no sooner were the walls raised up above the ground than all their work was overwhelmed and broken down by night invisibly, no man perceiving how, or by whom, or what. And the same thing happening again, and yet again, all the workmen, full of terror, sought out the king, and threw themselves upon their faces before him, beseeching him to interfere and help them or to deliver them from their dreadful work. Filled with mixed rage and fear, the king called for the astrologers and wizards, and took counsel with them what these things might be, and how to overcome them.	{ {'entity1': 'Vortigern', 'entity2': 'his master's sons', 'entity1Type': 'PER', 'entity2Type': 'PER', 'relation': 'enemy_of'}, {'entity1': 'Vortigern', 'entity2': 'castle', 'entity1Type': 'PER', 'entity2Type': 'FAC', 'relation': 'owns'}, {'entity1': 'Vortigern', 'entity2': 'astrologers and wizards', 'entity1Type': 'PER', 'entity2Type': 'PER', 'relation': 'companion_of'} }
"Thou art full young and tender of age," said King Arthur, "to take so high an order upon thee." "Sir," said Griflet, "I beseech thee make me a knight;" and Merlin also advising the king to grant his request, "Well," said Arthur, "be it then so," and knighted him forthwith. Then said he to him, "Since I have granted thee this favour, thou must in turn grant me a gift." "Whatsoever thou wilt, my lord," replied Sir Griflet. "Promise me," said King Arthur, "by the faith of thy body, that when thou hast jousted with this knight at the fountain, thou wilt return to me straightway, unless he slay thee."	{ {'entity1': 'King Arthur', 'entity2': 'Griflet', 'entity1Type': 'PER', 'entity2Type': 'PER', 'relation': 'mentor_of'}, {'entity1': 'Merlin', 'entity2': 'King Arthur', 'entity1Type': 'PER', 'entity2Type': 'PER', 'relation': 'advises'} }

F Dataset Collection - Titles and Authors

PG Book ID	Title	Author

106	Jungle Tales of Tarzan	Edgar Rice Burroughs
12371	The Experiences of a Barrister, and Confessions of an Attorney	Samuel Warren
12753	The Legends of King Arthur and His Knights	James, Sir Knowles
12807	Dick Prescott's Fourth Year at West Point - Or, Ready to Drop the Gray for Shoulder Straps	H. Irving (Harrie Irving) Hancock
1329	A Voyage to Arcturus	David Lindsay
134	Maria; Or, The Wrongs of Woman	Mary Wollstonecraft
14174	The Mating of Lydia	Humphry, Mrs. Ward
15284	The Tale of Johnny Town-Mouse	Beatrix Potter
1574	Historic Girls: Stories Of Girls Who Have Influenced The History Of Their Times	Elbridge S. (Elbridge Streeter) Brooks
1617	The Wind in the Rose-Bush, and Other Stories of the Supernatural	Mary Eleanor Wilkins Freeman
165	McTeague: A Story of San Francisco	Frank Norris
16630	Empire Builders	Francis Lynde
1881	The Call of the Canyon	Zane Grey
18873	Contes et légendes. 1re Partie	H. A. (Hélène Adeline) Guerber
21299	Blue Jackets: The Log of the Teaser	George Manville Fenn
21446	Favourite Fables in Prose and Verse	Harrison Weir
22066	The Long Roll	Mary Johnston
23060	The Unknown Masterpiece - 1845	Honoré de Balzac
24584	Man Overboard!	F. Marion (Francis Marion) Crawford
24714	Fairy Tales from Brazil: How and Why Tales from Brazilian Folk-Lore	Elsie Spicer Eells
25165	The Candy Country	Louisa May Alcott
25205	Light On the Child's Path	William Allen Bixler
25513	Edmund Dulac's Fairy-Book: Fairy Tales of the Allied Nations	Edmund Dulac
2662	Under the Greenwood Tree; Or, The Mellstock Quire - A Rural Painting of the Dutch School	Thomas Hardy
29452	The Wings of the Dove, Volume 1 of 2	Henry James
30365	In Desert and Wilderness	Henryk Sienkiewicz
31217	Household Papers and Stories	Harriet Beecher Stowe
31858	Ancestors: A Novel	Gertrude Franklin Horn Atherton
32543	The White Chief of the Caffres	Alfred W. (Alfred Wilks) Drayson
3322	East Lynne	Henry, Mrs. Wood
33382	Penny Nichols and the Black Imp	Joan Clark

34025	Ancient Rome: The Lives of Great Men	Mary Agnes Hamilton
35179	The Three Sapphires	William Alexander Fraser
35504	Miss Maitland, Private Secretary	Geraldine Bonner
35671	The Messenger	Elizabeth Robins
36684	Molly Brown's Freshman Days	Nell Speed
36703	A Bayard From Bengal - Being some account of the Magnificent and Spanking Career of Chunder Bindabun Bhosh,...	F. Anstey
37121	Charles Dickens' Children Stories	Charles Dickens
37251	In Touch with Nature: Tales and Sketches from the Life	Gordon Stables
39018	Mr. Marx's Secret	E. Phillips (Edward Phillips) Oppenheim
39375	Christmas-Tree Land	Mrs. Molesworth
396	The Lady, or the Tiger?	Frank R. Stockton
40033	The Missing Formula - Madge Sterling Series, 1	Mildred A. (Mildred Augustine) Wirt
40882	Felix Holt, the Radical	George Eliot
42455	The Mystery of the Sea	Bram Stoker
42934	Polly's Southern Cruise	Lillian Elizabeth Roy
43982	Stories of the Old World	Alfred John Church
44	The Song of the Lark	Willa Cather
44111	Red Dynamite - A Mystery Story for Boys	Roy J. (Roy Judson) Snell
4470	Diana of the Crossways — Complete	George Meredith
44872	The Man Who Fell Through the Earth	Carolyn Wells
45517	The Putnam Hall Cadets; or, Good Times in School and Out	Edward Stratemeyer
47139	Stories from Wagner	J. Walker (Joseph Walker) McSpadden
47634	Sons and Lovers	D. H. (David Herbert) Lawrence
5111	The Real Diary of a Real Boy	Henry A. (Henry Augustus) Shute
5182	The Old English Baron: a Gothic Story	Clara Reeve
51919	Rancho Del Muerto, and Other Stories of Adventure - by Various Authors, from "Outing"	Charles King
52610	Ward Hill, the Senior	Everett T. (Everett Titsworth) Tomlinson
52617	The Decameron (Day 1 to Day 5) - Containing an hundred pleasant Novels	Giovanni Boccaccio
52702	Mrs Peixada	Henry Harland
53920	Kittyboy's Christmas	Amy Ella Blanchard

540	The Red Fairy Book	Andrew Lang
55847	Known to the Police	Thomas Holmes
56085	The Silver Princess in Oz	Ruth Plumly Thompson
5658	Lord Jim	Joseph Conrad
56665	Tales and Stories - Now First Collected	Mary Wollstonecraft Shelley
59136	Finkler's Field: A Story of School and Baseball	Ralph Henry Barbour
6053	Evelina, Or, the History of a Young Lady's Entrance into the World	Fanny Burney
61457	Charley's Log: A Story of Schoolboy Life	Emma Leslie
619	The Warden	Anthony Trollope
62126	Captivating Bible Stories for Young People, Written in Simple Language	Charlotte M. (Charlotte Mary) Yonge
64264	Zero Hour	Ray Bradbury
653	The Chimes - A Goblin Story of Some Bells That Rang an Old Year out and a New Year In	Charles Dickens
66687	Fairy Tales for Workers' Children	Hermynia Zur Mühlen
6852	Venus in Furs	Leopold, Ritter von Sacher-Masoch
6941	Old Mortality, Complete	Walter Scott
6985	A Prefect's Uncle	P. G. (Pelham Grenville) Wodehouse
70653	Rattle of Bones	Robert E. (Robert Ervin) Howard
71864	The White Countess	Florence Warden
72063	Once Upon a Time Animal Stories	Carolyn Sherwin Bailey
72824	The Mystery of the Blue Train	Agatha Christie
73548	The Story of the Rhinegold (Der Ring des Nibelungen) Told for Young People	Anna Alice Chapin
74155	A Frontier Knight: A Story of Early Texan Border-Life	Amy Ella Blanchard
74440	Two Brave Boys, and, The Wrong Twin	Mary E. (Mary Emily) Ropes
74593	The Baseball Boys of Lakeport: Or, The Winning Run	Edward Stratemeyer
74763	Lost Gip	Hesba Stretton

Improving Hate Speech Classification with Cross-Taxonomy Dataset Integration

Jan Fillies[1,2] and Adrian Paschke[1,2,3]
[1]Institut für Angewandte Informatik, Leipzig, Germany
[2]Freie Universität Berlin, Berlin, Germany
[3]Fraunhofer-Institut für Offene Kommunikationssysteme, Berlin, Germany
jan.fillies@fu-berlin.de

Abstract

Algorithmic hate speech detection faces significant challenges due to the diverse definitions and datasets used in research and practice. Social media platforms, legal frameworks, and institutions each apply distinct yet overlapping definitions, complicating classification efforts. This study addresses these challenges by demonstrating that existing datasets and taxonomies can be integrated into a unified model, enhancing prediction performance and reducing reliance on multiple specialized classifiers. The work introduces a universal taxonomy and a hate speech classifier capable of detecting a wide range of definitions within a single framework. Our approach is validated by combining two widely used but differently annotated datasets, showing improved classification performance on an independent test set. This work highlights the potential of dataset and taxonomy integration in advancing hate speech detection, increasing efficiency, and ensuring broader applicability across contexts.

1 Introduction

Research has shown a direct link between the rise of online hate speech and offline events (Lupu et al., 2023), highlighting the growing impact of digital platforms on real-world occurrences. As of April 2023, there are an estimated 4.8 billion global social media users, making up about 59.9% of the world's population (Kemp, 2023). This massive reach underscores the scale of the problem, with Facebook alone removing 38.3 million instances of hate speech in the first three quarters of 2023 (Dixon, 2023). These numbers emphasize both the urgency and magnitude of the issue, making it a top priority for the research community. The challenge lies in balancing the preservation of free speech with the need to protect individuals from harm. While algorithms play a key role in addressing this issue, they are just one part of a broader, multifaceted approach. In this context, this research aims to develop efficient and effective algorithmic solutions for hate speech detection.

One main challenge in the field is that the understanding of hate speech varies and is influenced by factors such as topic (Wiegand et al., 2019), author (Nejadgholi and Kiritchenko, 2020), and time (Justen et al., 2022), among others. Even within the legal context, it is a complex process deciding whether a statement should be classified as hateful or not. In response, research, private, and public entities have developed their own definitions and community standards, legal frameworks, or annotation guidelines (MacAvaney et al., 2019).

Especially in the research field, the available datasets heavily depend on the annotation procedure and the definitions of hate speech provided to the annotators (Vidgen and Derczynski, 2020). This dependence and wide variety of definitions makes it challenging to compare (Fortuna and Nunes, 2018) or merge datasets annotated within different annotation schemas. While the field of available annotated hate speech corpora is limited to begin with, this additional limitation of incompatibility further complicates efforts to provide general and reliable hate speech detection.

This research addresses this gap by providing a machine learning structure that combines existing definitions and datasets. It identifies mismatches in definitions, faults during the annotation combining process, and missing labels in datasets. The study demonstrates the feasibility of merging annotation schemas and datasets to detect a wider variety of hate speech definitions using just one trained classifier. It establishes that a single general taxonomy can be created and employed for multi-label federated training of a classifier, thereby improving prediction quality.

The approach is evaluated using two standard research datasets and their respective definitions. The outcome involves the creation of a comprehensive hate speech taxonomy and the training of a

Proceedings of LaTeCH-CLfL 2025, pages 148–159

general hate speech classifier.

The scripts used for preprocessing, dataset construction, training, and evaluation are available as part of the paper.[1] This offers a deeper insight and facilitates the reproducibility of our work. Please note that the used datasets have to be obtained from the cited sources.

2 Related Work

Datasets - The field of hate speech datasets is rapidly growing. Established datasets include (Hosseinmardi et al., 2015; de Gibert et al., 2018; ElSherief et al., 2018), while newer, smaller datasets (Fillies et al., 2023b, 2025) continue to emerge. A comprehensive overview is provided by Vidgen and Derczynski (2020). Analysis of these datasets highlights diverse annotation schemes (Chung et al., 2019), from binary labels to multi-class hierarchies (Ranasinghe and Zampieri, 2020). Universal annotation frameworks are also recognized (Bartalesi et al., 2006). However, no single benchmark dataset or universally accepted definition of hate speech exists (MacAvaney et al., 2019). The wide range of definitions has been extensively studied by Stephan (2020).

Algorithmic Detection - For detecting hate speech, toxic speech, abusive language, and related areas, the predominant algorithmic approach has utilized supervised transformer-based architectures (Mozafari et al., 2020; Poletto et al., 2021; Plaza-del Arco et al., 2023). Fine-tuning transformer models, particularly BERT (Devlin et al., 2019), has demonstrated significant performance enhancements compared to other methods (Liu et al., 2019a; Kirk et al., 2022; Fillies et al., 2023a). Recently, the focus has shifted towards using pre-trained large language models combined with prompting techniques for hate speech detection (Kim et al., 2023; Plaza-del Arco et al., 2023; Fillies and Paschke, 2024).

Taxonomy and Ontology Matching - Several researchers have aimed to create general hate speech ontologies (Stranisci et al., 2022; Sharma et al., 2018) and taxonomies (Salminen et al., 2018; Zufall et al., 2022; Lewandowska-Tomaszczyk et al., 2023). Salminen et al. (2018) integrated their taxonomy into a transformer-based hate speech detection model, partially building on existing taxonomies and combining them to annotate a new dataset. The practice of merging ontologies is well established (Shvaiko and Euzenat, 2013). However, no research has yet combined hate speech taxonomies to make existing datasets suitable for iterative federated learning.

Federated and Continuous Learning - Federated learning for hate speech detection is crucial as it mitigates privacy concerns related to data sharing. A key development is Zampieri et al. (2024), which introduces a binary hate speech classifier using a decentralized architecture, demonstrating superior performance across datasets while preserving privacy. Another significant study, Gala et al. (2023), explores multi-class federated learning on a static dataset with uniform annotations, disregarding annotation mismatches and emphasizing distributed training benefits. In continuous learning, Omrani et al. (2023) propose a novel framework for detecting problematic content by integrating various datasets and treating each label as an independent classification task.

This research directly builds upon the work of Zampieri et al. (2024), Gala et al. (2023), and Omrani et al. (2023). It extends the findings of Zampieri et al. (2024) and Gala et al. (2023) by demonstrating that federated training for hate speech detection is feasible not only for binary classification but also for multi-label hate speech datasets with varying definitions of hate speech. In relation to Omrani et al. (2023), it advances the research by integrating labels into a unified taxonomy with hierarchical aspects, introducing a deeper semantic relationship model, and showing that this model can be continuously adapted.

3 Methodology

The research is divided into three main parts. First, a general hate speech taxonomy is created. Second, this taxonomy is used to fine-tune a pre-trained multi-label hate speech detection model multiple times on two different datasets (see Sections 4 and 6). Lastly, continuous evaluation is conducted after each training cycle. Each step is detailed in this section (see Figure 1), with selected datasets, taxonomies, and the models serving as examples to demonstrate the approach's functionality.

1. In the first step, the taxonomies are combined into one general taxonomy. Here, the general taxonomy should include all the classes proposed by the underlying concepts. A class hierarchy is introduced to represent and adjust to

[1] https://github.com/fillies/HateSpeechCrossTaxonomyDatasetIntegration

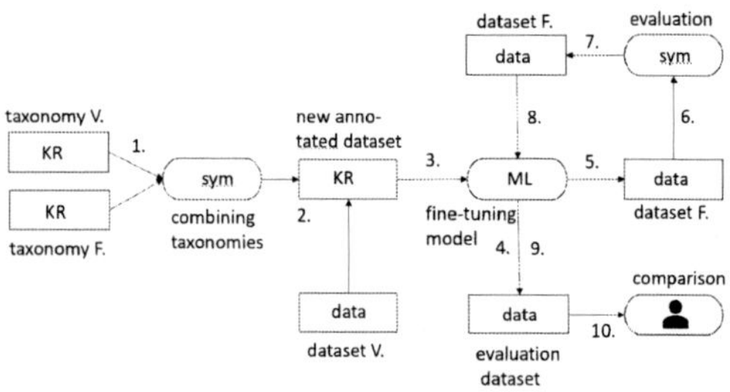

Figure 1: Boxology-Model of the Process. F. = Fanton et al. 2021, V. = Vidgen et al. 2021, sym = Symbolic Processing KR. = Knowledge Representation, ML = Machine Learning

different levels of abstraction (see section 5). In this step, classes that cannot be merged are identified and removed. A word-level matching of annotations between the original and the new general taxonomy is introduced. The class hierarchy of the general taxonomy is represented through a one-hot encoded vector; when a subclass is flagged as identified, the parent classes must be present too.

2. In the following step, one dataset is selected to have its annotations transferred into the new annotation format based on the general taxonomy. Here, it is expected that certain flags within the annotations are missing or, more precisely, incorrectly annotated.

3. Based on this newly annotated dataset, a multi-label classifier is trained (see section 6).

4. To validate the performance of the trained model and provide insight into the generalizability of the model, an external binary hate speech dataset is provided as an evaluation dataset, and the performance is measured (see section 6.6).

5. The trained classifier is now used to predict all known labels of the second dataset.

6. The True Positive, False Negative, False Positive, and True Negative distributions of the predictions generate insights into three main aspects regarding the annotations. Firstly, it can be observed where the definitions of concepts are not aligned. Secondly, it can be determined if the general taxonomy made a mistake in its hierarchical structure. Lastly, it can be identified which flags are not represented in the old annotation of the new dataset (see section 6.7).

7. After evaluation, the prediction scores and the human annotations of the second dataset can be combined. In the parts where the human annotation identified a hateful instance, they overwrite the given predictions. Classes that had to be excluded due to definition mismatches can be annotated, but only with the predictions of the network. The predicted values are normalized to [0,1], while the human annotations remain binary.

8. Based on this mix of predicted and human-based annotations, the original network is fine-tuned again on the new dataset (see section 6.6). Extra measures to prevent overfitting can be implemented.

9. The dataset is evaluated again using the same binary hate/no-hate external dataset (see section 6.6).

10. Lastly, the two measurements of prediction quality on the external dataset are compared to validate the performance and provide insight into generalizability (see section 6.7).

4 Datasets

Two primary datasets with different annotations were selected for this research, along with two additional datasets: one for evaluation and one for balancing the two main datasets during training with non-hateful statements.

The first main dataset, provided by Vidgen et al. (2021), is a large, dynamically generated collection of 41,255 entries created over four rounds, with 54% of the entries being hateful. The dataset includes 11 English-language training datasets for hate and toxicity from hatespeechdata.com. Its hierarchical taxonomy, based on Robert C Nickerson and Muntermann (2013), classifies entries into hate and no-hate categories. The hate entries are further divided into five types (Derogation, Animosity, Threatening Language, Support for Hateful Entities, Dehumanization). Additionally, 29 identities as hate targets are annotated. The annotations were performed by 20 trained annotators.

The second main dataset compiled by Fanton et al. (2021) is also a dynamically generated human-in-the-loop dataset, containing 5,000 hateful statements. Created over two cycles with human input in between, the initial dataset included 880 statements and was developed in collaboration with 20 experts from various NGOs. The annotations featured 10 labels ("DISABLED," "JEWS," "OVERWEIGHT," "LGBT+," "MUSLIM," "WOMEN," "PEOPLE OF COLOR," "ROMANI," "MIGRANTS," "OTHER"). Three trained students were involved in the annotation process.

The dataset from Fillies et al. (2023b) was selected for non-hateful statements, as only the hateful entries were selected from the two main datasets, and training a classifier solely on those would likely result in overfitting. This dataset, in English, includes annotated Discord messages collected between March 2021 and June 2022, comprising 88,395 chat messages. Around 6.42% of the messages were classified as hate speech.

The final support dataset, from Ljubešić et al. (2021), was chosen for validation and independent evaluation of the classifier's performance. It consists of YouTube comments collected between January and May 2020, with approximately 50% hate and 50% non-hateful examples.

5 General Taxonomy

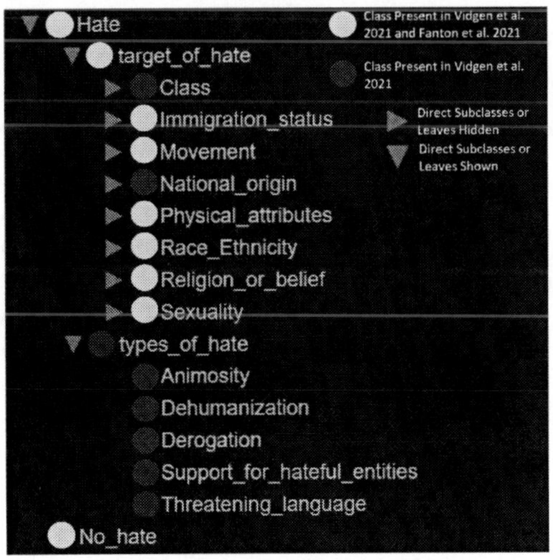

Figure 2: Overview General Taxonomy Level 1 - 3

This research explores merging multiple taxonomies into a central one to enable a single classifier to predict diverse definitions using differently annotated datasets. As a demonstration, two existing taxonomies were combined. The taxonomy was developed by a two-person team and is shown in Appendix A.1, with the first three levels in Figure 2. Shared classes and leaves (labels not further broken down) are highlighted in yellow, while those unique to Vidgen et al. (2021) are in red. Both taxonomies contributed different, identical, or new subclasses and leaves. The final taxonomy has five layers.

The taxonomy from Vidgen et al. (2021) formed the basis for the merge due to its thoroughness. It initially distinguishes between hate and non-hate statements.

Hate types from Vidgen et al. (2021) were grouped under the label "types_of_hate," which was absent in Fanton et al. (2021). Adjustments were made for hate targets, with seven out of 11 classes from Fanton et al. (2021) fitting directly into the new taxonomy. The remaining classes, like "Gender," "Intersectional," and "Disability," required modifications.

Due to Fanton et al. (2021) introducing the labels "Disabled" and "Overweight", a class regarding physical attributes was introduced, also containing the label "Gender," which then includes the class "Gender Minorities," unlike Vidgen et al. (2021) where it is independent. The last label from Vidgen et al. (2021), "Intersectional," was not included explicitly, as it is contained in the multi-label encodings (e.g., black women) that are represented in the taxonomy.

The classes ("Jews", "Muslim", "Women", "Romani", "Migrants") from Fanton et al. (2021) were already covered in the taxonomy. The label "People of color" from Fanton et al. (2021) was initially introduced as an independent label under the class "Physical_attributes/skin_color/" next to the labels "Black" and "White." However, the evaluation of the trained network's performance clearly showed this as a mistake, making it necessary to make "Black" a subclass of "People of Color."

The main challenge was the label "LGBT+" by Fanton et al. (2021) due to its covering of multiple aspects. It is first a political and social movement, standing for "lesbian, gay, bisexual, transgender, plus other sexual and gender identities," making it difficult to locate in the existing classes of gender and sexual orientation. The decision was made to include it in the taxonomy as a movement.

It is noteworthy that in the actual dataset annotations by Vidgen et al. (2021), labels appeared that were not represented in the provided taxonomy, such as "old.people," "russian," "lgbtq," "eastern.europe," and "non.white." These labels were included in the new general taxonomy with their own classes. However, the label "other" from Fanton et al. (2021) had to be disregarded. The final taxonomy consists of 23 classes and 43 leaves, merging labels from both taxonomies directly or through abstraction.

6 Experimental Classifier

This section describes the creation of an experimental classifier. The classifier proves the validity of the concept as a proof-of-work. As detailed in the methodology section (3), the labels in the existing datasets from Vidgen et al. (2021) can be matched to the labels of the new taxonomy, creating a new annotation schema for the dataset. The annotated dataset is then used to fine-tune a pretrained language model to be a multi-label hate speech classifier. After this initial training, the classifier is used to reannotate the second dataset from Fanton et al. (2021), introducing the new annotation schema and providing insights into the created taxonomy, missing labels, and different underlying definitions of hate contained in the two datasets.

The predicted annotations can then be merged with the existing human annotations and used to fine-tune the network again. If the approach holds merit, the minimum requirement is that the hate speech prediction quality of the network increases on an independent test set after the training cycles. This section describes the steps of this process.

6.1 Encoding

The goal is to map the taxonomy into a network-readable format while preserving class structure information and enabling the annotation of multiple definitions within a unified schema. The proposed encoding uses a sparse binary vector, where each position corresponds to a class or leaf in the taxonomy. This allows the network to learn parent-child relationships while capturing varying degrees of hate within a single framework.

For example, in the schema "Target_of_hate / Physical_attributes / Skin_color / People_of_color / Black," a statement expressing hate toward Black people would be encoded as [1,1,1,1,1], while hate toward people of color would be [1,1,1,1,0]. This approach enables the network to recognize hierarchical relationships and adapt to different depths of hate speech definitions.

6.2 Evaluation Metrics

Two evaluation metrics were used: accuracy and F-1 scores. For a deeper understanding of the results, the distributions of predictions in regard to the human-annotated labels were evaluated in the four groups: True Positive (TP), True Negative (TN), False Positive (FP), and False Negative (FN).

Accuracy is defined as the ratio of correct predictions to the number of total predictions. The F1-Score metric is beneficial in situations where datasets have imbalanced class distributions (Tsourakis, 2022), fitting the problem at hand. For the F-1 Score, a threshold of 0.5 was chosen.

6.3 Algorithm

As a base, the state-of-the-art model RoBERTa was chosen, first introduced by Liu et al. (2019b). It is a fine-tuned, improved version of the BERT model pretrained and introduced by Devlin et al. (2019). RoBERTa uses the same architecture as BERT but applies a different tokenizer and pretraining scheme. The research used the pretrained multi-label RoBERTa model for multi-label sequence classification provided through the platform HuggingFace.[2] In combination with the fitting tokenizer from "twitter-roberta-base-emotion".[3]. It is meant to be an example implementation to show merit.

6.4 Technical Setup

For training, Google Colaboratory (Colab) was used, providing a browser-based environment for writing and executing Python code in Jupyter notebooks. As noted by Kimm et al. (2021), Colab offers access to TPUs and GPUs without requiring additional configuration. For all training sessions, a cluster with Nvidia V100 GPUs, 12.7 GB System-RAM, 16 GB GPU-RAM, and 72.8 GB Storage was utilized. The first training cycle took 45 minutes, while the second cycle took 5 minutes. For both cycles, a fixed seed was used, with the evaluation step size set to 500, train and evaluation batch sizes set to 6, and the number of training epochs set to 4. Other hyperparameters followed the default recommendations from RoBERTa. To prevent overfitting during the second cycle, the dropout ratio for attention probabilities and the dropout probability for fully connected layers in embeddings, encoder, and pooler were both set to 0.5.

[2]https://huggingface.co/docs/transformers/model_doc/roberta#transformers. RobertaForSequenceClassification

[3]https://huggingface.co/cardiffnlp

6.5 Data preparation

As detailed in Section 6.1, both datasets were encoded using sparse one-hot encoding based on the taxonomy. They were cleaned of duplicates, missing data, and unusable annotations. Given the nature of BERT models, no additional text preprocessing was performed to preserve information. Since both datasets lacked non-hateful language, 30% non-hateful statements from Fillies et al. (2023b) were randomly added. Considering that only 6% of the 88,000 messages in Fillies et al. (2023b) contain hate, the risk of including complex cases like counter-hate speech was minimal. These non-hateful examples were also one-hot encoded. A 10% holdout set was reserved for evaluation, and both datasets were randomized.

After cleaning and adding 30% non-hate speech statements, the dataset from Vidgen et al. (2021) contained 18,380 instances, while the dataset based on Fanton et al. (2021) had 4,767 instances.

The annotation of the Fanton et al. (2021) dataset combined human annotations from Fanton et al. (2021) with predictions from the first training cycle. When the network failed to predict a label but an annotator identified it, the human annotation took precedence. This approach is justified, as human annotations rely on inter-annotator agreement, reducing the likelihood of false positives, since multiple annotators would need to select the same incorrect label. When no human labels were available or the human annotation didn't match the network's prediction, the network's predictions were used. This was necessary because certain labels were not annotated in the second dataset, and false negatives by annotators were more likely, given that inter-annotator agreement was reduced to binary decisions. For example, the network might predict a low likelihood of racism in a statement (e.g., a score of 0.2 on a scale from -1 to 1). However, human annotation, based on a binary majority agreement among three annotators (two say no racism detected, but one identifies racism), could be flawed. In such cases, the network's prediction is considered a more accurate reflection of reality than the potentially flawed binary annotation.

6.6 Results

The prediction results from the three fine-tuning experiments and their evaluation on the independent evaluation test set (ETS) are shown in Table 1. The details of these results are discussed individually in section 6.7.

Table 1: All Training and Evaluation Test Set Results

Cycle	Dataset	F1-Score	Accuracy
Cycle-1	Vidgen	0.89	0.46
Cycle-1	ETS	0.73	-
Cycle-1-A	Vidgen	0.89	0.55
Cycle-1-A	ETS	0.73	-
Cycle-2	Fanton	0.91	0.74
Cycle-2	ETS	0.84	-

Table 2: Display of selected classes from the class wise prediction's evaluation of RoBERTa-Cycle-1 on the dataset by (Fanton et al., 2021)

Class/Leaves	F1-Score	Instances
Hate	1.00	3539
Target_of_hate	0.99	3539
Movement	0.00	465
LGBTQ+	0.00	465
Physical_attri	0.90	1036
Skin_color	0.93	301
Black	0.00	0
Non_white	0.03	301
Religion/belief	0.99	1401
Jews	0.99	418
Muslims	0.98	983
Sexuality	0.00	0
Bisexual	0.00	0
Gay	0.00	0
Types_of_hate	0.00	0
Weighted avg	0.89	15017

6.6.1 RoBERTa-Cycle-1

In the first stage, the classifier (RoBERTa-Cycle-1) was trained on the dataset from Vidgen et al. (2021) and evaluated on the evaluation dataset from Ljubešić et al. (2021).

This training and evaluation were followed by an analysis of the classifier's predictions at the class level for the dataset from Fanton et al. (2021) (see Table 2). For each class, results were assessed, and performance drops, such as in the cases of 'Non_white' and 'LGBTQ+', were identified. Incorrectly associated labels were pinpointed (see Table 3 and 4). For instance, many statements labeled 'LGBTQ+' were misclassified under the "Sexuality" label. Table 3 shows the percentages of other classes predicted for the "LGBTQ+" label, while Table 4 shows the misclassification for "Non_white". The percentages do not add up to

Table 3: Display of selected classes where the class "LGBTQ+" gets miss labeled to. Using the RoBERTa-Cycle-1 model on the dataset by Fanton et al. (2021)

Class	Percentage
Physical_attri.	0.308
Gender	0.295
Gender_min.	0.189
Trans	0.166
Women	0.037
Sexuality	0.850
Gay	0.819

Table 4: Display of selected classes where "Non_white" is mislabeled, using the RoBERTa-Cycle-1 model on the dataset by (Fanton et al., 2021).

Class	Percentage
Black	0.882
Race_Ethnicity	0.078

1, as this is a multi-label prediction with binary annotations.

These misclassifications highlight the need for adjustments in the taxonomy, as "LGBTQ+" and "Non_white" are not correctly represented. This led to the need to relabel and retrain the model, resulting in RoBERTa-Cycle-1-A.

6.6.2 RoBERTa-Cycle-1-A

In the following, the model RoBERTa-Cycle-1-A and its performance on the Evaluation Test were established, see Table 1. It can be observed that the F-1 score remains stable while the accuracy increases significantly after adjusting the taxonomy. All prediction results for all classes of the datasets can be found on GitHub[4]. Table 5 displays a selection of classes important for evaluating the adjustment of the taxonomy in the previous step.

After the training of RoBERTa-Cycle-1-A, the same in-depth evaluation of the classifier's predictions on a class level for the dataset from Fanton et al. (2021) was performed, see GitHub[5].This time, no outlier class, in terms of prediction performance, was identified, indicating that there is no further need for adjustment.

[4]https://github.com/fillies/HateSpeechCrossTaxonomy DatasetIntegration

[5]https://github.com/fillies/HateSpeechCrossTaxonomy DatasetIntegration

Table 5: Display of selected classes from the class wise predictions evaluation of RoBERTa- Cycle-1-A on the dataset by (Fanton et al., 2021)

Class/Leaves	F1-Score	Instances
Hate	1.00	3539
Target_of_hate	0.99	3539
Skin_color	0.94	301
Non_white	0.94	301
Black	0.00	0
Weighted avg	0.91	-

6.6.3 RoBERTa-Cycle-2

Based on RoBERTa-Cycle-1-A and the merged machine and human annotations of the Fanton et al. (2021) dataset, the model RoBERTa-Cycle-2 was trained and evaluated on the Evaluation Test Set, see Table 1. A relevant increase in F1-Score (from 0.73 to 0.84) on the ETS can be observed, accompanied by a general increase in prediction quality on the new dataset (to a new F1-Score of 0.91 and an accuracy of 0.74).

Different from RoBERTa-Cycle-1 and similar to RoBERTa-Cycle-1-A, the evaluation of each annotated class and its prediction performance, see Table 6, did not produce noteworthy outliers in regard to underperformance. Therefore, no further adjustment of the taxonomy is necessary. All prediction results for all classes across all datasets can be found on GitHub[6].

6.7 Discussion of Results

6.7.1 RoBERTa-Cycle-1

After the first training cycle on the dataset from Vidgen et al. (2021), the results in table 1, particularly the F1-Score, show strong performance for the RoBERTa-Cycle-1 classifier. The notable difference between F1-Score and Accuracy highlights the class imbalance, which corresponds with the sparse input vectors and unbalanced class distributions in the dataset. The F1-Score of 0.73 on the Evaluation Test Set further confirms that the classifier successfully learned and generalized the key aspects of hate speech.

The predictions from RoBERTa-Cycle-1 on the Fanton et al. (2021) dataset (see Table 2) show that the model excels at identifying higher levels of abstraction, especially in binary hate speech classification, but struggles with more specific categories.

[6]https://github.com/fillies/HateSpeechCrossTaxonomy DatasetIntegration

Table 6: Display of selected classes from the class wise predictions evaluation of RoBERTa-Cycle-2 on the dataset from Vidgen et al. (2021)

Class/Leaves	F1-Score	Instances
Hate	1.00	14900
Target_of_hate	1.00	14780
Movement	0.00	0
LGBTQ+	0.00	0
Physical_attributes	0.93	7541
Skin_color	0.88	2918
Black	0.86	2553
Non_white	0.89	2918
Religion_or_belief	0.86	2529
Jews	0.87	1293
Muslims	0.84	1267
Sexuality	0.89	1552
Bisexual	0.00	110
Gay	0.87	1487
Types_of_hate	1.00	14900
Weighted avg	0.82	-

Three issues are observed. First, annotations, such as "types_of_hate," are missing from the Fanton et al. (2021) annotations.

Second, while the network performs well in predicting the "skin_color" class, it mislabels many "non_white" statements as "black," indicating a taxonomy error (see Table 4). The error rate of around 11% across other classes is acceptable given the network's overall performance. Lastly, the network significantly underperforms on the "Movement" class and the "LGBTQ+" leaf, with misclassifications spread across multiple leaves in different classes (see Table 3), suggesting a mismatch in definitions. The issue of mismatched definitions is a clear limitation at this stage. For cases like "black" and "non_white," taxonomy adjustments—such as making "non_white" the parent class of "black"—can help address misclassifications within leaves or subclasses. However, deeper issues, like the "LGBTQ+" misclassifications, may require more advanced solutions, potentially utilizing ontology matching techniques in the future.

6.7.2 RoBERTa-Cycle-1-A

After retraining the classifier with the new encoded filtered input, Table 1 shows improved accuracy for RoBERTa-Cycle-1-A and resolves the taxonomy issue for "black" and "non_white" classes (see Table 5). This performance increase is linked to the label adjustment based on the revised taxonomy. The network's prior learning that "black" is a leaf of "non_white" highlights the value of encoding semantic relationships into labels, enhancing label comparability and generalizability in future iterations.

6.7.3 RoBERTa-Cycle-2

RoBERTa-Cycle-2's class-wise performance on the dataset from Vidgen et al. (2021) (see Table 6) shows that, despite retraining, it preserves the original class definitions (e.g., "types_of_hate") while improving its general understanding of hate speech, as evidenced by the increase in prediction quality on the Evaluation Test Set from 0.73 to 0.84.

Although there is a slight decrease in the weighted average prediction quality from 0.89 to 0.82 on the Vidgen et al. (2021) dataset, this is reasonable given the complete fine-tuning. The model adapts well, correctly covering both new and old concepts, demonstrating that careful design and fine-tuning allow it to retain learned patterns while adapting to new definitions.

7 Conclusion and Outlook

The results of this research demonstrate the feasibility of combining different hate speech taxonomies into a single, general taxonomy, which can be used to train a classifier capable of predicting a broader range of hate speech definitions. This approach reduces the need for multiple niche models, minimizing computational resources, and allows for model training without sharing sensitive data, thus addressing privacy concerns. The semantic relationships encoded in the labels also enhance generalizability for further training, aligning with current research in federated learning and continuous learning for hate speech detection.

By iteratively fine-tuning a pre-trained multi-label classifier on two distinct datasets, the research shows that a general taxonomy can improve hate speech detection, leading to higher performance in classifying general hate speech, as demonstrated on an independent evaluation test set. This work serves as proof that a general taxonomy can be used in multi-label hate speech classification, integrating diverse datasets and definitions of hate speech. It also suggests that, in the future, only trained networks need to be exchanged, not the sensitive datasets, advancing federated hate speech detection.

Looking ahead, further research is needed to explore automatic matching of taxonomies on both logical and semantic levels, including detecting mismatches based on definitions. Validation with a broader variety of hate taxonomies, and possibly the creation of a hate speech ontology, is essential. Additionally, encoding structural knowledge through ontologies holds significant potential. Further work is needed on bias mitigation and quality assurance in the context of hate speech detection.

Limitations

The work has to address the following limitations. Firstly, it does not serve as a general proof that all datasets and all taxonomies can be combined into one. As seen in the work already, certain subparts of the two choose example taxonomies could not be merged. The problems seen here are similar to the problems arising and handled within the ontology matching community (Shvaiko and Euzenat, 2013), the found solutions from that field will greatly contribute to future development of the approach. Furthermore, a significant challenge is that at least the first round of training is done with possibly mislabeled data, which could lead to underperformance in the field. Similarly, the usage of algorithmically created annotations may propagate biases and underperformance, potentially even enhancing them. Lastly, the proposed iterative retraining could lead to the loss of the originally trained definitions of hate and functionality, if no countermeasures, such as more advanced subclass test sets and overfitting prevention, are conducted.

Ethical Considerations

Even though machine learning based applications to detect hate speech automatically online are not the solution to hate online, they are a fundamental tool in the process of combating online hate speech. this research advocated for a contextual aware human-in-the-loop strategy to counter online hate speech. The research is in the interest of society, and the public good is a central concern. The algorithmic detection of hate speech is necessary to provide a harm-free space, especially for demographic groups with special needs for protection, such as adolescents. The research is advancing the field in a more open but data-secure direction. While more diverse understandings of what constitutes hate speech is usable, the potential limitations are stated in section 7.

References

Valentina Bartalesi, Rachele Sprugnoli, Valentina Bartalesi Lenzi, and Giovanni Moretti. 2006. Cat: the celct annotation tool creep (cyberbullying effects prevention) view project it-timebank view project cat: the celct annotation tool.

Yi-Ling Chung, Elizaveta Kuzmenko, Serra Sinem Tekiroglu, and Marco Guerini. 2019. CONAN - COunter NArratives through nichesourcing: a multilingual dataset of responses to fight online hate speech. In *Proceedings of the 57th Annual Meeting of the Association for Computational Linguistics*, pages 2819–2829, Florence, Italy. Association for Computational Linguistics.

Ona de Gibert, Naiara Perez, Aitor García-Pablos, and Montse Cuadros. 2018. Hate speech dataset from a white supremacy forum. In *Proceedings of the 2nd Workshop on Abusive Language Online (ALW2)*, pages 11–20, Brussels, Belgium. Association for Computational Linguistics.

Jacob Devlin, Ming-Wei Chang, Kenton Lee, and Kristina Toutanova. 2019. BERT: Pre-training of deep bidirectional transformers for language understanding. In *Proceedings of the 2019 Conference of the North American Chapter of the Association for Computational Linguistics: Human Language Technologies, Volume 1 (Long and Short Papers)*, pages 4171–4186, Minneapolis, Minnesota. Association for Computational Linguistics.

Stacy Jo Dixon. 2023. Facebook hate speech removal per quarter 2023.

Mai ElSherief, Vivek Kulkarni, Dana Nguyen, William Yang Wang, and Elizabeth Belding. 2018. Hate lingo: A target-based linguistic analysis of hate speech in social media. In *Proceedings of the international AAAI conference on web and social media*, volume 12.

Margherita Fanton, Helena Bonaldi, Serra Sinem Tekiroğlu, and Marco Guerini. 2021. Human-in-the-loop for data collection: a multi-target counter narrative dataset to fight online hate speech. In *Proceedings of the 59th Annual Meeting of the Association for Computational Linguistics and the 11th International Joint Conference on Natural Language Processing (Volume 1: Long Papers)*, pages 3226–3240, Online. Association for Computational Linguistics.

Jan Fillies, Michael Peter Hoffmann, and Adrian Paschke. 2023a. Multilingual hate speech detection: Comparison of transfer learning methods to classify german, italian, and spanish posts. In *2023 IEEE International Conference on Big Data (BigData)*, pages 5503–5511. IEEE.

Jan Fillies and Adrian Paschke. 2024. Simple llm based approach to counter algospeak. In *Proceedings of the 8th Workshop on Online Abuse and Harms (WOAH 2024)*, pages 136–145.

Jan Fillies, Silvio Peikert, and Adrian Paschke. 2023b. Hateful messages: A conversational data set of hate speech produced by adolescents on discord. *Preprint*, arXiv:2309.01413.

Jan Fillies, Esther Theisen, Michael Hoffmann, Robert Jung, Elena Jung, Nele Fischer, and Adrian Paschke. 2025. A novel german tiktok hate speech dataset: far-right comments against politicians, women, and others. *Discover Data*, 3(1):4.

Paula Fortuna and Sérgio Nunes. 2018. A survey on automatic detection of hate speech in text. *ACM Comput. Surv.*, 51(4).

Jay Gala, Deep Gandhi, Jash Mehta, and Zeerak Talat. 2023. A federated approach for hate speech detection. *arXiv preprint arXiv:2302.09243*.

Homa Hosseinmardi, Sabrina Arredondo Mattson, Rahat Ibn Rafiq, Richard Han, Qin Lv, and Shivakant Mishra. 2015. Analyzing labeled cyberbullying incidents on the instagram social network. In *Social Informatics*, pages 49–66, Cham. Springer International Publishing.

Lennart Justen, Kilian Müller, Marco Niemann, and Jörg Becker. 2022. No time like the present: Effects of language change on automated comment moderation. In *2022 IEEE 24th Conference on Business Informatics (CBI)*, volume 01, pages 40–49.

Simon Kemp. 2023. Digital 2023 april global statshot report - datareportal – global digital insights.

Youngwook Kim, Shinwoo Park, Youngsoo Namgoong, and Yo-Sub Han. 2023. Conprompt: Pre-training a language model with machine-generated data for implicit hate speech detection. In *Findings of the Association for Computational Linguistics: EMNLP 2023*, pages 10964–10980.

Haklin Kimm, Incheon Paik, and Hanke Kimm. 2021. Performance comparision of tpu, gpu, cpu on google colaboratory over distributed deep learning. *2021 IEEE 14th International Symposium on Embedded Multicore/Many-core Systems-on-Chip (MCSoC)*, pages 312–319.

Hannah Rose Kirk, Abeba Birhane, Bertie Vidgen, and Leon Derczynski. 2022. Handling and presenting harmful text in nlp research. *arXiv preprint arXiv:2204.14256*.

Barbara Lewandowska-Tomaszczyk, Anna Bączkowska, Olga Dontcheva-Navrátilová, Chaya Liebeskind, Giedrė Valūnaitė Oleškevičienė, Slavko Žitnik, Marcin Trojszczak, Renata Povolná, Linas Selmistraitis, Andrius Utka, et al. 2023. Llod schema for simplified offensive language taxonomy in multilingual detection and applications. *Lodz papers in pragmatics*, 19(2):301–324.

Ping Liu, Wen Li, and Liang Zou. 2019a. NULI at SemEval-2019 task 6: Transfer learning for offensive language detection using bidirectional transformers. In *Proceedings of the 13th International Workshop on Semantic Evaluation*, pages 87–91, Minneapolis, Minnesota, USA. Association for Computational Linguistics.

Yinhan Liu, Myle Ott, Naman Goyal, Jingfei Du, Mandar Joshi, Danqi Chen, Omer Levy, Mike Lewis, Luke Zettlemoyer, and Veselin Stoyanov. 2019b. Roberta: A robustly optimized bert pretraining approach. *Preprint*, arXiv:1907.11692.

Nikola Ljubešić, Igor Mozetič, Matteo Cinelli, and Petra Kralj Novak. 2021. English YouTube hate speech corpus. Slovenian language resource repository CLARIN.SI.

Yonatan Lupu, Richard Sear, Nicolas Velásquez, Rhys Leahy, Nicholas Johnson Restrepo, Beth Goldberg, and Neil F. Johnson. 2023. Offline events and online hate. *PLOS ONE*, 18(1):1–14.

Sean MacAvaney, Hao-Ren Yao, Eugene Yang, Katina Russell, Nazli Goharian, and Ophir Frieder. 2019. Hate speech detection: Challenges and solutions. *PLOS ONE*, 14(8):1–16.

Marzieh Mozafari, Reza Farahbakhsh, and Noël Crespi. 2020. Hate speech detection and racial bias mitigation in social media based on bert model. *PLOS ONE*, 15(8):1–26.

Isar Nejadgholi and Svetlana Kiritchenko. 2020. On cross-dataset generalization in automatic detection of online abuse. In *Proceedings of the Fourth Workshop on Online Abuse and Harms*, pages 173–183, Online. Association for Computational Linguistics.

Ali Omrani, Alireza S Ziabari, Preni Golazizian, Jeffery Sorensen, and Morteza Dehghani. 2023. Towards a unified framework for adaptable problematic content detection via continual learning. *arXiv preprint arXiv:2309.16905*.

Flor Miriam Plaza-del Arco, Debora Nozza, Dirk Hovy, et al. 2023. Respectful or toxic? using zero-shot learning with language models to detect hate speech. In *The 7th Workshop on Online Abuse and Harms (WOAH)*. Association for Computational Linguistics.

Fabio Poletto, Valerio Basile, Manuela Sanguinetti, Cristina Bosco, and Viviana Patti. 2021. Resources and benchmark corpora for hate speech detection: a systematic review. *Language Resources and Evaluation*, 55:477–523.

Tharindu Ranasinghe and Marcos Zampieri. 2020. Multilingual offensive language identification with cross-lingual embeddings. In *Proceedings of the 2020 Conference on Empirical Methods in Natural Language Processing (EMNLP)*, pages 5838–5844, Online. Association for Computational Linguistics.

Upkar Varshney Robert C Nickerson and Jan Muntermann. 2013. A method for taxonomy development and its application in information systems. *European Journal of Information Systems*, 22(3):336–359.

Joni Salminen, Hind Almerekhi, Milica Milenković, Soon-gyo Jung, Jisun An, Haewoon Kwak, and Bernard Jansen. 2018. Anatomy of online hate: Developing a taxonomy and machine learning models for identifying and classifying hate in online news media. *Proceedings of the International AAAI Conference on Web and Social Media*, 12(1).

Sanjana Sharma, Saksham Agrawal, and Manish Shrivastava. 2018. Degree based classification of harmful speech using Twitter data. In *Proceedings of the First Workshop on Trolling, Aggression and Cyberbullying (TRAC-2018)*, pages 106–112, Santa Fe, New Mexico, USA. Association for Computational Linguistics.

Pavel Shvaiko and Jérôme Euzenat. 2013. Ontology matching: State of the art and future challenges. *IEEE Transactions on Knowledge and Data Engineering*, 25(1):158–176.

Adriana Stephan. 2020. Comparing platform hate speech policies: Reddit's inevitable evolution. A program of the Cyber Policy Center, a joint initiative of the Freeman Spogli Institute for International Studies and Stanford Law School.

Marco Antonio Stranisci, Simona Frenda, Mirko Lai, Oscar Araque, Alessandra Teresa Cignarella, Valerio Basile, Cristina Bosco, and Viviana Patti. 2022. O-dang! the ontology of dangerous speech messages. In *Proceedings of the 2nd Workshop on Sentiment Analysis and Linguistic Linked Data*, pages 2–8, Marseille, France. European Language Resources Association.

Nikos Tsourakis. 2022. *Machine Learning Techniques for Text: Apply modern techniques with Python for text processing, dimensionality reduction, classification, and evaluation*. Packt Publishing.

Bertie Vidgen and Leon Derczynski. 2020. Directions in abusive language training data, a systematic review: Garbage in, garbage out. *Plos one*, 15(12):e0243300.

Bertie Vidgen, Tristan Thrush, Zeerak Waseem, and Douwe Kiela. 2021. Learning from the worst: Dynamically generated datasets to improve online hate detection. In *Proceedings of the 59th Annual Meeting of the Association for Computational Linguistics and the 11th International Joint Conference on Natural Language Processing (Volume 1: Long Papers)*, pages 1667–1682, Online. Association for Computational Linguistics.

Michael Wiegand, Melanie Siegel, and Josef Ruppenhofer. 2019. Overview of the germeval 2018 shared task on the identification of offensive language. In *Proceedings of GermEval 2018, 14th Conference on Natural Language Processing (KONVENS 2018), Vienna, Austria – September 21, 2018*, pages 1 – 10. Austrian Academy of Sciences, Vienna, Austria.

Marcos Zampieri, Damith Premasiri, and Tharindu Ranasinghe. 2024. A federated learning approach to privacy preserving offensive language identification. *arXiv preprint arXiv:2404.11470*.

Frederike Zufall, Marius Hamacher, Katharina Kloppenborg, and Torsten Zesch. 2022. A legal approach to hate speech – operationalizing the EU's legal framework against the expression of hatred as an NLP task. In *Proceedings of the Natural Legal Language Processing Workshop 2022*, pages 53–64, Abu Dhabi, United Arab Emirates (Hybrid). Association for Computational Linguistics.

A Appendix

A.1 The General Taxonomy

The general taxonomy has on level 0 the classes Hate and No-hate. On level 1 it is further broken down into Target_of_hate and Types_of_hate.

1. No-hate
2. Hate
   (a) Target_of_hate
   (b) Types_of_hate

Target_of_hate is further broken down into:

1. Class
   (a) Working_class
2. Immigration_status
   (a) Asylum_seeker
   (b) Foreigner
   (c) Immigrants
   (d) Refugee
3. Movement
   (a) LGBTQ+
4. National_origin
   (a) China
   (b) Korea
   (c) Pakistan
   (d) Other_N
   (e) Poland
   (f) Russian
5. Physical_attributes
   (a) Age
      i. Old
      ii. Young
   (b) Disability
   (c) Gender
      i. Gender_minorities
         A. Trans

ii. Man
iii. Women
(d) Overweight
(e) Skin_color
i. Black
ii. Non_white
iii. White

6. Race_Ethnicity
(a) Arabs
(b) Asia
i. East_A
ii. South
iii. South_east
(c) Black_people
(d) Europe
i. East_E
(e) Hispanic
(f) Indigenous
i. Aboriginal_people
(g) Minority_groups
(h) Mixed_race
(i) People_from_Africa
(j) Travelers
i. Roma

7. Religion_or_belief
(a) Hindus
(b) Jews
(c) Muslims
(d) Other_R

8. Sexuality
(a) Sexuality
(b) Bisexual
(c) Gay
(d) Lesbian

Types_of_hate is further broken down into:

1. Animosity
2. Dehumanization
3. Derogation
4. Support_for_hateful_entities
5. Threatening_language

Classifying Textual Genre in Historical Magazines (1875-1990)

Vera Danilova and **Ylva Söderfeldt**
Uppsala University, Department of History of Science and Ideas, Uppsala, Sweden
{vera.danilova, ylva.soderfeldt}@idehist.uu.se

Abstract

Historical magazines are a valuable resource for understanding the past, offering insights into everyday life, culture, and evolving social attitudes. They often feature diverse layouts and genres. Short stories, guides, announcements, and promotions can all appear side by side on the same page. Without grouping these documents by genre, term counts and topic models may lead to incorrect interpretations. This study takes a step towards addressing this issue by focusing on genre classification within a digitized collection of European medical magazines in Swedish and German. We explore two scenarios: 1) leveraging the available web genre datasets for zero-shot genre prediction, 2) semi-supervised learning over the few-shot setup. This paper offers the first experimental insights in this direction. We find that 1) with a custom genre scheme tailored to historical dataset characteristics it is possible to effectively utilize categories from web genre datasets for cross-domain and cross-lingual zero-shot prediction, 2) semi-supervised training gives considerable advantages over few-shot for all models, particularly for the historical multilingual BERT. The models and code are available on GitHub[1].

1 Introduction

Quantitative processing of digitized archives referred to as "distant reading" helps historians in conducting large-scale analysis and categorization of their data (Moretti, 2000). However, it is of utmost importance to develop methods that can contribute to reliable interpretations (Da, 2019). This paper proposes genre[2] classification to improve reliability of distant reading interpretations for visually- and information-rich materials, such as historical magazines.

The ActDisease[3] Dataset is an extensive private collection currently being digitized as part of an ongoing project on the modern history of European medicine. It consists of medical magazines issued by ten European patient organizations in four languages (Swedish, German, French, and English) throughout the 20th century. Each magazine had a different publication frequency, resulting in a varying number of issues per year and featuring diverse page formats and visually complex layouts. Within the same page, these magazines often combine texts that carry different communicative purposes, such as personal narratives, advertisements, instructions, short stories, etc. Failing to group these texts hinders the accurate interpretation of term counts and topic models across historical periods, as results may be skewed toward the most frequent genres.

Moreover, grouping by genre enriches historical interpretations by providing a broader view of evolving communicative strategies over time (Broersma, 2010) and allowing for more fine-grained analyses of term distributions and topic models. In the historical research, these text groups are referred to as "epistemic genres" and have been recognized as a valuable conceptual tool for exploring cross-cultural history of medicine (Pomata, 2014; Hanson, 2022). Their use is linked to the development of knowledge communities, such as patient organizations in our case.

Due to scarcity of annotated data for our dataset, this paper explores the effectiveness of zero-shot learning using publicly available datasets annotated with web genres and registers, and assesses the mapping of the existing categories to our custom ones. We also investigate the impact of few-shot learning, comparing the standard approach with a semi-supervised method that incorporates prior

[1]https://github.com/veraDanilova/genre-classification-LaTeCH-CLFL2025

[2]We use the definition of genre as a class of documents that share a communicative purpose (Kessler et al., 1997)

[3]ActDisease project (ERC-2021-STG 10104099): http://actdisease.org

Proceedings of LaTeCH-CLfL 2025, pages 160–171
May 4, 2025 ©2025 Association for Computational Linguistics

fine-tuning on the full dataset to leverage broad knowledge and task-specific adaptation. Additionally, we compare the performance of models pretrained on modern versus historical data in classifying genres within historical materials.

The paper is organized as follows. Section 2 discusses work on genre classification for historical materials, as well as the recent advances in genre classification with LLMs. Section 3 provides definitions for genre categories. Section 4 gives details on the datasets used for zero-shot and few-shot experiments. Section 5 outlines the experimental setup: models and types of experiments. Section 6 discusses the results, and Section 7 concludes the paper.

2 Related Work

The application of classical machine learning (ML) methods to genre extraction from historical newspapers has been discussed in (Broersma and Harbers, 2018). Rather than proposing a specific algorithmic solution, the authors focus on the challenges of defining and annotating genres in historical newspapers, as well as the difficulties in transparently evaluating and comparing different algorithms.

While automatic genre classification for historical sources remains relatively unexplored, there is extensive research on automatic identification of web genres and registers (Kuzman and Ljubešić, 2023). The state-of-the-art textual genre classifier is a version of XLM-Roberta (Conneau et al., 2020) fine-tuned on a combination of web genre datasets with extensive genre category coverage (Kuzman et al., 2023).

We extend this work by comparing the performance of three multilingual encoders - XLM-Roberta, mBERT (Devlin et al., 2019) and historical mBERT (Schweter et al., 2022) - for zero-shot and few-shot genre classification of multilingual historical magazines.

3 Genre Categories

A set of genre categories was defined under the supervision of the main historian of the project who specializes in patient organizations. *Academic* reports about academic research or explains complex scientific ideas in an accessible way (research article, report or popular science article). *Administrative* reports about the activities or operations of the patient organizations (meeting minutes, financial reports, annual reports, editorial information, official correspondence and petitions, announcements). *Advertisement* promotes products or services with intent to sell them (promotion, advertisement). *Guide* provides advice or instructions for step-by-step implementation to achieve a certain goal or solve a problem related to health, legal issues or other (dietary advice, physical exercise instructions, recipe, procedural instructions, application guidelines). *Fiction* aims to entertain the reader, gives reading pleasure, engages the reader emotionally (poems, short stories, humor, myths, novel, novellas). *Legal* explains or informs about terms and conditions (contract, rules, amendment, general terms and conditions). *News* informs or reports about updates on recent events and important developments (daily news). *Nonfiction prose* (nf_prose) narrates about events or experiences from personal life or represents a description of cultural phenomena or history (historical narrative, auto(biography), memoire, travel note, personal letter, opinion essay, cultural article, documentary prose). *QA* is text structured in a question-answer format, for example questions from members and answers from medical professionals.

4 Datasets

For zero-shot prediction, we take advantage of the publicly available datasets used in the previous work for automatic genre identification (AGI) (Kuzman et al., 2023) and the investigation of cross-lingual genre transfer in dependency parsing (Danilova and Stymne, 2023).

The entire ActDisease Dataset is used to fine-tune the models for masked language modeling (MLM) in the semi-supervised few-shot scenario. A portion of it is annotated for the experiments.

4.1 AGI Datasets

Corpus of Online Registers of English (CORE) (Egbert et al., 2015) is a large dataset containing around 50k documents manually annotated with web registers. It uses a two-level label hierarchy: 8 main registers and 47 subregisters. Subregisters are fine-grained and are well-suitable for mapping to our categories. The mapping is discussed in detail in the next subsection that describes the historical dataset. Multilingual register corpora in Swedish, Finnish and French (Repo et al., 2021) are annotated only with the main registers and we leverage them for mapping only partially.

Functional Text Dimensions (FTD) is a dataset

Historical	CORE	UDM	FTD
academic	research article (RA)	academic	academic (A14)
administrative	-	parliament	-
advertisement	advertisement (AD), description with intent to sale (DS)	-	commercial (A12)
guide	how-to (HT), recipe (RE), other how-to/instructional (OH), how-to instructional (HI)	guide	instruct (A7)
fiction	poem (PO), short story (SS)	fiction	fictive (A4), poetic (A19)
legal	legal terms and conditions (LT)	legal	legal (A9)
news	news report / blog (NE)	news	reporting (A8)
nonfiction_prose	personal blog (PB), opinion blog (OB), travel blog (TB), historical article (HA), magazine article (MA)	nonfiction prose, blog	personal (A11), argumentative (A1)
QA	question/answer forum (QA), advice (AV)	QA	

Table 1: Mapping of genre categories between the AGI datasets and the ActDisease Dataset

DATA	*G*	*B*	*instances*	*tokens*
CORE	+	2	28.5K	7.5M
CORE	+	1	33.7K	8.7M
CORE	-	1	33.6K	8.7M
CORE	-	2	25.8K	6.7M
FTD	+	2	3.8K	1.0M
FTD	-	1	7.0K	1.7M
FTD	+	1	3.8K	1.0M
FTD	-	2	7.0K	1.7M
UDM	-	1	5.0K	1.0M
UDM	+	1	1.4K	0.3M
UDM	+	2	1.3K	0.3M
UDM	-	2	5.0K	1.0M
merged	+	1	40.2K	10.4M
merged	+	2	24.2K	6.3M
merged	-	2	40.1K	9.7M
merged	-	1	55.6K	13.8M

Table 2: Training data configurations for the AGI datasets. [B2] means balanced by two levels: our label and original dataset labels. [B1] means balancing by our labels only. [G+] means the filtering by language family is performed and only Germanic languages are present in the dataset. [G-] is for the case when all language families are included in the dataset

DATA	*language family*	*instances*	*tokens*
CORE	gem	3.9K	1041.1K
FTD	gem, sla	700	174.8K
UDM	gem, roa, sla, urj	720	156.9K
merged	gem, roa, sla, urj	4.6K	1084.4K

Table 3: Test data for intra-dataset evaluation of the classifiers. In the language family column, we use ISO codes of languages families: gem - Germanic, roa - Romance, sla - Slavic, urj - Uralic

of document-level annotations of web genres (Sharoff, 2021; Lepekhin and Sharoff, 2022). We use the available data for two languages: English and Russian. Documents belonging to multiple labels or annotated as "unsuitable" are discarded. The final dataset includes 1686 English and 1693 Russian documents labeled with 10 categories.

UD-MULTIGENRE (UDM) is a subset of Universal Dependencies (UD) in 38 languages enriched with genre annotations on sentence level (Danilova and Stymne, 2023). It uses 17 genre categories based on the original treebank-level UD labels and contains 657.4k sentences (11M tokens) in total.

X-GENRE dataset is a combination of English CORE, English FTD and Slovene Ginco (Kuzman et al., 2023). Since there already exists a model for genre classification fine-tuned on this dataset, we use it as a baseline for zero-shot prediction on comparable categories.

Genre Category Mapping. To map the categories of the datasets to genres of our historical dataset, two annotators independently reviewed the guidelines of each dataset and assigned the most suitable categories to our genre labels. The categories on which the annotators agree are grouped under the corresponding genres. The final mapping is presented in Table 1.

Dataset sampling configurations. We investigate two aspects of the training data: language selection and data balancing. For language selection, we consider two scenarios: training on the entire set of available languages and training exclusively on Germanic languages. In terms of data balancing, we implement two strategies. The first involves balancing the data at two levels: our genre labels and the corresponding AGI labels. This ensures that all AGI subcategories are equally represented. The second strategy focuses on balancing only by our genre labels, using downsampling to reduce the size of the largest genres. The configurations are shown in Table 2. *Merged* signifies that, for

Year	Volume	Issue_Nr	Title	Paragraph	academic	administrative	advertisement	fiction	guide	nf_prose	legal	QA	news
1958	vol008	nr001	THE ISLAND (Diabetes was not an obstacle	Thankfully, the Air Force Command agreed to the flight, and we were able to follow the doctor's advice. It was August when we left the Air Force base in California and were flown to the Philippines. Many people expressed the opinion that we were taking too great a risk to take Donna Sue on such a trip - but we felt that we must live a life that was in keeping with our way, with our father's profession, and our little girl should live that life with us.	0	0	0	0	0	1	0	0	0
1958	vol008	nr001	THE ISLAND (Diabetes was not an obstacle	My husband and I knew that we were in God's hands wherever we went and that there were great doctors and good hospitals everywhere! And insulin was available wherever we went. All we needed was faith in God and a little intelligence and certainly a few good people willing to help us.	0	0	0	0	0	1	0	0	0
1958	vol008	nr001	THE ISLAND (Diabetes was not an obstacle	But I was still scared. Especially because I had never seen the inside of an airplane, let alone flown in one. And now I was about to fly over 11,000 km. That's no small feat for a first trip in an airplane!	0	0	0	0	0	1	0	0	0

Figure 1: An example from the annotated subset of "Diabetiker Journal"

each genre, we aggregate the available data from all datasets.

Each model is fine-tuned on all the configurations resulting in 48 fine-tuned models. A random 10% portion of each training set with stratification by label is used for validation. For an intra-dataset evaluation of the models, we use a test set described in Table 3. This test set is shared by all configurations within the same dataset type (CORE, FTD, UDM, merged). Pre-processing of the data includes removal of web addresses, emails, XML-tags, and emoji.

4.2 ActDisease Dataset

The ActDisease Dataset is a private dataset currently undergoing digitization (Aangenendt et al., 2024). At this stage, the digitization process is completed for two languages, Swedish and German, and partially completed for French. In this paper, we focus on the magazines issued in German and Swedish. German data covers the 1875–1990 period and Swedish data—1938–1990. The dataset contains 64863 issues with a total size of 112M tokens.

Preprocessing for annotation. The dataset is initially represented as the XML output of the Optical Character Recognition (OCR) engine ABBYY Finereader 14[4] for each page. To facilitate the annotation process, we use the following procedure to extract continuous text fragments under each title in each issue.

For each recognized paragraph, font attribute patterns of its lines (size, font type, font size, bold, italic) are collected from the OCR output. Consequent lines with the font attribute pattern are merged into paragraphs and paragraphs containing only non-words are dropped. Content pages are identified using regex and the titles are collected.

Each issue's paragraphs are represented as a sequence of font sizes attributes and are clustered using GaussianHMM, which is a well-known method in speech pattern recognition (Bilmes, 2008). Clusters corresponding to titles are identified using fuzzy string matching: MinHash locality sensitive hashing (Broder, 1997) and TheFuzz[5], a tool based on the Levenstein distance. The cluster that follows the title cluster and contains the longest sequence of uniform font attribute patterns is consider to be part of text under this title. It is added to the dataset with year, volume, issue number and title as descriptors. The clusters that precede or follow this text cluster are added with the same title if they contain the same font attribute pattern.

Annotation. Annotation files (Numbers spreadsheets) are produced for two periodicals: the Swedish "Diabetes" and the German "Diabetiker Journal". To increase variation in content, we select the first and mid-year issues in each year. An example of annotations for several translated paragraphs from the "Diabetiker Journal" are shown in Figure 1. The annotation was performed by 4 historians and 2 computational linguists either native or proficient in Swedish and German. At least 2 annotations were collected for each paragraph. The average kappa agreement is 0.7. The final dataset includes only those paragraphs, for which at least two annotators agree.

Sampling Strategy. The annotated dataset is divided into a training set (1182 paragraphs) and a held-out set (552 paragraphs), with stratification based on labels. The distribution of paragraphs across languages and genres in these sets is illustrated in Figures 2 and 3.

For few-shot experiments, models are trained on six different training set sizes: 100, 200, 300, 400, 500, and 1182 instances. The subsets are randomly sampled from the training set, ensuring each is balanced by label. The held-out set is further divided into a validation set and a test set, each containing an equal number of instances and preserving label balance. The legal and news categories are

[4]`https://www.abbyy.com/company/news/abbyy-finereader-14-pdf-solution/`

[5]https://github.com/seatgeek/thefuzz

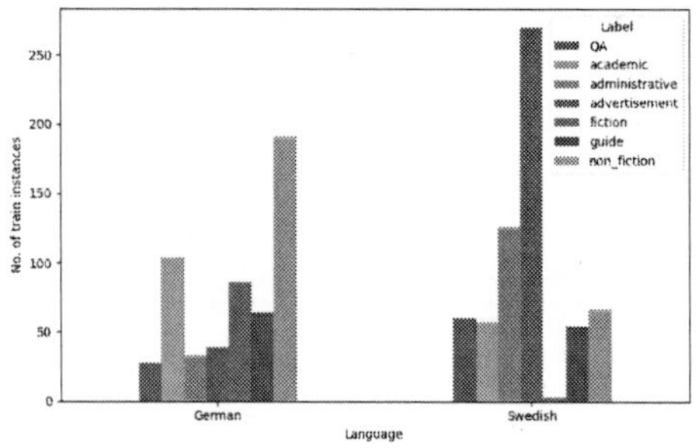

Figure 2: Genre distribution in languages in the training sample of the ActDisease Dataset

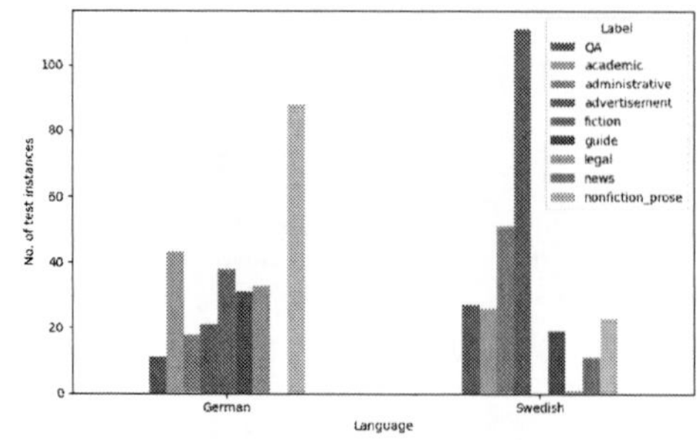

Figure 3: Genre distribution in languages in the held-out sample of the ActDisease Dataset

excluded from these experiments due to insufficient training data.

For zero-shot experiments, the entire test set is used as the test set.

5 Experimental Setup

The main goal of this study is to identify the optimal training dataset configurations and fine-tuning strategies for aligning with the annotated genre labels. We explore two scenarios: zero-shot prediction, where models predict genres using existing web genre datasets without seeing the target data, and few-shot vs. semi-supervised few-shot training. In the semi-supervised scenario, we examine if pre-training the models for MLM on the entire ActDisease Dataset improves their few-shot prediction performance.

5.1 Models

For fine-tuning, we utilize pre-trained base versions of mBERT, XLM-RoBERTa and historical multilingual model hmBERT on the AGI datasets. BERT-like models have been extensively used in the previous work for web register and genre classification (Lepekhin and Sharoff, 2022; Kuzman and Ljubešić, 2023; Laippala et al., 2023). XLM-RoBERTa outperformed mBERT on the XNLI benchmark (Conneau et al., 2020) and has recently been successfully applied for web genre classification in (Kuzman et al., 2023).

hmBERT is relevant for this work, since it is pre-trained on a large corpus of historical newspapers. The Swedish portion spans publications from 1900 to 1910, while the German dataset provides good coverage of the 19th and 20th centuries.

mBERT is used for comparison with hmBERT since both are based on BERT, while XLM-RoBERTa is not directly comparable.

5.2 Zero-Shot Prediction

In historical NLP, in-domain training data is often unavailable. To address this, we fine-tune our models on each out-of-domain AGI training dataset configuration individually, as well as on a merged version that combines all datasets. We begin by evaluating the classifiers' predictions on their respective native test sets. Since we map the original labels to our genre categories, this change in genre representation is likely to affect the models' inference.

Following this, we perform zero-shot prediction on the ActDisease Dataset's test set and compare the results to a baseline. This scenario is cross-lingual for the FTD and X-GENRE datasets because they lack German and Swedish instances. For the UDM and CORE datasets, the scenario is partially cross-lingual: UDM includes Swedish instances in guide, fiction, and administrative categories, and German - in news; CORE contains a small number of Swedish instances in the guide category.

Baseline. We use the state-of-the-art classifier of web genres - X-GENRE (Kuzman et al., 2023) as a baseline. We consider the predictions on the most similar labels that can be directly mapped to ours: Instruction (mapped to: guide), Legal, News, Promotion (advertisement), Prose/Lyrical (fiction).

5.3 Few-shot and semi-supervised training

In this experiment, we explore a scenario with a limited number of annotated training examples. We train the models on datasets of different sizes, ranging from 100 examples up to the full training dataset of 1182 paragraphs. The training is conducted in two modes: with and without an initial phase of MLM pre-training on the entire ActDisease Dataset.

	FTD		CORE		UDM		merged	
	ACC	Macro-F1	ACC	Macro-F1	ACC	Macro-F1	ACC	Macro-F1
hmBERT	0.66	0.68	0.75	0.75	0.68	0.69	0.67	0.68
mBERT	0.88	0.88	0.76	0.77	**0.82**	**0.83**	0.80	0.79
XLM-RoBERTa	**0.91**	**0.91**	**0.78**	**0.78**	**0.82**	**0.83**	**0.83**	**0.83**

Table 4: Intra-dataset evaluation of the classifiers. Average scores over the models trained on different dataset configurations.

		QA	academic	administrative	advertisement	fiction	guide	legal	news	nf_prose
	X-GENRE	-	-	-	0.69	0.39	0.59	0.66	0.08	-
FTD	hmBERT	-	0.37	-	0.56	0.43	0.33	**0.9**	0.38	0.47
	mBERT	-	0.61	-	0.62	0.40	0.47	**0.82**	0.34	0.54
	XLM-RoBERTa	-	0.57	-	0.74	0.49	0.57	**0.89**	0.28	0.56
CORE	hmBERT	0.1	0.45	-	0.07	0.41	0.23	**0.80**	0	0.20
	mBERT	0.18	0.48	-	0.10	0.32	0.26	**0.80**	0	0.34
	XLM-RoBERTa	0.35	0.50	-	0.11	0.46	0.30	**0.84**	0.07	0.33
UDM	hmBERT	0.1	0.04	**0.43**	-	0.27	0.26	0.09	0.01	0.03
	mBERT	0.16	0.25	0.25	-	0.17	0.29	0.16	0.04	0.01
	XLM-RoBERTa	**0.53**	0.21	0.30	-	0.30	0.31	0.14	0.05	0.08
merged	hmBERT	0.10	0.18	0.24	0.22	0.36	0.18	0.19	0.01	0.17
	mBERT	0.05	0.15	0.18	0.23	0.19	0.17	0.21	0.02	0.09
	XLM-RoBERTa	0.43	0.27	0.14	0.34	0.40	0.28	0.45	0.04	0.14

Table 5: Zero-shot per-category F1 scores averaged across dataset configurations. The highlighted values indicate cases where the highest average F1 performance for a certain category does not result from systematic overprediction of this category by the classifiers, as verified through our analysis of confusion matrices.

6 Results

6.1 Intra-Dataset Evaluation of the Classifiers

The evaluation of models fine-tuned on web genre datasets is presented in Table 4, where they are assessed against their corresponding native test sets. The results are averaged across dataset configurations. XLM-RoBERTa shows the best performance across all datasets. For UDM, both XLM-RoBERTa and mBERT greatly outperform hmBERT. hmBERT achieves the lowest scores on all datasets, which is expected in view of the nature of its historical training data. The best genre prediction capacity is observed on the FTD dataset with XLM-RoBERTa.

The scores of mBERT and XLM-RoBERTa on the CORE dataset with our genre mapping are noticeably lower than on other datasets. Moreover, during fine-tuning, overfitting occurs earlier for CORE (from the 3rd epoch on average) than for UDM or FTD (from the 5th epoch on average). This performance may indicate that our genre mapping for this dataset is inappropriate.

The results for the merged dataset are not surprising in view of the performance of the CORE dataset, since CORE instances dominate in the merged training data. Similarly to CORE, overfitting occurs earlier for the models trained on the merged dataset (from the 3rd epoch on average).

6.2 Zero-Shot Inference

Table 5 presents the zero-shot inference results (F1 scores) for various genres, averaged across different dataset configurations. Since each AGI dataset contains only a subset of the genres, it is not possible to directly compare the overall performance metrics of the classifiers. Instead, we evaluate the performance for each genre separately and analyze the confusion matrices[6] to mitigate potential biases.

In general, our analysis indicates that models trained on the FTD dataset configurations perform better with our genre mapping compared to models trained on other datasets. It also suggests that merging datasets necessitates a different approach to achieve optimal results.

Upon close examination of the results from models trained on the UDM dataset, we observe a class-specific bias. Despite applying downsampling, models trained on all dataset configurations tend to overpredict the news category. The average

[6]Appendix C contains confusion matrices that showcase the trends observed in zero-shot inference

accuracy of these models remains below 0.5. The proportion of news instances in the dataset configurations is consistent with other downsampled categories like academic, fiction, and legal, averaging around 15%. However, the news category includes the highest number of Germanic instances, most of which are in German, potentially explaining this bias.

Interestingly, the administrative category, when classified by hmBERT, is less affected by this bias compared to other categories. Furthermore, hmBERT correctly predicts on average 25 out of 69 administrative instances, outperforming mBERT (11) and XLM-RoBERTa (14). A possible explanation for this could involve two factors: 1) hmBERT's pre-training on historical newspapers, which extensively used the report genre—characterized by near-verbatim chronological documentation of meetings and events (Bødker, 2020), and 2) textual similarity between patient organization meeting records and European parliamentary meeting minutes in the UDM training set.

On a different note, XLM-RoBERTa shows superior performance in the QA category, averaging 16 correct predictions out of 38 instances, while mBERT and hmBERT achieve only 4 and 2 correct predictions, respectively.

Classifiers trained on FTD and CORE show strong performance in predicting the legal category with no biases detected in our confusion matrix analysis with respect to this category.

Table 6 illustrates the average impact of different configuration options on fine-tuning for each dataset. For the FTD dataset, additional balancing based on the original labels or filtering by language family does not enhance performance. Although the CORE dataset is predominantly English, the inclusion of a small number of Finnish and French instances slightly diminishes its performance. For the UDM dataset, the presence of other language families and balancing generally improve performance in terms of macro F1.

In summary, for cross-lingual zero-shot prediction, training on the FTD dataset using our genre mapping is more effective than training on CORE or UDM, or using a pre-trained multilingual genre classifier.

6.3 Few-Shot Inference

Fig 4 shows the trends in performance of the models on the multilingual historical test set after being fine-tuned on training sets of various sizes. Further pre-training with a MLM objective is clearly advantageous. F1 keeps increasing with the number of training instances but is still below 0.8 with 1182 training instances for all models. hmBERT-MLM outperforms XLM-RoBERTa-MLM and mBERT-MLM by a small margin. mBERT-MLM is very close to hmBERT-MLM with dataset size 500. For the dataset size of 400, a decline in performance is observed for XLM-RoBERTa, XLM-RoBERTa-MLM, and hmBERT-MLM. Particularly for XLM-RoBERTa, fine-tuning on this dataset portion greatly increases confusion between QA and academic, advertisement and guide, as well as nf_prose and fiction. For the models with MLM-pretraining, the confusion is less pronounced. Further investigation is needed to understand the un-

	configuration	*F1*
FTD	[B 2]	0.51
	[B 1]	**0.56**
	[G +]	0.52
	[G -]	**0.56**
CORE	[B 2]	0.32
	[B 1]	0.32
	[G +]	**0.32**
	[G -]	0.31
UDM	[B 2]	**0.19**
	[B 1]	0.18
	[G +]	0.14
	[G -]	**0.22**

Table 6: Macro F1 scores of models trained on the AGI datasets averaged by configuration settings. [B2] means balanced by two levels: our label and original dataset labels. [B1] means balancing by our labels only. [G+] means the filtering by language family is performed and only Germanic languages are present in the dataset. [G-] is for the case when all language families are included in the dataset

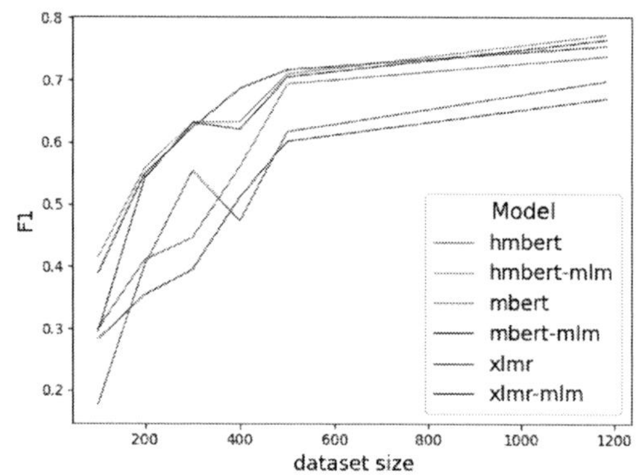

Figure 4: Performance of the models in a few-shot setting with and without MLM fine-tuning.

MODEL	XLMR		XLMR-MLM		hmBERT		hmBERT-MLM		mBERT		mBERT-MLM	
SIZE	500	1182	500	1182	500	1182	500	1182	500	1182	500	1182
QA	0.61	0.76	**0.77**	**0.84**	0.55	0.73	0.71	0.76	0.62	0.72	0.73	0.78
academic	0.63	**0.81**	0.75	**0.81**	0.62	0.76	0.70	0.78	0.75	0.77	**0.77**	**0.81**
administrative	0.78	0.84	0.79	0.84	0.70	0.82	0.77	**0.86**	**0.82**	0.82	0.80	**0.86**
advertisement	0.81	**0.93**	**0.90**	**0.93**	0.84	0.91	0.89	**0.93**	0.87	0.92	0.87	0.92
fiction	0.49	0.05	0.55	0.34	0.53	0.10	0.60	**0.51**	0.58	0.47	**0.62**	0.33
guide	0.67	0.76	**0.73**	**0.79**	0.52	0.58	0.64	0.72	0.68	0.68	0.67	**0.79**
nf_prose	0.30	0.72	0.42	0.77	0.42	0.74	**0.62**	**0.80**	0.51	0.75	0.53	0.78
accuracy	0.63	0.78	0.72	0.81	0.63	0.76	**0.73**	**0.82**	0.71	0.78	**0.73**	0.81
macro_F1	0.61	0.69	0.70	0.76	0.60	0.67	**0.71**	**0.77**	0.69	0.73	**0.71**	0.75

Table 7: Per-category F1 and overall metrics achieved by pre-trained models in a few-shot setting (with and without MLM fine-tuning) for two dataset sizes: 500 and 1182 training instances.

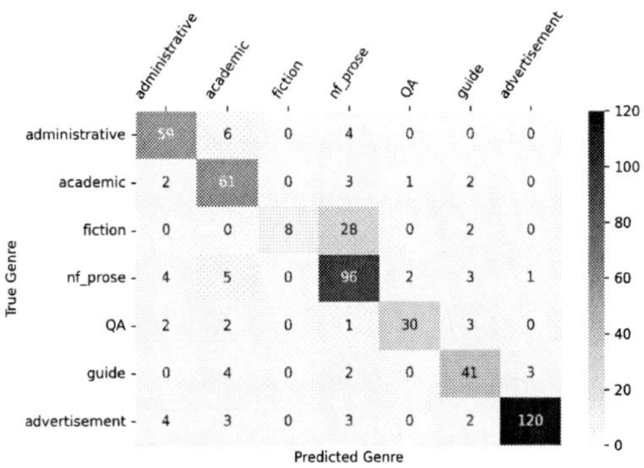

Figure 5: XLM-Roberta-MLM classification results with full-sized training dataset

derlying causes.

Table 7 provides further details on the label-wise F1 scores for dataset sizes 500 and 1182 (light grey columns). Although hmBERT outperforms other models in terms of overall accuracy and F1 score, label-wise F1 scores show that this is largely due to stronger prediction of fiction and nonfiction prose and a less drastic drop in fiction with the dataset size increase.

An analysis of confusion matrices, such as the one depicted in Figure 5 for XLM-Roberta-MLM, reveals that nonfictional prose is frequently overpredicted when the model is trained on the entire training dataset. This overprediction indicates that the fiction and nonfictional prose categories may be becoming increasingly similar, causing greater confusion for the classifiers and resulting in higher misclassification rates.

In contrast, hmBERT-MLM exhibits a lower susceptibility to this confusion compared to other models, suggesting it is better at distinguishing between these categories even as they become more similar.

Genre identification in this context is particularly challenging because all genres are confined to a specific domain: patient organizations' magazines focused on diabetes. This means that both fictional and (auto)biographical narratives frequently revolve around the experiences of diabetes patients, and are likely to share themes and narrative structures.

Among the models not further pre-trained on the ActDisease Dataset, mBERT achieves a surprisingly strong macro F1 score compared to the others.

Additional pre-training with a MLM objective enhances the quality of the few-shot learning for the three considered models. It results in considerable gains: on average 18.5% across models trained on all dataset sizes. The greatest average increase in macro F1 is observed for hmBERT-MLM (24% as opposed to 14.5% for mBERT-MLM and 16.9% for XLM-RoBERTa). For XLM-RoBERTa and hmBERT, the effect of over-fitting in the fiction category with the full-size dataset becomes less pronounced in the MLM-fine-tuned models. It is not the case in the mBERT though.

7 Conclusions

In this work, we address an underexplored problem of genre classification for historical magazines. First, we show that with a custom genre scheme based on the dataset properties it is possible to successfully leverage the categories available in the modern datasets in cross-domain and cross-lingual zero-shot prediction. Our analysis reveals that models trained on the FTD dataset configurations achieve better alignment with our genre mapping compared to those trained on other datasets.

Next, we highlight the advantages of few-shot learning using a small set of annotated instances. Even a limited annotated sample from the same data source greatly enhances genre classification performance on our historical test dataset. Furthermore, we find that prior MLM fine-tuning substantially improves few-shot learning across all models, with particularly strong gains for historical multilingual BERT.

For future work, we aim to expand annotation efforts to include new genre categories and languages (English and French). Once sufficient annotations are available, we will also explore monolingual few-shot experiments to compare the performance of monolingual and multilingual large language models on this task. In addition, we plan to investigate how linguistic similarities between training and test genre data are related to the classification performance.

8 Limitations

Our study acknowledges several limitations that should be addressed in future research. While we are actively working on expanding the dataset, the size of our annotated dataset in these experiments is relatively small, which may restrict the generalizability and robustness of our findings. A larger corpus would provide more comprehensive training data and potentially lead to more reliable model performance.

Additionally, the annotated dataset exhibits some degree of imbalance across different genres. This imbalance could introduce biases during the training process, affecting the overall performance and fairness of our models.

Moreover, due to the scarcity of annotated instances for individual languages, we do not cover the monolingual few-shot setup. It would involve fine-tuning language-specific pre-trained models for MLM and then performing few-shot training. However, in this scenario, much less data would be used for MLM-fine-tuning.

Lastly, our pre-processing for annotation extracts mostly clean paragraphs with low OCR error rate. In real-life cases, the paragraphs are often noisy and suffer from poor OCR, especially in case of unusual fonts or layouts. We plan to address this in the future research.

Acknowledgments

This research is funded by the European Union (ERC, ActDisease, ERC-2021-STG 10104099). Views and opinions expressed are, however, those of the author(s) only and do not necessarily reflect those of the European Union or the European Research Council. Neither the European Union nor the granting authority can be held responsible for them.

We would like to thank the **Centre for Digital Humanities and Social Sciences** at Uppsala University for providing us with the computational resources for training and evaluating our models. We are especially grateful to Dr. Maria Skeppstedt, Dr. Julia Reed, Dr. Andrew Burchell, and Gijs Aangenendt for their invaluable contributions to annotation, category definition, and mapping, as well as their feedback on the paper. We sincerely thank Dr. Maria Skeppstedt and the anonymous reviewers for their insightful comments and suggestions, which greatly enhanced the quality of the paper.

References

Gijs Aangenendt, Maria Skeppstedt, and Ylva Söderfeldt. 2024. Curating a historical source corpus of 20th century patient organization periodicals. In *Proceedings of the Huminfra Conference (HiC 2024)*, pages 76–82.

Jeff Bilmes. 2008. *Gaussian Models in Automatic Speech Recognition*, pages 521–555. Springer New York, New York, NY.

Andrei Z. Broder. 1997. On the resemblance and containment of documents. In *Proceedings of the Compression and Complexity of SEQUENCES 1997*, pages 21–29. IEEE. Cat. No.97TB100171.

Marcel Broersma. 2010. Journalism as a performative discourse: The importance of form and style in journalism. In Verica Rupar, editor, *Journalism and Meaning-Making: Reading the Newspaper*, pages 15–35. Hampton Press, Cresskill.

Marcel Broersma and Frank Harbers. 2018. Exploring machine learning to study the long-term transformation of news. *Digital Journalism*, 6(9):1150–1164.

Henrik Bødker, editor. 2020. *Journalism History and Digital Archives*, 1st edition. Routledge.

Alexis Conneau, Kartikay Khandelwal, Naman Goyal, Vishrav Chaudhary, Guillaume Wenzek, Francisco Guzmán, Edouard Grave, Myle Ott, Luke Zettlemoyer, and Veselin Stoyanov. 2020. Unsupervised cross-lingual representation learning at scale. In *Proceedings of the 58th Annual Meeting of the Association for Computational Linguistics*, pages 8440–8451, Online. Association for Computational Linguistics.

Nan Z. Da. 2019. The computational case against computational literary studies. *Critical Inquiry*, 45(3):601–639.

Vera Danilova and Sara Stymne. 2023. UD-MULTIGENRE – a UD-based dataset enriched with instance-level genre annotations. In *Proceedings of the 3rd Workshop on Multi-lingual Representation Learning (MRL)*, pages 253–267, Singapore. Association for Computational Linguistics.

Jacob Devlin, Ming-Wei Chang, Kenton Lee, and Kristina Toutanova. 2019. BERT: Pre-training of deep bidirectional transformers for language understanding. In *Proceedings of the 2019 Conference of the North American Chapter of the Association for Computational Linguistics: Human Language Technologies, Volume 1 (Long and Short Papers)*, pages 4171–4186, Minneapolis, Minnesota. Association for Computational Linguistics.

Jesse Egbert, Douglas Biber, and Mark Davies. 2015. Developing a bottom-up, user-based method of web register classification. *Journal of the Association for Information Science and Technology*, 66(9):1817–1831.

Marta Hanson. 2022. Epistemic genres as a conceptual tool in the history of chinese medicine. *Chinese Medicine and Culture*, 5(1):1–8.

Brett Kessler, Geoffrey Nunberg, and Hinrich Schutze. 1997. Automatic detection of text genre. In *35th Annual Meeting of the Association for Computational Linguistics and 8th Conference of the European Chapter of the Association for Computational Linguistics*, pages 32–38, Madrid, Spain. Association for Computational Linguistics.

Taja Kuzman and Nikola Ljubešić. 2023. Automatic genre identification: a survey. *Language Resources and Evaluation*.

Taja Kuzman, Igor Mozetič, and Nikola Ljubešić. 2023. Automatic genre identification for robust enrichment of massive text collections: Investigation of classification methods in the era of large language models. *Machine Learning and Knowledge Extraction*, 5(3):1149–1175.

Veronika Laippala, Samuel Rönnqvist, Miika Oinonen, Aki-Juhani Kyröläinen, Anna Salmela, Douglas Biber, Jesse Egbert, and Sampo Pyysalo. 2023. Register identification from the unrestricted open web using the corpus of online registers of english. *Language Resources and Evaluation*, 57(3):1045–1079.

Mikhail Lepekhin and Serge Sharoff. 2022. Estimating confidence of predictions of individual classifiers and TheirEnsembles for the genre classification task. In *Proceedings of the Thirteenth Language Resources and Evaluation Conference*, pages 5974–5982, Marseille, France. European Language Resources Association.

F. Moretti. 2000. Conjectures on world literature. *New Left Review*, 1(1):54–68.

Gianna Pomata. 2014. The medical case narrative: distant reading of an epistemic genre. *Literature and medicine*, 32(1):1–23.

Liina Repo, Valtteri Skantsi, Samuel Rönnqvist, Saara Hellström, Miika Oinonen, Anna Salmela, Douglas Biber, Jesse Egbert, Sampo Pyysalo, and Veronika Laippala. 2021. Beyond the English web: Zero-shot cross-lingual and lightweight monolingual classification of registers. In *Proceedings of the 16th Conference of the European Chapter of the Association for Computational Linguistics: Student Research Workshop*, pages 183–191, Online. Association for Computational Linguistics.

Stefan Schweter, Luisa März, Katharina Schmid, and Erion Çano. 2022. hmbert: Historical multilingual language models for named entity recognition. *CoRR*, abs/2205.15575.

Serge Sharoff. 2021. Genre annotation for the web: text-external and text-internal perspectives. *Register studies*, 3(1):1–32.

A Genre Annotation Guidelines

A.1 Genre Definitions

Academic reports about academic research or explains complex scientific ideas or discoveries in an accessible way.

Author : medical professionals, researchers

Target audience : physicians, researchers, patients, or other readers of the periodical.

Features : 1) high density of specialist language including domain-specific terms (e.g., "coronary angiography") and research terms (e.g., "experiment", "approach", "results", "method"); 2) references to academic works; 3) factual, often impersonal, narrative about an observation of a process (experiment/treatment/chemical reactions) and its outcomes.

Subgenres : academic article, academic report, popular science article

Administrative reports about the activities or discusses plans of the patient organization.

Author : directive authorities or members

Target audience : members, directive authorities of another organization/authority, politicians

Features : 1) presence of named entities referring to the organization and its directive members; 2) terms such as "annual meeting", "financial report", "association report", "association activities", "association meeting"; 3) detailed chronological reporting;

Subgenres : meeting minutes, financial reports, annual reports, editorial information, official correspondence and petitions, announcements

Advertisement promotion of products and services with intent to sell them, e.g.: sweeteners, injectors, alcohol, yoga, courses for nurses, lotteries. These texts aim to create awareness of brands, products, services, and ideas, as well as to persuade the public to respond in a certain way toward what is advertised.

Subgenres : advertisement, promotion, invitation

Guide recommends, provides advice or instructions for step-by-step implementation to achieve a certain goal or solve a problem related to health, legal issues or other. It can be one step-action or more.

Author : directive authorities, members of the organization, medical doctors, dieticians, patients, consultants

Target audience : members or other readers of the periodical

Features : 1) imperative modality expressed with auxiliary verbs such as "should", "must"; 2) itemized lists of actions; 3) addresses the reader in 2nd person plural; 4) chronological order; 5) presence of expressions similar to "It is recommended to"/"We recommend you to" or "It is advisable"/"We advise you"

Subgenres : dietary advice, physical exercise instructions, recipe, procedural instructions, application guidelines

Fiction aims to entertain the reader, gives reading pleasure, engages the reader emotionally.

Author : fiction authors

Target audience : members or other readers of the periodical

Features : 1) presence of imaginary elements, such as invented characters, events, worlds; 2) dense use of creative language such as tropes; 3) emotional engagement; 4) can include dialogue of characters

Subgenres : poems, short stories, humor, myths, novel, novella

Legal explains or informs about law.

Subgenres : contracts, terms and conditions

News report about recent events. Contains short factual text announcing an event with no analysis or literary narrative, not a long-read.

Subgenres : daily news reports

Nonfictional prose narrates/reports about events/experiences from personal life or represents a neutral description of cultural phenomena or history.

Author : members of the organization, patients

Target audience : members or other readers of the periodical

Features : 1) first-/third-person narrative; 2) chronological perspective; 3) references to time; 4) factual or opinion; 5) language is not rich in tropes; 6) informal or neutral language;

Subgenres : auto(biography), memoire, travel note, personal letter, opinion essay, cultural article, documentary prose

QA is text structured in a question-answer format, for example, questions from members and answers from medical professionals. Most frequently corresponds to the questions and answers section of the magazine.

A.2 Criteria for Genre Assignment

We base the categorization on concepts shared by these sources that closely align with the idea of communicative purpose. Although communicative purpose is itself a complex and multilayer concept, it has often been considered a key characteristic feature for genre identification and categorization.

We perform classification on the paragraph level. Each paragraph is part of a column text under a certain title. Title often indicates what type of text all the underlying paragraphs belong to. E.g., the "Våra lokalföreningar" will indicate that the following text discusses organizational activities.

The annotator is given a table where each row includes a paragraph with its identifiers (journal, year, volume, issue number), the corresponding title and empty genre category columns. The annotator should place his hard assignment (1) in the corresponding column in front of each paragraph.

B Fine-tuning Settings

The following hyper-parameters were used in our experiments for fine-tuning in the zero shot and few-shot settings:

- Number of epochs: 10
- Learning rate: $1e-5$
- Batch size: 8
- Weight decay: 0
- Maximum sequence length: 512

Other settings are set to default values in the Huggingface's Trainer[7].

For the MLM fine-tuning, we used the official script `run_mlm.py` available in the transformers GitHub[8] with batch size equal to 8.

[7] `https://huggingface.co/docs/transformers/main_classes/trainer`

[8] `https://github.com/huggingface/transformers/tree/main/examples/pytorch/language-modeling`

C Classifier Performance in Zero-Shot Evaluation

The following figures illustrate zero-shot performance of classifiers fine-tuned on existing datasets for web genre and register classification when applied to our historical test dataset, as discussed in Section 6.2.

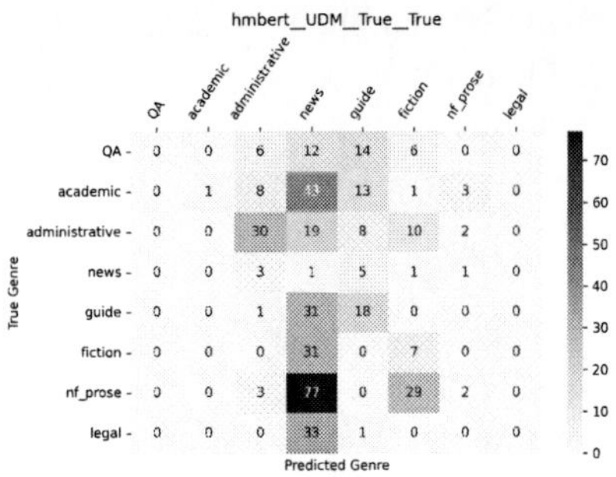

Figure 6: Classification results for hmBERT fine-tuned on UDM (B2 G+). The classifier recognizes 43% of paragraphs in the administrative genre.

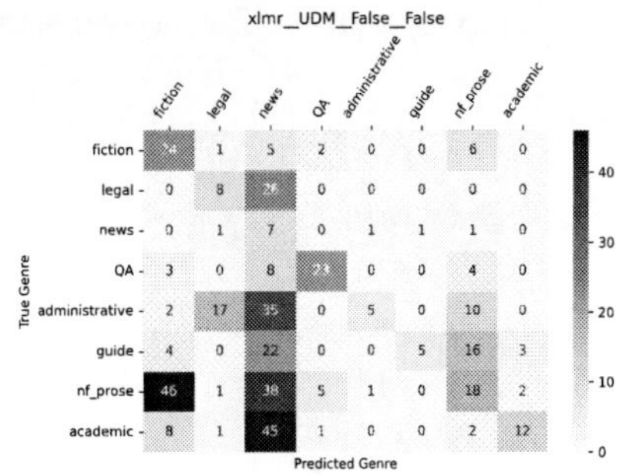

Figure 7: Classification results for XLM-RoBERTA fine-tuned on UDM (B1 G-). The classifier recognizes 60% of paragraphs in the QA genre.

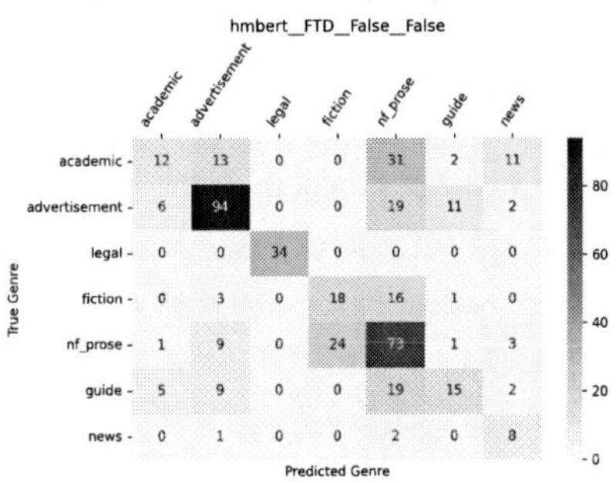

Figure 8: Classification results for hmBERT fine-tuned on FTD (B1 G-). The classifier recognizes 100% of paragraphs in the legal genre.

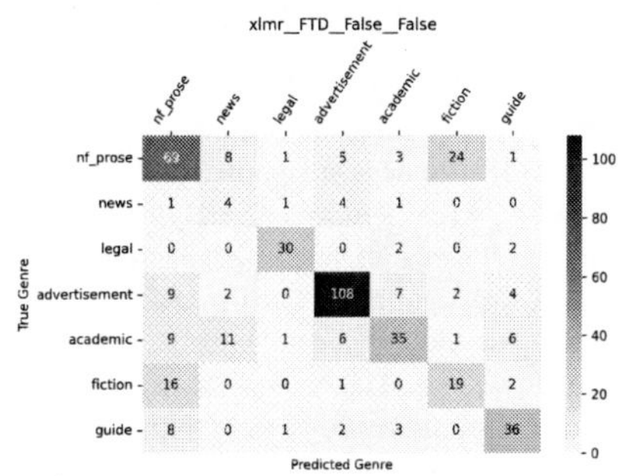

Figure 9: Classification results for XLMR-RoBERTA on FTD (B1 G-). The classifier recognizes 88% of paragraphs in the legal genre.

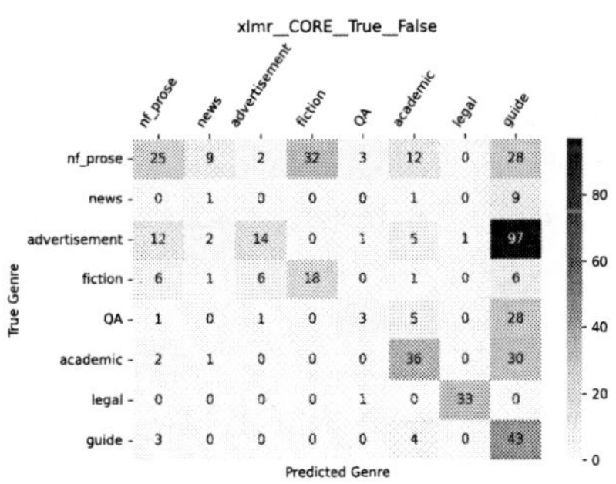

Figure 10: Classification results for XLM-Roberta fine-tuned on CORE (B1 G+). The classifier recognizes 97% of paragraphs in the legal genre.

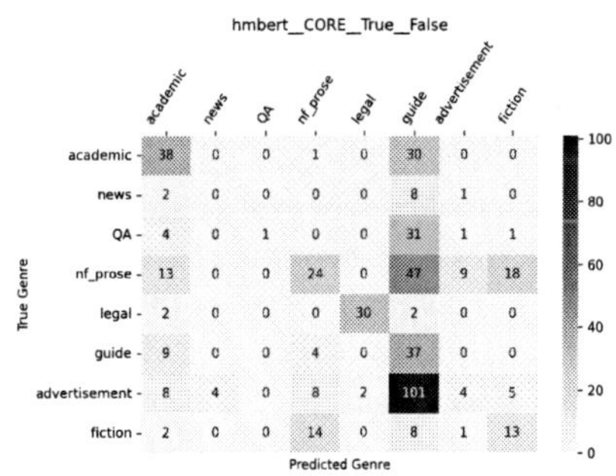

Figure 11: Classification results for hmBERT fine-tuned on CORE (B1 G+). The classifier recognizes 88% of paragraphs in the legal genre.

Lexical Semantic Change Annotation with Large Language Models

Thora Hagen
Leibniz Institute for the German Language (IDS), Mannheim, Germany
University of Würzburg, Germany
hagen@ids-mannheim.de

Abstract

This paper explores the application of state-of-the-art large language models (LLMs) to the task of lexical semantic change annotation (LSCA) using the historical German DURel dataset. We evaluate five LLMs, and investigate whether retrieval-augmented generation (RAG) with historical encyclopedic knowledge enhances results. Our findings show that the Llama3.3 model achieves comparable performance to GPT-4o despite significant parameter differences, while RAG marginally improves predictions for smaller models but hampers performance for larger ones. Further analysis suggests that our additional context benefits nouns more than verbs and adjectives, demonstrating the nuances of integrating external knowledge for semantic tasks.

1 Introduction

The increasing application of natural language processing (NLP) methods to the humanities presents a range of challenges, particularly when working with historical or non-standard language data. One such challenge is the detection of lexical semantic change (LSC) (Tahmasebi et al., 2021; Periti and Montanelli, 2024), i.e. how words have shifted in meaning due to cultural, social, or linguistic contexts. Although large language models (LLMs) have demonstrated considerable success in modern language tasks, their ability to effectively interpret historical texts is still limited. Many works show how language models struggle with such long-tail knowledge (Kandpal et al., 2023; Wang et al., 2023). Linguistic limitations in particular then influence other computational research fields, such as the analysis of literary texts, where subtle shifts in meaning must be captured to correctly interpret a historical text via the lens of a historical reader.

LLMs are predominantly trained on contemporary data, which may lack the necessary historical linguistic context to accurately process and interpret older texts. Many tasks in the humanities that employ LLMs are directly or indirectly dependent on historical knowledge, including the recognition of historical facts, events, and discourse, as well as changes in word meaning over time (e.g., *gay*, *awful*, *computer*). When working with older text collections, this impacts applications such as historical sentiment analysis, the classification of historical texts, the analysis of narrative and character descriptions, and even machine translation of older documents. Understanding how different LLMs represent historical semantics is crucial for researchers who work with historical texts, as it informs their choice of model for specific tasks.

This paper investigates the performance of multiple state-of-the-art LLMs on the task of LSC annotation for historical German. The goal is to evaluate the models' ability to detect semantic shifts, and therefore to potentially infer which of the models would be the best to represent historical semantics via this proxy task. The research questions of this paper are the following: RQ1: How well can the current state-of-the-art LLMs annotate lexical semantic change given two contexts and a target word? RQ2: Can historical, referential knowledge increase the performance of the lexical semantic change annotation task?

2 Lexical Semantic Change Detection

Lexical semantic change detection (LSCD) is a well-established subfield of computational linguistics and NLP. Given a large diachronic text corpus (i.e. a corpus is that is divided into two or more time slices), the goal is to automatically detect which words have changed in meaning. These results are then compared to manually annotated gold datasets of word meaning shift, where annotations are either on a binary or graded (1-4) scale of relatedness (Tahmasebi et al., 2021; Kurtyigit et al., 2021).

Typically, word embeddings are used to detect

Proceedings of LaTeCH-CLfL 2025, pages 172–178
May 4, 2025 ©2025 Association for Computational Linguistics

Table 1: One example of a context pair with target word highlighted in bold letters (engl. *the press* and *to press*) from the DURel dataset.

context 1	context 2	rating
V. Die Geschichte des Rechts der **Presse**. 1) Die Elemente der Geschichte.	[...] **Pressen** Sie mir kein offenherziger Bekenntniß ab. Jch liebe Sie, und bin ganz die Jhrige.	1 (Unrelated)

LSC; both contextualized approaches relying on transformer-based models or approaches based on static word vectors are possible. With static approaches, word embedding models of each corpus slice are created individually and are then aligned (e.g. through orthogonal Procrustes) (Hamilton et al., 2016; Wevers and Koolen, 2020). Contextualized approaches first calculate sets of token embeddings for every word in question, taking the surrounding context into account. Here, only one model is used, and one time slice corresponds to one set of token embeddings instead. The cosine distance of one word to itself in different time slices is then used to gauge its semantic "stableness", indicating whether the word has changed meaning or not. Contextualized approaches could either average embeddings beforehand or calculate average pairwise distances instead (Giulianelli et al., 2020; Laicher et al., 2021).

To evaluate LSCD approaches, some datasets were already manually created for different languages. Here, multiple contexts are strategically paired so that they contain the same word. Human annotators evaluate these pairs, assessing how stable the word meaning within these two contexts appears to be. Repeated annotation of these context pairs then results in a word usage graph, from which individual word senses or a single category of meaning shift can be inferred (Schlechtweg et al., 2018, 2020; Kurtyigit et al., 2021). In the remainder of the paper, this process will be referred to as lexical semantic change annotation (LSCA).

With the emergence of large decoder-only language models, such as ChatGPT, the view on LSCD has changed. Previously, embeddings were the only reliable way of detecting LSC, simply because not enough training data are available to fine-tune a model on the task. So, LSCD is currently a strictly unsupervised task. Now, LSCD can rely on the vast amount of knowledge that has been pre-trained into LLMs, which already show huge popularity with zero-shot (unsupervised) approaches. So far however, the results of using LLMs for LSCD have been mixed. Periti et al. (2024) compared BERT with GPT-3.5 for LSCD by having the models rank 37 target words by degree of change, finding comparable performance between the two. In contrast, Wang and Choi (2023) reported better performance when prompting GPT-4 to rate context pairs, outperforming the BERT-based embedding approach. However, their study was limited to the short-term change dataset, TempoWiC.

In this paper, the focus lies on LSCA, where we assess meaning change at the instance level by prompting LLMs to annotate context pairs, and we evaluate through correct classification, not ranking. By applying this approach to the long-range change, German dataset DURel, we aim to extend previous findings on the overall representation of semantic change in LLMs.

3 Experiments

3.1 Dataset

For this experiment we chose DURel (Schlechtweg et al., 2018), which is a manually annotated dataset for German LSCD. 22 target words were selected on the basis of previous intuitions that these words can represent change in meaning. Five annotators rated the context pairs on a scale of 1 to 4 (see example in Table 1). The contexts were derived from the DTA corpus (*Deutsches Textarchiv*), spanning roughly the 19th century.

3.2 Methods

First, we compiled all individual judgments of the context pairs in DURel. We averaged the scores for context pairs across the annotators and rounded the results, resulting in 1318 averaged use pairs (439 'identical', 413 'closely related', 303 'distantly related', 163 'unrelated'). Ratings of 0 ('unsure') were excluded. To assess the stability and generalizability of the experiment, rather than evaluating the model on the entire dataset once, we randomly sampled 30 instances 20 times, which allowed us to compute 20 F1 scores for model evaluation. The samples were randomized initially and then kept fixed across all experiments. This approach helps

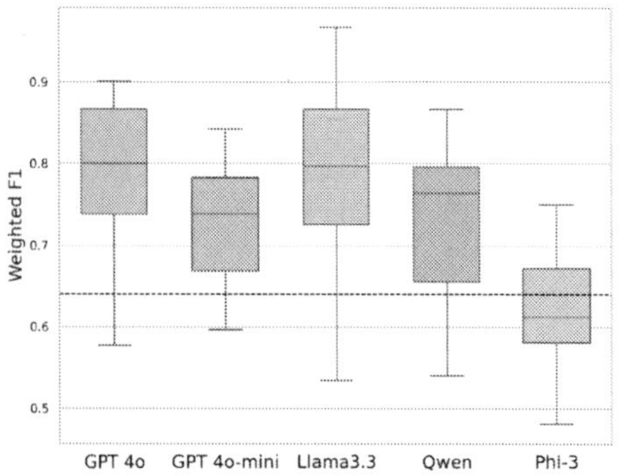

Figure 1: Binary LSCA results (F1) for 5 select models. Dotted line indicates majority baseline.

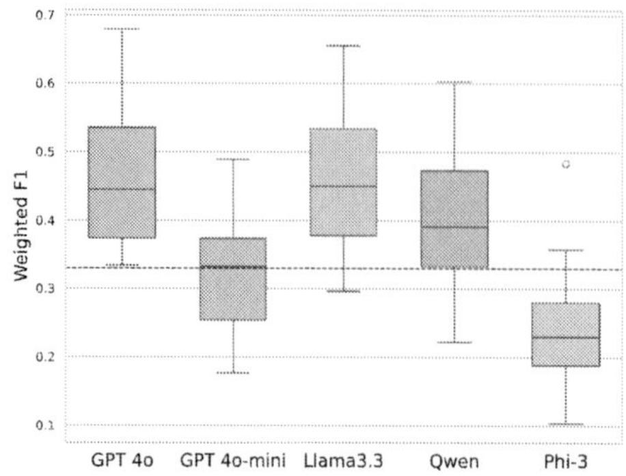

Figure 2: Graded LSCA results (F1) for 5 select models. Dotted line indicates majority baseline.

assess the consistency and reliability of the model's performance across different data subsets, offering a better indication of its overall effectiveness on new, unseen data.

Based on the results of Periti et al. (2024), the prompt was designed as a zero-shot approach, asking to rate the target word based on the two contexts for similarity (see Appendix A). DURel is constructed around comparing lexical items, not tokens, which means that target words may appear as different derivative or orthographical forms in two contexts. The prompt includes instructions not to base decisions on whether the same lexical item also happens to appear as the same token or not. Finally, the models are asked to first give a detailed explanation of their reasoning and then state their rating as one of the 4 relatedness categories, not their numerical equivalents. During the evaluation, the ratings were then extracted from the models responses with regular expressions. 5 different models were evaluated: GPT-4o-mini, GPT-4o, Llama3.3-70B, Phi3, and Qwen2.5-72B. With this selection of models, we mostly wanted to compare open vs. closed domain as well as larger vs. smaller LLMs.[1]

3.3 Results

For the results, we chose to look at the original 4-way classification as well as binary classification, where we labeled classes 1 and 2 as 'change' and 3 and 4 as 'no change', to simulate the two most prevalent evaluation strategies (Schlechtweg et al., 2020). As expected perhaps, the smaller models with 3B and 8B parameters (Phi and GPT-4o-mini) under perform compared to the larger models – for the case of Phi-3 even below the majority baseline (Fig. 1, 2). However, the Llama model demonstrates comparable performance to GPT-4o, despite the latter having 200B parameters. This trend is consistent across both binary and graded LSCA evaluations. The main differences are that the binary results exhibit higher volatility, which is mainly reflected in a larger first quartile, and the performance margin between large and small models is more noticeable for the graded task.

The relatively high spread of F1 scores across different sample sets suggests that model performance is highly dependent on the specific instances chosen. This variability implies that either certain target words or contexts are more challenging for the model or that the model struggles with consistent predictions. This highlights the need for more data annotations so that model performance can be evaluated on a more diverse and representative set of target words, reducing the impact of instance-specific variability and improving overall reliability.

3.4 Historical Prompt Augmentation

In this section, we evaluate whether providing additional lexical context may improve the LSCA task. Retrieval Augmented Generation (RAG) has widely been adopted because of its efficiency instead of fine-tuning when it comes to providing additional input to LLMs (Gao et al., 2023). We therefore turn to a historical German encyclopedia

[1]Embedding-based approaches are commonly used for LSCD, where the goal is to track semantic shift over time by comparing word distributions in different corpora. However, LSCA requires evaluating semantic change at the level of individual word instances in context. Since embedding models like BERT are not explicitly trained for this task and lack sufficient training data for reliable instance-level change detection, they are not directly applicable for LSCA.

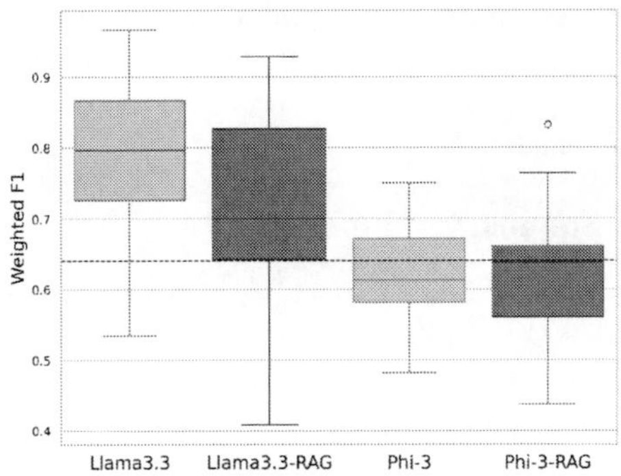

Figure 3: Binary LSCA results (F1) for Llama3.3 and Phi3 with their RAG equivalents. Dotted line indicates majority baseline.

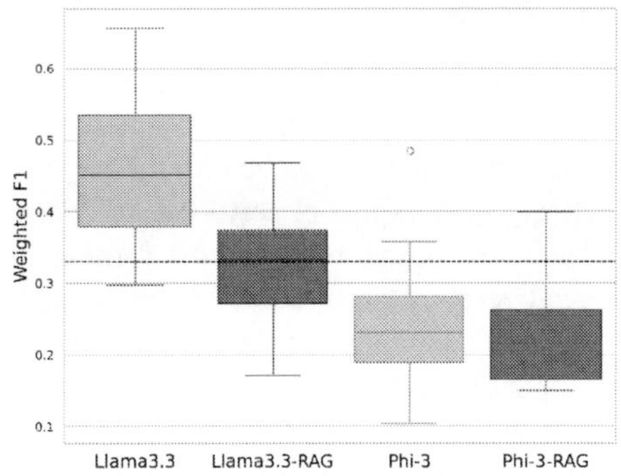

Figure 4: Graded LSCA results (F1) for Llama3.3 and Phi3 with their RAG equivalents. Dotted line indicates majority baseline.

of the early 20th century (Meyers' Großes Conversations Lexikon, 1905). We chose this resource for mainly two reasons: 1) encyclopedias generally contain a vast amount of referential knowledge that could help with providing more context to how a word was used and 2) this encyclopedia aligns with the DURel dataset time-wise. While LLMs are predominantly trained on contemporary data, the inclusion of an older encyclopedia provides the model with a historical perspective. This may allow the model to simultaneously process knowledge from the early 20th century and its own contemporary knowledge.

Instead of storing the entries in the RAG database as a whole, we have split the texts further in order to be able to carry out a more precise retrieval. We chose two approaches: context-sentence construction and triple construction. For the context sentences, we first split the encyclopedia corpus by sentence delimiters and added the entries' headword to every sentence as contextual information. One retrieved sentence is for example: *[Motivieren] in der Kunst, vor allem in der Dichtkunst: eine dargestellte Handlung oder Begebenheit [...].* Triples were extracted through diverse heuristics and regular expressions to condense the content of the encyclopedias further, e.g. *Motiv Synonym Beweggrund.* All texts are embedded using OpenAI's `text-embedding-3-small`. During inference, 5 instances per database per context (= 20 text instances) are retrieved as additional prompt information as follows:

Let the embeddings of a context sentence T and a target word W be represented as $\mathbf{e}_T$ and $\mathbf{e}_W$, respectively. The calculation of the final embedding $\mathbf{e}_{\text{final}}$ is given by:

$$\mathbf{e}_{\text{final}} = \frac{\mathbf{e}_T + w \cdot \mathbf{e}_W}{\|\mathbf{e}_T + w \cdot \mathbf{e}_W\|}$$

where: w is a fixed weight ($w = 1.5$ in our case), and $\|\cdot\|$ denotes the Euclidean norm. This means that for retrieval, more weight is given to the target word in relation to the surrounding context, so that similarity mostly considers the target word and is not as much influenced by other words in the context. The nearest neighbors are calculated from either database via cosine similarity.

Take, for instance, the target word *Vorwort*, which could mean both "preface"[2] or "preposition."[3] The retrieval produced *Preface Definition Vorrede* and *[Vorwort] Auch Vorrede eines Buches (praefatio)* as the two most relevant texts for the former, as well as *Vorwort verweist auf Präposition* and *[Präposition] (lat.), Vorwort, ein Redeteil, der entweder dem von ihm regierten Worte vorausgeht, z. B. mit Vernunft, oder, was seltener ist, nachfolgt, z. B. des Vaters wegen.* for the latter. In this case, even though the target word is the same, the query correctly produces differently contextualized documents for the two meanings, demonstrating that the approach is viable. This additional context is then integrated into the prompt as well (see Appendix A). The information is described as optional, meaning that the model should also assess whether the information is helpful or not.

[2]Context from DURel: "[...] und sprach im Vorworte ganz wie ein guter Landsmann der beiden Dänen. [...]"

[3]Context from DURel: "[...] und die Verhältnisse durch Vorwörter ausdrückt. So z. E. kann man anstatt hier, heute, rechts, bald, rc. sagen"

3.5 Results

The results of the RAG approach are mixed: For the smaller Phi3 model, some improvements could be observed while the approach for the larger model actively impairs model performance (Fig. 3, 4). This could be due to the fact that these models already capture the same kind of historical knowledge and additional context only provides noise. To better understand these changes, we analyzed the transition from the previous models to the RAG models at the level of individual target words, examining whether the new predictions correctly or incorrectly leaned towards similarity or dissimilarity.

Generally speaking, we find that the changes meant higher similarity predictions after RAG, and re-classification affected certain words disproportionally. Consequently, most errors occurred due to a higher similarity prediction, where especially the words *feine*, *flott*, and *packen* (*fine, fast, to pack*) were affected. These words accounted for 22 out of 49 new mistakes in this category. Now correctly assigned similarity scores due to higher similarity are mostly the words *Kinderstube*, *Anstellung*, und *Bilanz* (*nursery, employment, balance*). Changes towards dissimilarity mostly and erroneously affected *locker* (*loose; loosely*), while correct re-classification in the dissimilarity category seems evenly spread (but less likely overall).

It could be hypothesized that ingesting the encyclopedia generally benefits the contextualization of nouns rather than verbs and adjectives, also given the fact that encyclopedias typically focus on explaining concepts, while verbs and adjectives may not receive the same level of detailed explanation.

Furthermore, we observe that language models tend to overemphasize domain differences when annotating LSC, which remains largely unchanged even with the addition of RAG. For instance, in the case of *englisch*, the model classifies *englische Krankheit* ("English disease") and *Englische Flotte* ("English fleet") as having distantly related meanings explicitly due to being used in different domains, despite both usages fundamentally referring to England. While the two contexts indeed belong to different domains—medicine versus military—the core meaning of *englisch* remains stable. This suggests that the model relies heavily on contextual domain differences rather than recognizing the underlying semantic continuity of a word. The fact that this pattern persists with RAG indicates that additional historical context does not necessarily correct this bias, highlighting a potential limitation in how LLMs process lexical meaning across different domains.

4 Summary of Findings

We can conclude that the open-domain Llama3.3 model performs on par with the closed-domain GPT-4o model for the LSCA task (though larger models tend to perform better overall), suggesting that both models contain similar knowledge of historical semantics. Providing additional context through a historical encyclopedia yields mixed results: the augmentation only slightly positively impacts the smaller model, and the performance is highly dependent on the target word. Overall, we found that LLMs may process semantics differently than humans would, as the models put a larger emphasis on the domain in which a word is used. Future work will need to address this challenge, uncovering the reasoning for the models behavior as well as steering models more towards a human intuition of lexical semantics.

5 Limitations

This paper presents only a preliminary experiment on how to further explore the LSCA task using LLMs. First, the prompts could be further refined, potentially incorporating more of the original annotation guidelines from the DURel dataset. Similarly, the handling of additional context through RAG could be optimized, including adjustments to how the retrieved information is presented to the model. The preprocessing of encyclopedias for the RAG database, as well as the choice of retrieval strategy, could also be improved. In this study, several parameters were kept stable for pragmatic reasons—such as the weighting of the target word for embedding creation, the number of items retrieved, and the decision to retrieve two separate contexts—but these should be further evaluated and tuned in future experiments. Finally, the results and observed volatility highlight the need to study a larger set of target words and to explore how different external sources might influence the automatic annotation of lexical semantic change.

References

Yunfan Gao, Yun Xiong, Xinyu Gao, Kangxiang Jia, Jinliu Pan, Yuxi Bi, Yi Dai, Jiawei Sun, and Haofen

Wang. 2023. Retrieval-augmented generation for large language models: A survey. *arXiv preprint arXiv:2312.10997.*

Mario Giulianelli, Marco Del Tredici, and Raquel Fernández. 2020. Analysing lexical semantic change with contextualised word representations. In *Proceedings of the 58th Annual Meeting of the Association for Computational Linguistics*, pages 3960–3973.

William L. Hamilton, Jure Leskovec, and Dan Jurafsky. 2016. Diachronic Word Embeddings Reveal Statistical Laws of Semantic Change. In *Proceedings of the 54th Annual Meeting of the ACL (Volume 1: Long Papers)*, pages 1489–1501, Berlin, Germany.

Joseph Meyer, editor. 1905. *Meyers Großes Konversations-Lexikon*. Leipzig.

Nikhil Kandpal, Haikang Deng, Adam Roberts, Eric Wallace, and Colin Raffel. 2023. Large language models struggle to learn long-tail knowledge. In *International Conference on Machine Learning*, pages 15696–15707. PMLR.

Sinan Kurtyigit, Maike Park, Dominik Schlechtweg, Jonas Kuhn, and Sabine Schulte im Walde. 2021. Lexical semantic change discovery. In *Proceedings of the 59th Annual Meeting of the ACL and the 11th International Joint Conference on Natural Language Processing (Volume 1: Long Papers)*, pages 6985–6998.

Severin Laicher, Sinan Kurtyigit, Dominik Schlechtweg, Jonas Kuhn, and Sabine Schulte im Walde. 2021. Explaining and Improving BERT Performance on Lexical Semantic Change Detection. In *Proceedings of the 16th Conference of the European Chapter of the ACL: Student Research Workshop*.

Francesco Periti, Haim Dubossarsky, and Nina Tahmasebi. 2024. (Chat) GPT v BERT Dawn of Justice for Semantic Change Detection. In *Findings of the ACL: EACL 2024*, pages 420–436.

Francesco Periti and Stefano Montanelli. 2024. Lexical semantic change through large language models: a survey. *ACM Computing Surveys*, 56(11):1–38.

Dominik Schlechtweg, Barbara McGillivray, Simon Hengchen, Haim Dubossarsky, and Nina Tahmasebi. 2020. SemEval-2020 Task 1: Unsupervised Lexical Semantic Change Detection. In *Proceedings of the 14th Workshop on Semantic Evaluation*, pages 1–23, Barcelona (online). International Committee for Computational Linguistics.

Dominik Schlechtweg, Sabine Schulte im Walde, and Stefanie Eckmann. 2018. Diachronic Usage Relatedness (DURel): A Framework for the Annotation of Lexical Semantic Change. In *Proceedings of the 2018 Conference of the NAACL: Human Language Technologies, Volume 2 (Short Papers)*, pages 169–174, New Orleans, Louisiana. Association for Computational Linguistics.

Nina Tahmasebi, Lars Borin, Adam Jatowt, Yang Xu, and Simon Hengchen. 2021. *Computational approaches to semantic change*. Language Science Press, Berlin.

Jindong Wang, Xixu Hu, Wenxin Hou, Hao Chen, Runkai Zheng, Yidong Wang, Linyi Yang, Haojun Huang, Wei Ye, Xiubo Geng, et al. 2023. On the robustness of chatgpt: An adversarial and out-of-distribution perspective. *arXiv preprint arXiv:2302.12095.*

Ruiyu Wang and Matthew Choi. 2023. Large language models on lexical semantic change detection: An evaluation. *arXiv preprint arXiv:2312.06002.*

Melvin Wevers and Marijn Koolen. 2020. Digital begriffsgeschichte: Tracing semantic change using word embeddings. *Historical Methods: A Journal of Quantitative and Interdisciplinary History*, 53(4):226–243.

A Prompt Template

This is the prompt template used for both experiments. The parts highlighted in blue were used for the RAG experiment only:

"You are a knowledgeable linguistic assistant with expertise in lexical semantics. Your task is to analyze the meanings of words in different contexts to determine how related they are. You will be given a target word and two sentences/contexts where this word appears. Note that the word may not appear in the same token form in both contexts; it could be a different lexical form of the same word (e.g., an inflected or derived form). Carefully assess both the similarities and differences in meaning without assuming that they must be different. Additionally, you will be provided with information: 1. Knowledge graph triples related to each context. 2. Relevant encyclopedia sentences where the target word appears. These sentences may provide extra insights or cultural background but should not be used as the primary basis for comparison.

1. Carefully analyze each context independently to determine the target word's meaning. 2. Compare the meanings directly, focusing on their **core semantic similarities or differences**. 3. If the meanings are **exactly the same** or **completely different**, prioritize "Identical meanings" or "Unrelated meanings" over intermediate ratings. 4. Use the knowledge graph triples and encyclopedia sentences as **clarification tools**, but do not let overlaps influence your judgment unfairly.

Rating: - Identical meanings: The word's meaning is exactly the same in both contexts. - Closely related meanings: The word's meanings are very similar, with only minor differences in nuance or usage. - Distantly related meanings: The word's meanings are somewhat connected but show clear differences in usage or interpretation. - Unrelated meanings: The word's meanings have no apparent connection between the contexts.

Input:
Target Word: '{target_word}'
Context 1: '{sentence_1}'
Context 2: '{sentence_2}'
Relevant Knowledge Graph Triples for Context 1: {triples_1}
Relevant Encyclopedia Sentences for Context 1: {encyclopedia_sentences_1}
Relevant Knowledge Graph Triples for Context 2: {triples_2}

Relevant Encyclopedia Sentences for Context 2: {encyclopedia_sentences_2}

Output: Explanation: [Provide a detailed explanation of the relatedness of the target word in both contexts. Use the encyclopedic data as supplementary insights, but focus on comparing the meanings of the word as used in Context 1 and Context 2.] Rating: [Identical meanings, Closely related meanings, Distantly related meanings, or Unrelated meanings]"

AI Conversational Interviewing: Transforming Surveys with LLMs as Adaptive Interviewers

Alexander Wuttke[1], Matthias Aßenmacher[1,2], Christopher Klamm[2], Max M. Lang[3], Quirin Würschinger[1], Frauke Kreuter[1,2]

[1]LMU Munich, [2]Munich Center for Machine Learning (MCML), [3]University of Mannheim, [4]University of Oxford

Correspondence: a.wuttke@lmu.de

Abstract

Traditional methods for eliciting people's opinions face a trade-off between depth and scale: structured surveys enable large-scale data collection but limit respondents' ability to voice their opinions in their own words, while conversational interviews provide deeper insights but are resource-intensive. This study explores the potential of replacing human interviewers with large language models (LLMs) to conduct scalable conversational interviews. Our goal is to assess the performance of AI Conversational Interviewing and to identify opportunities for improvement in a controlled environment. We conducted a small-scale, in-depth study with university students who were randomly assigned to be interviewed by either AI or human interviewers, both employing identical questionnaires on political topics. Various quantitative and qualitative measures assessed interviewer adherence to guidelines, response quality, participant engagement, and overall interview efficacy. The findings indicate the viability of AI Conversational Interviewing in producing quality data comparable to traditional methods, with the added benefit of scalability. We publish our data and materials for re-use and present specific recommendations for effective implementation.

1 Introduction

Structured surveys are popular tools to assess public opinion (Groves, 2009; Kertzer and Renshon, 2022; Stantcheva, 2023). These surveys typically gather individual orientations through self-reports, asking respondents to select from predefined options on fixed questions. This method allows for efficient data collection across large populations, producing structured, tabular data that is straightforward to analyze and comparable across respondents (Krosnick, 1999; Groves, 2009). Due to these benefits, structured surveys hold a prominent position in both academic and commercial research.

Despite their established utility, structured surveys with predefined response options have significant limitations (Schwarz and Hippler, 1987; Kash, 2013). Their static and impersonal nature often leads to respondent fatigue, which can diminish engagement and, consequently, the quality of responses (Krosnick, 1999; Jeong et al., 2023). More critically, the rigid format of these surveys constrains respondents from fully expressing their thoughts, restricting them from offering responses that researchers may not have anticipated (Chang et al., 2021; Esses and Maio, 2002; Reja et al., 2003; Baburajan et al., 2022; Duck-Mayr and Montgomery, 2023).

This limitation hampers the discovery of new phenomena and prevents a comprehensive understanding of the full spectrum of people's attitudes. An alternative to structured surveys is conversational interviewing, sometimes called in-depth or semi-structured or qualitative interviewing (Adeoye-Olatunde and Olenik, 2021; Kallio et al., 2016; Adams, 2015). It involves interviewers engaging with respondents in a more open-ended format, allowing them to freely express their thoughts on topics of interest. The dynamic nature of conversational interviews helps alleviate respondent fatigue and permits the exploration of opinions beyond predefined response options. However, this approach requires skilled interviewers capable of conducting nuanced conversations, which limits its application to small sample sizes due to the associated costs.

So, survey research faces a trade-off between depth and scale: researchers must choose between conducting in-depth explorations with small groups through or large-scale but rigid surveys. However, recent advances in natural language processing (Dubey et al., 2024; Üstün et al., 2024; Workshop et al., 2023; Costello et al., 2024) present new possibilities for addressing this dilemma. The conversational capabilities of instruction-finetuned large

Proceedings of LaTeCH-CLfL 2025, pages 179–204
May 4, 2025

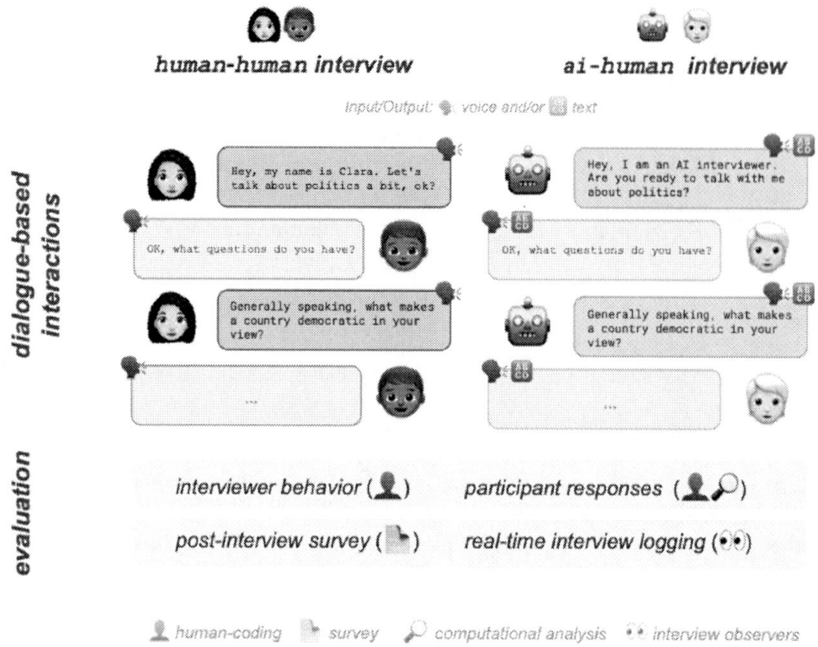

Figure 1: Illustration of the concurrent interview settings (human- vs. AI-conducted) and the various metrics (👤, 👁, 📄 and 🔍) applied to assess interview quality.

language models (Wei et al., 2022; Ouyang et al., 2022) have made them applicable across various academic and industrial domains. Because LLMs can engage in human-like conversations (Cai et al., 2024; di San Pietro et al., 2023; Palmer and Spirling, 2023), they have the potential to assist or even replace human interviewers in conducting conversational interviews. By eliminating the costly need for human interviewers, LLMs could enable scalable in-depth conversations, potentially resolving the trade-off between depth and scale.

Contributions We contribute to the emerging paradigm of AI Conversational Interviewing by conducting the first close-up investigation of its practical implementation and performance (cf. Figure 1):

- We provide a new comprehensive assessment pipeline of AI performance in conducting conversational interviews
- We document the practical challenges participants face when interacting with an AI interviewer
- We are the first to explore the performance of voice-assisted LLM-based interviewing
- We are the first to perform a detailed comparative analysis of AI-conducted versus human-conducted conversational interviews
- We pre-registered the study to ensure transparency in the research process
- We publish code and data for reuse: https://github.com/AIinterviewing/ai-conversational-interviewing-LaTeCH-CLfL2025

2 Related Work

To implement and evaluate AI Conversational Interviews this study combines insights from three distinct lines of work that have rarely been combined.

Advances in AI research have facilitated multiple ongoing commercial and academic projects that use LLM-powered chatbots for in-depth, qualitative, or semi-structured interviews, as they are interchangeably called (Chopra and Haaland, 2023; Weidmann et al., 2024). Although implementations vary, the studies collectively highlight the potential of LLMs for conducting conversational interviews. Yet, critical questions regarding the implementation remain unresolved and little is known about the relative performance compared with human-led interviews.

Qualitative studies have extensively explored best practices for conducting in-person interviews (Adams, 2015). Our approach is to build on these insights when implementing AI Conversational Interviewing.

Studies in survey methodology have extensively examined how different interview implementations influence responses. One line of research has focused on interviewer and mode effects (Mittereder et al., 2018; Malhotra and Krosnick, 2007). The presence of an interviewer significantly impacts respondents, often leading to greater engagement but also increasing the likelihood of socially desirable responses (Atkeson et al., 2014; West and Blom, 2016). In this vein, studies on conversational interviewing has shown that a more active and flexible interviewer who engages with questions from respondents can improve data quality (Schober and Conrad, 1997; Davis et al., 2024; Mittereder et al., 2018).[1] Another important factor is the input mode. Responses to open-ended questions vary depending on whether they are submitted via text or speech. Text input typically requires more effort, which can result in shorter but more carefully considered responses (Gavras et al., 2022; Höhne et al., 2024). So, the responses will not necessarily be better or worse depending on input mode, but they will differ predictably, as text- and speech-based interviews elicit distinct psychological reactions from participants (Gavras et al., 2022).

3 Study Design and Implementation

Our study pursues two goals: (a) Assess the performance of AI Conversational Interviewing (in comparison to human-led interviewing) and (b) Identify problems and opportunities for improvement of AI Conversational Interviewing.

We conducted a small-N study among university students in a controlled environment. Ahead of data collection, we pre-registered our research questions, research design, and evaluation metrics (cf. OSF Registry).

We conducted both AI-led and human-led interviews as part of a class activity, where students were randomly assigned to serve as either interviewers or respondents in the respective conditions. Identical questionnaires were used in both interview settings. After the interview, respondents filled out a structured questionnaire to evaluate their interview experience. In the AI interview condition, students monitored the interviewees in real-time to identify any technical issues.

3.1 Procedure

The study was embedded in a student seminar on survey methodology that was hosted via Zoom. Students were informed that they would participate in a pilot study of conversational interviewing. The seminar proceeded with a detailed script (cf. Appendix C.2), lasting about 120 minutes:

1. Participants were informed about the upcoming procedure, the technical requirements were laid out, and they were asked for consent to participate and collect their data.

2. As preparation for the upcoming tasks, an instructor gave a 10-minute presentation about scientific approaches to interview respondents, and rules for good interviewer behavior.

3. Students were paired up and randomly assigned different roles:

    (a) Students participated in both a human-conducted and an AI-conducted interview, with the sequence randomly assigned

    (b) In the human-conducted interviews, students took on roles as either respondents or interviewers

    (c) In the AI-conducted interviews, students served as either respondents or observers, monitoring for any technical issues during the interview

3.2 Model setup

We implemented a voice-assisted AI Conversational Interviewing pipeline with GPT-4[2] and a Chainlit-based user interface, using the following task-adapted prompts (cf. Appendix C):

1. The **system** instruction to act as an interviewer (*You are a survey interviewer named 'InterviewGPT', an AI interviewer, wanting to find out more about people's views [...]*)

[1] Our method is similar to traditional "conversational interviewing" in that it enhances flexibility during the interview. However, AI Conversational Interviewing differs by highlighting the flexibility of the respondents rather than the interviewer.

[2] GPT-4 turbo, version: 04/2024

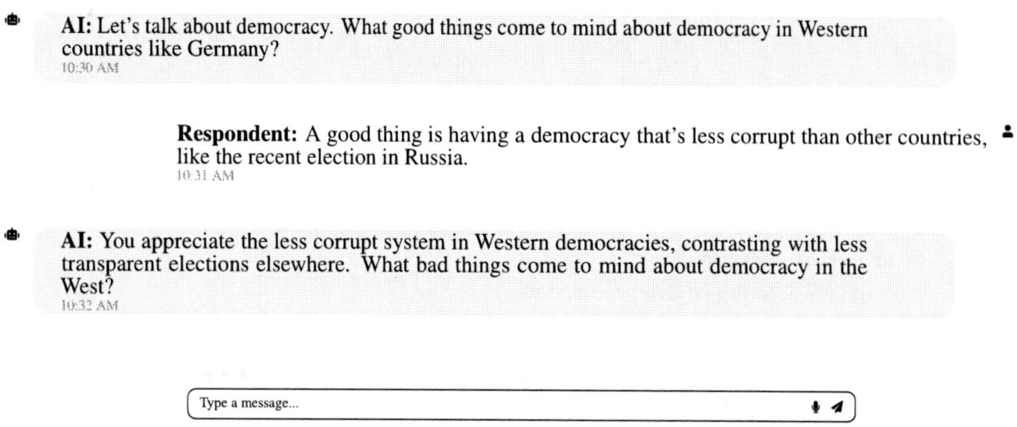

Figure 2: Illustrative example of our used Chat Interface structure (with an interaction between an AI agent and a user) of the AI in-depth interview, showcasing how the interviewer engages in *active listening* by occasionally rehearsing the preceding answer, as instructed (cf. Appendix C). The input field includes options for text input () and voice input ().

2. the **user** instructions with specific guidelines, derived from the qualitative literature on human in-depth interviewing (Adams, 2015), specifying desirable and undesirable interviewer behavior (*[...] Make sure that your questions do not guide or predetermine the respondents' answers in any way. Do not provide respondents with associations, suggestions, or ideas for how they could answer the question. [...]*)

3. a **task** questionnaire on politics and democracy, developed by a democracy researcher among the authors (e.g. *And what do you think "politics" is? How would you define this term?*)

3.3 User interface

To enable voice-assisted interviewing, we developed a user interface based on Chainlit[3], with customization for audio input and output as shown in Figure 2). Our voice-assisted implementation allowed respondents to choose between voice and text modes for both the model output (interviewer questions) and their input (responses). When respondents selected audio input, their speech was transcribed into text, which they could then review and edit before submitting their responses. This approach sought to blend the spontaneity and expressiveness of audio input with the precision and control offered by text-based refinements. For audio output, interviewer questions were displayed as text and could be delivered as voice upon the user's request. We utilized OpenAI Whisper (Radford et al., 2023) for text-to-speech transcriptions of model-generated text.

3.4 Interview Content

Human and AI in-depth interviews were conducted with an identical questionnaire in English (cf. Appendix D). The questionnaire concerned questions on politics and democracy (e.g. *Let us talk about democracy. When you think about how democracy works right now in Western countries such as Germany, what are the good things that come to mind?* or *And what do you think "politics" is? How would you define this term?*). Human-led interviews lasted 16 minutes, on average. AI-led interviews lasted 22 minutes, on average.

3.5 Evaluation Metrics

We computed a set of quantitative and qualitative measures, designed to evaluate the effectiveness, efficiency, and quality of AI-conducted interviews in comparison to traditional human-conducted interviews. Besides quantitative text-based metrics (), we evaluate indicators of participant engagement, response depth, and coherence (). Additionally, we gathered survey feedback () on the interview experience from participants in both interview settings.

Interviewer behavior: Human coding. We provided two research assistants with the interviewer guidelines, which outlined desirable and undesirable interviewer behaviors (cf. Appendix

[3] https://chainlit.io/

H). The research assistants then manually double-coded each conversational turn of the interviewer (e.g., a question) to identify any potential violations of these guidelines. In essence, we assessed whether the human and AI interviewers adhered to the instructions.

Interview responses: Human coding. Two research assistants were provided with a detailed coding manual to assess the quality of the participants' responses (cf. Appendix G). They assessed factors such as whether a response directly addressed the question, whether the participant appeared engaged, and the specificity and detail of the response. In essence, we evaluated whether the interviews elicited insightful responses from participants.

Interview responses: Computational analysis. We computed the Flesch Reading Ease scores on the transcribed interview data to evaluate response readability and length (Flesch, 1948). Additionally, we calculated the number of tokens per response to obtain a more granular measure of linguistic complexity and information density.

Structured post-interview survey. After each interview, the respondents were asked to fill out a survey on their experience (cf. Appendix K).

Real-time problem recording. During the AI interview, one student from each pair was assigned to observe the other student's interaction with the AI interviewer. The observer was given a form to document any technical difficulties or other issues the respondent encountered during the interview (cf. Appendix F).

4 Findings

We collected data on six human-led and five AI-conducted interviews. Human-led interviews were audio-recorded and then transcribed.

Figure 2 presents an example snippet from an AI conversational interview, showcasing how the interviewer engages in active listening by occasionally repeating the preceding answer, as instructed.

Qualitative inspection of the transcribed data shows that both the AI and human interviewers faithfully followed the provided questionnaire. Manual coding of all interviewer behavior shows that neither humans nor AI always acted in full accordance with the interview guidelines (Figure 6). Summarizing across all coded categories, we counted 72 violations per AI interview and 64 violations ($\downarrow$ -11.11%) per human interview, on average.

While error rates of human and AI interviewers were at similar levels, the nature of the errors differed. Contrary to instructions, human interviewers often failed to engage in active listening, which involves restating the respondent's answer to ensure proper understanding. Specifically, 94 percent of guideline violations related to active listening were committed by human interviewers, compared to only 6 percent by the AI interviewer (cf. Appendix I)). Conversely, and in contrast to internal pre-tests, the AI interviewer predominantly failed to follow the instruction to 'ask follow-up questions when a respondent gives a surprising, unexpected, or unclear answer,' with 88 percent of violations of this rule attributed to the AI interviewer. These findings highlight the challenge of finding the right balance between asking too many and too few follow-up questions in any in-depth interviewing setting. Moreover, the fact that the interviewer model had previously succeeded in asking appropriate follow-up questions during internal tests serves as a reminder that even minor modifications to prompts can lead to unintended side effects.

Another guideline was to avoid any behavior that could bias the respondents' answers. However, despite the instruction to 'not take a position on whether their answers are right or wrong,' the AI interviewer occasionally judged the respondent, typically in an encouraging manner (e.g., 'Your definition of politics is quite insightful', 67 percent attributed to the AI interviewer). In contrast, human interviewers sometimes erred by guiding respondents through associations or suggestions for their answers, accounting for 75 percent of such violations. Overall, while no interviewer setting perfectly adhered to the guidelines, these findings suggest that AI interviewers demonstrate a similar level of effectiveness to human student interviewers in following instructions for in-depth interviewing. However, achieving optimal performance relies on fine-tuning and thoroughly testing model instructions.

Turning from the interviewer's behavior to the participants' responses, we see that both interviewing settings succeeded in eliciting answers from respondents at substantial lengths. In the AI interviewer setting, the average response length was 52.39 words. In the human interview setting, the average response length was 32.81 words

	↓ ↑	**AI Interviewer**	**Human Interviewer**	Δ
Qualitative Assessments				
Clarity	↑	**4.3**	3.9	+0.4
Empathy	↑	2.6	**2.9**	-0.3
Engagement	↑	2.6	**3.2**	-0.6
Grammatical correctness	↑	**4.3**	3.8	+0.5
Relevance	↑	**4.6**	4.3	+0.3
Response complexity	↓	**1.9**	2.1	-0.2
Specificity	↑	3.1	**3.6**	-0.5
Tone of answers	↑	3.1	**3.3**	-0.2
Quantitative Assessments				
Tokens per answers	↑	**52.39**	32.81	+19.58
Readability	↑	**77.66**	62.22	+15.44
Survey Results				
Clarity	↑	1.5	**1.9**	-0.4
Interestingness	↑	2.5	**3.9**	-1.4
Repeatability	↑	2.5	**3.6**	-1.1
Overall Satisfaction	↑	**3.8**	**3.8**	+0.0
Understanding	↑	4.0	**4.3**	+0.3

Table 1: Comparison of AI-conducted vs human-conducted interviews: Qualitative assessments, quantitative measurements, and participant survey results where Δ shows the difference between AI and human scores (+ AI performed better and − showing where humans performed better) and we use arrows (↓ ↑) to indicate the desired direction for each metric - whether a higher ↑ or lower score ↓ is better.

(↓ -62.63%).

While participants' answers to the AI interviewer were substantial in length, were they also meaningful in substance? The transcribed responses were given to human coders to rate response quality. While we observe minor differences across setting, overall, the ratings indicate a similar response quality. Responses in human and AI interviews were rated as similarly *clear* (i.e., easy to understand), *empathetic* (i.e., sensitive towards the interviewer), *engaged* (i.e., high level of enthusiasm or interest), *complex* (i.e., advanced vocabulary), *grammatically correct* (i.e., error-free), *specific* (i.e., detailed information), and adequate in *tone* (i.e., suitable for the context).

One particularly important outcome is the assessed relevance of the responses—whether they are useful and directly related to the question asked. Once again, no substantial differences in relevance were observed between AI and human interviews. While these estimates should be interpreted with caution due to the considerable imprecision associated with the small sample size, the findings suggest that engaging with an AI interviewer does not lead to a significant decline in response quality compared to a human interviewer. We interpret this as a proof-of-concept, underscoring the general viability of AI Conversational Interviewing.

Our setup allowed for a close-up investigation of how our AI interviews unfolded in practice. Real-time problem recording during AI interviews showed that respondents interacted seamlessly with our user interface, which resembled familiar chat interfaces, indicating that no learning curve was necessary. Yet, occasionally, the latency of the GPT responses was criticized (e.g. "*Sometimes the time it takes to produce an answer is unexpectedly long. But it is not really off putting.*", "*run time is quite slow, it takes a couple (>5 seconds)*"). While this latency may reflect similar reaction times in human-to-human chat interactions, participants appeared to prefer shorter waiting times when they were aware they were interacting with an AI interviewer.

Our implementation was voice-assisted, allowing respondents to choose between text and speech for both the interviewer's output and their own input. While no issues were reported with the voice output of the interview questions, the real-time problem recording noted several instances where respondents reported technical issues with audio recording and transcription ("*Some problems*

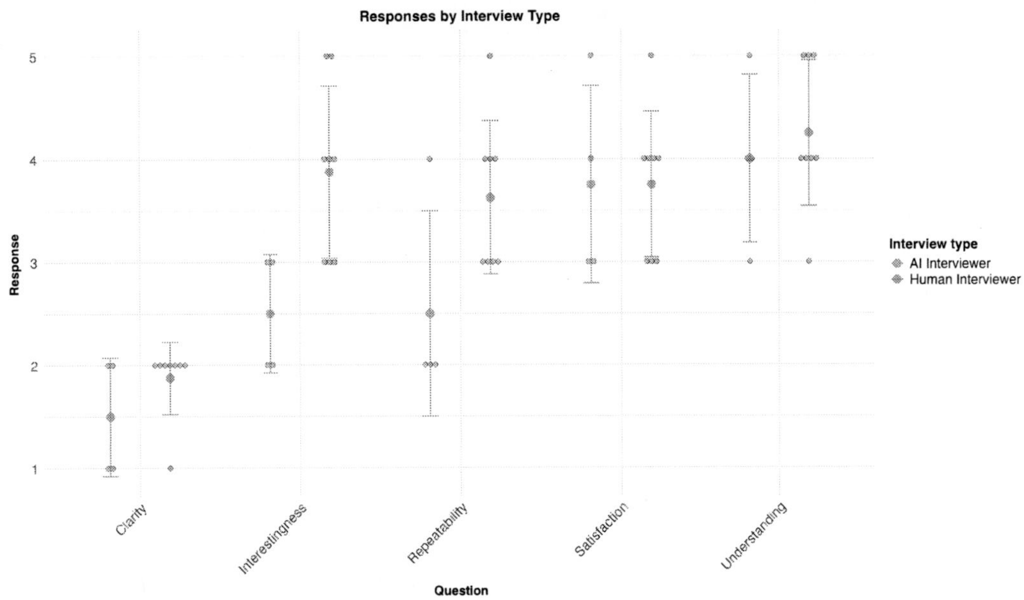

Figure 3: Evaluation for AI (green) vs Human Interviewers (orange), showing the scores (y-axis) across different interview assessment criteria for participants' evaluation of interview (x-axis).

with the microphone: Sometimes does not record, speech recognition sometimes recognises words incorrectly", "*small recurring problems with audio recording (not sure if it already runs, accidently stop in recording early*", "*recording just stopped completely for a couple seconds and interviewee was kinda mad about it*").

Our post-interview survey confirmed these issues. Although five AI interview participants reported trying the audio recording function, only one found it to work sufficiently well to rely on it primarily during the interview. The remaining respondents either partly or primarily preferred to provide written answers to the AI interviewer.

Although unintended, this presents an analytical opportunity to explore differences between written and audio-recorded responses in the AI interviewer setting. As the survey-methodological literature suggests, the answers of respondents who relied on text input were significantly shorter (on average, *21 tokens* per answer) than the answers by respondents who used audio-recorded throughout the AI interview (*63 tokens* per answer (↑ +67%). So, response length markedly varied with input mode.

However, the survey-methodological literature indicates that audio-recorded responses should not be considered inherently superior but rather qualitatively different from written responses. One student observing a respondent providing written input noted that "*the respondent does not have the opportunity to elaborate in a free way in the written answers. She was very focused on writing good sentences which hindered her in her elaboration*", highlighting the distinct psychological processes associated with each input mode.

Further qualitative observation indeed suggests that text-based inputs encourage respondents to think before writing, whereas audio recording tends to prompt respondents to "think out loud", allowing them to develop their thoughts while speaking (see Appendix F for an example). The response styles associated with audio- and text-based input modes are also reflected in objective measures we extracted from the transcribed interview data. Text-based AI interviews achieved a Flesch Reading Ease score of 77.66 while the fully audio-based AI interview scored at 48.32 (↑ +62,22%) (Flesch Reading Ease score for human interviews: 62; higher values indicate higher readability). Hence, compared to text input, audio input in AI interviews may be associated with longer but less elaborate answers. How did respondents experience the interviews? Participants felt that both the human and AI interviewers were clear in their questions and that each understood their responses (Figure 3). Respondents in both settings left the interview satis-

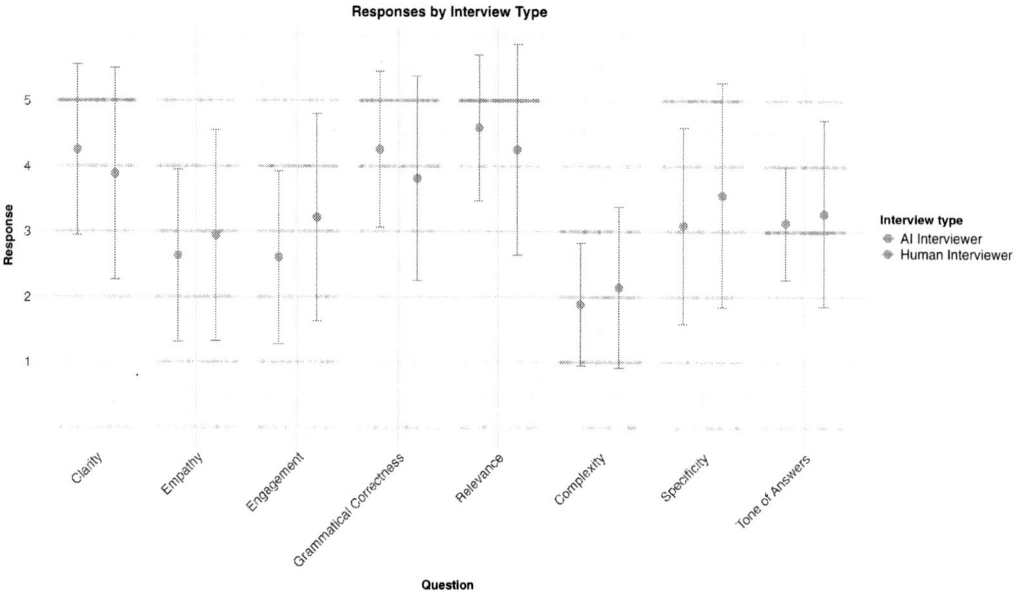

Figure 4: Evaluation for AI (green) vs Human Interviewers (orange), showing the scores (y-axis) across different interview assessment criteria for human-rated response quality (x-axis).

fied. However, participants found the AI interview less interesting and were less likely to repeat it, possibly due to the technical problems with the audio recording. While emphasizing that a satisfactory interview hinges on a flawless technical implementation of the interview process, these findings suggest that the absence of a human interviewer does not necessarily need to go along with a deteriorated interview experience for the respondents.

5 Discussion and Recommendations

Applying the questionnaire to a student sample with both human and AI interviewers demonstrates the general viability of AI Conversational Interviewing. When properly implemented, AI Conversational Interviewing can collect high-quality data. A comprehensive set of qualitative and quantitative metrics suggests that AI interviewing maintains quality comparable to that of human interviewing, but at significantly lower costs, thereby making in-depth interviews more scalable.

Although these findings highlight the potential of AI Conversational Interviewing, the success of the method depends on its precise implementation. Based on our comprehensive analysis, we present five recommendations for the future development and employment of AI-driven in-depth interviews:

Leverage existing knowledge. When specifying desired interviewer behavior, it is crucial to draw on established principles from survey methodology. These practices, developed through extensive research and practical experience, offer proven guidelines for effective implementation.

Context-specific definition of desired interviewer behavior. It is crucial to make deliberate judgment calls to tailor the desired interviewer behavior to your specific research context. This may involve decisions on aspects such as the importance or frequency of follow-up questions, the depth of probing on certain topics, or the level of formality in the interview tone (for example, Weidmann et al. (2024) demonstrated the effectiveness of empathy prompting). Each research project may require a unique approach to AI interviewer behavior to ensure the collection of appropriate data.

Consider user experience. The interface through which participants interact with the AI interviewer is crucial to the success of the interview. It is essential to rely on familiar and intuitive user interfaces that minimize cognitive load and technical barriers. Well-designed interfaces enable participants to focus on providing thoughtful responses rather than being distracted by technical difficulties.

Careful prompting. The prompts provided to the AI interviewer are crucial to its performance. Conduct thorough pre-testing to ensure that the AI's behavior aligns with your established guidelines. It is important to consider the potential unintended side-effects of modifying prompts, as even minor adjustments can lead to significant changes in interviewer behavior or question interpretation (Tam et al., 2024; Sclar et al., 2024; Zhu et al., 2024).

Input mode matters. Recognize that the chosen input mode (e.g., text or speech) will significantly influence participant behavior by eliciting different psychological responses. Response patterns may vary across several outcomes, sometimes in contrasting ways. For instance, spoken responses might be longer but less detailed, while written responses may be shorter yet more concise and thoughtfully constructed. The choice of input mode should be made with careful consideration of your research objectives and the type of data you aim to collect.

6 Conclusion

Our research contributes to the growing field of AI-supported interviewing by offering initial insights through an in-depth evaluation process. We assessed AI performance using a variety of quantitative and qualitative evaluation methods, documenting the challenges participants faced and comparing AI-conducted interviews with human-led ones. To ensure transparency, we have made our pipeline, questions, and data publicly available. Based on our preliminary findings, we propose five areas for consideration in future implementations: integrating established survey methodology principles, adapting AI behavior to different contexts, designing user-friendly interfaces, conducting comprehensive pre-testing, and being aware of input mode effects. While our results highlight the potential of AI Conversational Interviewing, it is important to recognize that outcomes are heavily dependent on the specific implementation methods used.

Limitations

Several limitations reflect our study's design of a close-up monitoring of AI interviewing in practice. The study's small sample limits the generalizability of the findings. Our decision to have students monitor the AI interviewing process impedes investigating whether the absence of a human being fosters respondents' proclivity to discuss sensitive topics which may be an additional advantage of AI Conversational Interviewing. Our participants were students with an interest in survey methodology which may have been more motivated than ordinary participants. Furthermore, the use of a closed model restricts the study's replicability compared to the transparency that could be achieved with an open-source model (Spirling, 2023). We chose GPT-4 because it was the state of the art at the time of the interviews and offered social science researchers the most accessible opportunity for application (Palmer et al., 2024). By showing the pitfalls of the best-performing model across several benchmarks, we aimed to provide a starting point for an open discussion on this type of model. For future research, we plan to compare the capabilities of different models, including strong open-source models such as Llama 3.1 (Dubey et al., 2024), to provide a more comprehensive and application-oriented view of AI interviewing techniques. Finally, our study concerned collecting data via AI Conversational interviews and not its analysis where researchers may rely on computational methods for text analysis (Baden et al., 2022; Banks et al., 2018; DiMaggio, 2015; Grimmer et al., 2022).

Ethics Statement

We affirm that our research adheres to the ACL Ethics Policy. To protect participant privacy, we ensure that no individuals are identifiable. To maximize the public value of our work, we make all underlying data and source code openly available for reuse. We declare that no conflicts of interest could influence the study's outcomes, interpretations, or conclusions. All funding sources supporting this research are acknowledged in the acknowledgments section. Furthermore, we have rigorously documented our methodology, experiments, and results to enhance the replicability of our findings.

Acknowledgements

We thank Laura Kiemes and Valeriya Barakhvostova for excellent research assistance. We are grateful for helpful comments we received at I2SC Saarbrücken Kick-Off Event, the Mainz Workshop on Citizen Perspectives on Demcracy, and the LMU MCMP seminar series. Alexander Wuttke was funded by LMU's Young Researcher Support Fund. Matthias Aßenmacher was funded by the Deutsche Forschungsgemeinschaft (DFG, German Research

Foundation) under the National Research Data Infrastructure – NFDI 27/1 - 460037581.

References

William C. Adams. 2015. Conducting Semi-Structured Interviews. In Kathryn E. Newcomer, Harry P. Hatry, and Joseph S. Wholey, editors, *Handbook of Practical Program Evaluation*, 1 edition, pages 492–505. Wiley.

Omolola A Adeoye-Olatunde and Nicole L Olenik. 2021. Research and scholarly methods: Semi-structured interviews. *Journal of the american college of clinical pharmacy*, 4(10):1358–1367.

Lonna Rae Atkeson, Alex N. Adams, and R. Michael Alvarez. 2014. Nonresponse and Mode Effects in Self- and Interviewer-Administered Surveys. *Political Analysis*, 22(3):304–320.

Vishnu Baburajan, João de Abreu e Silva, and Francisco Camara Pereira. 2022. Open vs closed-ended questions in attitudinal surveys–comparing, combining, and interpreting using natural language processing. *Transportation research part C: emerging technologies*, 137:103589.

Christian Baden, Christian Pipal, Martijn Schoonvelde, and Mariken AC G van der Velden. 2022. Three gaps in computational text analysis methods for social sciences: A research agenda. *Communication Methods and Measures*, 16(1):1–18.

George C Banks, Haley M Woznyj, Ryan S Wesslen, and Roxanne L Ross. 2018. A review of best practice recommendations for text analysis in r (and a user-friendly app). *Journal of Business and Psychology*, 33:445–459.

Zhenguang G. Cai, Xufeng Duan, David A. Haslett, Shuqi Wang, and Martin J. Pickering. 2024. Do large language models resemble humans in language use? *Preprint*, arXiv:2303.08014.

Arturo Chang, Thomas Ferguson, Jacob Rothschild, and Benjamin Page. 2021. Ambivalence about international trade in open-and closed-ended survey responses. *Institute for New Economic Thinking Working Paper Series*, 162.

Felix Chopra and Ingar Haaland. 2023. Conducting Qualitative Interviews with AI.

Thomas H Costello, Gordon Pennycook, and David G Rand. 2024. Durably reducing conspiracy beliefs through dialogues with ai. *Science*, 385(6714):eadq1814.

Rachel E Davis, Frederick G Conrad, Shaohua Dong, Anna Mesa, Sunghee Lee, and Timothy P Johnson. 2024. An ounce of prevention: using conversational interviewing and avoiding agreement response scales to prevent acquiescence. *Quality & Quantity*, 58(1):471–495.

Chiara Barattieri di San Pietro, Federico Frau, Veronica Mangiaterra, and Valentina Bambini. 2023. The pragmatic profile of chatgpt: assessing the pragmatic skills of a conversational agent. *PsyArXiv*.

Paul DiMaggio. 2015. Adapting computational text analysis to social science (and vice versa). *Big Data & Society*, 2(2):2053951715602908.

Abhimanyu Dubey, Abhinav Jauhri, Abhinav Pandey, Abhishek Kadian, Ahmad Al-Dahle, Aiesha Letman, Akhil Mathur, Alan Schelten, Amy Yang, Angela Fan, Anirudh Goyal, Anthony Hartshorn, Aobo Yang, Archi Mitra, Archie Sravankumar, Artem Korenev, Arthur Hinsvark, Arun Rao, Aston Zhang, Aurelien Rodriguez, Austen Gregerson, Ava Spataru, Baptiste Roziere, Bethany Biron, Binh Tang, Bobbie Chern, Charlotte Caucheteux, Chaya Nayak, Chloe Bi, Chris Marra, Chris McConnell, Christian Keller, Christophe Touret, Chunyang Wu, Corinne Wong, Cristian Canton Ferrer, Cyrus Nikolaidis, Damien Allonsius, Daniel Song, Danielle Pintz, Danny Livshits, David Esiobu, Dhruv Choudhary, Dhruv Mahajan, Diego Garcia-Olano, Diego Perino, Dieuwke Hupkes, Egor Lakomkin, Ehab AlBadawy, Elina Lobanova, Emily Dinan, Eric Michael Smith, Filip Radenovic, Frank Zhang, Gabriel Synnaeve, Gabrielle Lee, Georgia Lewis Anderson, Graeme Nail, Gregoire Mialon, Guan Pang, Guillem Cucurell, Hailey Nguyen, Hannah Korevaar, Hu Xu, Hugo Touvron, Iliyan Zarov, Imanol Arrieta Ibarra, Isabel Kloumann, Ishan Misra, Ivan Evtimov, Jade Copet, Jaewon Lee, Jan Geffert, Jana Vranes, Jason Park, Jay Mahadeokar, Jeet Shah, Jelmer van der Linde, Jennifer Billock, Jenny Hong, Jenya Lee, Jeremy Fu, Jianfeng Chi, Jianyu Huang, Jiawen Liu, Jie Wang, Jiecao Yu, Joanna Bitton, Joe Spisak, Jongsoo Park, Joseph Rocca, Joshua Johnstun, Joshua Saxe, Junteng Jia, Kalyan Vasuden Alwala, Kartikeya Upasani, Kate Plawiak, Ke Li, Kenneth Heafield, Kevin Stone, Khalid El-Arini, Krithika Iyer, Kshitiz Malik, Kuenley Chiu, Kunal Bhalla, Lauren Rantala-Yeary, Laurens van der Maaten, Lawrence Chen, Liang Tan, Liz Jenkins, Louis Martin, Lovish Madaan, Lubo Malo, Lukas Blecher, Lukas Landzaat, Luke de Oliveira, Madeline Muzzi, Mahesh Pasupuleti, Mannat Singh, Manohar Paluri, Marcin Kardas, Mathew Oldham, Mathieu Rita, Maya Pavlova, Melanie Kambadur, Mike Lewis, Min Si, Mitesh Kumar Singh, Mona Hassan, Naman Goyal, Narjes Torabi, Nikolay Bashlykov, Nikolay Bogoychev, Niladri Chatterji, Olivier Duchenne, Onur Çelebi, Patrick Alrassy, Pengchuan Zhang, Pengwei Li, Petar Vasic, Peter Weng, Prajjwal Bhargava, Pratik Dubal, Praveen Krishnan, Punit Singh Koura, Puxin Xu, Qing He, Qingxiao Dong, Ragavan Srinivasan, Raj Ganapathy, Ramon Calderer, Ricardo Silveira Cabral, Robert Stojnic, Roberta Raileanu, Rohit Girdhar, Rohit Patel, Romain Sauvestre, Ronnie Polidoro, Roshan Sumbaly, Ross Taylor, Ruan Silva, Rui Hou, Rui Wang, Saghar Hosseini, Sahana Chennabasappa, Sanjay Singh, Sean Bell, Seohyun Sonia Kim, Sergey Edunov, Shaoliang Nie, Sharan Narang, Sharath Raparthy, Sheng Shen, Shengye Wan, Shruti Bhosale, Shun

Zhang, Simon Vandenhende, Soumya Batra, Spencer Whitman, Sten Sootla, Stephane Collot, Suchin Gururangan, Sydney Borodinsky, Tamar Herman, Tara Fowler, Tarek Sheasha, Thomas Georgiou, Thomas Scialom, Tobias Speckbacher, Todor Mihaylov, Tong Xiao, Ujjwal Karn, Vedanuj Goswami, Vibhor Gupta, Vignesh Ramanathan, Viktor Kerkez, Vincent Gonguet, Virginie Do, Vish Vogeti, Vladan Petrovic, Weiwei Chu, Wenhan Xiong, Wenyin Fu, Whitney Meers, Xavier Martinet, Xiaodong Wang, Xiaoqing Ellen Tan, Xinfeng Xie, Xuchao Jia, Xuewei Wang, Yaelle Goldschlag, Yashesh Gaur, Yasmine Babaei, Yi Wen, Yiwen Song, Yuchen Zhang, Yue Li, Yuning Mao, Zacharie Delpierre Coudert, Zheng Yan, Zhengxing Chen, Zoe Papakipos, Aaditya Singh, Aaron Grattafiori, Abha Jain, Adam Kelsey, Adam Shajnfeld, Adithya Gangidi, Adolfo Victoria, Ahuva Goldstand, Ajay Menon, Ajay Sharma, Alex Boesenberg, Alex Vaughan, Alexei Baevski, Allie Feinstein, Amanda Kallet, Amit Sangani, Anam Yunus, Andrei Lupu, Andres Alvarado, Andrew Caples, Andrew Gu, Andrew Ho, Andrew Poulton, Andrew Ryan, Ankit Ramchandani, Annie Franco, Aparajita Saraf, Arkabandhu Chowdhury, Ashley Gabriel, Ashwin Bharambe, Assaf Eisenman, Azadeh Yazdan, Beau James, Ben Maurer, Benjamin Leonhardi, Bernie Huang, Beth Loyd, Beto De Paola, Bhargavi Paranjape, Bing Liu, Bo Wu, Boyu Ni, Braden Hancock, Bram Wasti, Brandon Spence, Brani Stojkovic, Brian Gamido, Britt Montalvo, Carl Parker, Carly Burton, Catalina Mejia, Changhan Wang, Changkyu Kim, Chao Zhou, Chester Hu, Ching-Hsiang Chu, Chris Cai, Chris Tindal, Christoph Feichtenhofer, Damon Civin, Dana Beaty, Daniel Kreymer, Daniel Li, Danny Wyatt, David Adkins, David Xu, Davide Testuggine, Delia David, Devi Parikh, Diana Liskovich, Didem Foss, Dingkang Wang, Duc Le, Dustin Holland, Edward Dowling, Eissa Jamil, Elaine Montgomery, Eleonora Presani, Emily Hahn, Emily Wood, Erik Brinkman, Esteban Arcaute, Evan Dunbar, Evan Smothers, Fei Sun, Felix Kreuk, Feng Tian, Firat Ozgenel, Francesco Caggioni, Francisco Guzmán, Frank Kanayet, Frank Seide, Gabriela Medina Florez, Gabriella Schwarz, Gada Badeer, Georgia Swee, Gil Halpern, Govind Thattai, Grant Herman, Grigory Sizov, Guangyi, Zhang, Guna Lakshminarayanan, Hamid Shojanazeri, Han Zou, Hannah Wang, Hanwen Zha, Haroun Habeeb, Harrison Rudolph, Helen Suk, Henry Aspegren, Hunter Goldman, Ibrahim Damlaj, Igor Molybog, Igor Tufanov, Irina-Elena Veliche, Itai Gat, Jake Weissman, James Geboski, James Kohli, Japhet Asher, Jean-Baptiste Gaya, Jeff Marcus, Jeff Tang, Jennifer Chan, Jenny Zhen, Jeremy Reizenstein, Jeremy Teboul, Jessica Zhong, Jian Jin, Jingyi Yang, Joe Cummings, Jon Carvill, Jon Shepard, Jonathan McPhie, Jonathan Torres, Josh Ginsburg, Junjie Wang, Kai Wu, Kam Hou U, Karan Saxena, Karthik Prasad, Kartikay Khandelwal, Katayoun Zand, Kathy Matosich, Kaushik Veeraraghavan, Kelly Michelena, Keqian Li, Kun Huang, Kunal Chawla, Kushal Lakhotia, Kyle Huang, Lailin Chen, Lakshya Garg, Lavender A, Leandro Silva, Lee Bell, Lei Zhang, Liangpeng Guo, Licheng Yu, Liron Moshkovich, Luca Wehrstedt, Madian Khabsa, Manav Avalani, Manish Bhatt, Maria Tsimpoukelli, Martynas Mankus, Matan Hasson, Matthew Lennie, Matthias Reso, Maxim Groshev, Maxim Naumov, Maya Lathi, Meghan Keneally, Michael L. Seltzer, Michal Valko, Michelle Restrepo, Mihir Patel, Mik Vyatskov, Mikayel Samvelyan, Mike Clark, Mike Macey, Mike Wang, Miquel Jubert Hermoso, Mo Metanat, Mohammad Rastegari, Munish Bansal, Nandhini Santhanam, Natascha Parks, Natasha White, Navyata Bawa, Nayan Singhal, Nick Egebo, Nicolas Usunier, Nikolay Pavlovich Laptev, Ning Dong, Ning Zhang, Norman Cheng, Oleg Chernoguz, Olivia Hart, Omkar Salpekar, Ozlem Kalinli, Parkin Kent, Parth Parekh, Paul Saab, Pavan Balaji, Pedro Rittner, Philip Bontrager, Pierre Roux, Piotr Dollar, Polina Zvyagina, Prashant Ratanchandani, Pritish Yuvraj, Qian Liang, Rachad Alao, Rachel Rodriguez, Rafi Ayub, Raghotham Murthy, Raghu Nayani, Rahul Mitra, Raymond Li, Rebekkah Hogan, Robin Battey, Rocky Wang, Rohan Maheswari, Russ Howes, Ruty Rinott, Sai Jayesh Bondu, Samyak Datta, Sara Chugh, Sara Hunt, Sargun Dhillon, Sasha Sidorov, Satadru Pan, Saurabh Verma, Seiji Yamamoto, Sharadh Ramaswamy, Shaun Lindsay, Shaun Lindsay, Sheng Feng, Shenghao Lin, Shengxin Cindy Zha, Shiva Shankar, Shuqiang Zhang, Shuqiang Zhang, Sinong Wang, Sneha Agarwal, Soji Sajuyigbe, Soumith Chintala, Stephanie Max, Stephen Chen, Steve Kehoe, Steve Satterfield, Sudarshan Govindaprasad, Sumit Gupta, Sungmin Cho, Sunny Virk, Suraj Subramanian, Sy Choudhury, Sydney Goldman, Tal Remez, Tamar Glaser, Tamara Best, Thilo Kohler, Thomas Robinson, Tianhe Li, Tianjun Zhang, Tim Matthews, Timothy Chou, Tzook Shaked, Varun Vontimitta, Victoria Ajayi, Victoria Montanez, Vijai Mohan, Vinay Satish Kumar, Vishal Mangla, Vítor Albiero, Vlad Ionescu, Vlad Poenaru, Vlad Tiberiu Mihailescu, Vladimir Ivanov, Wei Li, Wenchen Wang, Wenwen Jiang, Wes Bouaziz, Will Constable, Xiaocheng Tang, Xiaofang Wang, Xiaojian Wu, Xiaolan Wang, Xide Xia, Xilun Wu, Xinbo Gao, Yanjun Chen, Ye Hu, Ye Jia, Ye Qi, Yenda Li, Yilin Zhang, Ying Zhang, Yossi Adi, Youngjin Nam, Yu, Wang, Yuchen Hao, Yundi Qian, Yuzi He, Zach Rait, Zachary DeVito, Zef Rosnbrick, Zhaoduo Wen, Zhenyu Yang, and Zhiwei Zhao. 2024. The llama 3 herd of models. *Preprint*, arXiv:2407.21783.

JBrandon Duck-Mayr and Jacob Montgomery. 2023. Ends against the middle: Measuring latent traits when opposites respond the same way for antithetical reasons. *Political Analysis*, 31(4):606–625.

Victoria M Esses and Gregory R Maio. 2002. Expanding the assessment of attitude components and structure: The benefits of open-ended measures. *European review of social psychology*, 12(1):71–101.

Rudolph Flesch. 1948. A new readability yardstick. *Journal of Applied Psychology*, 32(3):p221 – 233.

Konstantin Gavras, Jan Karem Höhne, Annelies G. Blom, and Harald Schoen. 2022. Innovating the Collection of Open-Ended Answers: The Linguistic and Content Characteristics of Written and Oral

Answers to Political Attitude Questions. *Journal of the Royal Statistical Society Series A: Statistics in Society*, 185(3):872–890.

Justin Grimmer, Margaret E Roberts, and Brandon M Stewart. 2022. *Text as data: A new framework for machine learning and the social sciences*. Princeton University Press.

Robert M. Groves, editor. 2009. *Survey methodology*, 2nd ed edition. Wiley series in survey methodology. Wiley, Hoboken, N.J. OCLC: ocn302189175.

Jan Karem Höhne, Christoph Kern, Konstantin Gavras, and Stephan Schlosser. 2024. The sound of respondents: predicting respondents' level of interest in questions with voice data in smartphone surveys. *Quality & Quantity*, 58(3):2907–2927.

Dahyeon Jeong, Shilpa Aggarwal, Jonathan Robinson, Naresh Kumar, Alan Spearot, and David Sungho Park. 2023. Exhaustive or exhausting? evidence on respondent fatigue in long surveys. *Journal of Development Economics*, 161:102992.

Hanna Kallio, Anna-Maija Pietilä, Martin Johnson, and Mari Kangasniemi. 2016. Systematic methodological review: developing a framework for a qualitative semi-structured interview guide. *Journal of advanced nursing*, 72(12):2954–2965.

Gwen Kash. 2013. Open versus closed: effects of question form on transit rider expressions of policy preferences in arequipa, peru. *Transportation research record*, 2354(1):51–58.

Joshua D Kertzer and Jonathan Renshon. 2022. Experiments and surveys on political elites. *Annual Review of Political Science*, 25(1):529–550.

Jon A Krosnick. 1999. Survey research. *Annual review of psychology*, 50(1):537–567.

Neil Malhotra and Jon A Krosnick. 2007. The effect of survey mode and sampling on inferences about political attitudes and behavior: Comparing the 2000 and 2004 anes to internet surveys with nonprobability samples. *Political Analysis*, 15(3):286–323.

Felicitas Mittereder, Jen Durow, Brady T. West, Frauke Kreuter, and Frederick G. Conrad. 2018. Interviewer–respondent Interactions in Conversational and Standardized Interviewing. *Field Methods*, 30(1):3–21. Publisher: SAGE Publications Inc.

Long Ouyang, Jeffrey Wu, Xu Jiang, Diogo Almeida, Carroll Wainwright, Pamela Mishkin, Chong Zhang, Sandhini Agarwal, Katarina Slama, Alex Gray, John Schulman, Jacob Hilton, Fraser Kelton, Luke Miller, Maddie Simens, Amanda Askell, Peter Welinder, Paul Christiano, Jan Leike, and Ryan Lowe. 2022. Training language models to follow instructions with human feedback. In *Advances in Neural Information Processing Systems*.

Alexis Palmer, Noah A Smith, and Arthur Spirling. 2024. Using proprietary language models in academic research requires explicit justification. *Nature Computational Science*, 4(1):2–3.

Alexis Palmer and Arthur Spirling. 2023. Large language models can argue in convincing ways about politics, but humans dislike ai authors: implications for governance. *Political science*, 75(3):281–291.

Alec Radford, Jong Wook Kim, Tao Xu, Greg Brockman, Christine Mcleavey, and Ilya Sutskever. 2023. Robust Speech Recognition via Large-Scale Weak Supervision. In *Proceedings of the 40th International Conference on Machine Learning*, pages 28492–28518. PMLR.

Urša Reja, Katja Lozar Manfreda, Valentina Hlebec, and Vasja Vehovar. 2003. Open-ended vs. close-ended questions in web questionnaires. *Developments in applied statistics*, 19(1):159–177.

Michael F Schober and Frederick G Conrad. 1997. Does conversational interviewing reduce survey measurement error? *Public opinion quarterly*, pages 576–602.

Norbert Schwarz and Hans-J Hippler. 1987. What response scales may tell your respondents: Informative functions of response alternatives. In *Social information processing and survey methodology*, pages 163–178. Springer.

Melanie Sclar, Yejin Choi, Yulia Tsvetkov, and Alane Suhr. 2024. Quantifying language models' sensitivity to spurious features in prompt design or: How i learned to start worrying about prompt formatting. In *The Twelfth International Conference on Learning Representations*.

Arthur Spirling. 2023. Why open-source generative ai models are an ethical way forward for science. *Nature*, 616(7957):413–413.

Stefanie Stantcheva. 2023. How to run surveys: A guide to creating your own identifying variation and revealing the invisible. *Annual Review of Economics*, 15(1):205–234.

Zhi Rui Tam, Cheng-Kuang Wu, Yi-Lin Tsai, Chieh-Yen Lin, Hung yi Lee, and Yun-Nung Chen. 2024. Let me speak freely? a study on the impact of format restrictions on performance of large language models. *Preprint*, arXiv:2408.02442.

Jason Wei, Maarten Bosma, Vincent Y. Zhao, Kelvin Guu, Adams Wei Yu, Brian Lester, Nan Du, Andrew M. Dai, and Quoc V. Le. 2022. Finetuned language models are zero-shot learners. *Preprint*, arXiv:2109.01652.

Joshua Weidmann, Michael M. Bechtel, Aaron Cannon, and Michael Hess. 2024. Dialing Up the Empathy: Using AI Chatbots to Conduct Qualitative Interviews in Mass Surveys.

Brady T. West and Annelies G. Blom. 2016. Explaining Interviewer Effects: A Research Synthesis. *Journal of Survey Statistics and Methodology*, page smw024.

BigScience Workshop, :, Teven Le Scao, Angela Fan, Christopher Akiki, Ellie Pavlick, Suzana Ilić, Daniel Hesslow, Roman Castagné, Alexandra Sasha Luccioni, François Yvon, Matthias Gallé, Jonathan Tow, Alexander M. Rush, Stella Biderman, Albert Webson, Pawan Sasanka Ammanamanchi, Thomas Wang, Benoît Sagot, Niklas Muennighoff, Albert Villanova del Moral, Olatunji Ruwase, Rachel Bawden, Stas Bekman, Angelina McMillan-Major, Iz Beltagy, Huu Nguyen, Lucile Saulnier, Samson Tan, Pedro Ortiz Suarez, Victor Sanh, Hugo Laurençon, Yacine Jernite, Julien Launay, Margaret Mitchell, Colin Raffel, Aaron Gokaslan, Adi Simhi, Aitor Soroa, Alham Fikri Aji, Amit Alfassy, Anna Rogers, Ariel Kreisberg Nitzav, Canwen Xu, Chenghao Mou, Chris Emezue, Christopher Klamm, Colin Leong, Daniel van Strien, David Ifeoluwa Adelani, Dragomir Radev, Eduardo González Ponferrada, Efrat Levkovizh, Ethan Kim, Eyal Bar Natan, Francesco De Toni, Gérard Dupont, Germán Kruszewski, Giada Pistilli, Hady Elsahar, Hamza Benyamina, Hieu Tran, Ian Yu, Idris Abdulmumin, Isaac Johnson, Itziar Gonzalez-Dios, Javier de la Rosa, Jenny Chim, Jesse Dodge, Jian Zhu, Jonathan Chang, Jörg Frohberg, Joseph Tobing, Joydeep Bhattacharjee, Khalid Almubarak, Kimbo Chen, Kyle Lo, Leandro Von Werra, Leon Weber, Long Phan, Loubna Ben allal, Ludovic Tanguy, Manan Dey, Manuel Romero Muñoz, Maraim Masoud, María Grandury, Mario Šaško, Max Huang, Maximin Coavoux, Mayank Singh, Mike Tian-Jian Jiang, Minh Chien Vu, Mohammad A. Jauhar, Mustafa Ghaleb, Nishant Subramani, Nora Kassner, Nurulaqilla Khamis, Olivier Nguyen, Omar Espejel, Ona de Gibert, Paulo Villegas, Peter Henderson, Pierre Colombo, Priscilla Amuok, Quentin Lhoest, Rheza Harliman, Rishi Bommasani, Roberto Luis López, Rui Ribeiro, Salomey Osei, Sampo Pyysalo, Sebastian Nagel, Shamik Bose, Shamsuddeen Hassan Muhammad, Shanya Sharma, Shayne Longpre, Somaieh Nikpoor, Stanislav Silberberg, Suhas Pai, Sydney Zink, Tiago Timponi Torrent, Timo Schick, Tristan Thrush, Valentin Danchev, Vassilina Nikoulina, Veronika Laippala, Violette Lepercq, Vrinda Prabhu, Zaid Alyafeai, Zeerak Talat, Arun Raja, Benjamin Heinzerling, Chenglei Si, Davut Emre Taşar, Elizabeth Salesky, Sabrina J. Mielke, Wilson Y. Lee, Abheesht Sharma, Andrea Santilli, Antoine Chaffin, Arnaud Stiegler, Debajyoti Datta, Eliza Szczechla, Gunjan Chhablani, Han Wang, Harshit Pandey, Hendrik Strobelt, Jason Alan Fries, Jos Rozen, Leo Gao, Lintang Sutawika, M Saiful Bari, Maged S. Al-shaibani, Matteo Manica, Nihal Nayak, Ryan Teehan, Samuel Albanie, Sheng Shen, Srulik Ben-David, Stephen H. Bach, Taewoon Kim, Tali Bers, Thibault Fevry, Trishala Neeraj, Urmish Thakker, Vikas Raunak, Xiangru Tang, Zheng-Xin Yong, Zhiqing Sun, Shaked Brody, Yallow Uri, Hadar Tojarieh, Adam Roberts, Hyung Won Chung, Jaesung Tae, Jason Phang, Ofir Press, Conglong Li, Deepak Narayanan, Hatim Bourfoune, Jared Casper, Jeff Rasley, Max Ryabinin, Mayank Mishra, Minjia Zhang, Mohammad Shoeybi, Myriam Peyrounette, Nicolas Patry, Nouamane Tazi, Omar Sanseviero, Patrick von Platen, Pierre Cornette, Pierre François Lavallée, Rémi Lacroix, Samyam Rajbhandari, Sanchit Gandhi, Shaden Smith, Stéphane Requena, Suraj Patil, Tim Dettmers, Ahmed Baruwa, Amanpreet Singh, Anastasia Cheveleva, Anne-Laure Ligozat, Arjun Subramonian, Aurélie Névéol, Charles Lovering, Dan Garrette, Deepak Tunuguntla, Ehud Reiter, Ekaterina Taktasheva, Ekaterina Voloshina, Eli Bogdanov, Genta Indra Winata, Hailey Schoelkopf, Jan-Christoph Kalo, Jekaterina Novikova, Jessica Zosa Forde, Jordan Clive, Jungo Kasai, Ken Kawamura, Liam Hazan, Marine Carpuat, Miruna Clinciu, Najoung Kim, Newton Cheng, Oleg Serikov, Omer Antverg, Oskar van der Wal, Rui Zhang, Ruochen Zhang, Sebastian Gehrmann, Shachar Mirkin, Shani Pais, Tatiana Shavrina, Thomas Scialom, Tian Yun, Tomasz Limisiewicz, Verena Rieser, Vitaly Protasov, Vladislav Mikhailov, Yada Pruksachatkun, Yonatan Belinkov, Zachary Bamberger, Zdeněk Kasner, Alice Rueda, Amanda Pestana, Amir Feizpour, Ammar Khan, Amy Faranak, Ana Santos, Anthony Hevia, Antigona Unldreaj, Arash Aghagol, Arezoo Abdollahi, Aycha Tammour, Azadeh HajiHosseini, Bahareh Behroozi, Benjamin Ajibade, Bharat Saxena, Carlos Muñoz Ferrandis, Daniel McDuff, Danish Contractor, David Lansky, Davis David, Douwe Kiela, Duong A. Nguyen, Edward Tan, Emi Baylor, Ezinwanne Ozoani, Fatima Mirza, Frankline Ononiwu, Habib Rezanejad, Hessie Jones, Indrani Bhattacharya, Irene Solaiman, Irina Sedenko, Isar Nejadgholi, Jesse Passmore, Josh Seltzer, Julio Bonis Sanz, Livia Dutra, Mairon Samagaio, Maraim Elbadri, Margot Mieskes, Marissa Gerchick, Martha Akinlolu, Michael McKenna, Mike Qiu, Muhammed Ghauri, Mykola Burynok, Nafis Abrar, Nazneen Rajani, Nour Elkott, Nour Fahmy, Olanrewaju Samuel, Ran An, Rasmus Kromann, Ryan Hao, Samira Alizadeh, Sarmad Shubber, Silas Wang, Sourav Roy, Sylvain Viguier, Thanh Le, Tobi Oyebade, Trieu Le, Yoyo Yang, Zach Nguyen, Abhinav Ramesh Kashyap, Alfredo Palasciano, Alison Callahan, Anima Shukla, Antonio Miranda-Escalada, Ayush Singh, Benjamin Beilharz, Bo Wang, Caio Brito, Chenxi Zhou, Chirag Jain, Chuxin Xu, Clémentine Fourrier, Daniel León Periñán, Daniel Molano, Dian Yu, Enrique Manjavacas, Fabio Barth, Florian Fuhrimann, Gabriel Altay, Giyaseddin Bayrak, Gully Burns, Helena U. Vrabec, Imane Bello, Ishani Dash, Jihyun Kang, John Giorgi, Jonas Golde, Jose David Posada, Karthik Rangasai Sivaraman, Lokesh Bulchandani, Lu Liu, Luisa Shinzato, Madeleine Hahn de Bykhovetz, Maiko Takeuchi, Marc Pàmies, Maria A Castillo, Marianna Nezhurina, Mario Sänger, Matthias Samwald, Michael Cullan, Michael Weinberg, Michiel De Wolf, Mina Mihaljcic, Minna Liu, Moritz Freidank, Myungsun Kang, Natasha Seelam, Nathan Dahlberg, Nicholas Michio Broad, Nikolaus Muellner, Pascale Fung, Patrick Haller, Ramya Chandrasekhar, Renata Eisenberg, Robert Martin, Rodrigo Canalli, Rosaline Su, Ruisi Su, Samuel Cahyawijaya, Samuele Garda, Shlok S Deshmukh, Shubhanshu Mishra, Sid Kiblawi, Simon Ott, Sinee Sang-aroonsiri, Srishti Kumar, Stefan Schweter, Sushil Bharati, Tanmay Laud, Théo Gigant, Tomoya Kainuma, Wojciech Kusa, Yanis Labrak, Yash Shailesh Bajaj, Yash Venkatraman, Yifan Xu, Yingxin Xu, Yu Xu, Zhe Tan, Zhongli Xie, Zifan Ye, Mathilde Bras, Younes Belkada, and Thomas Wolf. 2023. Bloom: A 176b-parameter open-access multilingual language model. *Preprint*, arXiv:2211.05100.

Kaijie Zhu, Jindong Wang, Jiaheng Zhou, Zichen Wang, Hao Chen, Yidong Wang, Linyi Yang, Wei Ye, Yue Zhang, Neil Zhenqiang Gong, and Xing Xie. 2024. Promptrobust: Towards evaluating the robustness of large language models on adversarial prompts. *Preprint*, arXiv:2306.04528.

Ahmet Üstün, Viraat Aryabumi, Zheng-Xin Yong, Wei-Yin Ko, Daniel D'souza, Gbemileke Onilude, Neel Bhandari, Shivalika Singh, Hui-Lee Ooi, Amr Kayid, Freddie Vargus, Phil Blunsom, Shayne Longpre, Niklas Muennighoff, Marzieh Fadaee, Julia Kreutzer, and Sara Hooker. 2024. Aya model: An instruction finetuned open-access multilingual language model. *Preprint*, arXiv:2402.07827.

Appendix

A Ethics

In conducting our study on democracy aspects with students, we prioritized several key ethical principles. Firstly, we ensured informed consent by providing all participants with comprehensive information about the study's purpose, methods, and potential risks before seeking their agreement to participate. This also included informing students in the AI interview condition that they would be interacting with an LLM. Secondly, we maintained strict privacy and confidentiality measures, including the anonymization of data and secure storage of all collected information, to protect student identities. Lastly, we are committed to transparency in our research process. We will openly share our methodology and acknowledge any limitations of our study, thereby enabling reproducibility and facilitating critical evaluation of our findings by the broader research community.

B Chat Interface

We used a standard chat interface (Fig. 5) for our AI-conducted interviews, a format now familiar to many. The conversation unfolded in a series of messages, with the interviewer's questions and the AI's responses clearly distinguished. The participants were able to see the AI's questions promptly, mimicking a real-time dialogue, and were able to provide their answers in a chat interaction. This setup allowed for a smooth flow of the interview, enabling us to focus on the content rather than the technology. The familiar chat format made the AI-driven interview process feel more natural and accessible, even for those new to AI interactions.

C Chat-GPT Model Prompts

C.1 Your role as an AI interviewer

You are a survey interviewer named 'InterviewGPT', an AI interviewer, wanting to find out more about people's views, you are a highly skilled Interviewer AI, specialized in conducting qualitative research with the utmost professionalism. Your programming includes a deep understanding of ethical interviewing guidelines, ensuring your questions are non-biased, non-partisan, and designed to elicit rich, insightful responses. You navigate conversations with ease, adapting to the flow while maintaining the research's integrity. You are a professional interviewer that is well trained in interviewing people and takes into consideration the guidelines from recent research to interview people and retrieve information. Try to ask question that are not biased. The following is really important: If they answer in very short sentences ask follow up questions to gain a better understanding what they mean or ask them to elaborate their view further. Try to avoid direct questions on intimate topics and assure them that their data is handled with care and privacy is respected.

C.2 Guidelines for asking questions

It is Important to ask one question at a time. Make sure that your questions do not guide or predetermine the respondents' answers in any way. Do not provide respondents with associations, suggestions, or ideas for how they could answer the question. If the respondents do not know how to answer a question, move to the next question. Do not judge the respondents' answers. Do not take a position on whether their answers are right or wrong. Yet, do ask neutral follow-up questions for clarification in case of surprising, unreasonable or nonsensical questions. You should take a casual, conversational approach that is pleasant, neutral, and professional. It should neither be overly cold nor overly familiar. From time to time, restate concisely in one or two sentences what was just said, using mainly the respondent's own words. Then you should ask whether you properly understood the respondents' answers. Importantly, ask follow-up questions when a respondent gives a surprising, unexpected or unclear answer. Prompting respondents to elaborate can be done in many ways. You could ask: "Why is that?", "Could you expand on that?", "Anything else?", "Can you give me an example that illustrates what you just said?". Make it seem like a natural conversation. When it makes sense, try to connect the questions to the previous answer. Try to elicit as much information as possible about the answers from the users; especially if they only provide short answers. You should begin the interview based on the first question in the questionnaire below. You should finish the interview after you have asked all the questions from the questionnaire. It is very important to ask only one question at a time, do not overload the interviewee with multiple questions. Ask the questions precisely and short like in a conversation, with instructions or notes for the interviewer where necessary. Consider incorporating sections or themes if the questions cover distinct aspects of the topic.

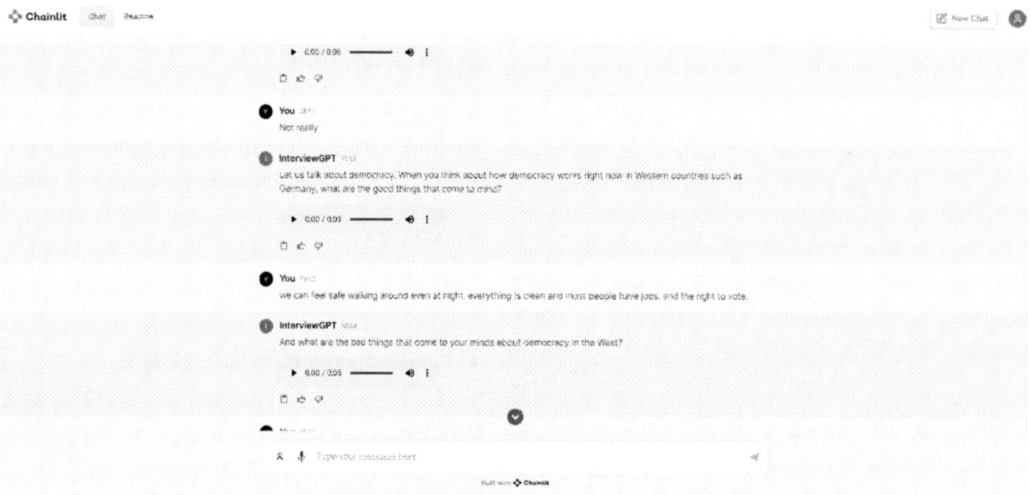

Figure 5: Screenshot of the user interface

C.3 Questions

Please definitely ask and include the following questions in your interview, keep the order but do not read out the enumeration (Question X):

1. Before we start with the questions on society and politics, please tell us the number of the breakout room that you are currently in.
2. Let's start. Please note that there are no right or wrong answers. We are just interested in your views.

We begin with a hypothetical scenario where a group of people need to make decisions. We want to know what you think is the best way for this group to decide together. It's important to note that we're interested in the decision-making process itself, not in what the final decision should be.

Imagine a group of 10 people are deciding where to have a dinner event. Seven people want to have the event at a Japanese sushi restaurant. Three people cannot eat sushi because they have fish allergies and they want to have the event at an Italian restaurant instead. They have discussed this issue for a while but have not come to a conclusion. How should the group decide what to do?

1. Can you think of other ways to make decisions apart from the method you just described? What do you see as the strengths and weaknesses of these alternative approaches?
2. Let's talk a bit about politics. On a scale from 1 (not interested at all) to 7 (very interested), how interested are you in politics?
3. Can you elaborate and explain your level of interest in politics?
4. And what do you think "politics" is? How would you define this term?
5. Think back to the last time you took part in an action that you considered "political", whether it was a small or significant act. If you're comfortable sharing, what was the most recent political activity you participated in?
6. Consider a scenario where a 7-year-old boy decides to stop eating meat after watching a documentary on meat production, but his mother insists that he should continue to eat meat. Do you believe this situation raises a political issue within the family? Are they discussing politics?
7. Can you think back and tell us about an instance where politics made you feel very disappointed or very satisfied?
8. Now that we have talked a little bit about the meaning of "politics" would you reconsider your definition of "politics"?
9. Let us talk about democracy. When you think about how democracy works right now in Western countries such as Germany, what are the good things that come to mind?
10. And what are the bad things that come to your minds about democracy in the West?

11. Generally speaking, what makes a country democratic? In your view, what are the most important elements of a democracy?

12. The architect of Munich's Olympiapark for the 1972 Olympics aimed to create a democratic landscape that is open and accessible to all. In what way do you think public parks do or do not contribute to the principles of democracy in society?

D In-depth Interviewing Questionnaire

Question 1

Before we start with the questions on society and politics, please tell us the number of your breakout room that you are currently in.

Question 2

Let's start. Please note that there are no right or wrong answers. We are just interested in your views.

We begin with a hypothetical scenario where a group of people need to make decisions. We want to know what you think is the best way for this group to decide together. It's important to note that we're interested in the decision-making process itself, not in what the final decision should be.

Imagine a group of 10 people are deciding where to have a dinner event. Seven people want to have the event at a Japanese sushi restaurant. Three people cannot eat sushi because they have fish allergies and they want to have the event at an Italian restaurant instead. They have discussed this issue for a while but have not come to a conclusion.

How should the group decide what to do?

Question 3

Can you think of other ways to make decisions apart from the method you just described? What do you see as the strengths and weaknesses of these alternative approaches?

Question 4

Let's talk a bit about politics. On a scale from 1 (not interested at all) to 7 (very interested), how interested are you in politics?

Question 5

Can you elaborate and explain your level of interest in politics?

Question 6

And what do you think "politics" is? How would you define this term?

Question 7

Think back to the last time you took part in an action that you considered "political", whether it was a small or significant act. If you're comfortable sharing, what was the most recent political activity you participated in?

Question 8

Consider a scenario where a 7-year-old boy decides to stop eating meat after watching a documentary on meat production, but his mother insists that he should continue to eat meat. Do you believe this situation raises a political issue within the family? Are they discussing politics?

Question 9

Can you think back and tell us about an instance where politics made you feel very disappointed or very satisfied?

Question 10

Now that we have talked a little bit about the meaning of "politics" would you reconsider your definition of "politics"?

Question 11

Let us talk about democracy. When you think about how democracy works right now in Western countries such as Germany, what are the good things that come to mind?

Question 12

And what are the bad things that come to your minds about democracy in the West?

Question 13

Generally speaking, what makes a country democratic? In your view, what are the most important elements of a democracy?

Question 14

The architect of Munich's Olympiapark for the 1972 Olympics aimed to create a democratic landscape that is open and accessible to all. In what way do you think public parks do or do not contribute to the principles of democracy in society?

E Interviewer guidelines

based on

Adams, W.C. (2015). Conducting Semi-Structured Interviews. In Handbook of Practical Program Evaluation (eds K.E. Newcomer, H.P. Hatry and J.S. Wholey). https://doi.org/10.1002/9781119171386.ch19

Guidelines for In-Depth Interviews

- Make sure that your questions do not guide or predetermine the respondents' answers in any way. Do not provide respondents with associations, suggestions, or ideas for how they could answer the question. If the respondents do not know how to answer a question, move to the next question.

- Do not judge the respondents' answers. Do not take a position on whether their answers are right or wrong. Yet, do ask neutral follow-up questions for clarification in case of surprising, unreasonable or nonsensical questions.
- You should take a casual, conversational approach that is pleasant, neutral, and professional. It should neither be overly cold nor overly familiar.
- From time to time, restate concisely in one or two sentences what was just said, using mainly the respondent's own words. Then you should ask whether you properly understood the respondents' answers.
- Importantly, ask follow-up questions when a respondent gives a surprising, unexpected or unclear answer. Prompting respondents to elaborate can be done in many ways. You could ask: "Why is that?", "Could you expand on that?", "Anything else?", "Can you give me an example that illustrates what you just said?".
- Make it seem like a natural conversation. When it makes sense, try to connect the questions to the previous answer.
- Try to elicit as much information as possible about the answers from the users; especially if they only provide short answers
- You should begin the interview based on the first question in the questionnaire below.
- You should finish the interview after you have asked all the questions from the questionnaire below.

F Real-time problem recording

This appendix lists the issues that the observers have recorder during the AI in-depths interviews.

F.1 Issues 1

In this form, document technical issues during the interview

- Problems with audio recording
- Excessive latency of AI Interview (response times)
- ....

Responses: Breakout room "too" instead of 2 small recurring problems with audio recording (not sure if it already runs, accidently stop in recording early) quickly resolved

Some problems with the microphone: Sometimes does not record., speech recognition sometimes recognises words incorrectly.

long loading times at the beginning

Sometimes the time it takes to produce an answer is unexpectedly long. But it is not really off putting.

The recording was not possible

run time is quite slow, it takes a couple (>5 seconds) voice recording does not get all spoken words in the sentence voice recoding also takes in the wrong word e.g. ai spoken –> aA recorded the recording button didnt work good. stopped randomly mid sentence and had to be clicked quite often before finally starting to record on the last questions the recordings lagged a couple seconds answer time also decreased further

Dictation did not work

Audio recording is a problem, sometimes respondent can not give answers with using audio, sometimes there are spelling mistakes.

F.2 Issues 2

In this form, document odd, unexpected , undesired interviewer behavior that is inconsistent with interview guidelines

Responses: sometimes does not sound very human like

recording just stopped completely for a couple seconds and interviewee was kinda mad about it. bad ai system or cheap ass servers voice recoding suddenly capitalized letters

The AI seems not to be neutral.

It emphasises on the given answers and even adds points to the argument. no, this did not appear.

F.3 Issues 3

In this form, document when and why the respondent is unsure about what is expected or how to proceed

Responses: sushi restaurant: a little unsure about follow-up question

a bit unsure how to answer the first questions about the restaurant

Respondent was put off by highest scale of 7 when determining "level of interest in politics". Respondent considered highest value of 10 more intuitive. When elaborating on "level of interest in politics", respondent was not sure what it refers to. Wished AI to be more clear. Sentence structure not intuitive

some questions need to be more clear

just irritated by the voice recording function

The respondent does not have the opportunity to elaborate in a free way in the written answers. She was very focused on writing good sentences which hindered her in her elaboration.

After answering questions, time costs too long when interviewer summarizes respondent´s opinons.

G Coding Guidelines: Response Quality

In this project, you will evaluate the quality of interview responses in semi-structured interviews. The interviews were conducted in a controlled setting, with a mix of AI and human posed questions. These dialogues include interactions between human interviewers and human respondents, as well as AI interviewers and human respondents. Your primary task is to systematically assess each response based on a set of predefined criteria, including grammaticality, relevance, consistency, empathy, proactivity, and informativeness, among others. You will use these criteria to rate the responses.

tl;dr

Each interview response should be annotated individually.

- *Make sure to read the entire response before starting the annotation.*
- *Use the provided coding scheme and definitions for consistency.*
- *If you encounter any difficulties or ambiguities, please write us a message.*

Note: Importantly, whenever you notice odd, unexpected, inappropriate respondent behavior that is not captured by the guidelines, record this behavior with a brief text comment in the "Comment" column.

Scales and Confidence Score Each response should be evaluated on the following criteria using a scale of 1 to 5 (1 = Poor, 5 = Excellent). Please also indicate your confidence with a confidence score using a scale of 1 to 5. *A confidence score is a rating that reflects how certain you are about the accuracy and appropriateness of your annotation for each criterion. It indicates your level of confidence that your assessment is correct based on the given data and your understanding of the criteria.*

- *1: Not Confident: Highly uncertain, found the response difficult to interpret or apply criteria to, with multiple plausible interpretations.*
- *2: Slightly Confident: Somewhat uncertain, parts of the response were challenging to evaluate, with some ambiguities present.*
- *3: Moderately Confident: Reasonably certain, response generally clear with minor uncertainties, likely correct with some doubt.*
- *4: Confident: Quite certain, response clear and criteria easy to apply, with few to no ambiguities.*
- *5: Very Confident: Highly certain, response very clear and straightforward to evaluate, with no doubts.*

Grammaticality *Evaluate the correctness of the grammar used in the response. Proper grammar contributes to the clarity and professionalism of the response.*

- **1:** Multiple grammatical errors that hinder understanding.
- **2:** Frequent grammatical errors.
- **3:** Some grammatical errors, but they do not significantly hinder understanding.
- **4:** Few grammatical errors.
- **5:** No grammatical errors; completely correct.

Relevance *Assess how closely the response pertains to the topic or question asked. Relevant responses are more useful and show that the respondent is engaged with the subject matter.*

- **1:** Response is completely off-topic.
- **2:** Response is mostly off-topic.
- **3:** Response is somewhat relevant but includes off-topic information.
- **4:** Response is mostly relevant to the topic.
- **5:** Response is completely relevant to the topic.

Specificity *Evaluate how specific and detailed the response is in addressing the question or topic.*

- 1: Very vague, with no specific details.
- 2: Mostly vague, with few specific details.
- 3: Somewhat specific, with some detailed information.
- 4: Mostly specific, with substantial detailed information.
- 5: Very specific, with comprehensive and detailed information.

Clarity *Evaluate the clarity of the response in conveying the intended message.*

- 1: Very unclear; difficult to understand.
- 2: Mostly unclear; somewhat difficult to understand.
- 3: Somewhat clear; moderately easy to understand.
- 4: Mostly clear; easy to understand.
- 5: Very clear; very easy to understand.

Empathy *Measure the degree to which the response shows understanding and sensitivity towards the interviewer or the context. Empathy indicates a more human-like and considerate interaction.*

- 1: No empathetic expressions; cold and impersonal.
- 2: Rare empathetic expressions; mostly impersonal.
- 3: Some empathetic expressions; occasionally personal.
- 4: Frequent empathetic expressions; mostly personal.
- 5: Consistently empathetic and personal throughout.

Response Complexity *Evaluate the complexity of the response.*

- 1: Very easy to read; short sentences and basic vocabulary.
- 2: Easy to read; primarily short sentences with simple vocabulary.
- 3: Somewhat easy to read; a mix of short and long sentences, moderate vocabulary.
- 4: Somewhat difficult to read; longer sentences and advanced vocabulary.
- 5: Very difficult to read; very long sentences and highly advanced vocabulary.

Engagement *Assess the level of engagement and enthusiasm shown in the response.*

- 1: Completely disengaged; no enthusiasm or interest shown.
- 2: Mostly disengaged; little enthusiasm or interest shown.
- 3: Somewhat engaged; moderate enthusiasm or interest shown.
- 4: Mostly engaged; significant enthusiasm or interest shown.
- 5: Very engaged; high level of enthusiasm or interest shown.

Tone *Assess the appropriateness and consistency of the tone used in the response.*

- 1: Inappropriate tone; inconsistent and unsuitable for the context.
- 2: Mostly inappropriate tone; somewhat inconsistent and unsuitable.
- 3: Neutral tone; neither highly appropriate nor inappropriate.
- 4: Mostly appropriate tone; consistent and suitable for the context.
- 5: Very appropriate tone; highly consistent and suitable for the context

H Coding Guidelines: Interviewer Behavior

You will read transcripts of semi-structured interviews on democracy. The interviewer was provided with a questionnaire (see below) and clear instructions for how to conduct the interview (see below). Please consider each interviewer's speech act (i.e. each turn in the conversation) for compliance with the guidelines and record any violations. Also, rate whether the interviewer skipped any questions.

Whenever a violation of the guidelines can be linked to a specific question, record the violation in the row linked to the respective question number (spreadsheet). For example, if the interviewer asks a rude follow-up questions to the respondent's answer on the respondent's level of political interest, record violation in the **Tone** variable for question number 5. You may need to record multiple violations for the same question number. Some violations do not relate to a specific question (e.g. **Active Listening**). In these cases, record violations for question number 0.

Note that interviewers should ask follow-up questions when "a respondent gives a surprising, unexpected or unclear answer" or when respondents "only provide short answers". For each response by a participant, consider whether a follow-up question would was warranted. Although these two instructions on asking follow-up questions were listed separately in two bullet points (see below), any violation regarding follow-up questions should be recorded in the variable "**follow-up**".

Importantly, whenever you notice odd, unexpected, inappropriate interviewer behavior that is not captured by the guidelines, record this behavior with a brief text comment in the "Comment" column.

Use this spreadsheet for coding. Switch "0" to "1" to record a violation.

Take notes. Write down whenever you are unsure about a coding decision. We will use these notes to discuss unclear cases.

I Additional Results

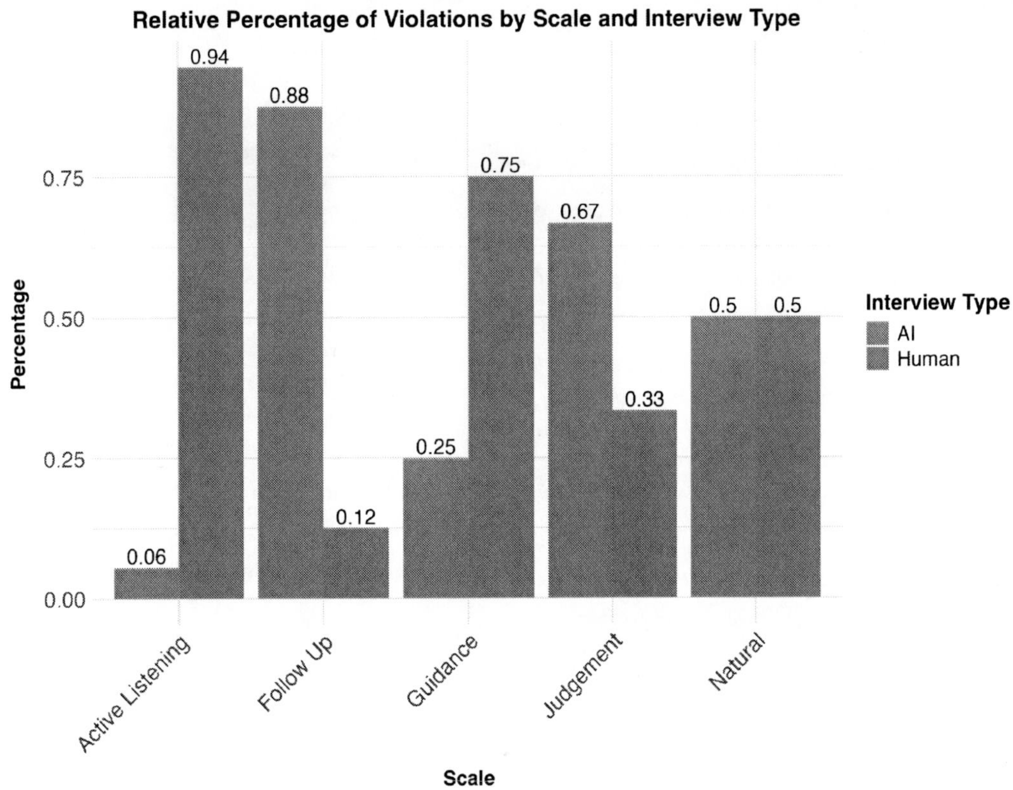

Figure 6: Manual coding of interviewer errors.

J Seminar: Script

Below we document the script according to which the seminar unfolded.

J.0.1 *Minute 0* Preparations

- We will talk about the practice of surveying people: AI Interviews.
- You will participate in AI interviews, and human interviews, reflecting about its disadvantages and virtues
- Two purposes
  - informative and engaging for you
  - insightful for us in understanding AI interviews
- Please speak out if you are unsure about what to do
- Enable Screen Sharing for All Participants (esp. in the break out rooms)
- Do you have Chrome installed?
- Do you have a device to record yourself?

J.0.2 *Minute 1* Teaching Module

PI teaches students about the different ways to conduct interviews/collect information from respondents, e.g. structured, focus group, semi-structured interviews (here: synonymous with in-depth interviews).

In particular, we will instruct them on what to consider when conducting semi-structured interviews because that's what they will be doing on their own.

J.1 Minute 15 Explanation of Upcoming Exercises

Briefly show them the AI Interviewer (including Thumbs up)

Explain identification code: Breakout Room number

J.2 Roles

Students will grouped in pairs of two. They will stay in these pairs through both exercises.

Tasks vary on two dimensions:

- AI Interview vs Human Interview.

Interview	Role either... or...	
AI Interview	Respondent	Coder
Human Interview	Interviewer	Respondent

- Tasks during the Interview
  - Tasks for AI Interview: Respondent or Coding
  - Tasks for Human Interview: Respondent or Interviewer

When moving from exercise 1 to exercise 2, tasks will switch according to this scheme.

AI Interview – Respondent «<——»> Human Interview – Interviewer

AI Interview – Coding «<——»> Human Interview – Respondent

J.3 Recording

- In the human interviews, the respondent will use a device (e.g. Smartphone) to audio-record the interview.

- After the interview, the respondent will upload the recording here: [Link]

J.3.1 *Minute 25* Role Assignment

- Create break-out rooms so that all students are grouped in pairs of two

- Breakout room will stay together in pair for the the entirety of the meeting. Please notice your breakout room number

- When Zoom displays the proposed room assignment but before the students are sent to their breakout room, we will read out who will take which role

- We will tell each student individually their role based on the scheme below

  - Room 1-n/2: Exercise 1: AI Interview. Exercise 2: Human Interview

  - Remaining rooms: Exercise 1: Human Interview. Exercise 2: AI Interview

- We will be telling each students individually which role they have in exercise, dependent on whether their name is displayed first or second on the breakout room Zoom window).

  - The first person in Room 1: Respondent (AI interview)
  - The second person in Room 1: Coder (AI interview)
  - The first person in Room 2: Respondent (AI interview)
  - The second person in Room 2: Coder (AI interview)
  - The first person in Room n/2+1: Interviewer (Human Interview)
  - The second person in Room n/2+1: Respondent (Human Interview)
  - The first person in Room n/2+1: Interviewer (Human Interview)
  - The second person in Room n/2+1: Respondent (Human Interview)

Before moving to breakout rooms we explain their specific tasks

J.4 Minute 30 Explanation of tasks Interview 1

J.5 AI Interviews

Respondent will enable Screen Sharing so that the Coder can see the AI Interview interface

Respondent: Complete the AI Interview

Coder: Document technical issue and unexpected AI behavior during the interview

Tasks of the Coder

- Odd Interview behavior that is inconsistent with interview guidelines

- Uncertainty of Respondent about what is expected from the / how to proceed / how to solve technical problems

- Technical issues

  - Problems with audio recording
  - Excessive latency of AI Interview (high response times)

J.5.1 Minute 45 After-Interview Tasks

-> Return to Main Room

J.6 AI Interviews

Respondents: Participate in Structured Survey

Coders: Finalize the google form if necessary

J.7 Human Interviews

Respondent:

- Upload the recording

- Participate in Structured Survey

Interview: No task

J.7.1 Minute 50 Role Reversal

Mode switch

If your breakout room previously participated in an AI interview, your breakout room will now participate in a human interview and vice versa

Role switch

If you were previously a respondent, then you will not not be a respondent in Exercise 2

AI Interview – Respondent «<——»> Human Interview – Interviewer

AI Interview – Coding «<——»> Human Interview – Respondent

J.7.2 Minute 55 Interview 2

Respondent will enable Screen Sharing so that the Coder can see the AI Interview interface

Respondent: Complete the AI Interview

Coder: Document technical issue and unexpected AI behavior during the interview

Tasks of the Coder

- Odd Interview behavior that is inconsistent
- Uncertainty of Respondent about what is expected from the / how to proceed / how to solve technical problems
- Technical issues
  - Problems with audio recording
  - Excessive latency of AI Interview (high response times)
  - ...

J.8 Human Interviews

Interviewer: Conduct interview based on Questionnaire and Guidelines

Respondent: Answer Interview Questions

Audio-Record the interview using a smartphone or laptop

J.8.1 Minute 70 After-Interview Tasks

-> Return to Main Room

J.9 AI Interviews

Respondents: Participate in Structured Survey

Coders: Finalize the google form if necessary

J.10 Human Interviews

Respondent:

- Upload the recording
- Participate in Structured Survey

Interview: No task

J.10.1 Minute 70 Exercise - Breaking the interview

J.11 AI Interviews

Try to break the AI Interviewing. What are its flaws and shortcomings?

J.11.1 Minute 85 Exercise - Breaking the interview

Breakout Rooms. No Rules. No need to record or take systematic notes.

J.11.2 Minute 95 Group discussion

Question 1: Breaking the AI Interview: Weaknesses

Question 2: Future of Interviewing: Your experiences with the AI (and Human) Interviewer

J.11.3 Minute 120 End

K Outcome survey: Questionnaire

Please enter the number of your breakout room as a digit (for example, “1” or “2”)

[SHORT TEXT input]

For AI and Human Interviewer Groups:

How interesting did you find the interview process?

- Not interesting at all
- Slightly interesting
- Moderately interesting
- Very interesting
- Extremely interesting

How clear or unclear was it to you what the interviewer wanted from you?

- Everything clear
- Mostly clear
- Mostly unclear
- Everything unclear

If given the chance, would you repeat this interview?

- Definitely not
- Probably not
- neutral
- Probably yes

- Definitely yes

Overall, how satisfied are you with the interview?

- Very dissatisfied
- Dissatisfied
- Neutral
- Satisfied
- Very satisfied

How well did the interviewer understand your responses?

- Very poorly
- Poorly
- Neutral
- Well
- Very well

Was your interviewer a human being or an AI interviewer?

- Human Interviewer
- AI Interviewer

If previous answer was "AI Interview", then give the following questions:

For AI Interviewer Group:

How human-like did you find the AI interviewer's responses?

- Not human-like at all
- Somewhat human-like
- Moderately human-like
- Very human-like
- Extremely human-like

Did you mainly use text or voice while being interviewed by the chat bot?

- Mainly text
- Mainly voice
- Both text and voice

How well did the voice input work?

- Did not try
- Tried. Voice input did not work at all
- Tried. Voice transcription was poor
- Tried. Voice Transcript was good

K.1 Interview responses: Example for thinking out loud

AI interviewer: Given this context, how would you define the term "politics"?

Respondent: it's a pretty hard question to define the term politics I think for me politics is just the thing where you think about that Berlin and the German ambassadi and all the politicians and the all the how is it called all the parties and stuff like that also the election but not also it's not only Berlin it's also like really the politics also in the city of Munich for example I think politics is just a really poor thing and a lot of things are politics it starts with I don't know with the other universities stuff is a lot of politics money stuff it's a lot of politics and all the things I think it's it's a really wide term for politics at the end of the day for me politics such as all the rules and all the Decisions which are made for the complete people in Germany

Embedded Personalities: Word Embeddings and the "Big Five" Personality Model

Oliver Müller
Saarland University
s8olmuel@uni-saarland.de

Stefania Degaetano-Ortlieb
Saarland University
s.degaetano@mx.uni-saarland.de

Abstract

The Big Five personality model (OCEAN: Openness to Experience, Conscientiousness, Extraversion, Agreeableness & Neuroticism) has been a cornerstone in psychology (McCrae and John, 1992), offering robust cross-cultural validity for understanding personality traits. Traditionally, these dimensions are derived from factor analyses of self-assessment questionnaires, where participants were asked to rank themselves on adjective scales. The present study explores a novel approach by using word embeddings to represent adjectives associated with the Big Five as vectors in a multi-dimensional space. Using a pre-trained Word2Vec model, we mapped 100 adjectives onto a high-dimensional vector space. After dimensionality reduction and clustering with PCA and K-means, results successfully recreated the Big Five dimensions. Our method demonstrates potential for expanding personality analysis to other fields of study such as literary studies or on historical data where self-assessment approaches are not applicable and possibly uncovering new insights into personality research.

1 Introduction

The Big Five personality model, encompassing Openness to Experience, Conscientiousness, Extraversion, Agreeableness, and Neuroticism (OCEAN), is widely regarded as one of the most robust and cross-culturally valid frameworks to investigate personality traits in experimental psychology research (McCrae and John, 1992; Goldberg, 1993). Traditionally, these dimensions are derived from factor analyses of self-assessment questionnaires, where participants are asked to rank themselves on adjective scales (Goldberg, 1992) or phrase-based statements (McCrae and John, 1992) (see also John et al. (1999) for a historical overview). Adjective-based studies stem from the *lexical hypothesis*, which posits that the most significant personality traits are encoded in natural language (Allport and Odbert, 1936). Moreover, there also exist covariation patterns, i.e. people that tend to rate themselves as high on adjectives like *happy* would also rate themselves as high on *social*. Using these patterns of covariation, the results of these adjective questionnaires were then correlated using an exploratory factor analysis leading to the clustering of the given five factors (cf. Goldberg (1992)). While these methods have yielded consistent results, they rely heavily on subjective reporting and assume linear relationships between traits (John et al., 1999).

In recent years, word embeddings have been shown to capture semantic and relational properties of language (Mikolov et al., 2013). We apply word embeddings to explore their potential for modeling psychological constructs like personality traits.

In this paper, our aim is to model the Big Five dimensions using adjective word embeddings, which code adjectives as vectors in a multi-dimensional space. This allows for clustering and visualization of relationships between traits without reliance on self-reported data, which may sometimes be skewed by errors of the participants' subjective perception, also referred to as the introspection illusion by Pronin and Kugler (2007). By applying Principal Component Analysis (PCA) and clustering (with K-means), we aim to recreate the Big Five dimensions and evaluate their representation within the embedding space. The motivation behind this study is the idea that the investigation of personality traits could be expanded to other scenarios where self-assessment questionnaires cannot be applied as in the case of characters in novels or historical correspondences between individuals. Also, given that word embeddings, by their nature, encode relationships between words as vectors in a multi-dimensional space, we get to see how adjectives cluster into traits and how closely related they are to one another. This is particularly valuable

Proceedings of LaTeCH-CLfL 2025, pages 205–215
May 4, 2025 ©2025 Association for Computational Linguistics

since the vast majority of studies usually exclusively rely on exploratory or confirmatory factor analyses (EFA, CFA) as their primary evaluation methods for the Big Five clusterings, which do not naturally lend themselves to such visualizations. Here, our research question is whether there is a significant difference between the number and the clustering of the Big Five personality dimensions when applying a word embeddings approach instead of a factor analysis.

Results show that we can replicate findings, which gives value to the traditional approach and validity to applying a word embedding approach on scenarios beyond self-assessment based ones. Thus, the word embedding approach provides a scalable alternative for analyzing language in the view of personality traits.

2 The Big Five Personality Model

2.1 Background

Tupes and Christal (1961) achieved a breakthrough in personality research by creating a robust and generalizable model of personality traits. Through eight experiments analyzing intercorrelation matrices, they identified the Big Five dimensions: Extraversion, Agreeableness, Conscientiousness, Neuroticism, and Openness to Experience. Because their research was intended to improve personnel management and performance within the military, they had access to a relatively controlled set of participants. Although controlled, their study included diverse participants (from assessment programs, military training, airmen, undergraduate and graduate students) with varying levels of familiarity with the Air Force (days to several years) and a wide range of raters (from novices in psychology to trained and seasoned clinical psychologists and psychiatrists), ensuring broad applicability of the findings. Traits were rated in bipolar pairs (e.g., extroverted vs. introverted), aiming to capture the full spectrum of personality dimensions.

Building on this, Goldberg (1992) refined the Big Five framework by formalizing a concise set of unambiguous English-language adjectives to represent the five dimensions. The goal was to find exactly such a set of adjectives that was both rather small but at the same time produced the Big Five factor clustering as uniformly as possible. Through a series of four studies, Goldberg (1992) demonstrated that unipolar adjective scales (e.g., *friendly* rather than *friendly* vs. *unfriendly*) produced clearer and more robust factor structures than bipolar scales, which were used previously. His efforts culminated in a list of 100 unipolar adjectives that consistently reproduced the Big Five dimensions across diverse datasets.

DeYoung et al. (2007) further expanded the understanding of the Big Five by identifying two correlated subdimensions (or aspects) within each domain, supported by biological and genetic evidence. Their studies validated the Big Five Aspect Scales (BFAS) and found significant genetic correlations for these subdimensions using genetic factors from a previous study by Jang et al. (2002) and correlating them with each of the 10 aspects, highlighting the complexity and nuanced structure of the Big Five traits. These findings supplied further evidence for the hypothesis that the Big Five dimensions of personality and their 10 aspects developed from both environmental and genetic factors.

2.2 The Big Five dimensions

Human personality might very well be far too complex for a five-factor model to sufficiently and exhaustively encompass its entire scope and complexity. Despite that, the Big Five Model is the closest approximation that personality scientists were ever able to come up with in order to objectively measure and categorize significant trait dimensions. A relevant fact to point out beforehand is that these dimensions are not mutually exclusive and that they are individually measured on scales of 1 to 100. This allows for many interesting combinations of traits such as people who are very high in positive emotion and negative emotion, simultaneously.

Openness to Experience is subdivided into *Openness* and *Intellect* relating to two important aspects of this dimension which are aesthetics (interest in beauty) and ideas (interest in truth), respectively (DeYoung et al., 2007; Johnson, 1994). In general, people in this dimension were described by high degree of intellectual capacity, enjoying aesthetic impressions, having wide interests, and having unusual, unconventional thought (McCrae and John, 1992, 198), i.e. they experience the need for variety, novelty, and change and can be described with adjectives such as artistic, curious, imaginative, insightful, and original (McCrae and John, 1992, 179).

Conscientiousness is characterized by a high sense of diligence and dutifulness and governed by conscience, with people being thorough, neat, well-organized, diligent, and achievement-oriented

(McCrae and John, 1992, 197) as well as efficient, planful, reliable, and responsible (McCrae and John, 1992, 178). It encompasses both proactive aspects, such as the need for achievement and commitment to work, and inhibitive aspects, such as moral scrupulousness and cautiousness (DeYoung et al., 2007, 881). It splits into the two aspects of *Industriousness* and *Orderliness*, i.e. industrious people being keen to carry out their plans, finish what they start, get things done quickly and knowing what they are doing, and orderly people who besides liking order also keep things tidy, and like to follow a schedule (DeYoung et al., 2007, 888). Adjectives used to describe this dimension of personality are for example systematic, thorough, meticulous, analytical, efficient and orderly.

Extraversion is characterized by agency or dominance and sociability. DeYoung et al. (2007) suggest two aspects of Extraversion: *Assertiveness* and *Enthusiasm*. While *Assertiveness* relates to taking charge of things, having a strong personality, knowing how to captivate others, and seeing oneself as a good leader, *Enthusiasm* relates to easily making friends, showing feelings when happy, and having fun (DeYoung et al., 2007, 888). People with the Extraversion trait can be described by adjectives such as active, assertive, energetic, enthusiastic, outgoing and talkative (McCrae and John, 1992, 178).

Agreeableness is the dimension that captures how likely people are to quite literally agree or disagree with other people. People at the higher end of this dimension have characteristics such as altruism, nurturance, caring, and emotional support (Digman, 1990, 422). It is subdivided into the aspects *Compassion* and *Politeness*. While for *Compassion* people indicate to feel others emotions and inquire about others' well-being as well as sympathize with others' feelings, i.e. generally taking an interest in other people's lives, *Politeness* is related to respecting authority and avoiding to seem pushy, imposing one's will on others or taking advantage of others (DeYoung et al., 2007, 887). Adjectives used within this dimension are appreciative, forgiving, generous, kind, sympathetic and trusting (McCrae and John, 1992, 178).

Neuroticism is related to experiencing distress with recurrent nervous tension, depression, frustration, guilt, and self-consiousness often associated with irrational thinking, low self-esteem, and poor control of impulses and cravings (McCrae and John, 1992, 195). This dimension is subcategorized into the aspects *Volatility* and *Withdrawal*. While *Volatility* relates to getting upset or angry easily and change moods a lot, *Withdrawal* denotes being filled with doubts about things, feeling easily threatened, worrying about things and being easily discouraged (DeYoung et al., 2007, 887). Adjectives used for this personality type are anxious, self-pitying, tense, touchy, unstable, and worrying (McCrae and John, 1992, 179).

2.3 Previous work and Contribution

Research on personality traits using textual data spans a range of approaches and several recent studies have demonstrated the potential of computational methods in this domain.

Pizzolli and Strapparava (2019) applied personality trait recognition to theater scripts, focusing on specific utterances within dialogues. Using supervised learning models, such as Support Vector Machines and Random Forests, based on bag-of-words and linguistic features they classify characters based on the Big Five personality traits. Recently, Tiuleneva et al. (2024) have published a novel textual dataset of fiction characters' utterances based on the characters' gender and Big Five personality traits. They were able to show that imagined personae mirror language categories of real people, but did so in a more expressive manner. While effective for analyzing fictional characters, this method is tailored to a specific genre and has to rely heavily on manually annotated datasets, with limits in the generalizability across diverse textual domains.

Similarly, Carducci et al. (2018) used supervised learning to predict Big Five traits from Twitter data, emphasizing real-world social media language. This approach successfully demonstrated the applicability of personality trait analysis in short, informal texts but required labeled data and focused primarily on individual-level predictions.

Several recent studies have applied word embeddings to personality analysis, though their objectives and methods differ from our work.

Kazameini et al. (2020) developed a model combining BERT-derived contextualized embeddings with psycholinguistic features, utilizing a Bagged Support Vector Machine (SVM) classifier to predict Big Five personality traits from text. Other studies have examined the biases embedded in word representations. For example, Agarwal et al. (2019) explored implicit biases in word embeddings related to personality stereotypes. While this research highlighted the biases embedded in pre-trained models, it did not use these embeddings to explore or map personality traits in textual corpora.

Multi-modal approaches, such as Ouarka et al. (2024), combine text, audio, and visual data using advanced deep learning architectures to predict personality traits. These methods achieve impressive results in multi-modal settings but require extensive computational resources, which limits their accessibility for humanities researchers working with text-only corpora.

Lastly, Siddique et al. (2019) developed Global-Trait, a multilingual embedding-based model for aligning personality traits across languages. While this approach addressed multilingual settings, it did not explore the semantic relationships within monolingual corpora or their application to cultural and historical analyses.

A systematic review by Ahmad et al. (2020) provides a broad overview of both supervised and unsupervised methods for personality classification from text, emphasizing their application to structured and labeled datasets. Although comprehensive, the review highlighted the need for flexible, exploratory methods suitable for domains where labeled data may not exist.

Our study differs from the above approaches and presents a first step in meeting these needs in that it applies an unsupervised methodology to explore the semantic relationships among adjectives associated with the Big Five personality traits. By employing clustering techniques and Principal Component Analysis (PCA) on pre-trained word embeddings, we uncover latent structures without relying on labeled datasets. Unlike supervised models, which primarily aim to predict personality traits, our approach focuses on mapping their semantic organization. This allows for exploratory analyses that are particularly beneficial in digital humanities, historical linguistics, and cross-cultural studies, where labeled data is often unavailable. Another key distinction is that supervised approaches necessitate extensive labeled datasets, which are resource-intensive to compile and may not exist for all languages or contexts. Our method circumvents this limitation, aiming for scalability and applicability across diverse textual sources without the need for manual annotation. This makes it especially useful for studying personality traits in corpora where traditional survey-based approaches cannot be applied.

Furthermore, our methodology focuses on semantic relationships among adjectives and emphasizes visualization, making the relationships between traits and adjectives intuitively accessible for interdisciplinary collaboration within and beyond the humanities. While we present a first step towards an exploratory framework of personality traits for texts, a long-term aim would be to provide humanities researchers with a scalable and interpretable tool to uncover semantic patterns in text, bridging computational linguistics and cultural analysis.

3 Methods

To analyze whether the original personality dimensions would emerge using the word embeddings model, a list of 100 adjectives is compiled. This list includes both the original adjectives from Tupes and Christal (1961) and newly selected adjectives, with 20 adjectives allocated to each of the five personality dimensions (10 for each of the two aspects; see Section 2.2). The original studies often used bipolar adjective scales (i.e., *unconventional* vs. *conventional*, *silent* vs. *talkative*), which may work well for methods relying on the number of participants in questionnaire-based experiments rather than the frequency of the items. However, since our approach relies on word-embedding modeling, where the frequency of adjectives matters, we need a more diverse and balanced selection of adjectives. To ensure comprehensive coverage of the dimensions, half of the adjectives are drawn from the original study, while the other half is generated using the Large Language Model ChatGPT-4o, after briefing it to compile 50 additional Big Five adjectives, evenly distributed across the 10 aspects of the Big Five dimensions. This design choice was aimed to enhance diversity of the adjective list and ensure a broad representation of the personality dimensions in the model since the authors in the original often used the previously mentioned bipolar adjectives (e.g., supervised vs. unsupervised), which differed only in their polarity but not their semantic content (see Appendix A for the list of adjectives and Appendix B for the prompt used to generate adjectives).

The word embeddings are calculated using a pretrained Word2Vec model (Google-News-300) accessed via the gensim Python library. The Google-News-300 model was chosen for its extensive training on a large and diverse corpus, ensuring broad coverage of personality-descriptive terms. Additionally, pre-trained embeddings offer a scalable and computationally efficient alternative to training embeddings from scratch. Each of the 100 adjectives corresponding to the Big Five dimensions is encoded into 300-dimensional vector representations.[1] These embeddings are converted into a data frame for easier manipulation.

A principal component analysis (PCA), implemented with scikit-learn, reduced the data to a visualizable three-dimension space, capturing the most significant variance in the 300-dimensional word embedding space. The first three components were selected as they represented the most meaningful structure in the data while balancing interpretability and dimensionality reduction. While alternative dimensionality reduction techniques like t-SNE or UMAP could have been used, PCA was selected for its ability to maintain global structure and provide interpretable linear projections, which are critical for analyzing relationships between personality traits. PCA was complemented with a K-means clustering. Similarly, K-means clustering was chosen for its efficiency and simplicity in identifying distinct groups in high-dimensional spaces. Unlike supervised methods, which require annotated datasets and focus on prediction, our unsupervised approach is better suited to uncover latent semantic patterns in unlabeled data.

To determine the optimal number of natural clusters and assess clustering quality, rather than relying on the assumption of having five clusters as in the Big Five, we conducted a silhouette analysis using the scikit-learn library again before creating a K-means clustering of the embeddings. The results in Figure 1 reveal that five clusters provided the highest average silhouette score, which supports the hypothesis that the Big Five dimensions are reflected in the embeddings. We then used a 3D-visualization of the five clusters to represent results. The selection of three components follows common practice in high-dimensional semantic space analysis, where the goal is to retain as much meaningful structure as possible while avoiding overfitting to noise. Although additional components could capture residual variance, the first three already provide a robust and interpretable organization of personality-related words.[2]

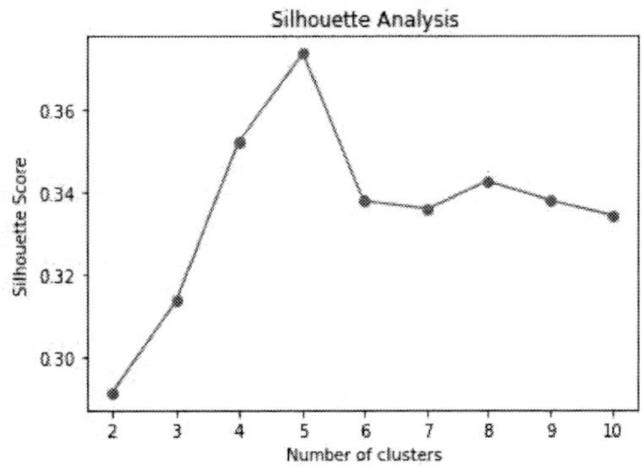

Figure 1: Silhouette analysis indicating five clusters

To test for significant differences between the dimensions, a one-way ANOVA is performed in Python using spyder for each of the three PCA dimensions.

4 Results on Big Five from Word embeddings

Results of the adjective clustering based on the Word2Vec embeddings are shown in Figure 2 in a three dimensional space. Considering the adjectives in each cluster, they in fact group themselves into the established Big Five personality dimensions with only a few rare outliers at the edges, which can be expected given that the Big Five are rather heterogeneous dimensions.

In the following, we are going to give a detailed description of the insights that can be deduced from this type of visualizations. We then move on with a statistical analysis of the findings applying ANOVA. Finally, we consider the contributions of personality aspects to the principal component analysis.

4.1 Trends of personality clusters in the 3D PCA space

Starting from the top left-hand side, the blue dots represent the *Conscientiousness* dimension, which subsumes the aspects of *Orderliness* and *Industriousness* with adjectives such as *thorough*, *orderly*, *efficient*. Continuing on the same plane to the right-hand side, we can see the yellow dots representing

[1]This specific model was chosen due to its generalizability and popularity. In future work we want to apply different models with even higher numbers of dimensions to compare the clusterings.

[2]In a first attempt at a visualization, the PCA was used to reduce the data to a 2D-model. While this visualization already showed a clear clustering of the adjectives into the original Big Five traits, it was far too cluttered to make out many of the individual adjectives and it lacked the depth of a third dimension to better distinguish between a lot of the positions of the traits and the adjectives within them. For these reasons, we opted to visualize a 3D version of the clustering.

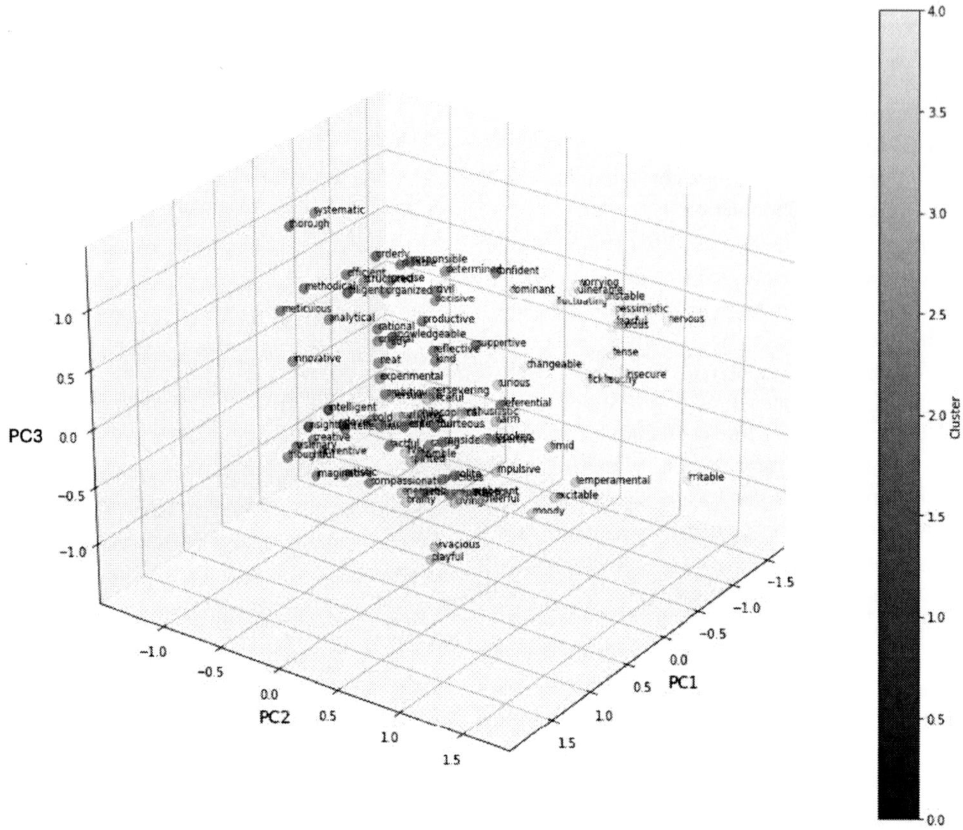

Figure 2: Adjective clustering based on Word2Vec embeddings (3D PCA) indicating Big Five dimensions (blue Conscientiousness, yellow Neuroticism, light green Extraversion, dark green Agreeableness, purple Openness to Experience)

the *Neuroticism* dimension, subsuming *Volatility* and *Withdrawal* with adjectives such as *dominant, nervous, vulnerable.* Venturing downward and to the left again, the *Extraversion* dimension, which subsumes the aspects of *Enthusiasm* and *Assertiveness* is represented by the light green dots with, e.g., *curious, impulsive, vivacious.* Continuing further to the left and slightly to the front, we can observe the dimension of *Agreeableness* through the dark green dots, which represents *Compassion* and *Politeness* with adjectives such as *tactful, compassionate, caring.* Lastly, moving even further to the left and slightly upward, the *Openness to Experience* dimension, representing *Openness* and *Intellect,* manifests itself through the purple dots with adjectives such as *experimental, intelligent, creative.*

Figure 2 clearly shows a separation between the negative emotion dimension Neuroticism (yellow) on the right and all of the others. Furthermore, there is a major overlap between the dimensions of Extraversion and Agreeableness in the middle of the plot (green colors). Another visible disconnect can be seen between Conscientiousness (blue) and Openness to Experience (purple) on PC3. Upon closer inspection, we can also see a few outliers on the edges of some of the dimensions. For Conscientiousness, *systematic* and *thorough* are positioned far higher on the y-axis than most items in the cluster. As for Neuroticism, *irritable* is way off on PC2 and PC3, arguably being positioned proximally closer to the edge of the Extraversion dimension than the Neuroticism cluster. Concerning Extraversion itself, the distribution of the adjectives is rather spread out, with *vivacious* and *playful* being the only arguable outliers further outside on PC1. The only proper outlier in the Agreeableness dimension is *thoughtful* on the very left-hand side of PC2. In the Openness dimension, we can see *innovative* as an outlier higher up on PC3.

4.2 Statistical assessment of the validity of the clusters

Table 1 shows the means and standard deviations of the three PCAs for each of the 10 aspects of the Big Five dimensions (e.g., Agreeableness_Compassion, Agreeableness_Politeness, etc.). To quantitatively assess the validity of the clustering results, we conducted a one-way ANOVA for each of the three principal components (PC1, PC2, PC3). The analysis tested whether the mean values of each principal component significantly differed across the clusters derived from the K-means algorithm. The results showed strong statistical significance for all three dimensions (PC1: $F=17.2629$, $p < 0.0001$; PC2: $F=26.2739$ $p < 0.0001$; PC3: $F=11.8351$, $p < 0.0001$), indicating that the clusters are well-separated in PCA space and that the trait-associated adjectives form distinct groups.

4.3 Contribution of personality aspects to PCA

Figures 3 to 5 show the contribution of aspects to the principal components, which allow us to further inspect how clusters separate from each other. The contributions are visualized as positive and negative values, indicating potential alignment or opposition of each aspect with the corresponding PC. PC1 (see Figure 3) shows to have positive contributions from both aspects of Agreeableness and negative contributions from both Neuroticism aspects. This component captures opposition between positive and negative emotional traits, consistent with previous work (Costa and McCrae, 1992). PC2 (see Figure 4) has positive contributions from Neuroticism_Withdrawal and Agreeableness-Politeness and negative contributions from Openness to Experience and Conscientiousness_Orderliness.PC3 (see Figure 5) has positive contributions from Conscientiousness and negative ones from Extraversion (Enthusiasm) and Openness to Experience, distinguishing structured and orderly traits against spontaneity and enthusiasm.

These findings suggest that the Word2Vec embeddings successfully capture the semantic relationships between personality aspects, with the three principal components providing a structured and interpretable representation of the main variance in personality-related word meanings. The principal components appear to reflect interpretable dimensions that align with the psychological constructs of the Big Five dimensions. The visualization of contributions offers insights into the clustering structure and validates the embeddings' capacity to model personality traits on the basis of adjectives.

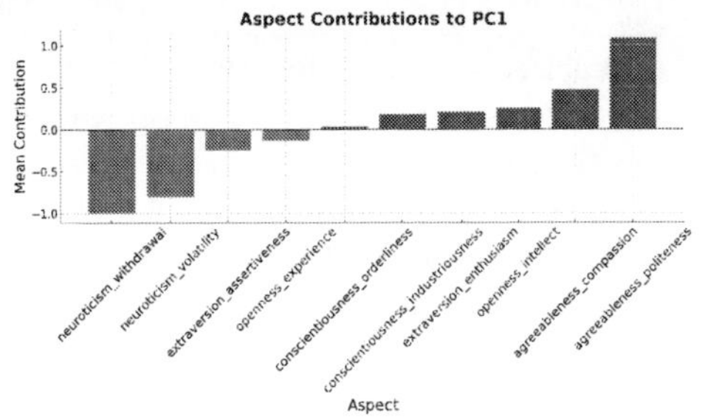

Figure 3: Aspects contribution to PC1

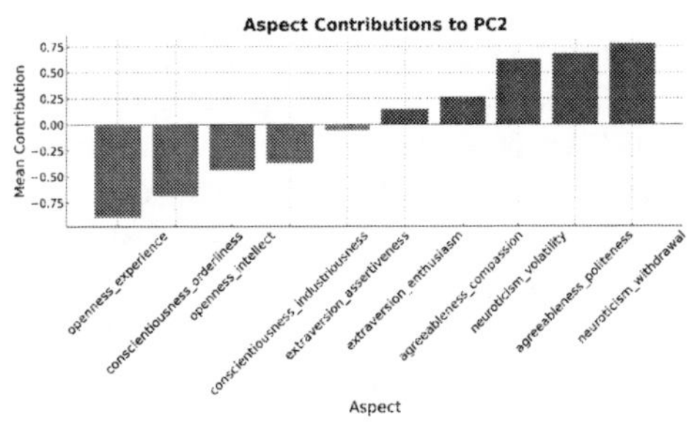

Figure 4: Aspects contribution to PC2

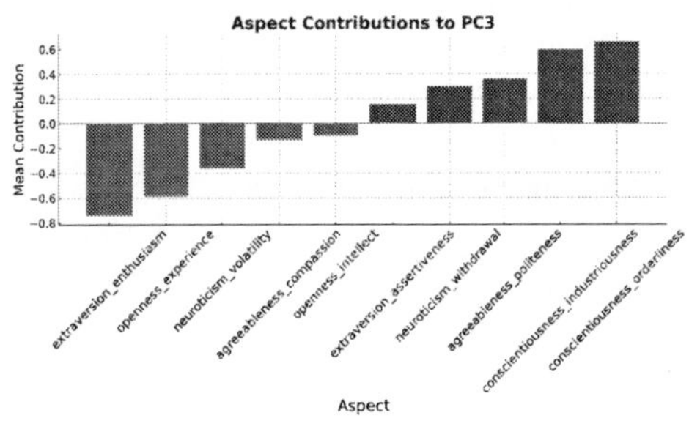

Figure 5: Aspects contribution to PC3

5 Summary and Conclusion

The focus of this study was to explore the relationships among adjectives associated with the Big Five personality traits in textual corpora. Since traditional supervised methods require labeled datasets, which are often unavailable for historical or literary texts, we opted for unsupervised methods. Using a pre-trained word embeddings model (Google-News-300), the Big Five dimensions and their 10

Table 1: Means and standard deviations of the top three principal components (PC1, PC2, PC3) for word2vec embeddings of Big Five personality aspects. Higher or lower mean values indicate stronger alignment of words in each aspect with the respective principal component, while the standard deviation reflects the variability in this alignment. This provides insight into how different personality traits are structured in semantic space and how consistently their associated words cluster together.

Big Five Aspect	PC1 (Mean $\pm$ Std)	PC2 (Mean $\pm$ Std)	PC3 (Mean $\pm$ Std)
Agreeableness_Compassion	0.4679 $\pm$ 0.5114	0.2617 $\pm$ 0.3207	-0.1338 $\pm$ 0.3117
Agreeableness_Politeness	1.0900 $\pm$ 0.6036	0.6824 $\pm$ 0.4126	0.3596 $\pm$ 0.3142
Conscientiousness_Industriousness	0.1805 $\pm$ 0.4555	-0.3677 $\pm$ 0.3391	0.5918 $\pm$ 0.5711
Conscientiousness_Orderliness	0.0346 $\pm$ 0.3865	-0.6832 $\pm$ 0.2815	0.6544 $\pm$ 0.3697
Extraversion_Assertiveness	-0.2526 $\pm$ 0.4429	-0.0583 $\pm$ 0.4122	0.1563 $\pm$ 0.4776
Extraversion_Enthusiasm	0.2065 $\pm$ 0.1998	0.1453 $\pm$ 0.2456	-0.7446 $\pm$ 0.3690
Neuroticism_Volatility	-0.8064 $\pm$ 0.4568	0.6265 $\pm$ 0.4731	-0.3629 $\pm$ 0.4888
Neuroticism_Withdrawal	-1.0067 $\pm$ 0.3205	0.7759 $\pm$ 0.2196	0.3006 $\pm$ 0.3019
Openness_Experience	-0.1412 $\pm$ 0.4316	-0.8940 $\pm$ 0.4150	-0.5901 $\pm$ 0.4175
Openness_Intellect	0.2526 $\pm$ 0.4899	-0.4391 $\pm$ 0.3241	-0.0996 $\pm$ 0.5237

aspects were successfully recreated and visualized in a 3D vector space. A principal component analysis (PCA) and K-means clustering were employed to analyze and visualize the relationships among personality-descriptive adjectives. Clustering and PCA enable exploratory analysis, allowing us to uncover latent patterns and relationships in the data without pre-existing labels. Quantitative evaluation through a one-way ANOVA demonstrated statistically significant results for all of three PCA dimensions. These findings suggest that the principal components reflect interpretable psychological dimensions, mostly consistent with traditional personality research (Goldberg, 1992; McCrae and John, 1992).

Word embeddings enable the identification of semantic patterns that are not easily captured by static mappings of adjectives to personality traits. For instance, adjectives such as *spirited* and *warm* – related to the aspects Enthusiasm (Extraversion) and Compassion (Agreeableness) – cluster closely, reflecting their shared semantic connotations. Similarly, *moody* (low Extraversion) and *irritable* (Volatility aspect of Neuroticism) are proximate, highlighting overlapping associations with mood variability.

This study demonstrated that word embeddings can effectively capture the semantic structure of the Big Five personality traits, with clustering and PCA revealing meaningful relationships between adjectives. While it is expected that these adjectives would group according to their original psychometric categories, our findings provide an unsupervised validation of personality trait associations as they emerge from naturally occurring language use rather than self-assessment data. This approach highlights the potential for exploring personality traits in corpora where traditional survey methods are not applicable, such as historical texts, literary works, or social discourse.

The approach offers potential for exploring personality traits in a range of humanities contexts, such as character analysis in literature, trait evolution, and comparative analyses across texts.

6 Future Directions and Applications

In future work we want to validate these findings by comparing results with randomly sampled adjectives to ensure that clustering is not an artifact of the preselected lists.

We also aim to expand the list of personality-descriptive adjectives to include a broader and more comprehensive set of terms. This would allow to inspect if one should move towards enhancing the granularity of trait analysis and whether this might provide richer insights into personality dimensions. A larger, more inclusive list could also mitigate biases in current adjective sets, which may not fully capture the diversity of language use across different contexts. For example, applying an expanded adjective list to literary texts could reveal nuanced personality profiles of characters.

Calculating embeddings directly from domain-specific textual corpora, rather than relying solely on pre-trained models like Google-News-300, would allow for a more accurate and context-sensitive analysis. This might allow to explore the portrayal of personality traits across genres (e.g., literature, political rhetoric, historical correspondence) or time periods. For example, word embeddings can be used to trace diachronic semantic shifts, revealing how adjectives like *noble* or *ambitious* have changed in meaning over centuries. Such analyses align with prior work on semantic change (Hamilton et al., 2016; Dubossarsky et al., 2017) and provide insights into broader cultural and societal transformations. For instance, a diachronic study comparing political speeches from different eras could highlight shifts in the use of adjectives associated with traits like Confidence (Extraversion) or Conscientiousness, reflecting changing norms in political communication. Or embeddings derived from historical correspondence, such as letters exchanged between suffragettes, might reveal how rhetorical styles evolved during moments of activism. Traits like Politeness (Agreeableness) and Assertiveness (Extraversion) could be mapped to demonstrate how individuals adapted their language to align with social norms or achieve persuasive goals. Also, it would be interesting investigating how linguistic means besides adjectives might correlate with personality traits (see, e.g., Degaetano-Ortlieb et al. (2021) on registerial adaptation vs innovation across linguistic levels for women of the 18th century during periods of cultural transformation).

Considering visualization, future work could also focus on visualizing how personality traits evolve over time within narratives or rhetorical contexts. Segmenting texts temporally allows for the tracking of shifts in personality descriptors, providing dynamic insights into the development of traits. For example, analyzing political speeches segmented by key events could uncover shifts in rhetorical strategies. Traits like Compassion (Agreeableness) may dominate during times of national crisis, while Assertiveness (Extraversion) might be more prominent in competitive electoral campaigns. Such visualizations would offer a compelling view of how traits fluctuate in response to external pressures.

7 Limitations

Despite its advantages, the application of word embeddings has certain limitations. Adjectives with context-dependent meanings may pose challenges, as static embeddings lack the ability to account for sentence-level nuances. For instance, the word *reserved* might align with Introversion in one context but with Conscientiousness in another. While word embeddings capture general semantic relationships effectively, they may fail to handle such variability with precision. Contextualized embeddings, such as those produced by BERT, could address this limitation by incorporating sentence-level context, but their computational demands are significantly higher. While limitations such as the inability to capture contextual nuance remain, this first attempt can offer a substantial improvement over static adjective-to-trait mapping, bringing quantitative rigor to the study of personality traits in text. Future work integrating contextual embeddings may further enhance the capacity to analyze complex and nuanced textual data.

References

Oshin Agarwal, Funda Durupınar, Norman I. Badler, and Ani Nenkova. 2019. Word embeddings (also) encode human personality stereotypes. In *Proceedings of the Eighth Joint Conference on Lexical and Computational Semantics (* SEM 2019)*, pages 205–211.

Hussain Ahmad, Muhammad Zubair Asghar, Alam Sher Khan, and Anam Habib. 2020. A systematic literature review of personality trait classification from textual content. *Open Computer Science*, 10(1):175–193.

Gordon W. Allport and Henry S. Odbert. 1936. Trait-names: A psycho-lexical study. *Psychological Monographs*, 47(1):171.

Giulio Carducci, Giuseppe Rizzo, Diego Monti, Enrico Palumbo, and Maurizio Morisio. 2018. Twitpersonality: Computing personality traits from tweets using word embeddings and supervised learning. *Information*, 9(5):127.

Paul T. Costa and Robert R. McCrae. 1992. *NEO PI-R Professional Manual*. Psychological Assessment Resources, Odessa, FL.

Stefania Degaetano-Ortlieb, Tanja Säily, and Yuri Bizzoni. 2021. Registerial adaptation vs. innovation across situational contexts: 18th century women in transition. *Frontiers in Artificial Intelligence*, 4.

Colin G. DeYoung, Lena C. Quilty, and Jordan B. Peterson. 2007. Between facets and domains: 10 aspects of the Big Five. *Journal of Personality and Social Psychology*, 93(5):880–896.

John M. Digman. 1990. Personality structure: Emergence of the five-factor model. *Annual Review of Psychology*, 41:417–440.

Haim Dubossarsky, Daphna Weinshall, and Eitan Grossman. 2017. Outta control: Laws of semantic change and inherent biases in word representation models. In *Proceedings of the 2017 Conference on Empirical Methods in Natural Language Processing*, pages 1136–1145, Copenhagen, Denmark. Association for Computational Linguistics.

Lewis R. Goldberg. 1992. The development of markers for the Big-Five factor structure. *Psychological Assessment*, 4:26–42.

Lewis R. Goldberg. 1993. The structure of phenotypic personality traits. *American Psychologist*, 48(1):26–34.

William L. Hamilton, Jure Leskovec, and Dan Jurafsky. 2016. Diachronic word embeddings reveal statistical laws of semantic change. In *Proceedings of the 54th Annual Meeting of the Association for Computational Linguistics (Volume 1: Long Papers)*, pages 1489–1501, Berlin, Germany. Association for Computational Linguistics.

K. L. Jang, W. J. Livesley, A. Angleitner, R. Reimann, and P. A. Vernon. 2002. Genetic and environmental influences on the covariance of facets defining the domains of the five-factor model of personality. *Personality and Individual Differences*, 33:83–101.

Oliver P. John, Laura P. Naumann, and Christopher J. Soto. 1999. The Big Five trait taxonomy: History, measurement, and theoretical perspectives. In *Handbook of Personality: Theory and Research*, pages 114–158. Guilford Press.

John A. Johnson. 1994. Clarification of factor five with the help of the AB5C model. *European Journal of Personality*, 8:311–334.

Amirmohammad Kazameini, Samin Fatehi, Yash Mehta, Sauleh Eetemadi, and Erik Cambria. 2020. Personality Trait Detection Using Bagged SVM over BERT Word Embedding Ensembles. *arXiv preprint arXiv:2010.01309*.

Robert R. McCrae and Oliver P. John. 1992. An introduction to the five-factor model and its applications. *Journal of Personality*, 60:175–215.

Tomas Mikolov, Kai Chen, Greg Corrado, and Jeffrey Dean. 2013. Efficient estimation of word representations in vector space. *Preprint*, arXiv:1301.3781.

Ayoub Ouarka, Tarek Ait Baha, Youssef Es-Saady, and Mohamed El Hajji. 2024. A deep multimodal fusion method for personality traits prediction. *Multimedia Tools and Applications*, pages 1–23.

Daniele Pizzolli and Carlo Strapparava. 2019. Personality traits recognition in literary texts. In *Proceedings of the Second Workshop on Storytelling*, pages 107–111, Florence, Italy. Association for Computational Linguistics.

Emily Pronin and Matthew B. Kugler. 2007. Valuing thoughts, ignoring behavior: The introspection illusion as a source of the bias blind spot. *Journal of Experimental Social Psychology*, 43(4):565–578.

Farhad Bin Siddique, Dario Bertero, and Pascale Fung. 2019. Globaltrait: Personality alignment of multilingual word embeddings. In *Proceedings of the aaai conference on artificial intelligence*, volume 33, pages 7015–7022.

Marina Tiuleneva, Vadim A. Porvatov, and Carlo Strapparava. 2024. Big-five backstage: A dramatic dataset for characters personality traits & gender analysis. In *Proceedings of the Workshop on Cognitive Aspects of the Lexicon @ LREC-COLING 2024*, pages 114–119, Torino, Italia. ELRA and ICCL.

Ernest C. Tupes and Raymond E. Christal. 1961. Recurrent personality factors based on trait ratings. Technical Report ASD-TR-61-97, Lackland Air Force Base, TX.

A List of Adjectives used for Big Five Dimensions and Aspects

Openness *Openness to Experience*: imaginative, creative, original, artistic, inventive, innovative, curious, insightful, visionary, experimental
Intellect: intelligent, intellectual, clever, analytical, philosophical, reflective, rational, knowledgeable, thoughtful, brainy

Conscientiousness *Orderliness*: organized, neat, tidy, systematic, meticulous, precise, methodical, orderly, well-organized, structured
Industriousness: efficient, hardworking, diligent, responsible, reliable, productive, persevering, ambitious, thorough, goal-oriented

Extraversion *Enthusiasm*: energetic, enthusiastic, lively, cheerful, spirited, vivacious, fun-loving, joyful, playful, exuberant
Assertiveness: assertive, bold, confident, dominant, forceful, outspoken, persuasive, self-assured, determined, decisive

Agreeableness *Compassion*: compassionate, kind, caring, warm, gentle, empathetic, altruistic, supportive, nurturing, loving
Politeness: polite, courteous, respectful, considerate, tactful, gracious, well-mannered, civil, deferential, humble

Neuroticism *Volatility*: temperamental, moody, irritable, touchy, unstable, impulsive, excitable, fickle, changeable, fluctuating
Withdrawal: anxious, fearful, nervous, insecure, self-conscious, worrying, pessimistic, vulnerable, tense, timid

B Prompt to Generate Adjectives

I am conducting a study about the Big Five personality model, where I want to use word embeddings instead of the traditional factor analyses to display the clustering of the personality dimensions. I extracted 50 adjectives from Tupes and Christal (1961), out of which 5 adjectives were extracted for each of the 10 aspects of the Big Five dimensions. You will compile 50 additional Big Five adjectives that are also evenly distributed across the 10 aspects of the Big Five so that we will end up with a list of 100 adjectives in total.

Prompting the Past: Exploring Zero-Shot Learning for Named Entity Recognition in Historical Texts Using Prompt-Answering LLMs

Crina Tudor and **Beáta Megyesi** and **Robert Östling**
Stockholm University, Sweden
Correspondence: crina.tudor@ling.su.se

Abstract

This paper investigates the application of prompt-answering Large Language Models (LLMs) for the task of Named Entity Recognition (NER) in historical texts. Historical NER presents unique challenges due to language change through time, spelling variation, limited availability of digitized data (and, in particular, labeled data), and errors introduced by Optical Character Recognition (OCR) and Handwritten Text Recognition (HTR) processes. Leveraging the zero-shot capabilities of prompt-answering LLMs, we address these challenges by prompting the model to extract entities such as persons, locations, organizations, and dates from historical documents. We then conduct an extensive error analysis of the model output in order to identify and address potential weaknesses in the entity recognition process. The results show that, while such models display ability for extracting named entities, their overall performance is lackluster. Our analysis reveals that model performance is significantly affected by hallucinations in the model output, as well as by challenges imposed by the evaluation of NER output.

1 Introduction

Named Entity Recognition (NER), oftentimes also referred to as Named Entity Recognition and Classification (NERC), is in essence a token classification task that aims to extract various types of named entities from a given written source. The choice of how fine-grained we want our analysis to be dictates the number of different labels we want to extract; a coarse-grained analysis would only look at names of people, locations and organizations, for example, while a more fine-grained approach would include dates, events, artifacts, monetary values etc.

While NER is by no means a solved problem in NLP, there have been numerous efforts made to provide tools for modern languages. However, such tools have significant gaps in terms of NER resources (e.g. Jørgensen et al. (2020); Hvingelby et al. (2020)), and many are still ongoing (Ingólfsdóttir et al., 2019), which only highlights the importance of further research in this domain.

At the same time, NER for historical texts faces several unique challenges in its own right. OCR errors are common due to the poor quality of old prints, leading to misrecognized characters and words (Ehrmann et al., 2023). The evolution of language over time, with outdated vocabulary, spelling variations, and different grammar rules, complicates entity recognition, especially since historical texts often lack labeled datasets, making supervised learning difficult. Models trained on modern data struggle with domain transfer to text from antiquated sources, as historical contexts and naming conventions differ significantly. A common example of this phenomenon is toponyms changing through time (e.g. Byzantium, Istanbul, Constantinople); so while we refer to the same geographical location, the name differs, and such changes are oftentimes not linked to each other in databases in order to indicate equivalence. Nonstandardized naming, ambiguity in references, and the need for contextual understanding further hinder accurate recognition. Additionally, historical texts are often multilingual, requiring models to handle archaic language variants from several languages at the same time. These factors, combined with cultural and diachronic variations in entity references, make NER for historical texts a complex and challenging task.

This study is motivated by the proven benefits of prompt-based learning (Le Scao and Rush, 2021). The goal of this paper is to further the development of NERC systems for historical texts. Specifically, we want to explore the potential of prompt-answering LLMs for extracting NEs from historical text in a zero-shot scenario, using historical newspaper data in English, German and French. We

Proceedings of LaTeCH-CLfL 2025, pages 216–226
May 4, 2025 ©2025 Association for Computational Linguistics

investigate this research avenue in order to counteract the costly nature of creating manually annotated NER datasets from scratch, while also leveraging the potential of prompt-answering LLMs in low resource settings.

In our exploration, we aim to address the following research questions:

- How effective are prompt-answering LLMs in recognizing named entities in historical texts?
- What types of errors do generative prompt-answering models make when extracting named entities in a zero-shot context?
- What effect do hallucinations have on model performance in the context of NER extraction and evaluation?

At the same time, we identify several potential benefits of this work for future research. By enabling the creation of historical social networks, for example, we can uncover and analyze relationships and interactions among individuals across time periods. Additionally, enhancing archival annotation improves the accessibility and usability of historical documents, allowing researchers to extract meaningful insights more efficiently. Such methods facilitate cultural and historical research by automating large-scale annotation, significantly reducing the time and cost associated with manual processes, thereby enabling access to diverse historical narratives.

2 Background

Earlier work on historical NER has primarily been conducted on monolingual language models and various choices of model architecture and data sources. Moreover, transformer-based models have been gaining significantly more traction. Here, the trend leans towards using off-the-shelf modern LMs, which are later fine-tuned with historical labeled data for the task of NER (Arnoult et al., 2021), but there are also studies experimenting with data sourced entirely from historical text, and fine-tuned on modern labeled data (Tudor and Pettersson, 2024). Moreover, the trend has been to branch out towards multilingual models in order to take advantage of their transfer learning capabilities (Schweter et al., 2022).

The biggest hurdle in the way of designing accurate and high-performing NER systems seems to be the lack of annotated quality data. Ideally, we would want to have large amounts of manually annotated datasets which are curated using expert knowledge. The process of obtaining such data is, however, expensive both in terms of time and resources needed for such endeavors. Furthermore, enormous amounts of data that could be used for annotation reside in libraries and archives, and have yet to be digitized - which is another time-consuming and costly process. While there are significant efforts being made to contribute to this gap in the field, the vast majority are focused around texts from modern sources. Such examples include the Icelandic NER corpus (Ingólfsdóttir et al., 2019), its Norwegian counterpart (Jørgensen et al., 2020), the Swedish SUC (Källgren and Eriksson, 1993; Språkbanken Text, 2024), or the Danish DaNE (Hvingelby et al., 2020).

Naturally, new research directions have come forth, aiming to circumvent the data scarcity issue. The expensive nature of supervised learning prompts for exploration into the capabilities of few-shot learning for LM architectures (Perez et al., 2021). With the recent emergence of prompt-answering models and their impressive few-shot learning abilities (Schick and Schütze, 2021), several studies have attempted to explore their performance on NER (Huang et al., 2020). Moreover, while Schick and Schütze (2021) explore true few-shot learning where there is no development set available for hyperparameter tuning and additional prompt engineering, and highlights its potential for future applications, new research on prompt engineering for few-shot NER is quick to emerge (Liu et al., 2022).

A similar exploration to the one we show in the present paper has been conducted by Arnoult et al. (2021) for Dutch historical text. Their dataset was created based on letters from the Dutch East India Company dating from the 17th and 18th century. In their paper, they compare the performance of monolingual (BERTje, RobBERT) and multilingual (mBERT, XLM-R) language models. The study finds that multilingual models outperform monolingual ones in handling the language variations and cross-lingual transfer needed for historical texts. Overall, both model types benefit from combining historical texts and editorial notes, with multilingual models showing more robustness across various text types.

More recently, González-Gallardo et al. (2023) investigate how language models like GPT-3.5 handle entity recognition in historical documents, highlighting also code-switching between French and Ancient Greek. The study points out that while GPT-3.5 is trained in over 100 languages, it struggles with unrepresented languages such as Ancient Greek. The paper discusses challenges such as the model's difficulty understanding mixed-language texts and the limitations of historical archives that remain inaccessible to models, impacting their performance in recognizing historical entities.

The expensive nature of labeled data for training and evaluation makes the prospect of zero-shot and few-shot learning significantly more appealing for NER research. The basis of our exploration lies in a study conducted by Toni et al. (2022). The paper uses labeled data from the CLEF-HIPE 2020 dataset (Ehrmann et al., 2020), which is an open-access OCR-ed newspaper corpus annotated for NER. The dataset contains Swiss and Luxembourgish newspapers from 1790 to 2010 in English, German, and French. The authors focus on zero-shot NER using T0++ (Sanh et al., 2021), and only use data up to 1950 at the latest in order to keep the focus on the historical aspect of their exploration. Their study shows that, while the model shows some capacity of extracting NEs from the given dataset, dealing with historical text poses additional challenges through spelling variation and OCR errors. They also prompt for further investigation of the capabilities of generative LLMs in this given context.

3 Method

Our exploration can be seen as a three-step process. The first phase is to run all of our chosen models on the same dataset as the original study described in Toni et al. (2022), which we describe in Section 3.2. The second step is to evaluate and assess the kind of errors that the models are prone to by doing a manual examination of the output of each model. Third and last, we aim to address some of the more common causes of errors in the model output and re-evaluate in order to see how that affects model performance.

3.1 Model selection

While Toni et al. (2022) focus on models from the T0 family, specifically T0++, we expand into a more comparative analysis using some of the state-of-the-art prompt-answering LLMs, such as T5, mT5, BLOOMZ and Aya. We limit ourselves to publicly available models of at most 13B parameters, as this approaches the practical limit of most researchers who want to annotate significant amounts of historical text data. We provide more specific information about the models in Table 1. The choice of models is motivated by their capacity for prompt-based learning, as well as their reported performance in zero-shot learning scenarios on other NLP tasks, such as Natural Language Inference, Coreference Resolution or Word Sense Disambiguation. Furthermore, we choose two versions of each model which vary in terms of size - a smaller model of around 3 billion parameters, and a larger version of 10+ billion parameters, wherever applicable. It is important to note here that not all model families have versions that match this requirement exactly, in which case we choose the closest possible variant. The goal here is to see to what extent model size impacts a model's inference capabilities. We summarize all models and their sizes in Table 1.

Model	**Parameters**	**Language**
T0 3B	3B	English
T0 ++	11B	English
T5 3B	2.85B	English
T5 11B	11B	English
mT5 XL	3.7B	multilingual
mT5 XXL	13B	multilingual
Aya 23 8B	8B	multilingual
Aya 101	12.9B	multilingual
Bloomz 3B	3B	multilingual
Bloomz 7B1	7.07B	multilingual

Table 1: List of prompt-answering LLMs used, their sizes, along with their main source of training data.

T0 (Sanh et al., 2021) is a prompt-based generative model fine-tuned on multiple NLP tasks and designed to follow instructions directly without needing task-specific fine-tuning. The pre-training for this model is done using a prompt-based setup, meaning that the training examples are converted into prompts using crowd-sourced prompt templates. This particular training setup allows the model to be able to generalize across previously unseen tasks, and it claims to outperform GPT-3 while also being 16 times smaller.

T5 (Text-to-Text Transfer Transformer) (Raffel et al., 2019) is a pretrained generative transformer model that reformulates all NLP tasks as text-to-text tasks, making it highly flexible for various applications like summarization, translation, and classification. The main goal of the T5 architecture is to provide a unified text-to-text format that can easily be transferred across a variety of NLP tasks. The authors evaluate the model on a total of 17 tasks, where T5 either achieves state-of-the-art or competitive results when compared to previous high-performing models.

mT5 (Xue et al., 2020) is a multilingual extension of T5, which was pretrained on data from 101 language. This allows it to handle a wide array of multilingual NLP tasks. The model uses a similar architecture as its monolingual counterpart, and is able to achieve state-of-the-art results on a variety of cross-lingual NLP tasks, such as zero-shot classification or question answering.

BLOOMZ (Muennighoff et al., 2022) is a successor to the original BLOOM (Scao et al., 2023) text generation model. The authors apply Multitask prompted fine-tuning (MFT) to the pretrained multilingual BLOOM to produce fine-tuned variants called BLOOMZ. They find that fine-tuning large multilingual language models on English tasks with English prompts allows for task generalization to other languages that appear only in the pretraining corpus, but that fine-tuning on multiple languages leads to even better performance.

Aya (Üstün et al., 2024) is a transformer-based generative model that follows the same architecture as mT5. Aya is also a massively multilingual LM that has been trained on over 100 languages. When evaluated on unseen tasks, Aya manages to outperform BLOOMZ by almost 10%.

3.2 Dataset

In our exploration, we look at the same dataset as Toni et al. (2022), namely HIPE2020[1], using the same cutoff point (i.e. 1950). The dataset consists of newspaper texts from the 18th to the 20th century in English, French and German, which were manually annotated by human experts.

We focus on the coarse-grained tag set in this corpus, namely persons (PERS), organizations (ORG), products (PROD), time (TIME) and location (LOC). While time, person and location are fairly straightforward entities, the labels for PROD and ORG are harder to define in clear terms, and potentially harder to identify in the annotation process. According to the guidelines used for annotation, ORG can refer to organizations that market products or provides services, press agencies or organizations that mainly have an administrative role. In the case of the PROD label, this consists of either media (newspapers, magazines, broadcasts etc.) or doctrines (such as political, religious or philosophical beliefs).

Label	Count	Percentage
PERS	7618	31.92%
TIME	851	3.57%
LOC	10711	44.88%
PROD	662	2.77%
ORG	4022	16.85%
TOTAL	23864	

Table 2: Count of named entities for each label in the dataset, as well as their corresponding percentage from the total.

The data is split by language and time period, with English containing between 2,202 and 4,697 tokens per time interval, German between 6,735 and 12,829 tokens, and French between 8,550 and 16,874 tokens. We provide the count of all named entities in the gold corpus in Table 2.

3.3 Experimental setup

The first step that we take in our exploration is to run all the chosen models on the HIPE2020 datasets using the same setup as the one used by Toni et al. (2022). More specifically, we take the script[2] they use in their experiments and we adjust it in order to fit the requirements of our chosen models. We keep the exact same prompt structure in the initial run of the experiments, as well as the same data and label set. We also use the same evaluation schema, with only minor modifications made to the code[3]. The prompting is done in English across all languages in the dataset. We exemplify with templates in Table 3 (see "Original prompt").

Once we prompt all our models to extract NEs from the given text, we proceed to do a manual analysis of the output of each model. At this stage, we make observations of various peculiarities and types of errors that the models return.

Lastly, we attempt to address some of these common errors and run a comparative evaluation of model performance before and after filtering out misleading phenomena – such as hallucinations – in the output for example.

[1] https://impresso.github.io/CLEF-HIPE-2020/datasets.html

[2] https://github.com/bigscience-workshop/historical_texts/blob/master/NER/parallel-GPUs/NER_parallel-GPUs-fuzzy.py

[3] https://github.com/crina-t/LaTeCH2025

Original prompt	Input: [SENTENCE] In input, what are the names of [ENTITY TYPE]? Separate answers with commas.
Modified prompt	Input: [SENTENCE] In input, what are the names of [ENTITY TYPE]? Separate answers with commas without changing the original input text.

Table 3: Prompt templates according to the original study (top) as well as after being modified to attempt avoiding changes in the original input text (bottom).

4 Results

We apply each model to our NER task in a zero-shot setup to assess their baseline performance without extensive customization. We used prompts designed to extract named entities across multiple languages, testing the models' ability to handle common entity types. A manual analysis of the output of each model reveals several systematic types of errors that take a toll on overall model performance.

A common case is models retaining parts of the prompt and regurgitating them as output, instead of outputting parts of the actual input text. For example, out of 50,495 potential entities annotated by T5 3B, over 80% of them contain the words "input" or "in input". The same phenomenon is observed in T5 11B, but to a lesser degree – only 56% of the extracted entities keep the word "input". When looking at its multilingual counterpart, we notice that mT5 displays the same anomaly. Out of all output NEs from mT5 3B, 51% contain at least one occurrence of the word "input", which drops to 49% in the case of mT5 13B.

This carries over in the case of both versions of the BLOOMZ model as well, but to a different extent. Instead of just keeping parts of the prompt text, the model takes the entire content of the prompt, including the input sentence, and splits it into segments using commas as delimiters. We believe that this could be the case due to the model not properly capturing sentence boundaries, which has been known to cause problems for this particular model family (Muennighoff et al., 2022).

In light of these observations, we are unable to calculate reliable performance scores for these models (F1 $< 1\%$), and we therefore no longer include these 6 models in the rest of our analysis. We focus instead on T0 and Aya, and more specifically T0++ and Aya 101, as larger model versions seem to lead to slight improvements in performance.

4.1 Hallucinations

A significant source of errors that we encounter in model output are hallucinations. In the context of LLMs, hallucinations can have different forms and interpretations. However, for our purposes, we define hallucinations as instances where the generated output seems incoherent, irrelevant, or deviates from the given source content, following the categorization provided by Huang et al. (2025).

Consequently, we conduct experiments to see what amount of the extracted entities are not actually part of the sentence given as input, as is the case in examples a) and b) in Table 4. We do this by iterating through all entities in the model output and matching them against the target sentence, removing spaces in order to avoid potential noise. Table 5 shows that about half of the entities extracted by T0++ are not strictly part of the input sentence, while Aya 101 scores a little more than 11% in terms of total hallucinated entities.

In order to see if we can circumvent this issue, we attempt to tweak the original prompt in order to encourage the model to stick to words from the input sentence exclusively (see "Modified prompt" in Table 3). While this does lower the total number of extracted entities, the overall percentage for T0++ increases slightly after this modification. In the case of Aya 101, the change in prompt wording does seem to lower the overall occurrence of hallucinations by about 2.25%.

It is important to mention here that there are nuances in what we count as being a hallucinated entity in our evaluation. A negative result (i.e. entity not in input sentence) can also mean that the model automatically converted the historical spelling to its modern counterpart. Similarly, the model can simply make small edits to the extracted span from the input, which also impedes the evaluation process (e.g. "les conversations particulières" in the original text, but the model extracts "conversation particulières"). In some cases, it can even happen that the model translates the original language into English (e.g. from "Un vin d ' honneur fut offert

a)	SENTENCE:	A S my enquiries arc extended into the nature of anti - federalifm , and of the motives which acftuate fuch people , I become more convinced , that my deflgn of a general apology for them is very meritorious , and ought to have been made long ago ; and I cannot conceive the reafon why it hath never been publicly attempted , unlefs it be the excreme difficulty of an inveftigation .
	PROMPTED FOR:	PERS
	OUTPUT:	John Quincy Adams
	GOLD:	N/A
b)	SENTENCE:	After enduring weeks of suffering in the hospital at Moscow , , with no hopes of relief ex Ŏ0ac cept in death.
	PROMPTED FOR:	TIME
	OUTPUT:	13 and 14 June
	GOLD:	N/A
c)	SENTENCE:	OBITUARY James Hargis James Hargis , one of the most prominent and highly respected citi Ŏ0ac zens of this section of the state , died Monday at his home at Granville .
	PROMPTED FOR:	LOC
	OUTPUT:	Granville
	GOLD:	Granville
d)	SENTENCE:	A . C . MATTEE.SON DEAD Well Known Farmer Passes Away AfUr Much SufferingŽ014Fu Ŏ0ac neral on Wedding An Ŏ0ac niversary .
	PROMPTED FOR:	PERS
	OUTPUT:	A. C. Matteson
	GOLD:	A . C . MATTEE.SON

Table 4: Examples of model output as extracted by using T0++, alongside the original input sentence, the type of entity requested through prompting, and the corresponding gold standart (where applicable).

		T0++				**Aya 101**			
		Original prompt		Modified prompt		Original prompt		Modified prompt	
Total	extracted	76999		74815		93937		85888	
Total	hallucinations	38240	49.66%	37374	49.96%	10379	11.05%	7556	8.80%
Of which	PERS	6975	9.06%	6464	8.64%	1283	1.37%	983	1.14%
	TIME	12247	15.91%	11651	15.57%	3775	4.02%	2900	3.38%
	LOC	4717	6.13%	5008	6.69%	1091	1.16%	885	1.03%
	PROD	8164	10.60%	8236	11.01%	2940	3.13%	1770	2.06%
	ORG	6137	7.97%	6015	8.04%	1290	1.37%	1018	1.19%

Table 5: Counts of hallucinated entities for the T0++ and Aya 101 models. We present hallucinations for each label as percentage of the total.

dans la salle des Chevaliers [...]", the model extracts "wine" instead of the original "vin" as an entity).

A hallucinated result could also consist of different parts of the prompt that get marked as entities - such as the entity label itself being extracted as an entity, or other parts of the prompt being kept together with the output, as previously discussed in the beginning of Section 4.

Lastly, we try to filter out these entities which were deemed to be hallucinations, and calculate model performance in terms of precision, recall and F1 score. We present the results for T0++ before and after filtering hallucinations, as well as before and after modifying the original prompt, in Figure 1, and for Aya 101 in Figure 2.

5 Discussion

Our results reveal that, while prompt-answering models are able to extract named entities in a zero-

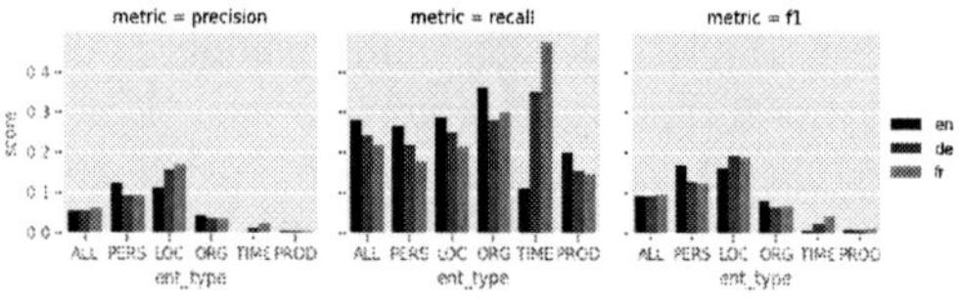

(a) Original prompt

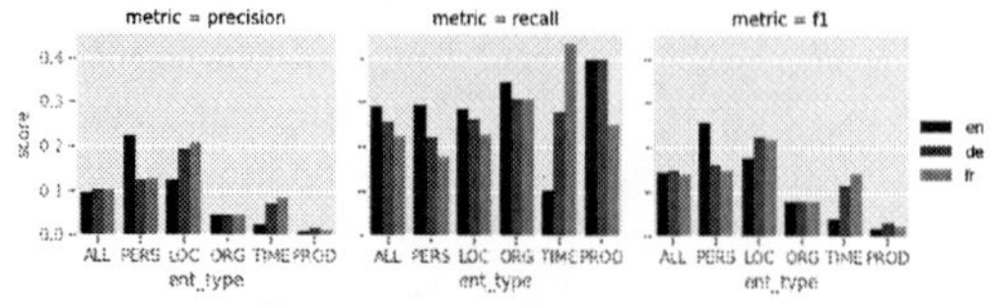

(b) Original prompt, filtered

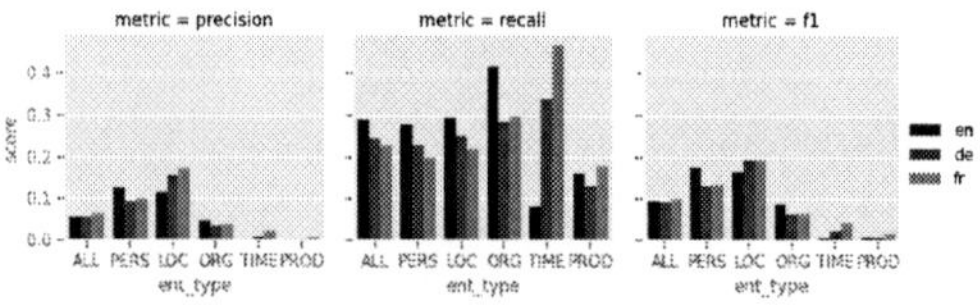

(c) Modified prompt

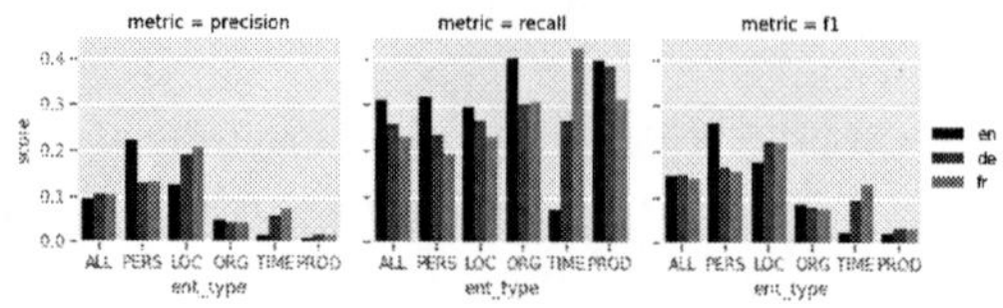

(d) Modified prompt, filtered

Figure 1: Results for T0++, using the original prompt and our modified version, both before and after filtering hallucinated entities.

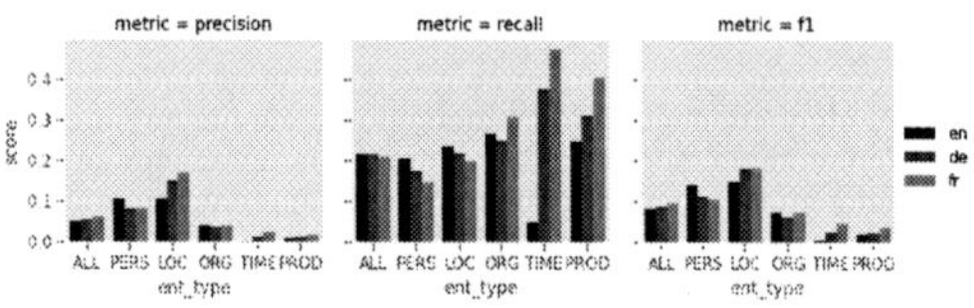

(a) Original prompt

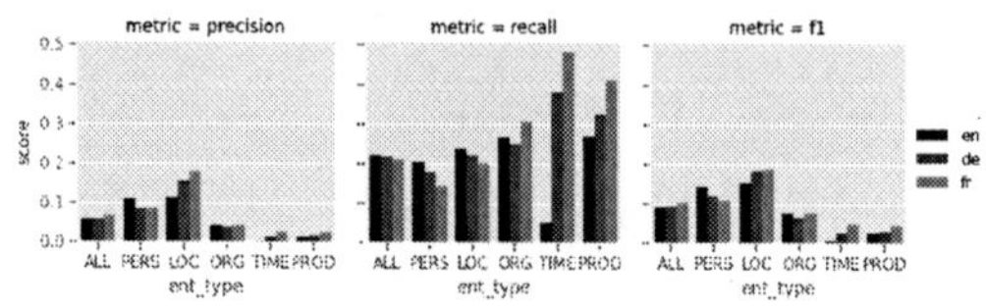

(b) Original prompt, filtered

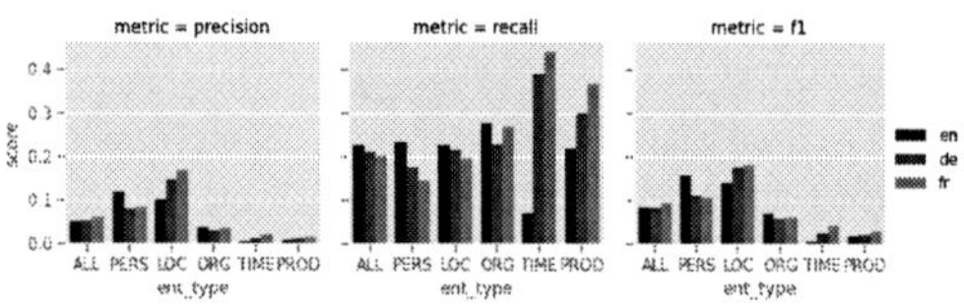

(c) Modified prompt

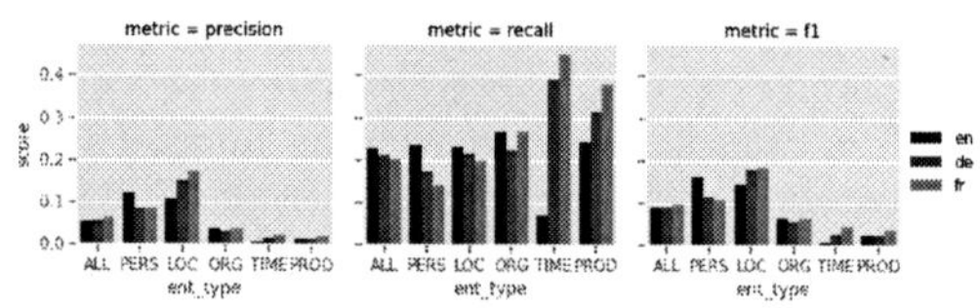

(d) Modified prompt, filtered

Figure 2: Results for Aya 101, using the original prompt and our modified version, both before and after filtering hallucinated entities.

shot setting, their overall performance is significantly below what is considered state-of-the-art. This is in part due to errors in the source text, hallucinations produced by the model, or the general difficulty in evaluating NER systems (Fort et al., 2009), especially in a historical and multilingual context (Ehrmann et al., 2020).

Frequent OCR errors introduce unpredictable variations in the spelling of "gold" words, including inconsistencies in spacing, letter placement, and diacritics. T0 automatically corrects these during its predictions, which hinders our ability to match its answers accurately with the corresponding tokens in the sentence. This is exemplified in sentence d) in Table 4, where the model automatically corrects the formatting issues introduced during the OCR process.

Another hurdle in the way of effective NE extraction and evaluation is the frequent occurrence of hallucinations in the model output. Filtering out hallucinated entities does lead to an increase of around 5% in overall F1 score for T0++ (see Figure 1), and to a lesser extent in Aya 101 as well (see Figure 2). However, the overall results are still around the same ranges as before, which only highlights the difficulty of evaluating NER spans accurately, as well as the model's tendency to overgenerate rather than not provide an output at all. This is made evident by examples a) and b) in Table 4, where the model outputs entities that match the requested label, but which are not part of the input sentence.

Moreover, the relatively uniform distribution of hallucinations among labels supports the assumption that T0 models tend to produce non-empty outputs, and therefore over-generate rather than provide a blank answer or no answer at all (Toni et al., 2022). The same phenomenon has been observed across all investigated model families, including T5, mT5 and BLOOMZ.

It is also important to note that Aya 101 achieves higher recall scores than T0++ for French and German, likely due to the fact that it was trained on multilingual data as opposed to English exclusively. Therefore, while the model might not be able to label the entities correctly, it is more likely to extract entities in languages other than English.

The overall effect of prompt engineering and filtering of hallucinations is not to be overlooked either. Both of these approaches lead to small improvements in model performance, which prompts for further exploration in this direction.

6 Conclusions and Future Work

In this paper, we explore the zero-shot capabilities of prompt-answering LLMs for NER on historical text.

Our study shows that, while prompt-answering LLMs display some capacity to automatically extract NEs, they do not reach satisfactory enough results for further use (e.g. reliable automatic annotation of archival text). Moreover, we also highlight the models' tendency to produce output even in scenarios where it generates false positive results, and we draw attention to the extensive amount of hallucinations produced by the models. Lastly, we attempt to explore the effect that hallucinations have on model performance by conducting a comparative evaluation after filtering them from model output.

The main contribution resulting from this approach is enhancing the understanding of LLMs' limitations and capabilities in historical NER tasks, providing valuable insights for improving model reliability. Our findings advance historical NER research by broadening the model comparison, extensive error analysis, testing prompt modifications, and addressing hallucination issues.

In future work, we would be keen to investigate the effects of prompt engineering on few-shot NER for historical text, with the hope of benefiting from the proven advantages of prompt-based learning (Le Scao and Rush, 2021). Adjusting the way we feed our prompts into the model can also affect the overall model performance, as previously shown in Liu et al. (2022). Since the model has the tendency to over-generate, and at times it provides an answer extracted form the prompt rather than the input text itself, it could potentially be more beneficial to treat prompting as a two-step process, where we first provide the model with the prompt, and then input the text we want to work with as a secondary step.

Another possible avenue for research is to look into what would be the minimum amount of data or examples required for few-shot or zero-shot learning in historical NER tasks using LLMs without having to compromise on performance. Lastly, since it is common practice for current state-of-the-art models to be released in "families" consisting of various sizes of the same ground architecture, it could also be relevant to experiment with how more variation in parameter size affects the capabilities of such prompt-answering LLMs – including, but not limited to, the model families already mentioned in this paper. A final way forward would be to ensure that the LLM used has seen sufficient amounts of historical text and, if possible, NER examples in historical texts during training.

This study highlights the potential of generative models in improving access to and the analysis of historical texts, aiding in digital humanities efforts, as well as in archival and historical research, while also drawing attention to some of their potential pitfalls.

Acknowledgments

The project is financed by the Swedish Research Council, partially by DECRYPT - Decryption of Historical Manuscripts (grant 2018-06074), and partially by The Swedish Graduate School of Digital Philology (grant 2022-06343). The computations were enabled by resources provided by the National Academic Infrastructure for Supercomputing in Sweden (NAISS), partially funded by the Swedish Research Council through grant agreement no. 2022-06725.

References

Sophie I. Arnoult, Lodewijk Petram, and Piek Vossen. 2021. "Batavia asked for advice. Pretrained language models for Named Entity Recognition in historical texts.". In *Proceedings of the 5th Joint SIGHUM Workshop on Computational Linguistics for Cultural Heritage, Social Sciences, Humanities and Litera-*

ture, pages 21–30, Punta Cana, Dominican Republic (online). Association for Computational Linguistics.

Maud Ehrmann, Ahmed Hamdi, Elvys Linhares Pontes, Matteo Romanello, and Antoine Doucet. 2023. Named entity recognition and classification in historical documents: A survey. *ACM Comput. Surv.*, 56(2).

Maud Ehrmann, Matteo Romanello, Alex Flückiger, and Simon Clematide. 2020. Overview of clef hipe 2020: Named entity recognition and linking on historical newspapers. In *Experimental IR Meets Multilinguality, Multimodality, and Interaction*, pages 288–310, Cham. Springer International Publishing.

Karen Fort, Maud Ehrmann, and Adeline Nazarenko. 2009. Towards a methodology for named entities annotation. *ACL-IJCNLP 2009 - LAW 2009: 3rd Linguistic Annotation Workshop, Proceedings*.

Carlos-Emiliano González-Gallardo, Emanuela Boros, Nancy Girdhar, Ahmed Hamdi, Jose G. Moreno, and Antoine Doucet. 2023. Yes but.. Can ChatGPT Identify Entities in Historical Documents? *Preprint*, arXiv:2303.17322.

Jiaxin Huang, Chunyuan Li, Krishan Subudhi, Damien Jose, Shobana Balakrishnan, Weizhu Chen, Baolin Peng, Jianfeng Gao, and Jiawei Han. 2020. Few-shot named entity recognition: A comprehensive study. *Preprint*, arXiv:2012.14978.

Lei Huang, Weijiang Yu, Weitao Ma, Weihong Zhong, Zhangyin Feng, Haotian Wang, Qianglong Chen, Weihua Peng, Xiaocheng Feng, Bing Qin, and Ting Liu. 2025. A survey on hallucination in large language models: Principles, taxonomy, challenges, and open questions. *ACM Transactions on Information Systems*, 43(2):1–55.

Rasmus Hvingelby, Amalie Brogaard Pauli, Maria Barrett, Christina Rosted, Lasse Malm Lidegaard, and Anders Søgaard. 2020. DaNE: A named entity resource for Danish. In *Proceedings of the Twelfth Language Resources and Evaluation Conference*, pages 4597–4604, Marseille, France. European Language Resources Association.

Svanhvít Lilja Ingólfsdóttir, Sigurjón Thorsteinsson, and Hrafn Loftsson. 2019. Towards high accuracy named entity recognition for Icelandic. In *Proceedings of the 22nd Nordic Conference on Computational Linguistics*, pages 363–369, Turku, Finland. Linköping University Electronic Press.

Fredrik Jørgensen, Tobias Aasmoe, Anne-Stine Ruud Husevåg, Lilja Øvrelid, and Erik Velldal. 2020. NorNE: Annotating named entities for Norwegian. In *Proceedings of the Twelfth Language Resources and Evaluation Conference*, pages 4547–4556, Marseille, France. European Language Resources Association.

Gunnel Källgren and Gunnar Eriksson. 1993. The linguistic annotation system of the Stockholm - Umeå Corpus project. In *Sixth Conference of the European Chapter of the Association for Computational Linguistics*, Utrecht, The Netherlands. Association for Computational Linguistics.

Teven Le Scao and Alexander Rush. 2021. How many data points is a prompt worth? In *Proceedings of the 2021 Conference of the North American Chapter of the Association for Computational Linguistics: Human Language Technologies*, pages 2627–2636, Online. Association for Computational Linguistics.

Andy T. Liu, Wei Xiao, Henghui Zhu, Dejiao Zhang, Shang-Wen Li, and Andrew Arnold. 2022. QaNER: Prompting Question Answering Models for Few-shot Named Entity Recognition. *Preprint*, arXiv:2203.01543.

Niklas Muennighoff, Thomas Wang, Lintang Sutawika, Adam Roberts, Stella Biderman, Teven Le Scao, M Saiful Bari, Sheng Shen, Zheng-Xin Yong, Hailey Schoelkopf, et al. 2022. Crosslingual generalization through multitask finetuning. *arXiv preprint arXiv:2211.01786*.

Ethan Perez, Douwe Kiela, and Kyunghyun Cho. 2021. True few-shot learning with language models. *Preprint*, arXiv:2105.11447.

Colin Raffel, Noam Shazeer, Adam Roberts, Katherine Lee, Sharan Narang, Michael Matena, Yanqi Zhou, Wei Li, and Peter J. Liu. 2019. Exploring the limits of transfer learning with a unified text-to-text transformer. *CoRR*, abs/1910.10683.

Victor Sanh, Albert Webson, Colin Raffel, Stephen H. Bach, Lintang Sutawika, Zaid Alyafeai, Antoine Chaffin, Arnaud Stiegler, Teven Le Scao, Arun Raja, Manan Dey, M Saiful Bari, Canwen Xu, Urmish Thakker, Shanya Sharma Sharma, Eliza Szczechla, Taewoon Kim, Gunjan Chhablani, Nihal Nayak, Debajyoti Datta, Jonathan Chang, Mike Tian-Jian Jiang, Han Wang, Matteo Manica, Sheng Shen, Zheng Xin Yong, Harshit Pandey, Rachel Bawden, Thomas Wang, Trishala Neeraj, Jos Rozen, Abheesht Sharma, Andrea Santilli, Thibault Fevry, Jason Alan Fries, Ryan Teehan, Stella Biderman, Leo Gao, Tali Bers, Thomas Wolf, and Alexander M. Rush. 2021. Multitask prompted training enables zero-shot task generalization. *Preprint*, arXiv:2110.08207.

Teven Le Scao, Angela Fan, Christopher Akiki, Ellie Pavlick, Suzana Ilić, Daniel Hesslow, Roman Castagné, Alexandra Sasha Luccioni, François Yvon, Matthias Gallé, Jonathan Tow, Alexander M. Rush, Stella Biderman, Albert Webson, Pawan Sasanka Ammanamanchi, Thomas Wang, Benoît Sagot, Niklas Muennighoff, Albert Villanova del Moral, Olatunji Ruwase, Rachel Bawden, Stas Bekman, Angelina McMillan-Major, Iz Beltagy, Huu Nguyen, Lucile Saulnier, Samson Tan, Pedro Ortiz Suarez, Victor Sanh, Hugo Laurençon, Yacine Jernite, Julien Launay, Margaret Mitchell, Colin Raffel, Aaron Gokaslan, Adi Simhi, Aitor Soroa, Alham Fikri Aji, Amit Alfassy, Anna Rogers, Ariel Kreisberg

Nitzav, Canwen Xu, Chenghao Mou, Chris Emezue, Christopher Klamm, Colin Leong, Daniel van Strien, David Ifeoluwa Adelani, Dragomir Radev, Eduardo González Ponferrada, Efrat Levkovizh, Ethan Kim, Eyal Bar Natan, Francesco De Toni, Gérard Dupont, Germán Kruszewski, Giada Pistilli, Hady Elsahar, Hamza Benyamina, Hieu Tran, Ian Yu, Idris Abdulmumin, Isaac Johnson, Itziar Gonzalez-Dios, Javier de la Rosa, Jenny Chim, Jesse Dodge, Jian Zhu, Jonathan Chang, Jörg Frohberg, Joseph Tobing, Joydeep Bhattacharjee, Khalid Almubarak, Kimbo Chen, Kyle Lo, Leandro Von Werra, Leon Weber, Long Phan, Loubna Ben allal, Ludovic Tanguy, Manan Dey, Manuel Romero Muñoz, Maraim Masoud, María Grandury, Mario Šaško, Max Huang, Maximin Coavoux, Mayank Singh, Mike Tian-Jian Jiang, Minh Chien Vu, Mohammad A. Jauhar, Mustafa Ghaleb, Nishant Subramani, Nora Kassner, Nurulaqilla Khamis, Olivier Nguyen, Omar Espejel, Ona de Gibert, Paulo Villegas, Peter Henderson, Pierre Colombo, Priscilla Amuok, Quentin Lhoest, Rheza Harliman, Rishi Bommasani, Roberto Luis López, Rui Ribeiro, Salomey Osei, Sampo Pyysalo, Sebastian Nagel, Shamik Bose, Shamsuddeen Hassan Muhammad, Shanya Sharma, Shayne Longpre, Somaieh Nikpoor, Stanislav Silberberg, Suhas Pai, Sydney Zink, Tiago Timponi Torrent, Timo Schick, Tristan Thrush, Valentin Danchev, Vassilina Nikoulina, Veronika Laippala, Violette Lepercq, Vrinda Prabhu, Zaid Alyafeai, Zeerak Talat, Arun Raja, Benjamin Heinzerling, Chenglei Si, Davut Emre Taşar, Elizabeth Salesky, Sabrina J. Mielke, Wilson Y. Lee, Abheesht Sharma, Andrea Santilli, Antoine Chaffin, Arnaud Stiegler, Debajyoti Datta, Eliza Szczechla, Gunjan Chhablani, Han Wang, Harshit Pandey, Hendrik Strobelt, Jason Alan Fries, Jos Rozen, Leo Gao, Lintang Sutawika, M Saiful Bari, Maged S. Al-shaibani, Matteo Manica, Nihal Nayak, Ryan Teehan, Samuel Albanie, Sheng Shen, Srulik Ben-David, Stephen H. Bach, Taewoon Kim, Tali Bers, Thibault Fevry, Trishala Neeraj, Urmish Thakker, Vikas Raunak, Xiangru Tang, Zheng-Xin Yong, Zhiqing Sun, Shaked Brody, Yallow Uri, Hadar Tojarieh, Adam Roberts, Hyung Won Chung, Jaesung Tae, Jason Phang, Ofir Press, Conglong Li, Deepak Narayanan, Hatim Bourfoune, Jared Casper, Jeff Rasley, Max Ryabinin, Mayank Mishra, Minjia Zhang, Mohammad Shoeybi, Myriam Peyrounette, Nicolas Patry, Nouamane Tazi, Omar Sanseviero, Patrick von Platen, Pierre Cornette, Pierre François Lavallée, Rémi Lacroix, Samyam Rajbhandari, Sanchit Gandhi, Shaden Smith, Stéphane Requena, Suraj Patil, Tim Dettmers, Ahmed Baruwa, Amanpreet Singh, Anastasia Cheveleva, Anne-Laure Ligozat, Arjun Subramonian, Aurélie Névéol, Charles Lovering, Dan Garrette, Deepak Tunuguntla, Ehud Reiter, Ekaterina Taktasheva, Ekaterina Voloshina, Eli Bogdanov, Genta Indra Winata, Hailey Schoelkopf, Jan-Christoph Kalo, Jekaterina Novikova, Jessica Zosa Forde, Jordan Clive, Jungo Kasai, Ken Kawamura, Liam Hazan, Marine Carpuat, Miruna Clinciu, Najoung Kim, Newton Cheng, Oleg Serikov, Omer Antverg, Oskar van der Wal, Rui Zhang, Ruochen Zhang, Sebastian Gehrmann, Shachar Mirkin, Shani Pais, Tatiana Shavrina, Thomas Scialom, Tian Yun, Tomasz Limisiewicz, Verena Rieser, Vitaly Protasov, Vladislav Mikhailov, Yada Pruksachatkun, Yonatan Belinkov, Zachary Bamberger, Zdeněk Kasner, Alice Rueda, Amanda Pestana, Amir Feizpour, Ammar Khan, Amy Faranak, Ana Santos, Anthony Hevia, Antigona Unldreaj, Arash Aghagol, Arezoo Abdollahi, Aycha Tammour, Azadeh HajiHosseini, Bahareh Behroozi, Benjamin Ajibade, Bharat Saxena, Carlos Muñoz Ferrandis, Daniel McDuff, Danish Contractor, David Lansky, Davis David, Douwe Kiela, Duong A. Nguyen, Edward Tan, Emi Baylor, Ezinwanne Ozoani, Fatima Mirza, Frankline Ononiwu, Habib Rezanejad, Hessie Jones, Indrani Bhattacharya, Irene Solaiman, Irina Sedenko, Isar Nejadgholi, Jesse Passmore, Josh Seltzer, Julio Bonis Sanz, Livia Dutra, Mairon Samagaio, Maraim Elbadri, Margot Mieskes, Marissa Gerchick, Martha Akinlolu, Michael McKenna, Mike Qiu, Muhammed Ghauri, Mykola Burynok, Nafis Abrar, Nazneen Rajani, Nour Elkott, Nour Fahmy, Olanrewaju Samuel, Ran An, Rasmus Kromann, Ryan Hao, Samira Alizadeh, Sarmad Shubber, Silas Wang, Sourav Roy, Sylvain Viguier, Thanh Le, Tobi Oyebade, Trieu Le, Yoyo Yang, Zach Nguyen, Abhinav Ramesh Kashyap, Alfredo Palasciano, Alison Callahan, Anima Shukla, Antonio Miranda-Escalada, Ayush Singh, Benjamin Beilharz, Bo Wang, Caio Brito, Chenxi Zhou, Chirag Jain, Chuxin Xu, Clémentine Fourrier, Daniel León Periñán, Daniel Molano, Dian Yu, Enrique Manjavacas, Fabio Barth, Florian Fuhrimann, Gabriel Altay, Giyaseddin Bayrak, Gully Burns, Helena U. Vrabec, Imane Bello, Ishani Dash, Jihyun Kang, John Giorgi, Jonas Golde, Jose David Posada, Karthik Rangasai Sivaraman, Lokesh Bulchandani, Lu Liu, Luisa Shinzato, Madeleine Hahn de Bykhovetz, Maiko Takeuchi, Marc Pàmies, Maria A Castillo, Marianna Nezhurina, Mario Sänger, Matthias Samwald, Michael Cullan, Michael Weinberg, Michiel De Wolf, Mina Mihaljcic, Minna Liu, Moritz Freidank, Myungsun Kang, Natasha Seelam, Nathan Dahlberg, Nicholas Michio Broad, Nikolaus Muellner, Pascale Fung, Patrick Haller, Ramya Chandrasekhar, Renata Eisenberg, Robert Martin, Rodrigo Canalli, Rosaline Su, Ruisi Su, Samuel Cahyawijaya, Samuele Garda, Shlok S Deshmukh, Shubhanshu Mishra, Sid Kiblawi, Simon Ott, Sinee Sang-aroonsiri, Srishti Kumar, Stefan Schweter, Sushil Bharati, Tanmay Laud, Théo Gigant, Tomoya Kainuma, Wojciech Kusa, Yanis Labrak, Yash Shailesh Bajaj, Yash Venkatraman, Yifan Xu, Yingxin Xu, Yu Xu, Zhe Tan, Zhongli Xie, Zifan Ye, Mathilde Bras, Younes Belkada, and Thomas Wolf. 2023. Bloom: A 176b-parameter open-access multilingual language model. *Preprint*, arXiv:2211.05100.

Timo Schick and Hinrich Schütze. 2021. It's not just size that matters: Small language models are also few-shot learners. In *Proceedings of the 2021 Conference of the North American Chapter of the Association for Computational Linguistics: Human Language Technologies*, pages 2339–2352, Online. Association for Computational Linguistics.

Stefan Schweter, Luisa März, Katharina Schmid, and Erion Çano. 2022. hmBERT: Historical Multilingual Language Models for Named Entity Recognition. *Preprint*, arXiv:2205.15575.

Språkbanken Text. 2024. Sucx 3.0.

Francesco De Toni, Christopher Akiki, Javier de la Rosa, Clémentine Fourrier, Enrique Manjavacas, Stefan Schweter, and Daniel van Strien. 2022. Entities, Dates, and Languages: Zero-Shot on Historical Texts with T0. *Preprint*, arXiv:2204.05211.

Crina Tudor and Eva Pettersson. 2024. People and places of the past - named entity recognition in Swedish labour movement documents from historical sources. In *Proceedings of the 8th Joint SIGHUM Workshop on Computational Linguistics for Cultural Heritage, Social Sciences, Humanities and Literature (LaTeCH-CLfL 2024)*, pages 185–195, St. Julians, Malta. Association for Computational Linguistics.

Linting Xue, Noah Constant, Adam Roberts, Mihir Kale, Rami Al-Rfou, Aditya Siddhant, Aditya Barua, and Colin Raffel. 2020. mt5: A massively multilingual pre-trained text-to-text transformer. *CoRR*, abs/2010.11934.

Ahmet Üstün, Viraat Aryabumi, Zheng-Xin Yong, Wei-Yin Ko, Daniel D'souza, Gbemileke Onilude, Neel Bhandari, Shivalika Singh, Hui-Lee Ooi, Amr Kayid, Freddie Vargus, Phil Blunsom, Shayne Longpre, Niklas Muennighoff, Marzieh Fadaee, Julia Kreutzer, and Sara Hooker. 2024. Aya model: An instruction finetuned open-access multilingual language model. *arXiv preprint arXiv:2402.07827*.

LLMs for Translation: Historical, Low-Resourced Languages and Contemporary AI Models

Merve Tekgürler
Stanford University
Department of History and Program in Symbolic Systems
mtekgurl@stanford.edu

Abstract

Large Language Models (LLMs) have demonstrated remarkable adaptability in performing various tasks, including machine translation (MT), without explicit training. Models such as OpenAI's GPT-4 and Google's Gemini are frequently evaluated on translation benchmarks and utilized as translation tools due to their high performance. This paper examines Gemini's performance in translating an 18th-century Ottoman Turkish manuscript, *Prisoner of the Infidels: The Memoirs of Osman Agha of Timișoara*, into English. The manuscript recounts the experiences of Osman Agha, an Ottoman subject who spent 11 years as a prisoner of war in Austria, and includes his accounts of warfare and violence. Our analysis reveals that Gemini's safety mechanisms flagged between 14% and 23% of the manuscript as harmful, resulting in untranslated passages. These safety settings, while effective in mitigating potential harm, hinder the model's ability to provide complete and accurate translations of historical texts. Through real historical examples, this study highlights the inherent challenges and limitations of current LLM safety implementations in the handling of sensitive and context-rich materials. These real-world instances underscore potential failures of LLMs in contemporary translation scenarios, where accurate and comprehensive translations are crucial—for example, translating the accounts of modern victims of war for legal proceedings or humanitarian documentation.

1 Introduction

Machine Translation (MT) has long been a cornerstone of Natural Language Processing (NLP), facilitating cross-linguistic communication and information accessibility. With the advent of Large Language Models (LLMs) such as OpenAI's GPT-4 and Google's Gemini, MT has seen significant advancements in both performance and adaptability. These models are not only evaluated on standard translation benchmarks, but are also deployed as translation tools across various domains. However, the translation of historical and low-resourced languages presents unique challenges that are often overlooked in mainstream MT research. Ottoman Turkish (OT), an extinct language with limited digital resources, exemplifies such a low-resourced language.

Translating OT manuscripts remains a labor-intensive task with limited scholarly resources. To the best of our knowledge, there is no MT system specifically designed for OT-to-English (OT-EN) translation. Current tools for Turkish-English translation are not directly adaptable for this task, despite Turkish being the most closely related living language to Ottoman. However, we know anecdotally that scholars in Ottoman studies have been using LLMs for translating their sources. Indeed, LLMs have the potential to act as first-pass translators of OT, reducing the time and effort needed to translate primary sources.

Accessible and reliable primary sources are indispensable for historians. However, in English-language instructional settings, the scarcity of translated non-English sources limits historians' ability to teach global histories. This skews students' perception of history, reinforcing a narrow view that excludes varied cultural perspectives and further marginalizing certain groups. Enhancing the availability of primary sources through effective translation is essential for diversifying history curricula and democratizing access to the past. By increasing the availability of multilingual primary sources, we can contribute to a more inclusive and comprehensive understanding of our shared history.

In addition to addressing the challenges of translating low-resourced historical languages, this study explores the ethical implications of integrating artificial intelligence (AI) safety mechanisms within Large Language Models (LLMs). These safety protocols are designed to mitigate the dis-

Proceedings of LaTeCH-CLfL 2025, pages 227–237
May 4, 2025 ©2025 Association for Computational Linguistics

semination of harmful content by flagging and restricting passages that contain violence, hate speech, or other sensitive topics. These protocols use algorithms to evaluate the contents of user prompts before these can be processed by LLMs, effectively content-moderating user prompts. Often there is little detail or clarity as to how these algorithms are implemented and what constitutes as inappropriate prompts. In the context of translation, such mechanisms can inadvertently impede sensitive narratives from being processed by the models. Translation requires accuracy and reliability, arguably even more when it comes to complex and difficult narratives of human experience.

AI safety and content moderation raises ethical issues regarding the use of LLMs for translation. Our work facilitates the examination of these ethical issues on real life data. As LLMs are increasingly incorporated into translation pipelines, it is crucial to understand how these safety mechanisms handle complex accounts from real sources, as opposed to synthetic texts created to test AI models. However, turning testimonies of contemporary individuals into AI test sets comes with its own set of ethical challenges, such as violations of privacy and consent. By testing LLMs on historical documents, we can assess the impact of these safety decisions without involving the stories of living individuals.

This paper investigates the performance of Google's Gemini in translating an 18th-century Ottoman Turkish manuscript, *Prisoner of the Infidels: The Memoirs of Osman Agha of Timișoara*, into English. By analyzing how AI safety settings influence the translation process, this study aims to uncover the limitations and potential biases introduced by these mechanisms when handling historical and context-rich materials.

2 Related Works

This research project is at the intersection of historical NLP, Digital History, machine translation, and NLP research on low-resourced languages. By historical NLP, we are referring to works like those on Coptic (Enis and Megalaa) or Latin (Martínez Garcia and García Tejedor, 2020) that study these historical languages within the field of NLP. The use of NLP methods in History research has increased in the recent years Jo (2020); de Bolla (2023); Guldi (2023). Our work recognizes the value that computational approaches add to History scholarship. At the same time, we argue that Digital History, much like NLP, has a bias towards English as non-English languages are extremely underrepresented in this field. Thus, we see similarities between our work and those of NLP researchers studying other non-English, low-resourced languages (Doumbouya et al., 2023).

2.1 Translation with LLMs

Some of the most intriguing challenges stem from the intersection of machine translation (MT) and LLMs. Tanzer et al. (2024) presents a remarkable case study and a new benchmark, Machine Translation from One Book (MTOB), which studies translation between Kalamang and English. Kalamang is a language with fewer than 200 speakers and no Internet presence, making it absent from any LLM training data. By providing reference materials such as a grammar book, word list, and example sentences, the researchers were able to prompt LLMs to achieve promising results. Another related area of research at the intersection of LLMs and MT is the use of dictionaries within the context window of LLMs. Ghazvininejad et al. (2023) argues that using bilingual dictionaries could effectively enable LLMs to correctly identify rare words and transfer their skills to low-resourced and out-of-domain MT settings. Translating a historical, extinct language like OT represents a new research horizons building upon these approaches.

2.2 Ottoman Turkish

Ottoman Turkish (OT) is a historical and primarily written language, which was the official language of the Ottoman Empire (1299-1923). OT was based on Anatolian Turkish, but contained many words and phrases borrowed and adapted from Arabic and Persian. Moreover, it displayed certain syntactic forms, such as the use of Persian genitive case *izafa*, which are no longer used in Turkish. Most importantly, OT was written in Arabo-Persian script (Buğday, 2009). After the dissolution of the Ottoman Empire, the newly-formed Republic of Turkey implemented series of civil and administrative laws, including the 1928 Alphabet Reform (Zürcher, 2004; Lewis, 1984). Also known as *Harf Devrimi* in Turkish, literally translated 'letter reform', this law resulted in a rapid transformation of the Turkish alphabet from Arabo-Persian to Latin script. Within 6 months of the law passing, the official script of the Republic was already latinized. The change of script was followed by the formation of a state-led language simplification committee.

Its mission was to invent "native" Turkish words to replace their Arabic and Persian counterparts. In the past century, the language changed enough that even native speakers of Turkish can no longer innately understand OT even in transliteration.

Due to the differences between Ottoman and Modern Turkish, NLP tools developed for Turkish are not directly applicable for OT. As such, OT remains an underrepresented language in NLP. To this day, there is only one paper in the Association of Computational Linguistics (ACL) Anthology that primarily deals with OT (Özateş et al., 2024).

2.3 AI Safety and Content Moderation

Google's report on Gemini 1.5 (Team, 2024) includes some broad descriptions of the company's safety related concerns and decisions. The Gemini Team lists 7 categories of harmful content: child sexual abuse and exploitation, revealing personal identifiable information that can lead to harm (e.g., Social Security Numbers), hate speech, dangerous or malicious content (including promoting self-harm, or instructing in harmful activities), harassment, sexually explicit content, and medical advice that runs contrary to scientific or medical consensus.

Despite outlining these categories, the Gemini Team has not publicly shared specific examples for each category beyond referencing standard benchmarks such as the BBQ benchmark (Parrish et al., 2022). The team employs strategies to cleanse pre-training data of harmful content and utilizes supervised fine-tuning, particularly Reinforcement Learning from Human Feedback (RLHF), to align the model's behavior with their safety criteria. When it comes to API interactions, Gemini's safety settings are streamlined into four harm categories: hate speech, dangerous content, harassment, and sexually explicit content.

Table 1: An Example of Safety Ratings for a Single Prompt

Metric	Hate Speech	Dangerous Content	Harassment	Sexually Explicit
Probability	Negligible	Negligible	Negligible	Medium
Probability Score	0.45075	0.29068	0.46023	0.77322
Severity	Low	Low	Low	High
Severity Score	0.37886	0.22085	0.20834	0.81757
Blocked	No	No	No	Yes

As depicted Table 1, each of the four harm categories is associated with two values: Severity Score and Probability Score. Severity score indicates the intensity of potential harm within the prompt. Probability score reports the model's confidence in this assessment. A prompt can be blocked for one category or a combination of categories.

Our research aligns closely with studies at the intersection of NLP and content moderation. As demonstrated by Gligoric et al. (2024), distinguishing reliably between the use and mention of harmful content using NLP methods is exceedingly challenging. Gligoric et al. (2024) argues that the use of words to convey a speaker's intent is traditionally distinguished from the mention of words for quoting or describing their properties. This distinction is pivotal for our research, as translation further complicates this issue.

In our study, Gemini is not prompted to generate 'harmful' language, but with translating it. Whether translation constitutes a case of mention remains debatable. However, it is indisputable that translation shares similarities with the act of mentioning. Various domains—such as legal testimonies, educational materials, news reports, and academic texts—rely on translation to report content. For instance, a legal testimony involving assault is expected to contain potentially harmful language, yet an accurate translation of this language is crucial for proper legal proceedings. Understanding how LLMs navigate the translation of sensitive content can be informative in improving both translation accuracy and content moderation strategies.

3 Data

3.1 Osman Agha: Person and Manuscript

Osman Agha was an Ottoman subject who spent 11 years as a prisoner of war in Austria during the Great Turkish Wars (1683-1699). His memoirs, *Prisoner of the Infidels: The Memoirs of Osman Agha of Timișoara*, completed on May 18, 1724, provide a detailed account of warfare, captivity, and diplomatic interactions. Despite the rich content, the manuscript remained relatively obscure during the Ottoman era, with only a single extant copy preserved in the British Library (MS. Or. 3213). This is extremely rare in the manuscript-centered literary culture of the Ottomans, where popular works typically had multiple copies by different scribes.

Richard F. Kreutel and Otto Spies published the first scholarly German translation of *Osman Agha* in 1954 (Kreutel and Spies, 1954). In the subsequent years, the manuscript was translated into Modern Turkish before it was transliterated into Latin script OT in 2020 (Koç, 2020). Giancarlo

Casale published the English translation (Casale, 2021) as a stand-alone work in 2021. The publication history of this manuscript shows that the original text and its translation have never been available within the same publication. This separation implies that while the transliteration and many translations may have been included in LLM training corpora, it was likely not presented in a parallel text format, presenting unique challenges for machine translation models tasked with translating low-resourced, historical languages like Ottoman.

3.2 Dataset

The dataset for this experiment contains the translations, English (Casale, 2021) and German (Kreutel and Spies, 1954), and transliteration (Koç, 2020) of the manuscript *Prisoner of the Infidels*. We scanned and OCR'ed these works and extracted the text at sentence level. We used SentAlign, a sentence alignment algorithm (Steingrimsson et al., 2023) to match the Ottoman Turkish and English texts to each other. SentAlign uses the language-agnostic BERT Sentence Embedding (LaBSE) model (Feng et al., 2022) to capture the meaning of sentences in parallel text corpora and identify which ones are translations of each other. This is a complex matching process that includes one-to-one, one-to-many, many-to-one, and many-to-many, based on similarity scores, and even removal of sentences with no matches. After alignment, we obtained the OT-EN dataset with 757 sentence pairs. We used VecAlign (Thompson and Koehn, 2019), another sentence alignment algorithm with the same LaBSE embeddings, to align the German translation with the English translation. After alignment, we had a second dataset of 1,699 DE-EN parallel sentences.

Table 2: Dataset Overview

Dataset Name	Number of Sentence Pairs
Ottoman Transliteration	1,095
English Translation	2,191
German Translation	2,101
OT-EN Parallel Text	755
DE-EN Parallel Text	1,699

4 Preliminary Experiments

While this paper deals with the performance of Gemini 1.5 Pro, we tested the performance of the following models on translating *Osman Aga*: GPT-3.5, GPT-4, Gemini 1.0, Cohere Aya, before conducting the experiments discussed in this paper, and GPT-4o, GPT-o3-mini, Gemini 2.0, and Claude Sonnet 3.7 leading up to the writing of this paper. We also tested a state-of-the-art translation model, Helsinki NLP Opus NMT model, for Turkish to English translation (Tiedemann, 2020) and fine-tuned this model on a custom dataset that we created from Turkish-English novels and handful Ottoman works with English translations. We report Bilingual Evaluation Understudy or BLEU scores (Papineni et al., 2002) and character n-gram F-score or chr-F (Popović, 2015) below.

Table 3: Osman Agha BLEU and chrF Scores

Model	BLEU	chrF
GPT-3.5	7.11	35.84
GPT-4	7.97	37.71
Gemini 1.0	7.85	36.61
Gemini 1.5	9.28	38.09
Cohere Aya	5.74	28.91
GPT-4o	8.74	38.38
GPT-o3-mini	6.02	35.67
Gemini 2.0 Pro	6.89	35.11
Claude Sonnet 3.7	9.74	40.32
Helsinki NLP OpusMT	2.83	19.39
Fine-tuned OpusMT	3.87	24.23

During our preliminary experiments, we discovered that Gemini 1.5 exhibited content moderation behavior despite relatively high scores and acceptable first-pass translations. These preliminary results prompted our investigations into Gemini 1.5 Pro as outlined below.

5 Methods

Since our research goal is to study Gemini's safety settings and its relation to translation, we searched for code examples written or approved by Google. We identified this notebook from Google Cloud Platform's GitHub repository. The first example in this notebook was translation of French into English, which we included as Figure 6 in the Appendix of this paper. We modified this code to save the output of the model, safety ratings, and the other values into a CSV.

For our experiments, we used Gemini Pro 1.5 through API calls. We prompted the model to translate the manuscript sentence by sentence. We ran a first pass in which we sent requests for the entire manuscript. Of the 755 sentences in OT-EN dataset, 208 sentences, or 27%, were not translated. We know from previous experiments that sometimes these models can behave in an unexpected way and simply not translate. Thus, we ran a second pass on these 208 sentences using the same translation prompt. In the second pass, 34 more sentences were translated and we ended up with a total of 174 untranslated sentences, which represents about 23% of the entire dataset.

Our quantitative analysis focused on these 174 untranslated sentences. We extracted the safety rating information for each sentence and plotted the severity and probability scores. We studied the relationship between how severe the predicted harm in a given sentence is with how confident the model is with its assessment. Additionally, we realized that each sentence can be blocked for one, two, three, or all four categories. We ran further analysis to identify which of these 4 categories and their exclusive combinations are seen in these 174 sentences. We also mapped these on an histogram across the entire manuscript. The sentences in the dataset are in the order in which the manuscript was originally written. We grouped the sentences into bins of 25 sentences and colored the histogram bins based on exclusive combinations of harm categories observed in that 25 sentence chunk.

We ran the same translation prompt on the German translation of the manuscript and followed the same model of doing 2 passes. As we stated above, we want to understand if these trends regarding safety are a result of the contents of the manuscript or related to the fact that Ottoman Turkish is a low-resourced language. The original DE-EN dataset consisted of 1699 sentences. In the first pass, 363 sentences, or 21% of the dataset, was not translated. In the second pass, 36 more sentences were translated, meaning that only 328 sentences, or 19% of the original dataset, were left untranslated. One sentence was not translated without triggering any safety flags or returning any response from the model in both passes. We removed that sentence from the untranslated sentences dataset and ended up with 327 sentences for analysis. We ran the same quantitative analysis on this dataset as with its Ottoman counterpart.

6 Results

Figures 1 and 2 report the relationship between the severity and probability scores for OT-EN and DE-EN datasets, respectively. Increasing severity score strongly indicates an increase in model confidence for both OT and DE cases, with a coefficient of 0.914 for OT and 0.935 for DE. In both cases we see similar trends in the model being less confident in its classification of dangerous content and more confident in its classification of harassment.

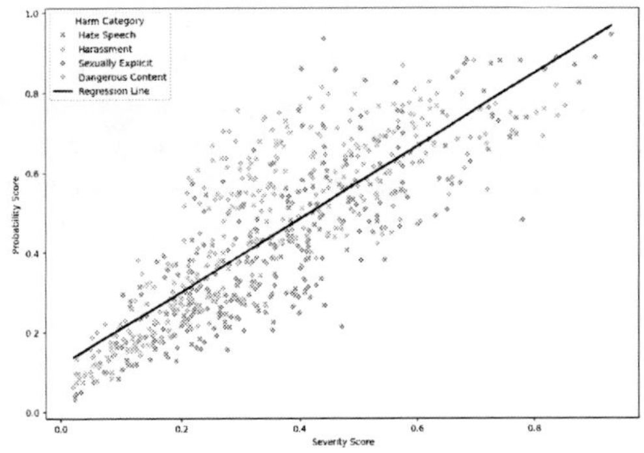

Figure 1: Severity Score - Probability Score Plot for Flagged Ottoman Turkish Sentences

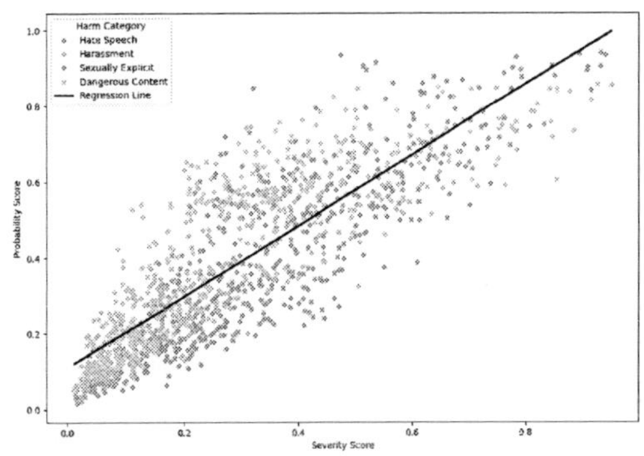

Figure 2: Severity Score - Probability Score Plot for Flagged German Sentences

The main difference between the two languages is in the classification of severity. For the exact same manuscript, Gemini classified more of the flagged sentences with less severity for German than for Ottoman Turkish in 3 harm categories, shown in the severity comparison in Figure 3. Note that the difference is not statistically significant.

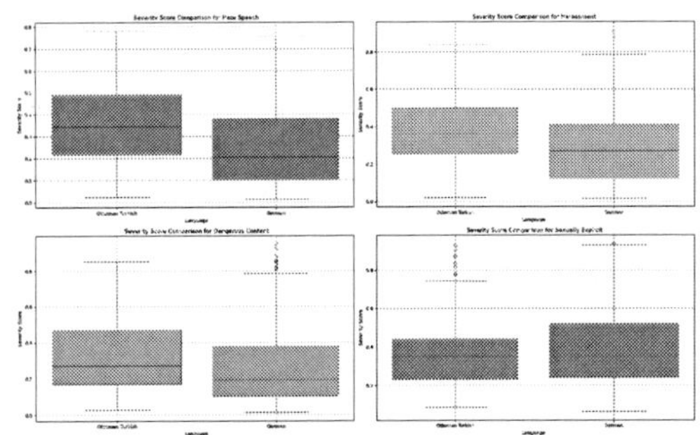

Figure 3: Comparison of the Severity Scores in Ottoman and German Datasets

Table 4 shows that the number of sentences flagged for each category or combinations of categories follow a similar trend between OT and DE datasets. In neither of them is there a sentence flagged exclusively for hate speech and dangerous content, or for hate speech, dangerous content and harassment. The distributions of flags per category and category combinations are broadly similar.

Table 4: Blocked Sentences Summary by Categories

Category(ies)	Ottoman Turkish	German
Hate Speech	0	7
Dangerous Content	6	19
Harassment	46	69
Sexually Explicit	36	110
Hate Speech, Dangerous Content	0	0
Hate Speech, Harassment	41	46
Hate Speech, Sexually Explicit	0	1
Dangerous Content, Harassment	21	34
Dangerous Content, Sexually Explicit	2	6
Harassment, Sexually Explicit	4	9
Hate Speech, Dangerous Content, Harassment	10	14
Hate Speech, Dangerous Content, Sexually Explicit	0	0
Hate Speech, Harassment, Sexually Explicit	6	6
Dangerous Content, Harassment, Sexually Explicit	1	6
All Four Categories	1	0
Total Number of Blocked Sentences	**174**	**327**

The similarity in the broader trends across these two datasets supports our hypothesis that the flagging of these sentences is indeed related to the contents of the manuscript and not due to Ottoman Turkish being a low-resourced language.

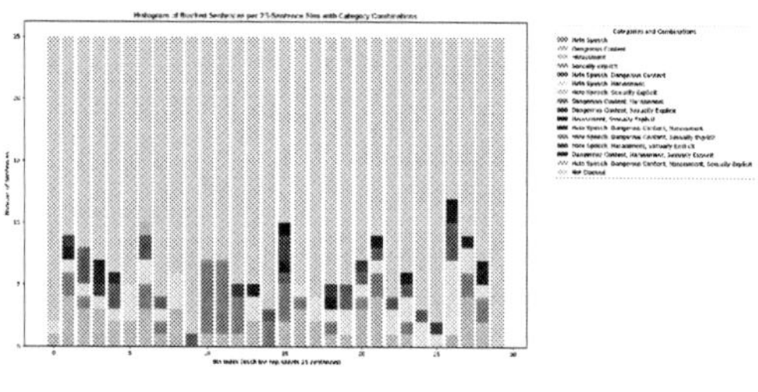

Figure 4: Distribution of Flagged Sentences across the entire Ottoman Manuscript

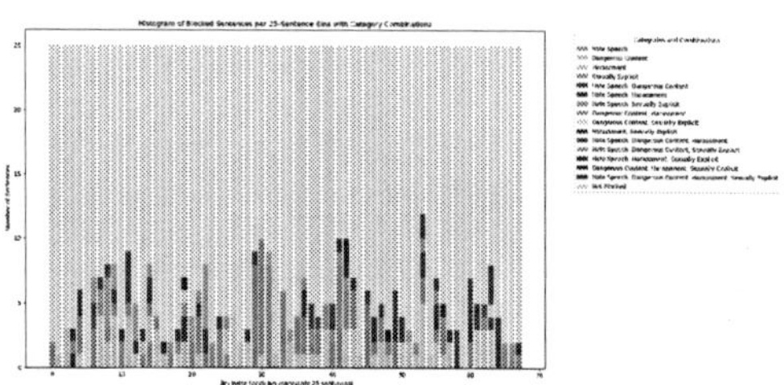

Figure 5: Distribution of Flagged Sentences across the entire German Manuscript

As shown in Figures 4 and 5, our findings with the distribution of the blocking across the manuscript show that the safety triggers are not random. Looking at the OT histogram, we see that hate speech, dangerous content and harassment category is more prevalent towards the beginning and the end of the manuscript. Those are the sections where Osman Agha is on the move: he is captured early in the narrative and towards the end, he flees captivity in disguise, traveling across Austria. The parts marked as sexually explicit correspond to the parts of Osman's story when he is developing a relationship with an Austrian noblewoman, after the woman's husband passed away. The categories harassment and hate speech and harassment are distributed all across the manuscript. Considering the nature of the story, it makes sense to see these two distributed across rather than clustered. These factors reaffirm our proposition that there is a relationship between the contents and the safety flags.

7 Analysis

Below we offer a close analysis of three examples of blocked sentences in the OT-EN dataset.

Example 1

Ottoman Turkish: "Tamâm istedüğü kadar döğdükden sonra kapuyu açub bizi ol Hırvatlar ile temürcü kerhânesine gönderüb ayağımıza bir çift esîr prangası tokuyub ol sâʻat derûn kalʻaya zindâna gönderdi."

Ground Truth English: "Finally, when he had beaten me quite as much as he wanted, he opened the door and had the Croatians take me down to the blacksmith's workshop, where I was fitted with a pair of shackles. Then he sent me to the jail in the inner fortress."

This was the only sentence which was flagged in all 4 of the harm categories. While it clearly depicts violence, evident in the references to beating and shackling, there is no clear description of sexual contents. Yet this sentence was marked as medium harm severity (0.637) for sexually explicit content. We believe that this mistake arose from the word *kerhâne* in the Ottoman sentence. In Modern Turkish, *kerhâne*, refers exclusively to a place of sex work. However in OT it refers to a place of work more generally. Moreover, this example deals with a compound noun *temürcü kerhânesi* where *temürcü* means blacksmith, which is why it is translated into English as *blacksmith's workshop*.

With safety setting turned off, Gemini successfully translated this word in this sentence as *forge*. This examples indicates that even though Gemini is able to recognize the context of a word, the content moderation algorithm cannot, which results in unnecessary blocking of user prompts. One of the promises of using LLMs was the context awareness and the potential of these models to understand nuances even in settings unseen at training time. Content moderation is preventing access to the model and thus to the potential that this technology offers.

Example 2

Ottoman Turkish: "Ben dahî dedim ki, "Ne olsa gerek? Kızın bikrini alub bozmuşsuz! Kız şimdi hâmileyim deyü havf eder."

Ground Truth English: "“What do you think happened?” I said. “You've taken her maidenhood and ruined her, and now she's afraid that she may be pregnant."

This sentence is flagged as sexually explicit and dangerous content as well as harassment. Such classification is misleading. This sentence refers to a young woman's experience of sexual assault and her fears of becoming pregnant as a result. As a matter of fact, it is a conversation between two individuals, in which the speaker is accusing the listener of violating a young woman. Sexual assault is not sexually explicit content; the model's classification of this sentence as high severity sexually explicit content with 0.867 severity score indicates issues with the safety settings.

Example 3

Ottoman Turkish: "Nemçe zâbitleri ne kadar men' eylemek murâd eyledilerse mümkin olmayub hattâ gördüğümüz üzre cenerallar at üzerinde müselmân soyub katl edenlerin bir kaçını tüfenk ile urub öldürmüşlerdir. Gine sâ'irleri mukayyed olmayub garet eylemişlerdir."

Ground Truth English: "The Austrian officers did try to prevent all of this, but it was impossible. I even saw mounted officers who fired and killed a few of their own troops as they despoiled and murdered the Muslims, but this did not prevent the rest, who continued as before."

This sentence was flagged for harassment and hate speech both with low severity, 0.282 and 0.357, respectively. However in both cases, the model was over 60% certain of its decision, resulting in a block. This sentence is a complicated account of warfare. It depicts Austrian officers killing their own troops because those troops have gone rogue. They are committing extrajudicial murder, which is restricted even in warfare. Moreover, it is narrated from the victims' perspective. Flagging such complicated narratives further silences victims.

Example 4

Ottoman: Bir gün 'ale's-seher cümle halk hâbda iken kadınımızın kaftancı kızı Margot ismiyle müsemmâ on beş yaşında bir mahbûbe, kara gözlü, memeleri iki dâne turunca benzer, gayet latîf sıfatlı kız idi, gelüb yatağımıza binüb yanımızda yatub beni iki kollarıyla kuçub bûs eylemeğe başlayınca gözümü açub ne görsem! Hiç me'mûl olunmayan bir kaziyye vâki' olub, "'Acabâ bu şey düş müdür, hayâl midir?" tefekkür ederdim.

Ground Truth English: One day, just before daybreak, while everyone was still asleep, I was visited by one of my lady's handmaidens, a girl named Margot. She was fifteen years old, a darling dark-haired beauty with breasts like two oranges and a delightful figure. She climbed right into my bed and lay beside me, embraced me with both arms, and started kissing me! I opened my eyes, and could hardly believe the situation in which I found myself.

This sentence remained untranslated even after turning the model safety settings off. We believed that the reference to Margot's age *She was fifteen years old* coupled with the sexual contents in the passage triggered deeper, unchangeable settings. We tested this further by changing the age reference in the original passage from fifteen to twenty. The model then translated the edited sentence. This example prompted us to further investigate how Gemini handles age. We created a simple test sentence in Turkish which translated to English as "I am a 15 year old girl and I was sexually assaulted." Gemini 1.5 did not translate this sentence either, even with the safety settings off. This example shows how a real, historical example could help identify an aspect of model behavior that merits further investigation.

8 Discussion

Osman Agha offer a unique opportunity for investigating the relationship of translation and AI safety. This manuscript is not calling for violence or depicting gory scenes. But it contains descriptions of warfare and death, which are despite their saddening nature, part of the realities of life in the past as well as today. This manuscript does not contain any pornographic depictions, but it does mention sexual assault and at times narrates sexual affairs. Osman Agha does not call for hate towards any particular group, but he does use historical terms, like infidel, which are not appropriate to use in reference to people today. The diversity of themes covered in this manuscript means that there are a variety of sections that can helped us infer more about the AI safety implementations behind Gemini.

We recognize the importance of AI safety settings, especially when it comes to incredibly large models like Gemini. However, translation and chat are not equivalent tasks. Google is actively encouraging the use and deployment of Gemini in translation, evident in their report (Team, 2024) and in their investment in developing the MTOB benchmark (Tanzer et al., 2024). Translation is a standard use case in their basic usage examples. Yet, the company does not offer any details about how they see their safety settings interacting with translation.

With an ever-increasing context window, it will be remarkably easy to miss a few sentences that were left untranslated. And those sentences might be exactly the ones that a victim of personal or structural violence needed to express to the rest of the world. Mistakes in translation stand out. Refusals to translate however can be hidden away, behind code that is designed to move onto the next sentence if it encounters an 'error'. Osman Agha's experiences, although sometimes not very pleasant to read, are not far from the experiences of Palestinians or Ukrainians, among other groups experiencing warfare in today's world. We need to ensure that AI safety implementations do not silence victims and underprivileged groups.

9 Implications

LLMs are useful tools to historians, especially for those working with languages like OT that are otherwise not served by existing language technologies. Historical research, whether it is testing LLMs on real, historical data instead of fictional test cases, or applying historical critical thinking to technologies, offers a unique perspective to computational studies.

In lieu of a conclusion, we would like to offer some thoughts regarding the implications of our work. On January 28, 2025 Guardian reported an interesting finding about how DeepSeek did not answer questions about Tiananmen Square in its chat interface. Many reputable news agencies conducted their own analysis into this issue, including the CNN World, which used this title in its reporting: "DeepSeek is giving the world a window into Chinese censorship and information control." On February 12, 2025, OpenAI released an updated model spec. [1] This document contains several examples of prompts that highlight how the OpenAI models are supposed to respond in different scenarios. These scenarios include political and politicized questions that offer insights into OpenAI policies.

In conjuncture with these developments, our research offers an in-depth study of one model, Gemini 1.5, and through our examples, we offer a window into information control in a closed source model. Users can indeed change the safety settings of Gemini in API calls, much like they can run their own instance of DeepSeek without the layer that prevents it from responding to questions related to Tiananmen Square. In either case, however, studying these models as artifacts from the perspective of History and Philosophy of Science tells us something about the production context and use cases of these models. Who is designing these technologies and for whom are these technologies designed? Whose experiences do not meet the threshold of safety requirements or information policies of companies and governments? These questions are central for our understanding and evaluation of ethics of science and technology, and their impact on society today.

10 Ethical Considerations

Our work enables the examination of ethical issues related to AI safety and content moderation in AI models without posing risks to contemporary individuals. It is crucial to understand how these safety mechanisms handle complex accounts that may contain harmful content. By testing LLMs on historical accounts, we can study the impact of these safety decisions without exposing the stories of people who are alive today to these models. Osman Agha's account is over 300 years old and his immediate relatives passed away long ago. This minimizes the risk associated with incorporating his experiences, however challenging they may be, into these models. Additionally, we address concerns related to the use of the translation. While the original manuscript is no longer under copyright, its translations are protected. Therefore, we must ensure that the data is shared in a manner that prevents the illegal recreation of the translation. We are committed to handling the translated material responsibly to avoid any unauthorized distribution

[1] https://model-spec.openai.com/2025-02-12.html

or misuse.

11 Acknowledgments

The author designed and conducted the experiments and wrote the entire paper. The original inspiration to focus on translation of Ottoman Turkish as a valuable task comes from Umar Patel. This research was supported at various stages by professors Mark Algee-Hewitt, Chris Manning, Dan Jurafsky, and Diyi Yang at Stanford University. The author used ChatGPT Plus for debugging code, visualization support, and copy editing purposes. The author thanks Chloé Brault for help in revising. They are also grateful for the generations of scholars who meticulously transcribed, transliterated, and translated Osman Agha's memoirs.

References

Korkut Buğday. 2009. *The Routledge Introduction to Literary Ottoman*. Routledge, New York.

Giancarlo Casale. 2021. *Prisoner of the Infidels: The Memoir of an Ottoman Muslim in Seventeenth-Century Europe*. University of California Press, Oakland.

Peter de Bolla. 2023. *Explorations in the Digital History of Ideas: New Methods and Computational Approaches*. Cambridge University Press, Cambridge.

Moussa Koulako Bala Doumbouya, Baba Mamadi Diané, Solo Farabado Cissé, Djibrila Diané, Abdoulaye Sow, Séré Moussa Doumbouya, Daouda Bangoura, Fodé Moriba Bayo, Ibrahima Sory 2. Condé, Kalo Mory Diané, Chris Piech, and Christopher Manning. 2023. Machine translation for nko: Tools, corpora and baseline results. *Preprint*, arXiv:2310.15612.

Maxim Enis and Andrew Megalaa. Ancient voices, modern technology: Low-resource neural machine translation for coptic texts. In *Coptic Translator*, pages 1–15.

Fangxiaoyu Feng, Yinfei Yang, Daniel Cer, Naveen Arivazhagan, and Wei Wang. 2022. Language-agnostic BERT sentence embedding. In *Proceedings of the 60th Annual Meeting of the Association for Computational Linguistics (Volume 1: Long Papers)*, pages 878–891, Dublin, Ireland. Association for Computational Linguistics.

Marjan Ghazvininejad, Hila Gonen, and Luke Zettlemoyer. 2023. Dictionary-based phrase-level prompting of large language models for machine translation. *Preprint*, arXiv:2302.07856.

Kristina Gligoric, Myra Cheng, Lucia Zheng, Esin Durmus, and Dan Jurafsky. 2024. Nlp systems that can't tell use from mention censor counterspeech, but teaching the distinction helps. *Preprint*, arXiv:2404.01651.

Jo Guldi. 2023. *The Dangerous Art of Text Mining: A Methodology for Digital History*. Cambridge University Press, Cambridge.

Eun S. Jo. 2020. *Foreign Relations of the United States Series, 1860-1980: A Study in New Archival History*. Ph.D. thesis, ProQuest Dissertations and Theses. Copyright - Database copyright ProQuest LLC; ProQuest does not claim copyright in the individual underlying works; Last updated - 2023-06-21.

Uğur Koç. 2020. *Bir Osmanlı Türk askerinin maceralı esirlik hikayesi: Temeşvarlı Osman Ağa'nın Esaretnâmesi'nin orijinal ve sadeleştirilmemiş Latin harfleriyle transkripsiyonu*. Unknown, Istanbul.

Richard F. Kreutel and Otto Spies. 1954. *Leben und Abenteuer des Dolmetschers Osman Ağa: Eine türkische Autobiographie aus der Zeit der großen Kriege gegen Österreich*. Selbstverlag des Orientalischen Seminars der Universität Bonn, Bonn.

Geoffrey L. Lewis. 1984. Atatürk's language reform as an aspect of modernization in the republic of turkey. In Jacob M. Landau, editor, *Atatürk and the Modernization of Turkey*, 1st edition, page 19. Routledge, New York. First published 1984. eBook published 16 June 2019.

Eva Martínez Garcia and Álvaro García Tejedor. 2020. Latin-Spanish neural machine translation: from the Bible to saint augustine. In *Proceedings of LT4HALA 2020 - 1st Workshop on Language Technologies for Historical and Ancient Languages*, pages 94–99, Marseille, France. European Language Resources Association (ELRA).

Şaziye Özateş, Tarık Tıraş, Efe Genç, and Esma Bilgin Tasdemir. 2024. Dependency annotation of Ottoman Turkish with multilingual BERT. In *Proceedings of The 18th Linguistic Annotation Workshop (LAW-XVIII)*, pages 188–196, St. Julians, Malta. Association for Computational Linguistics.

Kishore Papineni, Salim Roukos, Todd Ward, and Wei-Jing Zhu. 2002. Bleu: a method for automatic evaluation of machine translation. In *Proceedings of the 40th Annual Meeting of the Association for Computational Linguistics*, pages 311–318, Philadelphia, Pennsylvania, USA. Association for Computational Linguistics.

Alicia Parrish, Angelica Chen, Nikita Nangia, Vishakh Padmakumar, Jason Phang, Jana Thompson, Phu Mon Htut, and Samuel R. Bowman. 2022. Bbq: A hand-built bias benchmark for question answering. *Preprint*, arXiv:2110.08193.

Maja Popović. 2015. chrF: character n-gram F-score for automatic MT evaluation. In *Proceedings of the Tenth Workshop on Statistical Machine Translation*, pages 392–395, Lisbon, Portugal. Association for Computational Linguistics.

Steinthor Steingrímsson, Hrafn Loftsson, and Andy Way. 2023. SentAlign: Accurate and scalable sentence alignment. In *Proceedings of the 2023 Conference on Empirical Methods in Natural Language Processing: System Demonstrations*, pages 256–263, Singapore. Association for Computational Linguistics.

Garrett Tanzer, Mirac Suzgun, Eline Visser, Dan Jurafsky, and Luke Melas-Kyriazi. 2024. A benchmark for learning to translate a new language from one grammar book. *Preprint*, arXiv:2309.16575.

Gemini Team. 2024. Gemini 1.5: Unlocking multimodal understanding across millions of tokens of context. *Preprint*, arXiv:2403.05530.

Brian Thompson and Philipp Koehn. 2019. Vecalign: Improved sentence alignment in linear time and space. In *Proceedings of the 2019 Conference on Empirical Methods in Natural Language Processing and the 9th International Joint Conference on Natural Language Processing (EMNLP-IJCNLP)*, pages 1342–1348, Hong Kong, China. Association for Computational Linguistics.

Jörg Tiedemann. 2020. The Tatoeba Translation Challenge – Realistic data sets for low resource and multilingual MT. In *Proceedings of the Fifth Conference on Machine Translation*, pages 1174–1182, Online. Association for Computational Linguistics.

Erik J. Zürcher. 2004. *Turkey: A Modern History*, 3rd edition. I.B. Tauris, London, UK.

A Appendix: Figures

Vertex AI SDK basic usage

Below is a simple example that demonstrates how to prompt the Gemini 1.5 Pro model using the Vertex AI SDK. Learn more about the Gemini API parameters.

```
# Load a example model with system instructions
example_model = GenerativeModel(
    MODEL_ID,
    system_instruction=[
        "You are a helpful language translator.",
        "Your mission is to translate text in English to French.",
    ],
)

# Set model parameters
generation_config = GenerationConfig(
    temperature=0.9,
    top_p=1.0,
    top_k=32,
    candidate_count=1,
    max_output_tokens=8192,
)

# Set safety settings
safety_settings = {
    HarmCategory.HARM_CATEGORY_HARASSMENT: HarmBlockThreshold.BLOCK_LOW_AND_ABOVE,
    HarmCategory.HARM_CATEGORY_HATE_SPEECH: HarmBlockThreshold.BLOCK_LOW_AND_ABOVE,
    HarmCategory.HARM_CATEGORY_SEXUALLY_EXPLICIT: HarmBlockThreshold.BLOCK_LOW_AND_ABOVE,
    HarmCategory.HARM_CATEGORY_DANGEROUS_CONTENT: HarmBlockThreshold.BLOCK_LOW_AND_ABOVE,
}

prompt = """
  User input: I like bagels.
  Answer:
"""

# Set contents to send to the model
contents = [prompt]

# Counts tokens
print(example_model.count_tokens(contents))
```

```
# Prompt the model to generate content
response = example_model.generate_content(
    contents,
    generation_config=generation_config,
    safety_settings=safety_settings,
)

# Print the model response
print(f"\nAnswer:\n{response.text}")
print(f'\nUsage metadata:\n{response.to_dict().get("usage_metadata")}')
print(f"\nFinish reason:\n{response.candidates[0].finish_reason}")
print(f"\nSafety settings:\n{response.candidates[0].safety_ratings}")
```

```
total_tokens: 14
total_billable_characters: 29


Answer:
J'aime les bagels.


Usage metadata:
{'prompt_token_count': 14, 'candidates_token_count': 8, 'total_token_count': 22}

Finish reason:
1

Safety settings:
[category: HARM_CATEGORY_HATE_SPEECH
probability: NEGLIGIBLE
probability_score: 0.15077754855155945
severity: HARM_SEVERITY_NEGLIGIBLE
severity_score: 0.07821868986494064
, category: HARM_CATEGORY_DANGEROUS_CONTENT
probability: NEGLIGIBLE
probability_score: 0.06730107963085175
severity: HARM_SEVERITY_NEGLIGIBLE
severity_score: 0.09089674800634384
, category: HARM_CATEGORY_HARASSMENT
probability: NEGLIGIBLE
probability_score: 0.12527924776887727
severity: HARM_SEVERITY_NEGLIGIBLE
severity_score: 0.08525123447179794
, category: HARM_CATEGORY_SEXUALLY_EXPLICIT
probability: NEGLIGIBLE
probability_score: 0.21068390770435333
severity: HARM_SEVERITY_NEGLIGIBLE
severity_score: 0.11260009557008743
]
```

Figure 6: Gemini Example Code

Optimizing Cost-Efficiency with LLM-Generated Training Data for Conversational Semantic Frame Analysis

Shiho Matta†, Yin Jou Huang†, Fei Cheng†, Hirokazu Kiyomaru*, Yugo Murawaki†
†Kyoto University
*NII LLMC
{matta, huang, feicheng, murawaki}@nlp.ist.i.kyoto-u.ac.jp,
kiyomaru@nii.ac.jp

Abstract

Recent studies have shown that few-shot learning enables large language models (LLMs) to generate training data for supervised models at a low cost. However, for complex tasks, the quality of LLM-generated data often falls short compared to human-labeled data. This presents a critical challenge: how should one balance the trade-off between the higher quality but more expensive human-annotated data and the lower quality yet significantly cheaper LLM-generated data? In this paper, we tackle this question for a demanding task: conversational semantic frame analysis (SFA). To address this, we propose a novel method for synthesizing training data tailored to this complex task. Through experiments conducted across a wide range of budget levels, we find that smaller budgets favor a higher reliance on LLM-generated data to achieve optimal cost-efficiency.

1 Introduction

It is costly to construct training data with human annotation for supervised learning models (SLMs). In recent years, large language models (LLMs) like GPT-4 have demonstrated remarkable abilities in generating coherent text, understanding context, and following complex specifications to accomplish tasks (Brown et al., 2020; OpenAI, 2024). Therefore, there have been many attempts to leverage existing LLMs as data synthesizers to generate training data for SLMs, aiming to reduce data costs. Studies have indicated that using LLM-generated data can cut costs significantly while achieving a comparable performance against human-annotated data for certain tasks (Wang et al., 2021; Ding et al., 2023).

In this paper, we explore the feasibility of synthesizing training data for conversational semantic frame analysis (SFA). SFA captures knowledge exchanged between speakers by extracting semantic frames, which consist of a **trigger** (the main action) and its **arguments** (details of the event). For example, in Figure 1, the triggers "line up" (*PLACE*) and "fry" (*BAKE_FRY*) are annotated, with corresponding arguments like *Object*, *Time*, and *Temperature* linked to them. An important characteristic of these dialogues is the frequent repetition and confirmation of technical details. For example, in Figure 1, the interviewer's question introduces a new argument to an existing frame. Refer to Figure 12 in Appendix for a longer and more complex annotation example.

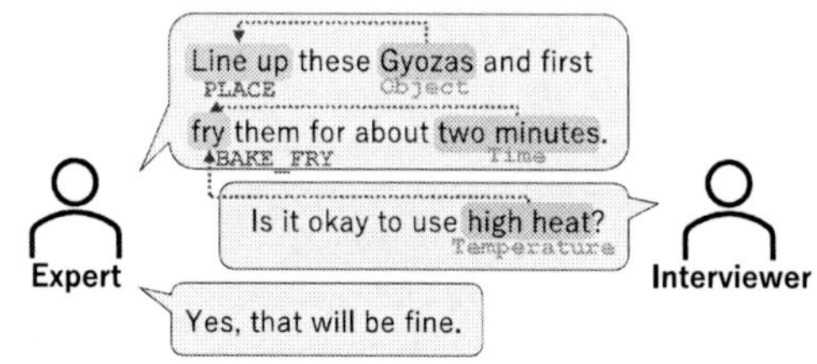

Figure 1: A dialogue piece with semantic frame annotation. Green indicates a trigger, and orange indicates an argument. The argument-trigger relation is illustrated with arrows. This is a simplified demonstration translated from Japanese.

We expect LLM-generated data for SFA to be of lower quality than human-annotated data, as SFA is significantly more complex than the tasks typically addressed in previous LLM-based data synthesis studies (Wang et al., 2021; Ding et al., 2023; He et al., 2024; Josifoski et al., 2023). These studies have primarily focused on simpler tasks such as sentence-level labeling, extracting relation triplets, or tasks with fewer recurring entities and relations. Furthermore, Ma et al. (2023) demonstrated that few-shot LLMs generally underperform in many information extraction tasks, such as named entity recognition, compared to supervised baselines. Given these findings, it is reasonable to expect that LLM-generated data for SFA will also be of lower quality than human-annotated data.

Given that LLM-generated data for SFA may

Proceedings of LaTeCH-CLfL 2025, pages 238–251
May 4, 2025 ©2025 Association for Computational Linguistics

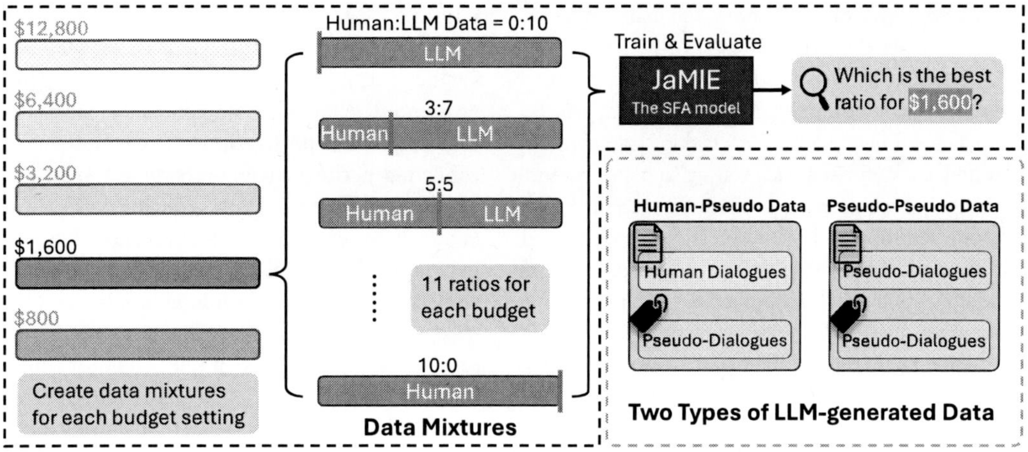

Figure 2: The overview of the cost-efficiency analysis. We mixed human data and LLM-generated data to create data mixtures up to a specific budget. The ratio of human data to LLM-generated data was adjusted in increments of 0.1. These data mixtures were then used to train our SFA model to identify the ratio that achieves optimal cost-efficiency.

be of lower quality compared to human data, it is not feasible to simply replace all human data with LLM-generated data, despite the latter being significantly cheaper. Instead, it becomes essential to consider the **trade-off** between the higher quality of human data and the lower cost of LLM-generated data. This trade-off is particularly relevant in scenarios where the budget is limited. This raises the research question: How to adjust the ratio of human to LLM-generated data within a fixed budget for optimal performance?

We address this question by synthesizing LLM-generated training data and combining it with human-annotated data to train the SLM, evaluating whether this combination achieves optimal performance within the budget (Figure 2). This process is repeated across a wide range of budget settings, from as low as $200 to as high as $12,800. For each budget level, we experiment with different ratios of human and LLM-generated data to identify the combination that maximizes cost-efficiency.

We propose a novel method for synthesizing training data using an LLM for the challenging task of SFA, generating two types of data: Human-Pseudo (HP) and Pseudo-Pseudo (PP). PP data comprises pseudo-dialogues and pseudo-labels that are both synthesized by an LLM, whereas HP data combines human dialogues sampled from a human-annotated dataset with pseudo-labels generated by the LLM. By comparing the performance of models trained on HP and PP data, we aim to determine whether the text component (dialogues) or the label component plays a more critical role in improving SFA performance in this situation.

Our empirical results reveal a clear trend across various budget levels: as the budget decreases, the optimal ratio shifts toward relying more on LLM-generated data. Conversely, when the budget is sufficiently large, incorporating LLM-generated data can actually harm performance. Another key contribution of our work is the direct comparison between HP and PP data. Our findings demonstrate that PP data is highly competitive with HP data, indicating that, in this context, replacing human-generated text with LLM-generated text is a viable and cost-effective option. We believe our findings can be applied to SFA in other technical domains or similar tasks (e.g., frame semantic parsing).

2 Related Work

Semantic Frame Analysis (SFA) / Frame Semantics in Dialogues Semantic frame analysis is a task inspired by frame-semantic parsing (FSP) and semantic role labeling (SRL). Unlike the FrameNet project used in FSP (Baker et al., 1998) or PropBank used in SRL (Kingsbury and Palmer, 2002), the frame design in semantic frame analysis differs in two ways: (1) the trigger types are domain-specific and predicate-centered, and (2) the argument types are frame-agnostic and domain-agnostic, meaning that a fixed set of argument types is used across various technical domains. Here, we refer to the process of identifying the span and type of triggers and arguments as **Trigger Detection** and **Argument Detection**.

Frame semantics can be used to capture critical information in dialogue situations. Skachkova and

Kruijff-Korbayova (2021) proposed using frame semantics in the domain of disaster response. The extracted information is used to capture and interpret verbal team communication for mission process assistance. Ebner et al. (2020) tackled argument detection in a multi-sentence setting to better capture events that span across sentences, which is similar to our setting that is done on the dialogue level. In this study, we focus on conversational SFA in Japanese interview dialogues, using the cooking section of the EIDC dataset (Okahisa et al., 2022; Chika et al., 2024) for the experiments and analyses.

Supervised Learning Models (SLMs) for SFA Previous studies have employed probabilistic model (Das et al., 2010) and RNN-based model (Swayamdipta et al., 2017) as SLMs for FSP. Kalyanpur et al. (2020) introduced Transformer-based models (Vaswani et al., 2017) to FSP, utilizing a sequence-to-sequence Transformer model and framing FSP as a text generation task by tagging entities with index numbers for tokens. In Matta et al. (2023), an encoder transformer model was used to address SFA in a cascaded manner: first, a trigger detection model identifies triggers within the context, and then a separate argument detection model determines the arguments for each trigger. However, we are concerned that this cascaded approach might introduce error propagation. Therefore, in this paper, we adopt JaMIE (Cheng et al., 2022), an encoder-centric model that simultaneously detects entities and their relations, offering an end-to-end solution for SFA.

LLMs for SFA-like tasks While no existing work directly targets SFA using LLMs, recent studies have explored related tasks, such as named entity recognition (NER) and relation extraction (RE). Wang et al. (2023a) reformulated NER as a text-generation task by wrapping entities in tag pairs, allowing LLMs to process them efficiently. Zhang et al. (2023) and Wan et al. (2023) enhanced LLM performance on RE tasks by improving prompt design. Sun et al. (2023) tackled various NLP tasks, including NER and RE, by utilizing improved prompting and few-shot retrieval methods, similar to the approaches in Wang et al. (2023a) and Wan et al. (2023). These studies, along with the method proposed by Kalyanpur et al. (2020), have inspired our prompt design for SFA using an LLM (Figure 4).

LLMs as Data Synthesizers There have been numerous efforts to utilize LLMs for generating synthetic data to train SLMs. Wang et al. (2021) utilized few-shot GPT-3 to generate labels for natural language understanding and generation tasks, achieving performance comparable to human labeling while significantly reducing costs. Ding et al. (2023) explored various methodologies for generating labeled data using GPT-3 and demonstrated results on par with human-labeled data in tasks such as sentiment triplet extraction. He et al. (2024) employed GPT-3.5 with chain-of-thought reasoning (Wei et al., 2023) as an alternative to crowdsourced annotators, demonstrating performance that was either superior to or on par with human annotators. However, these studies focus on tasks that are less complex than SFA. They either involve a single label per sequence, extract fewer entities, or do not include relations. Additionally, they do not provide an analysis of the trade-off between human and LLM-generated data.

3 Preliminaries

We define Semantic Frame Analysis (SFA) and introduce the EIDC dataset (Okahisa et al., 2022; Chika et al., 2024), which contains SFA annotations and is used in this study.

3.1 Semantic Frame Analysis (SFA)

Semantic frame analysis aims to extract semantic frames, which represent events, in a given context. The core of a semantic frame is a **trigger**, which is a predicate and the main action of the event. Since each frame has only one trigger, we refer to the frame type by the trigger type from now on without further notice. The event can also include associated details, such as the object, instrument, or temperature, referred to as frame **arguments**, linked to the event-evoking trigger. Note that different from frame designs such as the FrameNet project (Baker et al., 1998), argument types in the EIDC dataset are designed to be both frame-agnostic and domain-agnostic, meaning all frames can accept arguments such as *Object*, *Time*, *Manner*, etc.

SFA consists of two parts: **Trigger Detection** and **Argument Detection**. In trigger detection, the task is to identify the spans of triggers and classify their types, which functions similarly to a named entity recognition task. In argument detection, the goal is not only to identify the spans and types of arguments but also to determine their associated triggers. During evaluation, an argument prediction is considered incorrect if its association with a trigger is wrong, even if the span and type are correctly identified. Additionally, a single trigger can have multiple associated arguments. Our proposed data synthesis method (Section 4.2) can generate data for SFA while adhering to these conditions.

3.2 Technical Interview Dialogue Dataset with SFA Annotation

In this paper, we utilize the *cooking* section of the EIDC dataset (Okahisa et al., 2022; Chika et al., 2024). Note that when referring to the EIDC dataset, we specifically mean the cooking section unless stated otherwise. Examples of dialogues and SFA annotations in this domain are presented in Figure 1 and 12.

Technical Interview Dialogues The EIDC dataset contains interview dialogues where an expert discusses cooking processes with an interviewer. The expert introduces and explains a recipe spontaneously or in response to the interviewer's questions. The interviewer is asked to actively elicit knowledge about the cooking process through interactions, such as asking questions.

Annotation for Semantic Frame Analysis Each dialogue in the EIDC dataset comes with manual annotations of SFA. Human annotators manually assign labels to the dialogues with reference to the annotation guideline, which defines how to label entities and relations in the context and provides demonstrations. We also extracted these information from the annotation guideline and used them in the system prompt for the LLM. The trigger types represents cooking actions such as bake frying and cutting because the semantic frames are designed to capture cooking-related events. A complete list of entity types can be found in Appendix A.6. The original paper by Chika et al. (2024) presents inter-annotator agreement scores, including Cohen's kappa, to demonstrate annotation quality.

4 Data Synthesis With an LLM

This section presents our methodology for constructing training data for conversational semantic frame analysis using an LLM.

4.1 Pseudo-dialogue Generation

To generate pseudo-dialogues, the LLM is prompted with few-shot dialogues and asked to generate new ones that are close to the few-shots in format but contain different contents (Figure 3). For the few-shot examples, we not only sample from a preserved pool of human dialogues but also adopt the self-instruct strategy (Wang et al., 2023b) to sample from the previously generated pseudo-dialogues to increase diversity. The pre-filtering and post-filtering methods, along with the detailed settings for the self-instruction of pseudo-dialogues, are explained in Section 5.1.

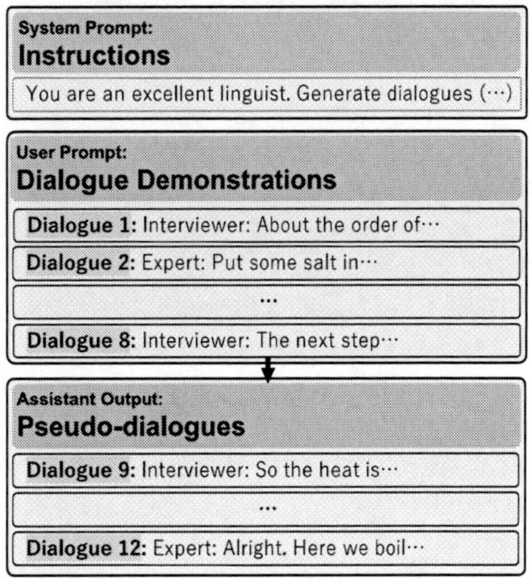

Figure 3: The overview of the prompt design for pseudo-dialogue generation. Refer to the actual prompt design in Appendix A.3.

4.2 Pseudo-labels by LLM

We apply pseudo-labels to the dialogues via a novel three-step tagging and labeling prompting scheme that converts SFA into a text generation task. An example of this pseudo-labeling process is illustrated in Figure 4. The steps are as follows, given an input context:

1. **Entity Tagging**: Insert entity tags (<En> and </En>, $n \in \mathbb{N}$) to mark the start and end of entities.

2. **Trigger Detection**: Identify the triggers among the entities tagged in Step 1.

3. **Relation Detection**: Determine argument relations among the entities tagged in Step 1.

This output format captures multiple entities and relations simultaneously and can be easily converted into the data format required by the SLM. We provide type definitions as outlined in the annotation guidelines within the system prompt and

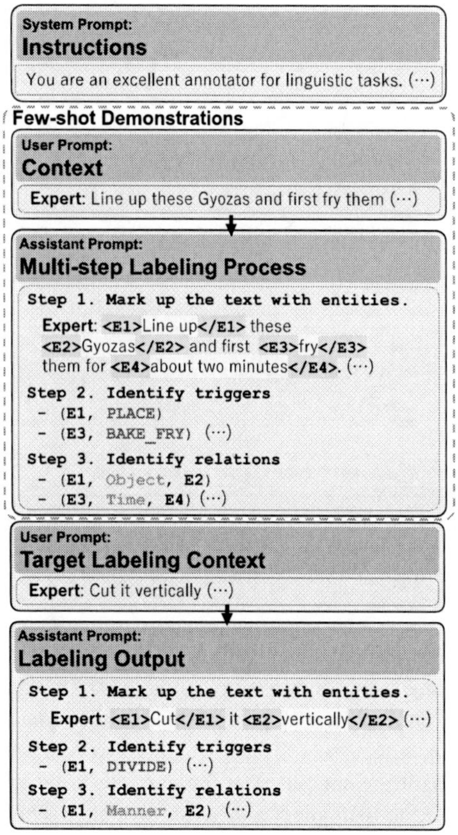

Figure 4: We designed a novel multi-step labeling scheme for LLMs to handle SFA in text generation. Refer to the full prompt design in Appendix A.4.

demonstrate the tagging process using a few-shot approach.

4.3 Data Variants

We construct three data variants used in this study: Human-Human (HH), Human-Pseudo (HP), and Pseudo-Pseudo (PP). In this context, "Human" refers to data collected from humans, while "Pseudo" denotes data generated by an LLM. We did not consider a Pseudo-Human variant because human annotation is too precious to be assigned to lower-quality LLM-generated dialogues.

Human-Human (HH) We sampled human dialogues and labels directly from the EIDC dataset and formed HH data. The Human-Human data is the most expensive and is also expected to have the highest label accuracy, closely aligning with the desired standards defined in the annotation guidelines.

Human-Pseudo (HP) In HP data, SFA labels are assigned by an LLM to human dialogues sampled from the EIDC dataset using the pseudo-labeling method from Section 4.2.

Pseudo-Pseudo (PP) PP data is fully synthesized, with LLM-generated dialogues and labels.

5 Experimental Settings

To study how to achieve optimal cost-efficiency by collecting both human and LLM-generated data with a fixed budget, we conducted the following steps for the experiments.

1. **Collecting data**: Sample/synthesize Human-Human (HH), Human-Pseudo (HP), and Pseudo-Pseudo (PP) data.

2. **Defining budget settings**: Define a range of budgets to simulate the fixed budget scenario.

3. **Creating HH+HP and HH+PP mixtures**: For each budget setting, construct human and LLM-generated data mixtures to simulate budget allocations.

4. **Training and evaluating the SFA model**: Train the SFA model using the data mixtures and evaluate its performance to identify the optimal data ratio.

In the following sections, we provide detailed descriptions of these steps. An overview of the cost-efficiency analysis is demonstrated in Figure 2.

5.1 Details of Data Synthesis Procedures

We provide details on the data synthesis procedures. We reserved 3 dialogues[1] from the EIDC training data as few-shot examples for both the pseudo-dialogue generation and pseudo-labeling process.

Pseudo Dialogue Generator As introduced in Section 4.1, we adopted the self-instruct strategy (Wang et al., 2023b) to bootstrap pseudo-dialogue generation. Following the settings in their work, we provide the model with 6 human dialogues and 2 pseudo-dialogues as few-shots. We synthesized the first 100 pseudo-dialogues with only human dialogues as few-shots. Afterward, we moved on to mixing few-shot examples. Before adding pseudo-dialogues back into the dialogue pool, we filtered them by ROUGE-L score (<0.7) against

[1] To fit within the context length limits of both the LLM and the SLM, we divide dialogues into smaller **sessions** using a heuristic method. Hereafter, a 'dialogue' will refer to a 'dialogue session' unless otherwise specified. Each session consists of up to 10 utterances.

Data Type	Data Size (Sessions)	Cost		
		Text ($)	Label ($)	Total ($)
Human-Human	1,472	6.4k	6.4k	12.8k
Human-Pseudo	2,858	12.4k	0.37k	12.8k
Pseudo-Pseudo	4,293	0.28k	0.56k	0.84k

Table 1: The size and cost statistics of the three data variants.

existing dialogues to ensure that the newly generated ones were not extremely similar to the existing ones. None of the pseudo-dialogues exceeded this limit. We then filtered the most similar ones using ROUGE-L to reduce them to the desired size shown in Table 1, which ended with a max ROUGE-L score of 0.52. We used GPT-4-0613 (accessed 01/2024) and set the generation temperature to 0.7, the presence penalty to 2.

Pseudo SFA Labeler We adopted GPT-4-0613 (accessed 01/2024) to generate pseudo-labels for SFA. For few-shots, we sampled 3 complete human dialogues, then filtered them to remove sessions with too few entities, resulting in 37 dialogue sessions. For each labeling target, we used 3 few-shots: the top 2 most similar dialogue sessions, determined by the ROUGE-L score to ensure similarity to the target, and 1 specially preserved dialogue session containing as many as 30 entities. This special few-shot was included in all cases because we empirically observed that GPT-4 tends to overlook entities if the few-shots lack sufficient entities.We conducted an ablation study to determine this prompt design, which we report in Appendix A.1. We further provide a case analysis of LLM-generated labels in Appendix A.2.

5.2 Data and Budget Settings

We provide details on the data statistics, data mixtures, and budget settings.

Data Statistics As shown in Table 1, we collected up to $12,800 for both HH and HP data, which roughly aligns with the three-year total of scholarship funds for a PhD student at a Japanese university.[2] For HH data, we sampled $12,800 worth of human dialogue and label pairs from the EIDC dataset, out of a maximum of 4,600 instances and a total cost of $40,000 of the original dataset. For HP data, we repeatedly sampled human dialogues in the EIDC dataset and then applied pseudo-labels to them until the cost reached $12,800, which was calculated based on the cumulative costs of the human dialogues and OpenAI API usage. For PP data, due to the low cost of both pseudo-dialogue and pseudo-labels, we collected 1.5x times the data size compared to HP data while only costing $840. The costs for pseudo-dialogues and pseudo-labels were also calculated from the token usage of the OpenAI API service. We ceased further collection of PP data upon discovering that performance had reached saturation and would not improve with additional data.

We conducted a quantitative analysis comparing human dialogues and pseudo-dialogues. We found that the average length of pseudo-dialogues generated by GPT-4 was similar to that of human dialogues (127 tokens vs. 136 tokens) and exhibited fewer extreme outliers in terms of length. By comparing the label density of HP and PP data, we observed that pseudo-dialogues tended to contain more entities than human dialogues, leading to a higher count for certain label types. For more details on the length and label distributions of pseudo-dialogues, refer to Appendix A.5 and Appendix A.6.

Data Mixtures We create two types of data mixtures: **HH+HP**[3] and **HH+PP mixtures**, to simulate the situation where one collects human data and LLM-generated data at the same time. Refer to Appendix A.8 for a demonstration of the budget allocation between the two types of data.

Budget Settings We set different budget ranges for the HH+HP mixture and the HH+PP mixture, with the budget range for the latter being lower due to the significantly lower cost of PP data. For each budget, we adjust the proportion of HH data within the budget from 0 to 1 with an interval of 0.1, creating 11 ratio variants for each budget level.

- For HH+HP mixture ($):
  800, 1,200, 1,600, 3,200, 6,400, 12,800

[2]We excluded the collection cost of few-shot examples sampled from the training split of the EIDC dataset, as well as the instructions derived from the annotation guidelines.

[3]When creating HH+HP mixtures, we avoided choosing data with the same human dialogues to avoid confusion to the SFA model.

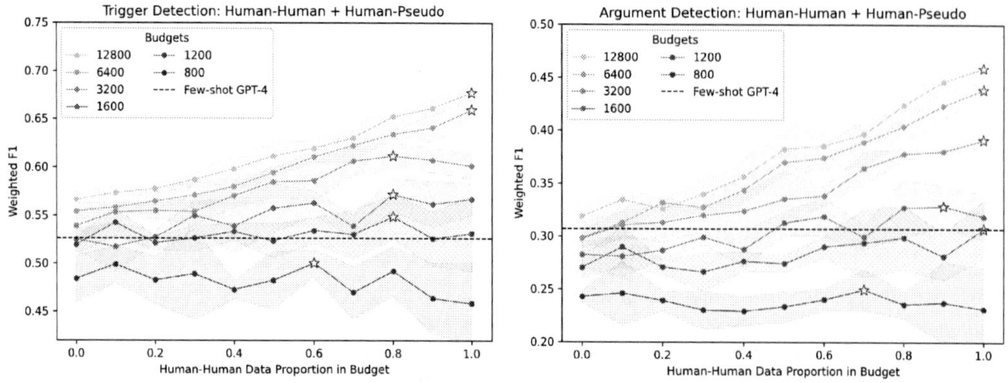

Figure 5: The cost-efficiency plot for HH+HP mixture. The black dotted line represents the performance of few-shot GPT-4. Each budget curve features a star marking its optimal point. The shaded region around each curve indicates the standard deviation across five different seeds.

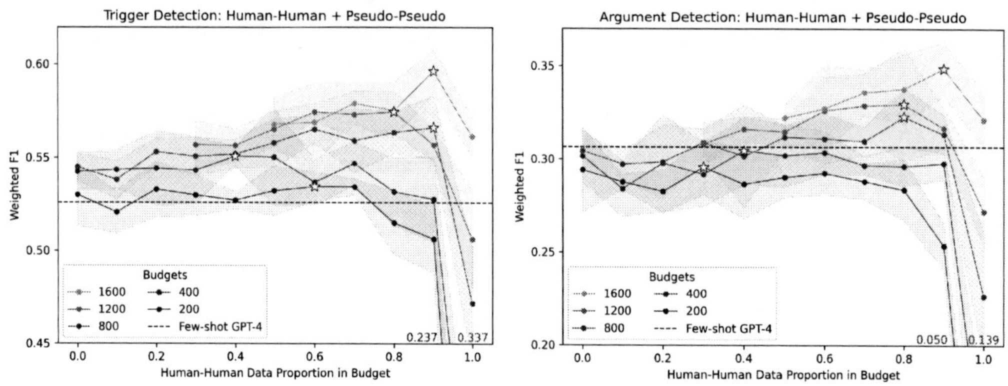

Figure 6: The cost-efficiency plot for HH+PP mixture. Due to the collection limit of $840 worth of PP data, the plot only shows the right portion of the curve for budgets $1,200 and $1,600, where the data is combined with HH data. The values of some outlier points are displayed on the plot with colors corresponding to the budget curve.

- For HH+PP mixture ($):
  200, 400, 800, 1,200, 1,600

5.3 Supervised Learning Model and Evaluation Metrics for SFA

We adopt JaMIE (Cheng et al., 2022) as our supervised learning model (SLM) for SFA. JaMIE is an architecture featuring one transformer encoder and multiple decoding heads for sequence labeling and can handle relation extraction by design. We employ the Japanese DeBERTa-V2-base as the pretrained encoder for JaMIE and train the decoding heads from scratch.[4] Refer to the training hyperparameters in Appendix A.7.

We evaluated the performance of Trigger Detection and Argument Detection using a classification metric that accounts for both the type and span accuracy of entities.[5] Correct predictions require both the entity's type and span to be accurate. We award partial scores if the predicted entity's type is correct but the span only overlaps with the true answer. Argument predictions are marked false if their associated trigger is incorrect.[6] The overall performance is measured using a weighted F1 score, aggregated from the F1 scores of each class.

6 Results and Analyses

The objectives of the cost-efficiency analysis are as follows:

1. **Optimal Data Ratio**: What is the optimal ratio for combining human data and LLM-generated data within a limited budget? Is the ratio budget-dependent?

2. **HP vs. PP**: Should one pay more to collect human-dialogues instead of pseudo-dialogues

[4] https://huggingface.co/ku-nlp/deberta-v2-base-japanese

[5] We modified the evaluation code from seqeval (https://github.com/chakki-works/seqeval).

[6] In addition to semantic frames, the data also included Event Coreference Relations (ECR). We did not evaluate ECR directly, however, we evaluated argument detection by allowing the target trigger to be any of the events on the same ECR event sequence in the true labels.

for a potential performance increase?

We analyze the experimental results to answer these objectives in the following sections.

6.1 Cost-efficiency Analysis

In this section, we address the first objective: optimal data ratio for HH+HP and HH+PP mixtures, and if it is budget-dependent.

HH+HP Mixture In Figure 5, we observe that when the budget is lower than \$6,400 for trigger detection and \$3,200 for argument detection, optimal cost-efficiency is achieved by combining HH and HP data. The lower the budget is, the more HP data should be included for best performance. In this case, the trade-off between human data and LLM-generated data has a positive impact on the performance.

On the other hand, we see that when the budget is higher than above, the optimal cost-efficiency is brought by using 100% HH data. This shows that LLM-generated data cannot be used in all situations because it may harm the performance.

HH+PP Mixture In Figure 6, we see that for all the budgets we set, the optimal performance was achieved by combining HH and PP data. We specifically observed that since PP data is so much cheaper, allocating 10% of the budget to PP data in budget \$1,600 brought a significant performance boost for both trigger and argument detection. Although we did not further raise the budget for PP data, we can estimate that the optimal will be achieved by using 100% HH data if we raise the budget to \$6,400 and above. Therefore, we conclude that when the budget is not high enough to reach saturation (optimal performance by using 100% HH data), one should combine human and LLM-generated data and adjust the ratio to using more LLM-generated data as the budget declines.

6.2 Human-Pseudo vs. Pseudo-Pseudo

We further investigated the second objective: is HP data better than PP data for having human dialogues instead of pseudo-dialogues?

We observed no significant disadvantage caused by replacing human dialogues with pseudo-dialogues for LLM-generated data. In fact, with the same budget of \$1,600, one could achieve a slightly higher performance in trigger detection using PP data compared to HP data (0.596 in Figure 6 vs. 0.571 in Figure 5). Therefore, from a cost-sensitive perspective, PP data is a superior option.

6.3 Data Augmentation for Low-resource Setting

We review the effectiveness of LLM-generated data from a data augmentation perspective (Figure 7). In this setting, we trained the SLM first using all LLM-generated data, i.e., either all HP or PP data, then continued training it on different costs of HH data, ranging from \$800 to \$12,800. The result shows that when the amount of HH data is limited (lower than \$3,200), both HP and PP data help boost performance. The effectiveness of LLM-generated data is more significant when the budget for HH data is low. Notably, while the cost of PP data is significantly cheaper than HP data in this setting (\$840 vs. \$12,800), the former is arguably competitive against the latter as the max performance gap (green line vs. red line) is less than 0.02 F1 score.

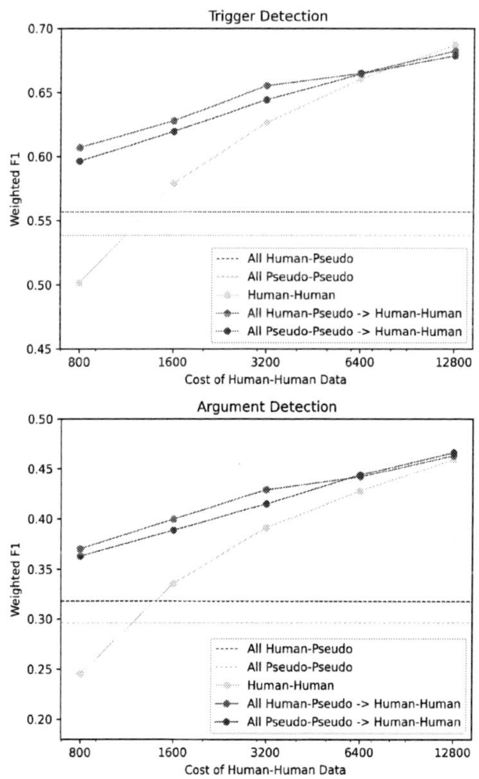

Figure 7: The effectiveness of LLM-generated data from a data augmentation perspective. We trained the SLM on all HP or PP data (blue and orange dotted lines), then continued training on different sizes of HH data (red and green lines).

7 Conclusion

In this paper, we conducted a comprehensive analysis to evaluate the cost-efficiency to combine

LLM-generated data with human-annotated data for Japanese conversational semantic frame analysis under various budget constraints. We proposed a novel method to synthesize two types of training data: Human-Pseudo (HP) data and Pseudo-Pseudo (PP) data, for the experiments and analyses. Our findings indicate that the ideal ratio to combine human and LLM-generated data is budget-dependent, with a tendency to favor a higher proportion of LLM-generated data as the budget decreases. Furthermore, our results suggest that fully synthesized data (PP data) is a viable option, as it is significantly cheaper while maintaining comparable performance levels to the half-synthesized counterpart (HP data). In future work, we aim to extend our analysis to other domains and tasks to validate the generalizability of our findings.

Limitations

While we believe our conclusions are comprehensive within our experimental settings, our work has several limitations. Firstly, determining the **exact** ratio of human to LLM-generated data remains challenging, as it depends on factors such as the specific task, dataset characteristics, and budget constraints. Secondly, we only focused on the task of SFA in the cooking domain in this work. We hope that future work could extend the findings of our work to other domains and related tasks.

References

Collin F. Baker, Charles J. Fillmore, and John B. Lowe. 1998. The Berkeley FrameNet project. In 36th Annual Meeting of the Association for Computational Linguistics and 17th International Conference on Computational Linguistics, Volume 1, pages 86–90, Montreal, Quebec, Canada. Association for Computational Linguistics.

Tom Brown, Benjamin Mann, Nick Ryder, Melanie Subbiah, Jared D Kaplan, Prafulla Dhariwal, Arvind Neelakantan, Pranav Shyam, Girish Sastry, Amanda Askell, et al. 2020. Language models are few-shot learners. Advances in neural information processing systems, 33:1877–1901.

Fei Cheng, Shuntaro Yada, Ribeka Tanaka, Eiji Aramaki, and Sadao Kurohashi. 2022. Jamie: A pipeline japanese medical information extraction system with novel relation annotation. In Proceedings of the Thirteenth Language Resources and Evaluation Conference (LREC 2022).

Taishi Chika, Taro Okahisa, Takashi Kodama, Yin Jou Huang, Yugo Murawaki, and Sadao Kurohashi. 2024. Domain transferable semantic frames for expert interview dialogues.

Dipanjan Das, Nathan Schneider, Desai Chen, and Noah A. Smith. 2010. Probabilistic frame-semantic parsing. In Human Language Technologies: The 2010 Annual Conference of the North American Chapter of the Association for Computational Linguistics, pages 948–956, Los Angeles, California. Association for Computational Linguistics.

Bosheng Ding, Chengwei Qin, Linlin Liu, Yew Ken Chia, Boyang Li, Shafiq Joty, and Lidong Bing. 2023. Is GPT-3 a good data annotator? In Proceedings of the 61st Annual Meeting of the Association for Computational Linguistics (Volume 1: Long Papers), pages 11173–11195, Toronto, Canada. Association for Computational Linguistics.

Seth Ebner, Patrick Xia, Ryan Culkin, Kyle Rawlins, and Benjamin Van Durme. 2020. Multi-sentence argument linking. In Proceedings of the 58th Annual Meeting of the Association for Computational Linguistics, pages 8057–8077, Online. Association for Computational Linguistics.

Xingwei He, Zhenghao Lin, Yeyun Gong, A-Long Jin, Hang Zhang, Chen Lin, Jian Jiao, Siu Ming Yiu, Nan Duan, and Weizhu Chen. 2024. AnnoLLM: Making large language models to be better crowdsourced annotators. In Proceedings of the 2024 Conference of the North American Chapter of the Association for Computational Linguistics: Human Language Technologies (Volume 6: Industry Track), pages 165–190, Mexico City, Mexico. Association for Computational Linguistics.

Martin Josifoski, Marija Sakota, Maxime Peyrard, and Robert West. 2023. Exploiting asymmetry for synthetic training data generation: SynthIE and the case of information extraction. In Proceedings of the 2023 Conference on Empirical Methods in Natural Language Processing, pages 1555–1574, Singapore. Association for Computational Linguistics.

Aditya Kalyanpur, Or Biran, Tom Breloff, Jennifer Chu-Carroll, Ariel Diertani, Owen Rambow, and Mark Sammons. 2020. Open-domain frame semantic parsing using transformers. Preprint, arXiv:2010.10998.

Paul Kingsbury and Martha Palmer. 2002. From Tree-Bank to PropBank. In Proceedings of the Third International Conference on Language Resources and Evaluation (LREC'02), Las Palmas, Canary Islands - Spain. European Language Resources Association (ELRA).

Yubo Ma, Yixin Cao, Yong Hong, and Aixin Sun. 2023. Large language model is not a good few-shot information extractor, but a good reranker for hard samples! In Findings of the Association for Computational Linguistics: EMNLP 2023, pages 10572–10601, Singapore. Association for Computational Linguistics.

Shiho Matta, Yin Jou Huang, Hirokazu Kiyomaru, and Sadao Kurohashi. 2023. Utilizing pseudo dialogue in conversational semantic frame analysis. ANLP2023.

Taro Okahisa, Ribeka Tanaka, Takashi Kodama, Yin Jou Huang, and Sadao Kurohashi. 2022. Constructing a culinary interview dialogue corpus with video conferencing tool. In Proceedings of the Thirteenth Language Resources and Evaluation Conference, pages 3131–3139, Marseille, France. European Language Resources Association.

OpenAI. 2024. Gpt-4 technical report. Preprint, arXiv:2303.08774.

Natalia Skachkova and Ivana Kruijff-Korbayova. 2021. Automatic assignment of semantic frames in disaster response team communication dialogues. In Proceedings of the 14th International Conference on Computational Semantics (IWCS), pages 93–109, Groningen, The Netherlands (online). Association for Computational Linguistics.

Xiaofei Sun, Linfeng Dong, Xiaoya Li, Zhen Wan, Shuhe Wang, Tianwei Zhang, Jiwei Li, Fei Cheng,

Lingjuan Lyu, Fei Wu, and Guoyin Wang. 2023. Pushing the limits of chatgpt on nlp tasks. Preprint, arXiv:2306.09719.

Swabha Swayamdipta, Sam Thomson, Chris Dyer, and Noah A. Smith. 2017. Frame-semantic parsing with softmax-margin segmental rnns and a syntactic scaffold. Preprint, arXiv:1706.09528.

Ashish Vaswani, Noam Shazeer, Niki Parmar, Jakob Uszkoreit, Llion Jones, Aidan N. Gomez, Lukasz Kaiser, and Illia Polosukhin. 2017. Attention is all you need. Preprint, arXiv:1706.03762.

Zhen Wan, Fei Cheng, Zhuoyuan Mao, Qianying Liu, Haiyue Song, Jiwei Li, and Sadao Kurohashi. 2023. Gpt-re: In-context learning for relation extraction using large language models. In Proceedings of the 2023 Conference on Empirical Methods in Natural Language Processing, pages 3534–3547.

Shuhe Wang, Xiaofei Sun, Xiaoya Li, Rongbin Ouyang, Fei Wu, Tianwei Zhang, Jiwei Li, and Guoyin Wang. 2023a. Gpt-ner: Named entity recognition via large language models. arXiv preprint arXiv:2304.10428.

Shuohang Wang, Yang Liu, Yichong Xu, Chenguang Zhu, and Michael Zeng. 2021. Want to reduce labeling cost? GPT-3 can help. In Findings of the Association for Computational Linguistics: EMNLP 2021, pages 4195–4205, Punta Cana, Dominican Republic. Association for Computational Linguistics.

Yizhong Wang, Yeganeh Kordi, Swaroop Mishra, Alisa Liu, Noah A. Smith, Daniel Khashabi, and Hannaneh Hajishirzi. 2023b. Self-instruct: Aligning language models with self-generated instructions. In Proceedings of the 61st Annual Meeting of the Association for Computational Linguistics (Volume 1: Long Papers), pages 13484–13508, Toronto, Canada. Association for Computational Linguistics.

Jason Wei, Xuezhi Wang, Dale Schuurmans, Maarten Bosma, Brian Ichter, Fei Xia, Ed Chi, Quoc Le, and Denny Zhou. 2023. Chain-of-thought prompting elicits reasoning in large language models. Preprint, arXiv:2201.11903.

Kai Zhang, Bernal Jiménez Gutiérrez, and Yu Su. 2023. Aligning instruction tasks unlocks large language models as zero-shot relation extractors. arXiv preprint arXiv:2305.11159.

A Appendix

A.1 Ablation for Prompt Design for Pseudo-labeling

We conducted an ablation study to determine the impact of different prompt design choices on pseudo-labeling performance and adopted one of the top-performing prompt designs. We evaluate the effects of varying instruction styles and few-shot selection strategies by measuring the performance of few-shot LLMs on the validation dataset, as detailed below:

- **Instruction Style**
  - w/ entity demo.: The instruction includes entity demonstrations.
  - wo/ entity demo.: The instruction only has a description for each entity type, but no examples are provided (Figure 13).
- **Few-shot Selection Methods**
  - By ROUGE-L: Examples are selected based on the highest ROUGE-L similarity score to the input.
  - Mandatory: A single hand-picked example that is entity-rich, containing up to 30 entities, is always included.
  - Random: Examples are randomly selected from the few-shot pool.

We observed that enabling ROUGE-L-based few-shot retrieval, incorporating the mandatory few-shot example, and providing entity demonstrations in the instruction generally improved performance. Additionally, not all LLMs performed well on SFA. For instance, GPT-4-1106-preview occasionally failed to recognize entities in the context, even when they were present. GPT-3.5-turbo-0125 exhibited similar errors but also struggled with output formatting, sometimes producing invalid outputs that had to be evaluated as empty predictions. Moreover, it suffered from hallucinations, generating non-existent entity types. Based on these observations, we conclude that SFA requires LLMs at least at the GPT-4 level to achieve reliable performance.

A.2 Case Analysis on LLM-generated labels

We conduct an error case analysis on two common types of mistakes made by the LLM during the

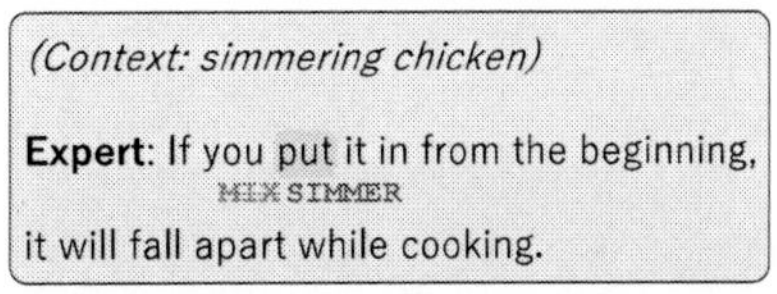

Figure 8: It is difficult for LLM to label correctly when it is necessary to infer the entity type from the context.

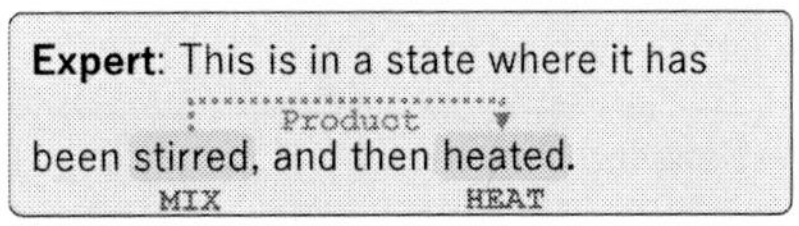

Figure 9: It is difficult for LLM to handle complex relations, such as *Product*.

pseudo-labeling process. These cases were identified by comparing HH and HP data, both of which contain the same human dialogues.

In the first case (Figure 8), the expert and interviewer discuss a simmering process in the preceding context. In this context, the action of *put* refers to placing something into boiling water and should therefore be labeled as *SIMMER*. However, the LLM tends to interpret the word literally, labeling it as *MIX* instead. It is challenging to instruct the model to account for this type of inference accurately.

Another common challenge for the LLM is handling complex argument relations, such as *Product*. *Product* is a unique type of argument that requires the argument itself to be an existing trigger. In Figure 9, the predicate *stirred* functions both as a *MIX* type trigger and as a *Product* argument for the trigger *heated*. However, the LLM failed to recognize the *Product* argument relation.

A.3 Prompt For Pseudo-dialogue Generation By LLM

An example of the prompt for pseudo-dialogue generation is shown in Figure 14.

A.4 Prompt For LLM SFA Labeling

The adopted prompt design for SFA labeling is shown in Figures 15, 16, and 17.

A.5 Length Distribution of Pseudo-dialogues

We present the length distributions of human dialogues and pseudo-dialogues in Figure 11. We observed that GPT-4 generally followed the length specification in the instruction, resulting in an average length of 127 tokens (token count by Japanese DeBERTa-V2 tokenizer) compared to an average of 136 tokens in human dialogue sessions. Moreover, pseudo-dialogues have a more short-tailed distribution, which means there are fewer extremely short or long outliers.

A.6 Label Distribution in Pseudo-dialogues

We present the label distributions across three data types: Human-Human, Human-Pseudo, and Pseudo-Pseudo in Figure 10. When comparing Human-Human to Human-Pseudo, we observe that replacing human labelers with GPT-4 leads to fluctuations in certain label types. Specifically, there is a decrease in types such as "BAKE_FRY" and "SIMMER" in triggers and "Manner" in arguments, and an increase in types like "PLACE" in triggers and "Instrument" in arguments. While we believe that these fluctuations will not be a significant issue, it is important to point out that in addition to the fluctuations, the labels generated by GPT-4 may not be accurate either.

When comparing Human-Pseudo to Pseudo-Pseudo, we observe that replacing human dialogues with pseudo-dialogues leads to a higher frequency of certain types than in human dialogues. For example, types like "MIX" and "BAKE_FRY" in triggers and all argument types appear more frequently. This increase occurs because GPT-4 tends to fit a whole story into a pseudo-dialogue, resulting in a higher overall entity count. In contrast, human dialogues are heuristically cut into smaller sessions, which can lead to fewer entities per session. Also, the increase in trigger types "MIX" and "BAKE_FRY" indicates that GPT-4 tends to mention these specific events, creating a bias toward specific topics.

A.7 Training Hyperparameters for the SLM

We adopted JaMIE (Cheng et al., 2022) as our SLM for SFA. For the encoder, we used a pre-trained Japanese DeBERTa-V2-base model with an encoder learning rate of 2e-5 and a relation decoder learning rate of 1e-2, without a learning rate schedule.[7] The model was trained for up to 30 epochs, and the best checkpoint was selected based on the highest validation weighted F1 score. The validation and test sets are defined in the EIDC dataset with sizes of 269 and 379 dialogue sessions, respectively.

[7]https://huggingface.co/ku-nlp/deberta-v2-base-japanese

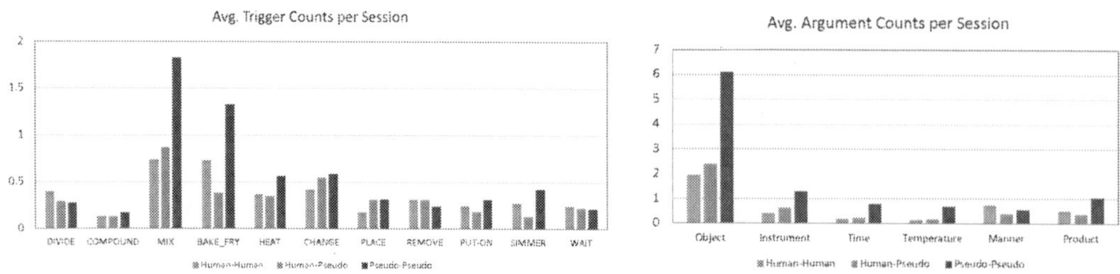

Figure 10: Trigger and argument label distribution.

LLM	Instruction	Few-shot Selection	T. F1	Arg. F1
GPT-3.5-turbo-0125	w/ entity demo.	2 by ROUGE-L + 1 mandatory	0.434	0.170
GPT-4-1106-preview	w/ entity demo.	2 by ROUGE-L + 1 mandatory	0.484	0.256
GPT-4-0613	w/ entity demo.	3 random	0.484	0.269
	w/ entity demo.	3 by ROUGE-L	0.519	0.277
	w/ entity demo.	2 random + 1 mandatory	0.513	0.293
	w/ entity demo.	1 by ROUGE-L + 1 mandatory	**0.519**	0.303
	w/o entity demo.	2 by ROUGE-L + 1 mandatory	0.460	0.245
GPT-4-0613†	w/ entity demo.	2 by ROUGE-L + 1 mandatory	0.514	**0.314**

Table 2: Ablation study on prompt design for pseudo-labeling. T. F1 and Arg. F1 denote the weighted-F1 scores for trigger and argument detection, respectively. † indicates the final prompt design chosen for pseudo-labeling. Performance is measured on the validation set.

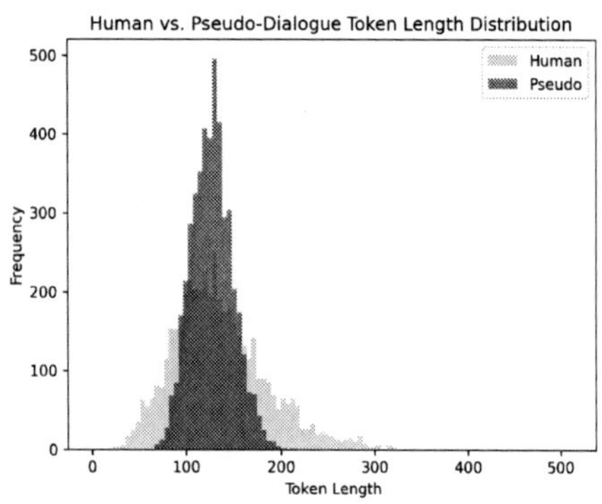

Figure 11: The length distributions of human and pseudo-dialogues.

A.8 Demonstration for Budget Allocation

For example, when one has $1,600 of budget and wants to allocate 30% ($480) of that to HH data and 70% ($1,120) to HP data, the final mixture will contain 55 instances of HH data and 250 instances of HP data.

- $1,600 (30% HH, 70% HP) = 55 ($480) HH + 250 ($1,120) HP

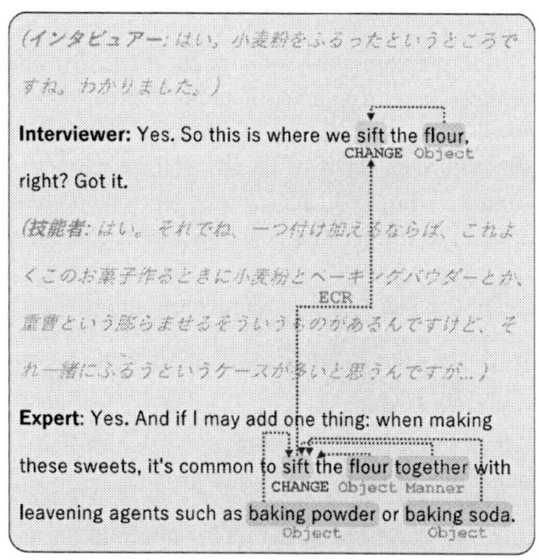

Figure 12: This human-annotated data example demonstrates that (1) the same event is mentioned across multiple utterances, (2) a single trigger can have multiple same type arguments, and (3) an ECR relation is present, although it is not directly evaluated in this paper. The example is translated from Japanese, and the original text is provided in gray italic font.

BAKE_FRY: 油を用いて火や熱源で調理する。~~（例：焼く、揚げる、炒める、焦がす、ローストする）~~

Figure 13: Without entity demonstration means to remove ~~the examples~~, only keeping the description.

```
System Prompt:

You are an excellent linguist.
Generate dialogues that are similar to the given dialogue
context's length, but have different content.
The dialogue should include an interviewer (インタビュアー)
and an expert (技能者), who will talk about the cooking
process of a dish.
The expert will try to explain the details of the cooking
process, and the interviewer will ask questions to clarify
the details.
Try to add details to the dialogue, such as the tools,
techniques, time, temperature, etc.
Dialogues can start or end halfway through the cooking
process.
Make sure each dialogue contains more than 3 turns.
Do NOT copy from existing dialogue context, make sure each
dialogue is diverse and creative.
Each dialogue must be in a single line, like the
demonstration from the user. Only start new lines when you
want to start a new dialogue piece.
The user will provide you with 8 example dialogue pieces.
You must continue generating from Dialogue 9 to Dialogue 12.

Few-shots:

Dialogue 1: 技能者:これは先ほどのレンコンのみじん切りと、あと長ネギ2
分の1本ぐらいを、これもみじん切りにしておきます。インタビュアー:うん、2
分の1本結構ね量を使われるんですね。技能者:そうですね、はい。インタビュ
アー:ヘルシー。技能者:はい。インタビュアー:もしネギ、青ネギとかでも大丈
夫なんですかね？技能者:もちろん大丈夫です。インタビュアー:大丈夫ですか。
技能者:はい。あと玉ねぎでも大丈夫です。インタビュアー:玉ねぎでも。いろ
いろ使えますね。家にある、あるものをなんか。

Dialogue 2: インタビュアー:このパスタソースの作り方について教えていた
だけますか？技能者:まずオリーブ油とにんにくをフライパンに入れ、香ばしい
匂いが立つまで炒めます。次にトマト缶を加えて5分ほど煮込みます。インタ
ビュアー:その後に塩コショウで調味するんですよね？技能者:はい、そして最
後にベーシックなパスタソースが完成します。あとはお好みでバジルやチーズ
を加えることもできます。インタビュアー:パスタは何分茹でると良いですか？
技能者:袋に記載されている時間通りに茹でると最適な硬さになりますよ。
(…)

Model Output:

Dialogue 9: インタビュアー:この焼き鳥の作り方について教えてもらえます
か？技能者:まず、鶏肉を一口大に切り分け、竹串に刺します。次に塩とコショ
ウで下味をつけ、炭火でじっくりと焼き上げます。インタビュアー:それはどれ
くらいの時間焼くのですか？技能者:各面がキツネ色になるまで約5分間ほど焼
きます。そして最後に特製のたれを塗って仕上げます。インタビュアー:その特
製のたれは何を使っていますか？技能者:主にしょうゆ、みりん、砂糖を基本と
しており、あとは秘密のスパイスが入っていますよ。
(…)
```

Figure 14: The prompt design for pseudo-dialogue generation. In this example, Dialogue 1 is a human dialogue, and Dialogue 2 is a previously generated pseudo-dialogue.

```
System Prompt:
You are an excellent annotator for linguistic tasks. You will be provided
with a piece of Japanese dialogue. Your task is to annotate it with labels
for semantic frame analysis.

Step 1. Mark up the text with entities.
Mark up the text using the following tags:
- <En>: The start of the n-th entity
- </En>: The end of the n-th entity

2. Identify triggers
Identify triggers from the extracted entities. Trigger types include:
- BAKE_FRY: 油を用いて火や熱源で調理する。（例: 焼く、揚げる、炒める、焦がす、ローストす
る）
- DIVIDE: 何かの全体ないしは部分を2つ以上に分ける。（例: 切る、刻む、割く、ほぐす、割る、
砕く、カットする、スライスする）
- CHANGE: 形状・向き・温度を変化させる。（例: 擦る、溶かす、冷ます、ひっくり返す、泡立て
る、潰す、広げる、伸ばす、こねる、発酵させる）
(…)
3. Identify Relations
Identify relations between entities. There are 3 categories of relations:
Argument, ECR and Product. Arguments should be further determined by types:
- Object: 当該の料理イベントの主たる材料を表す要素。（例: 豆腐、人参、お肉、じゃがいも、
葉っぱ）
- Instrument: 当該の料理イベントを実行するために用いる道具や調理器具を表す要素。（例: 包
丁、フライパン、冷水、泡立て器、鍋、ベーキングシート）「包丁で切る」、「泡立て器でよくかき
混ぜる」、「ひじきを冷水で戻す」などの形で現れる。
(…)
If two event triggers indeed refer to the same event/action, you should
label their relation as ECR. As for Product, if E2 uses the outcome from E1,
then you should label the two (E2, Product, E1).
```

Figure 15: The system prompt for the LLM. Some type definitions are omitted.

```
Few-shots:
user
技能者:これは豚挽肉をボウルに入れたところです。はい。
インタビュアー:お願いします。
技能者:はい。室温にし、室温でよくこねておきます。はい。
インタビュアー:はい。よくこねるというのは、だいたいどの状態が目安になりますか？
技能者:そうですね、ちょっとモチモチってなるぐらいまでこねていただければ。はい、そんなにハン
バーグのときほどこねないんですけれども。はい。
インタビュアー:はい。ハンバーグほどではない、なく、でもしっかりとこねる。
assistant
Step 1. Mark up the text with entities.
技能者:これは<E1>豚挽肉</E1>を<E2>ボウル</E2>に入れたところです。はい。
インタビュアー:お願いします。
技能者:はい。室温にし、<E3>室温</E3>で<E4>よく</E4><E5>こねて</E5>おきます。はい。
インタビュアー:はい。よくこねるというのは、だいたいどの状態が目安になりますか？
技能者:そうですね、ちょっとモチモチってなるぐらいまで<E6>こねて</E6>いただければ。はい、
そんなに<E7>ハンバーグのときほど</E7><E8>こね</E8>ないんですけれども。はい。
インタビュアー:はい。ハンバーグほどではない、なく、でも<E9>しっかりと</E9>こねる。

Step 2. Identify triggers (trigger entity, type).
- (E5, CHANGE)
- (E6, CHANGE)
- (E8, CHANGE)

Step 3. Identify argument and ECR relations (entity1, relation, entity2).
- (E5, Object, E1)
- (E5, Instrument, E2)
- (E5, Temperature, E3)
- (E5, Manner, E4)
- (E6, Manner, E9)
- (E6, ECR, E5)
- (E8, Manner, E7)
- (E8, ECR, E6)
```

Figure 16: The few-shot demonstration for the LLM. We show one example here.

```
Labeling Target:
user
技能者: 今日はフライドポテトの作り方についてお話します。
インタビュアー：さいの目に切ったジャガイモを直接揚げていくんですか？
技能者: 実はそうではありません。先に70～80℃でじっくりと揚げて水分を飛ばすのがポイントです。
インタビュアー：その後はどうすればいいんですか？
技能者: 一度取り出して油を切ったら、今度は180℃でサクッと揚げます。これにより外側はパリッ
と、中はホクホクのフライドポテトが完成します。
======================
Model output:
assistant
Step 1. Mark up the text with entities.
技能者: 今日は<E1>フライドポテト</E1>の作り方についてお話します。
インタビュアー：<E2>さいの目に切ったジャガイモ</E2>を直接<E3>揚げ</E3>ていくんですか？
技能者: 実はそうではありません。先に<E4>70～80℃</E4>でじっくりと<E5>揚げ</E5>て水分を
飛ばすのがポイントです。
インタビュアー：その後はどうすればいいんですか？
技能者: <E6>一度</E6><E7>取り出し</E7>て油を切ったら、今度は<E8>180℃</E8>でサクッと
<E9>揚げ</E9>ます。これにより外側はパリッと、中はホクホクのフライドポテトが完成します。

Step 2. Identify triggers (trigger entity, type).
- (E3, BAKE_FRY)
- (E5, BAKE_FRY)
- (E7, REMOVE)
- (E9, BAKE_FRY)

Step 3. Identify argument and ECR relations (entity1, relation, entity2).
- (E3, Object, E2)
- (E5, Temperature, E4)
- (E5, ECR, E3)
- (E7, Time, E6)
- (E9, Temperature, E8)
- (E9, Product, E7)
```

Figure 17: The input labeling target and an actual labeling output from the LLM. This is an example from the Pseudo-Pseudo data.

Don't stop pretraining! Efficiently building specialised language models in resource-constrained settings.

Sven Najem-Meyer[1], Frédéric Kaplan[1], Matteo Romanello[2]

[1]Digital Humanities Laboratory, EPFL, Lausanne, Switzerland
[2]Institute of Archeology and Classical Studies, University of Lausanne, Lausanne, Switzerland
{sven.najem-meyer,frederic.kaplan}@epfl.ch
matteo.romanello@unil.ch

Abstract

Developing specialised language models for low-resource domains typically involves a trade-off between two specialisation strategies: adapting a general-purpose model through continued pretraining or retraining a model from scratch. While adapting preserves the model's linguistic knowledge, retraining benefits from the flexibility of an in-domain tokeniser – a potentially significant advantage when handling rare languages. This study investigates the impact of tokenisation, specialisation strategy, and pretraining data availability using classical scholarship – a multilingual, code-switching and highly domain-specific field – as a case study. Through extensive experiments, we assess whether domain-specific tokenisation improves model performance, whether character-based models provide a viable alternative to subword-based models, and which specialisation strategy is optimal given the constraints of limited pretraining data. Contrary to prior findings, our results show that in-domain tokenisation does not necessarily enhance performance. Most notably, adaptation consistently outperforms retraining, even with limited data, confirming its efficiency as the preferred strategy for resource-constrained domains. These insights provide valuable guidelines for developing specialised models in fields with limited textual resources.

1 Introduction

Transformer-based language models have achieved remarkable success through transfer learning, where models pretrained on large general-purpose corpora are fine-tuned for downstream tasks. Though relatively straightforward, this approach proves more challenging for tasks involving highly domain-specific fields or rare languages. In such settings, it might be beneficial – if not essential – to develop specialised language models (e.g. Lee et al., 2019; Chalkidis et al., 2020; Schweter et al., 2022; Yamshchikov et al., 2022). However, there is no consensus on the optimal specialisation strategy – whether to pretrain a model from scratch or to adapt an existing one.

Adapting involves further pretraining a generic model on domain-specific data. The approach has been shown to increase downstream performance (e.g. Peters et al., 2019; Gururangan et al., 2020), while preserving the broad linguistic knowledge acquired during the initial pretraining phase. However, this strategy does not grant infinite flexibility. A key obstacle to specialisation often lies in the model's predefined vocabulary. Commonly used subword tokenisation methods (e.g. Wu et al., 2016; Kudo and Richardson, 2018) tie the model to a fixed vocabulary, which can be suboptimal or utterly inappropriate for certain languages. Thus, several tokenisation-free models have been developed to address this issue. CANINE (Clark et al., 2022) and CHARFORMER (Tay et al., 2022) use a broad set of Unicode points as a vocabulary. However, while they circumvent tokenisation issues, these models often perform below their subword-based counterparts and significantly limit the maximum input sequence length.

While domain-specific tokenisation may improve model performance, modifying the model's vocabulary and embeddings requires retraining from scratch. This creates a critical trade-off between optimising tokenisation at the cost of pretrained knowledge or leveraging existing models despite suboptimal tokenisation. As the decision is constrained by the availability of pretraining data, the dilemma is particularly crucial in low-resource settings. Studies reporting superior results from retraining domain-specific models (e.g. Lee et al., 2019; Schweter et al., 2022) often have access to extensive training resources. While some studies claim better results with smaller pretraining datasets (Riemenschneider and Frank, 2023; Manjavacas Arevalo and Fonteyn, 2021), many

Proceedings of LaTeCH-CLfL 2025, pages 252–260

advocate for adapting over retraining (Konle and Jannidis, 2020; Gururangan et al., 2020), but few systematically control for tokenisation, leaving its precise role in model performance an open question.

This study examines these specialisation strategies in the context of classical scholarship, a field characterised by intense multilingualism, frequent code-switching, and highly domain-specific vocabulary. These factors, along with the extensive use of rare characters and diacritics, pose significant tokenisation challenges, particularly for texts with a high proportion of Latin and ancient Greek, which are often absent from generic multilingual models, making the field an ideal case study for tokenisation and specialisation strategies. While character-level models may offer greater adaptability, subword tokenisers often struggle with historical texts due to transcription errors, spelling variations, and morphological inconsistencies. Retraining also remains impractical given the scarcity of clean textual data. Although this study assembles the largest classics-related corpus to date, it remains constrained to 1.4B tokens for six languages, less than half the 3.3B tokens used by the first monolingual BERT (Devlin et al., 2019). This study assesses the impact of tokenisation, specialisation strategy, and the availability of domain-specific data. It asks three research questions: What are the benefits of in-domain tokenisation? Do character-based models provide a viable and more adaptable alternative to subword models? Finally, which specialisation strategy is most effective given the constraints of available data?

2 Related work

Domain- and language-specific tokenisation Rust et al. (2021) investigated the impact of tokenisation on the performance of various monolingual and multilingual language models. The authors found a beneficial impact in utilising dedicated monolingual tokenisers. More specifically, their research reveals that languages well-represented within the multilingual model's (mBERT) training data (e.g. English or Japanese) suffer minimal performance loss when compared to their monolingual counterparts. However, for languages less represented in the multilingual training data such as Finnish, the multilingual model's tokeniser performed worse than its monolingual counterpart. Consequently, mBERT performed significantly worse than the ad-hoc pretrained Finnish BERT, with an average drop of 3.8 points in F1 and accuracy across multiple downstream tasks. Detailing these analyses for large language models, Ali et al. (2024) show that the size and specificity of the vocabulary as well as the tokenisation method could account for differences of 5% to 15% in a wide variety of downstream tasks. Their study further demonstrates that while multilingual tokenisers are more efficient with a larger vocabulary (82,000 to 100,000), English monolingual tokenisers find an optimal range between 33,000 and 45,000 tokens. Table 1 provides a general comparison between models, pretraining and adapting data as well as tokenisation and specialisation strategies.

Table 1: Overview of domain-specific language models. Tok. indicates whether the tokeniser is Generic or In-Domain. Str. indicates the (best) specialisation strategy used: Re-Training or Adapting. Gen. and Spec. refer to the size of the generic and domain-specific pretraining data (in billion words).

Paper	Lang.	Tok.	Dom.	Gen.	Spec.	Str.
Devlin (2019)	Eng	G	Gen.	3.3	-	-
Liu (2019)	Eng	G	Gen.	33	-	-
Conneau (2020)	Multi	G	Gen.	250	-	-
Beltagy (2019)	Eng	ID	Science	3.3	3.17	RT
Lee (2019)	Eng	G	Medical	3.3	18	AD
Chalkidis (2020)	Eng	G	Law	3.3	2.5	AD
Manjavacas (2021)	Eng	ID	History	-	3.9	RT
Schweter (2022)	Multi	ID	History	-	30	RT
Gabay (2022)	Fra	ID	History	-	0.19	RT
Hosseini (2021)	Eng	G	History	3.3	5.4	AD
Brandsen (2021)	Dut	G	Archeo.	2.4	0.66	AD
Bamman (2020)	Lat	ID	Anc. Lg.	-	0.64	RT
Singh (2021)	Gre	ID	Anc. Lg.	-	<0.1	RT
Yamshchikov (2022)	Gre	G	Anc. Lg.	3.0	0.01	AD
Riemenschneider (2023)	Multi	ID.	Anc. Lg.	-	0.57	RT

Byte- and character-level tokenisation In an exploratory study, Choe et al. (2019) showed that byte-level language models could match the perplexity of word-level models when given the same parameter budget. Building upon their research, Clark et al. (2022) released CANINE, which shows gains over mBERT (Devlin et al., 2019) by working with characters instead of subword tokens. While different character-level tokenisation strategies have been proposed by competing models such as CHARFORMER (Tay et al., 2022) and CharacterBERT (Boukkouri et al., 2020), ByT5 (Xue et al., 2022) is the first to show that byte-level tokenisation can outperform word-level tokenisation on a wide range of tasks. The authors argue that byte-level tokenisation is more efficient than character-level tokenisation, given that it allows for a smaller vocabulary size and a more efficient use of the model's parameters. In their experiments, ByT5 outperformed T5 (Raffel et al., 2020) on a wide range of tasks, including translation, summarisation, and question answering. Furthermore, the authors show that ByT5 is more robust to out-of-domain data than T5, suggesting that byte-level tokenisation can improve the generalisation capabilities of language models.

Domain-Specific Language Modelling Domain-specific language models have been developed for law (Chalkidis et al., 2020), biomedicine (Lee et al., 2019), science (Beltagy et al., 2019), history (Schweter et al., 2022), and classical philology (Riemenschneider and Frank, 2023). BioBERT (Lee et al., 2019), trained on 18B tokens of biomedical texts, retained BERT's vocabulary and weights, while SciBERT (Beltagy et al., 2019) explored both an adapted and a fully retrained model, demonstrating a slight superiority of in-domain tokenisation. In the legal domain, Chalkidis et al. (2020) compared retraining and adapting strategies for LegalBERT. However, the authors only assessed the performance of their adapted model on downstream legal tasks, allowing no comparison with the retrained model. Manjavacas Arevalo and Fonteyn (2021) compared the performance of a generic BERT, a historical-adapted BERT (Hosseini et al., 2021) and MacBERTh, a model pretrained on a corpus of 3.9B tokens composed of historical English exclusively. Despite sharing the same architecture, MacBERTh outperformed the two other models across a range of historical NLP tasks. This aligns with broader findings indicating that domain-specific models generally surpass generic ones within their fields (Schweter et al., 2022; Gabay et al., 2022; Konle and Jannidis, 2020; Manjavacas and Fonteyn, 2022; Gururangan et al., 2020).

Modelling classical scholarship and ancient languages In the field of classical studies, the development of domain-specific language models is made particularly crucial by the under-representation – if not the complete absence – of ancient languages in generic pretraining corpora. This absence is especially problematic in the case of ancient Greek, which exhibits a complex morphology, a rich inflectional system, and profuse usage of diacritics which radically distinguishes it from modern, simplified Greek. Recent years have therefore seen several efforts to develop language models tailored to ancient languages. Bamman and Burns (2020) released a LatinBERT which outperformed the state of the art. Most interestingly, these results are obtained with a relatively small pretraining corpus of 640M tokens gathered from diverse sources, showing that a dataset roughly one-fourth the size of BERT's could be leveraged to train a model achieving state-of-the-art performance. For ancient Greek, two notable studies stand out. Yamshchikov et al. (2022) adapt a modern Greek BERT to ancient Greek, while Singh et al. (2021) leverage online available corpora to train an ancient Greek model from scratch. Both studies show that language-specific models outperform generic monolingual and multilingual models on ancient Greek NLP tasks. Finally, in a more recent study, Riemenschneider and Frank (2023) released a collection of BERT- and T5-based ancient Greek and trilingual (Latin, Greek and English) models geared towards philology. Trained on slightly more data than the previous studies, the authors demonstrate that their models outperform the former models by a considerable margin across a range of philology-related tasks.

3 Pretraining data

In order to amass sufficient in-domain pretraining data to conduct our experiments, numerous classics-related corpora are gathered in a new Classical Scholarship Corpus (CSC). The final Classical Scholarship Corpus contains 1.4B tokens of domain-specific clean texts written in ancient Greek, Latin, English, French, German, and Italian. At the time of writing, our CSC is likely the largest corpus of clean texts gathered in the field so far. Texts are sourced through agreements with major publishers and providers or via web scraping. Hence, some corpora contain copyright-protected material. In total, 30 corpora are marshalled including notably Brill-KIEM[1], Internet Archive[2], the Corpus Thomisticum[3], Perseus and First1KGreek[4], and JSTOR[5]. The many challenges and peculiarities of classics-related data make data-cleaning a critical pre-processing step. This step notably involves the removal of documents with a high rate of optical character recognition errors. This is achieved by filtering out texts containing a low proportion (<65%) of alphanumeric characters or

[1] https://github.com/kiem-group/pdfParser
[2] https://web.archive.org/
[3] https://www.corpusthomisticum.org/
[4] https://www.opengreekandlatin.org/
[5] https://www.jstor.org/

a high proportion (>30%) of words not found in standard dictionaries. Corpora are also cleaned from recurring text spans such as headers, footers or webpage trademarks.

4 Methods

4.1 Evaluation methods

In line with Ali et al. (2024) and Rust et al. (2021), tokenisation is evaluated both intrinsically and extrinsically. Intrinsic evaluation is conducted using fertility, a widely adopted metric defined as the average number of tokens required to represent a word and measured on a 32M-tokens left-out set of the CSC. Extrinsic evaluation is established by the models' performance on downstream tasks.

These include four classics-related token classification tasks, all evaluated using macro-average F1 score, precision and recall. The first task involves Latin part-of-speech tagging with EvaLatin (Sprugnoli et al., 2020), a dataset comprising about 300,000 tokens. The second involves bibliographical entity recognition with EpiBau[6], a dataset of 1.1M English tokens annotated with ca. 37k entity mentions. Third comes multilingual named entity recognition with AjMC-NE-Corpus (Romanello and Najem-Meyer, 2024), a dataset of 111k tokens annotated with 7.3k named entities in English, German and French (AjNER$_{(de|en|fr)}$). Finally, text anchors recognition is evaluated with the AjMC-LL-Corpus[7], a dataset of 145k tokens annotated with 9.1k entity mentions in English, German and French (AjLR). Text anchors (lemmata) are specific to classical commentaries, and serve the purpose of linking commentary glosses to their corresponding text.

4.2 Base models

Two multilingual transformer encoders are retrained, adapted, and fine-tuned in our experiments: XLM-RoBERTa-base (Conneau et al., 2020), a subword-based, multilingual transformer encoder featuring a 250,000 SentencePiece tokeniser (Kudo and Richardson, 2018) and trained on 100 languages, including Latin and modern Greek, and CANINE-C (Clark et al., 2022), a character-based transformer encoder featuring a 40,000 Unicode points vocabulary and trained on 104 languages, including Latin and modern Greek[8]. Though CANINE's architecture necessarily differs from XLM-RoBERTa's, both models use the same 12-layers transformer stack and feature comparable parameter counts (121M vs 125M). Though these differences hamper an absolutely controlled comparison, our goal is also to provide researchers with an investigation of existing solutions and their respective upsides and shortcomings. Therefore, we also fine-tune two additional models for broader comparison purposes: hmBERT (Schweter et al., 2022), a BERT-based subword model trained on a 130GB corpus of historical texts and newspapers, including German, French, Swedish, Finnish and English, and PhilBERTa (Riemenschneider and Frank, 2023), a BERT-based model trained for classical scholarship, primarily geared towards Latin and ancient Greek, but also including English.

	hmB.	PhilB.	XLM-R	XLM-R (In-domain)		
Size (k)	33	64	250	250	82	33
Fertility	2.05	1.93	2.08	1.52	1.61	1.80

Table 2: Fertility scores of in-domain and generic tokenisers. Lower fertility scores indicate that fewer tokens are required to represent a word.

5 Experiments and results

5.1 What are the benefits of in-domain tokenisation?

Fertility To assess the benefits of specialised tokenisers, three XLM-R tokenisers are trained on the CSC: a large tokeniser of 250,000 tokens, equating XLM-R's original vocabulary size, an intermediary tokeniser of 82,000 tokens, and a small tokeniser of 33,000 tokens. Fertility scores are displayed in Table 2. As expected, fertility decreases (i.e. improves) with the domain-specificity of the tokeniser and its vocabulary size, showing that a larger specialised vocabulary requires fewer tokens to represent the same word.

5.1.1 Extrinsic evaluation

Models To evaluate the effects of tokenisation extrinsically, four XLM-R models are pretrained from scratch on in-domain data exclusively, with the different tokenisers. XLM-R$_{\text{RT-G-250}}$ is ReTrained using XLM-R's original Generic vocabulary. XLM-R$_{\text{RT-ID-(250|82|33)}}$ are ReTrained using In-Domain vocabularies of 250,000 82,000, and 33,000 tokens

[6] `https://github.com/mromanello/EpibauCorpus`

[7] Unpublished at time of writing as partially copyrighted.

[8] Since the authors did not release their implementation, a customised pretraining pipeline is used to train CANINE on in-domain data (See `https://github.com/sven-nm/shiba-canine`).

respectively. All models are pretrained for three epochs on the CSC and fine-tuned on each downstream task for 40 epochs, leaving other recommended hyperparameters unchanged.

Results Results are shown in Table 3. Surprisingly, the model retrained with the generic tokeniser (XLM-$R_{RT\text{-}G\text{-}250}$) outperforms those trained with in-domain tokenisers on all tasks, with an overall improvement of 8.4 points in F1 score over XLM-$R_{RT\text{-}ID\text{-}250}$. This result is particularly unexpected as the in-domain tokenisers are specifically designed to improve model performance on classical scholarship tasks. Interestingly, we observe a negative correlation between F1 scores and vocabulary sizes which is also incoherent with the fertility scores presented above: a better (i.e. lower) fertility usually implies a better tokeniser.

Analyses As no straightforward explanation justifies this result, further analyses are conducted. Our hypothesis is that in-domain tokenisation results in a substantially sparser token distribution, as specialised vocabularies contain more tokens fitting the precise needs of a relatively small domain-specific corpus. Hence as more tokens are used, their average frequency across the corpus diminishes. Token frequency was measured on a 300M subset of the CSC for each tokeniser and supports this hypothesis. While XLM-R's generic tokeniser only needs 95,754 of its 250,000 tokens in its vocabulary to segment the corpus, its in-domain counterpart uses 246.864 tokens. Hence, the model based on the former benefits from 6,137 token occurrences on average, while the model based on the latter must learn from a much sparser distribution of tokens, averaging to 1,701 occurrences per unique token. Furthermore, quantiles show that the generic vocabulary also leads to a much higher concentration of used tokens, with 75% of used tokens having over 1.1k occurences, versus 0.5k for XLM-R-ID-250.

While XLM-$R_{RT\text{-}ID\text{-}33}$ performs significantly better than its 250 and 82 counterparts, it still does not surpass the model based on the generic tokeniser. This result raises two considerations. First, it supports the idea that enhancing token density leads to significantly better results, especially in the case of relatively limited pretraining data. While intrinsic evaluation metrics such as fertility may provide a valuable insight on tokeniser performance in domains provided with abundant training data, the results provided here show token density to be a significantly more reliable predictor of extrinsic performance. Hence, researchers working in resource-limited environments should be advised to take this metric into account when choosing the vocabulary size of an in-domain tokeniser. Second, it shows that contrary to a generally supported claim (Rust et al., 2021; Beltagy et al., 2019; Ali et al., 2024), in-domain tokenisation does not necessarily imply better model performance. One possible explanation for this outcome is that the tokeniser's training corpus may simply be too limited in size to support the development of robust subword units. While in-domain tokenisers may lead to the best performance when given sufficient token density, they still do not outperform the generic tokeniser, suggesting that a more robust tokenisation might be obtained by training the tokeniser on larger corpora.

5.2 Do character-based models provide a viable and more adaptable alternative to subword models?

This second series of experiments provides a comparison between generic and adapted versions of CANINE (character-based) and XLM-R (subword-based). Generic versions (XLM-R and CANINE) use the checkpoints provided by each model's authors. Adapted versions (XLM-R_{AD} and CANINE-C_{AD}) are further pretrained on the CSC for three epochs. The last adapting checkpoints were shown by pre-tests to yield the best downstream results and are therefore fine-tuned for 40 epochs on each downstream task. Though XLM-R largely outperforms CANINE-C on all tasks, the latter shows much higher gains from adaptation, with improvements up to 15% F1 score for $AjNER_{en}$. Though the model's performance is still lower than XLM-R's, the gap is significantly reduced. Interestingly, adaptation significantly degrades the performance of CANINE-C on lemma recognition, while it generally benefits on all other tasks and models. Error analysis shows this effect to be due only to a significant precision drop on greek-only entities.

Discussion It remains to be seen whether the higher adaptability of CANINE-C is due to its character-based tokenisation or to other factors such as the model's architecture or pretraining objectives, which are not controlled in these experiments. However, these results confirm the model's claimed adaptability across languages (Clark et al., 2022) and suggest that researchers thoroughly de-

Model	EpiBau	EvaLat.	AjLR	AjNER_{de}	AjNER_{fr}	AjNER_{en}	Avg
hmBERT	0.847	0.934	0.889	0.904	0.835	0.846	0.876
PhilBERTa	0.781	0.925	0.619	0.775	0.602	0.690	0.732
CANINE-C	0.729	0.890	0.749	0.809	0.712	0.616	0.751
$\text{CANINE-C}_{\text{AD}}$	0.794	0.899	0.708	0.824	0.789	0.766	0.796
XLM-R	0.854	0.944	0.875	0.907	0.856	0.838	0.879
$\text{XLM-R}_{\text{RT-G-250}}$	0.818	0.912	0.807	0.879	0.802	0.794	0.835
$\text{XLM-R}_{\text{RT-ID-250}}$	0.788	0.895	0.668	0.809	0.722	0.683	0.761
$\text{XLM-R}_{\text{RT-ID-82}}$	0.769	0.900	0.668	0.824	0.783	0.735	0.780
$\text{XLM-R}_{\text{RT-ID-33}}$	0.787	0.905	0.761	0.848	0.814	0.795	0.818
$\text{XLM-R}_{\text{RT-G-250-300M}}$	0.623	0.684	0.578	0.670	0.587	0.542	0.614
$\text{XLM-R}_{\text{RT-G-250-600M}}$	0.734	0.771	0.711	0.786	0.701	0.687	0.732
XLM-R_{AD}	0.844	0.948	0.896	**0.935**	0.871	0.869	0.894
$\text{XLM-R}_{\text{AD-EP5}}$	**0.868**	**0.952**	0.896	0.924	**0.895**	**0.886**	**0.903**
$\text{XLM-R}_{\text{AD-300M}}$	0.860	0.948	0.897	0.911	0.886	0.867	0.895
$\text{XLM-R}_{\text{AD-600M}}$	0.858	0.947	**0.909**	0.923	0.886	0.875	0.900

Table 3: F1 scores of all models across downstream tasks. Results are reported for models with three epochs of pretraining. The average F1 score is equally weighted across all tasks. The best results across all models are highlighted in bold.

prived of generic subword models usable in their research field may find significant benefits in adapting CANINE-C to their domain. However, in the current state, CANINE remains significantly less capable than XLM-R.

5.3 Which specialisation strategy is most effective given the constraints of available data?

The goal of this last series of experiments is to determine whether retraining or adapting yields best results depending on the quantity of available data. Although limited to the case of classics, these experiments may provide valuable insights for other domains with similar characteristics.

Models To address the question, six variants of XLM-R are trained, each being either ReTrained or ADapted on 300M, 600M or 1.4B tokens ($\text{XLM-R}_{\text{(RT|AD)-(300M|600M|}\emptyset\text{)}}$). As the generic tokeniser has been shown to yield the best results in the first research question, it is used for the three retrained models, also allowing for a fairer comparison with adapted models, as the latter necessarily keeps the model's original vocabulary. In the experiments involving a subset of the pretraining data, model checkpoints are compared after an equal number of training steps as opposed to an equal number of epochs. This method is chosen in order to keep the amount of pretraining tokens the only changing variable.

Results XLM-R_{AD} outperforms all other models trained on the entirety of CSC by a significant margin. This result shows the superiority of adapted models over both retrained and generic models. As XLM-R_{AD} performs best, it is also further pretrained for two additional epochs, reaching a total of five epochs ($\text{XLM-R}_{\text{AD-EP5}}$), showing an overall improvement in performance and producing the best model overall. Table 3 also shows the results of models pretrained on 300M, 600M, and 1.4B tokens. Surprisingly, results show that 300M and 600M models yield even better results than the model trained on the entire corpus (XLM-R_{AD}). This unexpected outcome might be due to the fact that models are here compared at an equal number of training steps, and not at an equal number of training epochs. This implies that data-ablated models have been exposed to fewer distinct examples but have encountered these examples with greater frequency. When compared with a model trained for an approximately equal number of epochs on the entire corpus, the latter overtakes the former. Hence, the model trained on the entire corpus continues to improve after three epochs and finally yields the best results at five epochs, which corresponds approximately to the number of epochs run by XLM-R$_{\text{AD-300M}}$. In any case, the observed differences are very small, and lead to the more reasonable conclusion that the model's performance is not significantly affected[9] by the amount of in-domain data it is further pretrained on. This very encouraging result suggests that researchers working in resource-constrained environments can still benefit from adapting models to their domain, even if they only have access to a small amount of data.

This is not the case with retrained models, whose performance pronouncedly drops when further pretrained on ablated data. This result is consistent with the trend observed in recent years, which shows that the results of pretrained models are very sensitive to the amount of data they are pretrained on. Hence, while adapting XLM-R with 1.4B as opposed to 300M tokens causes the model's average performance to drop 0.1%, retraining, the same deprivation implies a remarkable drop of 22.9% F1 score on average.

6 General discussion

The importance of tokenisation The conclusions of these experiments are multifaceted. First, experiments confirm previous findings on the critical role of tokenisation (Ali et al., 2024; Rust et al., 2021). Our experiments compare the performance of two XLM-R models pretrained on the same data but using two distinct tokenisers of equal size: a generic and a domain-specific tokeniser. As shown in Table 3, our results reveals differences ranging up to 7% on average downstream F1 scores. This substantial difference underscores the necessity of a meticulous examination of this oft-overlooked stage of model development.

Second, unlike previous studies, these experiments illustrate that in-domain tokenisation does not necessarily lead to better performance. Analyses indicate that intrinsic tokenisation evaluation methods relying on fertility do not correlate with downstream results. On the contrary, in a resource-limited environment, lower (i.e. better) fertility also leads to a lower average token frequency and less performant models. We argue that in low-resource settings, tokenisation should balance input sequence length and token-type density. While high-fertility, small-sized tokenisers produce longer input sequences by breaking words into smaller subwords, they also enable more frequent representation of each token within the corpus, which correlates with model performance. This study therefore advocates the adoption of token density as a novel intrinsic evaluation metric.

Although smaller in-domain tokenisers consistently yield better results than their larger in-domain counterparts, they still do not surpass the performance of a larger, generic tokeniser. This improved performance may be attributable to the substantially larger size training corpus, which could favour a more robust and efficient vocabulary. This hypothesis is left for future research.

The potential of character-based models The second series of experiments consistently shows that CANINE-C is outperformed by XLM-R across all downstream tasks. However, the limits of this comparison must be highlighted. Notably, the two models are pretrained on different corpora with distinct training objectives and exhibit slight architectural differences, with CANINE-C incorporating downsampling and upsampling convolutional layers around its central transformer blocks. Thus, the findings merely indicate that even in a domain where tokenisation is suboptimal, XLM-R achieves better performance than CANINE-C.

Second, the results demonstrate CANINE-C's strong adaptability to the domain, with the adapted model yielding an average improvement of 5% in F1 score over the generic model. This improvement is substantial when compared to XLM-R's average improvement of 1.5% in F1 score. Researchers working with highly specific or underrepresented languages not covered by large multilingual models may therefore find character-based models like CANINE-C advantageous when adapted to their domain.

The superiority of adapted models Finally, the third series of experiments shows an undeniable superiority of adapted models over retrained and generic models, regardless of the amount of available pretraining data. This result aligns with the principle that adaptation preserves the extensive linguistic knowledge embedded in the generic base-model, a solid foundation difficult to replicate when training from scratch on limited resources. Although retraining has shown success

[9]McNemar's tests show average differences above 0.038% in F1 score to be statiscally significant ($p < .05$). Thus, the difference between XLM-R$_{\text{AD-EP5}}$ and XLM-R$_{\text{AD-600M}}$ is not statistically significant, as is the difference between XLM-R$_{\text{AD}}$ and XLM-R$_{\text{AD-300M}}$.

in domain-specific fields with ample pretraining corpora, such as biomedical or legal domains, resource-constrained fields appear to benefit most by leveraging the power of scale utilised by the model during its original pretraining. The findings also reveal that an adaptation corpus of 300M tokens already achieves 75% of the overall performance gains, indicating adaptation as an efficient and resource-effective specialisation strategy. As the superiority of adaptation over retraining is especially evident in data-ablation scenarios, it suggests that researchers and practitioners working with limited pretraining data should prioritise this approach. Moreover, adaptation may offer the only viable pathway to specialising large language models, an approach also left for future work.

7 Conclusion

This study provides a comprehensive analysis of the impact of tokenisation and specialisation strategies on the performance of language models in the field of classical scholarship. Our results show that in-domain tokenisation does not necessarily lead to better model performance in a resource-constrained environment, and that token density is a more reliable predictor of extrinsic performance. Our experiments also show that character-based models can offer a viable alternative to subword models, especially when adapted. Finally, we show that adaptation is the most effective specialisation strategy in a resource-constrained environment, and that even relatively small adaptation corpora can yield significant performance gains. These findings provide valuable insights for researchers working in resource-limited environments and highlight the importance of tokenisation and specialisation strategies in the development of large language models. We leave the investigation of our findings in other historical domains for future work, make our models available to the research community[10].

Acknowledgments

This research has been supported by the Swiss National Science Foundation under an Ambizione grant PZ00P1_186033.

[10]See `XLM-R-for-classics*` models at `https://huggingface.co/sven-nm/`.

References

Mehdi Ali, Michael Fromm, Klaudia Thellmann, Richard Rutmann, Max Lübbering, Johannes Leveling, Katrin Klug, Jan Ebert, Niclas Doll, Jasper Schulze Buschhoff, Charvi Jain, Alexander Arno Weber, Lena Jurkschat, Hammam Abdelwahab, Chelsea John, Pedro Ortiz Suarez, Malte Ostendorff, Samuel Weinbach, Rafet Sifa, Stefan Kesselheim, and Nicolas Flores-Herr. 2024. Tokenizer choice for llm training: Negligible or crucial? *Preprint*, arXiv:2310.08754.

David Bamman and Patrick J. Burns. 2020. Latin bert: A contextual language model for classical philology. *arXiv:2009.10053 [cs].*

Iz Beltagy, Kyle Lo, and Arman Cohan. 2019. Scibert: A pretrained language model for scientific text. *arXiv:1903.10676 [cs].*

Hicham El Boukkouri, Olivier Ferret, Thomas Lavergne, Hiroshi Noji, Pierre Zweigenbaum, and Junichi Tsujii. 2020. Characterbert: Reconciling elmo and bert for word-level open-vocabulary representations from characters. *Preprint*, arXiv:2010.10392.

Ilias Chalkidis, Manos Fergadiotis, Prodromos Malakasiotis, Nikolaos Aletras, and Ion Androutsopoulos. 2020. Legal-bert: The muppets straight out of law school. *Preprint*, arXiv:2010.02559.

Dokook Choe, Rami Al-Rfou, Mandy Guo, Heeyoung Lee, and Noah Constant. 2019. Bridging the gap for tokenizer-free language models. *Preprint*, arXiv:1908.10322.

Jonathan H. Clark, Dan Garrette, Iulia Turc, and John Wieting. 2022. Canine: Pre-training an efficient tokenization-free encoder for language representation. *Transactions of the Association for Computational Linguistics*, 10:73–91.

Alexis Conneau, Kartikay Khandelwal, Naman Goyal, Vishrav Chaudhary, Guillaume Wenzek, Francisco Guzmán, Edouard Grave, Myle Ott, Luke Zettlemoyer, and Veselin Stoyanov. 2020. Unsupervised cross-lingual representation learning at scale. *Preprint*, arXiv:1911.02116.

Jacob Devlin, Ming-Wei Chang, Kenton Lee, and Kristina Toutanova. 2019. Bert: Pre-training of deep bidirectional transformers for language understanding. *arXiv:1810.04805 [cs].*

Simon Gabay, Pedro Ortiz Suarez, Alexandre Bartz, Alix Chagué, Rachel Bawden, Philippe Gambette, and Benoît Sagot. 2022. From freem to d'alembert: A large corpus and a language model for early modern french. In *Proceedings of the Thirteenth Language Resources and Evaluation Conference*, pages 3367–3374, Marseille, France. European Language Resources Association.

Suchin Gururangan, Ana Marasović, Swabha Swayamdipta, Kyle Lo, Iz Beltagy, Doug Downey, and Noah A. Smith. 2020. Don't stop pretraining: Adapt language models to domains and tasks. *Preprint*, arXiv:2004.10964.

Kasra Hosseini, Kaspar Beelen, Giovanni Colavizza, and Mariona Coll Ardanuy. 2021. Neural language models for nineteenth-century english. *Journal of Open Humanities Data*, 7(0).

Leonard Konle and Fotis Jannidis. 2020. Domain and task adaptive pretraining for language models. In *Proceedings of the Workshop on Computational Humanities Research (CHR 2020)*.

Taku Kudo and John Richardson. 2018. Sentencepiece: A simple and language independent subword tokenizer and detokenizer for neural text processing. *Preprint*, arXiv:1808.06226.

Jinhyuk Lee, Wonjin Yoon, Sungdong Kim, Donghyeon Kim, Sunkyu Kim, Chan Ho So, and Jaewoo Kang. 2019. Biobert: A pre-trained biomedical language representation model for biomedical text mining. *Bioinformatics*, page btz682.

Enrique Manjavacas and Lauren Fonteyn. 2022. Adapting vs. pre-training language models for historical languages. *Journal of Data Mining & Digital Humanities*, NLP4DH(Digital humanities in languages).

Enrique Manjavacas Arevalo and Lauren Fonteyn. 2021. Macberth: Development and evaluation of a historically pre-trained language model for english (1450-1950). In *Proceedings of the Workshop on Natural Language Processing for Digital Humanities*, pages 23–36, NIT Silchar, India. NLP Association of India (NLPAI).

Matthew E. Peters, Sebastian Ruder, and Noah A. Smith. 2019. To tune or not to tune? adapting pretrained representations to diverse tasks. *arXiv:1903.05987 [cs]*.

Colin Raffel, Noam Shazeer, Adam Roberts, Katherine Lee, Sharan Narang, Michael Matena, Yanqi Zhou, Wei Li, and Peter J. Liu. 2020. Exploring the limits of transfer learning with a unified text-to-text transformer. *arXiv:1910.10683 [cs, stat]*.

Frederick Riemenschneider and Anette Frank. 2023. Exploring large language models for classical philology. In *Proceedings of the 61st Annual Meeting of the Association for Computational Linguistics (Volume 1: Long Papers)*, pages 15181–15199, Toronto, Canada. Association for Computational Linguistics.

Matteo Romanello and Sven Najem-Meyer. 2024. A named entity-annotated corpus of 19th century classical commentaries. *Journal of Open Humanities Data*, 10(1):1.

Phillip Rust, Jonas Pfeiffer, Ivan Vulić, Sebastian Ruder, and Iryna Gurevych. 2021. How good is your tokenizer? on the monolingual performance of multilingual language models. *Preprint*, arXiv:2012.15613.

Stefan Schweter, Luisa März, Katharina Schmid, and Erion Çano. 2022. hmbert: Historical multilingual language models for named entity recognition. In *Proceedings of the Working Notes of CLEF 2022 - Conference and Labs of the Evaluation Forum*, volume 3180 of *CEUR Workshop Proceedings*, pages 1109–1129, Bologna, Italy. CEUR.

Pranaydeep Singh, Gorik Rutten, and Els Lefever. 2021. A pilot study for bert language modelling and morphological analysis for ancient and medieval greek. In *Proceedings of the 5th Joint SIGHUM Workshop on Computational Linguistics for Cultural Heritage, Social Sciences, Humanities and Literature*, pages 128–137, Punta Cana, Dominican Republic (online). Association for Computational Linguistics.

Rachele Sprugnoli, Marco Passarotti, Flavio Massimiliano Cecchini, and Matteo Pellegrini. 2020. Overview of the evalatin 2020 evaluation campaign. In *Proceedings of LT4HALA 2020 - 1st Workshop on Language Technologies for Historical and Ancient Languages*, pages 105–110, Marseille, France. European Language Resources Association (ELRA).

Yi Tay, Vinh Q. Tran, Sebastian Ruder, Jai Gupta, Hyung Won Chung, Dara Bahri, Zhen Qin, Simon Baumgartner, Cong Yu, and Donald Metzler. 2022. Charformer: Fast character transformers via gradient-based subword tokenization. *Preprint*, arXiv:2106.12672.

Yonghui Wu, Mike Schuster, Zhifeng Chen, Quoc V. Le, Mohammad Norouzi, Wolfgang Macherey, Maxim Krikun, Yuan Cao, Qin Gao, Klaus Macherey, Jeff Klingner, Apurva Shah, Melvin Johnson, Xiaobing Liu, Łukasz Kaiser, Stephan Gouws, Yoshikiyo Kato, Taku Kudo, Hideto Kazawa, Keith Stevens, George Kurian, Nishant Patil, Wei Wang, Cliff Young, Jason Smith, Jason Riesa, Alex Rudnick, Oriol Vinyals, Greg Corrado, Macduff Hughes, and Jeffrey Dean. 2016. Google's neural machine translation system: Bridging the gap between human and machine translation. *arXiv:1609.08144 [cs]*.

Linting Xue, Aditya Barua, Noah Constant, Rami Al-Rfou, Sharan Narang, Mihir Kale, Adam Roberts, and Colin Raffel. 2022. Byt5: Towards a token-free future with pre-trained byte-to-byte models. *Preprint*, arXiv:2105.13626.

Ivan Yamshchikov, Alexey Tikhonov, Yorgos Pantis, Charlotte Schubert, and Jürgen Jost. 2022. Bert in plutarch's shadows. In *Proceedings of the 2022 Conference on Empirical Methods in Natural Language Processing*, pages 6071–6080, Abu Dhabi, United Arab Emirates. Association for Computational Linguistics.

"... like a needle in a haystack": Annotation and Classification of Comparative Statements

Pritha Majumdar[1], Franziska Pannach[1], Arianna Graciotti[2], Johan Bos[1]
[1]University of Groningen, [2]University of Bologna
Correspondence: p.majumdar@rug.nl

Abstract

We present a clear distinction between the phenomena of *comparisons* and *similes* along with a fine-grained annotation guideline that facilitates the structural annotation and assessment of the two classes, with three major contributions: 1) a publicly available annotated data set of 100 comparative statements; 2) theoretically grounded annotation guidelines for human annotators; and 3) results of machine learning experiments to establish how the–often subtle–distinction between the two phenomena can be automated. For the purpose of automatic classification, we present a baseline system (SVM), as well as experiments with large language models. We achieve 82% accuracy on the best performing model-Llama 3.3-70b-instruct following a few shot prompting strategy.

1 Introduction

The automatic processing of figurative language is a challenge that has long been a focal point of research in natural language processing (Ge et al., 2023; Rai and Chakraverty, 2020; Joshi et al., 2017; Amin and Burghardt, 2020). One of the tasks in dealing with comparative statements is to find clear boundaries between two very similar phenomena: that of comparison and simile.

The term *comparison* describes a linguistic unit that is used to convey similarities and dissimilarities between two entities. Even though comparisons in general are understood to be syntactic, they can in effect harmonize much more relevant semantic knowledge in everyday language. Comparisons are used in everyday communication, e.g., in a debate when one has to put across a point, or when pointing out a similarity or difference between entities that share some property. *Similes* on the other hand are special structures that are derived from comparisons and can also be called *figurative comparisons*. A simile can be defined as a figure of speech that is used to draw a parallel between two dissimilar entities or processes that have some shared properties. Let's consider the two examples:

(1) He is as tall as his brother.

(2) He is as tall as the tower.

In (1), the comparison is drawn between two brothers' physical size, while (2) draws a comparison between a human (he) and an object (tower) which makes the comparison figurative. This leads to an important consideration in the distinction between comparisons and similes: Comparisons can be drawn between any two entities, while a comparison only becomes figurative (simile), if the two entities belong from different semantic categories.

This paper presents an annotation methodology that allows us to distinguish if a comparative statement is a *literal comparison* or a *figurative comparison* (simile). To the best of our knowledge this is the first work that focuses on step-by-step annotation guidelines for comparison vs. simile, taking into account various features of comparative statements.

Similes are a particularly interesting phenomenon in the domain of literature, because they often carry subtle meaning that can be overlooked if a statement is treated as a simple comparison: "Poor Dorothea felt that every word of her uncle's was about as pleasant as a grain of sand in the eye to Mr. Casaubon." (Eliot, 1994, p.335). The former statement contains a simile. It carries more meaning than a simple comparison, i.e., it requires the reader to acknowledge that a grain of salt in the eye is very unpleasant and thus the statements that Dorothea's uncle makes in front of Mr. Casaubon are evoking a negative emotion in the listener.

In fiction, simile's are often used to transport subtle meaning and therefore particularly interesting to study. However, similes are a sparse phenomenon with rare occurrence in everyday usage, their annotation is time-consuming and often yields very little data per literary work. Therefore, this

Proceedings of LaTeCH-CLfL 2025, pages 261–271

work presents straightforward annotation guidelines by defining *nine* categories (subject of comparison, object of comparison, nature, categories, feature matching, symmetry, salience, broad unifying concept and domain incongruence) to distinguish similes from non-figurative comparisons, together with machine learning experiments that can help automatically annotating larger corpora of fictional texts for further studies in the domain of computational literary studies. The data set and gold standard annotation can be found here[1].

2 Related Work

The study of comparison in rhetoric can be dated as back as Aristotle (Freese et al., 1926), who highlighted the importance of using comparisons in everyday life (Seh, 2016). However, computational studies addressing the distinction between figurative and literal comparisons are scarce, since both phenomena follow a similar structure, and consist of the same constituents (Niculae and Danescu-Niculescu-Mizil, 2014). Niculae (2013) proposed a "similarity based approach" that aided in measuring the degree of figurativeness of a comparison which by extension can be used as a means of identification of similes. Since there is a lack of annotated corpora of comparisons, Niculae (2013) used the VUAMC corpora (Steen et al., 2010) to extract the comparison patterns of "like". They then annotated it for the task of simile identification. Since similes are a form of comparisons, Niculae and Yaneva (2013) contributed to computational research on simile by focusing on comparison recognition through the use of syntactic patterns. Most work on automatic detection and analysis of figurative language targets metaphors (Li et al., 2023; Boisson et al., 2024) and idioms (De Luca Fornaciari et al., 2024; Chakrabarty et al., 2022), but only few recent studies investigate similes as special comparative statements.[2] More recent exceptions are Liu et al. (2018); Wang et al. (2022), in which neural and transformer-based models are used in a multi-task setting to identify similes and their components in Chinese texts.

3 Annotation Guidelines

The guidelines that are presented here is developed based on Seh (2016), in which Seh dedicates a complete chapter in understanding comparisons and their distinction from similes. Before we introduce the annotation guidelines, we must first discuss the syntactic structure and the semantic particularities of different types of comparative statements. We will then discuss the steps involved in distinguishing a literal comparison from a simile. This paper does not focus on the merits of the individual underlying theories[3] of comparison. Instead, its main contribution is building a concise annotation guidelines that is derived from the theories for the task of identifying and distinguishing comparisons and similes.

3.1 Comparisons and Similes

Typically, a comparative structure consists of two elements that are the focus of a comparison, i.e., the (two or more) elements being compared, e.g., *he, his brother*, and the property, e.g., *tall*, with regard to which they are compared (Dixon, 2018). The other components of a comparative structure are:

(1) The item that is compared or *subject of comparison*;

(2) The standard of comparison against which the item is compared or *object of comparison*;

(3) The quantity or quality, i.e. the property used for the comparison or *parameter*;

(4) The standard marker which states the relationship between the subject and object of comparison or *mark*;

(5) The degree marker which states the extent of the comparison or *index*.

Table 1 illustrates an example of these components.[4] While a comparison is the phenomena of formally likening one thing to another that resemble each other in some properties, a simile is a figure of speech which generally relies on a linguistic marker to draw a parallel between two or more semantically distant entities or processes based on stated or implied (dis)similarities, so as to produce a particular image in a person's mind (Seh, 2016).

[1] `https://github.com/prithamajumdar/Annotation-Classification-of-Comparative-Statements`

[2] A comprehensive survey of computational approaches towards similes is accepted and currently undertaken by the authors in `https://direct.mit.edu/coli`.

[3] The theories are discussed in Seh (2016).

[4] Some sources such as Dixon (2018) and Seh (2016) refer the subject of comparison as *comparee* and object of comparison as *standard*

Table 1: Illustration of terminologies in comparisons

Sentence	Subject of Comparison	Index	Parameter	Mark	Object of Comparison
Max is more intelligent than George	Max	more	intelligent	than	George

For example[5],

(1) This book is *more* interesting than that one.

(2) The Earth is round *like* an orange.

Both the examples imply a *comparative degree of adjective*. For comparisons, the structures indicate *equality, superiority or inferiority* which means that all these comparisons are *scalable* (De Mille, 2024). In similes, we consider the similarity concept as a *spectrum*, wherein it can range from "some" similarity to "more than/less than" similarities (Cohen, 1968). Thus, comparisons are usually *quantitative*, while similes are *qualitative* by nature.

Furthermore, for a comparison to be a simile, the two elements of the simile should "differ in kind" (Bain, 1890), or to be "of different kind" (Waddy, 1889) or to be "drawn from one species of things to another" (Jamieson, 1823).

Categories This leads us to the next consideration in distinguishing a literal comparison from similes: the (semantic) *categories*. A category may be defined as "a number of objects which are considered equivalent" (Rosch, 1978). Aristotle defined ten categories into which each single concept may fit: Substance, Quantity, Quality, Relation, Where, When, Position, Possession, Action and Passion (Aristotle et al., 1889). The task of this categorisation is however not done haphazardly, but is "based on specific perceptible or known attributes and most times, it is either intuitive, used in a specialised context or rooted in a culture." (Seh, 2016). Rosch (1978) list three levels of natural categories:

(a) *basic-level category* that consists of basic objects like car,

(b) *super-ordinate category* to which the basic objects belong, like vehicle for car,

(c) *sub-ordinate category* are the types of basic objects, like SUV for car,

Therefore, comparisons generally concern entities that are at the same level of categorization and belong to the same super-ordinate category, while similes involve entities that are on different levels of categorization. For example,

[5]All the examples discussed in this section are taken from the thesis of Seh (2016).

(3) *Spoons are like forks.*

(4) *The girl is like a lily.*

In (3), spoons and forks are basic objects that have several subordinate categories (dessert spoon, teaspoon, soup spoon, fish fork, salad fork etc.) and belong to the same super-ordinate category, cutlery. Thus (3) is a *comparison*. On the other hand, girl and lily in (4) do not belong to a common category and a very high level of abstraction is required to find a shared super-ordinate category. Thus, (4) is a *simile* (Seh, 2016).

Feature Matching The next important step is to perform *feature matching*. On this level of annotation, similes can be identified by measuring similarity of two elements, taking into account their similarities and differences. For example,

(5) *The chair is like an armchair.*

(6) *This chair is like a boulder.*

Example (5) is a *comparison*, since they share many similar features (both are used for sitting and belong to the same super-ordinate category-furniture). The similarities are more prominent than the differences. However in (6), the similarity between a chair and boulder is much lower, the differences are more prominent than similarities. Therefore, it shows features of a *simile* (Seh, 2016).

Symmetry The next concept that we use to differentiate comparison and simile is *symmetry*. Comparisons are symmetrical in nature, which means that you can alter the order of subject of comparison and object of comparison. However, similes are asymmetrical in nature which means that changing the position of the subject and object can affect the meaning. For example,

(7) *Spoons are like forks* has the same meaning as *forks are like spoons* making the statement a *comparison*.

(8) *A girl is like a lily* is not the same as *A lily is like a girl*, making the statement a *simile*.

In (8), a descriptive quality of *a girl* is conveyed, but less so a quality of *a lily*.

Salience The next distinction between a comparison and simile is *salience*. In similes, the shared features of subject and object should show low salience in the subject of comparison, and high salience in the object of comparison.

(9) *Spoons are like forks*, both concepts show high salience, i.e., both are utensils and both are held by hand and are used for eating). Thus, this is a *comparison*.

(10) *The girl is like a butterfly*, the concepts have different levels of salience, e.g. the *butterfly* signifies fluidity, flittiness, lightness and transience, features that are more readily associated with butterflies than with girls. Thus, this makes it a *simile*.

Meaningfulness For a statement to be considered a simile, it should also be meaningful. That is, the items compared–while potentially from different domains–should still be relatable under a broader, unifying concept or category, e.g.,

(11) *Billboards are like spoons.*

(12) *Sally is like a block of ice.*

From the above example, (11) lacks a meaningful semantic connection because billboards and spoons cannot be easily grouped under a shared domain or concept–at least not without a further explanation. This makes the statement a *comparison*. While in (12), even though *Sally* and *a block of ice* come from different domains, they can still be compared through an abstract quality, e.g. *stiffness/metaphorical or actual coldness*. This broader concept allows for a reasonable connection between the two and makes the comparison a *simile*.

Domain Incongruence The last phenomenon to consider is *domain incongruence*. In our case, this means that the elements of comparison must belong to distinct categories or semantic domains, e.g. person and object). A statement can only qualify as a simile when the attributes shared by the subject of comparison and the object of comparison are not strictly identical.

(13) *Max is like the Empire State Building* is a *simile*.

(14) *Max is as tall as George* is a *comparison* because both are human.

3.2 Annotation Methodology

In this section we present the annotation methodology that allows us to decide if a statement is a *comparison, simile* or if the distinction is *Not Applicable* (see Table 2).

3.2.1 Identification

The first step in the annotation process is to identify the *subject of comparison* and *the object of comparison*. For example,

Max is as tall as George.

Tom is as fast as a leopard.

The subject of comparisons are *Max* and *Tom*, while the objects they are being compared to are *George* and *a leopard*.

Contextual Span We need to consider how much context should be included as the *subject* and *object of comparison*. In our annotation, we include the *noun*, the whole *noun phrase* or even the complete *clause* in situations where it is applicable. For example,

(1) In *Tom is as fast as a leopard*, we annotate *Tom* as the subject of the comparison, and *a leopard* as the object of the comparison.

(2) In *Few treasures are worth as much as a friend who is wise and helpful*, *Few Treasures* is the subject of the comparison, and the whole clause *a friend who is wise and helpful* is the object of comparison.

(3) *Better is the poor who walks in his integrity, than he who is perverse in his ways, and he is rich.* Here, we annotate *The poor who walks in his integrity* as the subject and *The rich who is perverse in his ways* as the object of the comparison.

Contraction In cases of contraction, we reduce the form to the root word. For example,

(4) In *I'm as hungry as a bear*. The subject of comparison is *I* instead of I'm.

Co-reference In cases of co-reference, we identify the subject/object of comparison as the noun/noun phrases. For example,

(5) *Tom is a solid and determined man, but sometimes he's as impetuous as a river of molten lava.* We resolve *Tom* as the subject of comparison instead of *he's*.

Multiple Components In cases of statements with multiple components in the subject or object of comparison, we mark all of them. For example,

(6) *Her mouth is smoother than oil, but in the end she is as bitter as wormwood, and as sharp as a two-edged sword.* Here, *her mouth* is the subject of comparison and *oil, wormwood, two-edged sword* are the objects of comparison.

Dialogues In case of dialogues, we reconstruct the subject/object of comparison to the most meaningful form. For example,

(7) *So February's policy note is a stunning reversal – as close as an institution can come to*

Table 2: Snippet of the method of annotation

Sentence	Subject of comparison	Object of comparison	Nature	Categories	Feature matching	Symmetry	Salience	Broad, unifying concept	Domain Incongruence	Result
Tom is as fast as a leopard	Tom	a leopard	Qualitative	Different basic level category (human, animal)	More prominent differences	Asymmetrical	High salience in object of comparison	Meaningful	Distinct	Simile
An elephant isn't as big as a whale	An elephant	a whale	Quantitative	Same superordinate category (animal)	More prominent similarities	Asymmetrical	Same salience	Meaningful	Similar	Comparison
I'll send it out as soon as the machine is available	It	-	-	-	-	-	-	-	-	Not Applicable

recanting without saying, "Sorry, we messed up". Here, we annotate the subject of comparison as *February's policy note*, and assign *an institution can come to recanting without apologizing* instead of *an institution can come to recanting without saying, "Sorry, we messed up."* as the object of comparison.

Exceptional cases In statements such as:

(8) *He paid as much as a million dollars for the painting*. There is no object of comparison. This statement merely is a form of emphasis and the marker *as much as* in this context does not compare two entities. In such cases, we mark the subject of comparison (if it is clear, i.e. *he*) and the object of comparison as *Not Applicable*.

However, this does not mean that all statements that contain the phrase *as much as* should be discarded. For example,

(9) In *She enjoys reading as much as watching movies*, we have a subject of comparison *reading* and an object of comparison *watching movies* which highlights and quantifies what *she* likes doing better by the phrase *as much as*.

3.2.2 Annotating the Characteristics

The second step of the annotation process is to annotate the characteristics derived from the subject and object of comparison. In this step we consider the factors introduced in Section 3.1 and establish them as the seven categories to make the final judgement of whether a statement is a simile or not. These seven categories are: *nature, categories, feature matching, symmetry, salience, broad unifying concept and domain incongruence*. See Table 3.

From the aforementioned considerations, the most important characteristics that enable us to decide if a statement is a comparison or a simile are:

(1) *Categories*: If the subject and object of comparison belong to the same super-ordinate category, more often than not, the statement is a *comparison*.

The category of domain incongruence is directly dependent on the characteristic of the category.

(2) *Feature matching*: A statement can be a simile if there are more prominent differences than similarities.

(3) *Broad unifying concept*: Since comparisons can practically be drawn from any two concepts, we need to establish if the comparison makes sense for it to be a simile.

However, as mentioned above, we still need to annotate the other characteristics since in some cases, we need to go beyond main three characteristics to assess the comparative statement.

Based on these relevant characteristics, we decide if a statement is a comparison or a simile.

For example,

(1) *Better is the poor who walks in his integrity, than he who is perverse in his ways, and he is rich* (see Table 4). The subject of comparison is *The poor who walks in his integrity* and the object of comparison is *The rich who is perverse in his ways*. This statement is a *comparison*. In this example, we can see there is an equal number of characteristics for the statement to be a comparison or simile. In such cases, we will concentrate more on the characteristics *category, feature matching* and *broad unifying concept* to determine if we annotate it as a comparison or a simile. Through this example we can see that not all comparisons have to be symmetrical or quantitative in nature.

(2) *The root of a flower is as weak as a baby's finger.* In this case, the subject of comparison is *The root of a flower* and the object of comparison is *a baby's finger*. This statement is a *simile*. In this example, we can see that the subject of comparison and the object of comparison are

Table 3: Characteristics of Comparisons and Similes

Characteristic	Comparison	Simile
Nature	Quantitative	Qualitative
Categories	Can belong to the same superordinate category	Should belong from different basic objects
Feature matching	More prominent similarities than differences between entities	High prominent differences than similarities between entities
Symmetry	Symmetrical	Asymmetrical
Salience	High salient in subject of comparison than object of comparison	High salient in object of comparison than subject of comparison
Broad concept	Can be any comparison (even nonsensical)	Should be a meaningful comparison
Domain incongruence	Similar semantic domains	Distinct semantic domains

Table 4: Example 1: Better is the poor who walks in his integrity, than he who is perverse in his ways, and he is rich

Attribute	Value
Nature	Qualitative
Category	Same superordinate category (human nature)
Feature matching	More prominent differences than similarities
Symmetry	Asymmetrical
Salience	Both have the same salience
Broad concept	Meaningful
Domain incongruence	Similar

symmetrical, i.e. they can be used interchangeably. This is a typical characteristic of comparisons. We also have the same salience for this statement. For example, the root of a flower is small and fragile, which are also both typical characteristics of a baby's finger. In such cases (as discussed above), we prioritize the characteristics *category, feature matching* and *broad, unifying concept* to aid us in deciding. According to those three characteristics, the statement qualifies as being a simile.

(3) *So February's policy note is a stunning reversal – as close as an institution can come to recanting without saying, "Sorry, we messed up." But it parallels a general shift in economists' opinion* (see Table 5). The subject of comparison is *February's policy note* and the *object of comparison* is *an institution can come to recanting without apologizing*. As we mentioned above, the most important characteristics when deciding between comparison or simile are *categories, feature matching, broad unifying concept*. If we have a different basic level category, more prominent differences and a meaningful concept, we annotate the statement as a *simile*. However, here we have another step that we need to consider before deciding if the statement is a simile or not, i.e. *the nature*. If the nature is quantitative, chances are high that there is no shared property, and the comparison between the subject and object of comparison are drawn just to quantify the relevance of the comparators. In such cases, we would identify the statement as a *comparison*. This is especially easy if we have an "as ... as" construction.

Table 5: Example 3: So February's policy note is a stunning reversal – as close as an institution can come to recanting without saying, "Sorry, we messed up." But it parallels a general shift in economists' opinion

Attribute	Description
Nature	Quantitative
Category	Different basic level category (politics, human nature)
Feature matching	More prominent differences
Symmetry	Symmetrical
Salience	Same salience
Broad concept	Meaningful
Domain incongruence	Distinct

(4) *It's as lovely as a rose.*

In such cases, we cannot annotate the subject of comparison in a meaningful way, since "it" and could signify anything. In such cases we will leave the annotation of the characteristics blank and classify the statement as *Not Applicable*.

However, in statements where we have a context following the undefined subject of comparison, we might be able to resolve it. For example,

(5) *"What are the twelve signs of the Zodiac, in the order in which the sun passes them by in the course of a year?" - "Um, let me think for a minute!" - "No thinking! It's got to come as quick as a shot!"* In this case, we can reconstruct the unspecified subject of comparison *it* to *the answer*.

(6) *He is a figment as much as a figure.*

This example is an idiomatic expression. Even though they have the structure of a comparison, subject and object of comparison cannot be derived in a meaningful way. We annotate such cases as *Not Applicable*.

4 Data

The data for the annotation study was extracted from the English data present in the Parallel Meaning Bank (PMB) (Abzianidze et al., 2017) and filtered by the simple regular expression: `as [a-z]* as an?`. We then manually clean the data to remove duplicate instances, shorten the sentences to simplify annotation and split complex sentences with multiple comparative structures into shorter sentences. For example, *"I am as light as a feather, I am as happy as an angel, I am as merry as a school-boy"* was split into three simple comparative sentences. Furthermore, all instances of "as well as" were removed as those are usually synonymous to statements containing *too* or *also*. We eventually gather a data set of 100 sentences. The statistics of our gold standard annotation can be found in Table 6.

Table 6: Results of Gold Standard Annotation

Class	Count
Simile	63
Comparison	19
Not Applicable	18

4.1 Annotation procedure

Subsequently, we conducted annotations based on the above presented annotation guidelines with two expert annotators[6]. It is to be mentioned here that the first-language of the annotators are Bengali and Italian, and none of them use English as their first language. This led to variation in understanding and interpreting many statements caused by a language barrier. The annotators were presented with 100 sentences and were asked to annotate the nine categories. Table 2 presents a snippet of such an annotation. After independent annotation, the gold standard was derived through resolving cases where Annotator 1 and 2 disagreed in their judgement by discussion between the experts.

4.2 Inter-annotator Agreement

We have analyzed the inter-annotator agreement using Cohen's κ across the following pairs (see Table 7). The annotation by the LLM is the result of prompting (that is discussed in section 5). The highest agreement is achieved between the LLM using different prompts, i.e. 64%. We have noted interesting differences of opinion between our human annotators, see subsection 6.1.

Table 7: Inter-annotator agreement

Comparison	Cohen's κ
Annotator 1 vs Annotator 2	0.62
Annotator 1 vs Zero-shot	0.47
Annotator 2 vs Zero-shot	0.39
Annotator 1 vs Few-shot	0.52
Annotator 2 vs Few-shot	0.55
Zero-shot vs Few-shot	0.64

5 Experiments

In correspondence to the human annotation, we also conduct machine learning experiments to help determine if and how the process of classifying a comparative statement into comparison or simile can be automated. For that purpose, we use a simple support vector machine (SVM) as our baseline (with support vector classification (SVC), a linear kernel, and the default regularization parameter (C=0.1)). The data was split into a training set and test set of 80%-20% and Tf-idf vectorizer was used as the feature extractor.

[6]Author 1 and Author 3

We then conduct two experiments with the Large Language Model (LLM) LLama-3.3-70b-instruct[7].

We perform the first experiment using zero-shot prompting, in which the LLM is asked to judge if a comparative statement is a *simile, comparison* or *Not Applicable*, see Table 9. In the second experiment, we apply a few-shot prompting method to the same model, see Table 10.

We test the performance against the gold standard annotated data.

6 Results

In this section, we report the results on the annotation task (inter-annotator agreement, Cohen's κ), and the machine learning experiments, i.e. the SVM baseline and LLM annotations that were conducted on the curated data set.

6.1 Error Analysis for Human Annotations

In this section, we will examine interesting differences noticed between the judgements of the two annotators. We categorize the differences into the following:

Stock similes: Certain comparisons are perceived as a proverb to one annotator while the other perceives it simply a simile (according to the annotation guideline). In figurative language such proverbial comparisons are called stock similes (Norrick et al., 2010). As Seh (2016) says, "The simile is so ancient a figure of speech that several comparee NP/quantity or quality-standard of comparison combinations have become an integral part of the language, losing in the process their initial figurative flavour". Stock similes thus have such familiar associations through the passing of time that they fail to impress or not even seen as figurative to the common folk (De Mille, 2024). Some of the examples of such disagreements from our data are:

(1) I am as healthy as a horse.

(2) Tom is as fast as a fiddle.

Cultural implications: Different cultural background has affected the decision of annotators in some cases. In such instances we see one annotator labels a comparison as a simile and the other (by perceiving the comparison quite literally) labels the same as Not Applicable. In such cases, difference in interpreting the construction literally vs. figuratively plays a role in the decision of the annotator.

(3) The child is as neat as a pin.

(4) He is as nutty as a fruitcake.

For (3), the annotator cannot associate the shared property *neat* with the object of comparison *pin*. The annotator perceives them as very different concepts and fails to have a meaningful relationship, i.e. a child can can be neat, but neat cannot be associated with a pin. Here, we can see how one annotator has annotated the sentences strictly according to the guidelines, while the other favored a more holistic perspective.

Syntactic Structure: In this category, we see that sometimes the syntactic structure of having "like" or "as" leads to misinterpretation. For example,

(5) Having eluded killers like malaria and AIDS, one should not then be killed prematurely by cancer – especially a form of cancer that could have been prevented with something as simple and as affordable as a vaccine.

In the (5), one annotator annotates it as *Not Applicable*, while the other annotates it as a simile. The annotator choosing simile as a category was also influenced by the widely spread metaphorical use of "illness as a killer", "illness as a war", which is also attested in the cognitive metaphor literature (Sontag, 1978; Lakoff and Johnson, 2008).

Metaphorical Influence: We have some interesting cases of metaphorical influence. For example,

(6) He is as innocent as a child.

(7) Her skin is as firm as a teenager's.

While on the surface level it seems like a comparison (since they belong to the same category), it is not always simple even though the subject and object of comparison are both humans. Here, we are comparing an adult to a child. The annotators disagree in this case, wherein one perceives it as a mere comparison, while the other thinks it's a simile. During discussion, the annotator said that metaphorical expression had an influence on the decision. We plan to look into more of these cases the future. For that purpose, we need to find more fine-grained way of annotating such cases, e.g. by looking at similar forms of expression from different domains like fiction.

[7] https://www.llama.com/docs/model-cards-and-prompt-formats/llama3_3/

6.2 Results of the Machine Learning Experiments

In this section, we report the results of our SVM baseline and the LLM- Llama 3.3-70b-instruct on our curated data set. In Table 8 we compare the results of all three experiments that we evaluate on our gold standard data. We see that in the third experiment, i.e. prompting the model with proper examples as illustration (see Section 5), the LLM is able to massively improve the accuracy from 72% to 82%.

Table 8: Baseline vs. LLM performance

Model	Accuracy
SVM	75%
Llama-3.3-70b (zero-shot)	72%
Llama-3.3-70b (few-shot)	82%

While the performance is encouraging, we also see some cases where the LLM takes some unexpected decisions (see Table 11). Even with clear prompts such as Instruction Prompt 2 (*If the subject and object of comparison belong to the same category, you should mark as a Comparison*), the LLM annotated the Example 1 as a *simile*. Interestingly, even though Instruction Prompt 1 says (*if there is unspecified subject or object of comparison you should mark it as Not Applicable*), the LLM judges Example 2 as *simile* and Example 4 as *comparison*.

6.3 Discussion

As pointed out by the Perspectivist Data Manifesto[8], linguistic annotation follows four basic components. A *set of instances* to annotate, followed by a *target phenomena* which is described in detail with guidelines and examples, an *annotation schema* that defines the phenomenon to annotate and finally a *group of annotators* who are deemed fit to carry out the annotation based on their expertise. In this paper, we follow the same procedure to make a distinction between when a comparative structure is called a comparison, and when it becomes it's figurative counterpart, simile. We begin with first defining the phenomena, comparison and simile, followed by the illustrations on what to annotate and a step-by-step process on how to annotate the comparative structures. Our fine-grained annotation guideline allows annotators to take a well-formed decision on whether a comparative statement is a literal comparison or a simile.

As discussed in section 6.1, the annotation of figurative language can be influenced by many factors, with cultural differences playing a significant role in shaping perspectives. This phenomenon of difference in perspective is reflected in the score of our inter-annotator agreement between our human annotators. We use the Cohen κ metric to track how similar the answers of our annotators are to the same set of questions. The final data set contains 63 instances of *Simile*, 19 instances of *Comparison* and 18 instances of *Not Applicable* on our gold standard annotation. Subsequently, our machine learning experiments also yield interesting results. From the performance of our baseline (SVM) and LLM (Llama-3.3-70b-instruct), we can clearly see that our baseline performs better than the zero-shot prompt with the LLM. This raises the interesting question of how well we can trust the judgments of LLMs, especially in subjects that require taking world knowledge into account. Our best performing model is the few-shot prompting with an accuracy of 82% which clearly indicates that by prompting a few examples the performance of the LLM can be boosted for such a classification task, showing the benefit of prompt engineering.

7 Conclusion and Future Work

This work is the first step towards building a pipeline to automatically detect and annotate similes in fiction. It is essential to first draw a clear distinction between a comparative structure as a literal comparison and as a simile, which is what we aimed through this work. The next focus of our project is to develop a fine-grained annotation guideline to annotate similes in literature. We also aim to make the guidelines largely language-agnostic, with a focus on English that will be refined for other languages, such as Bengali, that come from a completely different language family with a different word order. Furthermore, the final objective is to perform a quantitative and contrastive analysis to uncover cultural narratives and values depicted in simile usage in literature and the way of expression of humans in general.

[8] https://pdai.info/

8 Appendices

Table 9: Zero-shot prompt

Zero-shot Prompt:
Does the sentence contain a comparison, a simile, or not applicable? Answer with "Comparison," "Simile," or "Not Applicable" only. Do not write anything else.

Table 10: Prompt for the few-shot experiment

Few-shot prompting:
Here are some examples to guide your response:
1. Tom is as fast as a rabbit – *Simile*
2. He donated as much as 50,000 dollars to the charity – *Not Applicable*
3. An elephant isn't as big as a whale – *Comparison*
Instruction:
1. If there is an unspecified subject or object you should mark it as *Not Applicable*
Some examples:
a. Nothing is as good as a breath of fresh air
b. It's as beautiful as ever
2. If the subject or object of comparison belongs to the same category (human-human, animal-animal, celestial body, social gathering) **you should mark it as *Comparison***
Some examples:
a. I am as beautiful as my mother
b. She is as strong as her father
c. He was as drunk as the guitarist
d. The Earth looks as round as the Sun
e. Her eyes are as beautiful as a child's
f. The surface was as white as the wall
3. If there is an idiomatic expressions you should mark it as *Not Applicable*[9].
Some examples:
a. I am feeling under the weather today
4. If there is "like" as an example in the sentence you should mark it as *Not Applicable*
Some examples:
a. I feel like an ice cream

References

Lasha Abzianidze, Johannes Bjerva, Kilian Evang, Hessel Haagsma, Rik Van Noord, Pierre Ludmann, Duc-Duy Nguyen, and Johan Bos. 2017. The parallel meaning bank: Towards a multilingual corpus of translations annotated with compositional meaning representations. *arXiv preprint arXiv:1702.03964.*

Miriam Amin and Manuel Burghardt. 2020. A survey on approaches to computational humor generation. In *Proceedings of the 4th Joint SIGHUM Workshop on Computational Linguistics for Cultural Heritage, Social Sciences, Humanities and Literature*, pages 29–41.

Octavius Freire Aristotle et al. 1889. The organon, or logical treatises, of aristotle: With introduction of porphyry.

Alexander Bain. 1890. *English composition and rhetoric.* Longmans, Green & Company.

Joanne Boisson, Zara Siddique, Hsuvas Borkakoty, Dimosthenis Antypas, Luis Espinosa Anke, and Jose Camacho-Collados. 2024. Automatic extraction of metaphoric analogies from literary texts: Task formulation, dataset construction, and evaluation. *arXiv preprint arXiv:2412.15375.*

Tuhin Chakrabarty, Yejin Choi, and Vered Shwartz. 2022. It's not rocket science: Interpreting figurative language in narratives. *Transactions of the Association for Computational Linguistics*, 10:589–606.

Jean Cohen. 1968. La comparaison poétique: essai de systématique. *Langages*, (12):43–51.

Francesca De Luca Fornaciari, Begoña Altuna, Itziar Gonzalez-Dios, and Maite Melero. 2024. A hard nut to crack: Idiom detection with conversational large language models. In *Proceedings of the 4th Workshop on Figurative Language Processing (FigLang 2024)*, pages 35–44, Mexico City, Mexico (Hybrid). Association for Computational Linguistics.

James De Mille. 2024. *The elements of rhetoric.* BoD–Books on Demand.

Robert MW Dixon. 2018. Comparative constructions in english. In *Language at Large*, pages 472–493. Brill.

George Eliot. 1994. *Middlemarch.* Blackwood. Public domain.

John Henry Freese et al. 1926. *Aristotle, with an English Translation: The" Art" of Rhetoric*, volume 22. W. Heinemann.

Mengshi Ge, Rui Mao, and Erik Cambria. 2023. A survey on computational metaphor processing techniques: From identification, interpretation, generation to application. *Artificial Intelligence Review*, 56(Suppl 2):1829–1895.

Table 11: Some mismatched examples of few shot prompting

No	Sentences	LLM	Gold Standard
1	I am as giddy as a drunken man	Simile	Comparison
2	It's as lovely as a rose	Simile	Not Applicable
3	He is a figment as much as a figure	Comparison	Not Applicable
4	Nothing is as hard as a diamond	Comparison	Not Applicable
5	Tom isn't as naive as a lot of people think he is	Comparison	Not Applicable

Alexander Jamieson. 1823. *A Grammar of Rhetoric and Polite Literature: Comprehending the Principles of Language and Style, the Elements of Taste and Criticism, with Rules for the Study of Composition and Eloquence. Illus by Appropriate Examples, Selected Chiefly from the British Classics, for the Use of Schools Or Private Instruction.* G. & WB Whittaker.

Aditya Joshi, Pushpak Bhattacharyya, and Mark J Carman. 2017. Automatic sarcasm detection: A survey. *ACM Computing Surveys (CSUR)*, 50(5):1–22.

George Lakoff and Mark Johnson. 2008. *Metaphors we live by*. University of Chicago press.

Yucheng Li, Shun Wang, Chenghua Lin, and Frank Guerin. 2023. Metaphor detection via explicit basic meanings modelling. In *Proceedings of the 61st Annual Meeting of the Association for Computational Linguistics (Volume 2: Short Papers)*, pages 91–100, Toronto, Canada. Association for Computational Linguistics.

Lizhen Liu, Xiao Hu, Wei Song, Ruiji Fu, Ting Liu, and Guoping Hu. 2018. Neural multitask learning for simile recognition. In *Proceedings of the 2018 Conference on Empirical Methods in Natural Language Processing*, pages 1543–1553, Brussels, Belgium. Association for Computational Linguistics.

Vlad Niculae. 2013. Comparison pattern matching and creative simile recognition. In *Proceedings of the Joint Symposium on Semantic Processing. Textual Inference and Structures in Corpora*, pages 110–114.

Vlad Niculae and Cristian Danescu-Niculescu-Mizil. 2014. Brighter than gold: Figurative language in user generated comparisons. In *Proceedings of the 2014 conference on empirical methods in natural language processing (EMNLP)*, pages 2008–2018.

Vlad Niculae and Victoria Yaneva. 2013. Computational considerations of comparisons and similes. In *51st Annual Meeting of the Association for Computational Linguistics Proceedings of the Student Research Workshop*, pages 89–95.

Neal R Norrick, Armin Burkhardts, and Brigitte Nerlich. 2010. *Pear-shaped and pint-sized: Comparative compounds, similes and truth*. na.

Sunny Rai and Shampa Chakraverty. 2020. A survey on computational metaphor processing. *ACM Computing Surveys (CSUR)*, 53(2):1–37.

Eleanor Rosch. 1978. Principles of categorization. In *Cognition and categorization*, pages 27–48. Routledge.

Suzanne Patience Mpouli Njanga Seh. 2016. *Automatic annotation of similes in literary texts*. Ph.D. thesis, Université Pierre et Marie Curie-Paris VI.

Susan Sontag. 1978. Illness as metaphor. *Farrar, Straus and Giroux*, 3.

Gerard J Steen, Aletta G Dorst, J Berenike Herrmann, Anna A Kaal, Tina Krennmayr, and Tryntje Pasma. 2010. *A method for linguistic metaphor identification: From MIP to MIPVU*. John Benjamins Publishing Company.

Virginia Waddy. 1889. *Elements of Composition and Rhetoric: With Copious Exercises in Both Criticism and Construction*. American Book Company.

Xiaoyue Wang, Linfeng Song, Xin Liu, Chulun Zhou, Hualin Zeng, and Jinsong Su. 2022. Getting the most out of simile recognition. In *Findings of the Association for Computational Linguistics: EMNLP 2022*, pages 3243–3252, Abu Dhabi, United Arab Emirates. Association for Computational Linguistics.

Identifying Small Talk in Natural Conversations

Steffen Frenzel[1] **and Annette Hautli-Janisz**[2]
[1]University of Potsdam, [2]University of Passau
steffen.frenzel@uni-potsdam.de, annette.hautli-janisz@uni-passau.de

Abstract

Small talk is part and parcel of human interaction and is rather employed to communicate values and opinions than pure information. Despite small talk being an omnipresent phenomenon in spoken language, it is difficult to identify: Small talk is situated, i.e., for interpreting a string of words or discourse units, outside references such as the context of the interlocutors and their previous experiences have to be interpreted. In this paper, we present a dataset of natural conversation annotated with a theoretically well-motivated distillation of what constitutes small talk. This dataset comprises of verbatim transcribed public service encounters in German authorities and are the basis for empirical work in administrative policy on how the satisfaction of the citizen manifests itself in the communication with the authorities. We show that statistical models achieve comparable results to those of state-of-the-art LLMs.

1 Introduction

Small talk is an omnipresent phenomenon when people interact with each other. There is a variety of reasons why people engage in small talk, for instance to exhibit politeness, to build a connection with strangers or to start a conversation. From a linguistic point of view, small talk is a highly interesting type of conversation, for it is not primarily focused on the exchange of information – one could even argue that the topic of the conversation does not really matter – but rather about the exchange of values and opinions. From a computational point of view, small talk is a challenging phenomenon because it is highly context dependent, i.e., the individual background of the interlocutors together with the situational context determines the scope and content of the small talk. The genre they mostly appear in, namely conversations, is underrepresented in terms of resources overall, but in terms of small talk in particular.

But small talk is crucial for socio-linguistic analyses of conversations. The source of the data in this paper are public service encounters in Germany (Espinoza et al., 2024), i.e., direct conversations between citizens and representations of the state where citizens ask for support or benefits from the representatives. Previous work in administrative policy shows that even if the decision of the state is not in favor of the citizen, emphatic communication yields satisfaction scores that parallel those of favorable decisions (Guy et al., 2014). Therefore, being able to measure and identify relation-building blocks of conversation paves the way for meaningful sociolinguistic analyses of conversations at scale. The challenges are two-fold: From a theoretical point of view, concrete definitions for the concept of small talk are lacking, making the process of generating annotation guidelines tricky. Moreover, small talk is mostly performed in conversations – those are time-consuming to record and to transcribe, making sufficient training data expensive.

The contributions of this paper are three-fold: First, we put forward theoretically-motivated annotation guidelines that can be used to annotate small talk in transcribed conversations. We also present a new, human-annotated small talk dataset containing more than 2,600 utterances from German public service encounters. Lastly, we show that statistical models such as Logistic Regression or Support Vector Machines achieve results comparable to state-of-the-art LLMs after thorough training. Our error analysis demonstrates the difficulties of classifying small talk automatically.

2 Background

2.1 Theoretical conceptions of small talk

There is an abundance of literature on naming and defining the concept of small talk. It is investigated with a focus on its social functions (Fried-

Proceedings of LaTeCH-CLfL 2025, pages 272–277
May 4, 2025 ©2025 Association for Computational Linguistics

laender, 1922; Malinowski, 1949; Ventola, 1979; Coupland et al., 1992; Eggins and Slade, 2004; Senft, 2009; Chen et al., 2022), its impact on conversational structures (Laver, 1975; Edmondson and House, 1981; Schneider, 1988) and with respect to cultural differences (Isbister et al., 2000; Endrass et al., 2011). Regarding the topics covered in small talk, Schneider (1988) develops a taxonomy of topics distinguishing between topics concerning the immediate situation, the external situation and the communication situation. Isbister et al. (2000) shows that certain conversational topics are perceived as safe or unsafe depending on the cultural background of the subjects. In a follow-up study, Endrass et al. (2011) investigate how the prototypical distribution of conversation topics turns out for German and Japanese.

An example of what we consider small talk is shown in Figure 1. Prototypical topics according to Schneider's (1988) taxonomy appear ('family' and 'holidays'), but they are dependent on situational context (here, pre-christmas). These topics appear frequently in our dataset since they are connected to the main purpose of the conversation (applying for family benefits, for example). Other topics from Schneider's taxonomy (e.g., 'music' or 'sports') appear rarely or not at all. For the purpose of the annotation guidelines, we apply the theoretical concept of small talk topics to the conversational and cultural context of our dataset.

1. **Citizen:** Yes, in four weeks!
2. **Official:** Crazy, completely crazy!
3. **Citizen:** [laughs] And the children are already going crazy at home. I mean it's not normal anymore!
4. **Official:** Already? Because of Christmas?
5. **Citizen:** Yes, well I have decorated the house already, you know? So yes, they are really exited.
6. **Official:** Ah, nice!

Figure 1: Example of small talk (translated, German original transcript id: `202111240815el4d0y4nMAYMS`)

2.2 Small talk in NLP

With the rise of conversational AI systems there has been a growing interest in modeling and generating small talk (also under the labels 'chitchat', 'informal conversation', 'off-topic' talk etc.) (Sun et al., 2021; Choudhary and Kawahara, 2022; Stricker and Paroubek, 2024b,a, inter alia). Different attempts were made to equip conversational agents with small talk functions (Bickmore and Cassell, 2001; Cavazza et al., 2010; Mattar and Wachsmuth, 2012; Zhao et al., 2022) since several studies indicate they can help establishing a personal bond with the user (Reeves and Nass, 1996; Morkes et al., 1998; Chao et al., 2021). Chiu et al. (2022) and Liu et al. (2023) focus on generating transitions from small talk to task-oriented dialogue.

For English, a few attempts to classify small talk have been made. Stewart et al. (2006) detect small talk in conversational telephone speech using supervised models, based on their taxonomy on simple lexical and syntactic features. Arguello and Rosé (2006) employ lexical and syntactic features into their classification model. Joty et al. (2013) develop an unsupervised topic segmentation model that detects small talk as 'off-topic' segments. Konigari et al. (2021) test for the first time a transformer-based model for off-topic detection in open-domain conversations. Lai et al. (2022) introduce a human-annotated dataset for chit-chat detection in English livestreaming videos.

For German, similar work is lacking. This carries over to studies using the latest generation of LLMs, which have not been tested on such a task and also not against traditional text classification models. This is the starting point of this paper: We introduce a novel dataset for German small talk[1] and show that statistical models are on a par with the latest generation of LLMs for predicting small talk in natural conversation.

3 Annotation study

3.1 Dataset

Our experiments are conducted on the PSE v1.0 dataset (Espinoza et al., 2024), a collection of verbatim transcribed Public Service Encounters in various German authorities that were recorded between 2021 and 2023. The dataset consists of 106 conversations with a total of more than 31,000 speaker turns and 433,780 tokens. PSEs are usually initiated by a citizen's application for social benefits. During those meetings the public official has to determine eligibility and extent of the support, which means that the conversations cover highly personal topics. The representatives are therefore interested in creating an open conversational atmo-

[1]The dataset and the full annotation guidelines are available on Github: `https://github.com/steffrenzel/naacl_2025_smalltalk_detection`

sphere, with small talk being one of the linguistic mechanisms to achieve this goal.

3.2 Manual annotation of small talk

For the scope of this paper, small talk is assumed to be polite conversation about light topics (Schneider, 1988). We refine the concept by having its purpose be the maintenance of social relations which are used to create a basis for the main discussion of a conversation. This kind of conversation is technically not restricted to certain topics, but it is usually about things that the speakers can easily agree on. Situational context and cultural background of the speakers can have an influence on the form of small talk, both on the length and the primary goal, as well as the choice of topics (Isbister et al., 2000; Mattar and Wachsmuth, 2012). We do not assume a constraint on the timing of small talk in conversations, because interlocutors can structure a conversation by continually inserting small talk sections (Schneider, 1988; Chen et al., 2022).

Based on these aspects we iteratively derive annotation guidelines by conducting manual multiple-person annotation rounds. Initial attempts with a 6-step Likert scale yield only slight agreement across annotators on individual speaker moves (on average 0.24 Cohen's Kappa). For the final dataset, we use complete conversations and subsequently annotate each speaker move with a binary value ('no small talk', 'small talk'), enabling the use of context in the prediction (more on this in Section 4). With this adjustment, agreement between the two annotators of the main study is 0.534 Cohen's Kappa for 700 speaker moves, which corresponds to moderate agreement (Viera and Garrett, 2005). Overall, Both annotators are native speakers of German and students in computational linguistics.

4 Predicting small talk

4.1 Training

We use four different models to identify small talk, two statistical models (Logistic Regression and SVM) and two language models (GBERT, GPT-4) to see how more expensive models fare in comparison with smaller models.

The baseline is Logistic Regression, with tf-idf vectorization for training and test set (German stopwords are removed by the vectorizer) and with sentence embeddings from `paraphrase-multilingual-MiniLM-L12-v2` (Reimers and Gurevych, 2019). For SVM, we again use tf-idf versus sentence embeddings and conduct 5-fold cross-validation with `StandardScaler` from `scikit-learn`. Fine-tuning is performed using `GridSearchCV`. Again, both tf-idf vectors and sentence embeddings are used for vectorization.

The first language model is GBERT, a BERT model specifically trained on German data (Chan et al., 2020), with the optimal settings determined by `GridSearchCV` (see Table 1). We also use GPT-4.o (OpenAI and et al., 2024) with zero-shot, few-shot and task framing prompting.

4.2 Results

The classification models show moderate performances. Interestingly, the final results of the different models are fairly close together, despite differing model complexity fine-tuning options. The full results are listed in Table 1. The weighted average F1-score is used here as the main evaluation metric.

LR needs thorough fine-tuning to achieve good results. Since we are dealing with an imbalanced dataset (the negative class is much more frequent than the positive class), the model tends to over-fit quickly and develops a bias to the majority class. To mitigate this, instead of the classes, the probabilities for each class are extracted and a manual decision boundary is applied to balance the output. This works fairly well and the final runs lead to the best overall results in the model comparison.

SVM performs slightly different in comparison to LR. In both cases, embeddings work significantly better than tf-idf vectors, which is to be expected. Despite the tf-idf vectors being less meaningful, SVM can still get reasonable results from them. In combination with sentence embeddings, the models performance is only slightly worse than the best run of LR.

The GBERT model leads to the worst overall performance. Training epochs and batch-size have to be kept small in order to mitigate over-fitting. The relatively small size of the training dataset in combination with the class imbalance again led to a biased classification. Several attempts were made to mitigate this effect, using class weights as well as minority class oversampling using SMOTE (Blagus and Lusa, 2013). However, these attempts did not lead to better performance.

Finally, we also test GPT-4.o using different prompting strategies. For the zero-shot runs, we just provide instructions but do not give any examples from our dataset, resulting in an F1-score

Model	Vectorization	Hyperparameters	Acc	Prec	Rec	F1	Support (0 / 1)
LR	tf-idf	`penalty=L2, solver=liblinear, boundary=0.16`	0.51	0.75	0.51	0.56	514 (417/97)
	distilbert	`penalty=L2, solver=liblinear, boundary=0.2`	0.71	0.75	0.71	**0.73**	514 (417/97)
SVM	tf-idf	`C=2.0, kernel='poly', gamma='auto', weight='balanced'`	0.60	0.62	0.57	0.59	514 (417/97)
	distilbert	`C=.0, kernel='poly', gamma='auto', weight='balanced'`	0.70	0.69	0.67	0.68	514 (417/97)
GBERT	-	`epochs=3, batch-size=16, warm-up-steps=500`	0.61	0.66	0.53	0.59	514 (417/97)
GPT-4.o	-	`Few-Shot, temp=0.3`	0.65	0.72	0.65	0.68	514 (417/97)

Table 1: Best results across models and configurations, weighted average is used to account for class imbalance.

of 0.62. In the few-shot approach we add a few examples for both classes to the prompt. This approach works best, with an F1-score of 0.68. In the chain-of-thought run, we asks the model to explain its decisions, which does not work well since the model constantly predicts the negative class. For all these runs, the temperature is set to 0.3 – higher temperatures lead to less reproducible results and do not improve performance.

4.3 Error analysis

Both the manual annotation and the automatic classification show the difficulties in identifying small talk in our dataset. A qualitative analysis of the results shows major differences in how the classes are distributed over the course of a conversation.

Since the human annotators were given transcripts of complete conversations and their task was to classify on utterance level, they were aware of the conversational context. In both manual annotations, it is rare for a single utterance to be classified as small talk, while the surrounding utterances are not small talk. Instead, usually longer sections of a conversation are continuously identified as small talk - these occur particularly frequently at the beginning and end of a conversation. The biggest discrepancies between the two human annotators arise when identifying the transitions between small talk and other parts of the conversation. This shows once again that it is difficult to clearly distinguish small talk from other parts of conversation - there is often a 'transition zone' that can be interpreted differently despite comprehensive annotation guidelines.

Classification models that learn the concept of small talk only indirectly from the training data, on the other hand, often classify stand-alone utterances positively, while the surrounding utterances are classified negatively. Presumably, lexical and semantic criteria are more important here than the position in the conversation and the contextual utterances.

5 Conclusion

The error analysis has shown which problems remain in the classification of small talk. Complex classification models such as neural networks and transformer-based models are less suitable for this task until more training data is available. LLMs achieve in general good results in classifying the data, but prompting is the only way to control the classification. Simple classification models are labor-intensive as they have to be precisely fine-tuned. Ultimately, however, they provide the most transparent classifications and - at least in our study - achieved results comparable to those of LLMs.

Limitations

Operationalizing the concept of small talk for this task remains the biggest challenge. We learned in the process of (re-)designing the manual annotation that conversational context is key information for the human annotators. However, this kind of information needs to better implemented into the automatic classification, e.g. by engineering additional features.

Acknowledgments

We would like to thank our student assistants Simon Bross, Jana-Linn Lauruschkus, Klymentii Myslyvyi and Anna-Kezia Rosenbauer for annotating the dataset and additional model testing. We would like to thank Diego Frassinelli for additional supervision and the reviewers for their helpful feedback.

The work reported on in this paper was funded by the Deutsche Forschungsgemeinschaft (DFG – German Research Foundation) under Germany's Excellence Strategy – EXC-2035/1 – 390681379 as part of the project "Inequality in Street-level Bureaucracy: Linguistic Analysis of Public Service Encounters" at the University of Konstanz.

References

Jaime Arguello and Carolyn Rosé. 2006. Topic-segmentation of dialogue. In *Proceedings of the Analyzing Conversations in Text and Speech*, pages 42–49, New York City, New York. Association for Computational Linguistics.

Timothy Bickmore and Justine Cassell. 2001. Relational agents: a model and implementation of building user trust. In *Proceedings of the SIGCHI Conference on Human Factors in Computing Systems*, CHI '01, page 396–403, New York, NY, USA. Association for Computing Machinery.

Rok Blagus and Lara Lusa. 2013. Smote for high-dimensional class-imbalanced data. *BMC bioinformatics*, 14:106.

Marc Cavazza, Raul Santos de la Camara, and Markku Turunen. 2010. How was your day? a companion eca. In *Proceedings of the 9th International Conference on Autonomous Agents and Multiagent Systems: Volume 1 - Volume 1*, AAMAS '10, page 1629–1630, Richland, SC. International Foundation for Autonomous Agents and Multiagent Systems.

Branden Chan, Stefan Schweter, and Timo Möller. 2020. German's next language model. In *Proceedings of the 28th International Conference on Computational Linguistics*, pages 6788–6796, Barcelona, Spain (Online). International Committee on Computational Linguistics.

Chi Hsiang Chao, Xi Jie Hou, and Yu Ching Chiu. 2021. Improve chit-chat and QA sentence classification in user messages of dialogue system using dialogue act embedding. In *Proceedings of the 33rd Conference on Computational Linguistics and Speech Processing (ROCLING 2021)*, pages 138–143, Taoyuan, Taiwan. The Association for Computational Linguistics and Chinese Language Processing (ACLCLP).

Jiaxin Chen, Yudong Guo, and Jinyun Duan. 2022. How and when phatic communion enhances advice taking. *Asian Journal of Social Psychology*, 25(4):611–622.

Ssu Chiu, Maolin Li, Yen-Ting Lin, and Yun-Nung Chen. 2022. SalesBot: Transitioning from chit-chat to task-oriented dialogues. In *Proceedings of the 60th Annual Meeting of the Association for Computational Linguistics (Volume 1: Long Papers)*, pages 6143–6158, Dublin, Ireland. Association for Computational Linguistics.

Ritvik Choudhary and Daisuke Kawahara. 2022. Grounding in social media: An approach to building a chit-chat dialogue model. In *Proceedings of the 2022 Conference of the North American Chapter of the Association for Computational Linguistics: Human Language Technologies: Student Research Workshop*, pages 9–15, Hybrid: Seattle, Washington + Online. Association for Computational Linguistics.

Justine Coupland, Nikolas Coupland, and Jeffrey Robinson. 1992. "how are you?": Negotiating phatic communion. *Language in Society*, 21:207 – 230.

W. Edmondson and J. House. 1981. *Let's Talk, and Talk about it: A Pedagogic Interactional Grammar of English*. U-&-S-Pädagogik. Urban & Schwarzenberg.

S. Eggins and D. Slade. 2004. *Analysing Casual Conversation*. Equinox Textbooks and Surveys in Linguistics. University of Toronto Press.

Birgit Endrass, Yukiko Nakano, Afia Akhter Lipi, Matthias Rehm, and Elisabeth André. 2011. Culture-related topic selection in small talk conversations across germany and japan. In *Intelligent Virtual Agents*, pages 1–13, Berlin, Heidelberg. Springer Berlin Heidelberg.

Ingrid Espinoza, Steffen Frenzel, Laurin Friedrich, Wassiliki Siskou, Steffen Eckhard, and Annette Hautli-Janisz. 2024. PSE v1.0: The first open access corpus of public service encounters. In *Proceedings of the 2024 Joint International Conference on Computational Linguistics, Language Resources and Evaluation (LREC-COLING 2024)*, pages 13315–13320, Torino, Italia. ELRA and ICCL.

Violet Helen Friedlaender. 1922. *Pied Piper's Street and Other Essays*. Arrowsmith.

Mary Guy, Meredith Newman, and Sharon Mastracci. 2014. *Emotional Labor. Putting the Service in Public Service*. Routledge.

Katherine Isbister, Hideyuki Nakanishi, Toru Ishida, and Cliff Nass. 2000. Helper agent: designing an assistant for human-human interaction in a virtual meeting space. In *Proceedings of the SIGCHI Conference on Human Factors in Computing Systems*, CHI '00, page 57–64, New York, NY, USA. Association for Computing Machinery.

S. Joty, G. Carenini, and R. T. Ng. 2013. Topic segmentation and labeling in asynchronous conversations. *Journal of Artificial Intelligence Research*, 47:521–573.

Rachna Konigari, Saurabh Ramola, Vijay Vardhan Alluri, and Manish Shrivastava. 2021. Topic shift detection for mixed initiative response. In *Proceedings of the 22nd Annual Meeting of the Special Interest Group on Discourse and Dialogue*, pages 161–166, Singapore and Online. Association for Computational Linguistics.

Viet Lai, Amir Pouran Ben Veyseh, Franck Dernoncourt, and Thien Nguyen. 2022. BehanceCC: A ChitChat detection dataset for livestreaming video transcripts. In *Proceedings of the Thirteenth Language Resources and Evaluation Conference*, pages 7284–7290, Marseille, France. European Language Resources Association.

John Laver. 1975. Communicative functions of phatic communion. In Adam Kendon, Richard M. Harris, and Mary R. Key, editors, *Organization of Behavior in Face-to-Face Interaction*, pages 215–238. De Gruyter Mouton, Berlin, New York.

Ye Liu, Stefan Ultes, Wolfgang Minker, and Wolfgang Maier. 2023. System-initiated transitions from chitchat to task-oriented dialogues with transition info extractor and transition sentence generator. In *Proceedings of the 16th International Natural Language Generation Conference*, pages 279–292, Prague, Czechia. Association for Computational Linguistics.

Bronislaw Malinowski. 1949. The problem of meaning in primitive languages. In *The meaning of meaning*. Routledge & Kegan Paul.

Nikita Mattar and Ipke Wachsmuth. 2012. Small talk is more than chit-chat. In *KI 2012: Advances in Artificial Intelligence*, pages 119–130, Berlin, Heidelberg. Springer Berlin Heidelberg.

John Morkes, Hadyn K. Kernal, and Clifford Nass. 1998. Humor in task-oriented computer-mediated communication and human-computer interaction. In *CHI 98 Conference Summary on Human Factors in Computing Systems*, CHI '98, page 215–216, New York, NY, USA. Association for Computing Machinery.

OpenAI and Josh Achiam et al. 2024. Gpt-4 technical report. *Preprint*, arXiv:2303.08774.

Byron Reeves and Clifford Nass. 1996. The media equation: How people treat computers, television, and new media like real people and pla. *Bibliovault OAI Repository, the University of Chicago Press*.

Nils Reimers and Iryna Gurevych. 2019. Sentence-bert: Sentence embeddings using siamese bert-networks. In *Proceedings of the 2019 Conference on Empirical Methods in Natural Language Processing*. Association for Computational Linguistics.

K.P. Schneider. 1988. *Small Talk: Analyzing Phatic Discourse*. Linguistic (Hitzeroth). Hitzeroth.

Gunter Senft. 2009. Phatic communion. In *Culture and language use*. John Benjamin.

Robin Stewart, Andrea Danyluk, and Yang Liu. 2006. Off-topic detection in conversational telephone speech. In *Proceedings of the Analyzing Conversations in Text and Speech*, pages 8–14, New York City, New York. Association for Computational Linguistics.

Armand Stricker and Patrick Paroubek. 2024a. Chitchat as interference: Adding user backstories to task-oriented dialogues. In *Proceedings of the 2024 Joint International Conference on Computational Linguistics, Language Resources and Evaluation (LREC-COLING 2024)*, pages 3203–3214, Torino, Italia. ELRA and ICCL.

Armand Stricker and Patrick Paroubek. 2024b. A few-shot approach to task-oriented dialogue enhanced with chitchat. In *Proceedings of the 25th Annual Meeting of the Special Interest Group on Discourse and Dialogue*, pages 590–602, Kyoto, Japan. Association for Computational Linguistics.

Kai Sun, Seungwhan Moon, Paul Crook, Stephen Roller, Becka Silvert, Bing Liu, Zhiguang Wang, Honglei Liu, Eunjoon Cho, and Claire Cardie. 2021. Adding chit-chat to enhance task-oriented dialogues. In *Proceedings of the 2021 Conference of the North American Chapter of the Association for Computational Linguistics: Human Language Technologies*, pages 1570–1583, Online. Association for Computational Linguistics.

Eija Ventola. 1979. The structure of casual conversation in english. *Journal of Pragmatics*, 3.

Anthony Viera and Joanne Garrett. 2005. Understanding interobserver agreement: The kappa statistic. *Family medicine*, 37:360–3.

Xinyan Zhao, Bin He, Yasheng Wang, Yitong Li, Fei Mi, Yajiao Liu, Xin Jiang, Qun Liu, and Huanhuan Chen. 2022. UniDS: A unified dialogue system for chit-chat and task-oriented dialogues. In *Proceedings of the Second DialDoc Workshop on Document-grounded Dialogue and Conversational Question Answering*, pages 13–22, Dublin, Ireland. Association for Computational Linguistics.

Why Novels (Don't) Break Through: Dynamics of Canonicity in the Danish Modern Breakthrough (1870–1900)

Alie Lassche[1], **Pascale Feldkamp**[1], **Yuri Bizzoni**[1], **Katrine Baunvig**[2] and **Kristoffer Nielbo**[1]

[1] Center for Humanities Computing, Aarhus University

[2] Center for Grundtvig Studies, Aarhus University

{a.w.lassche, pascale.feldkamp, yuri.bizzoni, baunvig, kln}@cas.au.dk

Abstract

Recent studies suggest that canonical works possess unique textual profiles, often tied to innovation and higher cognitive demands. However, recent work on Danish 19th century literary novels has shown that some non-canonical works shared similar textual qualities with canonical works, underscoring the role of text-extrinsic factors in shaping canonicity. The present study examines the same corpus (more than 800 Danish novels from the Modern Breakthrough era (1870–1900)) to explore socio-economic and institutional factors, as well as demographic features, specifically, book prices, publishers, and the author's nationality – in determining canonical status. We combine expert-based and national definitions of canon to set up a classification experiment to test the predictive power of these external features, and to understand how they relate to that of text-intrinsic features. We show that the canonization process is influenced by external factors – such as publisher and nationality – but that text-intrinsic features nevertheless maintain predictive power in a dynamic interplay of text and context. To ensure reproducibility, code and raw data are available at `https://github.com/centre-for-humanities-computing/text-extrinsic-canon`.

1 Introduction

Why do some novels have an enduring status in literary cultures while others remain outside the canon? The question of how novels achieve – or fail to achieve – canonical status has long fascinated literary scholars, generating a rich field of study. Recent work suggests that the textual features of literary works hold significant predictive power in determining their canonicity. Compared to non-canonical works, canonical works exhibit a unique textual profile (Barré et al., 2023; Brottrager et al., 2021; Porter, 2018), with stylistic characteristics connected to a higher cognitive load on the reader (Bizzoni et al., 2024; Wu, 2023; Wu et al., 2024).

Moreover, recent studies have gone beyond stylistic analysis to examine representations of canonical novels in semantic space. For example, Barré (2024), working with a corpus of historical French fiction, demonstrated that canonical works are often more deeply integrated into an intertextual network after publication. Similarly, in Feldkamp et al. (2024b) we examined textual embeddings of late 19th-century Danish novels, revealing that canonical novels distinguish themselves through innovation and impact. These novels not only stand out from their contemporaries but also appear to be literary trendsetters of their time.

Although previous studies have reaffirmed the role of textual features in determining a novel's canonicity, they do not fully explain the phenomenon. Either the features selected for analysis or the definition of the "canon" appear to create blind spots. For instance, in Feldkamp et al. (2024b) we identified a category of novels with textual profiles similar to canonical works, which, however, remain lesser known today. This suggests that textual qualities alone may not be sufficient to explain canonicity. The inability of these "non-canonical canonicals" (i.e., novels with textual profiles similar to canonical works) to achieve widespread recognition implies that other factors – beyond the textual features – play a crucial role in shaping canonicity.

Previous research has emphasized the importance of text-extrinsic factors such as the spread of novels, their accessibility to readers, and the socio-economic conditions surrounding their production (Heydebrand and Winko, 1996; Guillory, 1995). These aspects may influence canonization processes, where evaluation plays a role at every level, from publisher to reviewer and reader (Heydebrand and Winko, 1996; Brottrager et al., 2021) and where institutions also create and maintain the

Proceedings of LaTeCH-CLfL 2025, pages 278–290
May 4, 2025 ©2025 Association for Computational Linguistics

canon (Guillory, 1995). Such factors may be key to understanding why some works with seemingly "canonical" characteristics fail to enter the canon.

Thus, the case of Feldkamp et al. (2024b)'s non-canonical novels raises an important question: are models which focus primarily on text-intrinsic features overlooking key factors related to a novel's dissemination and reception? To answer this question, we investigate the broader socio-economic and institutional contexts of literary production, focusing on text-extrinsic factors – specifically, book prices, publishing houses, and the author's nationality – as predictors for a novel's canonicity.

We test the strength of text-extrinsic features for determining the canonical status of a novel in a classification task. We compare this to the performance of exclusively text-intrinsic features as used in Feldkamp et al. (2024b), as well as the combination of text-extrinsic features and text-intrinsic features. We propose two hypotheses:

H1: Novels that achieve canonical status are more strongly associated with a combination of text-intrinsic and text-extrinsic features (than with, e.g., text-intrinsic features alone).

H2: Novels that achieve canonical status are more strongly associated with either text-intrinsic or text-extrinsic features (such that the addition of, e.g., text-extrinsic features does not significantly improve the prediction of canonicity).

Our classification task with different text-intrinsic and text-extrinsic settings will give us an idea of how these factors interact in literary canon formation. Moreover, we inspect models based on all possible feature combinations individually and analyse misclassifications in depth to gauge what they can tell us about the boundaries of the literary canon.

For this study, we use the same corpus of novels from the Modern Breakthrough (*det Moderne Gennembrud*, 1870-1900) as we did in Feldkamp et al. (2024b), to examine them in a controlled context. This period is ideal for our study because it offers exhaustive coverage of literary production within a short timeframe, situating the novels within a small, relatively contained literary field (the Danish). This approach is significant because previous efforts to examine canonicity often struggle to account for the "dark numbers" of literary production – i.e., the forgotten or "great unread" works (Moretti, 2000). By focusing on a small, restricted, yet exhaustive setting, we can directly compare canonical novels to the contemporary production, avoiding the potential biases introduced by spuriously selected control groups.

This paper is structured as follows: Section 2 reviews related work on text-intrinsic and text-extrinsic features of canonical works, as well as the literary context of our corpus. Section 3 provides an overview of the corpus used in this study and explains how the canonicity of a novel was defined. Section 4 details our methodological pipeline, covering the creation of document representations, selection of text-extrinsic features, preparation of classification tasks, execution of experiments, and analysis of false positives. Section 5 presents the results, beginning with descriptive statistics, followed by the classification outcomes and an in-depth analysis of false positives. This is followed by a discussion in Section 6, and concluding remarks in Section 7.

2 Related Work

2.1 Features of the canon

The discussion about canon has often focused on the tension between two perspectives: one that views canonicity as conferred "from above", based on cultural, political, or institutional factors (Guillory, 1995), and another that sees it as a reflection of the inherent excellence of the works "from below", grounded in text-intrinsic features (Bloom, 1995). Recent studies have offered a more nuanced view of this debate. They demonstrate that text-extrinsic features[1] are strong predictors of canonicity (Brottrager et al., 2021), but also confirm that canonical works possess distinctive text-intrinsic characteristics compared to non-canonical works (Feldkamp et al., 2024b; Barré et al., 2023; Brottrager et al., 2021; Porter, 2018). Furthermore, canonical works exhibit textual profiles that differ not only from non-canonical works but also from other categories of literary recognition, such as bestselling or prize-winning novels (Bizzoni et al., 2024; Wu et al., 2024). For distinguishing canonical works on the large scale, studies have mainly focused on stylistic or syntactic features (Algee-Hewitt et al., 2016; Brottrager et al., 2021), such as linguistic measures related to a novel's complexity (Wu et al., 2024). Notably, this has been an attempt to gauge stylistic/syntactic differences between canon and non-canon overall, and not within a given field or period. As such, the more contex-

[1] I.e., cultural, political, or market traits, as in Wang et al. (2019).

tual, but also the semantic aspects of literary texts have been relatively overlooked. Still, recent studies like Barré (2024) use text embeddings to show how canonical works appear to have a stronger echo in the literary field after their publication than non-canonical works have – perhaps a stronger presence in shaping norms and trends for literature, which can here be interpreted as semantic.

Considerable recent work has examined indicators of canonicity, shedding light on their interrelations (Brottrager et al., 2022, 2021; Feldkamp et al., 2024a; Barré et al., 2023; Algee-Hewitt et al., 2016). For instance, school-based and scholarly indicators of canonicity appear more closely linked, while prize lists tend to be more disparate, revealing a complex interplay of actors in canonization (Barré et al., 2023; Feldkamp et al., 2024b).

However, little data-driven research has investigated how a work's canonization relates to factors of literary production in its historical context, such as the role of its publishing house. Prominently, Winko (2002) describes canonization as an emergent process shaped by numerous uncoordinated yet intentional actions, where individual choices accumulate over time. While some actors, such as institutions, play a more influential role as guardians or shapers of the canon, the impact of different actor types remains conjectural, and even recent studies question the role of text-intrinsic features (Herrmann, 2011).[2]

Building on this literature, the present study firstly tests the relative influence of text-intrinsic features in the process of canonization. Secondly, it compares and examines how specific aspects of the literary system – particularly the role of publishers, accessibility (e.g., prices), and author profile (nationality) – shape the canonization of a work within its historical context.

2.2 The Danish Modern Breakthrough

The Modern Breakthrough was a transformative period in Danish literature, marking the shift from romanticism to realism and naturalism. Spearheaded by Georg Brandes,[3] the movement emphasized literature's role in societal critique, focusing on social issues, individualism, and science (D'Amico, 2016; Bjerring-Hansen and Wilkens, 2023).

At the same time, literary tastes shifted: realist novels rose to prominence, while historical novels, like those by B.S. Ingemann, lost their earlier popularity (Bjerring-Hansen and Rasmussen, 2023; Martinsen, 2012). This polarization between realist and historical literature highlights the evolving dynamics of literary authority, market forces, and reader reception. Realist novels gained a place in the literary canon, while genres like the historical novel declined (Bjerring-Hansen and Wilkens, 2023). Canonicity, therefore, may have been shaped by more than just textual qualities; socio-economic factors, market dynamics, and reader demographics also seem to have played a significant role.

Overall, the Modern Breakthrough was composed by three interdependent shifts: one in literary production (subject and volume of printed literature), one in the literary field (rise and fall of publishers), and one in literary culture (changing reader tastes and demand for accessible literature). The Modern Breakthrough likely led to the rise of certain textual profiles and a more heterogeneous corpus, reflecting the dominance of Realism. Moreover, changes in publishing dynamics and reader preferences may complicate the modeling of the canon. This also means that the period of the Modern Breakthrough, though relatively short in duration (30 years), is anything but a minor period in terms of complexity.

3 Data

Our dataset comprises 838 original Danish and Norwegian novels published between 1870 and 1900, accompanied by metadata such as page count, (original) book price and publishing house. All novels, including those by Norwegian authors, were published in Danish and by Danish publishers. The corpus includes all first-edition novels from Danish publishers during this period, excluding non-novel works like short story collections.[4]

We use the categorization of novels' canonical status in Feldkamp et al. (2024b).[5] Their list of

[2]Herrmann (2011) argues that the idea of textual factors influencing all forms of canon formation is an implicit assumption, neither empirically proven nor accounted for in theoretical descriptions.

[3]Brandes' Copenhagen lecture (1871) and J.P. Jacobsen's *Mogens* (1872) are often considered the start of the Modern Breakthrough (Bjerring-Hansen and Rasmussen, 2023).

[4]This compilation – the MiMe-MeMo corpus – was developed by J. Bjerring-Hansen, P. Diderichsen, D. Haltrup, and N.E.D. Jørgensen, based on the Danish book index. For details, see Bjerring-Hansen et al. (2022). Version 1.1, utilized in this study, is accessible at: `https://huggingface.co/datasets/MiMe-MeMo/Corpus-v1.1`.

[5]Note that the categorization in Feldkamp et al. (2024b) is author-based, meaning that all books in the corpus by an author mentioned in their canon-list are tagged as canonical, even if it is not the author's most prominent work.

	titles	*authors*
Corpus	838	361
Canon	114	20
Other	724	342

Table 1: Statistics on the corpus.

the canon included authors indexed in the Educational Canon (*Undervisningskanon*) and the Cultural Canon (*Kulturkanon*), introduced by the Danish government in the early 21st century to promote Danish literature and standardize school curricula (Harbild et al., 2004). However, the government-defined canons exclude Norwegian authors and are likely driven by political agendas. To provide a more expert-driven perspective, Feldkamp et al. (2024b) collected a canon list from on the encyclopedia *Den Store Danske*, specifically its entry on 'det moderne gennembruds litteratur.'[6] Novels featured in the Cultural Canon, written by authors mentioned in the Educational Canon, or listed in the entry of 'det moderne gennembruds litteratur' in *Den Store Danske* are labeled as *Canon*, while all others are categorized as *Other*. (See corpus statistics and category details in Table 1.[7])

4 Methods

To test our hypotheses, we take the following approach in this paper:

1. Creating document representations. To build a compact representation of the texts, we use a large language model to create a semantic embedding of each novel – the `m-e5-large-instruct` model.[8] Previous work has tested this model against three other SOTA models for Danish in creating embeddings that would perform well generally and across historical Danish documents for this particular corpus (Feldkamp et al., 2024b).[9] Each novel is divided into chunks of the same size,[10] and embeddings were created for every chunk. The average embedding of all chunks of a novel is then used as a representative embedding for that novel.

2. Selection of text-extrinsic features. For each novel, we collect its first edition price, the editor that published it, and the nationality of the author, to represent some aspects of the novels' text-extrinsic profile. Price and editor could be causes of a novel's canonization, or consequences of the very qualities that ensured its canonization. Nationality, on the other hand, can only act as 'cause' in the selection pattern. We selected these features as a starting point because we expected them to have the strongest impact on canonization and because they exhibit a reasonable distribution across the two classes. Other relevant elements, like reprint history, had to be excluded due to data availability.

3. Preparing classification tasks. We perform a classification task using a simple Random Forest model. Random Forest was chosen for this task because it shows robust performance with mixed data types (continuous and categorical) and, through its ensembling, effectively mitigates overfitting. It is also a robust model, well suited for handling outliers. The two classes we are working with are *Canon* and *Other*.

4. Sampling. Because our two classes are unbalanced, we randomly downsample the larger class (*Other*). In order to guarantee robustness, we repeat the majority class downsampling (and training/testing) 50 times and take the average precision, recall, and F1-score across all 50 runs as our results. In each run, we reserve 10% of the data for testing.

5. Experiments. First, we perform a baseline task in which we use the average sentence length as a feature, we assume this to be a relatively simplistic representation of a novel text. Second, to model the impact of text-intrinsic and text-extrinsic features on the process of canonization, we experiment with the following features: (1) text-intrinsic features, i.e., embeddings, and (2) text-extrinsic features, i.e., price, publisher, and nationality. We run experiments with all possible combinations of these four features.

6. False positives analysis. To detect non-canonical novels that contain a textual profile similar to canonical novels, we closely analyse the false positives from the experiments that result from run-

[6] See `https://denstoredanske.lex.dk/det_moderne_gennembruds_litteratur`. Note that while government canons and *Den Store Danske* index various genres,this paper focuses solely on novels.

[7] An extended dataset with additional tags is available on `https://huggingface.co/datasets/chcaa/memo-canonical-novels`.

[8] `https://huggingface.co/intfloat/multilingual-e5-large-instruct`.

[9] The four models that were tested included the historical Danish `MeMo-BERT` model (Al-Laith et al., 2024), the best-performing Danish sentence encoder `DFM-large` (Enevoldsen et al., 2023), and the two best-performing open-weight models on SEB, `m-e5-large` and its prompt based version `m-e5-large-instruct` (Wang et al., 2024). For a detailed description of the task, see Appendices F and G in Feldkamp et al. (2024b).

[10] Since the maximum chunk size includes the length of the prompt, we use a chunk size of 512 - 87 = 425 characters.

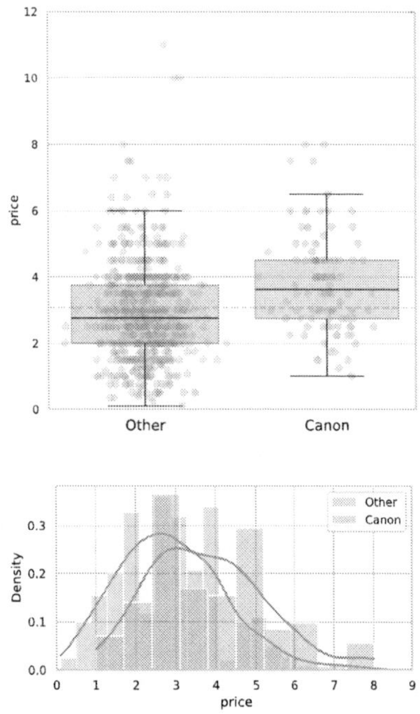

Figure 1: Boxplot (upper) and distribution (KDE) plot (lower) of book price across categories.

ning the model only on text-intrinsic features, i.e., embeddings. That is, we are interested in false positives where *Other* books were misclassified as *Canon*. In order to secure robustness of our results, we run enough iterations to obtain 12 predictions for each novel.[11]

5 Results

5.1 Descriptive statistics

Inspecting the descriptive statistics, we find that both the distribution of publishing houses and original book price vary between categories. The upper plot in Figure 1 shows the distribution of book prices per label category, depicted in two boxplots. The bottom figure shows a kernel density estimate (KDE) plot of each label category. On average, prices of canonical books are higher than those of non-canonical books. The heatmap in Figure 3 in Appendix A shows that almost all canonical books are published by a handful of the largest publishing houses (Gyldendal, Reitzel, Schubothe, Det Nordiske Forlag, Schou, and Philipsen). Together, these six publishing houses are responsible for 94% (107) of all canonical novels. However, this does not immediately imply that the larger the publishing house, the higher the chance a novel becomes canonical. There are other large publishing houses where no canonical novels were published (Jyds Forlags-forretning and A. Behrend, for example), and smaller publishing houses with a more even canon/non-canon ratio. Furthermore, these statistics show that publishing houses that are responsible for a large part of the canon production, also publish non-canonical books.

	Canon		Other	
	titles	*authors*	*titles*	*authors*
Danish	68%	70%	86%	89%
Norwegian	32%	30%	13%	10%
German	0%	0%	1%	1%

Table 2: Distribution of author nationalities within the corpus, based on number of authors and novels.

In Table 2, we present the distribution of author nationalities within our corpus, including both the distribution of unique authors and the distribution of all novels. Beyond Danish authors, the corpus includes works by Norwegian authors and a few German authors. The proportion of canonical novels written by Norwegian authors is notably higher than in the non-canonical group (32% versus 13%). In our classification tasks, we further examine the influence of the author's nationality on a novel's likelihood of achieving canonical status.

5.2 Classification tasks

The average performances of the classification experiments are summarized in Table 3. In nearly all experiments, the baseline performance based on average sentence length is surpassed. Embeddings alone appear to be strong predictors for canonicity, yielding F1-scores of 0.728 for the *Canon* class and 0.677 for the *Other* class. This aligns with the findings of Feldkamp et al. (2024b), suggesting that canonical novels possess a distinctive textual profile that sets them apart from the broader literary corpus. This result becomes even more impressive when we take into account that we are using an very rough representation of the novels – the texts are reduced to a set of semantic embeddings (of which we cannot say with certainty what exactly they do and do not capture), of which we then take the average.

However, several text-extrinsic features or com-

[11]In other words, we run enough iterations of our embedding-based classification model to ensure that every ' *Other* book is included in a test-set 12 times.

Type	Feature set	Precision		Recall		F1-score	
		Canon	*Other*	*Canon*	*Other*	*Canon*	*Other*
Baseline	avg_sentence_length	0.511	0.514	0.828	0.213	**0.585**	0.222
Text-extrinsic	price	0.551	0.553	0.560	0.534	**0.545**	0.534
	publisher	0.647	0.864	0.909	0.501	**0.753**	0.620
	nationality	0.633	0.549	0.293	0.839	0.389	**0.662**
	price_publisher	0.648	0.676	0.683	0.622	**0.658**	0.638
	price_nationality	0.580	0.580	0.551	0.601	0.554	**0.581**
	publisher_nationality	0.647	0.857	0.905	0.505	**0.752**	0.624
	price_publisher_nationality	0.657	0.684	0.691	0.637	**0.667**	0.652
Text-intrinsic	embeddings	0.681	0.764	0.795	0.624	**0.728**	0.677
Combination	embeddings_price	0.685	0.754	0.780	0.639	**0.723**	0.683
	embeddings_publisher	0.684	0.738	0.772	0.627	**0.718**	0.667
	embeddings_nationality	0.693	0.764	0.790	0.642	**0.731**	0.686
	embeddings_price_publisher	0.694	0.775	0.804	0.641	**0.739**	0.692
	embeddings_price_nationality	0.688	0.756	0.782	0.642	**0.726**	0.685
	embeddings_publisher_nationality	0.691	0.756	0.783	0.643	**0.728**	0.686
	embeddings_price_publisher_nationality	0.690	0.749	0.778	0.643	**0.726**	0.684

Table 3: Performance of Random Forest models based on a baseline (avg. sentence length) and different feature sets: text-extrinsic features only, text-intrinsic feature (embeddings), and a combination of text-extrinsic and -intrinsic features. The dataset is down-sampled to have balanced classes (114 data points per class). Values represent average results across 50 iterations. In green: the best settings for that class. In **bold**: the best predicted class for those settings.

binations thereof also obtain a high performance when predicting canonicity in our corpus. The average F1-scores range between 0.389 and 0.753. Some of these outperform the text-intrinsic features: the highest performance for the *Canon* class is achieved using the publishing house as the sole feature (0.753), followed closely by the combination of publisher and nationality (0.752). This reveals that text-extrinsic features also serve as good predictors for a novel's inclusion in the canon.

When text-extrinsic features are combined with embeddings, F1-scores for the *Canon* class fall within the range of 0.718 to 0.739, suggesting that together they achieve a similar performance in predicting canonicity. Across experiments – regardless of whether they rely on text-intrinsic or text-extrinsic features – the *Canon* class consistently exhibits better predictive outcomes. Exceptions arise when nationality alone, or in combination with price, are used as features.

To evaluate whether these results are disproportionally influenced by the very long tail of smaller publishing houses – each publishing only one novel – we conduct the same classification experiments on a subset of the corpus. This subset includes novels from the eight publishing houses that each contribute to the dataset with more than 25 novels (see Figure 3). The performance metrics for these experiments are shown in Table 4. Notably, the performance of the text-intrinsic features (embeddings) remain stable, with F1-scores stabilize at 0.713 for both classes. The F1-scores of the text-intrinsic features are slightly lower than in the experiments with the full corpus, and the same goes for the performances in experiments with both text-intrinsic and -extrinsic features. The pattern, observed in Table 3, remains the same: together, these features achieve a similar performance in predicting canonicity as in experiments with only text-intrinsic features.

These findings reinforce the robustness of embeddings in predicting canonicity and suggest that the textual characteristics distinguishing canonical novels are not merely artifacts of data imbalance among publishing houses.

5.3 Not breaking through

As much as these results show us that both text-extrinsic and text-intrinsic features play a role in the process of canonization, they also highlight novels that do not conform to this pattern. The F1-score of 0.728 when using embeddings as feature for the classification task, suggests there are novels with a textual profile similar to canonical works, but that remain lesser known today. In this section, we dive deeper into these false positives (incorrectly classified as *Canon*), to better understand why they failed to achieve canonical status. After predicting each novel 12 times, we filtered for non-canonical novels that were incorrectly labeled as *Canon* when

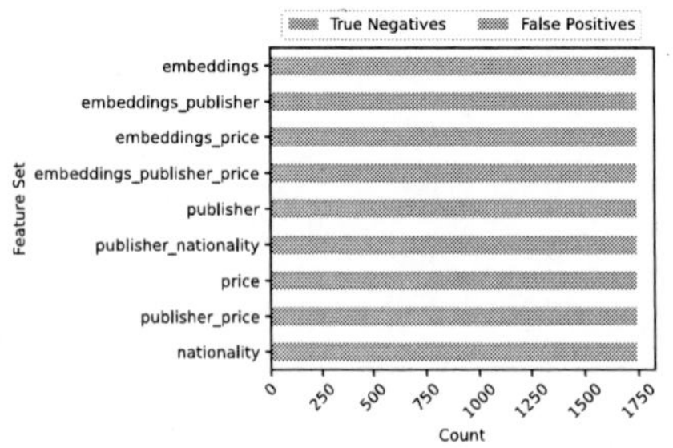

Figure 2: Ratio of true negatives (TN) and false positives (FP) of non-canonical novels that are incorrectly classified as canonical based on $embeddings$, when using other feature sets. We only include novels of which 75% of the predictions for $embeddings$ are FP. The unique number of novels is 145.

embeddings were used as features. We then applied a second filter, retaining only novels labeled as FP at least 9 times (75%). This resulted in a list of 145 novels, each predicted 12 times.

Figure 2 shows how these 145 novels are predicted when using different sets of features. The stacked bar plots show that when using text-extrinsic features such as publisher, price, nationality, or combinations thereof, the frequency of incorrect predictions for these 145 novels decreases substantially. In other words, text-extrinsic features make it easier to correctly predict these novels as non-canonical compared to embeddings. These false positive novels were published by 32 different publishing houses. Among them, 97 novels (67%) were published by the six houses responsible for most canonical novels: Gyldendal (54), Schubothe (14), Schou (11), Det Nordiske Forlag (9), Reitzel (7), and Philipsen (2). The remaining 48 novels were published by 26 smaller houses, most of which are represented by only one book in our dataset. To explore this phenomenon at the level of individual novels, we created the heatmap in Figure 4 in Appendix B. This visualization includes all 145 false positive novels (as identified using embeddings) and shows how often they were incorrectly classified as canonical when other feature sets were used. A cell value of 1 indicates that the novel was predicted as a false positive in all 12 predictions for that feature set, while a value of 0.5 indicates it was a false positive in 6 out of 12 predictions. Novels are sorted by the sum of their row values (excluding embeddings). The higher a novel appears in this heatmap, the more often our model correctly predicted it as *Other* based on its publisher, price, and the author's nationality.

Two novels that appear prominently in the heatmap (*Forfløjne Pile* and *På Solsiden*) are by Carl Muusmann (1863–1936), a Danish author and journalist who worked for various newspapers, including *Berlingske Tidende* and *Nationaltidende*. Muusmann was particularly known for his crime novels and was considered a pioneer in the genre. The textual style of these two novels is highly similar to canonical works, but they lack the correct combination of publisher, price, and other text-extrinsic features. Interestingly, another of Muusmann's novels, *Bondekunstneren*, appears lower in the heatmap, as its publisher and price align more closely with those of canonical works.

While many non-canonical novels were printed in lower-cost formats, some authors, such as Carl Muusmann, had works produced with considerable material quality. For example, Ilsøe (2014) notes that Muusmann's *Det lille Paradis* (1911) was published by Kunstforlaget Danmark with decorative endpapers designed by Axel Hou, indicating a level of aesthetic investment. This suggests that book material quality alone did not determine canonicity, and that institutional factors may have played a larger role in excluding certain works. Notably, Muusmann never remained with a single publisher; instead, his five novels in the dataset were published by four different houses, suggesting a lack of the institutional backing that often contributes to literary canonicity. Other authors with multiple novels high in the heatmap include Axel Betzonich (*Don Juans Efteraar*, *Peter Jensen*), Jakob Hansen (*Karen Hav*, *Ved Højvande*), and Otto Møller (*Lys over Landet!*, *Overmennesker*, *Millionærens Pilegrimsfærd*). These cases point in the direction of the hypothesis that writing in the correct textual style is insufficient for achieving canonical status; a novel must also have the right publisher, price, and potentially many other contextual attributes.

Conversely, novels at the bottom of the heatmap in Figure 4 exhibit the correct textual profile, publisher, price, and nationality, yet they are still excluded from contemporary canonical lists. This highlights, amongst other things, the inherent limitations of the canon itself. Despite expanding the canon by incorporating expert opinions (e.g., based on *Den Store Danske*), the presence of Norwegian author Jonas Lie in this heatmap (with his novels *Faste Forland*, *Livsslaven*, *Et Samliv*, *Niobe*, *Kommandørens Døttre*, *Thomas Ross*, and *Gå På*) underscores how perceptions of the canon differ

Type	Feature set	Precision		Recall		F1-score	
		Canon	*Other*	*Canon*	*Other*	*Canon*	*Other*
Baseline	avg_sentence_length	0.512	0.667	0.936	0.142	**0.656**	0.200
Text-extrinsic	price	0.536	0.544	0.516	0.564	0.518	**0.546**
	publisher	0.540	0.622	0.729	0.376	**0.599**	0.428
	nationality	0.627	0.537	0.302	0.807	0.393	**0.642**
	price_publisher	0.571	0.605	0.638	0.516	**0.596**	0.543
	price_nationality	0.559	0.547	0.540	0.564	0.538	**0.546**
	publisher_nationality	0.573	0.571	0.576	0.556	**0.562**	0.549
	price_publisher_nationality	0.573	0.588	0.618	0.527	**0.585**	0.542
Text-intrinsic	embeddings	0.719	0.738	0.724	0.709	**0.713**	**0.713**
Combination	embeddings_price	0.698	0.715	0.709	0.685	**0.695**	0.691
	embeddings_publisher	0.692	0.706	0.711	0.671	**0.694**	0.681
	embeddings_nationality	0.722	0.726	0.720	0.711	**0.713**	0.712
	embeddings_price_publisher	0.701	0.714	0.715	0.684	**0.700**	0.691
	embeddings_price_nationality	0.703	0.730	0.735	0.676	**0.710**	0.692
	embeddings_publisher_nationality	0.705	0.715	0.716	0.685	**0.703**	0.692
	embeddings_price_publisher_nationality	0.698	0.737	0.747	0.667	**0.714**	0.692

Table 4: Performance of Random Forest models based on a baseline (avg. sentence length) and different feature sets: text-extrinsic features only, text-intrinsic features (embeddings), and a combination of text-extrinsic and -intrinsic features. **The dataset only includes the novels of large publishing houses of which we have more than 25 novels in our dataset.** We have down-sampled to have balanced classes (107 data points per class). Numbers represent average results across 50 iterations. In green: the best settings for that class. In **bold**: the best predicted class for those settings.

across national boundaries. While Lie holds canonical status in Norway, he is not included in the version of the Danish canon that was used in this study.

6 Discussion

The results of our classification tasks show that both the text-intrinsic features and (a subset of) the text-extrinsic features provide predictive value of canonicity. In our experiments based on the full corpus, the text-extrinsic features outperform the embeddings. This confirms H2. However, when we only look at the performances of the experiments based on the subset of large publishing houses, text-intrinsic features outperform text-extrinsic features, which confirms our H2 in the opposite direction. A combination of both embeddings and nationality, or all features together, result in similar performances. This does not provide strong support for H1, but since a combination of features does not lower the predictive performance either, it is neither a rejection of this hypothesis. Additional experiments are required to be able to either confirm or reject H1.

In sum, the misclassification of novels, as discussed in the previous section, suggests that textual similarity to canonical works alone is not sufficient for inclusion in the canon: the lack of editorial support or limited distribution due to price choices might impact their status since their first publication. The presence of false positives having the 'right profile' in terms of price, editor and nationality, on the other hand, might indicate two different phenomena: *(i)* there are other text-extrinsic features that impact their canonical status, such as institutional support, inclusion in specific literary trends, and so forth; *(ii)* there are some essential text-intrinsic features, not captured by textual embeddings, that could explain their exclusion from the canonical group. Whether Muusmann and the other mentioned authors were excluded from our canonical lists for the first or the second order of reasons is probably a question for a next study.

There are several directions in which future research could develop. Firstly, the definition of canonicity could be refined, for example by using alternative lists, and by replacing categorical labels with a more continuous metric that better accounts for degrees of recognition. Expanding the range of text-extrinsic features could improve our understanding of how text and context interact with each other in the process of canonization. Additionally, a more detailed analysis of false positives – including their commercial success and literary afterlife – would help contextualize these works. One approach to this would be to do a text re-use study and investigate which novels are more often discussed in public debate – either cited in newspapers or mentioned in the works of influential critics such as Georg Brandes and Søren Kierkegaard. Moreover, it would be equally worthwhile to investigate the false negatives – canonical novels that were not classified as such based on their embeddings. Such an analysis could enhance our understanding of factors such as the role of publishers in the canonization process. Finally, further exploration is needed to understand why certain publishers are so closely linked to canon formation and how their role has evolved over time.

In terms of the methods we used, improving our sampling techniques (both through downsampling and upsampling) and refining our approach to text embeddings could enhance our results. Rather than averaging vectors, alternative approaches could be explored to experiment with different aggregation strategies. Further research is still needed to develop a more comprehensive understanding of what embeddings capture – and what they overlook. This could involve not only comparing embeddings with other textual features, such as syntactic complexity, cognitive processing difficulty, and stylistic patterns, but also employing these features as standalone text-intrinsic measures. Future work could also explore experiments with Generalized Additive Models (GAMs) to analyze potential non-linear relationships between features and classification outcomes, providing a more flexible yet interpretable alternative to linear models. Additionally, simpler and more interpretable methods, such as TF-IDF, could serve both as points of comparison and as alternative ways to analyze textual characteristics.[12]

7 Conclusion

This paper has examined the roles of text-extrinsic and text-intrinsic features in shaping a novel's canonicity, using the Danish Modern Breakthrough era (1870-1900) as a case study. We employed embeddings generated with the multilingual `m-e5-large-instruct` model as text-intrinsic features, while our text-extrinsic features included the novel's price, publisher, and the author's nationality. Using a Random Forest classification model, we predicted whether a novel belonged to the *Canon* or *Other* category based on various feature sets. Our findings demonstrate that text-extrinsic features are strong predictors of a novel's canonicity, suggesting that external dynamics play a significant role in canon formation. At the same time, embeddings alone emerged as robust predictors for canonicity, both on their own and when combined with text-extrinsic features. Importantly, we show that these results are not disproportionately influenced by the many small publishing houses that each published a single non-canonical novel.

We also explored what misclassifications reveal about the boundaries of the literary canon. By focusing on non-canonical novels with textual profiles similar to canonical works, we investigated why these novels failed to achieve canonical status. Our analysis seems to show that, for many authors, text-intrinsic characteristics were insufficient to secure a place in the canon. Conversely, we demonstrated that some novels exhibiting the correct textual profile, publisher, and price still failed to achieve canonical recognition.

Limitations

Creating embeddings

Prompts: This work utilizes the prompt-based embedding model `m-e5-large-instruct`. It is likely that embeddings could be notably different when using a different prompt. The chosen prompt was based on the tests in Feldkamp et al. (2024b), where the prompt '*Identify the author of a given passage from historical Danish fiction*' was used in the clustering task for historical Danish. Further prompt variations and variation effects on embeddings were presented in Feldkamp et al. (2024b).
Occurrence in training data: Canonical works may appear more frequently online or in varied contexts, potentially influencing embeddings in web-trained models. However, this effect is likely minor, as historical novels make up a small fraction of online discourse – especially in Danish, which represents a tiny portion of the multilingual model's training data. Ideally, training data should be examined, but this is often unfeasible due to limited access and computational constraints. The frequent rewriting of historical canons further complicates such efforts.

Canon definition

The concept of canonicity is inherently vague and subject to various interpretations. In our study, we adopt a binary categorization (canon/non-canon) as a pragmatic choice, acknowledging that the boundary between these categories is more fluid than

[12] A comparison between embeddings and TF-IDF representations was included in Feldkamp et al. (2024b).

our classification suggests. Our goal is to estimate broad distinctions rather than capture the full complexity of canon formation.

However, this approach may obscure cases where works occupy an ambiguous position within the literary field or where different actor types exert conflicting influence. In fact, this binary categorization simplifies a phenomenon that may be better represented as a continuous or multi-dimensional variable (Brottrager et al., 2022). One key issue with continuous canon variables is that they often assume independence between different actor evaluations – for instance, treating scholarly recognition and institutional adoption as separate yet equally weighted factors. In practice, these evaluations are often highly collinear, as institutional canons tend to reflect scholarly assessments, and vice versa (Feldkamp et al., 2024a; Barré et al., 2023). A more refined approach would account for these dependencies, potentially assigning different weights based on the extent to which one form of recognition reinforces another.

A further complication is whether canonicity should be treated as a singular phenomenon – one that different actor evaluations, such as scholars, institutions, etc., provide partial windows onto – or as multiple, overlapping but distinct processes. In our case, we implicitly conflate expert and government evaluations, assuming they reflect the same underlying phenomenon of "canon". This may not always hold, and future research could explore whether different forms of recognition should be treated as separate dimensions of canonicity or as interrelated signals of a shared phenomenon.

Acknowledgments

The authors of this paper were supported by grants from the Carlsberg Foundation (*The Golden Array of Danish Cultural Heritage*) and the Aarhus Universitets Forskningsfond (*Golden Imprints of Danish Cultural Heritage*).

Part of the computation done for this project was performed on the UCloud interactive HPC system, which is managed by the eScience Center at the University of Southern Denmark.

References

Ali Al-Laith, Alexander Conroy, Jens Bjerring-Hansen, and Daniel Hershcovich. 2024. Development and evaluation of pre-trained language models for historical Danish and Norwegian literary texts. In *Proceedings of the 2024 Joint International Conference on Computational Linguistics, Language Resources and Evaluation (LREC-COLING 2024)*, pages 4811–4819, Torino, Italia. ELRA and ICCL.

Mark Algee-Hewitt, Sarah Allison, Marissa Gemma, Ryan Heuser, Franco Moretti, and Hannah Walser. 2016. *Canon/Archive. Large-scale Dynamics in the Literary Field.* Stanford Literary Lab.

Jean Barré. 2024. Latent Structures of Intertextuality in French Fiction: How literary recognition and subgenres are framing textuality. In *Proceedings of the Computational Humanities Research Conference 2024*, volume 3834, pages 21–36, Aarhus, Denmark. CEUR-WS.

Jean Barré, Jean-Baptiste Camps, and Thierry Poibeau. 2023. Operationalizing Canonicity: A Quantitative Study of French 19th and 20th Century Literature. *Journal of Cultural Analytics*, 8(3).

Yuri Bizzoni, Pascale Feldkamp, Ida Marie Lassen, Mia Jacobsen, Mads Rosendahl Thomsen, and Kristoffer Nielbo. 2024. Good Books are Complex Matters: Gauging Complexity Profiles Across Diverse Categories of Perceived Literary Quality. *Preprint*, arXiv:2404.04022.

Jens Bjerring-Hansen, Ross Deans Kristensen-McLachlan, Philip Diderichsen, and Dorte Haltrup Hansen. 2022. Mending Fractured Texts. A heuristic procedure for correcting OCR data: 6th Digital Humanities in the Nordic and Baltic Countries Conference, DHNB 2022. In *CEUR Workshop Proceedings*, volume 3232, pages 177–186, Uppsala, Sweden.

Jens Bjerring-Hansen and Sebastian Ørtoft Rasmussen. 2023. Litteratursociologi og kvantitative litteraturstudier: Den historiske roman i det moderne gennembrud som case. *Passage - Tidsskrift for litteratur og kritik*, 38(89):171–189.

Jens Bjerring-Hansen and Sebastian Ørtoft Rasmussen. 2023. Litteratursociologi og kvantitative litteraturstudier: Den historiske roman i det moderne gennembrud som case. *Passage - Tidsskrift for litteratur og kritik*, 38(89):171–189. Number: 89.

Jens Bjerring-Hansen and Matthew Wilkens. 2023. Deep distant reading: The rise of realism in Scandinavian literature as a case study. *Orbis Litterarum*, 78(5):335–352.

Harold Bloom. 1995. *The Western Canon: The Books and School of the Ages*, 1st riverhead ed edition. Riverhead Books, New York, NY.

Judith Brottrager, Annina Stahl, and Arda Arslan. 2021. Predicting Canonization: Comparing Canonization Scores Based on Text-Extrinsic and -Intrinsic Features. In *Proceedings of the Computational Humanities Research Conference 2021*, volume 2989, pages 195–205.

Judith Brottrager, Annina Stahl, Arda Arslan, Ulrik Brandes, and Thomas Weitin. 2022. Modeling and predicting literary reception. *Journal of Computational Literary Studies*, 1(1):1–27.

Giuliano D'Amico. 2016. Modern Breakthrough. In *Routledge Encyclopedia of Modernism*, 1 edition. Routledge, London.

Kenneth Enevoldsen, Lasse Hansen, Dan S. Nielsen, Rasmus A. F. Egebæk, Søren V. Holm, Martin C. Nielsen, Martin Bernstorff, Rasmus Larsen, Peter B. Jørgensen, Malte Højmark-Bertelsen, Peter B. Vahlstrup, Per Møldrup-Dalum, and Kristoffer Nielbo. 2023. Danish foundation models. *Preprint*, arXiv:2311.07264.

Pascale Feldkamp, Yuri Bizzoni, Mads Rosendahl Thomsen, and Kristoffer L. Nielbo. 2024a. Measuring Literary Quality. Proxies and Perspectives. *Journal of Computational Literary Studies*. Forthcoming.

Pascale Feldkamp, Alie Lassche, Jan Kostkan, Márton Kardos, Kenneth Enevoldsen, Katrine Baunvig, and Kristoffer Nielbo. 2024b. Canonical Status and Literary Influence: A Comparative Study of Danish Novels from the Modern Breakthrough (1870–1900). In *Proceedings of the 4th International Conference on Natural Language Processing for Digital Humanities*, pages 140–155, Miami, USA. Association for Computational Linguistics.

John Guillory. 1995. *Cultural Capital: The Problem of Literary Canon Formation*. University of Chicago Press.

Steen Harbild, Stefan Hermann, and Steen Lassen, editors. 2004. *Dansk litteraturs kanon: rapport fra kanonudvalget*, 1. udg. ; 1. opl edition. Undervisningsministeriets forlag, København.

Leonhard Herrmann. 2011. System? Kanon? Epoche? Perspektiven und Grenzen eines systemtheoretischen Kanonmodells. In Matthias Beilein, Claudia Stockinger, and Simone Winko, editors, *Kanon, Wertung und Vermittlung*, pages 59–76. DE GRUYTER.

Renate von Heydebrand and Simone Winko. 1996. *Einführung in die Wertung von Literatur: Systematik - Geschichte - Legitimation*. 1953. Schöningh, Paderborn München.

Harald Ilsøe. 2014. Bogligt undertøj. Lidt om danske bogforsatser ca. 1880-1920. *Fund og forskning i det Kongelige Biblioteks samlinger*, 53:209–209.

Lone Kølle Martinsen. 2012. Bondefrihed og andre verdensbilleder. idehistorisker studier af b.s. ingemanns danmarkshistorie 1824-1836. *Temp - tidsskrift for historie*, 3(5):75–103.

Franco Moretti. 2000. Conjectures on World Literature. *New Left Review*, (1):54–68.

Jack Douglas Porter. 2018. Popularity/prestige. Technical report, Stanford Literary Lab.

Liang Wang, Nan Yang, Xiaolong Huang, Linjun Yang, Rangan Majumder, and Furu Wei. 2024. Multilingual e5 text embeddings: A technical report. *arXiv preprint arXiv:2402.05672*.

Xindi Wang, Burcu Yucesoy, Onur Varol, Tina Eliassi-Rad, and Albert-László Barabási. 2019. Success in books: predicting book sales before publication. *EPJ Data Science*, 8(1):31.

Simone Winko. 2002. Literatur-Kanon als 'invisible hand'-Phänomen. In *Literarische Kanonbildung*, pages 9–24. TEXT+KRITIK.

Yara Wu. 2023. Predicting the Unpredictable. Using Language Models to Assess Literary Quality. Master's thesis, Uppsala University, Uppsala.

Yara Wu, Yuri Bizzoni, Pascale Moreira, and Kristoffer Nielbo. 2024. Perplexing canon: A study on GPT-based perplexity of canonical and non-canonical literary works. In *Proceedings of the 8th Joint SIGHUM Workshop on Computational Linguistics for Cultural Heritage, Social Sciences, Humanities and Literature (LaTeCH-CLfL 2024)*, pages 172–184, St. Julians, Malta. Association for Computational Linguistics.

A Number of novels per publishing house

The heatmap with number of novels in each category published by a given publishing house can be found in Figure 3.

B Non-canonical canonical novels

The heatmap with non-canonical novels incorrectly classified as canonical based on text-intrinsic features can be found in Figure 4.

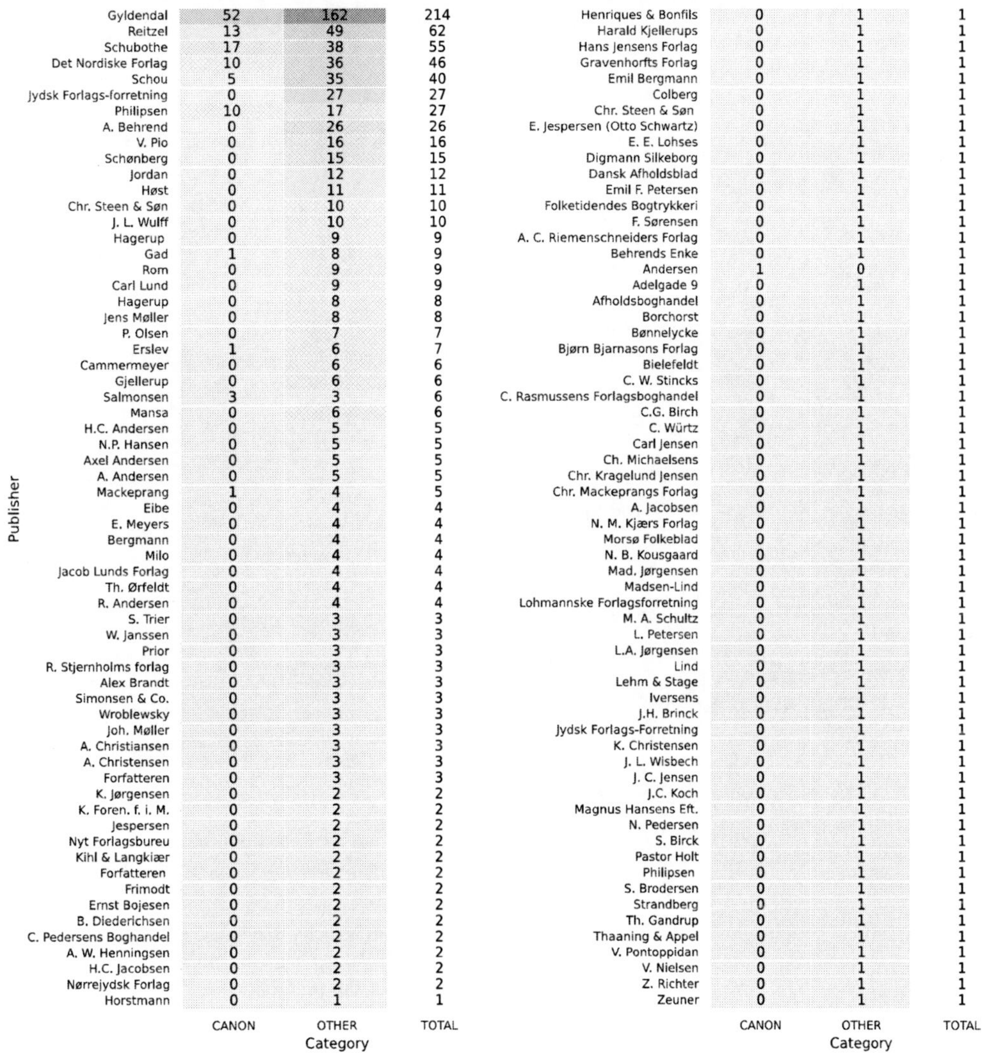

Figure 3: Number of novels in each category published by a given publishing house. Note that overall, the *Other* category generally has a higher entropy in its distribution over publisher than the *Canon* category. Entropy, $Other = 3.66$, $Canon = 1.72$. This difference persists when downsampling the majority group.

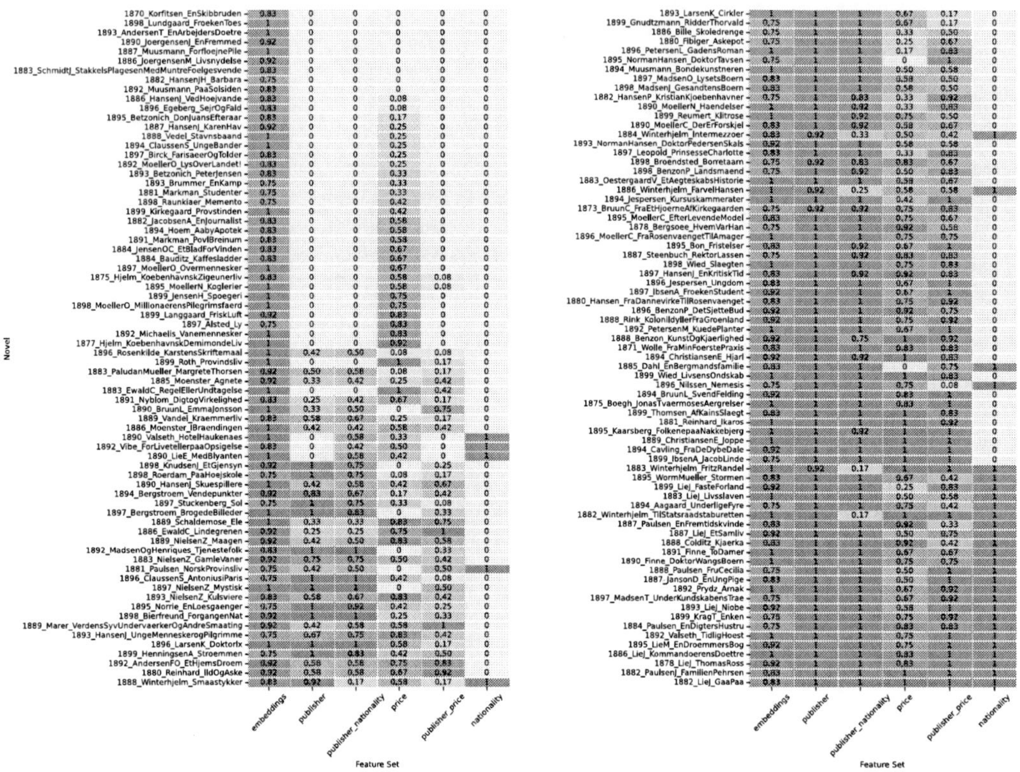

Figure 4: Heatmap of false positives (FP): non-canonical novels incorrectly classified as canonical based on $embeddings$ as features. Columns represent feature sets, with cell values showing normalized false positive counts ($FP/(TN + FP)$). We only include novels of which 75% of the predictions for $embeddings$ are FP ($embeddings >= 0.75$). The unique number of novels is 145, and every novel is predicted 12 times.

Adapting Multilingual Embedding Models to Historical Luxembourgish

Andrianos Michail
University of Zurich
andrianos.michail@cl.uzh.ch

Corina Julia Raclé
University of Zurich
corinajulia.racle@uzh.ch

Juri Opitz
University of Zurich
jurialexander.opitz@cl.uzh.ch

Simon Clematide
University of Zurich
simon.clematide@cl.uzh.ch

Abstract

The growing volume of digitized historical texts requires effective semantic search using text embeddings. However, pre-trained multilingual models face challenges with historical content due to OCR noise and outdated spellings. This study examines multilingual embeddings for cross-lingual semantic search in historical Luxembourgish (LB), a low-resource language. We collect historical Luxembourgish news articles from various periods and use GPT-4o for sentence segmentation and translation, generating 20,000 parallel training sentences per language pair. Additionally, we create a semantic search (Historical LB Bitext Mining) evaluation set and find that existing models perform poorly on cross-lingual search for historical Luxembourgish. Using our historical and additional modern parallel training data, we adapt several multilingual embedding models through contrastive learning or knowledge distillation and increase accuracy significantly for all models. We release our adapted models and historical Luxembourgish-German/French/English bitexts to support further research. [1]

1 Introduction

Exploration possibilities of historical texts, such as newspapers, have advanced rapidly due to digitization efforts by libraries and archives (Ehrmann et al., 2023a). Traditionally, tools relied on keyword-based searches, often enhanced with semantic enrichment techniques such as named entity recognition (Ehrmann et al., 2023b).

Recent embedding benchmarks (Muennighoff et al., 2023; Enevoldsen et al., 2025) show that massively multilingual embedding models, trained on diverse multilingual corpora, perform well in both multilingual and cross-lingual semantic search. These models have also become integral in Retrieval-Augmented Generation (RAG), where they help retrieve more relevant and contextually appropriate documents, thereby improving the faithfulness of generated responses.

However, for low-resource languages like Luxembourgish (LB), where multilingual models have limited exposure, their performance remains uncertain. Applying these models to semantic search in imperfectly digitized historical collections introduces additional challenges, as they must handle OCR errors and historical spelling variations. The disparity between these noisy, historical texts and the clean, modern digital-born data used to train multilingual models, combined with their limited support for Luxembourgish, complicates the development of effective exploration tools for historical Luxembourgish newspaper archives.

To address this issue, we compile 2,338 historical Luxembourgish news articles from different time periods and use GPT-4o to segment and translate them into modern French (FR), English (EN) and German (DE). The resulting parallel sentences serve as fine-tuning data to adapt existing multilingual embedding models for imperfectly digitized historical Luxembourgish.

Our main contributions:

(1) We adapt multilingual embeddings for digitized historical Luxembourgish by generating training data through a prompt-based translation approach with GPT-4o.

(2) We define a historical bitext mining task and create a high-quality cross-lingual semantic search test set with 233 source news articles (LB-DE: 2,127; LB-FR: 2,157; LB-EN: 2,105 sentences).

(3) We fine-tune and evaluate off-the-shelf models – *M-MPNet* (Reimers and Gurevych, 2020), *LaBSE* (Feng et al., 2022), *M-GTE* (Zhang et al., 2024), and *LuxEmbedder* (Philippy et al., 2025) – to as-

[1] See https://github.com/impresso/histlux_emb for our released models, data and source code.

Proceedings of LaTeCH-CLfL 2025, pages 291–298

sess our adaptation methods.
(4) We propose and evaluate a 1:1 data mixing strategy that balances noisy historical texts with clean modern texts to minimize performance degradation on modern Luxembourgish benchmarks.

2 Related Work

This section reviews relevant embedding models that support Luxembourgish semantic search, including monolingual Luxembourgish models and multilingual embeddings.

Reimers and Gurevych (2020) use knowledge distillation through a strong paraphrase-trained English embedding model and parallel data to create cross-lingually aligned models. Multiple instances of such models have been open sourced and a particularly powerful and popular one is *paraphrase-multilingual-mpnet-base-v2* (**M-MPNet**) which was trained on over 50 languages. Later within this work, we will explain how we extend this model to also support Luxembourgish.

The multilingual bitext mining model **LaBSE** (Feng et al., 2022) is trained with translation ranking loss and negative samples. It has been trained roughly on less than 100 Luxembourgish-English sentence pairs and specializes in zero-shot bitext mining.

A recent model is GTE Multilingual (**M-GTE**) (Zhang et al., 2024), a multilingual embedding model designed for long context text representation and reranking. *M-GTE* has been trained with hard negatives and has included 50,000 Luxembourgish pairs within its contrastive pre-training.

Specific model adaptations to Luxembourgish have also been developed. One example is **LuxemBERT** (Lothritz et al., 2022), a monolingual BERT model pre-trained for Luxembourgish using augmented data, partially generated by translating texts from closely related languages and incorporating relevant text sources.

Closely related to our work, **LuxEmbedder** (Philippy et al., 2025) used OpenAI's *text-embedding-3-small* and *LaBSE* to mine a set of parallel sentences for each pair of languages between Luxembourgish, English, and French. These parallel sentences (up to 20,000 per pair) were then used to further fine-tune *LaBSE*, improving performance on modern Luxembourgish evaluation sets. However, its ability to handle Luxembourgish texts from different historical periods—potentially affected by digitization errors common in large-scale historical text collections, remains unclear.

Our work aims to extend existing embedding models to better perform cross-lingual semantic search within a collection of historical, OCR-noisy Luxembourgish texts. The conditions of these texts combined with the different spelling variations[2] poses an interesting generalization challenge to the models.

3 Method

To adapt and evaluate embedding models for digitized historical Luxembourgish news articles, we create parallel texts by translating them into modern German, French, and English. This allows the models to learn cross-lingual representations and improves their ability to align historical Luxembourgish with contemporary languages for semantic search.

3.1 Parallel Historical Luxembourgish

We build our translated parallel data sets LB-DE, LB-FR and LB-EN from monolingual Luxembourgish texts sourced from the publicly available BNL newspaper archive.[3] Our data consists of articles from newspapers published between 1841 and 1948. To select diverse samples for translation, we first cluster the articles into 2,000 groups by K-Mean on a 100-topics LDA model output[4] and keep the 605 clusters with more than 20 articles.

We select articles through a two-step process, resulting in a total of 2,340 articles, as shown in Figure 1. First, we retrieve the most representative article from each cluster, ensuring it contains between 5 and 20 sentences (cutting of the remaining sentences). In a second round, we randomly sample three additional articles per cluster under the same length conditions.

We prompt GPT-4o to segment historical Luxembourgish articles and generate sentence-level translation pairs separately for German, French and English (see Prompt 2). The model is instructed to preserve the original meaning and structure as closely as possible while reconstructing sentences affected by OCR errors that could hinder translation. This process yields approximately 22,500 sentence pairs for the LB-DE, LB-FR and LB-EN pair. Notably, GPT-4o appears to perform sentence

[2]Luxembourgish had no standardized spelling until 1946 and underwent multiple further reformations (eg. in 1999)

[3]https://data.bnl.lu/data/historical-newspapers

[4]Taken from the impresso-project.ch (Ehrmann et al., 2020).

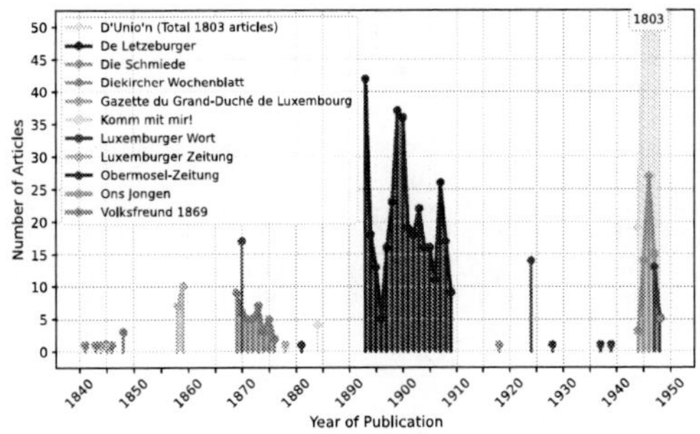

Figure 1: Source LB articles per newspaper per year.

segmentation consistently resulting in 65.0% of sentences forming exact quadruplets (4-way parallel) across the four languages.

To ensure fidelity to the original articles, we calculate the percentage of regenerated Luxembourgish sentences that do not exactly match their source texts. These account for 1.4% of all historical Luxembourgish sentences per language pair, which we manually correct. Most mismatches result from missing or added punctuation, modernized spelling, and, in rare cases, errors caused by the LLM not adhering to the instructed format.

To assess translation quality, a quadrilingual native speaker of Luxembourgish (LB) annotated 100 randomly selected sentence quadruplets after removing 15 samples with severe OCR problems. Of the 100 LB sentences presented without context, 88 were judged to be comprehensible or at least confidently guessable (23). The remaining 12 were considered incomprehensible due to OCR errors and archaic spellings, and their translations were not evaluated.

For the comprehensible and confidently guessable sentences, the German translations were rated as adequate in 78 cases (88.6%), with missing minor details in 9 cases and 1 case of inadequate translation. The French translations showed a similar pattern: 78 were adequate (88.6%), 9 were missing minor details, and 1 was inadequate. The English translations were also adequate in 78 cases (88.6%), with 10 missing minor details. A sample of the annotated dataset is available in the appendix (Table 2).

3.2 Framing an Evaluation Task: Historical LB Bitext Mining

From our parallel dataset, we set aside a held-out test set of 233 articles (2,127 sentences) to establish a historical semantic search benchmark for Luxembourgish-to-German, French, and English bitext mining (LB<->DE/FR/EN). A prediction is considered a true positive if the embedding model assigns a higher similarity to the correct parallel sentence than to any of the 2k alternative candidates. We report the bidirectional average accuracy. To minimize false negatives caused by near-identical sentences, we exclude candidate sentences with a Levenshtein similarity score above 0.85 to the source sentence, after removing non-alphanumeric characters from both. This filtering affects 57 source-candidate pairs (2.7%) in German, 65 (3%) in French, and 76 (3.6%) in English. A human review at different thresholds confirms the appropriateness of the filtering process and the chosen threshold.

3.3 Modern LB Evaluation Tasks

We replicate two evaluation tasks on modern Luxembourgish from Philippy et al. (2025).

ParaLux is a monolingual paraphrase detection test set designed to evaluate embedding models. Performance is measured by the proportion of cases (a total of 312 triplets) in which an embedding model assigns a higher similarity to an anchor-positive pair than to an anchor-negative pair. The negative sentences are adversarially generated to maintain high lexical similarity and manually verified to ensure they are true negatives.

SIB 200 (LB) is a repurposed subset of the 'Flores' dataset (NLLB Team et al., 2022; Adelani et al., 2024), used for monolingual zero-shot topic classification. In this task, texts are assigned to template sentences representing candidate topics based on embedding similarity.

3.4 Adapting Multilingual Embedding Models to Historical LB

3.4.1 Datasets

Historical: We use 2,105 historical LB newspaper articles (excluding held-out articles) with their sentence-level translations to create a parallel training set for the following language pairs: LB-DE (20,092), LB-FR (20,010), and LB-EN (19,054) sentences.

Modern: Philippy et al. (2025) extracted 89,405 LB-FR and 28,172 LB-EN parallel sentence pairs from RTL.lu, a trilingual news platform. This dataset was used to fine-tune the *LuxEmbedder* model.

Model	Training Data	Historical LB Bitext Mining				Modern LB		
		LB↔FR	**LB↔EN**	**LB↔DE**	**AVG**	**SIB 200 (LB)**	**ParaLux**	**AVG**
Random Baseline	–	00.00	00.00	00.00	45.97	14.28	50.00	32.14
text-embedding-3-small	–	78.36	75.08	82.33	78.59	40.20	15.71	27.96
text-embedding-3-large	–	86.18	83.63	88.15	85.99	58.82	26.28	42.55
M-MPNet	–	46.32	45.04	46.55	45.97	24.71	26.60	25.66
M-MPNet(+LB Distilled)	LB↔EN (Hist)	87.23	87.53	89.14	87.97	42.65	56.09	49.37
	LB↔EN (Modern)	75.55	77.03	78.09	76.89	**59.51**	80.13	69.82
	LB↔EN (Mixed)	**89.32**	**89.55**	**91.44**	**88.79**	59.41	**80.45**	**70.48**
LaBSE	–	93.12	95.27	94.01	94.13	43.24	**38.14**	40.69
LaBSE (Hist)	LB↔FR	**97.73**	97.22	98.10	97.68	39.61	25.00	32.31
	LB↔EN	97.24	97.44	97.96	97.54	41.76	22.44	32.10
	LB↔DE	97.08	97.01	**98.52**	97.54	34.02	14.74	24.38
LaBSE (Mixed)	LB↔FR	97.40	**97.55**	98.22	97.35	**45.69**	31.73	47.66
	LB↔EN	96.80	97.34	97.82	**97.75**	45.59	36.86	**50.23**
LuxEmbedder	–	84.49	85.09	85.48	85.02	**65.59**	**52.24**	**58.92**
LuxEmbedder (Hist)	LB↔FR	**97.47**	97.51	98.24	97.74	50.39	32.37	41.38
	LB↔EN	97.18	97.29	98.26	97.58	54.12	28.85	41.49
	LB↔DE	97.25	**97.72**	**98.43**	**97.80**	46.76	26.60	36.68
LuxEmbedder (Mixed)	LB↔FR	96.97	97.32	97.77	97.72	56.86	38.46	38.71
	LB↔EN	97.41	97.58	98.26	97.32	56.86	43.59	41.23
M-GTE	–	83.68	80.12	87.55	83.78	55.78	**70.51**	63.20
M-GTE (Hist)	LB↔FR	95.18	94.23	96.05	95.15	59.12	57.05	58.09
	LB↔EN	**95.81**	95.56	96.52	**95.96**	54.71	55.77	55.24
	LB↔DE	95.23	94.61	**97.65**	95.83	45.29	42.31	43.80
M-GTE (Mixed)	LB↔FR	95.53	95.11	96.78	95.80	60.98	60.26	60.62
	LB↔EN	95.48	**95.58**	96.55	95.87	**67.84**	64.10	**65.70**
M-GTE (Hist, Modern: 120k)	LB↔DE/FR/EN	**96.83**	**97.15**	**97.93**	**97.30**	62.16	62.82	62.75

Table 1: Performance (accuracy) of the examined models and our adapted variants within the Historical and Modern Luxembourgish evaluation sets. The last row shows an adapted model trained on the maximum available data, with details found at the end of Section 4.

Training Data Configurations We investigate three data mixing strategies for model training:
(1) *Hist*orical: 20,000 translated sentence pairs (LB↔FR, LB↔EN, or LB↔DE) from historical texts.
(2) *Modern*: 20,000 bitext-mined sentence pairs (LB↔FR or LB↔EN) from modern Luxembourgish news.
(3) *Mixed*: 20,000 *Hist* sentence pairs with 20,000 *Modern* sentence pairs in mixed batches.

3.4.2 LB Knowledge Distillation

We adapt *M-MPNet* for historical LB using multilingual knowledge distillation (Reimers and Gurevych, 2020). The original English model *paraphrase-mpnet-base-v2* serves as a frozen teacher, while LB-EN parallel sentences are used to train the *M-MPNet* student model to embedded LB sentences similar to their English translations. We fine-tune *M-MPNet* for five epochs using each of the three data mixing strategies: (1) *Hist*orical, (2) *Modern*, and (3) *Mixed*.

3.4.3 Contrastive Loss

We adapt *LaBSE*, *LuxEmbedder*, and *M-GTE* to historical LB using contrastive learning. Specifically, we fine-tune these embedding models using *MultipleNegativesRankingLoss* (Henderson et al., 2017), with a batch size of 8 for one epoch. For fine-tuning, we apply two of the previously defined data mixing strategies: (1) *Hist*orical and (3) *Mixed*.

4 Results

Table 1 shows the performance of the off-the-shelf and adapted models on the historical Luxembourgish bitext mining and the modern LB evaluation tasks.

Among the off-the-shelf(in cursive) models, *LaBSE* is the strongest model in all three languages. Surprisingly, *LuxEmbedder*, a LB-tuned version of *LaBSE*, shows an average performance drop of 9pp across language pairs in our bitext mining task, despite improved performance on the modern LB tasks. Similarly, *M-GTE* underperforms *LaBSE* by 10.4pp. Both OpenAI embedding models (*text-embedding-3-small/large*) show moderate performance.

Among the models contrastively adapted using the *Hist* pairs, the performance in historical bitext mining improves significantly, reaching up to 97.8% accuracy. Notably, after domain adaptation, *LuxEmbedder* matches the adapted *LaBSE*, reaching over 97.8% accuracy and closing the performance gap observed in the standard models. Meanwhile, the customized *M-GTE* models lag behind by about 2pp. Interestingly, across all model architectures, training on any language pair improves performance similarly across all pairs, showing a positive cross-lingual transfer.

These models experience significant performance drops in modern LB evaluations, particularly in *ParaLux*. However, adapting these models with mixed batches of *Hist* and *Modern* sentence pairs partially mitigated performance loss on the Modern LB evaluation tasks. Within *LaBSE* and *M-GTE*, this adaptation even improved the performance on SIB-200 topic classification, while sacrificing only up to 1% of the performance on historical bitext mining. These mixed-data adapted models provide an overall stronger general backbone for cross-lingual semantic searching within collections containing both historical and modern Luxembourgish.

The *M-MPNet* model, before distilling EN-LB knowledge, performs poorly in all LB evaluations, despite its proven exact matching capabilities in other languages, confirming its lack of support for the language. After distilling LB with any dataset, the model performs magnitudes better across the board. When distilled with a single dataset, the model performs best on historical semantic search tasks with the *Hist* sentence pairs. In contrast, when distilled with *Modern* sentence pairs, the model excels on modern LB tasks, achieving 80% accuracy on ParaLux[5] and outperforming the second-best *M-GTE*, which achieves 70%. Finally, distilling with the mixed data set yields the best results in all evaluations, demonstrating the synergy between the two sources.

However, even the *Mixed*-data distilled *M-MPNet* model only achieves an average accuracy across pairs of 90% in historical bitext mining, trailing the contrastive domain-adapted *LaBSE* and *LuxEmbedder* by 8pp and the off-the-shelf *LaBSE* model by 4pp.

The Final Model: Mix it All For a final all-purpose model covering both historical and modern LB, we contrastively adapt *M-GTE* to all language pairs of *Hist* while preserving an equal number of *Modern* sentence pairs, regardless of language. The adaptation dataset consists of 20,000 LB-FR/EN/DE (*Hist*), 20,000 LB-EN (*Modern*), and 40,000 LB-FR (*Modern*), for a total of 120,000 sentence pairs.

It is the best-performing historical semantic search *M-GTE* model, achieving an average accuracy of 97.5% across all language pairs. This model outperforms the adapted *LaBSE* and *LuxEmbedder* models on SIB-200 (+6pp) and ParaLux (+20pp), while performing similarly to them in the historical bitext mining evaluations.

5 Conclusions

In this work, we explore the adaptation of multilingual embedding models to digitized historical LB texts, a task where off-the-shelf models struggle due to limited exposure and their reliance on clean modern data. To address this issue, we generate parallel sentence-segmented documents by translating historical Luxembourgish newspaper articles into French, English, and German using GPT-4o.

To evaluate the effectiveness of adaptation, we design a historical bitext mining task with a held-out test set of 233 articles. Our results show that adaptation to parallel historical data improves retrieval accuracy by up to 13pp. However, this adaptation introduces trade-offs, particularly reducing performance on modern LB tasks that require high semantic precision, such as adversarial paraphrase detection. We mitigate this problem through a balanced data mixing strategy that helps preserve modern LB performance while improving historical text semantic search capabilities.

These results demonstrate the effectiveness of domain adaptation for historical text processing and suggest that such approaches could benefit low-resource languages facing digitization challenges. Such improvements are particularly relevant for libraries and archives, where effective cross-lingual semantic search can improve the discoverability of historical documents and support digital exploration.

[5]As shown in recent work (Michail et al., 2025), results on adversarial paraphrase discrimination test sets might not accurately reflect performance on semantic search in general. Therefore, this result should be interpreted with caution.

Limitations

Our findings paves the way for better semantic search systems within Luxembourgish archives. On the one hand, our method demonstrates clear benefits for the targeted use case, effectively embedding heterogeneous digitized historical texts and revealing shortcomings in off-the-shelf models. Through our exploration of adaptation methodologies, we have produced practical embeddings for semantic search while mostly preserving modern LB performance. On the other hand, we have not strictly reached a single best model across all evaluation sets. For example, in all of our adapted models, performance on *ParaLux* declines, possibly indicating interference with modern LB understanding and reduced sensitivity to semantic nuances.

Overall, we have applied a single adaptation method for each model type across all available data mixes, ensuring alignment with the models' initial training methods. Exploring alternative adaptation approaches may reveal additional patterns.

One problem with our evaluation is that they are all at the sentence level, whereas applications of such models would often be at the paragraph, article, or document level. The hypothesis that our improved performance would be reflected when embedding longer segments of text is possible, but not guaranteed. Lastly, while our research focuses on historical Luxembourgish, our methodology may also be useful for developing semantic search models in other underrepresented languages, which we do not examine in this study.

Acknowledgments

We would like to thank Fred Phillipy for helping with the human annotation. This research is conducted under the project *Impresso – Media Monitoring of the Past II Beyond Borders: Connecting Historical Newspapers and Radio.* Impresso is a research project funded by the Swiss National Science Foundation (SNSF 213585) and the Luxembourg National Research Fund (17498891).

References

David Adelani, Hannah Liu, Xiaoyu Shen, Nikita Vassilyev, Jesujoba Alabi, Yanke Mao, Haonan Gao, and En-Shiun Lee. 2024. SIB-200: A simple, inclusive, and big evaluation dataset for topic classification in 200+ languages and dialects. In *Proceedings of the 18th Conference of the European Chapter of the Association for Computational Linguistics (Volume 1: Long Papers)*, pages 226–245, St. Julian's, Malta. Association for Computational Linguistics.

Maud Ehrmann, Estelle Bunout, and Frédéric Clavert. 2023a. *Digitised Historical Newspapers: A Changing Research Landscape*, pages 1–22. De Gruyter Oldenbourg, Berlin, Boston.

Maud Ehrmann, Ahmed Hamdi, Elvys Linhares Pontes, Matteo Romanello, and Antoine Doucet. 2023b. Named entity recognition and classification in historical documents: A survey. *ACM Comput. Surv.*, 56(2).

Maud Ehrmann, Matteo Romanello, Simon Clematide, Phillip Benjamin Ströbel, and Raphaël Barman. 2020. Language resources for historical newspapers: the impresso collection. In *Proceedings of the Twelfth Language Resources and Evaluation Conference*, pages 958–968, Marseille, France. European Language Resources Association.

Kenneth Enevoldsen, Isaac Chung, Imene Kerboua, Márton Kardos, Ashwin Mathur, David Stap, Jay Gala, Wissam Siblini, Dominik Krzemiński, Genta Indra Winata, Saba Sturua, Saiteja Utpala, Mathieu Ciancone, Marion Schaeffer, Diganta Misra, Shreeya Dhakal, Jonathan Rystrøm, Roman Solomatin, Ömer Veysel Çağatan, (...), and Niklas Muennighoff. 2025. MMTEB: Massive multilingual text embedding benchmark. In *The Thirteenth International Conference on Learning Representations*.

Fangxiaoyu Feng, Yinfei Yang, Daniel Cer, Naveen Arivazhagan, and Wei Wang. 2022. Language-agnostic BERT sentence embedding. In *Proceedings of the 60th Annual Meeting of the Association for Computational Linguistics (Volume 1: Long Papers)*, pages 878–891, Dublin, Ireland. Association for Computational Linguistics.

Matthew Henderson, Rami Al-Rfou, Brian Strope, Yun hsuan Sung, Laszlo Lukacs, Ruiqi Guo, Sanjiv Kumar, Balint Miklos, and Ray Kurzweil. 2017. Efficient natural language response suggestion for smart reply. *Preprint*, arXiv:1705.00652.

Cedric Lothritz, Bertrand Lebichot, Kevin Allix, Lisa Veiber, Tegawende Bissyande, Jacques Klein, Andrey Boytsov, Clément Lefebvre, and Anne Goujon. 2022. LuxemBERT: Simple and practical data augmentation in language model pre-training for Luxembourgish. In *Proceedings of the Thirteenth Language Resources and Evaluation Conference*, pages 5080–5089, Marseille, France. European Language Resources Association.

Andrianos Michail, Simon Clematide, and Juri Opitz. 2025. PARAPHRASUS: A comprehensive benchmark for evaluating paraphrase detection models. In *Proceedings of the 31st International Conference on Computational Linguistics*, pages 8749–8762, Abu Dhabi, UAE. Association for Computational Linguistics.

Niklas Muennighoff, Nouamane Tazi, Loic Magne, and Nils Reimers. 2023. MTEB: Massive text embedding benchmark. In *Proceedings of the 17th Conference of the European Chapter of the Association for Computational Linguistics*, pages 2014–2037, Dubrovnik, Croatia. Association for Computational Linguistics.

NLLB Team, Marta R. Costa-jussà, James Cross, Onur Çelebi, Maha Elbayad, Kenneth Heafield, Kevin Heffernan, Elahe Kalbassi, Janice Lam, Daniel Licht, Jean Maillard, Anna Sun, Skyler Wang, Guillaume Wenzek, Al Youngblood, Bapi Akula, Loic Barrault, Gabriel Mejia Gonzalez, Hansanti, (...), and Jeff Wang. 2022. No language left behind: Scaling human-centered machine translation. *arXiv preprint arXiv:2207.04672*.

Fred Philippy, Siwen Guo, Jacques Klein, and Tegawende Bissyande. 2025. LuxEmbedder: A cross-lingual approach to enhanced Luxembourgish sentence embeddings. In *Proceedings of the 31st International Conference on Computational Linguistics*, pages 11369–11379, Abu Dhabi, UAE. Association for Computational Linguistics.

Nils Reimers and Iryna Gurevych. 2020. Making monolingual sentence embeddings multilingual using knowledge distillation. In *Proceedings of the 2020 Conference on Empirical Methods in Natural Language Processing (EMNLP)*, pages 4512–4525, Online. Association for Computational Linguistics.

Xin Zhang, Yanzhao Zhang, Dingkun Long, Wen Xie, Ziqi Dai, Jialong Tang, Huan Lin, Baosong Yang, Pengjun Xie, Fei Huang, Meishan Zhang, Wenjie Li, and Min Zhang. 2024. mGTE: Generalized long-context text representation and reranking models for multilingual text retrieval. In *Proceedings of the 2024 Conference on Empirical Methods in Natural Language Processing: Industry Track*, pages 1393–1412, Miami, Florida, US. Association for Computational Linguistics.

A Appendix

System:

You are a professional translator specializing in the translation of historical Luxembourgish newspaper articles into modern Standard {German/French/English}.
Your task is to translate paragraphs from such newspapers, provided to you by the user. These paragraphs may contain old spellings, outdated expressions, and likely a lot of OCR errors, as they are extracted from 19th-century LB newspapers. Please translate each sentence individually into modern Standard {German/French/English}. Prioritize retaining the original meaning, expressions, and any nuanced tone in each translation, even if the result sounds somewhat unconventional or even bad in {German/French/English}. If an expression is ambiguous due to its historical nature or OCR errors, attempt to reconstruct the most probable meaning based on linguistic context. Ensure that all punctuation and whitespace is preserved exactly. Do not add any extra formatting such as backticks, markdown, or additional symbols.

Please return the source sentences and your translations in the following format as JSON:

```
{"translation": [
{"lb": "lb_sent1", "{de}": "{de}_sent1"},
{"lb": "lb_sent2", "{de}": "{de}_sent2"},
{"lb": "lb_sent3", "{de}": "{de}_sent3"},
...]}
```

Figure 2: Zero-shot prompt template given to GPT-4o for the segmentation and translation of historical Luxembourgish newspaper articles to modern French(fr)/English(en)/German(de).

Newspaper	Year	Sentence	LB Compr.	FR Compr.	EN Compr.	DE Compr.
D'Union	1946	**LB**: Si bestét aus 18 000 tuben, weit 30 tonnen a kascht 400 000 dollar. **FR**: Elle est composée de 18 000 tubes, pèse 30 tonnes et coûte 400 000 dollars. **EN**: It consists of 18,000 tubes, weighs 30 tons, and costs 400,000 dollars. **DE**: Sie besteht aus 18.000 Röhren, wiegt 30 Tonnen und kostet 400.000 Dollar.	Comprehensible	Adequate	Adequate	Adequate
Ons Jorgen	1946	**LB**: „Daf net, mais ech hu kc properen Teller me'," **FR**: "Certainement pas, mais je n'ai plus d'assiette propre," **EN**: "Not really, but I don't have a single clean plate anymore." **DE**: „Das nicht, aber ich habe keinen sauberen Teller mehr.	Comprehensible	Adequate	Adequate	Adequate
De Letzeburger	1893	**LB**: De Batti: Elo hätte mer d'Stemmung gut eriwer, hätte mer elo och nach Rén. **FR**: Le Batti : Maintenant, nous aurions bien passé l'ambiance, si seulement nous avions aussi encore Rén. **EN**: Batti: Now we would have a good atmosphere if we also had some rain. **DE**: Der Batti: Jetzt hätten wir die Stimmung gut geschafft, hätten wir jetzt auch noch Regen.	Confidently Guessable	Adequate	Adequate	Adequate
De Letzeburger	1905	**LB**: Op d'Weis: Das ist im Lehen hfisslich eingerichtet. **FR**: À la manière de : Cela est arrangé vilaine dans la vie. **EN**: To the tune: It is poorly arranged in life. **DE**: Zur Melodie: Das ist im Leben hässlich eingerichtet.	Confidently Guessable	Adequate	Adequate	Adequate
De Letzeburger	1893	**LB**: Wann och d'Liss'ché wéss ze feischtren. **FR**: Même si Liss'ché sait lutter. **EN**: Even if Lisette knows how to flirt. **DE**: Wenn auch die Liss'ché weiß zu feilschen.	Incomprehensible	/	/	/
Obermosel-Zeitung	1924	**LB**: In vielen vorkern Bincl alle Krank, 80 cla,BB «lie ?eläer nicdt deBtellt terrien Können. **FR**: Dans de nombreux villages, tous sont malades, si bien que les champs ne peuvent pas être cultivés. **EN**: In many places, all are sick, so that the fields cannot be tended. **DE**: In vielen Dörfern sind alle krank, so dass die Felder nicht bestellt werden können.	Incomprehensible	/	/	/

Table 2: Sample of quadruplets of parallel sentence as used within our human evaluation of the dataset quality.

Author Index

Association for Computational Linguistics
209 N. Eighth Street
Stroudsburg, Pennsylvania 18360

ISBN 979-8-3313-1921-2

9 798331 319212

CURRAN ASSOCIATES INC.
proceedings.com